HAND BOOK OF POLYMER & PLASTICS TECHNOLOGY

HAND BOOK OF POLYMER & PLASTICS TECHNOLOGY

Written By :

EIRI Consultants and Engineers

ENGINEERS INDIA RESEARCH INSTITUTE

4449, Nai Sarak, Main Road, Delhi-110 006 (India)

Ph. : 91-11-23918117, 23916431, 23840361

Fax : 91-11-23916431, 23918117

* **E-Mail :** eirisidi@bol.net.in

* **Website :** www.eiriindia.org

Sole Distributor :

INDIAN INSTITUTE OF CONSULTANTS,

4/27, Roop Nagar, Delhi-110007

Printed and Published by :

ENGINEERS INDIA RESEARCH INSTITUTE

4449, Nai Sarak, Main Road, Delhi-110 006 (India)
Ph. : 91-11-23918117, 23916431, 23840361
Fax : 91-11-23916431, 23918117
★ **E-Mail :** eirisidi@bol.net.in
★ **Website :** www.eiriindia.org

Distributed by :

SMALL INDUSTRY RESEARCH INSTITUTE
INDIAN INSTITUTE OF CONSULTANTS

ISBN : 81-86732-92-6
Printed in New Delhi (India)

Rs. 950

Printed and Published by Sudhir Gupta for
"Engineers India Research Institute", 4449, Nai Sarak, Main Road,
New Delhi-110 006 and Printed at Swastik Offset, Delhi

Preface

The past few years have seen the development of many new polymeric materials, some of them, such as polypropylene and polyisoprene rubber, being the results of completely new polymerization techniques. There have also been corresponding advances in processing techniques. It seemed to us, however, that there was still room for a book which would cover the most important of these developments in a single volume and incorporate them into the general framework of plastics & polymer technology.

The prospect of getting new polymers via synthesis and polymerization of new monomers appears to have crossed the peak. Much brighter prospects of material development lie with approaches relating to preparing polymer blends, including interpenetrating polymer networks (IPNs) and also polymer composites based on reinforcement of polymers by proper incorporation of particulate and fibrous reinforcing agents. Adoption of novel synthetic routes for making new monomers and oligomers and for novel modification of polymers also appears attractive in this context. Moreover, with most common polymers being electrical insulators, prospects of synthesizing or formulating the conducting polymer systems have also generated wide interest.

*The book '**Hand Book of Polymer & Plastics Technology**' covers various methods including basic concept of High Polymer Systems, Raw Materials, Phenoplasts, Aminoplasts, Polyesters, Epoxy Resins, Silicones, Polyurethanes, Polyulefins, Polyvinyls, Polyamides, Acrylic Polymers, High Performance Thermoplastics, Natural and Modified Rubbers, Plasticisers, Stabilisers, and Related Additives, Fillers, Colourants, and Special Additives, Extrusion, Injection Molding and Blow Molding, Thermoforming, Powder Coating, Miscellaneous Processing Techniques, Physical and Chemical Testing of Plastics.*

The book has been written for the benefit and to prove an asset and a handy reference guide in the hands of new entrepreneurs and well established industrialists.

Director

ENGINEERS INDIA RESEARCH INSTITUTE

Nai Sarak, Main Road,
Delhi-110 006 (India)
E-mail : eirisidi@bol.net.in

CONTENTS AND SUBJECT INDEX

1

Basic Concepts of High Polymer Systems

1.1 Introduction and Historical Background

The quest for new materials has been with us from ancient times. Polymers, though introduced in the materials field in a meaningful manner only very recently, occupy a major place and pivotal position in the materials field today. In performance characteristics and applications prospects and diversity, they offer novelty and versatility not found in any other kind of materials.

Till about the first two decades of the twentieth century, confusion prevailed over the basic understanding of polymer molecules. They were recognised more as colloids or associated molecules. Attempts to determine their molecular weights using solutions in suitable solvents by cryoscopy often gave confusive, irreproducible, uncertain and sometimes very high values. For starch, natural rubber and cellulose, derivatives, molecular weights ranging up to 40,000-50,000 or even more were obtained. Such high values implied existence of very large molecules. But this was not accepted in view of the total lack of structural concepts about such large molecules. The chemists continued to favour the concept of large association of much smaller molecules of short chain or cylic structures.

1.2 Macromolecular Concept

The realisation of the macromolecular concept of polymeric materials in 1920s proved to be a vital turning point. Accumulated confused ideas of the earlier decades became meaningful and they were then translated into the production of a large variety of materials of hitherto unknown structures through polymerisation and copolymerisation of olefinic, diolefinic and vinylic compounds and combination thereof, and through polycondensation reactions between in large variety of bi- or polyfunctional compounds bearing well characterised chemical functional groups.

The macromolecular concept came into wide acceptance and appreciation soon after it was propounded by Staudinger in 1920. He advanced long- chain structural formulas for polystyrene, natural rubber, etc. Long sequences of simple chemical units linked with each other with covalent bonds came into recognition as the basic structural feature of a polymer molecule. The polystyrene obtained from polymerisation of styrene (CH_2+CH) came to be recognised to have the formula—(CH_2—CH)$_n$—where

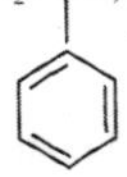

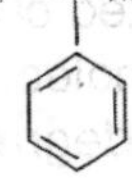

had a large value. Staudinger was not sure about the terminal points or end groups of the long-chain polymer molecules. He was of the view that there was no need to saturate the terminal valences and suggested that no end groups were needed. However, development and elucidation of the chain reaction theory and mechanism of vinyl and related polymerisation by Flory and others clearly established that polymer materials consisted of long chain molecules with well characterised end groups. Another distinctive feature of the same decade was the pioneering work of Carothers in the area of polycondensation and towards the first rational synthesis of linear macro molecules, polyester and polyamides.

A stage was reached by the middle of the 20th century, when the possibility of attaining almost any conceivable material property of structural importance through polymerisation, copolymerisation of polycondensation and through modification of available polymers by chemical treatment, reinforcements, compounding or blending, thermal or mechanical treatment, irradiation etc., appeared to be within our competence. We had reached the era of tailor-made polymers in a comprehensive sense. Material prospect brightened through what may be called "molecular engineering". Nowdays, through proper selection of monomers and their combinations, catalysts and other additives and adopting appropriate polymerisation conditions and techniques, experts are able to construct polymer molecules of almost any desired size, shape and complexity and of any desired chemical structure suited to almost any comtemplated end use.

1.3 Structural Features of a Polymer

The word polymer literally means many (*poly*) units (*mer*). A simple chemical unit repeats itself a very large number of times in the structure of a polymer molecule; this unit may consist of a single atom, or more commonly, a small group of atoms linked chemically. An example of the first kind (repeat units consisting of a single atom) is the well known plastic sulphur, -S-S-S-S-S-S-, in the molecules of which the repeating S atoms are joined together by covalent bonds. This polymeric sulphur is, however, unstable and it slowly changes back to the powdery form of sulphur on keeping at room temperature.

In bulk of the polymers, the repeating unit or simply the repeat unit is constituted of a small group of atoms combined in a specific fashion. The simple molecule from which its polymer is obtained or to which a polymer may be degraded is called the monomer. Table 1.1 lists some polymers and structures of the respective monomers and repeat units.

The number of repeat units in a given polymer molecule is known as its chain length or degree of polymerisation(DP). The molecular weight of the polymer is the product of the molecular weight of the repeat unit and DP.

When more than one kind of repeat units are present in a polymer, it is known as a copolymer. Polymers having molecular weight roughly in the range of 1000-20,000 are called low polymers and those having molecular weights higher than 20,000 as high polymers.

Table 1.1 Some polymers and respective monomers and repeat units.

Polymer	*Monomer*	*Repeat Unit*
Polyethylene	**Ethylene,** $CH_2 = CH_2$	$—CH_2 + CH_2—$
Polypropylene	**Propylene,** $CH_2 = CH(CH_3)$	$—CH_2—CH(CH_3)—$
Polystyrene	**Styrene,** $CH_2 = CH(C_6H_5)$	$—CH_2—CH(C_6H_5)—$
Poly (vinyl chloride)	**Vinyl chloride** $CH_2 = CH(Cl)$	$—CH_2—CH(Cl)—$
Poly (viny acetate)	**Vinyl acetate,** $CH_2 = CH(OCOCH_3)$	$—CH_2—CH(OCOCH_3)—$
Polyacrylonitrilte	**Acrylonitrite** $CH_2 = CH(CN)$	$—CH_2—CH(CN)—$

Table 1.1 *(Contd.)*

Polymer	*Monomer*	*Repeat Unit*
Poly (acrylic acid)	Acrylic acid, $CH_2=CH$ $\vert$ $COOH$	$-CH_2-CH-$ $\vert$ $COOH$
Poly (methacrylic acid)	Methacrylic acid, $CH_2=C(CH_3)$ $\vert$ $COOH$	$-CH_2-C(CH_3)-$ $\vert$ $COOH$
Poly (methyl acrylate)	Methyl acrylate, $CH_2=CH$ $\vert$ $COOCH_3$	$-CH_2-CH-$ $\vert$ $COOCH_3$
Poly (methyl methacrylate) Poly (tetrafluoroethylene)	Methyl methacrylate, CH_3 $CH_3=C$ $\vert$ $COOCH_3$	CH_3 $\vert$ $-CH_2-C-$ $\vert$ $COOCH_3$
Poly (tetrafluoroethylene)	Tetrafluoroethylene,	
Poly (oxymethylene)	$CF_2=CF_2$	$-CF_2-CF_2-$
Poly (oxymethylene)	Formaldehyde, $CH_2=O$	$-CH_2O-$
1,4 Polyisoprene	Isoprene, CH_3 $\vert$ $CH_2=C-CH=CH_2$	CH_3 $\vert$ $-CH_2-C=CH-CH_2-$
Polycaprolactam (Nylon 6)	Caprolactam, HN ⌐- - - - - - -¬ $HN-(CH_2)_5-C=O$	O ‖ $-HN-(CH_2)_5-C-$

1.4 Length to Diameter Ratio

Length to diameter ratio of a polymer molecule is very high compared to that of a simple molecule. If a small molecule such as the ethylene molecule is represented by a dot (·), then the molecule of a polymer, say polyethylene of 1000 DP will be represented by a line (—) formed by addition of sticking together of 1000 dots in a linear fashion. This characteristic difference in length to diameter ratio between a small molecule and a polymer or a high polymer molecule makes all the difference in their physical properties.

Due to their long lengths, molecules in a given sample of a polymer material remain in a state of entanglement, both intermolecular and intramolecular. High melting or softening temperature, high melt or solution viscosity exhibited by polymer materials arise as a consequence of the big size of their molecules and the entanglements of the molecular chains.

1.5 Classification of Polymers

Important classifications of polymers are shown in Table 1.2. The basis of classification and major classes of polymers along with examples are given below :

Table 1.2 Classification of polymers

Basis of Classification	*Polymer Tubes*
Origin	Natural, semisynthetic, synthetic
Thermal response	Thermoplastic, thermosetting
Mode of formation	Addition, condensation
Line structure	Linear, branched, cross linked
Application and physical properties	Rubbers, plastics, fibres
Tracticity	Isotactic, syndiotactic, atactic
Crystallinity	Non-crystalline (amorphous), semi-crystalline, crystalline.

The basis of classification and major classes of polymers along with examples are also given below.

1.5.1 Origin

(a) Natural Polymers They are available in nature. Examplex of such polymers are : natural rubber (1, 4-cis-polyisoprene), natural silk, cellulose, starch, proteins, etc.

(b) Semisynthetic Polymers They are chemically modified natural polymers such as hydrogenated, halogenated or hydro-halogenated natural rubber cellulosics, i.e. esters and ethers of cellulose such as cellulose nitrate, methyl cellulose, etc.

(c) ***Synthetic Polymers*** They are man-made polymers prepared synthetically. Polyethylene, polystyrene, poly (vinyl chloride), polyesters, phenol-formaldehyde resins etc., are example of synthetic polymers.

1.5.2. Thermal Response

(a) Thermoplastic Polymers They can be softened or plasticized repeatedly on application of thermal energy, without much change in properties if treated with certain precautions, e.g., polyolefins, polystyrene, nylons, linear polyesters and polyethers, poly (vinyl chloride), etc. They normally remain soluble and fusible after many cycles of heating and cooling.

(b) Thermosetting Polymers They can be obtained in soluble and fusible forms in early or intermediate stages of their synthesis, but they get set or cured and become insoluble and infusible when further heated or thermally treated; the curing or setting process involves chemical reactions leading to further growth and cross linking of the polymer chain molecules and producing giant molecules, e.g. phenolic resins, urea/melamine resins, epoxy resins, diene rubbers, unsaturated polyesters, etc.

1.5.3. Mode of Formation

(a) Addition Polymers They are formed from olefinic, diolefinic,vinylic and related monomers. They all have —C—C— linkage along the main chains of the polymers molecules and usually no other atom appears in the main chain. These polymers are formed by simple additions of monomers molecules to each other in quick succession by a chain mechanism. This is known as addition polymerisation or chain-growth polymerisation. The examples of such polymers are : polyethylene, polypropylene, ploystyrene, polybutadiene, poly (vinyl chloride), etc.

(b) Condensation Polymers They are formed from intermolecular reactions between bifunctional or polyfunctional monomer molecules having reactive functional groups such as —OH, —COOH, —NH_2, —NCO, etc. The related functional groups react with each other in a stepwise manner producing condensed structural linkages, usually with the elimination of a simple, small byproduct molecule in each step in reaction. Besides —C—C— linkages, they contain such atoms as O,N,S, etc. at regular intervals in the main chain. The process of their formation is called condensation polymerisation or step-growth polymerisation. Polyamides, polyesters, polyethers, polyurethanes, phenolics, epoxy resins, etc. are examples of condensation polymers.

1.5.4. Line Structure

(a) Linear Polymers They can schematically be represented by lines of finite lengths (Fig. 1.1) They are formed from olefinic, vinyl or related polymerisation under suitable conditions or by condensation polymerisation of bifunctional monomers. Linear polymers such as high density polyethylene, poly (vinyl chloride), polystyrene, nylon 6, etc. are soluble and fusible.

(b) Branched Polymers They can be schematically represented by lines of finite lengths with short or long branch structures of repeat units (Fig. 1.1). The branches appear as a consequence of uncontrolled side

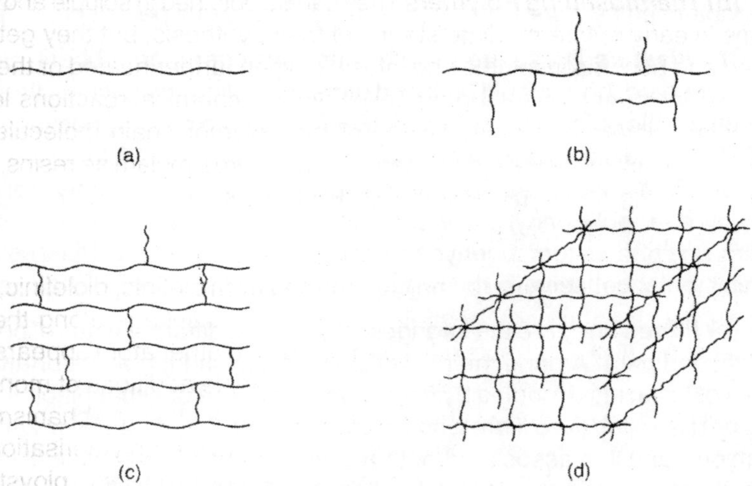

Fig. 1.1 *Schematic representation of (a) linear (b) branched (c) planar network, and (d) space network polymer structures*

reactions during polymerisation or by design of polymerisation. Branched polymers are usually more readily soluble and fusible than linear polymers of comparable chain length or moleular weight.

(c) Cross-linked or Network Polymers They can be represented by a network structure, planer-network as in graphite or space-network as in diamond (Fig. 1.1). Cross linked polymers are insoluble and infusible as the molecules in them are giant molecules, often of unusually high in infinite molecular weight. Depending on the nature and frequency of cross-links, such polymers may show different orders of swelling in solvents. Examples are: phenol-formaldehyde resins, epoxy resins, vulcanized rubber etc.

1.5.5 Application and Physical Properties

(a) Rubbers These polymers are characterised by long-range elasticity. On consideration of mechanical strength, they are rather weak, dimensionally unstable and undergo high elongations even on application of low stresses. They exhibit tensite strengths in the range of 300-3000 psi and elongation at break ranging between 300-1000%. Examples are natural rubber and synthetic rubbers. They are also known as elastomers. Technically, rubbers become useful if cross-linked to the desired extent. The cross-linking of rubber is commonly known as vulcanisation. The rubbery polymers are characterised by low molar cohesion (< 2 kcal/g mol per 5Å chain length).

(b) Plastics These are usually much stronger than rubbers. Some of them are hard, horny, rigid, stiff and dimensionally stable, while others may be soft and flexible. Plastics exhibit tensile strength ranging between 4,000-15000 psi and elongation at break ranging usually from 20 to 200% or even higher. The examples of plastics are polyethylene, polypropylene, polystyrene, poly (vinyl chloride), nylon polyamides, urea-formaldehyde resins and phenol-formaldehyde resins, polyarbonates, etc. Plastics usually exhibit molar cohesive in the range of 2-5 kcal/gmol per 5Å chain length.

(c) ***Fibres*** They are the strongest of the three different types of polymers mentioned here. Among the natural polymers of industrial importance, the foremost place is occupied by fibres, which may be of either plant or animal origin. The suitability of fibres, natural or synthetic, for use as textile materials is unique and it is associated not only with their high mechanical strength (tensile strength in the range of 20,000-150,000 psi) but also with other useful properties such as warmth or thermal insulation, softness and flexibility. Cotton cellulose, wool, silk, synthetic polyamides and plyester fibres, and acrylic fibres fall in this clan of polymers. They usually exhibit molar cohesive in the range of 4-10 kcal/g mol per 5 Å chain length.

1.5.6 Tacticity

A vinyl polymer, $—(CH_2—CHR)_n—$ is characterised by an asymmetric carbon atom in each of the repeat units of the chain molecules, and a type of stereochemical difference that they arise in the segments of the chain is *d, l* isomerism. In a polymer of this kind, such as polypropylene or polystyrene (Fig. 1.2), every alternate carbon atom indicated by an asterisk along the chain backbone is asymmetric.

Considering head to tail linkage of the repeat units, the first two asymmertic carbon atoms in each case (Fig. 1.2) have a different configuration in comparison with the last two, giving stereochemical sequence represented as *–d–d–l–l*. Depending on the tacticity or spatial disposition of the substituents attached to the asymmetric carbon atoms in the chain, we can have three major and distinctive sequence, (i) isotactic sequence represented as *–d–d–d–d–d–* or *–l–l–l–l–l*, giving similar or identical spatial disposition of the substituent in the repeat units (ii) syndiotactic sequence represented as *–d–l–d–l–d–l–* where the steric placements of the substituent are such as to give strictly alternating *d* and *l* configurations, and (iii) completely random placements of the *d* and *l* configurations giving what is known as the atactic structure represented as *–d–l–d–d–l–l–l–l–d–l–d–d–*, which ultimately turns out to be a combination of isotactic and syndiotactic sequences of varying lengths. Because of high order of steric regularity in isotactic structures fostering close packing

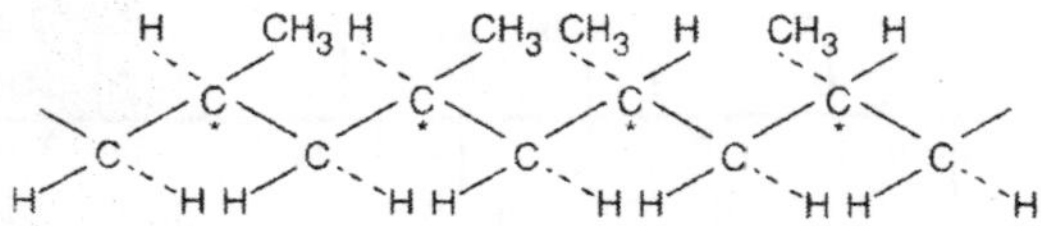

Polypropylene

(a)

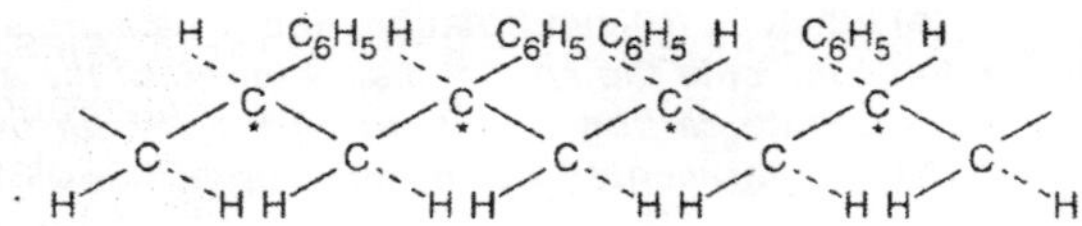

Polystyrene

(b)

Fig. 1.2 *Structures showing stereochemically similar and different sequences of repeat units for (a) polypropylene and (b) polystyrene*

of molecular chains, isotactic polymers are usually highly crystallines, whereas the randomness in placements of *d* and *l* configurations hinders molecular packing and hence development of crystallinity in atactic polymers. Syndiotactic structure, being also regular through alternation of d and l configurations, shows good tendency to crystallise. Differences in molecular structure due to tacticity difference may be understood from the line structures (Fig. 1.3.)

1.5.7. Crystallinity

When cooled from molten state, different polymers exhibit different tendencies to crystallise at different rates depending on many factors including prevailing physical conditions, chemical nature of the polymers, their molecular symmetry and structural regularity or irregularity. Bulky pendent groups or short-chain branches of different lengths hinder molecular packing and inhibit crystallisation. The nature of the crystalline state of polymers is not simple and it should not be confused with the regular geomatry of the crystal of low molecular weight compounds such as sodium chloride and benzoic acid. There are polymers which are, by the large,

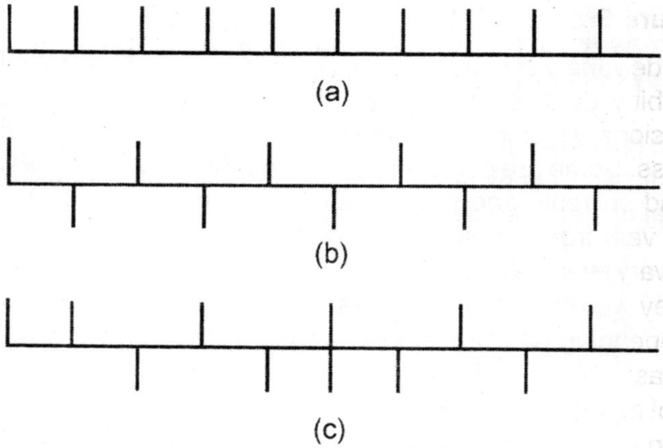

Fig. 1.3 Line structures for (a) isotactic (b) syndiotactic, and (c) atactic sequences. Small branches or vertical lines indicate the spatial dispositions of the substituent groups (R) attached to the alternate carbon atoms along the length of the vinyl polymer chain, —(CH_2—CHR)$_n$—, represented by the horizontal line.

amorphous and have very poor tendency to get transformed into ordered or oriented structure on cooling to near or even below room temperature. Natural or synthetic rubbrs, and glassy polymers such as polystyrene, acrylate and methacrylate polymers are polymers of this nature. In a crystalline polymer, a given polymer chain exists in or passes through several crystalline and amorphous zones. The crystalline zones are made up of intermolecular/intramolecular alignment or orderly (and hence closely packed) arrangement fo molecules or chain segments, and a lack of it leads to formation of amorphous zones. Polymers showing a high extent of crystallinity (>60%) are commonly known as crystalline polymers and those showing a significant but relatively poor degree of crystallinity are termed as semicrystalline polymers. Stress-incuded molecular orientation in a polymeric system is schematically represented in Fig. 1.4.

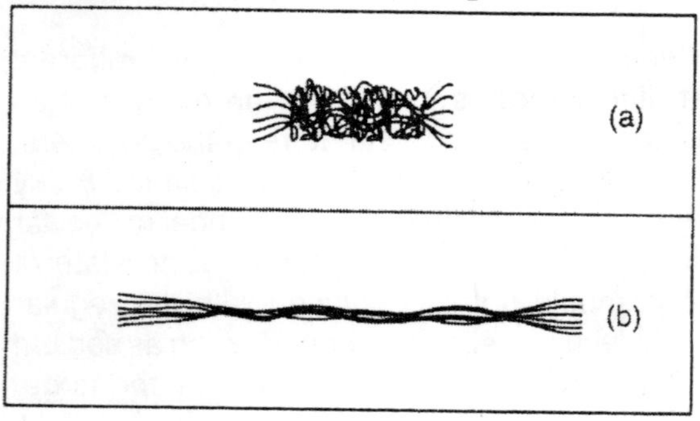

Fig. 1.4 Schematic representation of (a) unoriented (melt normally cooled), and (b) oriented (cold drawn from melt) structures of polymer molecules, orientation having taken place in the direction of the applied stress.

1.6 Structure-Property Relationship

The wide variety of natrual, semisynthetic and synthetic polymers known today exhibit wide diversity of properties. Some are rigid, hard and strong and dimensionally stable, while others are soft, flexible or largely deformable under stress. Some are soluble and fusible while others are more resistant to heat and solvents and may be even insoluble and infusible. All such properties vary from a polymer of one type to a polymer of another type. They may vary even between samples of the same type of polymer depending on how they were prepared and treated thermomechanically before being tested. Depending on the property ranges they exhibit, the polymers are classified as rubbers, plastics and fibres. To find a relation between the structure of a polymer and its physical properties, the factors which largely influence in properties should be primarily considered. These factors are: molecular weight, polarity, crystallinity, molar cohasion, linearity and non-linearity of polymeric chains, thermomechanical history of the polymer and temperature of observation, etc. The simple consideration of chemical structure of the repeat units to predict properties, particularly the mechanical behaviour has certain limitations. This is because the chemical structure of individual molecules or segments thereof contributes partly and often indirectly to mechanical properties and a more consequential and direct role is very often played by the supramolecular structure, i.e. the physical arrangement of the chain molecules with respect to each other, more so for crystalline polymers.

1.6.1 Molecular Weight

The molecular weight and molecular weight distribution in polymer systems play an important role in determining their bulk properties. Higher molecular weight permits greater degree of chain entanglements in higher melting or softening temperature and tensile strength. The general trend of variation of melting (softening) point and tensile strength of a polymer is shown in Fig. 1.5.

1.6.2. Linearity and Non-linearity of Polymer Chains

The properties of a polymer would largely depend on whether its chains are predominantly linear, branched to different extents or cross-linked. Linear polymers are mostly soluble and fusible. Small extents of branching make the otherwise equivalent polymer less resist to solvents, chemicals and heat, owing to enhanced molecular mobility manifested through the brances or pendent groups. High degrees of branching and ultimate cross-linking make the polymer relatively stiff through greater of chain entanglements

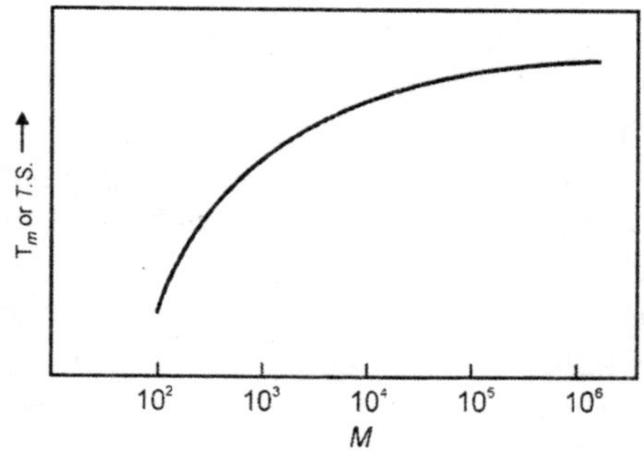

Fig. 1.5 General trend of variation of melting (softening) temperature, (T_m) and tensile strength (T.S.) of a polymer with variation of molecular weight (M)

and ultimately forming giant molecules of a network structure, thus restraining large scale molecular mobility or chain slippage and improving dimensional stability. Polymers thereby become less soluble and less fusible, and ultimately, insoluble and infusible. The mechanical strength increases substantially due to crosslinking which is clearly examplified by the curing or cross-linking of a host of thermosetting polymer systems such as the curing of penolic and urea resins, vulcanisation of rubbers etc.

Through establishment of cross-links, basic structural changes in the polymers are introduced and consequently, basic changes or improvements in properties are often achieved. By proper design of the process and according to the set objectives, different levels of cross-linking, low or high, may be achieved (Fig. 1.6).

In most commercial cross-linkable polymer systems, the established cross-links are covalent bonds and the process limitation is that the shaping of the polymer to a useful article must be accomplished before completion of the cross -linking. The process is mostly irreversible, and regeneration of the heat softenable uncross-linked structure for reprocessing is seldom possible.

1.6.3. Molar Cohesion, Polarity and Crystallinity

These factors or parameters are interrelated. A chain molecules having a strong polar structure for each repeat unit exerts strong attractive force on molecules around it. In the absence of such polar structures, the molar cohesion would be weak. Let us consider the two polymers; polyethylene, $—(CH_2—CH_2)_n—$, and nylon 6 polyamide. $[—(CH_2)_5—\overset{\overset{\displaystyle O}{\|}}{C}—\underset{\underset{\displaystyle H}{|}}{N}—]_n$ The methylene links in each polymer are practically non-polar, whereas the interunit linkage (—CONH—) in the polyamide is strongly polar. Assuming degree of polymerisation such that the chains are of equal lengths, the forces of attraction between the polyamide chains will be very much stronger than those between the polyethylene chains. This is reflected in much higher rigidity, tensile strength, melting point and crystallising tendencies of the polyamide. Moreover, extensive intermolecular hydrogen bond formation takes places in the polyamide, particularly on stretching it from the melt condition as it is cooled, resulting in the formation of the polyamide fibre.

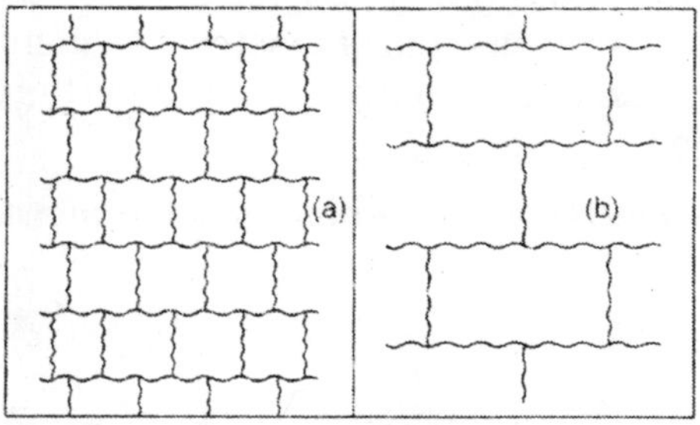

Fig. 1.6 *Schematic representation of cross-linked polymer structures: (a) high cross-link density, and (b) low cross-link density*

Again, though polyethylene has a weak molar cohesion which is of the same order as for the various rubbers, natural and synthetic, it does not really exhibit rubbery proprties; instead it is one of the most useful plastics known. Its improved physical (mechanical) properties are basically due to its very simple chemical structure. The architectural symmetry of its molecules facilitates close packing of the chains into a lattice structure, inducing crystallinity and strength. Besides the architectural symmetry, recurrence symmetry is also improved in determining the total forces of attraction between chains, particularly when oriented. This is very often illustrated by copolymerisation of two monomers leading to loss of recurrence symmetry, and also by chain branching. Thus, polyethylene prepared by the high-pressure method (free radical mechanism) and the one by the low-pressure method (anionic co-ordination mechanism) greatly differ in their properties; the low-pressure polyethylene being higher melting, its density and rigidity being higher and this polymer having higher degree of crystallinity. The reason is that the low-pressure polyethylene is predominantly linear and hence it has high degree of molecular symmetry, while the high pressure polyethylene is fairly branched, thus poorer in molecular symmetry.

The influence of molecular symmetry on polymer properties is also exemplified by the chemical modification of cellulose. Cellulose, originally an infusible fibre of good strength, resistant to solvents and having a good degree of crystallinity due to extensive intermolecular hydrogen bonds through the hydroxyl groups, is easily transformed into useful plastic products with good solubility in selected solvents and more or less well defined softening or melting points on progressive substitution of OH groups by esterification and etherification. As the consequence of these reactions, the high architectural and recurrence symmetry of cellulose chain molecules are progressively lost and hydrogen bonds are destroyed considerably. The completely modified cellulose, giving a degree of substitution equal to three, would normally have better strength characteristics than the incompletely modified products, because by complete modification the overall molecular symmetry is regained.

It is apparently surprising that the melting points of most linear aliphatic polyesters $HO{-}[(CH_2)_x{-}O\overset{\displaystyle O}{\underset{}{\overset{\|}{C}}}{-}(CH_2)_y{-}\overset{\displaystyle O}{\overset{\|}{C}}O]_n{-}H$ having polar $-\overset{\displaystyle O}{\overset{\|}{C}}-O-$ interunit linkages lie well below that of polyethylene[6] (Fig. 1.7). This may be partly explained considering that the contributions of the polar $(-\overset{\displaystyle O}{\overset{\|}{C}}-O-)$ groups in enhancing molar cohesion are far outweight by the flexibility effects imparted to the chains through the oxygen linkages in the chain backbone. The

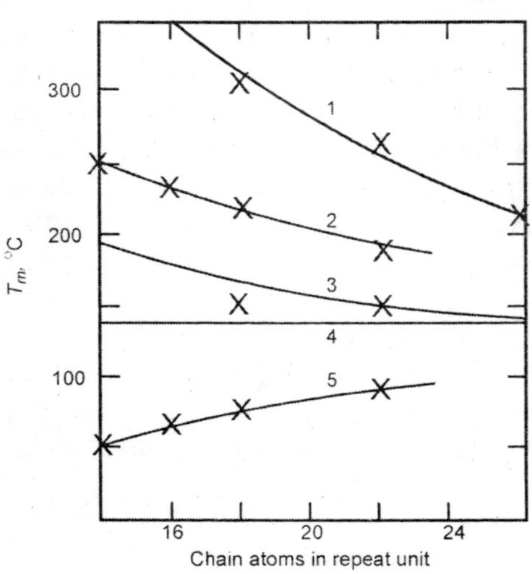

***Fig. 1.7** Trend of change of melting point (T_m) with variation of number of chain carbon atoms in repeat units in several linear (aliphatic) condensation polymers, viewed against the melting point of linear polyethylene (Curve-4) : Curves 1,2,3 and 5 are for polyureas, polyamides, polyurethanes and polyesters respectively. The melting points approach that of polyethylene as spacing between the polar interunit linkage is increased.*

increase in chain flexibility and hence lowering of melting point by oxygen linkages in the main chain is also illustrated by a much lower melting point (nearly 150°C) for the polyurethane $[\text{—(CH}_2)_5\text{—N(H)—C(=O)—O—}]_n$ than that for the analogous polyamide $[\text{—(CH}_2)_5\text{—N(H)—C(=O)—}]_n$ having melting point of 215°C.

Incorporation or rigid bulky groups such as an aromatic ring in the chain makes the polymer stiff and hence higher melting. Thus, while linear aliphatic polyesters are highly flexible and low melting polymers (Fig. 1.7.) the aromatic linear polyester, poly (ethylene terephathalate), H—[OOC—C_6H_4—COO—$(CH_2)_2$]n—OH is a relatively rigid polymer of high melting point (>250°C) and it can be readily drawn into a fibre of high strength, crystallinity and resistance to solvents and weathering conditions. Its improved physical properties are not due to enhanced molar cohesion, since an aromatic ring has nearly the same molar cohesion as six linear methylene groups, but are mostly due to the bulk and rigidity of the aromatic ring in each repeat unit, resulting in great hindrance to rotation and thus, reducing chain flexibility and at the same time enhancing chain stiffness enormously. Symmetrical structure of the terephathalic acid units also permits a close fitting of the chain molecules into a crystal lattice. On the other hand aromatic bifunctional compounds having functional groups in the *ortho* and *meta*

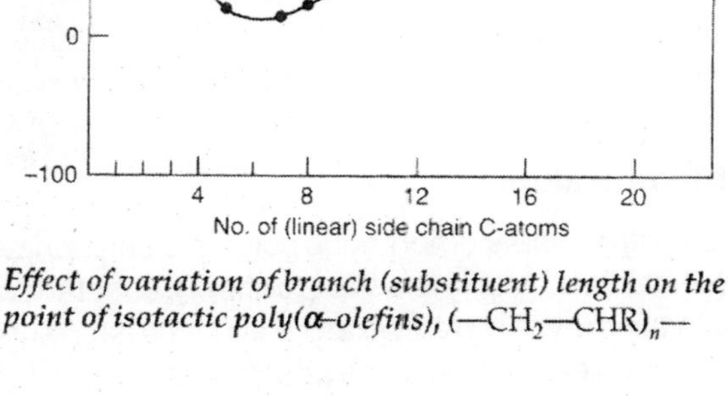

Fig. 1.8 *Effect of variation of branch (substituent) length on the melting point of isotactic poly(α-olefins),* $(\text{—CH}_2\text{—CHR})_n\text{—}$

positions yield similar polymers with inferior physical and mechanical properties mainly due to their poor molecular symmetry, resulting in their inability to fit into a lattice structure as closely as for polymers from the corresponding aromatic bifunctional compounds with functionalities in the *para* positions.

The intermolecular forces are opposed by thermal agitation. The effect of chain length is mainly extensive, i.e. total force of intermolecular attraction increases owing to greater molecular surface while the force per unit length or area remains constant. But contrast, polarity is intensive; more polar the structure, greater the attractive force per unit length on area. It is important to note that the effects of these factors are relatively short range and hence, minor and subtle variations in chemical structure may notably affect the physical behaviour of polymers.Structure-property relationship highlighting differences affected by aliphatic and aromatic structural units and the effect of flexible (—O—, —S—) and polar (—SO_2—) interunit linkages can be further appreciated by examining Table 1.3.

The polymer properties are also highly dependent on the spatial disposition of the side groups or side chains. The stereoregular (isotactic) polymers are of high degree of crystallinity and they exhibit higher strength and melting point than those exhibited by the corresponding random (atactic) polymers. The lengthening of the substituent group of the higher isotactic poly (α-olefin) homologoes decreases the melting point up to polyheptene; from this point the melting point curve follows on increasing trend (Fig. 1.8). The initial falling trend in melting point is due to repulsion of the bulky side groups in the crystalline region. The upward trend in melting point is probably a result of developing trends in crystallinity involving the relatively long flexible side groups, i.e. a case of side chain crystallinity. Further, dependence of physical properties on structural isomerism is vividly reflected in the well-known examples of 1,4-*cis*-polyisoprene (natural rubber) and 1,4-trans-polyisoprene (gutta percha) (See also Sec. 5.9); the former, being normally devoid of or poorer in crystallinity, is more flexible and behaves as a rubber, while the latter is a good plastic having good order of crystallinity in the normal condition.

1.6.4. Effect of Temperature

Roughly speaking, all linear amorphous polymers can behave as Hookian elastic (glassy) materials, highly elastic (rubbery) substances or viscous melts according to the prevailing temperature and time-scale of experiments. Different property profiles for the same polymer at different temperatures

Table 1.3 Thermal properties of some aliphatic and aromatic polymers (thermoplastics)

Polymer	*Repeat Unit*	T_g,°C	T_m,°C	*Remarks*
Polyethylene (linear, PE)	$—CH_2—CH_2—$	—115, —60	137	General puprose, low modulus polymer with good degree of toughness; excellent electrical insulator
Polystyrene, PS	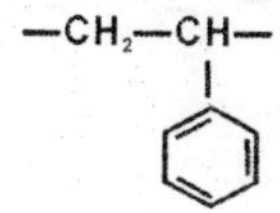	80 to 100	240	Rigid, brittle transparent polymer; excellent insulator
Poly (vinyl naphthalene), PVN	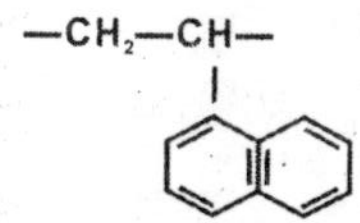	150	360	Highly rigid, brittle polymer, excellent insulator
Poly (para-phenylene), PPP		—	530	Tough, thermostable, intractable polymer with semiconducting or even good conducting (when doped) properties with electrical conductivity in the range 10^{-18} to 10^{2} $(\Omega cm)^{-1}$
Poly (tetramethylene oxide) PTMO	$—(CH_2)_4—O—$	-80	60	Weak, flexible polymer
Poly (phenylene ether), PPE	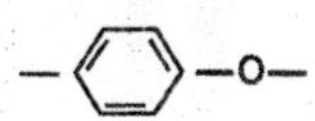	80	300	A good engineering thermoplastic, having high strength and toughness
Poly (phenylene oxide), PPO	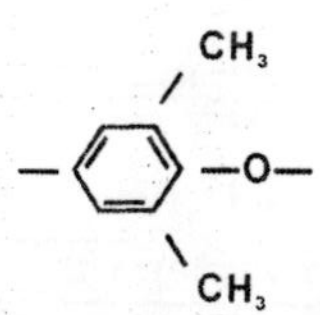	209	—	Very low water absorption; more resistant (chemically, mechanically and thermally) than PPE

(Contd.)

Table 1.3 (Contd.)

Polymer	*Repeat Unit*	T_g, °C	T_m, °C	*Remarks*
Poly (tetramethylene sulphide), PTMS	$—(CH_2)_4—S—$	—	70	Weak flexible polymer
Poly(phenylene sulphide), PPS	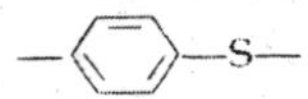	90	295	Strong, tough, thermally resistant polymer. Normally a good insulator, but when properly doped, say with 2–5% AsF_5, it assumes a semiconducting character
Poly(tetramethylene sulphone), PTMSO	$—(CH_2)_4—SO_2—$	—	270	Presence of strongly polar sulphone ($—SO_2—$) links makes the polymer mechanically strong and thermally more stable, as can be realized by comparing PTMSO with PTMS or PTMO
Poly(phenylene sulphone), PPSO	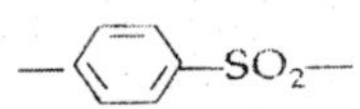	350	525	Mechanically very strong and thermally stable up to 500 °C; high-performance plastic
Poly(ether sulphone), PES	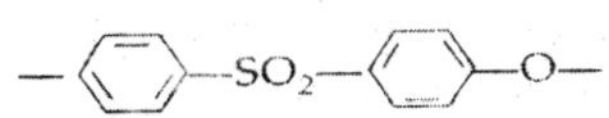	230	—	Thermostable, high performance transparent thermoplastic with improved processability in comparison with PPSO
Poly(ether ketone), PEK	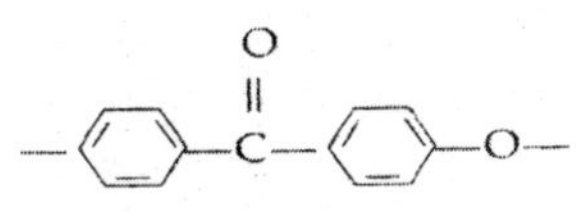	155	365	High performance thermoplastic with excellent environmental stress cracking resistance; continuous use temperature nearly 275°C
Poly(ether ether ketone) PEEK	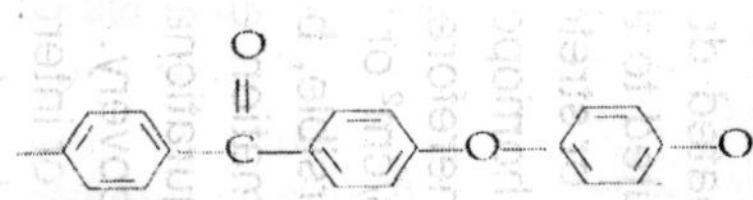	140	343	High performance, chemical resistant thermoplastic, showing a high continuous use temperature (250°C)

are related to variation in the physical structures or arrangements of the chain molecules as a consequence of different types and degrees of deformation.

1.6.5 Survey of Deformation Behaviour in the Amorphous State

An idealised graph of log (shear) modulus vs. temperature is shown in Fig. 1.9. The modulus curve usually shows a number of transitions each of which is connected with the gradual development of a specific kind of molecular movement.

At a temperature below the corresponding transition temperature, the molecular processes in question are frozen in. With rise in temperature, and in the vicinity of a transition point, an additional molecular movement begins to contribute to the deformation mechanism and hence lowers the resistance to deformation, i.e. the modules.

At very low temperatures, the only deformation occurring is Hookian elastic deformation which is time-independent and mechanically reversible. It takes place almost instantaneously and the deformation recovers instantaneously and completely on removal of the force or stress applied. The deformation is also thermodynamically reversible, as no energy is dissipated during the stress-strain cycle. The Hookian deformation is attributed to the small changes in valence angles and valence distances (bend or stretch of bonds) that take place against the strong binding forces of the homopolar bonds (dissociation energy, 30-200 kcal/mol), (Table 1.4), and therefore, it is associated with a high modulus in the region of 10^{10} dynes/cm^2 or higher. At sufficiently high temperatures, flow which is totally irreversible, both mechanically and thermodynamically, takes place. The deformation energy is dissipated as heat in the viscous melt and little configurational free energy is left after the deformation and hence there is no recovery. The polymer melt may be viewed as a cluster of randomly coiled or intercoiled molecules with very limited or no restriction on rotation of molecular segments due to closely neighbouring molecules. the deformation mechanism involved at this stage is slippage of molecular chains relative to each other but at the same time large scale displacement of chain segments normal to their chain axes is restricted, thereby giving rise to high melt viscocity. Cross-linked polymers are not expected to exhibit the flow phenomenon.

1.6.6 Transitions and Rubbery Region

The intermediate regions present some interesting deformation behaviours. The different transitions, shown schematically in Fig. 1.9, are

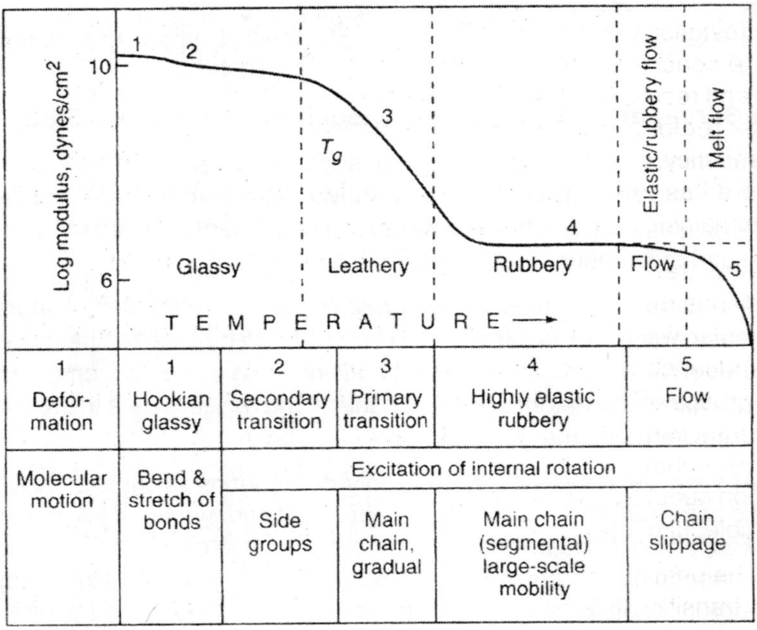

Fig. 1.9 ***Temperature dependence of log (shear) modulus in polymer system showing molecular mechanism of the deformations taking place at different points***

Table 1.4 Characteristics of typcial primary valence bonds.

Nature/Type of Bond	Average Bond Distance, A	Average Dissociation Energy, Kcal/mol
C—H	1.10	98
C—C	1.54	80
C=C	1.34	145
C—O	1.46	85
C=O	1.21	180
C—N	1.47	75
C≡N	1.15	215
C—Cl	1.77	80
C—F	1.32-1.40	100-125
O—H	0.96	110
N—H	1.01	92
O—O	1.32	34

manifestations of viscoelastic deformations which are time dependent in nature, reaching at the respective point an equilibrium value after a certain time and recovering after a time of the same magnitude. The deformation in these regions is often mechanically reversible, but owing to time-dependency, thermodynamically irreversible. A part of the deformation energy is stored as free energy which takes care of mechanical reversibility and the remaining part of the deformation energy is dissipated as heat.

The transitions schematically shown as primary and secondary transitions may be close or widely separated depending on the nature and molecular weight of the polymer. The secondary transition(s) arise as a consequence of inducement of thermal excitations involving rotation of the side groups of the polymeric chains and it generally leads to relatively small decrease in modules. Although, inception of rotation of small segments of the main chains is also attributed to such transitions but by the large the rotation about the bonds of the backbone chain is still strongly hindered and the molecular chains as a whole remain stiff.

The primary transition corresponds to what is commonly known as the glass transition temperature (T_g), and this transition arises as a consequence of excitation of rotation of segments of the main chains. Almost all polymers show a primary transition or a characteristic glass transition, but many of them may not exhibit a distinct secondary transition. Through the glass transition or primary transition, the polymers suffers a sharp and large change in modulus.

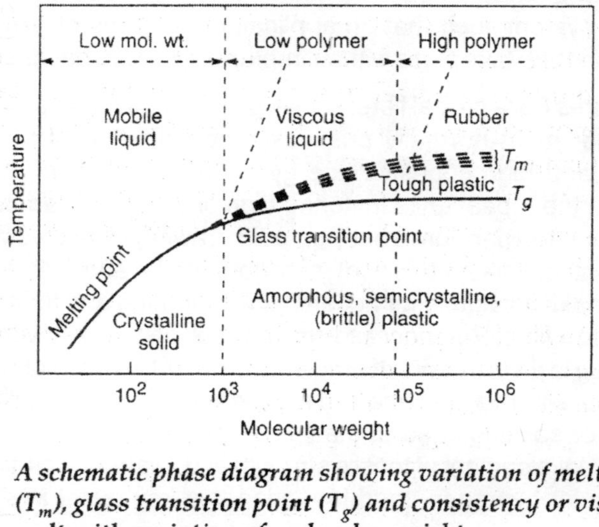

Fig. 1.10 ***A schematic phase diagram showing variation of melting point (T_m), glass transition point (T_g) and consistency or viscosity of melt with variation of molecular weight***

1.6.7. Property Demand and Polymer End-Use

A schematic though rough and approximate phase diagram for polymers is given in Fig. 1.10. It shows (i) how the melting temperature (T_m) and the glass transition temperature (T_g) vary and tend to level off with increase in molecular weight, (ii) how viscocity of melts varies with extension of chain lengths and (iii) the different regions or zones over which properties typical of plastics, rubbers, viscous fluids, etc. may be found.

(a) ***Elastomers or Rubbers*** It is apparent from the diagram that while useful plastic properties may be exhibit by polymers of wide molecular weight range (low polymer and high polymer), good useful rubbery properties are exhibited by polymers which are essentially high polymeric in nature. For revelation of rubberiness, the polymers must be far above their T_g and for practical advantage and common use, T_g for elastomers or rubbers should be in the range-40 to 80°C. This is very commonly attained in systems of low cohesive energy density (Table 1.5) and poor molecular symmetry resulting in amorphousness, at least in the unstrained state and permitting enough freedom of molecular motion so that deformation of high magnitude take place rapidly. Although, these requirements and features for elastomers imply high local or segmental mobility, the gross or full scale mobility as in the flow region must be low in practical elastomers. Restricted chain slippage must be assured in view of property demand in the form of regain of original shape and dimension on release of stress. This restriction is technically achieved through introduction of widely spaced primary valence cross-links in the chain molecular system such that on application of forces of extension, large deformations can take place without rupture of primary bonds.

(b) ***Fibres*** For a typical fibre, showing high tensile strength and modulus, the polymer must normally possess a combination of high molecular symmetry and high cohesive energy density manifested through polar structure in the repeat units fostering high order of permanent crystallinity (in the useful temperature zone) on cold drawing. The crystalline melting point, T_m (without decomposition) must normally be above 200°C and below 300°C to make it suitable for hot pressing or ironing and for its trouble-free spinning into a fibre. Resistance to common solvents is an advantage keeping dry cleaning in view. Again, the molecular weight should not be too high for synthetic fibre-forming polymers to ensure speedy and trouble free spinning from melt or solutions and at the same time it should be high enough to ensure full development of tensile strength and related properties. Extensive intermolecular hydrogen bond formation is a key factor in synthetic fibre technology.

(c) ***Plastics*** In general, the properties of plastics are more or less intermediate between those of fibres and elastomers, with good amount of overlap on one or the other side. Plastics are put to use in a wide range of applications and hence a wide variety of property combinations is associated with them. Consequently, a wide variety of structure may adequately describe them. Some polymers having high cohesive energy density such as nylon polyamides, behave as plastics when used without orientation of the molecules by stretching. But on orientation of the molecules by stretching or cold drawing major changes in the structure of their physical agglomerates take place leading to high order to crystallisation and the respective polymers then behave as excellent fibres.

The difference between rubbers, plastics and fibres is not really basic or very intrinsic, it is rather a matter of degree. Small or minor variations in chemical structure or physical conditioning often bring about significantly property variations and may transform a rubber to a resin or a plastic or vice-versa and a plastic to a fibre or vice versa. Thus, (i) moderate to extensive cyclisation, hydro-halogenation or halogenation of natural rubber, transforms it into a resinous product; (ii) limited chlorosulphonation of polyethylene introducing Cl atoms and $-SO_2Cl$ groups in the chain molecule through simultaneous treatment with chlorine and sulphur dioxide gas under pressure breaks its molecular symmetry and transforms this general purpose plastic into a synthetic rubber despite enhancement of polarity; blending or mixing with a liquid plasticiser readily transforms and hard rigid plastic poly (vinyl chloride), PVC into a leathery or rubbery product; (iii) limited N-alkylation of nylon polyamides makes them stretchable even when made into a fibre, and highly N-alkylated polyamides of comparable chain length become very soft or even liquids. Cellulose, an insoluble and infusible fibre, is readily transformed into good plastics on esterification or etherification. N-alkylation for the aliphatic polyamides and substitution of OH groups in cellulose reduce intermolecular hydrogen bond formation, resulting in weakening of the polymer systems.

1.6.8 Nature of Intermolecular Forces

Between molecules or chain segments not connected by primary (covalent) bonds, the so-called secondary bonds or Van der Walls forces give rise to attractive forces. The energy of the intermolecular attractive forces varies as the inverse sixth power of the intermolecular separation. It is nearly two orders of magnitude weaker than the covalent bonds. The cohesive energy amounts to the total energy required to remove a molecule in a liquid to a position far from its neighbours. The cohesive energy per unit volume, widely referred to as the cohesive energy density for a few commonly

Table 1.5 *Cohesive energy densities of some linear polymers* [8,9]

Polymer	*Repeat Unit*	*Cohesive Energy Density, Cal/cm³*
Polyethylene	$—CH_2—CH_2—$	56-64
Polystyrene	$—CH_2—CH\ (C_6H_5)—$	75-88
Polyisobutylene	$—CH_2—C(CH_3)_2—$	56-64
Polyisoprene (natural rubber)	$—CH_2—C(CH_3)C{=}CH—CH_2—$	60-67
Poly (vinyl acetate)	$—CH_2—CH\ (OCOCH_3)—$	82-94
Poly (vinyl chloride)	$—CH_2—CHCl—$	85-95
Poly (methyl methacrylate)	$—CH_2—C(CH_3)\ (COOCH_3)—$	78-85
Poly (ethylene terephthalate)	$—OCH_2CH_2OOCC_6H_4CO—$	90-115
Poly (hexamethylene adipamide, nylon - 66	$—HN(CH_2)_6NHCO(CH_2)_4CO—$	180-220
Polyacrylonitrile	$—CH_2—CH(CN)—$	150-230

used polymers is listed in Table 1.5 which clearly shows how variation in this parameter depends on molecular structure.

Among the different types of secondary valence forces known, one type arises from polarity of the molecules and it is manifested through interaction of dipoles. The magnitude of such interaction energy is dependent on the mutual alignment of the interacting dipoles. As molecular alignments are opposed by thermal agitation, the dipole forces are very much dependent on temperature.

Another kind of intermolecular interaction is that induced by polar molecular or segments through the dipoles on surrounding molecules or segments that do not have permanent dipoles.

The secondary bond forces consequent to interaction between permanent dipoles and induced dipoles are known as the induction forces.

The cohesive energy corresponding to the induction force is small and it does not depend on temperature.

There are also dispersion forces which are not dependent on polarity or permanent dipoles but which are consequences of different instantaneous configuration of electrons and nuclei of all kinds of molecules, resulting in time varying dipole moments that average out to zero. The dispersion forces exist in all molecular systems, polar or non-polar and constitute a major part of the cohesive forces except in systems having strong dipoles. In non-polar materials the molar cohesion is due only to the dispersion forces which are also independent of temperature. The energy of all the above secondary valence forces usually ranges between 2-5 kcal/mol.

A fourth but an important and major kind of intermolecular attraction, particularly in polar molecules containing fluorine, nitrogen, oxygen and occasionally chlorine atoms is due to hydrogen bonding. The energy of *hydrogen bonds* usually ranges between 5-10 kcal/mol and its overall cumulative effect in polymer material systems is very pronounced and sometimess overwhelming, so much so that suitable polymers having frequently and extensive hydrogen bonds along the chains, such as cellulose, polyamides, polyacrylonitrile, etc. are inherently crystalline and resistant to heat and solvents (see the idealised structure of pairs of molecules in each case in Fig. 1.11.). The exact nature of the hydrogen bond depends on the chemical nature and environment of the concerned polar groups and it is considered, in most systems, electrostatic or ionic and character. The average attractive force between section of polymer molecules in an oriented domain or crystal lattice is higher than that between sections that are not in a lattice. Crystallites are usually 10-15% more dence than the supercooled melt at the same temperature.

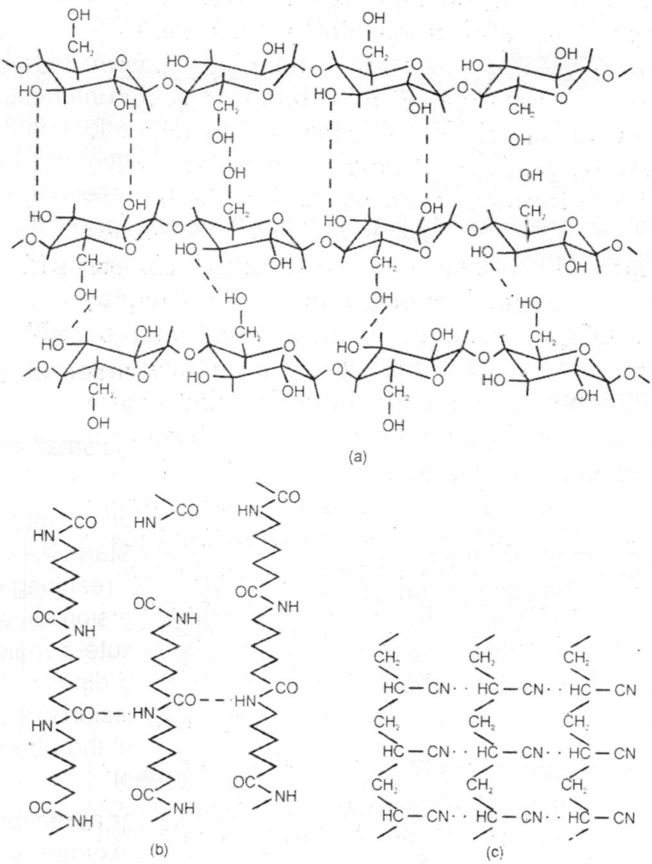

***Fig. 1.11** Idealised representation of segments of chain molecules of (a) cellulose fibre (b) (melt drawn) oriented nylon 6 polyamide fibre, and (c) oriented polyacrylonitrile fibre, showing formation of intermolecular hydrogen bonds in each case.*

2

Raw Materials

General

In addition to the developments in new products and techniques, outlined in the previous chapter, there has been a gradual evolution in the raw material used for the manufacture of plastics and rubbers. The original plastic, cellulose nitrate, was based on cellulose, usually in the form of wood-pulp, while the phenol and formaldehyde needed for the early phenol-formaldehyde resins were obtained from coal. Today, the emphasis has shifted very largely to petroleum and natural gas, especially in the U.S.A., where the larger part of plastics production is based on these materials.

In general, then, we may classify the main raw materials for plastics and rubbers into three groups :

(a) Natural products (cellulose, casein, etc.)

(b) Coal

(c) Petroleum and natural gas.

The members of the first group are, on the whole being replaced continuously, but the last two groups were both formed earliers in the earth's history and are irreplaceable.

The number of polymers and their intermediates is so great as to render it impossible to describe the manufacture of all the necessary raw materials in one chapter. Brief notes on the most important are given, therefore supplemented by diagrams showing the main routes by which polymers can be obtained from various raw materials.

Natural Products

Nature has conveniently provided for our use many excellent materials with long-chain structures eminently suitable for modification to useful polymers. The manufacture of cellulose nitrate is, of course, the earliest example of such a modification, other examples being cellulose acetates (also from cellulose) and casein plastics from milk.

Cellulose

Cellulose is a carbohydrate and occurs as the base material of all vegetable matter although not always in a form readily available for the manufacture of industrially useful plastics. Cotton linters and wood are both commercial sources of cellulose and were in early use for the manufacture of cellulose nitrate.

Wood was also extensively used at the one time for the production (by destructive distillation) of methyl alcohol and formaldehyde, both of them very useful intermediates in the manufacture of plastics. Little use is now made of this method as other cheaper and more plentiful sources have since been founds.

Materials Containing Starch or Pentoses

Starch is another long chain carbohydrate but its utilisation by the plastics industry has been small, although it has been used as the adhesive for paper and as a size for fibres. These are theoretical methods for converting starch and certain pentoses into polymeric materials but they are not always practical and little commercial use has been made of them. A typical series of conversions is shown in Fig. 2.1.

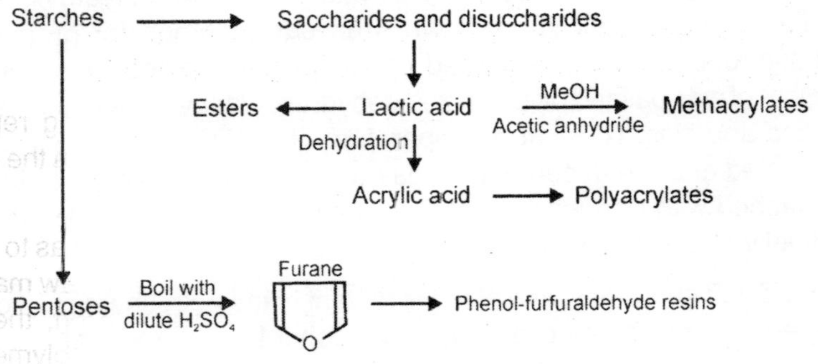

Fig. 2.1

Pentoses may be obtained from many agricultural residues such as corn waste (oat husks), furfuraldehyde being economically obtained in this way. Furfuraldehyde reacts with phenol to form resins in a manner similar to that of the better known reaction of phenol with formaldehyde.

Corn waste and other agricultural residues, such as bagasse and straw waste, can also be made to provide an alternative route to nylon 6,6. The conventional method utilises phenol as the starting point while the alternative route from agricultural residues utilises furfural.

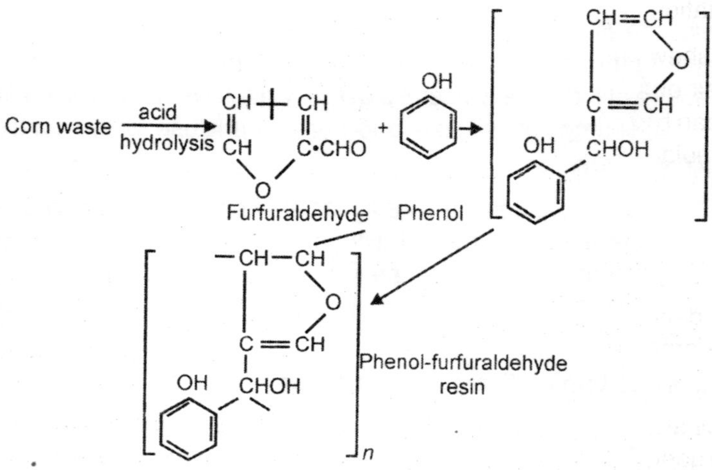

Ethyl alcohol is also readily obtainable from a variety of agricultural materials (a fact well knwon in many parts of the world, including the Scottish Highlands and the mountains of Kentucky!) among them being potatoes, corn barley, can sugar, beet sugar and molasses. Ethyl alcohol from molasses provided the ethylene for the original manufacture of polyethylene, and butadiene for synthetic rubbers while an early method for producing a synthetic rubber in Russia utilised ethyl alcohol obtained from potatoes. The alcohol was passed over a mixed dehydration/dehydrogenation catalyst (alumina and zinc oxide) at a temperature of 400°C. The reactants were then cooled and the uncondensed gas, containing most of the butadiene, was washed with turpentine or petrol. The butadiene removed in this way was finally separated by distillation.

Foodstuff shortages, and also the advent of the petrochemical industry, have led to large scale production of alcohol by this method becoming obsolete.

Materials Containing Proteins, Fats, or Oils

Ground Nuts and Cashew Nuts. The value of ground nuts as a source of food protein is well known, but at one time ground nuts were expected to be of even greater importance as a source of fibres which have properties akin to those of wool. In the initial stages of development such fibres were considered to have a bright future, but the subsequent development of acrylonitrile and polyester fibres rendered the protein fibres obsolete. The protein is obtained from ground nuts by alkaline extraction followed by acid precipitation.

Cashew nuts are of interest to the plastics industry by virtue of the fact that their out shell contains a dark-colored oil referred to as C.N.S.L. from which can be obtained an unsaturated phenol known as cardinol which has the formula.

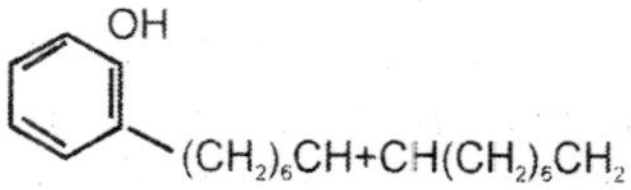

Cardanol will condence with formaldehyde to produce resins similar to phenol-formaldehyde resins but with somewhat inferior physical properties.

Zein. This material is a protein which occurs in maize. It is soluble in aqueous alcohols and can, therefore, be readily spun into fibres. The fibres are hardened in formaldehyde and then exhibit excellent resistance to solvents and greases. Unfortunately the extraction process is rather costly, which has militated against wider use of zein as a raw material.

Casein. This is the chief protein extracted cow's milk and is composed of α-amino acids. It may be precipitated from skimmed milk by either an acid or by the enzyme, rennet, the latter giving the protein in the most suitable form for plastics production. After precipitation the casein is first washed, pressed and dried. After extrusion into the required from, the material is hardened by immersion in formalin.

The main sources of casein are France, Argentina, and New Zealand.

Castor Oil. The material has assumed a particular importance in recent years as a source of one of the nylon (nylon 11 or 'Rilsan'). The castor is reacted with methanol, alcoholysis occurring to give methyl ricionleate. Particulars of the manufacturing process are given in the chapter on polyamides, but briefly the sequence of operations is pyrolysis of the methyl ricinoleate to give methyl andecylenate and hydrolysis of this to undecylenic acid. The acid is then reacted with ammonia to give the amino acid, 11-amino-undecanoic acid, which is then made to undergo a plycondensation reaction to give nylon 11.

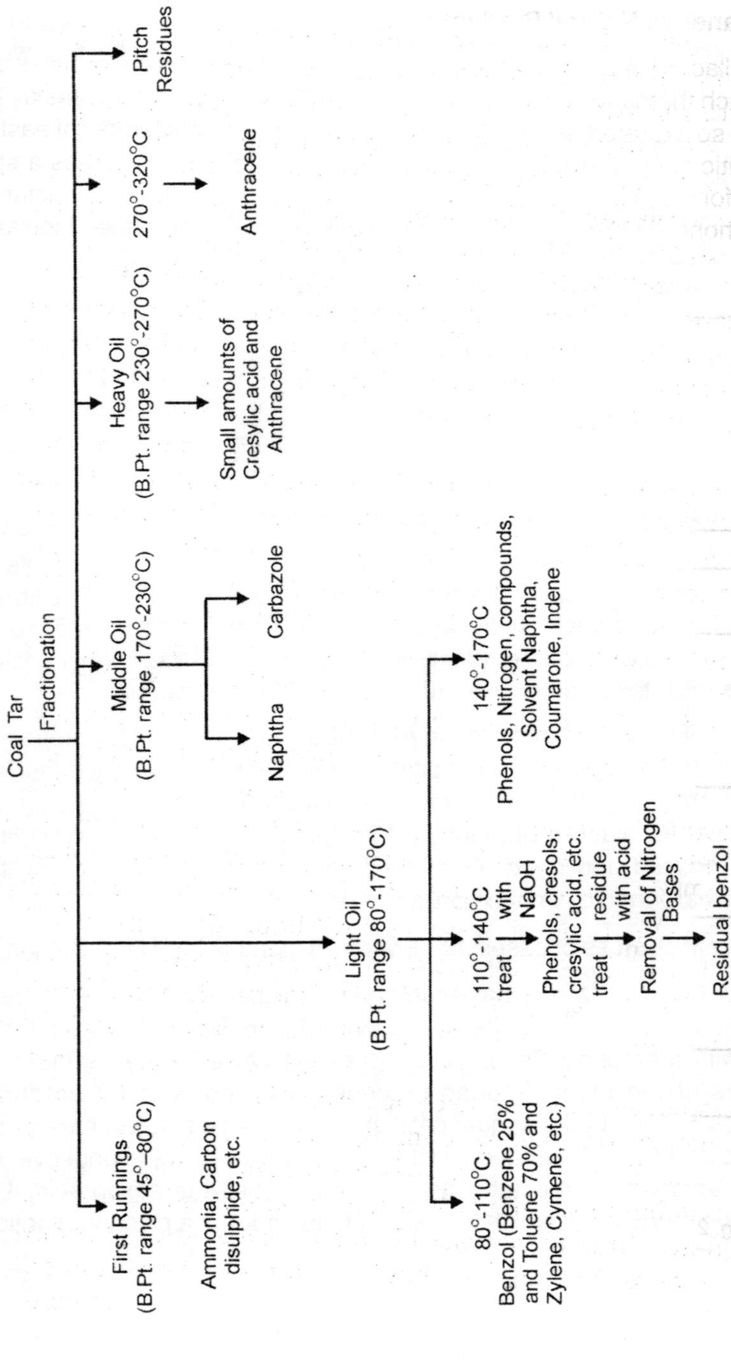
Coal Tar
Fractionation
First Runnings
(B.Pt. range 45°–80°C)
Ammonia, Carbon
disulphide, etc.
Light Oil
(B.Pt. range 80°-170°C)
80°-110°C
Benzol (Benzene 25%
and Toluene 70% and
Zylene, Cymene, etc.)
110°-140°C
treat with NaOH
Phenols, cresols,
cresylic acid, etc.
treat residue with acid
Removal of Nitrogen
Bases
Residual benzol
140°-170°C
Phenols, Nitrogen, compounds,
Solvent Naphtha,
Coumarone, Indene
Middle Oil
(B.Pt. range 170°-230°C)
Naphtha
Carbazole
Heavy Oil
(B.Pt. range 230°-270°C)
Small amounts of
Cresylic acid and
Anthracene
270°-320°C
Anthracene
Pitch
Residues

Fig. 2.2

Miscellaneous Natural Products

Shellac. Shellac is the protective covering produced by the scale insects that attach themselves to certain trees found mainly in Southern Asia. The material so excreted is not a definite polymer but consists largely of easters of aleuritic acid. The refined material has a long history of use as a spirit lacquer for wood and has also been extensively used for the manufacture of gramophone records, as a bonding agent for mica, and as an insulating varnish.

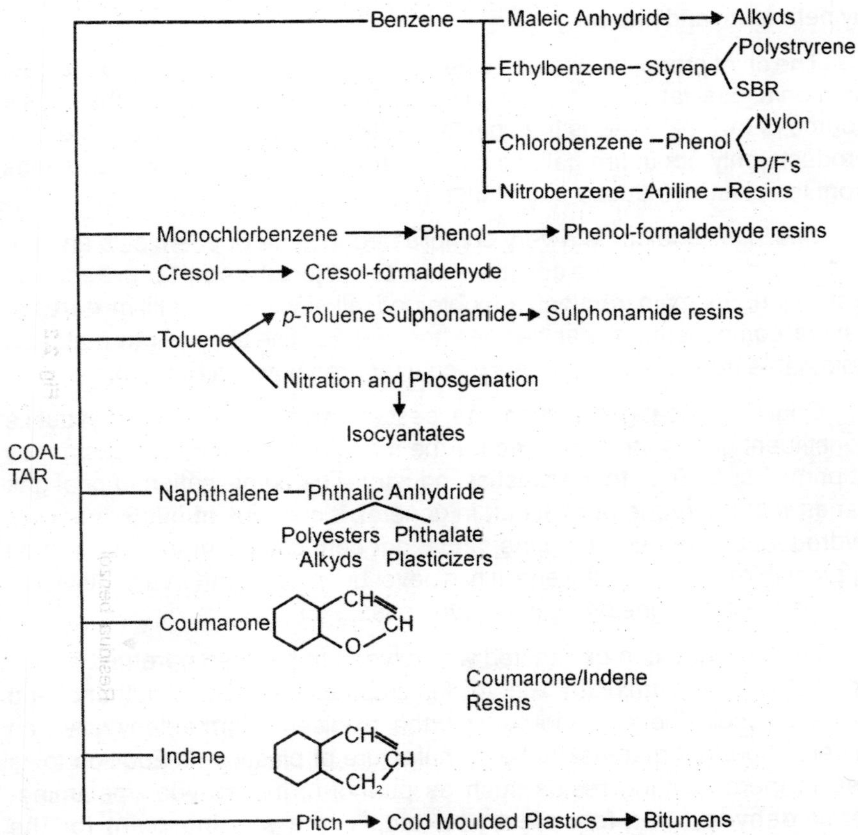

Fig. 2.3 Polymers, intermediates, and raw materials from coal tar fractions

Natural Rubber. Certain trees and other plants (of which the tree *Hevea brazilliensis* is the best-known) contain a milky white latex which can be trapped by making an incision in the bark. After collection this latex can be coagulated, washed and rolled into the crepe sheets of rubber with which are all family.

Coal

Coal was the first source of the raw materials used in the manufacture of synthetic polymers but it has now been superseded as the main sources by petroleum and natural gas.

The chief products obtained when coal is destructively distilled are gas, ammonia, coal tar and a residue of coke. The most important of these as a source of raw materials is the coal tar fraction. Since each tone of the coal products only about ten gallons of coal tar it is easy to see why demands from the plastics industry soon outstripped the supply.

Coal Tar. Coal tar is a very complicated mixture of chemicals and the first step of separating the constituents is to subject the coal tar to fractional distillation. Six main fractions are obtained, all of which are still mixtures of several components, as can be seen from Fig. 2.2 The plastics raw materials obtainable from the constituents of coal tar are shown in Fig. 2.3.

Coal Gas. Coat gas is of course, best known as a source of fuel but its constituent gases are also used for the manufacture of many substances of prime importance to the plastics industry. The complication of coal gas varies with the grade of coal but, in general, it contains about 50 per cent hydrogen, 30 per cent methane, and 8 per cent carbon monoxide with an appreciable amount of ethylene. It has never been a main source of ethylene, however, a better one being coke-oven gas.

The methane can be reacted with oxygen at high temperature, and in contact with an aluminium oxide/nickel catalyst it produces methanol and higher alcohols, the methanol being further oxidised to formaldehyde, which is very important material in the manufacture of plastics. In addition to its use in thermosetting resins such as phenol-formaldehyde, melamine-formaldehyde, urea-formaldehyde, etc. it is a starting point for the production of a family of polymers known as polyacetals (including polyformaldehyde itself), while we have already noted its use as a hardening agent for certain natural polymers such as casein and zein.

Ammonia Ammonia is of importance because of its conversion into urea and various amines. The urea is used for the manufacture of urea formaldehyde resins while amines have a variety of uses in the polymer industry, among the most important being their employment as curing agents for epoxy resins.

$$2NH_3 + CO_2 \xrightarrow{\text{Pressure}} \underset{\text{Urea}}{NH_2{\cdot}CO{\cdot}NH_2} \xrightarrow{\text{H·CHO}} \text{U/F resins}$$

Coke. Apart from its widespread use as a fuel, the importance of coke lies in its conversion to calcium carbide with subsequent reaction with water to produce acetylene. For many years coke was the main source of acetylene, but with the development of the petroleum cracking industry its global importance has greatly diminished although at the present time the carbide process is still the only one employed in the U.K.

Other chemicals obtained directed or indirectly from coke are shown in Fig. 2.4.

Petroleum

The production of chemicals from petroleum has reached immense proportions since its inception after the First World War and even an elementary account of the so-called petro-chemical industry would fill a book on its own. Some idea of the many materials of importance to the plastics industry which are now obtainable from petroleum can be seen by reference of Fig. 2.5, 2.6 and 2.7

There are three main methods by which petroleum fractions can be utilised in the production of chemical intermediates of importance to the polymer industries, and these may be summarised as follows :

1. The most important process is the cracking of various hydrocarbon feed stocks to give high yields of unsaturated gases such as ethylene, propylene, butylene, acetylene, the particular feedstock used being dictated by availability and the type of end-product required. In the U.K. the usual feedstock employed is a light pahtha distillate and at least 98 per cent of the present U.K. capacity for ethylene is based on naphtha. Other feed stocks which may be used are saturated refining gases such as propane and butane.

The feedstock is vaporized, diluted with stem, and heated rapidly to the cracking temperature. It is held at this temperature for a very short time, then rapidly cooled by quenching to prevent further reaction. The various products are then separated by fractionation.

2. Chemical intermediate are also formed during certain refining operations desiged to convert naphtha feedstocks to gasolines with high

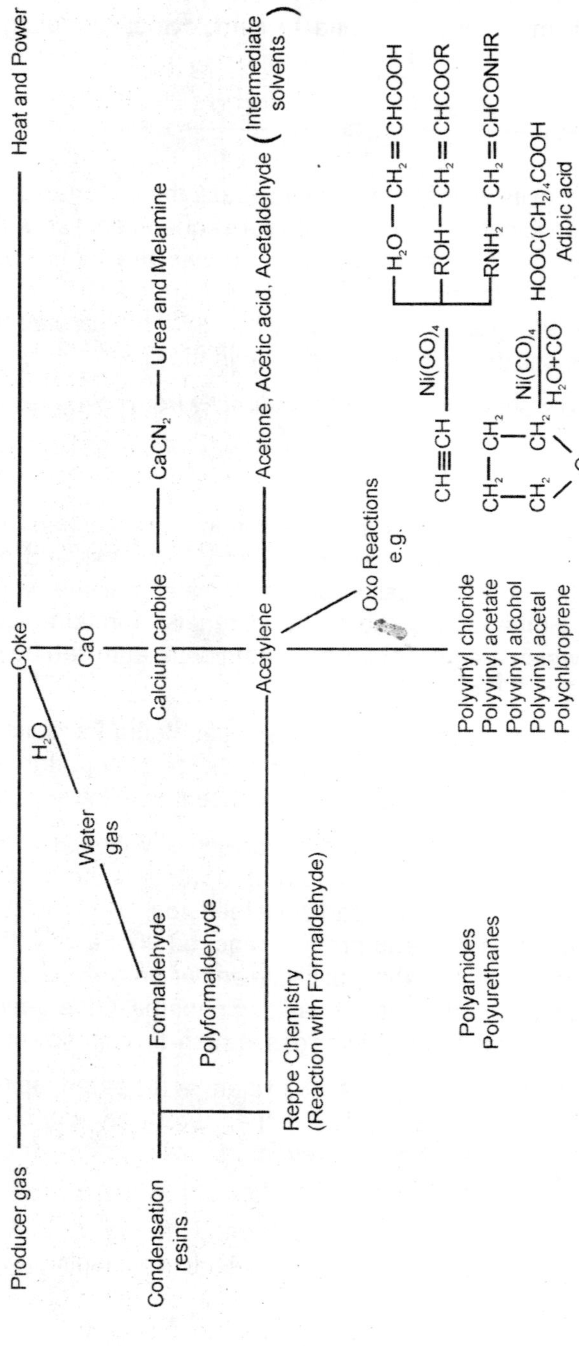

Fig. 2.4 Polymers, intermediates, and raw materials from coke

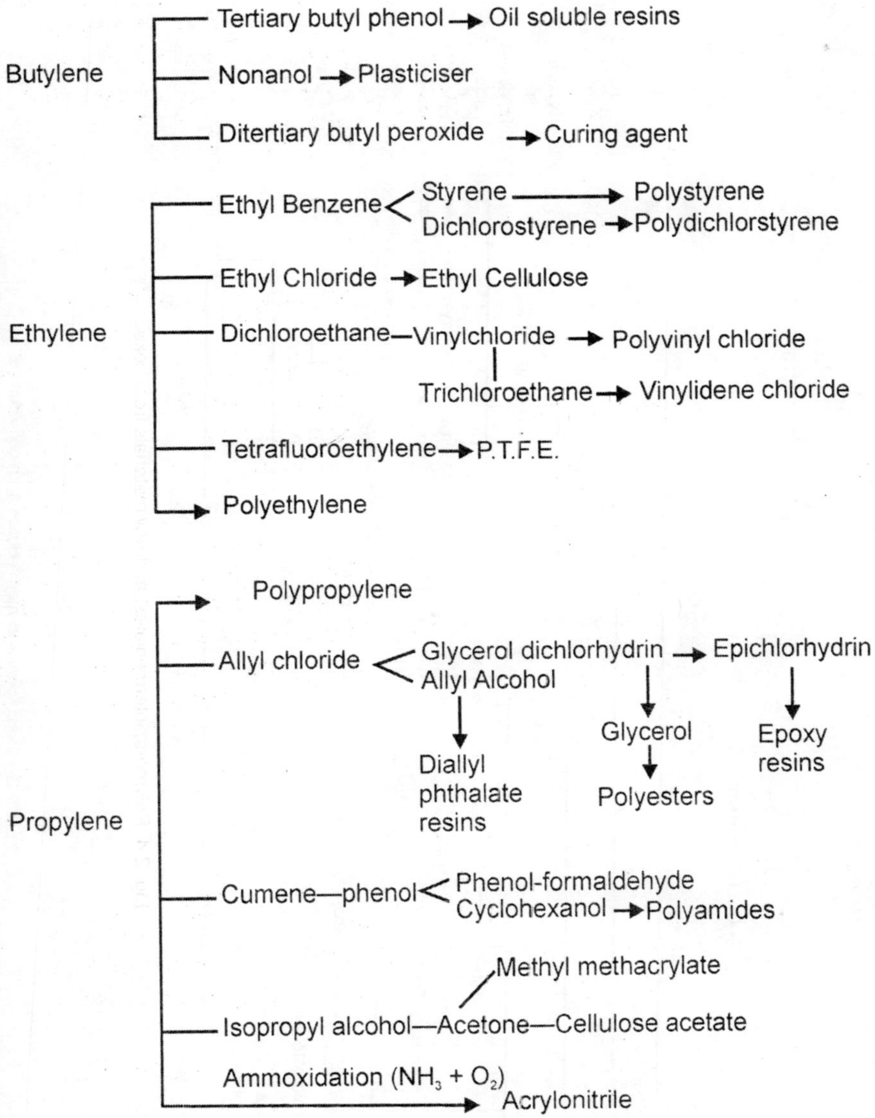

Fig. 2.5. Plastics from petroleum–polymers, intermediates, and ancillary materials

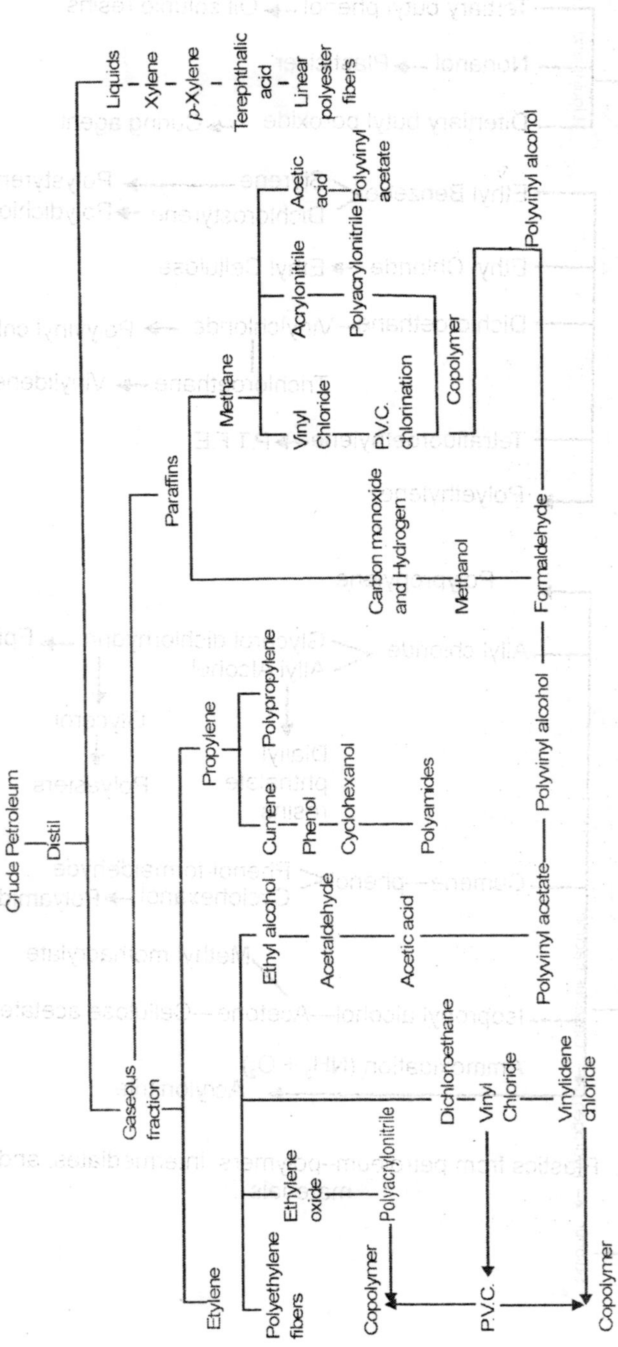

Fig. 2.6 Synthetic fibers and intermediates from petroleum

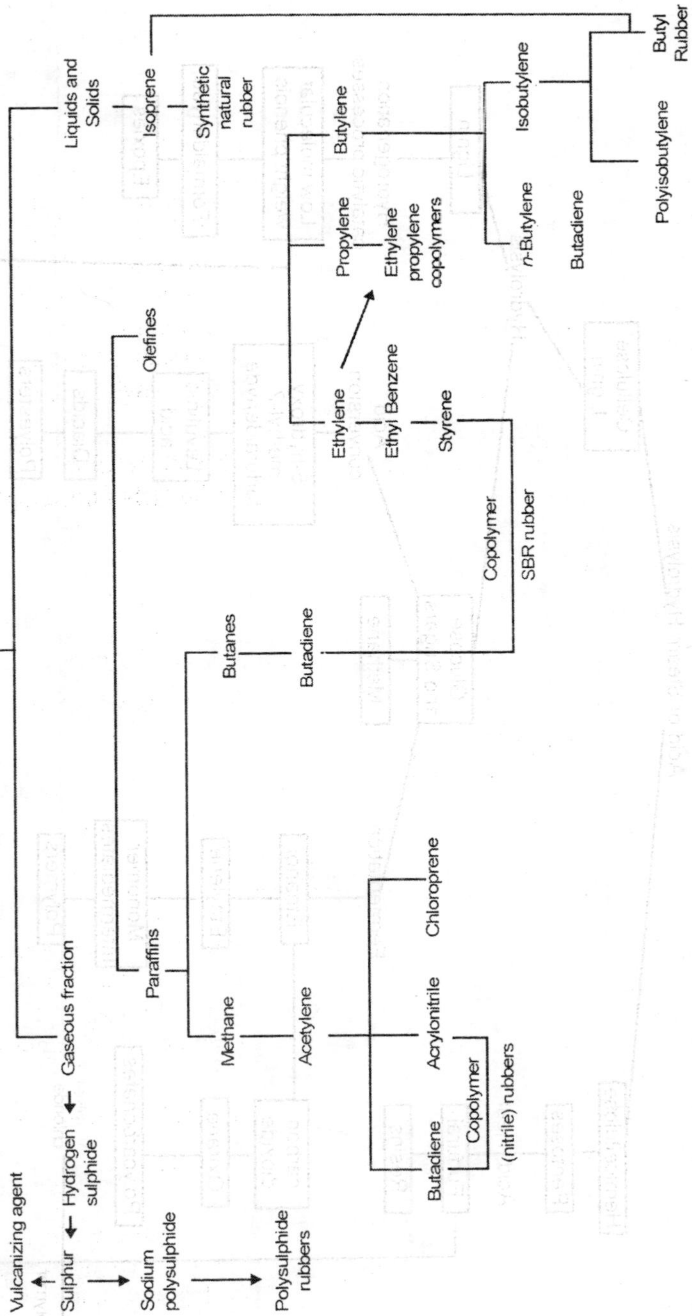

Fig. 2.7 Synthetic rubbers and ancillary materials from petroleum

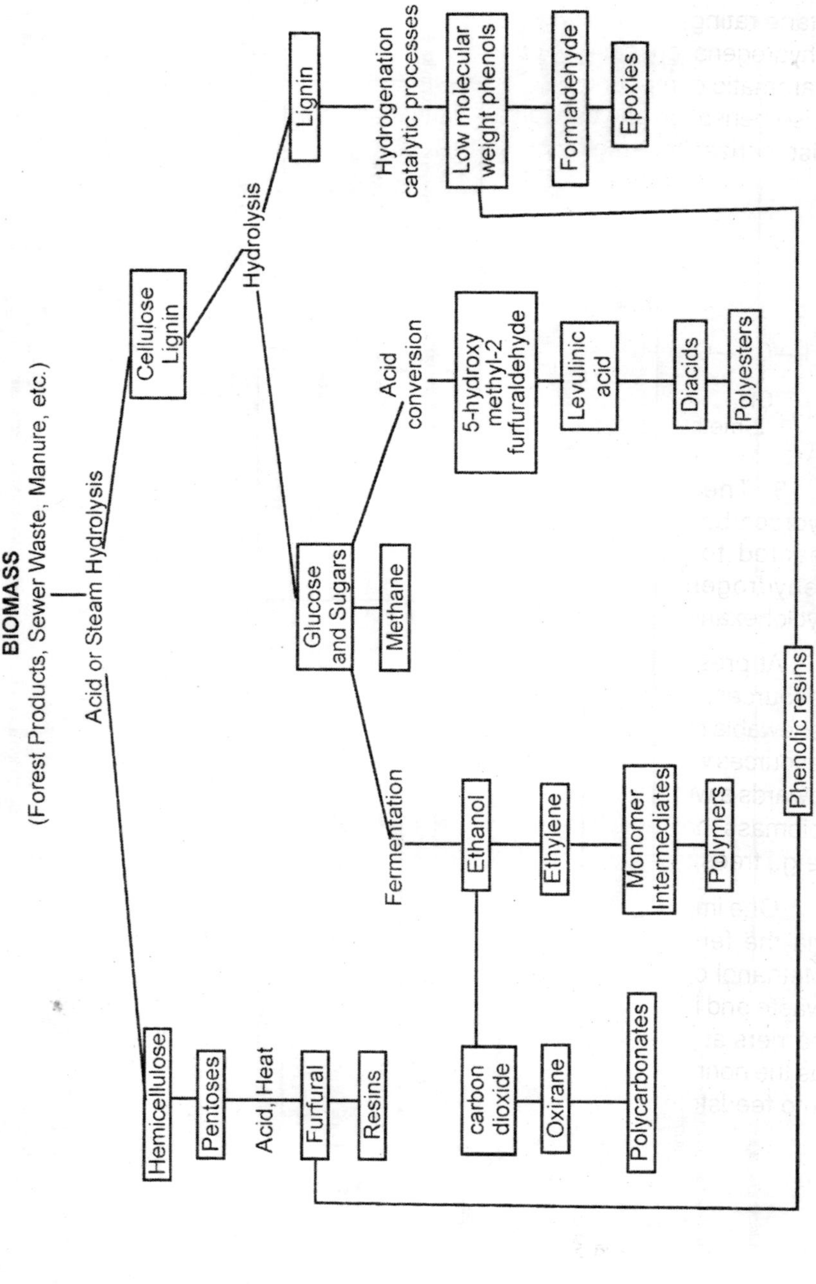
BIOMASS
(Forest Products, Sewer Waste, Manure, etc.)
Acid or Steam Hydrolysis
Hemicellulose
Cellulose Lignin
Hydrolysis
Lignin
Pentoses
Acid, Heat
Furfural
Resins
Glucose and Sugars
Methane
Fermentation
Ethanol
carbon dioxide
Oxirane
Polycarbonates
Ethylene
Monomer Intermediates
Polymers
Acid conversion
5-hydroxy methyl-2 furfuraldehyde
Levulinic acid
Diacids
Polyesters
Hydrogenation catalytic processes
Low molecular weight phenols
Formaldehyde
Epoxies
Phenolic resins

Fig. 2.8

octane ratings. In addition to this basic function, which is fundamentally a dehydrogenation reaction, converting cyclohexane and similar cyclo-parafins to aromatic compounds, such as benzene, there are minor reactions such as isomerisation and dehydrocyclisation of paraffin. n-Hexane, for example, is isomerized to 2-methylpentane or dehydrolyzed to benzene.

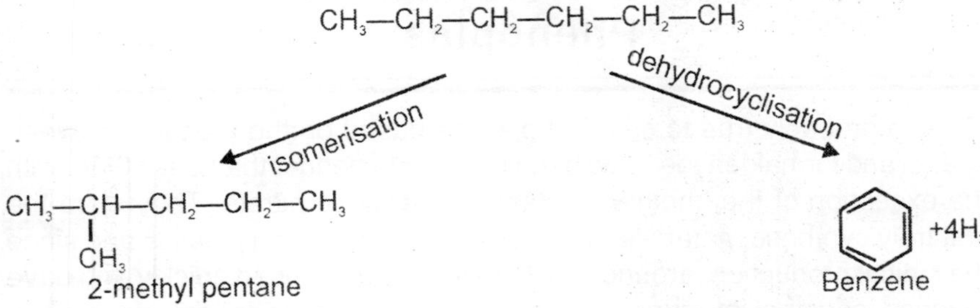

3. The third process used is the isolation of certain individual hydrocarbons from crude oil fractions which are subsequently chemically reacted to give the desired intermediate. Butane, for instance, is dehydrogenated to give butadiene, while cylohexane is oxidised to cyclohexanone.

At present there is an overwhelming dependence on non-renewable resources, particularly petroleum. As limitations on the availability of non - renewable resources increase, so the production of polymers from re-newable resources will become more attraction. Attention is being increasingly directed towards a wide range of re-newable resources and for convenience the name 'biomass' has been given to renewable resources with the biological basis (e.g., trees, seaweed, field crops, sewer waste, etc.)

One important monomer is ethylene which can be derived from ethanol via the fermentation of sugars from plant juices, cellulose, and starch. Methanol can be made from agricultural residues or from municipal solid waste and is important because it is the source of formaldehyde. The major barriers at present are economic rather than technical but this will change as the nonrenewable resources become source. The conversion of biomass into feedstocks and plymers of interest is outlined in Fig. 2.8

3

Phenoplasts

It is probably true to say that plastics based on the reaction between phenol and formaldehyde have been used for far longer than any others with the exception of the 'mother of plastics', cellulose nitrate. They were the first truly synthetic materials to be used in the producing plastics and since their initial production, around 1912, they have developed quickly and have reached industrial importance for a diverse number of applications in many countries. Although their consumption has not grown so rapidly over the past ten years as many of the thermoplastic polymers, they still remain one of the most important polymers of the plastics industry.

The history of the phenolic plastics dates back to the 1870's wher Baeyer studied the reaction of phenol with certain aldehydes and discarded the tar-like products because he was looking for pure and well-defined products. Little interest, therefore, was shown in this group of materials until the beginning of the twentieth century, when they were reinvestigated and their potential as the shellac substitute and a molding composition was realized. Many scientists had been interested in the reaction of phenols with various aldehydes but no great success was achieved until the classical work of L.H. Baekeland, which was made known in a series of papers and patents. His initial work was mainly carried out in the period 1905-1910 and its significance lay in his discoveries of how to control the phenol-aldehyde reaction by adjusting the ratio of the two reactants. The reaction could thus be controlled and stopped at an intermediate stage.

His work was the basis of the phenolic resins manufactured today for such used as adhesives, laminating resins, molding compositions, castings, surface coatings, forms, and ion-exchange resins. The development of these polymers did not proceed speedly for it was some 20 years before oil-soluble phenolics, suitable for surface coatings, were introduced. This new applications was followed by the introduction, in 1935, of the possible ion-exchange properties of phenolic resins. The popularity of these materials for this application was stimulated initially by the purification of sea water in war time and it has subsequently led to a fairly extensive commercial development.

Very little new development has occurred with this family of resins over the past 25 years although the introduction of the Xylok resins around the middle of the 1960's is considered a breakthrough in the technology of achieving high heat-resistant, phenolic materials.

RAW MATERIALS

Phenol (C_6H_5OH)

In its pure from phenol consists of white crystals that melt at about 41°C. For the manufacture of synthetic resins the phenol is normally used in the form of 90 per cent phenol and ten per cent orthocresol or in the ratio of 80/20. The phenol can be obtained either in the natural state or by synthetic means. The so-called natural phenol is obtained from coal tar by distillation, extraction of the middle oil cut by caustic soda, then acidification and finally distilling. The basic raw material for synthetic production is benezene, which may be converted to phenol by the Sulfonation, Raschig, or Cumene Processes.

(a) Sulfonation Process. Benzene is first sulfonated with sulfuric acid, then fused with caustic soda to form sodium phenate and sodium sulfite. The resultant mixture is then treated with further sulfuric acid, when phenol is liberated.

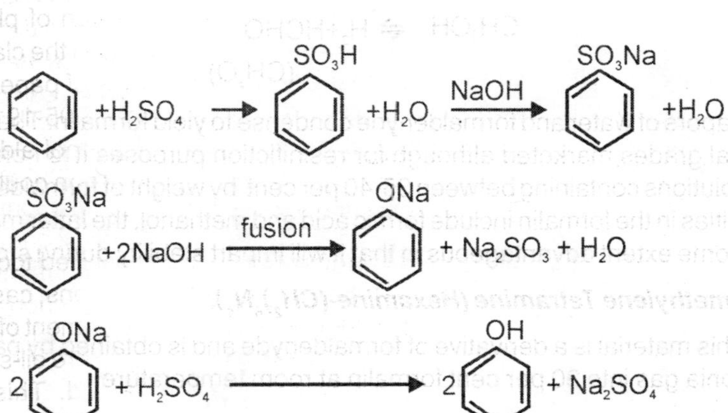

(b) Raschig Process. Benezene, hydrogen chloride, and air are passed over a heated copper-iron catalyst at 200-230°C. The resultant product is chlorobenzene and water in the gaseous state, which is then passed over a silica catalyst at about 500°C. The water hydrolyses the chlorobenezene to phenol and hydrochloric acid, which material can then be used for futher chlorination of the benzene.

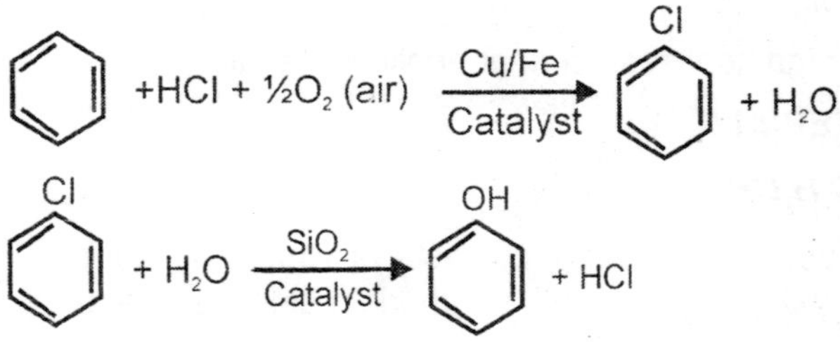

(c) Cumene Process. The catalytic reaction of benzene with propylene yields isopropyl benzene (Cumene) which oxidises to the hydroperoxide which is then broken down by acid to give phenol and acetone.

Formaldehyde (HCHO)

Formaldehyde is a gas which, on chilling, will condense to give a liquid boiling at — 19°C. This aliphatic aldehyde is prepared by the controlled catalytic oxidation of methyl alcohol. The procedure normally adopted is to pass a mixture of the alcoholic vapor and air over a heated catalyst, usually copper, the probable reaction being one of the dehydrogenation.

$$CH_3OH \rightleftharpoons H_2 + \underset{(CH_2O)}{HCHO}$$

Vapors of water and formaldehyde condense to yield formalin. There are several grades marketed although for resinifiction purposes it is normal to use solutions containing between 35-40 per cent by weight of formaldehyde. Impurities in the formalin include formic acid and methanol, the latter material is to some extent advantageous in that it will impart stability during storage.

Hexamethylene Tetramine (Hexamine-$(CH_2)_6N_4$).

This material is a derivative of formaldehyde and is obtained by passing ammonia gas into 30 per cent formalin at room temperature.

$$6CH_2O + 4NH_3 \rightarrow N_4(CH_2)_6 + 6H_2O$$

RESINIFICATION

Liquid or solid phenol-formaldehyde resins can be manufactured from the reaction of phenols with certain aldehydes. The process consists essentially of heating the reactants until condensation takes place, and effect which can be speeded up by the addition of catalysts. The catalysts may be either acids or bases, and depending on which type is used so will the end product differ. However, the same basic reaction takes place in both cases, which is the straightforward addition reaction between phenol and formaldehyde to give phenol alcohols. Thereafter the phenolic resins can be broadly classified either as one-stage or as two stage resins. If the molar ratio of formaldehyde to phenol is 1 : 1 or greater (i.e. molar excess of formaldehyde) and an alkaline catalysts such as ammonia or caustic soda is used, then a one stage resin is formed, generally called a resol. The resins so formed have reactive mehtylol (—CH_2OH) groups available in the molecule, and, on heating, the resol molecules condense together forming larger molecules without the addition of hardening agents :

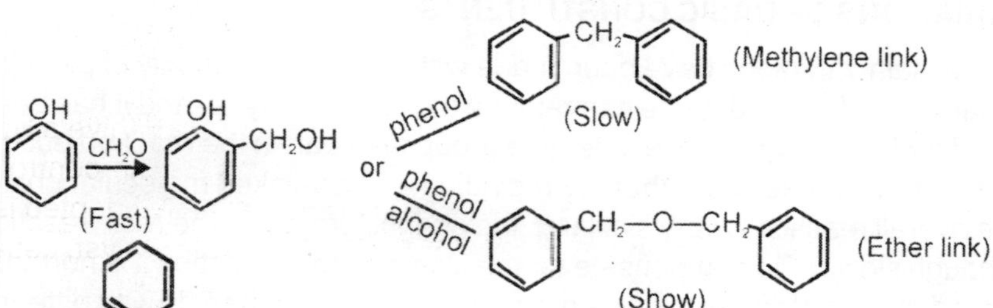

If the molar excess of phenol and an acid catalyst are used then a two - stage resin called a novolak is produced. These are resins which have no reactive methylol groups in the molecule and, on heating, are incapable of condensing with other novolak molecules without the addition of hardening agents. Therefore, to cross-link such materials to form insoluble and infusible resins it is usual to mix, during the compounding stages, materials capable of liberting further formaldehyde, e.g., hexamethylene tetramine or paraformaldehyde.

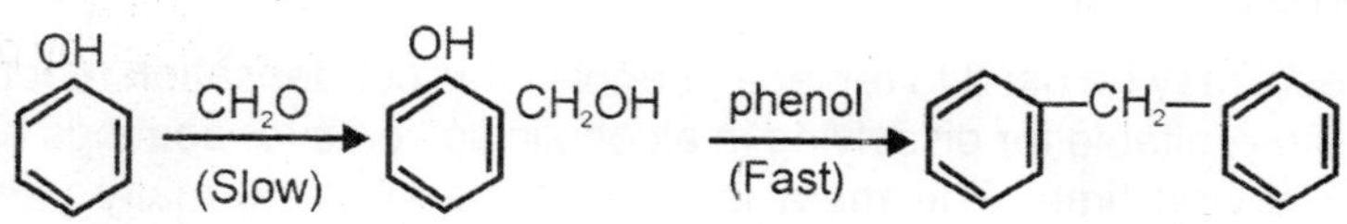

The final curing or heat hardening is considered to be a further condensation process. The following represents the building-up of one only of the simplest types of macromolecule and is shown in two dimensions.

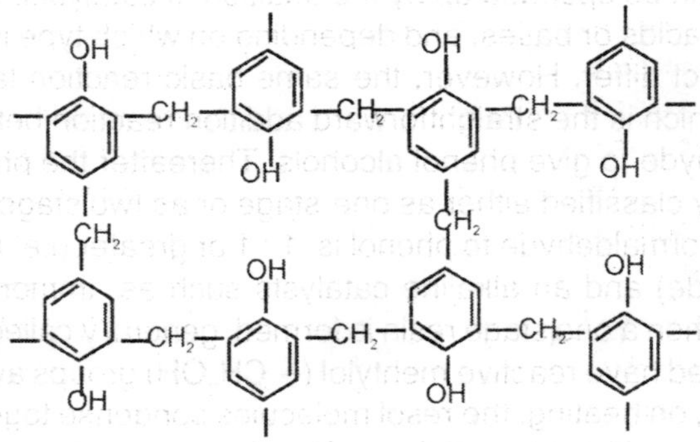

VARIATIONS OF BASIC CONSTITUENTS

Certain variations have been made with the phenolic family of plastics. In particular, furfuraldehyde can replace the formaldehyde, and it has been found that not only does the aldehyde group take part in the reaction but the furan ring also takes part, thereby providing a cross-linked molecular chain. The overall reaction is very similar to the phenol formaldehyde resin reaction although slower. To compensate for the slow speed of reaction it is normally carried out in a strongly alkaline medium. A range of materials with differing properties can be obtained by varying the molar ratio of phnol to furfural. The furfural can be obtained relatively cheaply from certain waste products of agricultural industry such as oat husks. The resins obtained by reacting phenol with furfural have excellent impact resistance as well as very good chemical resistance. They cure very quickly at high temperature and possess good flow characteristics. One of their main uses is for modifying conventional phenolic resins, an addition which enables higher loadings of filler to be used with these resins. Other applications include a limited use as temperature-resistant surface coatings. This family is discussed more fully at the end of this chapter.

Cresol may be used to replace phenol in this condensation reaction to give resins suitable for dissolving in alcoholic solvents for coatings having a quick drying time. The meta isomer of cresol is normally used for resinification.

If phenol is replaced by resorcinol then the reaction takes place at a considerably increased rate. This is only to be expected and is due to the fact that the resorcinol possesses two activated-formaldehyde resins are generally prepared by using a molar excess of resorcinol, and cure is effected by addition further aldehyde, usually in the form of paraformaldehyde. These resins cure at relatively low temperatures but unfortunately they are rather more expensive than the phenolic type and subsequently they are used conjunction with the latter materials. They have similar physical properties to the phenolics but give superior properties for certain specific applications such as in the field of adhesives. Recorcinol resins are used in the preparation of plywood; they possess excellent resistance to fungi and mold attack, also to the effect of boiling water. The fact that they may be cured at low temperatures makes them extremely attractive for bonding difficult types of applications such as arches and other curved structures.

There are other types of resins which cannot be classified as phenoplasts but as we have described the manufacture of formaldehyde in this chapter it is convenient to briefly mention them. Formaldehyde can be reacted with cyclohexanone and methyl cyclohexanone. Such resins are the CRF and MS2 types made by Laporte Industries U.K. They can be used as overcoating varnishes, tackifiers, and have a host of printing applications. Another type is the condensation product of high-boiling, aromatic solvents with formaldehyde. This type of resin is designated Knflex. (Kenrich Corp.).

The final variation of some interest is that of replacing phenol with the dark-colored oil known as cashew nutshell liquid, which contains an unsaturated phenol called cardanol. Cardanol condenses with formaldehyde in a similar manner to phenol and may be cured either by heating or by adding paraformaldehyde. The end-product has similar properties to the other pehnolic resins except they are somewhat more rubbery. They have found limited use in brake linings, adhesives and flexible insulating varnishes. Greater use of these cashew nutshell resins has been somewhat limited by their relatively low tensile strength.

MANUFACTURE

The reaction of phenol with formaldehyde is of the condensation type and is therefore normally carried out in resin kettles fitted for vaccum distillation (Fig. 3.1.) Several metals may be used in the construction of the resin kettle, the most popular being mild steel, although stainless steel, copper, iron and nickel have been used.

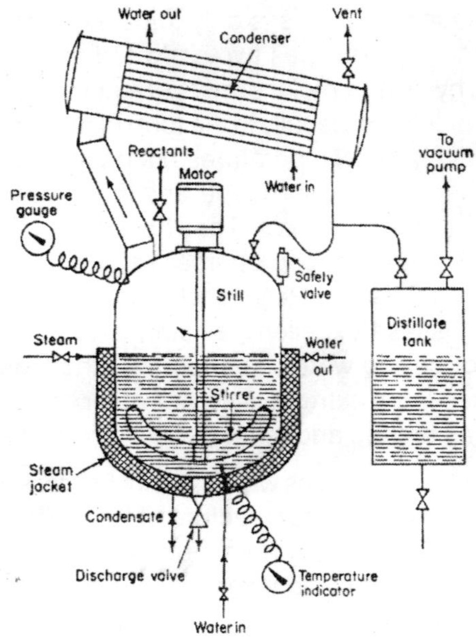

Fig. 3.1 Reaction vessel for manufacture for phenol-formaldehyde resins.

Where colour is important, as with the novolaks, it is essential to use stainless steel or nickel although for resols, where color is not so important mild steel, iron, or copper can be used. For the aminoplasts, which are described in the next chapter, the reaction kettle is very similar, and it is even possible to use glass -lined kettles.

The course of the reaction m y be followed by measuring the amout of free formaldehyde or by viscocity measurements. On completion of the condensation reaction, which is determined by suitable tests, the resin is then ready for discharging or blending as necessary.

Molding Powders

The novolak is prepared using the formulation details described previously and while the resin is still hot it is run into large shallow trays and allowed to cool. On cooling the resin is ground to a find powder and is then compounded with curing agent (hexamine), filler (woodflour), mold lubricant (stearates) and pigments. The properties of a molding powder are largely determined by the type of filler, which can constitute about 50 percent of the powder. Woodflour is normally used as a general-purpose filler but other materials are employed to give improved shock resitance (chopped fabric) electrical properties (mica) and water resistance (silica and mica). These ingredients are premixed and then compounded either on rolls or in a mixer with which a mill is associated. Both types of equipment are steam heated so that the product partly cures during compounding. The final curing is, of course, effected during the actual molding operation. After compounding, the product is ground to the correct particle size, blended and tested.

Laminating Resins

These are based on resols, the manufacturing details of which have been described previously. The condensation reaction is carried out until a specific degree of polymerisation has been reached, the resin being then run out and cooled if a solid resin is required, or a solvent added to the hot resol if a varnish-type material is required.

Casting Resins

These are prepared in a manner similar to resols although in this specific case a large excess of formaldehyde is used, with sodium hydroxide as the catalyst, and the reaction is usually carried out at about 65°C. This encourages the formation of the hydrophilic phenol alcohols, of low molecular weight. The alkaline catalyst is then neutralised with lactic acid, the resultant product is vaccum distilled, a plasticiser wuch as glycerol is added, and the mix is run into molds and slowly cured at temperature around 75°C. Oil solubility can normally be achieved by using substituted phenols such as *p*-tertiary butyl phenol or using higher aldehydes like acetaldehyde.

Coatings and Varnishes

Resol resins used for making varnishes suitable for coil impregnation, but resins of the novolak and resol type can be obtained. These are soluble in conventional paint-drying oils and thereby provide varnishes with excellent water resistance.

Adhesives

The resins normally used for the adhesive applications are the liquid resol types with an alkaline catalyst. They may be mixed with certain thermoplastics by a variety of methods of give adhesive suitable for bonding metal to metal. The phenolic plywood glues consist of resols and can either be cured by heat alone at 135°C or by adding small amounts of paraformaldehyde at temperature as low as 115°C. The methods of manufacture is similar as for the aminoplasts described.

PROCESSING

Molding Powders

Phenol formaldehyde molding powders may be processed by the conventional techniques of compression and transfer molding. The temperature range is normally between 150-180°C at pressures around 1 ton/in^2 or even higher. The molding powders are then fed to the mold either as cold powders or cold or preheated preforms. Phenolic molding powders of the wood flour type can also be extruded using specialised techniques.

Adhesives

Phenolic resins are used extensively in the production of plywood and comply with B.S. 1203, type WBP. An interesting technique used in the production of these wood laminates is that of impregnating a thin tissue paper with an alcoholic solution of a resol, placing it between wood veneers, and hot pressing it at 150°C. The actual wood veneers themselves can be impregnated and then compressed during the hot bonding process to produce a denser product which is commonly known as 'compreg'. This material is nearly isotropic and possesses exceptional mechanical properties.

Laminating/Impregnating Resins

Alcoholic solutions of resols can be used for impregnating fabric and paper to give laminated broads. Various methods of impregnating are used, including 'premix' technique, dipping, coating, or spreading. In the premix process the actual phenolic resin is added to the paper base during the papermaking process. The dipping process is carried out by passing the filler material through a bath containing the varnish, and then on to a drying oven. Coating, as can be seen from Fig. 3.2, is carried out by passing the filler material round one rill and picking the varnish up from an adjacent roll. The spreading methods the resin is introduced to the upper surface of the filler material, which is then passed between the rollers or under a scraper blade. This results in the resin being spread evently over the surface and removes any excess varnish.

The so-formed treated base must now be consolidated into the finished laminate. For molded shapes, a mold is obviously required and can be either of the open flash or open plunger type. The base-impregnated materials are to appropriate shapes and molded at temperatures around 150-180°C with pressures up to 3 ton/in^2. Boards or sheets can also be prepared by pressing the laminated structure between platens in multi-daylight presses under the above temperatures and pressure conditions. Tubes and cylinders can also

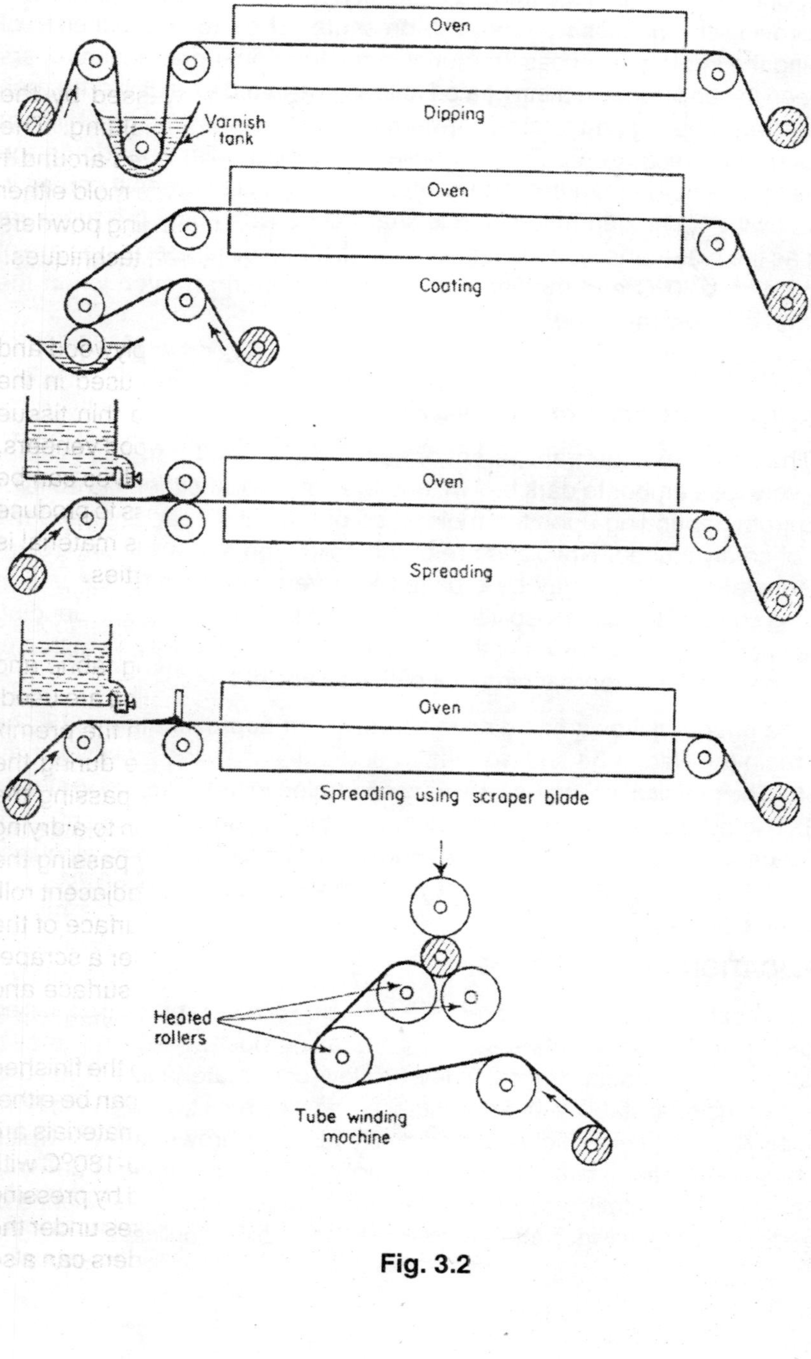
Oven
Varnish tank
Dipping
Oven
Coating
Oven
Spreading
Oven
Spreading using scraper blade
Heated rollers
Tube winding machine

Fig. 3.2

be produced by winding the treated base on a mandrel in a machine which can provide the necessary heat and pressure. The process consists of passing the impregnated base material in roll from over preheating rollers between the end frame to main heated rollers. The mandrel is driven through a universal coupling and rotates between the main rollers with which it is in contact. The pressure required is applied by a third roller bearing on the opposite side of the mandrel. The resin is partially cured when it comes in contact with the heated rollers and is finally consolidated by the pressure roller as the material is wound on the mandrel. Main roll temperatures are of the order of 160°C and the final curing is effected in an oven when the mandrel is finally removed.

PROPERTIES

Appearance and Form of Phenolic Resins

The resins may be transparent or nearly translucent, ranging in color from very pale amber to dark brown, and they may exist either in a solid or liquid from depending upon the molar ratio of the initial reactants and the type of catalyst used. Novolaks are of the solid type and are brittle rosin-like substances which may be crushed to a very fine powder for use in molding compositions or dissolved in an organic solvent for certain bonding application. The liquid resins of the resol type vary in viscosity from that of water to something approaching that of thick treacle.

The phenol novolak has a specific gravity of approximately 1.25, the cast resin (unfilled) 1.34 and wood-flour or α-cellulose filled moldings 1.35 to 1.4.. The physical properties will vary according to the fillers used (Table 3.1.). The cured resins are practically insoluble in common solvents, hot oils, aqueous acid, and salts, but are, however, slightly swollen by alcohols, water and dilute acids and alkalis. They decompose in concentrated oxidising acids and hot alkalis.

APPLICATIONS

The applications of phenolic resins for molding powders may be classified according to their final end-use i.e. general purpose, heat and impact resistance or electrical grades. They are low-cost materials, possessing good dimensional stability, heat resistance and also resistance to cold flow. The resultant molded articles are normally black or brown in color which has to some extent limited their wider applications. The general purpose compounds are usually wood-flour filled and possess a popular balance of properties/price for a wide variety of applications. Typical applications include

TABLE 3.1

PHYSICAL PROPERTIES OF PHENOLIC RESINS

	Cast resin	Molding resins			Laminating resins		
	(unfilled)	Wood-flour filled	Chopped cotton fabric	Mineral filled	Paper	Fabric	Asbestos
Specific gravity	1.34	1.35-1.4	1.34-1.38	1.9-2.0	1.24-1.38	1.34-1.38	1.6-1.8
Tensile strength (lb/in^2)	4-10,000	5-8000	5-8000	3-8000	7-20,000	8-20,000	6-12,000
Flexural strength (lb/in^2)	7-12,000	8-12,000	8-12,000	8-12,000	10-30,000	12-30,000	12-20,000
Shear strength (lb/in2)	6-8000	8-10,000	10-15,000	4-15,000	5-12,000	5-12,000	4-8000
Compressive strength (lb/in_2)	10-25000	15-35,000	20-32,000	20-32,000	20-40,000	25-40,000	20-40,000
Impact strength (ft. lb/in. notch)	0.2-0.6	0.1-0.5	0.3-3.0	0.25-1.5	0.3-1.5	1-4	0.5-1.5
Specific heat	0.4	0.35	0.34	0.3	0.35	0.35	0.3
Coefficient of Thermal expansion (°C)	3-8	3-6	2-6	2-4	2-3	2-3	2-3

TABLE 3.1 (Cont'd)

	Cast resin	Molding resins			Laminating resins		
	(unfilled)	Wood-flour filled	Chopped cotton fabric	Mineral filled	Paper	Fabric	Asbestos
Dielectric constant (10^3 c/s)	4 plus	5-15	5-10	5-10	4-8	6-12	10-18
Dielectric strength (V/mil)	200-300	100-300	100-250	100-250	250-750	100-500	50-100
Volume resistivity (ohm/cm)	1×10^{12}-10^{14}	1×10^{9} - 10^{12}	1×10^{8} - 10^{12}	1×10^{9} - 10^{12}	1×10^{10} - 10^{12}	1×10^{10} - 10^{12}	1×10^{9} - 10^{10}
Chemical resistance							
Weak acids	*R*	*FR*	*FR*	*R*	*FR*	*FR*	*R*
Strong acids		Decomposed by	oxidising acids	resistant	to reducing	organic	acids
Weak alkalis	*R*	*R*	*R*	*R*	*R*	*R*	*R*
Strong alkalis	*A*	*A*	*A*	*A*	*A*	*A*	*A*
Solvents	*R*	*R*	*R*	*R*	*R*	*R*	*R*

Key

R-resistant
FR-fairly resistant
A-attacked

telephone hand-sets, steering wheels, and fascia panels although the former application is being replaced quite extensive by thermoplastics. The impact resistant grades contain chopped fabric and can be used for pump impellers, washing machine agitators, lavatory seats, and electricals switches. Heat-resistant grades containing asbestos fillers are used in aircraft and missile applications. The electrical resistant grades are used for automobile ignition parts, coil formers, etc. Phenolic molding powders can be used in electrical equipment where insulation requirements are hot too stringent, such as plugs, switches, switch gear cases, and covers.

The ability of phenolic resins to impregnat and bond such materials as wood, paper and certain fabrics has led to their widespread use for various laminates, not only decorative but also for industrial purposes. Their use for impregnating a wood veneer has been limited to a certain extent by color, and they have a colored glue line which is not always, desirable. Industrial laminates are used as gear wheels, bushings, and dollies, and the somewhat thinner ones on which a layer of copper has been deposited, are now employed in the manufacture of grinding wheels by wetting an abrasive grit and then rolling it into a powdered phenolic resin which forms a putty which can be pressed into a mold to give a preform and finally cured.

As we have seen, casting resins are of the liquid type and prepared by using a large molar excess of formaldehyde and an alkaline catalyst. The resultant resin is normally neutralised by adding in lactic acid, and is plasticised with glycerol. They may be prepared in a wide range of colors but are to some extent being replaced by other plastic materials such as the polyester resins and polymethyl methacrylate for certain application. It is for this reason that cast phenolic resins have never developed as was originally hoped, but they still continue to find uses in such applications as billiard balls, umbrella handles, furniture handles, pipe and pen stems as well as cutlery handles, etc.

A comparatively recent development with this group of materials is that of the foamed pehnolics. The type of resin suitable for foaming would be the casting type and the foaming action is normally effected by the chemical liberation of gases from blowing agents. The usual blowing agents include the metals that react with acids to liberate hydrogen or certain nitrogen-containing compounds. The curing reaction is exothermic, which facilitates the rapid foaming desirable in order to obtain form of fine cell size. Lightweight foams with a density less than 1 lb/ft^3 may be produced, although for structural purposes higher density forms have been in the field of insulation for buildings, and transport vehicles. The main attractions of these foams are that they may be foamed *in situ* and possess good chemical, fire and heat resistant. Other applications include packaging, buoyancy, handicraft and decorative materials for stage and movie cinema scenery.

An even later development along this line is that of the syntactic foams, which may be prepared from microscopic hollow spheres of phenolic resins containing nitrogen, and subsequently mixed with phenolic, polyester, or epoxy resins. The resultant product is a putty like mass which can be trowelled, in a similar manner to cement into cavities, and finally cured. The end product has very high strength-to-weight ratio. Applications include fillers for acoustic tiles, concrete, and plaster.

FURANES

These resins have been around for 25 years for use essentially as corrosion-resistant mortars. There were many early unsuccessful attempts in utilise these resins in glass-reinforced laminates. They were used, however, as heat-resistant coatings for polyester and epoxy laminates especially in ballistic missile applications. The quaker Oats Company in the U.S.A. has been responsible for much of the development of these resins.

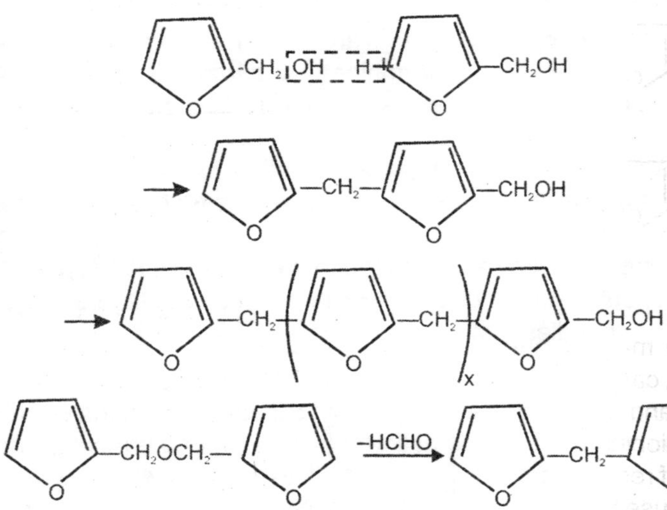

It has been shown on Raw Materials that furane resins can be obtained from a variety of naturally occurring materials. The main furane resins involve furfuryl alcohols as the sole polymeric constituent although there are other possibilities with combination of urea or phenol-formaldehyde.

Furfuryl alcohol can be resinified in the presence of acid catalysts. The system thus formed is neutralised and the water of condensation formed is removed by vaccum distillation to give a stable resin.

This resin can be further recatalysed by acid media (e.g., phosphoric acid, *p*-toluene sulfonic acid etc.) The resultant product is cross linked to form extremely chemically resistant materials. These cured resins are dark in color with a high degree of heat and chemical resistance.

Several theories of cross-linking have been postulated but one accepted suggestion is that the loss of unsaturation during cross-linking indicates the reaction is essentially a double bond polymerisation.

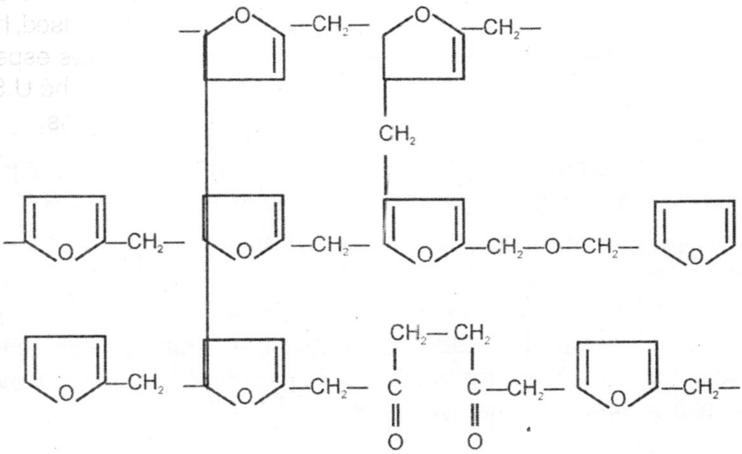

The main field of applications for these resins are as foundry core binders, carbon-graphite binders, and chemically resistant mortars. Phenol furfural and urea-formaldehyde, furfuryl alcohol have been used for adhesive applications, e.g., in plywood. The quaker Oats Company has developed a series of resins which can now be used in conjunction with glass laminates. Typical uses for such laminates are fume ducts, chemically resistant tanks, scrubbers and effluent tanks.

PHENOL-ARALKYL

All self-respecting organic chemistry students should be aware of the classical work carried out by Friedel and Crafts. This reaction involves the introduction of an alkyl or acyl group into an aromatic ring in the presence of a catalyst such as aluminium chloride.

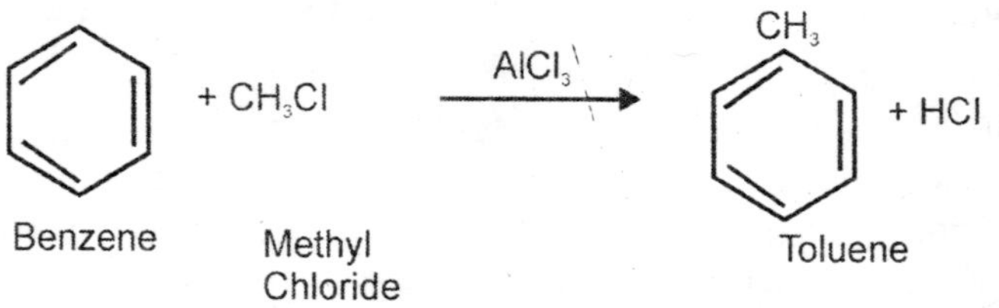

This work was followed by their attempts to heat benzyl chloride in the presence of aluminium chloride to form resinous materials. The resultant product was an insoluble infusible mass.

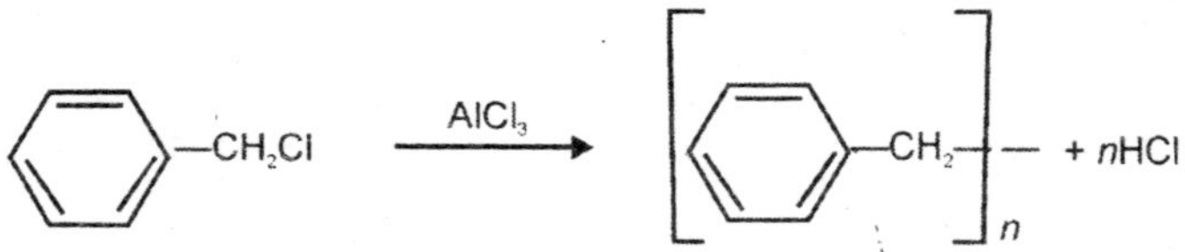

It is clear from our theories of functionality that the resultant product is not thermosetting because it cannot cross-link. Later it was proved that the end product was simply a highly branched molecule.

Many years later when the interest to develop polymers with heat resistance in excess of 200°C for space exploration became necessary work was revived both in the U.K. and the U.S.A. Work began around the 1950's but it was not until 1964 that a solid breakthrough was acheived. Originally the concept was the produce true thermosets by using compounds having two or three chlromethyl groups.

A typical reaction is as follows :

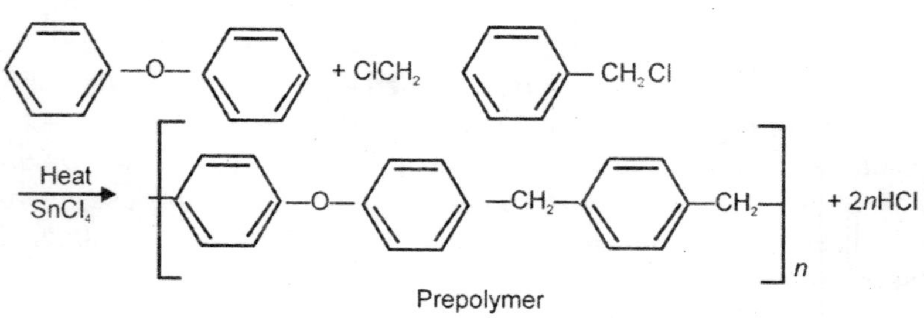

A prepolymer is formed by condensing diphenyl ether with dichloro-*p*-xylene in the presence of stannic chloride. Cross linking is achieved by adding more of the latter reactant. In 1964 both chemists at the Royal Aircraft Establishment, Farnborough and Albright and Wilson discovered the aralkyl ethers. They found these materials reacted in a similar manner to the chloromethyl compounds but the by-products were alcohols. This type of reaction is illustrated as follows by reacting naphthalene with dimethoxy-*p*-xylene with the elimination of methanol.

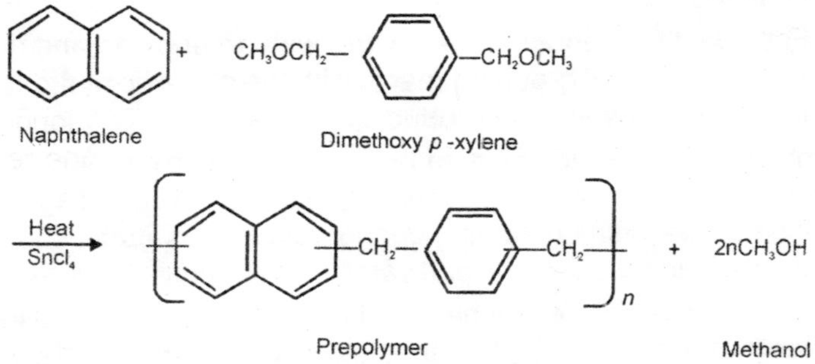

A prepolymer is also formed and the cross-linking is achieved by the addition of further aralkyl ether and heating in the presence of ferric chloride. Curing using this type of process is relatively slow and the degree of cross-linking is not high. Therefore applications for these type of resins have been limited to requirements of just high heat stability without high mechanical strength.

Albright & Wilson, Ltd. concentrated their efforts on the cross-linking reaction and found that by condensing the aralkyl ethers with phenolic compounds a prepolymer was formed which could be cross-linked with a variety of techniques. A simple example is shown as follows :

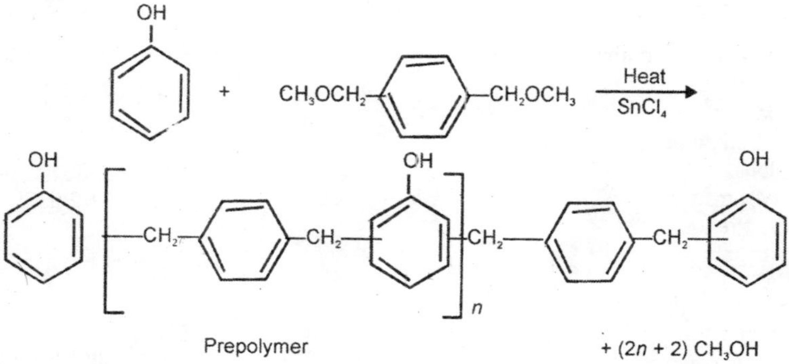

These materials are now sold by this company using the registered trade mark of Xylok resins.

There are two main methods of achieving cross-linking.

(1) *Hexamine.* The prepolymer is heated with hexamine which attacks the vacant ortho and para position on the phenolic muclei to form methylene or dimethylene amino linkages. Such a reaction is accompanied by the release of ammonia.

(2) *Epoxide.* the prepolymer is heated with an epoxide and a suitable accelator. This chemical grouping reacts with the phenolic hydroxyl to form cross-links without any volatile products being evolved.

Commercial resins include a base resin supplied as a 100% solid pre - polymer without curing agent, solid prepolymer without curing agent, a one-pack laminating varnish containing curing agent in a ketonic solvent such as methyl ethyl ketone, and a one part varnish, which cures by epoxy addition.

The applications for hexamine cured resins are for electrical insulation both for laminates and moldings. Asbestos filled Xylok resins have resulted in commutators with greatly improved lives. Graphite filled resins are used for the moldings in hot water pumps.

Resins cured by epoxides have higher heat resistance and thermal mechanical strength than hexamine cured types. (See table 3.2). The electrical industry is the obvious, largest potential user. Typical uses include high performance printed circuit boards; the easy processing characteristics of these resins should prove useful in structural materials (in the aircraft industry), heavy electrical insulation, and components for chemical plants.

Table 3.2

PHYSICAL PROPERTIES OF THE GLASS CLOTH REINFORCED FRIEDEL-CRAFTS LAMINATE

Properties	*Value*	*Test method*
Specific gravity	1.80	
Tensile strength at room temperature		
lbf in $^{-2}$	58,000	BS 2782, 301C
MN m^{-2}	404	
Tensile strength at 200°C		
lbf in $^{-2}$	40,800	BS 2782, 301C
MN m^{-2}	282	
Crushing strength		
lbf in $^{-2}$	69,500	BS2782, 303B
MN m^{-2}	480	
Izod impact stregth		
ft lb 0.5 in	10.7	BS 2782, 306A
Flammability oxygen index	32	ASTM D2863-70
Water absorption (%)	0.18	ASTM D570

4

Aminoplasts

The reaction between urea and formaldehyde has been known since Holzer first isolated methylene urea in 1884. Synthetic production of urea was achieved some fifty years earlier, in 1828, when Wohler, preparing ammonia cyanate, unexpectedly obtained urea. Commercial interest was not aroused in the reactions between urea and formaldehyde until a patent was granted to a Czechoslovak scientist named Hans John, in 1918. Other patent claims followed from two Austrians, Ripper and Pollak, and the Germans, Goldschmidt and Neuss. The patent issued to Pollak served as an ideal basis for the commercial development of 'organic glass'. His efforts were directed mainly to the casting of liquid resins whereas Goldschmidt and Neuss saw the potentialities of the resinous products as hotpress molding compounds.

The chemical, melaminė (2,4,6-triamino-1,3,5 triazine) was first prepared shortly after the discovery of urea, in 1843, by Liebig. It was first neglected as a commercial material and it was not until a century later that Henkel, in 1835, patented its resinous condensations with formaldehyde. Melamine when reacted with formaldehyde produces resins similar in appearance to those to urea but superior in respect to water resistance.

Thiourea, another chemical used on a somewhat smaller scale for producing aminoplasts was manufactured in this country, in 1924, by British Cyanide Ltd. (later to be known as British Industrial Plastics Ltd.) E.C. Rossiter studied the condensation reactions of this material and, in particular, those of thiourea and urea with formaldehyde. This work was followed, in 1926, by the introduction of the mixed urea-thiourea resin moulding powders. Such resins have never formed the basis of a satisfactory molding material, owing to their brittleness and relatively poor water and heat resistance.

The next few years saw consolidation of the early development work on the aminoplasts and large-scale production of urea formaldehyde moulding powders began in 1938; extension to wood glues followed soon after. The use of such resins has now become firmly established for such applications as molding powders, adhesives, textile treatments, and surface coatings.

Another member of a family which has attracted considerable interest over recent years is benzoguanamine-formaldehyde resin. Benzoguanamine is a triazine, closely resembling melamine although the resins produced from it are more water resistant than the melamine condensates. At present bonzoguanamine is more expensive than melamine and this prevents its wider use.

In recent years we have seen the development of aminoplasts in the field of injection molding. The ability to injection mold these plastics have resulted in a stimulated interest.

RAW MATERIALS

Urea (NH_2CONH_2) is a white crystalline solid melting at 132.6°C and having the empirical formula CON_2H_4. It can be produced by various methods, of which probably the most important is the reaction under pressure of carbon dioxide with ammonia is silver-lined autoclaves.

$$CO_2 + 2NH_3 \xrightarrow[70\text{-}230\ atm]{135\text{-}195^\circ C} CO(NH_2) + H_2O$$

There has been a more recent trend to stainless steel which is passivated by incorporating oxygen in the reactant steam. This allows higher operating conditions with improved degrees of conversion thereby reducing production costs.

Urea may also be synthesised by the acid hydrolysis of cyanamide. Calcium cyanamide is first extracted with water and the soluble lime is precipitated with sulfuric acid.

$$CO_2 + 2NH_3 \xrightarrow[70\text{-}230\ atm]{135\text{-}195^\circ C} CO(NH_2)_2 + H_2O$$

Melamine ($C_3H_6N_6$) is a white crystalline solid, sparingly soluble in water, and melts just above 350°C. It can be produced on a commercial scale by heating dicyandiamide under pressure with ammonia or by fusion with guanidine salts. Chemically it is the triamine of cyanuric acid ($C_3H_3O_3N_3$) and may also be considered as the trimer of cyanamide. It is generally represented by a triazine structure :

$$\underset{\text{Calcium Cyanamide}}{CaCN_2} + H_2SO_4 \longrightarrow CaSO_4 + \underset{\text{Cyanamide}}{NH_2CN} \xrightarrow{H_2O} \underset{\text{Urea (Carbamide structure)}}{NH_2CONH_2}$$

The reaction between lime and coke has also formed the basis of the commercial production of melamine as follows :

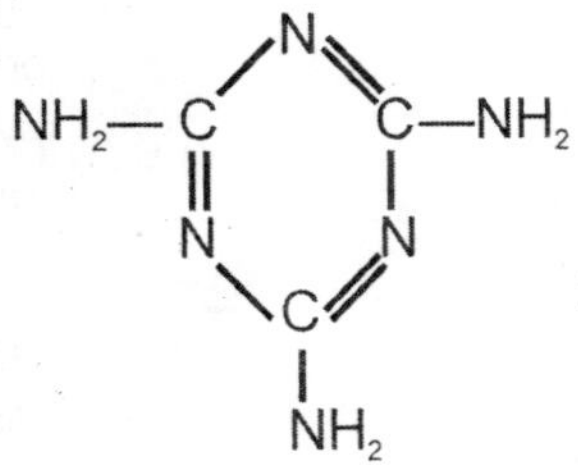

2,4,6-triamino-1,3,5, triazine

However, during the last ten years there has been a very considerable move towards manufacturing melakine from urea :

$$6CO\ (NH_2)_2 \longrightarrow C_3H_6N_6 + 3CO_2 + 6NH_3$$

The process is used in the U.S.A. and by many manufacturers in Europe, although British Oxygen Co. in the U.K. are still using the dicyandiamide route.

Thiourea ($CS(NH_2)_2$) in the pure state is a colorless crystalline compound melting at 182°C, and is soluble in water. It can be manufactured from ammonium thiocyanate or by the action of hydrogen sulfide on a solution of cyanamide obtained by extraction of calcium cyanamide.

$$NH_2CN + H_2S \longrightarrow CS(NH_2)_2$$

Benzoguanamine ($C_3H_4H_5C_6H_5$) is a white crystalline solid which melts at 227°C and is sparingly soluble in water. The guanamines can be prepared by heating dicyandiamide with a nitrile and a catalyst such as metallic sodium or sodium hydroxide.

Formaldehyde (CH_2O) is discussed fully in Chapter 3.

RESINIFICATION

The basis of the chemistry of the interaction of urea and formaldehyde is the formation of monomethylol and dimethylol urea. Monomethylol urea is obtained after mixing equimolar proportions of urea and formaldehyde to give a neutral solution. Dimethylol urea is prepared in a similar manner using 2 mols of formaldehyde per mol of urea. On a commercial scale the formalin (35-40 per cent w/v formaldehyde in water) is adjusted to a pH of 7.5 using sodium or potassium hydroxide. The reactions are as follows :

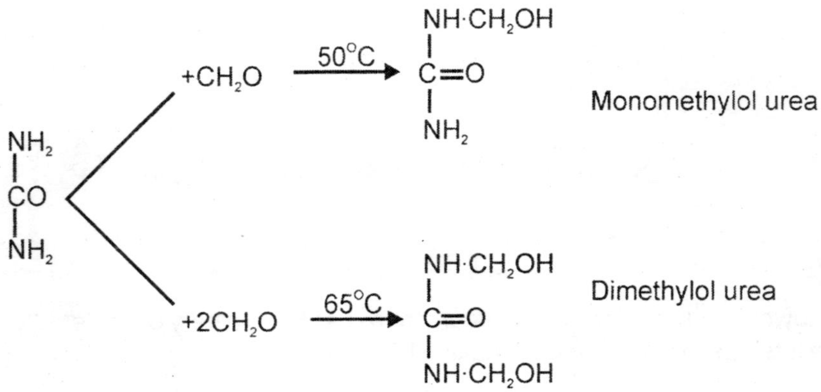

The methylol compounds so formed are relatively unstable and condense in the presence of a catalyst or on heating to produce methylene derivatives which ultimately become cross-linked and infusible products.

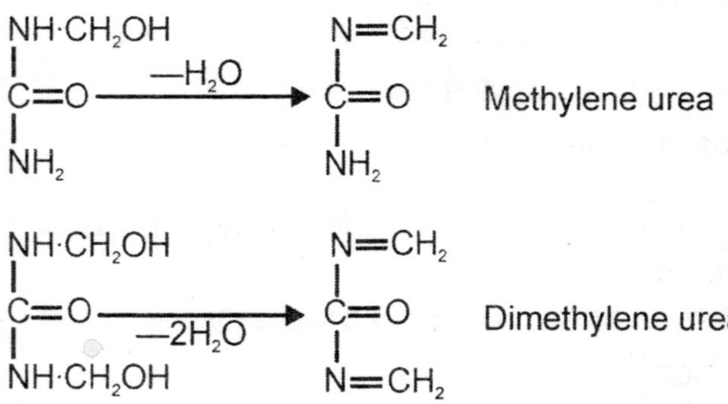

The functionality of monomethylol urea can be considered as 2 and that of formaldehyde as 2. Therefore, as discussed previously, the system will not cross lin. Dimethylol urea, formed from two mols of formaldehyde has a functionality of 4 and cross-links to give thermosetting resins of the following possible structure :

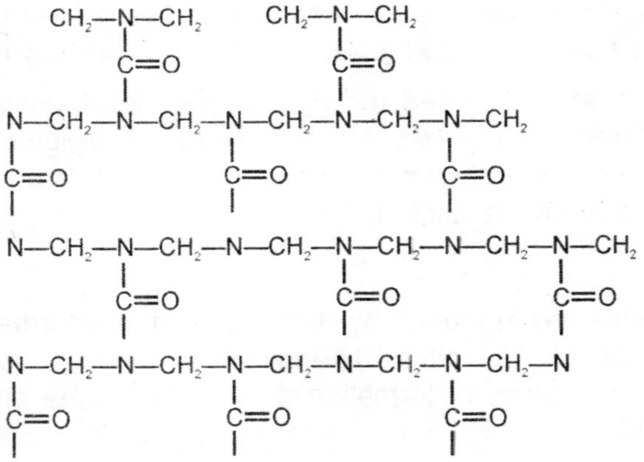

The condensation reactions between melamine and formaldehyde resemble those with urea but compared with the two methylol derivatives of urea, 1 mol of melamine can combine with 1-6 mols of formaldehyde. A similar reaction is also obtained with benzoguanamine and formaldehyde. The resultant resins can be cured by adding acid catalysts such as phthalic anhydride.

MANUFACTURE

The base resins are normally manufactured in a reaction kettle similar to that for phenol/formaldehyde resins described in chapter 3.

Molding Powders

The base resin, either urea or melamine, is produced in a fairly low state of condensation. Urea formaldehyde molecular ratios of about 1 : 1.5 are preferred, while melamine-formaldehyde molecular ratios very from 1 : 1.5 to 1 : 3.0. The condensation is carried out under faintly alkaline conditions, and although the actual process of resin manufacture is quite simple, rigid control of the pH is essential. There are two general methods used for converting the resin into a molding powder. One, which is termed the wet process, consists of kneading the filler (wood-flour or bleached wood pulp) with the aqueous resin until the filler becomes thoroughly impregnated. The resultant mix is then broken up into fine crumbs and dried to the required plasticity. At this stage the material is in a for similar to coarse desiccated coconut and is placed in a ball-mill together with catalyst (acidic, e.g., hexamine), lubricants (stearates) and pigments. It is then ground to a find powder and finally sieved to remove any coarse particles. The resultant molding powder may be too bulky for certain application and can be densified by granulating either on heated mixing rolls or on a Banbury mixer.

The other methods, termed and dry process, merely consists of mixing the condensed resin with fillers, catalyst, lubricants, and pigments on heated mixing rolls. At the correct temperature the mix resinifies and can then be sheeted off and finally granulated.

Adhesive

These resins are produced by reacting urea and formaldehyde in a molecular ratio of 1 : 2. The initial pH of the reaction medium is usually neutral or slightly alkaline to allow the formation of the methylol urea, and then raised to a mildly acid medium (pH = 5) to ensure a steady rate of condensation. The reaction can be followed by viscosity measurements and the tendency of the resin to be hydrophobic. At a predetermined stage the process is stopped by neutralisation and the resin is then either dehydrated under vaccum, to give a viscous product of 1-10 poises and 60-70 per cent solids content, or spray dried to give a resin powder. The resin syrup can then be stabilised by the addition of weak bases or by protective colloids such as starch. The liquid product has a shelf-life of between 3-9 months whereas the spray dried powder is usable for periods of up to two years.

Laminating Resins

For this application the resin is taken to a fairly advanced state of condensation. Urea-formaldehyde resins may require an acid catalyst to effect hardening. Melamine formaldehyde laminating resins are more popular and are obtained in the form of a dry powder by spray-drying the resultant condensation resin. The subsequent powders have a relatively long shelf-life and can be used as and when required by dissolving in water or water/alcohol mixtures, and heating to 60°C to give a solids content of 40-50 per cent.

The resin can be applied to fabric or paper by direct immersion or by roller coating. The resultant sheets must be cut into appropriate sizes and the laminates can then the build up from numerous sheets. The resultant laminate can be cured by pressing at 120-150°C under a pressure of 500-2000 lb/in_2. In the preparation of many of the well known decorative laminates the printed pattern layer is inpregnated either with a urea-melamine condensate or, as is more common, a phenolic resin, and a protective translucent overlay sheet, treated with melamine resin, superimposed.

Surface Coatings

Such resins are usually prepared by reacting urea and formalin together with an excess of a monohydric alcohol acidic conditions. The water of condensation so formed is distilled off. The most popular alcohol is butanol, and the resultant resin can be blended with equal parts of a glycelol/phthalic anhydride alkyd resin or a hydroxyl containing acrylic.

This reaction is generally referred to as etherification and sometimes these products are loosely referred to as "blocked" amino resins. On heating to about 150°C the alcohol splits off and the resin undergoes self-condensation and coreaction with the pendent hydroxyl groups of the alkyd or acrylic resin.

Etherification or alkylation with the lower alcohols such as methanol, generally leads to water soluble resins which have found considerable use in textile finishing but unfortunately are in compatible with hydrocarbon solvents.

One member of this family which has been widely used over the past years is the hexamethyl ether of hexamethylol melamine (HMEHMM). The structure is as follows :

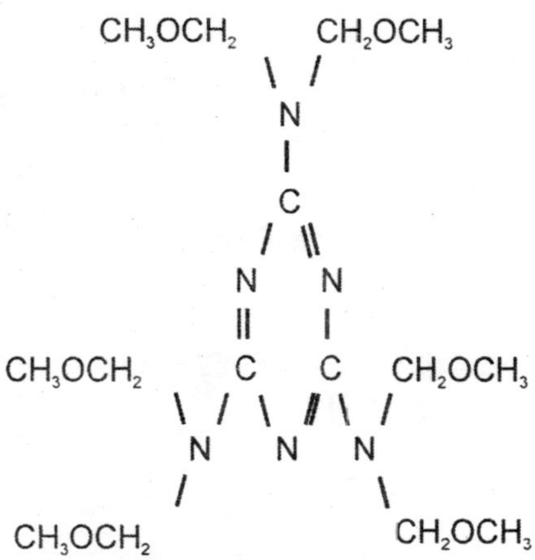

Typical commercial products of this family are cymel 300 and 301 manufactured by American Cyanamid. A general process would be to dissolve one mole of melamine in excess formalin (9 mol CH_2O) at about 60°C with the pH being kept at alkaline (9.0-9.5). On cooling the hexamethylol melamine separates out and is then filtered, washed with water, and even dried at temperatures not in excess of 40°C. Excess methanol is then added to the resultant dried hexamethylol melamine under acid conditions until dissolution is complete when the solution is neutralised and then filtered with the excess methanol being removed by vaccum distillation. The resultant pure ether is a crystalline solid, colorless, with a melting point temperature of 55°C.

This ether has limited solubility in water but dissolves readily in water containing methanol. It has the ability to react with groups containing a reactive hydrogen atom and its wide range of solubility and polymer compatability renders it a very versatile cross-linking agent for many potential surface coating polymers. If no catalyst are used then the cure times are lengthy but by the addition of strong acid catalysts such as p-toluene sulfonic acid the cycles are reduced considerably. This resin can also be used to react with epoxide groups where they react with hydroxyl groups. The resultant cured films have good flexibility with a high degree of resistance of alkalies.

This etherified melamine has been widely used as the cross linking agent for water soluble alkyds and acrylics. These water-based coating resins are now finding use in the autcmotice industry.

$$\underset{\text{Alkyd or acrylic}}{R{-}CH_2{-}CH_2{-}OH} + \underset{\text{Amino resin}}{R'{-}\underset{H}{N}{-}CH_2{-}OH} \longrightarrow$$

$$R{-}CH_2{-}CH_2{-}O{-}CH_2{-}\underset{H}{N}{-}R' \xrightarrow{\text{Heat}}$$

$$R{-}CH_2{-}CH_2{-}\underset{H}{N}{-}R' + CH_2 = O$$

Textile Finishing

Many years ago it became apparent that the tendency of cellulosic fabrics to crease when folded could be covercome by treatment with amino resins. These resins also impart a relatively high degree of resistance to shrinkage on washing. It is also better to first desize and scour the fabric (cotton) before impregnating. This allows the amino resin, which should also be of comparatively low molecular weight, to penetrate the cellulose fibres. Simply, the process consists of padding the fabric through an aqueous solution of amino resin containing an acid or acid liberating catalyst such as magnesium chloride. Excess resin is removed by passing through mangle rolls, which also ensures further penetration. The fabric can then be dried on a stenter with hot air and then passed through an oven at 140-160°C to cure the resin. Washing with alkaline can be used to neutralise the acid catalyst but this is not always done.

In concluding this section some different types of amino resins are discussed.

Ethylene Urea

This is made from reacting urea with ethylene diamine.

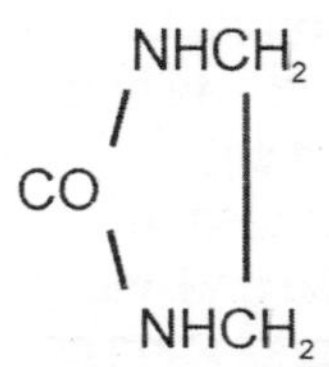

It will react with formaldehyde to form a dimethylol derivative which has ampt of 133°C and is readily soluble in water. This resin has been found to give good crease resistance and there is evidence to suggest that the dismethylol ethylene (DMEU) cross-links with adjacent cellulose molecules.

Propylene Urea

This is made by reacting urea and 1,3 diamine propane.

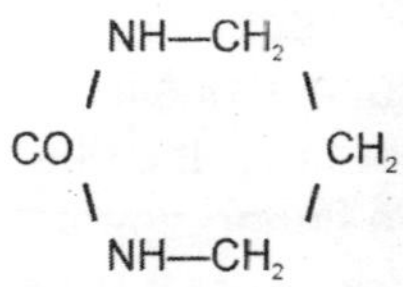

This product also react with formaldehyde to form the dimethylol derivative which is more resistant to laundering then the DMEU but more expensive.

Dihydroxyethylene Urea

This is made by reacting glyoxal with urea, although it is more common to form the dimethylol derivative by coreacting urea, glyoxal, and formaldehyde in 1 : 1 : 2 mol ratio yet without isolating the (DEU). This is probably the most widely used of the cyclic urea finishes and the cross-linking occurs

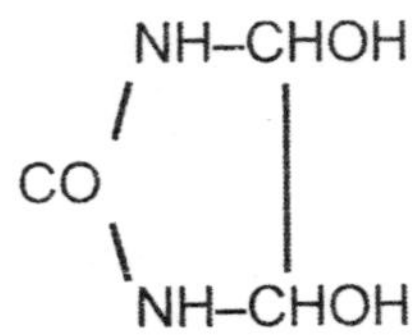

not only by the methylol groups but also via the ring hydroxyls. This product is noted for its absence of formaldehyde odor when finishing fabrics and curing.

The dimethylol dihydroxy ethylene urea (DMDHEU) has been found to be suitable in durable press processes. One of the best known types of processes in the Koratron process. This was introduced in the early 1960's by the Koret Company of California, U.S.A. The process simply consists of impregnating fabrics (blends of cotton or rayon with polyester) with a solution of ramino resin and a metal salt catalyst. The resultant impregnating fabric is then dried carefully to avoid resin fixation. The fabric is then made into garments which are hot pressed and finally baked for 10-20 minutes at 145-155°C. This process is ideal for placing creases and pleats where desired. It must be made clear that in this process no crosslinking must take place on the stored fabric and the reaction must go to completion in the baking oven. DMDHEU has been found to be very suitable for this process because it is capable of existing in the unreacted state for very long periods in the presence of metallic salts such as zinc nitrate or magnesium chloride.

Curing or Hardening Agents

Although certain urea formaldehyde resins will cure solely by the action of heat it is essential on an industrial scale to add materials which will speed up this process. For such resins it is essential that setting up will not take place in storage and, therefore, the effect should preferably be carried out by the action of heat on a curing agent. Many different materials have been used for molding powders from the inorganic material zinc sulfate to organic materials such as chloroacetamide. Other materials used include dichlorhydrin, triethyl phosphate and chloro acetone.

Hardeners are nearly always used for urea-formaldehyde resins in adhesive/laminating applications. They are usually acidic or acid liberating-substances. No alkaline hardeners, as far as present knowledge goes, have been used for curing urea-formaldehyde wood adhesives although certain such materials have been used for fixing urea condensates in the treatment of textiles. Ammonium salts are very popular hardening agents and these will react with the free formaldehyde present in the resin to give hexamine and free acid. The reaction is somewhat complex and may briefly by represented as follows :

$$4NH_4Cl + 6CH_2O \rightarrow N_4(CH_2)_6 + 6H_2O + 4HCl$$

There are other materials that can be used satisfactorily, including phosphoric acid, hydrogen peroxide, ethylene, thiocyanate, and glyceryl phthalates.

PROCESSING TECHNIQUES

Molding Powders

Aminoplasts can be molded by the conventional thermosetting molding techniques of compression and transfer molding described in Chapter 23. The thermosetting molding powders can be molded in the temperature range 135-170°C, using pressures of 1-3 ton/in2, depending on the complexity of the mold. Mold design is virtually the same as for the phenoplasts and, as with the latter materials, care must be exercised in allowing for the bulk factor of the molding powder. It has been found in practice that the UF's are somewhat more critical to mold than the MFs due to the fact that they have less flow and a tendency to set and cure faster in the mold.

Adhesives/Laminates

Urea-formaldehyde resins may be used for gluing wood by a variety of techniques and have now around a major outlet in the hot-press bonding of plywood. This process consists essentially of spreading the adhesive/hardener mixture on to the base wood veneers at a controlled rate and building up the laminate by placing the veneers on top of each other with the grain crossed each time. The resultant plywood laminate is then consolidated by pressing at 30-200 lb/in2 at temperature between 95-110°C. The glueline of the plywood is virtually colorless, which is an advantage over the phenolic adhesives, it does not support mold growth, and it will comply with certain sections of B.S. 1203 and 1204.

In certain constructional applications it is not always convenient to apply heat to the structure and techniques have now been developed whereby cold setting urea-formaldehyde adhesives can be used, pressure being applied by jigs and clamps.

Another interesting techniques is one in which the hardener is applied to the face of one adherend, resin to the face of the other; when the two faces are mated the resin is hardened and the adherends are satisfactory bonded. This is attractive because the limitations on pot-life are reduced.

In industry which has grown to considerable magnitude over the past few years is based on the manufacture of certain constructional materials from wood-waste and urea-formaldehyde adhesives. The resultant product is more commonly known as 'chipboard'. The boards are made by mixing 5-10 per cent of the resin with wood chips and pressing at 200-1000 lb/in^2 at a temperature of 100-110°C.

The use of melamine and urea-formaldehyde resins as laminating materials has already been discussed but we should mention here that the resultant laminate is normally pressed between 2000-3000 lb/in^2 at temperatures between 140-160°C.

PROPERTIES

The base resins are usually clear water-white syrups or white powders. Correctly cured moldings are odorless and tasteless which makes them eminently suitable for domestic articles. A specification is available covering such molding, viz. B.S. 1322: 1956, 'Aminoplastic Moulding Materials'. The

Table 4.1

TYPICAL PROPERTIES OF UF AND MF MOLDING POWDERS

Property	*U/F*	*U/F*	*M/F*
S.G. at 15°C		1.48-1.52	1.47-1.52
Tensile strength (lb/in^2)		5000-7000	7000-10,000
Elongation at Break (%)		0.6	0.7
Impact strength ft lb. notch		0.26	0.3
Compressive strength (lb/in^2)		25-35,000	25-40,000
Flexural strength (lb/in^2)		10-16,000	10-16,000
Thermal conductivity (cal/s/ cm^2/°C/cm X 10^{-4})		7-10	7-10
Heat Destortion temperature (°F)		270-280	380
Volume resistivity (ohm/cm)		10^{12}-10^{13}	10^{12}-10^{14}
Dielectric strength (V/mil)		300-400	300-400
Dielectric constant 10^6 c/s		6-7	7-8
Chemical resistance			
Strong acids		Decomposed	Decomposed
Weak acids		Resistant	Resistant
Strong alkalis		Attacked	Attacked
Weak alkalis		Slightly attacked	Resistant
Solvents		Resistant	Resistant

synthetic resin adhesives are covered by B.S. 1203: 1956, 'Synthetic Resin Adhesives for Plywood (phenol and urea-formaldehyde)' and B.S. 1204: 1956 'Synthetic Resin Adhesive (phenol and urea-formaldehyde) for Constructional Work in Wood'. Urea formaldehyde resins are less resistant to water than the melamine and phenol types. B.S. 1203 specific three types of adhesives– Type MR, Type WBP and Type BR. It has been established in practice that the phenolic resins meet the specification for Type WBP, melamine/urea resins for type BR and urea-formaldehyde resins for Type MR.

Aminoplasts are relatively unaffected by common organic solvents, oils, greases, cold water and cold dilute acids and alkalis. Urea resins are very slightly swollen by water and polyhydric alcohols whereas the melamines show practically no swelling. Both resins are attacked by acids and alkalis. Typical properties of urea and melamine formaldehyde molding powdes (α-cellulose filled) are given in Table 4.1.

APPLICATIONS

Although urea-formaldehyde resins were first used as molding powders it is not this application which absorbs the greater part of the resins used today. Many of the end-uses which were once exclusively applied to ureaformaldehyde resins are now being replaced by thermoplastic, materials. The reason is not always due to material performance, but with thermoplastics the injection molding techniques allow for rapid cycles and therefore higher production rates. However, urea/formaldehyde moldings powders are still used extensively for the production of electrical accessories due to the fact that in addition to having the required mechanical strength and rigidity they can also be molded round metallic inserts. Urea formal dehyde molding powders are one of the lowest priced nonflammable and nontracking molding materials at present available. Urea-formaldehyde molding powders are cheaper than melamine and are, therefore, generally favored for nearly all electrical accessories except for lampholders, for which MFs are used because of their greater resistance to embrittlement on prolonged exposure to high temperatures.

Urea-formaldehyde is used quite extensively for closures in the cosmetic industry because of its wide color range, its high degree of resistance to solvents, greases and oils, and its surface hardness. Such properties also make it eminently suitable for use in domestic goods such as hair dryer and mixer housings, clock cases, lavatory seats, and even buttons.

The application for which the melamine-formaldehyde molding powders are best known, and which accounts for probably the largest single outlet, is that of fine-quality tableware. The moldings are tasteless, odorless, nontoxic and will withstand staining from coffee, tea and fruit juices. For this application the molding powders are filled with α-cellulose. Other uses include cutlery handles, aerosol dispensers and domestic kitchen utensil housings.

It is probably true to say that the product life of the aminoplasts has been revitalised with the development of the technology for the injection molding thermosets. This new technique has so speeded up the molding process that these older materials can now complete with the newer thermoplastics on an equal footing.

Suggestions have been made in the literature that cellulose-filled-molding powders based on a cocondensation product of melamine-benzoguanamine and formaldehyde give moldings with better water resistance as well as resistance to stain by tea and coffee then melamine-formaldehyde. It has been mentioned previously that benzoguanamine is more expensive than melamine and thus these cocondensates are more costly molding materials.

The amino resins have now gained wide acceptance in the wood, furniture and allied industries. They are used largely in the production of plywood and 'chipboard', and their use in general constructional work is of some importance. The melamines are preferred where better strength and water-resistant characteristics are required.

The main outlet for these resins in the laminating field is in a production of decorative paper-based laminates. For this particular application the melamines are the preferred materials because of their good water-and heat resistance. Little description is necessary for the wide application of such laminates for surfacing wood, plaster and 'hardboard'. Melamine formaldehyde resins are also used in conjunction with glass-mat and cloth, cotton, asbestos and certain synthetic fibres. Such laminates in general possess high mechanical strength, good heat resistance, and good electrical insulating properties, for these reasons they are used in printed circuit panels and electrical switchgear.

The amino resins have also been used quite widely in the textile industry, originally to improve the crease-resistance of cellulose fabrics. The now well-known 'drip-dry' fabrics owe their existence largely to such resins. Fabrics can also be made partially waterproof by treatment with certain amino resins, although the silicone treatment is, in general, now to be preferred.

The tanning process of leather can be greatly accelerated by treatment with solutions of methylol melamines or other low condensed amino resins.

Both urea and melamine-formaldehyde resins have been used to overcome the well-known disadvantage of paper, that of losing its strength when wet. It has been found that treatment with melamine resins makes it longer-lasting though move expensive.

In conjunction with alkyds and acrylics they provide coatings which can be baked to give highly durable and mar-resistant finishes, indoor applications of which include coatings for kitchen and refrigerator cabinets. Melamine/alkyds and acrylics have also been used in automobile finishes, being applied by spray techniques and subsequently stoved (cured) at temperatures around 130°C. Butylated benzoguanamine resins are also used for stoving enamels and when plasticised with oil modified alkyds they cure more slowly than urea-formaldehydes and melamine formaldehydes, though they give films with better gloss and alkali resistance.

Mention should also be made of another application of urea-formaldehyde, a foamed material which is made by vigorously mixing an aqueous solution of a detergent, an acid catalyst, with a urea-formaldehyde condensate. After foaming, the material is discharged from mixer, where it sets rapidly, and then allowed to dry out slowly. Densities around 0.8 lb/ft3 can be obtained. Prefoamed slabs are used as thermal insulants for refrigerators and houses. A disadvantage of this material is the difficulty of handling it due to its relatively low strength. This is partly overcome in buildings where it can be foamed in situ between walls or under floors to improve thermal insulation.

UF foams were originally developed in Germany around the 1940s as heat insulating materials, using the trade name "IPORKA". It was not until some ten years later that this application came to the forefront of the insulation industry.

Not only can this foam be used in new brick houses but it can also be used in older types by drilling holes in the bricks and filling the cavities by injecting foam from a gun.

These foams are cheap, nonflammable and hydrophobic with low densities (0.5 lb/ft^3) although more dense products can be made by using more concentrated resin solution and different hardeners.

Other uses for these foams are holding blocks for foral arrangements, artificial snow for film and television scenery, also arrester beds at the end of airway runs.

5

Polyesters

The name polyester is used to describe a diverse group of materials formed as a result of a condensation reaction between a polyhydric alcohol and a polybasic acid. The history of these materials can be traced back to as early as 1847, when a Swedish scientist, J.J. Berzelius, obtained a white amorphous solid of a resinous nature on heating glycerol with tartaric acid. The reaction was subsequently modified later, in England, by replacing the tartaric acid with phthalic andydride (acid.) This particular work was carried out by Watson Smith who, in 1902, obtained a wide range of resinous products from such reactions, which he named 'glyptal.' The name was in use until made virtually obsolete by the introduction of 'alkyd', which is derived from a combination of the words Alcohol-aCID. The term 'alkyd' was originally coined by R.H. Kienle who carried out many classes polymerisation studies on polyesters used for surface coatings and molding powders.

A great advance was considered to have been made in 1937 when Carlton Ellis. In America, discovered that by adding unsaturated monomers to unsaturated polyesters the setting (curing) time was substantially reduced. This made the polyester resins attractive for use on a commercial basis, in addition to stimulating further interest.

The industry founded on polyester resins has been relatively slow in growing although, from the period 1919-1926, there was considerable industrial development of these resins in varnishes and paints. The use of polyesters for purposes other than surface coatings can be considered to have started at the outbreak of the Second World War when the first industrial uses of polyester as laminating resins were seen in the U.S.A. Developments were even later in this country, for it was not until 1946 that polyester resins were first offered to specialised industries such as the aircraft industry. Alkyd molding materials were first produced in the U.S.A. in 1948 and then later in Great Britain (1952).

During W.H. Carother's classical work on polymer formation, he investigated a large number of polyesters. He recognised the ability of certain linear polymers to form fibres and subsequently patents were taken out defining the conditions for fiber-forming polyesters. In particular, fibers formed from dibasic acids and glycols were mentioned. His basic work was to be later substantiated by two British scientists, Whinfield and Dickson who, in 1941, discovered that on reacting terephthalic acid with ethylene glycol, a resinous mass was formed which could be subsequently drawn into fibers. This was the beginning, in the U.K. of the synthetic fiber now of world renown, namely Terylene and Dacron in the U.S.A.

Since the early 1960's we have seen the introduction of several new types of polyesters. The alkyl and alkyl resins have developed in the molding field and the use of water soluble and air drying alkyds have also become well established. Around 1966 polyethylene terephthalate was developed for molding applications such as by the injection technique and later in 1969 came the introduction of polybutylene terephthalate and polymethylene terephthalate. In recent years we have seen the introduction of aromatic polyesters for heat temperature applications in the 1970's the vinyl esters were introduced into the field of laminating and casting.

CLASSIFICATION

Polyesters can be broadly classified into unsaturated, saturated, and the more recent vinyl ester polymers. These broad divisions can then be further subdivided as follows :

1. Unsaturated

(a) Laminating and Casting Resins. Probably the oldest member of this group is a type based on the reaction product of dibasic acids and dihydric alcohols. The polyesters units so formed must be capable of copolymerising with a vinyl-type monomer, thereby yielding a vinyl-polyester copolyser or simply a cured polyester with a thermoset structure. Included in this group are also the alkyl resins based on diallyl phthalate and diallyl isophthalate. These have found wide range casting as well as laminating resins.

The newest member of this group is the resins based on vinyl ester. These form a range of thermosetting resins which find wide use in fabricating reinforced plastic structures. While these materials may be regarded as unsaturated, the unsaturation does not occur along the polymer backbone and is terminal. The structure of these resins is discussed more fully later but basically it is as follows:

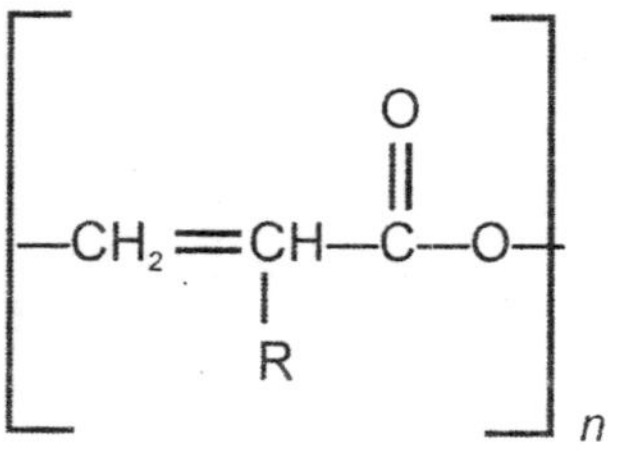

(b) Surface Coatings. The alkyds are the oldest member of this particular group and probably the oldest commercially available type of polyester. These resins are, in general, of the same type as (a) although the 'glyptal' (surface coatings) types are modified with oils or fatty acids.

Considerable work has been carried out to develop solventless wood lacquers in attempts in replace nitrocellulose. Single coats give a very high gloss surface but they suffer from air inhibition and remain permanently soft and tacky. This tackiness can be overcome by the addition of wax but the result is a dull finish. Wax-free polyester resins have now been developed and an early technique was employed to modify the polyester with a glyceryl α-alkyl ether. An interesting product which has found some use in this application is the tetra alkyl ether of sorbitol.

In recent years work has been carried out for developing water soluble alkyds. The approach was to build acid groups in excess by the use of polyfunctional acids such as trimellitic anhydride and then to neutralize the residual acid groups with an amine thereby rendering them water soluble.

2. Saturated

(a) Fibers and Films. These are based on the reaction of terephthalic acid with ethylene glycol and are linear, high molecular weight polymers which do not undergo any cross-linking reactions.

(b) Thermoplastic Molding Resins. The polyethylene terephthalate (P.T.E.) polymers as described in 2 (a) have expanded their uses into applications other than films and fibers, particularly in extrusion rather than injection molding. Polyester which have found extensive use in injection molding are polybutylterephthate (P.B.T.) and polytetramethylene terephthalate (P.T.M.T.) Similar materials have found use in powder coatings and hot melt adhesive. For this latter application there has been a move to using copolyesters utilising mixtures of varying carboxylic acids and glycols in certain critical proportions.

Another type is classified as aromatic polyesters and is described in the chapter on high temperature polymers.

(c) Molding Materials. Alkyd is also used to describe a group of thermosetting molding materials based on the reaction of a dihydric alcohols with an unsaturated acid such as maleic or fumaric in place of the more conventional phthalic acid (anhydride). A vinyl-type monomer is also necessary to effect speedy cross linking and curing. These materials, when suitably modified with certain fillers, are used as molding powders for compression and transfer-molding techniques similar to those used for the pheno-and amino plasts.

The resins discussed in 1 (a) for casting and laminating can also be used in conjunction with chopped glass fiber for dough molding compounds (DMC) as can be the resins based on allyl derivatives and vinyl esters.

(d) Polyester/Polyurethanes. Certain polyesters having a high hydroxyl, content can be reacted with various isocyanates to form polyurethanes, which are used extensively as foams, elastomers, surface coatings and adhesive. Such polyester are high viscous liquids or waxy solids at room temperature.

Polyesters formed from the ring opening of lactones such as the polycoprolactone from Union Carbide may be used as flesibilisers or the high molecular weight types as modifiers for high density polyethylene.

(e) Plasticisers. These can be polyesters which are completely saturated, normal referred to as polymeric plasticisers. A description of them is given later in this book, under the relevant section on plasticisers.

RAW MATERIALS

The many base raw materials used for manufacturing polyester resin can at times be confusing and, therefore, the preparation of the more important constituents is described.

Saturated Alcohols (Glycols)

(a) Ethylene glycol $[(CH_2)_2(OH)_2]$, is the first member of the glycol series which contains no double bond unsaturation. It is derived from ethylene via ethylene dichlorhydrin and ethylene oxide, or straight from ethylene oxide. The ethylene it self is obtained by the catalytic cracking of petroleum.

(i)

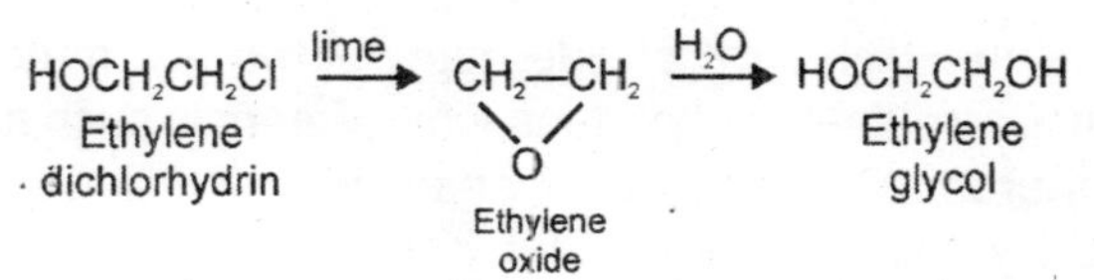

(ii)

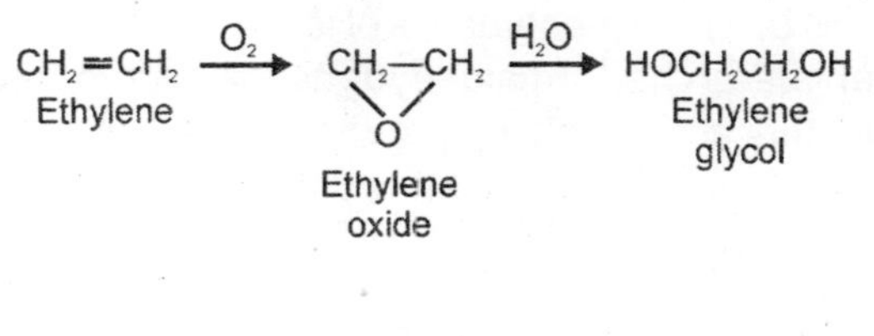

(b) Propylene glycol [$CH_3CHOHCH_2OH$]. Two isomers exist for this material although only 1,2 propanediol is commercially availabe. Propylene glycol is obtained from propylene via a similar set of reactions as for ethylene glycol. Propylene is a further product of the catalytic craking of petroleum.

(c) Diethylene glycol [$HOCH_2CH_2OCH_2CH_2Oh$] is produced either as a by-product in the manufacture of ethylene glycol or by reacting the latter material with ethylene oxide.

(d) Glycerol [$OHCH_2CHOHCH_2OH$] is used in the production of polyester resin employed as surface coatings. Traditionally, glycerol has been produced from vegetable oils as a by-product during saponification:

$$\text{vegetable oil} \xrightarrow[H_2O]{NaOH} \text{glycerol} + \text{soap}$$

An entirely different method is also used and is based on molasses, as follows :

$$\begin{matrix}\text{sugar} \\ \text{(molasses)}\end{matrix} \xrightarrow[\substack{\text{high pressure} \\ \text{catalyst}}]{\text{hydrogen}} \text{glycerol} + \text{other polyols}$$

The most common method, however, is to use propylene which is still the preferred commercial method. The propylene is first converted to allyl chloride, then to glycerol dichlorhydin and finally to glycerol.

There are many other saturated alcohols used in the manufacture of polyester resins although space does not permit a lengthy description. These include dipropylene glycol, mannitol, sorbitol, and 1,4 butanediol.

Mannitol and sorbitol are related to the sugar family but apart from these the remainder are products of the ever-growing petrochemicals industry. The largest two feedstocks are propylene and ethylene, previously discussed.

A reaction which can provide many of the raw materials for polyester production is an aldol-type condensation. Materials such as neopentyl glycol, trimethylol propane, hexantriol, penta erythritol, and many more can be produced by this reaction. The actual reaction involves aldol-type condensations between preparations of formaldehyde and other low molecular weight aldehydes. The formaldehyde takes part in the condensation and also reduces the 'end' aldehyde group.

$$2CH_2O + CH_3 \cdot CH_2 \cdot CHO \xrightarrow{\text{alkali}} (HO \cdot CH_2)_2\, C \cdot Me \cdot CHO \cdot$$

$$(HO \cdot CH_2)_2\, CMe \cdot CHO + CH_2O + MeOH \longrightarrow$$

$$CMe(CH_2 \cdot OH)_3 + H \cdot CO_2Me.$$

Another interesting reaction is in the manufacture of 1-4 butane diol. This involves the hydrogeneration of 1-4, butyne idol using a nickel-copper manganese catalyst. The 1,4-butyne diol is first obtained from the reaction between acetylene and formaldehyde.

With such a multitude of raw materials the polymer chemist has a wide range of functionalities and molecular weight to enable him to build in many different characteristics into the polyester resins. Commercial materials with functionalities *(f)* varying from 2 up to 6 are used. The following are some of the alcohols which are used showing their functionality.

(i) $HOH_2C—CH_2OH$

$f = 2$

Ethylene glycol

(ii)

H
|
HC — OH
|
HC — OH
|
HC — OH
|
H

$f = 3$

Glycerol

(iii)

CH_2OH
|
$HOH_2C—C—CH_2OH$
|
CH_2OH

$f = 4$

Pentaerythritol

(iv) $HOCH_2(CHOH)_4CH_2OH$

$f = 6$

Sorbitol

Unsaturated Alcohols

Allyl alcohols [$CH_2 = CHCH_2OH$] is prepared by the oxidation of propylene to acrolein, followed by reduction or by the isomerisation of propylene oxide.

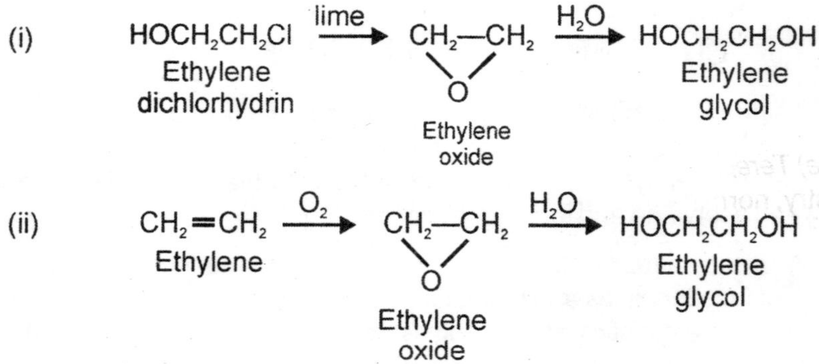

Other unsaturated alcohols used in polyester production include 2 butene-1,4 diol, and 2,5 dimethyl 3 hexyne, 2,5 diol and 3,6 dimethyl 4, octyne-3,6 diol.

Saturated Acids

(a) Phthalic acid [$C_6H_4(CODH)_2$] is normally produced and used in the form of the anhydride by the controlled oxidation of naphthalene or *o*-xylene.

(b) Adipic acid [$HOOC(CH_2)_4COOH$] is also an important raw material for the manufacture of polyamides, and its production is covered in Chapter 12, along with sebacic acid.

(c) Sebacic acid [$HOOC(CH_2)_8COOH$] is normally prepared from castor oil by treatment with hot caustic soda. The castor oil is 80 to 90 per cent the glyceride of ricinoleic acid:

$$\left[CH_3(CH_2)_5CHOHCH_2CH{=}CH(CH_2)_7COO\right]_3C_3H_5 + 6NaOH + 2H_2O \xrightarrow{\text{Heat}}$$

$$\underset{\text{2-Octanol}}{3CH_3(CH_2)_5\underset{\displaystyle OH}{\underset{|}{C}}HCH_3} + 3NaOOC(CH_2)_8COONa + \underset{\text{Glycerol}}{C_3H_3(HO_3)} + 3H_2$$

$$3NaOOC(CH_2)_8COONa \xrightarrow{HCl} \underset{\text{Sebacis acid}}{HOOC(CH_2)_8COOH}$$

(d) Azelaic acid [$HOOC(CH_2)_7COOH$] is made by the ozonolysis of oleic acid:

$$CH_3(CH_2)_7CH{=}CH(CH_2)_7COOH \xrightarrow[\text{Solvent}]{O_2,\ O_3,\ H_2O}$$

$$\underset{\text{Pelargonic acid}}{CH_3(CH_2)_7COOH} + \underset{\text{Azelaic acid}}{HOOC(CH_2)_7COOH}$$

(e) Terephthalic acid [$C_6H_4(COOH)_2$] is a product of the coal and petrolium industry, normally prepared by the oxidation of *p*-xylene.

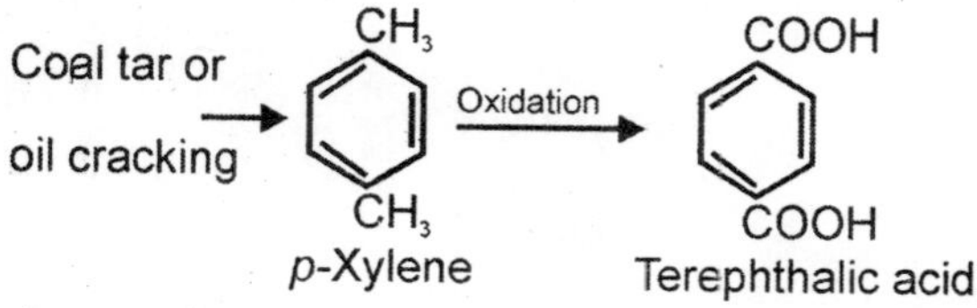

Dimethyl terephthalate is the ester normally used as the intermediate in the production of linear polyester for films and fibers, and it is produced by reacting terephthalic acid with methyl alcohol in the presence of sulfuric acid. There are two isomers of phthalic in general use for the production of polyester resins and their structural formula should not be confused.

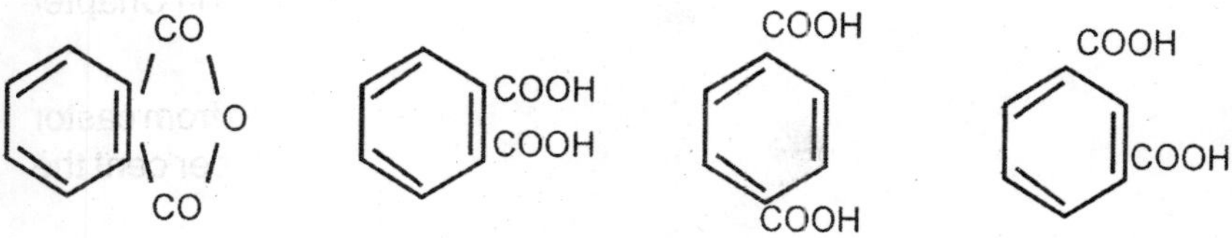

Phthalic anhydride | Phthalic acid (i) | Terephthalic acid (ii) | Isophthalic acid (iii)

Isophthalic acid is prepared industrially by the oxidation of *m*-xylene, which is obtained as a by-product in the manufacture of *p*-xylene. By using this saturated acid it is possible to obtain polyester resins with molecular weights higher than normal. Such resins exhibit superior strength characteristics, toughness and increased heat and chemical resistance over the standard phthalic acid resins.

Like a polyfunctional alcohols it is also possible to use polycarboxylic acids such as

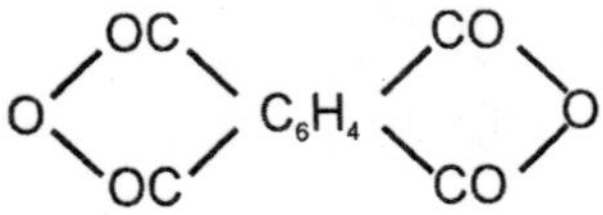

1,2 : 4, 5

$f = 4$

Pyromellitic anhydride

(i)

$C_6H_3(COOH)_3$

$f = 3$

Benzene tricarboxylic acid

(ii)

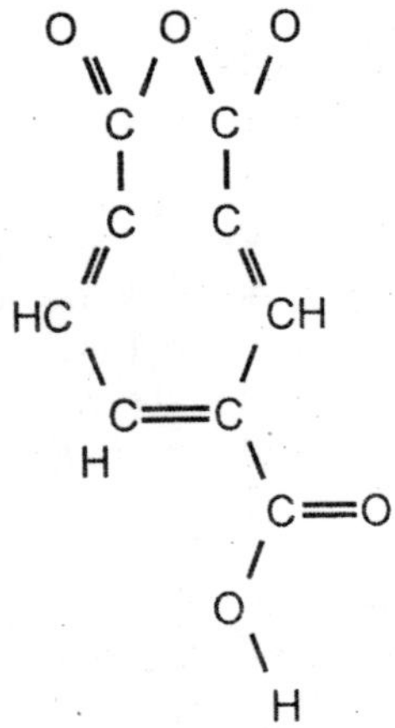

Trimellitic anhydride

$f = 3$

(iii)

Unsaturated Acids

The most commonly used acids are the cis-trans isomers maleic acid and fumaric acid. Maleic acid is used in the form of its anhydride.

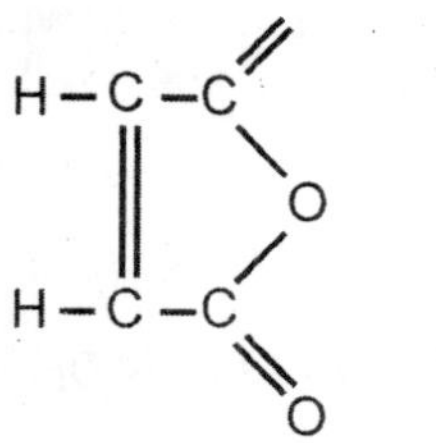
Maleic anhydride
(i)

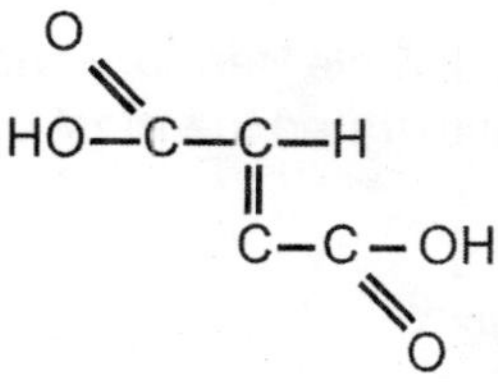
Fumaric acid
(ii)

Maleic anhydride is produced commercially by the catalytic oxidation of benzyene with a vanadium catalyst or by the vapor phase oxidation of butylene. Fumaric acid may be produced either by heating maleic acid or as a by-product in the manufacture of maleic anhydride. Both these unsaturated acids are relatively cheap and are the most popular of this group mainly due to price and the fact that more expensive acids do not offer significant advantages in properties. One exception, however, is chlorendic anhydride (hexachloro endomethylene tetra hydro phthalic acid), which is prepared by a Diels-Alder reaction between maleic anhydride and hexachlorocyclopentadiene. This product possesses double bonds which are not reactive under the usual conditions for preparing polyesters and they are therefore used in conjunction with maleic anhydride or fumaric acid in order to achieve cross-linking. Such a material is used when a high degree of flame resistance is required. The chlorendic anhydride is fumaric acid in order to achieve cross-linking. Such a material is used when a high dergree of flame resistance is required. The chlorendic anhydride in actual fact rapidly absorbs water from the air becoming "chlorendic acid" or more commonly referred to as HET acid.

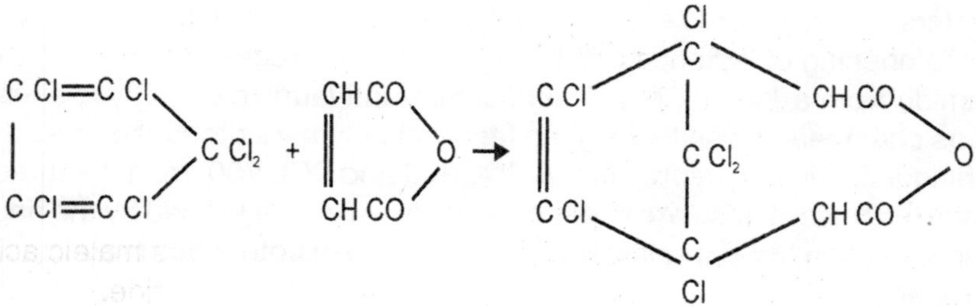

Chemistry of the Production of Polyesters

There is considerable literature and patents associated with this subject but the following illustrated the most common reactions available.

(a) Acid and glycol.

$$HO_2C \cdot R \cdot CO_2H + HOR'OH \rightleftharpoons HO_2C \cdot R \cdot CO_2 \cdot R'OH + H_2O$$

(b) Ester interchange.

$$MeO \cdot OC \cdot R \cdot CO \cdot OMe + HO \cdot R' \cdot OH \rightleftharpoons MeO \cdot OC \cdot R \cdot O \cdot R'OH + MeOH$$

(C) Acid chloride and glycol.

$$Cl \cdot OC \cdot R \cdot COCl + HO \cdot R' \cdot OH \longrightarrow Cl \cdot OC \cdot R \cdot CO_2 \cdot R'OH + HCL$$

(d) Ring opening of lactones (cyclic ester).

$$x\left[\begin{array}{c} CO \cdot O \\ \\ (CH_2)n \end{array}\right] + HO \cdot R \cdot OH \longrightarrow HO \cdot R[O_2C(CH_2)n]x\ OH$$

The first two reactions are reversible and continued reaction only occurs if the water or alcohol of condensation is removed completely. The ester interchange process is used mainly for the preparation of saturated polyesters of very high molecular weight suitable for fibers, film, or moldings. The ring opening of lactones can be likened to the process of preparing a polyamide from a lactam, e.g., caprolactum and laurilactum. Glycols are used as chain reaction initiates. One family of polymers produced by such a technique is the polycaprolactone PCL 300 and PCL 700, manufactured by Union Carbide. These are linear polyesters which are formed by the ring opening reaction of ε-caprolactone. The structure of both these products is given later.

Table 5.1

REACTIVE MONOMERS FOR POLYESTERS

Monomer	*Formula*	*Characteristics*
Styrene	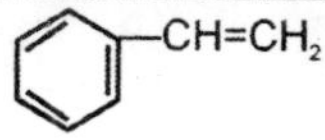	Relatively cheap, reduces viscosity, compatible
Methyl methacrylate	$CH_2{=}C(CH_3)\text{—CO—OCH}_3$	Good weathering
Vinyl toluene	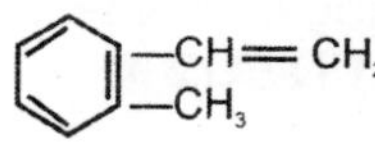	Similar in chemical-behavior to styrene-low vol-ability
α-Methyl styrene	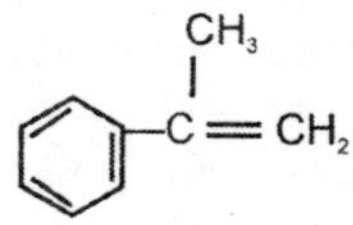	Reduces reactivity
Divinyl benzene	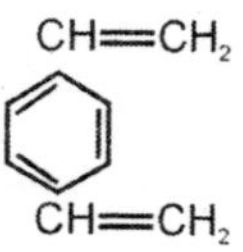	Difficult to blend with the poly-ester-reduces volatility
Dichlorostyrene	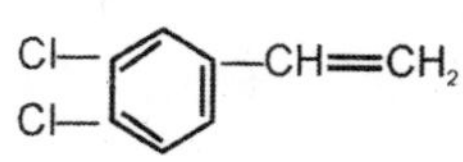	Good heat and fire resistance
Diallyl phthalate	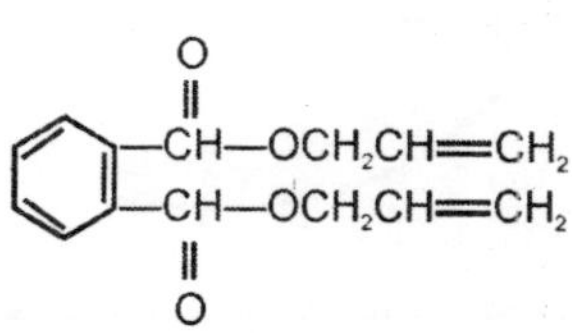	Slow-curing-flexi ble-low volatility
Triallyl cyanurate	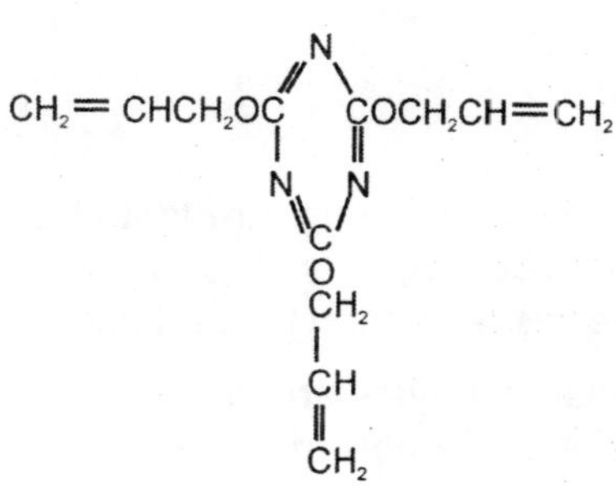	Heat resistance

Low molecular weight polyesters used for polyurethane technology and flexibilising cycloaliphatic epoxies are produced by the simple direct esterification process. These are regarded as diols and include such materials as Desmophen 2000 (from Bayer Chemicals, Germany) and Niax Polyols (Union Carbide, U.S.A.).

CROSS LINKING MONOMERS

It has been stated previously that for certain applications of polyester resins it is essential to convert the so-called linear polyester structure into the three-dimensional one commonly associated with thermosetting resins. This is normally achieved by adding a polymerisable vinyl type monomer; the more popular ones are listed in Table 5.1.

RESIN PREPARATION

Normally, all polyesters are prepared by using the same basic type of condensation reaction carried out in a resin kettle similar to the one described for phenol-formaldehyde in Chapter 3. The main difference is that the esterification reaction is carried out under a blanket of inert gas, such as nitrogen or carbon dioxide, whereas this precaution is unnecessary for pheno- and aminoplasts.

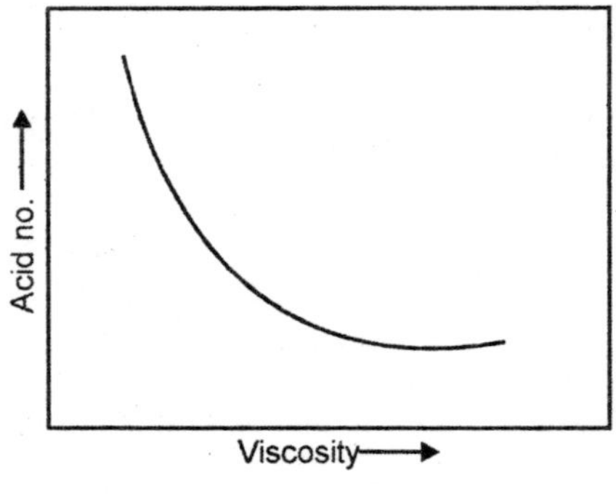

Fig. 5.1

The alcoholic and acidic constituents are first charged into the resin kettle and the temperature raised slowly to 140°C, with continuous stirring. The oxygen present in the vessel is then flushed out by the inert gas.

Sometimes esterification catalysts are introduced at the beginning of the reaction which brings about a considerable reduction in the reaction time. Suitable catalysts are *p*-toluene sulfonic acid or sulfuric acid. The reactants are refluxed and an inert solvent such as xylene is added to distill off azeotropically the water of reaction. The temperature is then slowly raised to 190°C until the acid value of the resin reaches 38-45. The acid value is an indication of the amount of free unreacted acid remaining, and is expressed

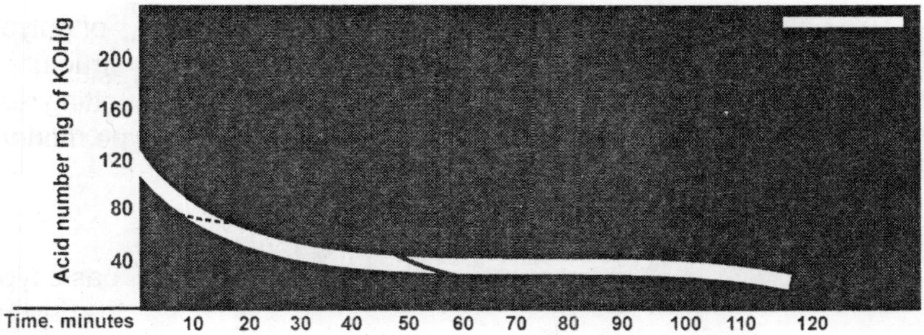

Fig. 5.2 Esterification rate of acids and anhydrides.

as the number of milligrams of potassium hydroxide required to neutralise one gram of sample. The viscocity increases throughout the reaction and the reaction is halted at a predetermined acid value. The relationship between viscocity and acid valve can be seen in Fig. 5.1. The esterification rate of acids and anhydrides is given in Fig. 5.2 The rate of reactions of polybasic acids with polyols can also be monitored by measuring the hydroxyl value and these tests are described in greater detail in the chapter entitled 'Physical and Chemical Testing of Plastics.'

On the reaching the required acid value the reactants are cooled to below 150°C, when the resin is ready for mixing with the reactive monomer. These resins, when dissolved in this monomer are highly reactive, and the cross-linking reaction can be started off by a free redical mechanism, and will gel. This can, however, be stopped by adding chemicals which prevent the free radicals from reacting. Such materials are quinone, hydroquinone, catechol, and teritiary butyl catechol.

Thus, before adding the resin from the kettle to another kettle containing the reactive monomer it is essential first to dissolve in inhibitor in the monomer. When the inhibitor has been well disappeared the polyester resin is added an stirred thoroughly. Finally, the resin is ready for discharging into containers. A flow diagram of the process can be seen in Fig. 5.3.

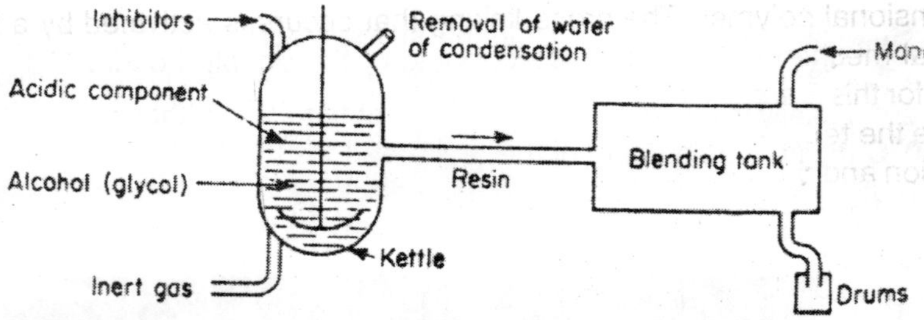

Fig. 5.3 Flow diagram for production of a polyester resin

The following formulation has been found suitable for the production of polyester resin for use in laminating the casting applications :

Materials		*Quantity (parts)*
Propylene glycol		*160*
Maleic anhydride		*115*
Phthalic anhydride		*85*
Xylene		*20*
Hydroquinone	*Inhibitors*	*0.5*
Quinone	*Inhibitors*	*0.005*
Styrene monomer		*150*

It is interesting to examine the graph in Fig. 5.2 which shows the rate of esterification of varying acids of differing structure. The acids used are phthalic anhydride, isophthalic acid, maleic anhydride, terephthalic acid, and trimellitic anhydride. It can be seen that the trimellitic anhydride reacts faster than the isophthalic or terephthalic acid and processes to the low acid number more rapidly than phthalic anhydride.

POLYMER STRUCTURE AND CHEMICAL TECHNIQUES

Laminating and Casting Resins

The typical procedure for the preparation of a polyester resin has been described earlier. The chemical reaction mechanism of the typical formulation quoted can now be looked at more closely.

The liquid resin obtained by such a reaction can be converted into the solid state by a further chemical reaction termed copolymerisation. This latter term is normally used more with thermoplastics than with the thermoset type of resins. The copolymerisation is effected by dissolving the resin in a reactive solvent which reacts with the unsaturated groups to form a three-dimensional polymer. The cross-linking that occurs is activated by a free radical mechanism which cause opening of the double bonds. Materials used for this reaction are sometimes called catalysts, although in the strictest sense the term is incorrect because they do, in actual fact, take part in the reaction and do not remain unchanged strucrtually.

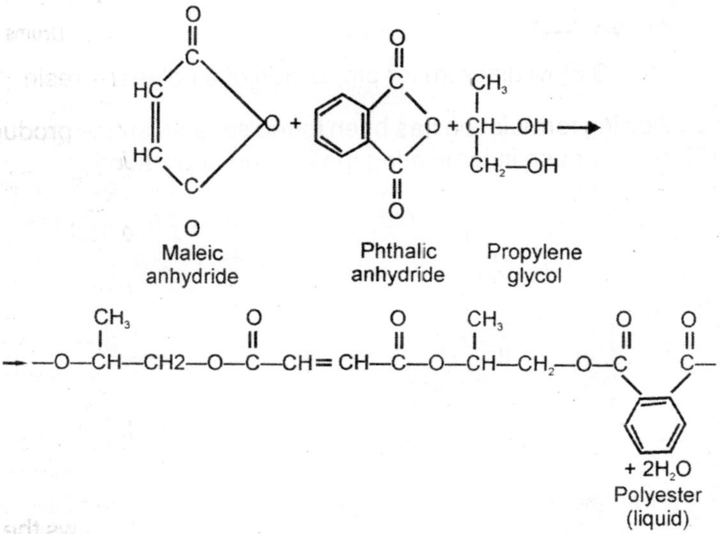

They are now more generally referred to as initiators and are usually organic peroxides. Two very popular materials are bnzoyl peroxide and methyl ethyl ketone peroxide. The speed of dissociation of these peroxides can be accelerated by the use of certain metallic salts or amines. The most popular accelerator for general use is cobalt naphthenate, which is normally used in conjunction with mehtyl ethyl ketone peroxide.

The polyesters can be cured either by hot or cold techniques, and for the former, benzoyl peroxide or teritiary butyl hydroperoxide are preferred while, for the cold-cure, methyl ethyl ketone peroxide or cyclohexanone peroxide are more commonly used.

The overall curing action can be schematically represented as follows, where M represents the maleic residue of the previous reaction described, P and pthththalic residue, G the glycol, and X the reactive monomer (such as styrene) :

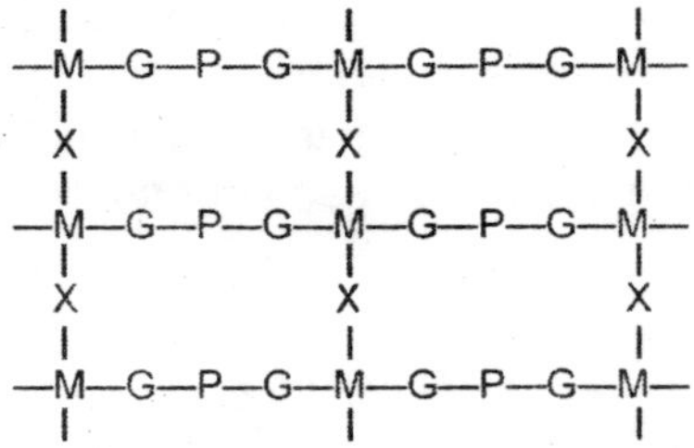

(cured polyester resin)

Vinyl Esters

A typical example of the molecular structure of a typical vinyl ester can be achieved by reacting two mols of methacrylic acid with a polyepoxide. The structure is as follows :

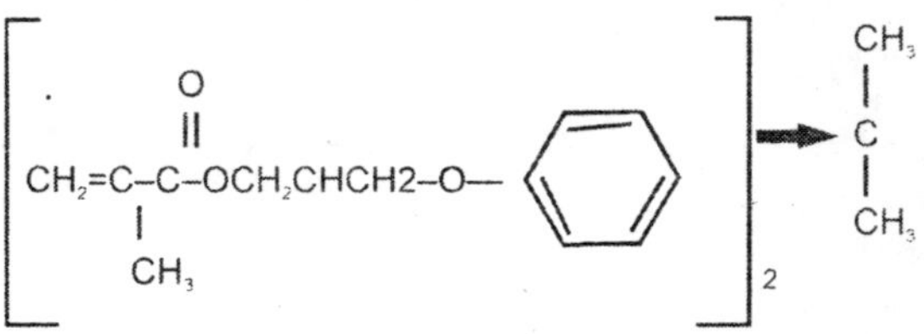

The derakane resins (Dow Chemical Co. U.S.A.) are the best known of this family and in practice they are diluted, like the unsaturated polyestes, with styrene to about 45-50% and curing is carried out using cobalt naphthenate, peroxides and dimethyl aniline.

Let us examine the molecular structure of a vinyl ester resin in comparison to a bisphenol *A*-fumaric acid polyester and a isophthalic acid polyester. It can be seen that chemical attack on all these types of resins occurs through hydrolysis of ester groups or the splitting of carbon to carbon double bonds (unsaturation). Such attack could be achieved by oxidation, halogenation, or by exposure to electron beam. As can be seen from the schematic structure of the cured bisphenol *A*-fumaric acid polyesters and isophthalic polyesters, ester linkages (O=C-O) occur throughout the molecular chain, making the resin very susceptible to attack by hydrolysis. In addition to these ester groups there are carbon to carbon (-C=C-) double bonds randomly spaced along the two nonvinyl polyesters. These double bonds are also very suceptible to attack but the vinyl ester resins have double bonds at the end of the molecular chain which react completely on polymerisation, giving a more chemically resistant structure.

(a) Vinyl ester.

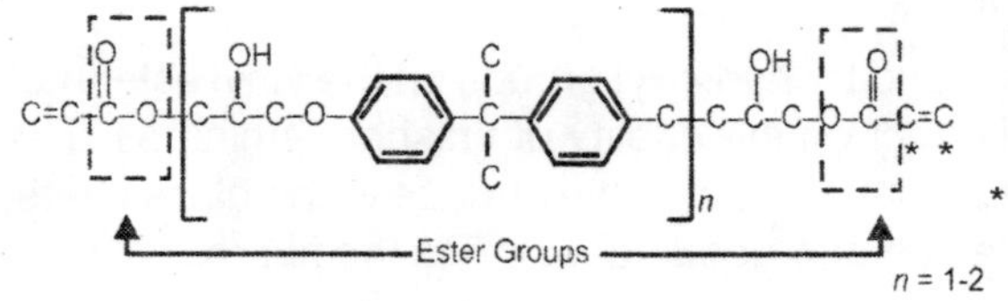

(b) Bisphenol A-fumaric acid polyester.

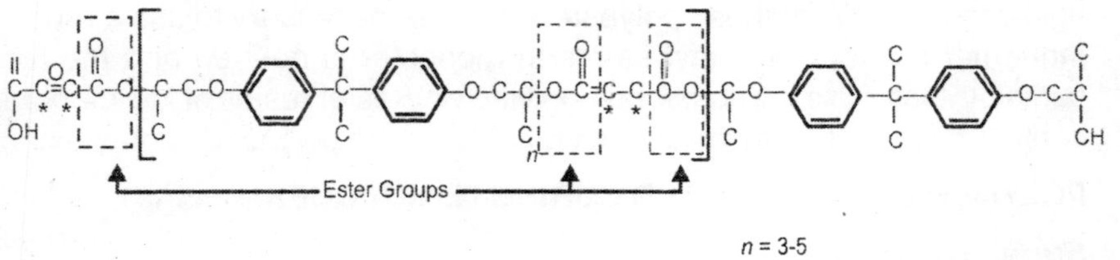

(c) Isophthalic polyester

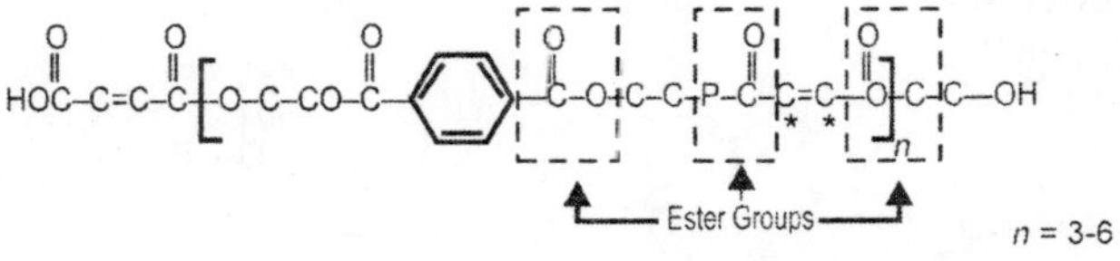

It has also been established that the number and arrangement of polar groups on vinyl ester resins make them less polar than polyester resins. They are thus less prone to the effect of water when cured by organic peroxides such as benzoyl peroxide. Any water present in peroxide cured polyesters affects the quality of the finished product. The water is absorbed at the polar sites but the vinyl esters absorption does not occur and the cure is unaffected.

* denotes reactive sites

The unsaturation on the vinyl esters is at the end and beginning of the chains and this makes the carbon-to-carbon double bonds exceptionally active. The derakane resins therefore cure rapidly with superior physical characteristics.

The secondary hydroxyl groups on the vinyl ester molecule also have a beneficial effect on the quality of finished laminates. The hydroxyl groups react with similar groups on the surface of the glass fibers, resulting in good surface wetting and good adhesion to the fibers.

It is also believed that because the cured vinyl ester resins contain only terminal cross-linking, the entire length of the molecular chain is not restricted and can therefore elongate under stress which makes it suitable to absorb mechanical or thermal shocks. The more conventional polyesters with the cross-linking taking place along the entire chain length are far more rigid and brittle. With these polyesters it is also necessary to use a reactive monomer but with the vinyl esters to monomer is needed and the resin cures by itself. This is another reason why vinyl ester resins of low monomer content have better corrosion resistance than the polyacid/alcohol esters.

POLYMER STRUCTURE AND CURING TECHNIQUES

Surface Coatings

Polyesters formed by reacting dibasic acids with dihydric alcohols consists of long-chain linear molecules, and they are themoplastic. If, however, the functionality *(f)* is above 2 : 2, i.e. 3 : 2 as it would be if glycerol were reacted with phthalic anhydride, then more complex resins are produced, which are essentially thermosetting and are referred to as alkyds. This latter reaction can be represented diagrammatically as follows, 'G' representing glycerol unit and 'P' phthalic acid.

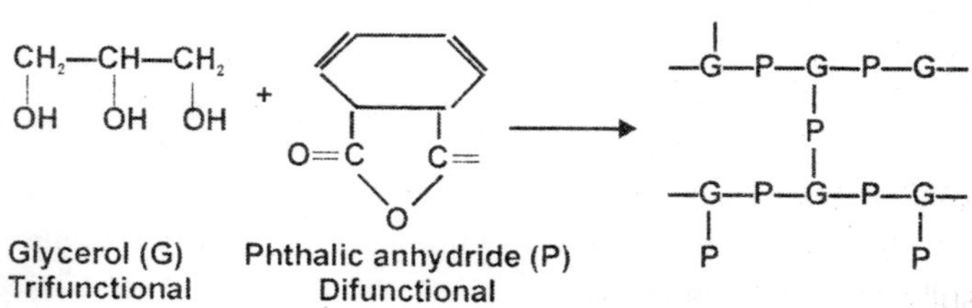

Glycerol (G) Trifunctional   Phthalic anhydride (P) Difunctional

A further alteration to this structure can be achieved by oil modification, which is of immense importance to the paint industry. Oil modification alkyd resins of the air-drying type cure by virtue of the oxidation of the drying oil added. The heat-cured types, in which the oil modification may or may not be oxidising, cure by heat alone or can be cocondensed with amino resins. Nondrying oils are coconut and castor oil, and the drying oil include linseed oil and dehydrated castor oil. These reactions can be illustrated as follows:

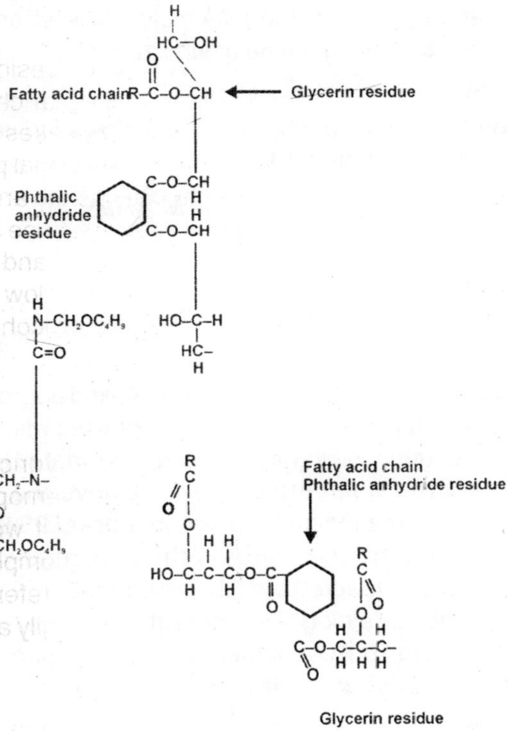

Butyland urea resin
Residual-OH groups or alkyd resin react with alkoxy groups of U-F or M-F resins to liberate alcohol and form an either linkage.

The resultant modified surface coating resins are conveniently classified according to their oil length, which is approximately the ratio of oil to resin.

Short oil alkyd	-	-	-	20-40 per cent oil
Medium oil alkyd	-	-	-	40-60 per cent oil
Long oil alkyd	-	-	-	greater than 60 per cent

Water Soluble Alkyds

Polyfunctionality of certain acids makes possible the synthesis of a wide variety of polymers useful in formulating paints and a wide variety of coatings. Particularly interesting is trimellitic anhydride (TMA) where the third functional carboxyl groups is used as the solubilising site.

The simplest water soluble resin prepared from TMA consists of polymer chains in which the third carboxyl group of the TMA molecule is left unreacted. This grouping is then neutralised by an amine or similar base which renders the polymer soluble in water.

A typical formulation for a baking enamel is as follows indicating the use of TMA as made by Amoco Chemical Corporation, U.S.A.

Materials	*Mol Ratio*
Trimellitic anhydride (TMA)	3
Neopentryl glycol (NPG)	8
Isophthalic acid (IPA)	2
Tall oil fatty acid (TOFA)	3

The alkyl resin is made by first charging the NPG, IPA, and approximately half the TMA into a reaction kettle. The reaction is then purged with nitrogen and partial condensation is begun. The ingredients are than heated to around 240°C and the speed depends upon the ability to remove the water of condensation. The contents are maintained at a temperature of 95-98°Cuntil the acid number is less than ten. The TOFA is then charged when the temperature reaches 230°C and reacted until the acid number is less then ten. Cool to 200°C and add the remaining TMA. Hold at this temperature until an acid number of 42-44. Cool to 160°C and then reduce to 80 percent NVM using a suitable solvent such as butoxyethanol and neutralise to a pH of 8.0-8.5 dimethylamino ethanol.

A suitable baking formulation can be obtained by adding water to give a viscocity of 100-120 s No. 4 Ford Cup. Then the alkyd is mixed with a suitable amino resin, e.g., Cymel 301, in a ratio 85/15 using titanium dioxide in a pigment/ binder ratio 0.98/1.0. The resultant paint must then be ground in a pebble mill or similar machinery until the correct degree of dispersion has been achieved. The resultant product then gives satisfactory results when baked 30 minutes at 150°C.

As previously discussed, solvent soluble air-dry alkyds were the first cross-linking coatings and are still used widely as exterior house paints as well as industrial coatings. The early attempts to incorporate water-sulubilising functionality into industrial drying-oil based resins resulted in coating which took hours to dry and thus were unacceptable. Added to this was poor physical characteristics such as low hardness and poor outdoor wealtherability. The use of linseed fatty acids and trimethylol propane as opposed to linseed oil with its natural glycerine content was found to yield air-dry alkyds with excellent hardness and flexibility and resonable drying times.

Miscellaneous Polyesters for Surface Coatings

A technique which has commanded considerable interest in the coating industry is the electrophoretic technique. By means of electrical charges coatings can be applied to metal and both water-soluble and solvent-soluble systems can be used. A water soluble formulation has already been discussed and the following is one suitable for both water and solvent techniques in electrophoretic coatings.

Material	*Mol ratio*
Tall oil fatty acid (TOFA)	6
Styrene allyl alcohols copolymer (SAAC)	2
Trimellitic anhydride (TMA)	2

The TOFA and SAAC is charged to a reaction kettle and then purged with nitrogen. The temperature is raised to 230°C and maintained for four hour until an acid number of less than ten is reached. It is then cooled to 165°C, the TMA is added, and the temperature is raised to 200°C until an acid value of 38 is reached. The resin is then cooled to below 150°C and is reduced to 80 percent NVM with butoxy ethanol and filtered wile warm. The pH can be adjusted to 7.5 with triethylamine if it is required for water solubilisation and then cured by a suitable amino resin.

Oil free polyester coatings can also be made and they provide useful materials for coil coating and gloss enamels by baking techniques. A suitable formulation can be using either neopentyl or propylene glycol with adipic and isophthalic acid as well as trimellitic anhydride. A hydroxyl excess of 15 per cent is achieved and the polyester resin can be cured with amino resins in a ratio of 4 : 1.

One other interesting group, which was touched on earlier, is the air drying polyesters which are wax free. One big problem in the early developments was air inhibitors and consequently the surface remained tacky. One method which overcome this effect was to modify the polyester with glyceryl α-allyl ether, or it is possible to replace the styrene with the adipic ester of glyceryl α, α'diallyl ether.

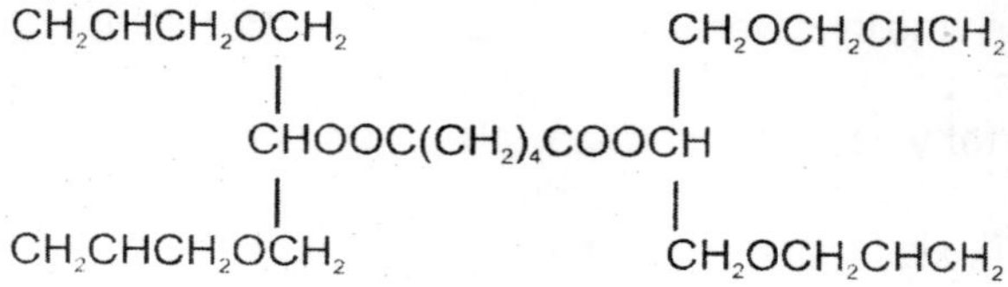

The liquid allyl ethers may be therefore used as reactive solvents in conjunction with conventional alkyds, forming solventless systems. The allyl ether groups may also be incorporated into water soluble alkyds and has provided a basis for a range of water thinnable air-drying and stoving media.

These allyl ethers dry by oxidation in air but in comparison with drying oils and polymerisation mechanism involved is more efficient. Some of the simpler products yield films which tend to embrittle but films have the great attraction of a reduced tendency to yellow in the absence of light.

Other allyl ethers suitable for use are α-allyl glycerol, pentaerythritol diallyl ether and sorbitol tetra allyl ether.

A typical formulation for an air drying system is as follows :

Material	*Mold ratio*
Sorbitol tetra-allyl ether	5
Diethylene glycol	2
Adipic acid	2
Trimellitic anhydride	3
(Excess hydroxyl-8 per cent)	

A water soluble type wold be

Material	Mol ratio
Pentaerythritol diallyl ether	8
Adipic acid	2
Trimellitic anhydride	3
(Excess hydroxyl-23 per cent)	

Molding Powders

It is now evident that glyptals (alkyds) are thermosetting resins, but unfortunately the time required to effect a final cure for certain applications is far too long to be practical. To obtain resins suitable for molding powders it has therefore been found necessary to replace the phthalic acid with an unsaturated material such as maleic acid. The resultant unsáturated polyester can then be made to cross-link rapidly via the ethylene link ages at temperatures in the region 150°C or even lower by using initiators such as benzoyl peroxide, as already mentioned. The curing action is also effected with an unsaturated monomer, such as styrene, vinyl toluene, or diallyl phthalate.

$$\underset{\text{Maleic acid}}{HOOCCH{=}CHCOOH} + \underset{\text{Ethylene glycol}}{OHCH_2{-}CH_2OH} +$$

$$+ HOOCCH{=}CHCOOH \rightarrow$$

$$\underset{\text{Ethylene glycol maleate}}{{-}OOCCH{=}CH{-}COO{-}CH_2{-}CH_2{-}OOC{-}CH{=}CHCOO{-}}$$

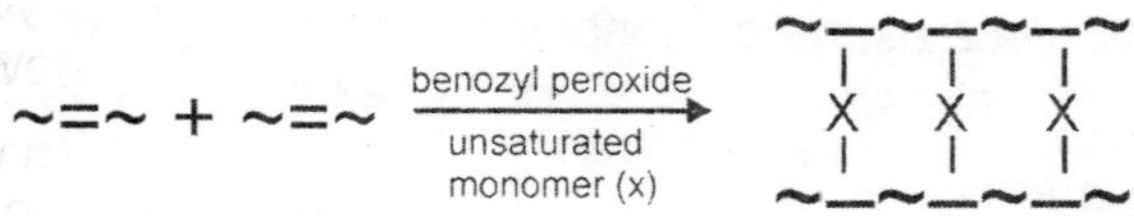

Molding powders have also been produced by using an unsaturated alcohols instead of the more conventional saturated type. For example, phthalic may be esterified with allyl alcohols to produce the ester, diallyl phthalate, which is cross linked by using an organic peroxide and opening up the double bonds in the vinyl groupings.

This group of resins is referred to as the "allyl" family. The esters formed from mono or dibasic acids are available as low viscosity monomers and thermoplastic prepolymers. The allyl monomers and prepolymers find use as cross linking agents for unsaturated polyester resins and in molding compounds. Typical monomers are triallyl cyanurate, diallyl chlorendate and diallyl maleate.

Typical commercial products include diethylene glycol bis (allyl carbonate), it is designated CR-39 Allyl Diglycol Carbonate made by PPG industries Inc. (U.S.A.). It can be prepared in the following manner.

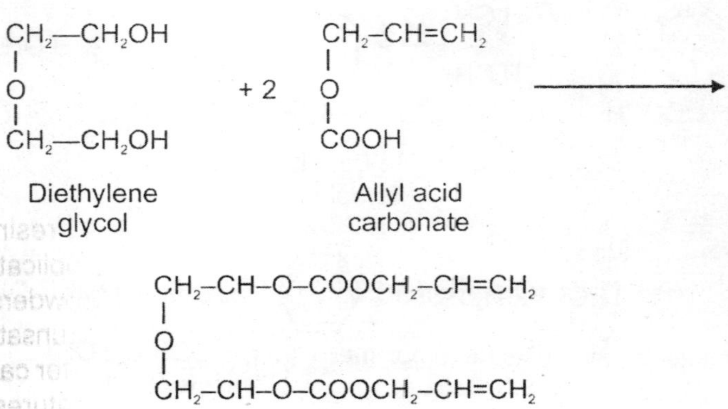

Other materials are Dapon 35 which is the prepolymer derived from diallyl orthophthalate and Dapon M is the isophthalate analogue (both manufactured by FMC Corp. U.S.A.). They are solid, linear, internally cyclised thermoplastics with unreacted allylic groups spaced at regular intervals along the polymer backbone.

The U.K. took another approach in attempts to produce low pressure resins. They utilised mixed esters in which the unsaturation was obtained either from acrylic acid (CH_2 : CH CO_2H) or methacrylic acid (CH_2 : CCH_3 CO_2H). Such products included a dimethacrylate glycol phthalate using n-butyl methacrylate as the comonomer. These resins were relatively slow and difficult to make which restricted their exploitation.

Surface Coatings

The processing techniques as applied to polyesters for surface coatings need very little further elaboration. Very nearly all gloss or enamel paints are today based upon alkyds, not white lead as was customary, and most readers will be fully conversant with the technique of applying them as well as with the basic details of such mechanized techniques as sparying. Certain specialized techniques are employed in spraying alkyd paints and this process can be carried out either by air atomizing or airless spray equipment. A recent advance in this field is the introduction of a surface coating based upon a polyester resin, suitable for use with wood, which cures in the cold by oxidation or air inhibition.

Fibers and Films

These materials are based on linear polyesters which are formed from the condensation reaction between dimethyl terephthalate and ethylene

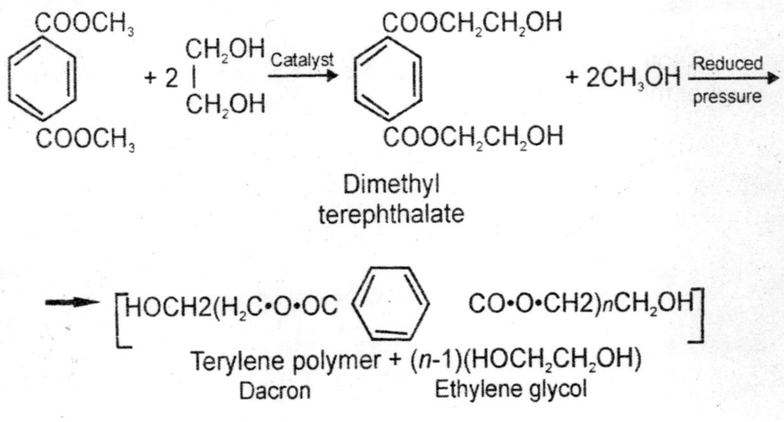

glycol. The reaction is actually an ester interchange process and, unlike the nylon polymers, this type of polyester is amorphous on cooling. The reaction can be catalysed by materials such as sodium methoxide and is normally carried out between 190-280°C.

The preparation of thermoplastic polyester molding materials is similar to the techniques used for fibers and film however different basic raw materials are used. Therefore no further description of the chemistry of these materials and the polyester structural foams of the same family is given.

Polyester/Polyurethanes. No elaboration is needed for this type of polyester because it is the standard reaction of a dicarboxylic acid with a dihydric alcohol. However, the structure of the polycarprolactones is more interesting and is described in a little more detail.

Polycaprolactones. It has been shown previously that polyesters can be made by the ring opening of lactones. A series of such resins have been made by the ring opening of ε-caprolactone. The polymers so formed are thermoplastic crystalline materials. These materials are manufactured by Union Carbide Corporation, U.S.A.

On such product is polycaprolactone diol (m.w. 10,000) which is designated PCL 300 with the following structure.

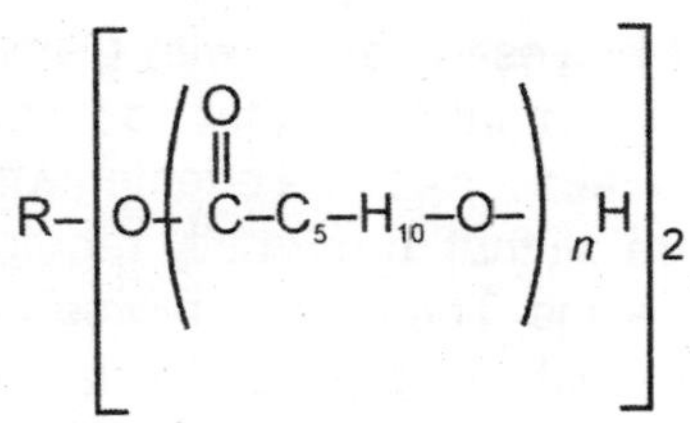

Another in this family with the same basic structural formula but this a higher molecular weight is PCL 700.

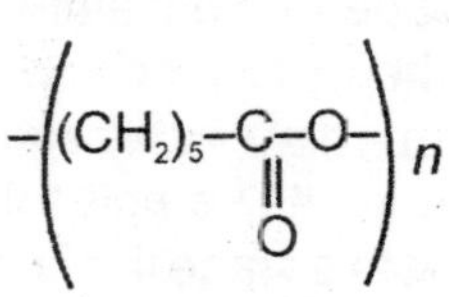

PROCESSING TECHNIQUES

Laminating and Casting Resins

In general, all thermosetting resin laminates are produced by impregnating the base material with a synthetic resin and then consolidating by applying heat and/or pressure. The degree of impregnating affects the characteristics of the final laminate, which is dependent upon such variable as the type of the base material and resin solvent (if any), resin characteristics (e.g., solids content and viscocity), or impregnanting time. The production techniques can be conveniently classified as either (a) high pressure or (b) low pressure. The fact that no by-products are evolved on curing polyester resins, as with epoxy resins, means that the low pressure process is more commonly used. The high-pressure is used with polyesters for dough or gunk moldings, which is described later. The casting techniques are very similar for polyesters as are used for epoxy resins, which are described in detail in Chapter 6.

Molding Powders

The materials are processed by the conventional thermosetting molding techniques such as compression and transfer molding. Specific details of these processes are given in the relevant chapter.

LOW PRESSURE PROCESS

The molding of polyester resins with glass fibers by this process is made simpler by virtue of the facts that no volatiles are evolved or curing needed, and that the reaction can be effected without heat. Pressures from zero to 500 lb/in^2 are all that in normally required consolidate these low-pressure (contact) resins. The term reinforced plastics' has now become virtually synonymous with low-pressure or cantact laminates.

1. Wet Lay-up Technique

A mold is first constructed out of wood, plaster of paris, metal, or epoxy resin reinforced and cheapened with aluminium powder. The surface of the mold must first be smoothed, polished and then treated with a release agent which may be hard was or a film former such a polyvinyl alcohol. A 'gel' coat is then applied, which is usually a polyester or an epoxy resin allowed to harden to a tacky state. At this stage the first layer of fibrous reinforcement is applied; the various types of reinforcement are described in Chapter 19. It is also possible to use thixotropic agents if vertical drainage is required. Further resin is then applied to other layers of reinforcement and worked into the interstices of the fibers, usually with a paint brush. This practice is repeated

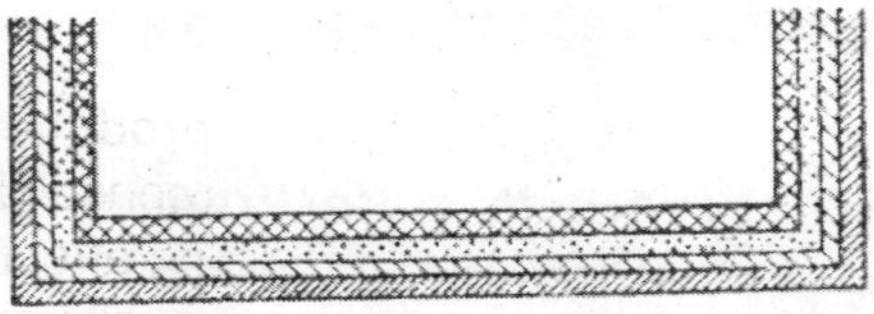

Fig. 5.4 Build-up of fiberglass reinforced laminate

several times until the required thickness is obtained (Fig. 5.4). The resultant laminated structure may then be cured be the placing it in a rubber bag and applying a vaccum (the vaccum-bag technique is described more fully. This process is one of the most popular methods used for reinforced plastics because there is virtually no limit to the size or complexity of the final molding. Mold costs are relatively, low, but the main disadvantage is that it is essentially a hand method and is therefore dependent on the skill of the operator. The process is extremely popular for manufacturing shell structure such as automobile bodies and parts, boats and chemical tanks.

2. Matched Metal Molding

This is essentially a performing technique used where large runs of small components are required. The productivity rate is comparable to that of the conventional molding techniques used for plastics. Basically the method consists of producing a 'preform' of the component using chopped glass fibers and impregnating by the following methods.

(a) *Plenum Chamber Technique*. In this method the fiber reinforcement takes a form of chopped glass fibers ½-2 in. in length which are passed into a chamber, and vaccum applied. Resin is then sprayed on to the fibers and the impregnated fibers thus assume the shape of the preform. The preform is finally withdrawn and cured.

(b) *Direct Fiber Method.* The resin binder and the glass fibers are sprayed on to a preform screen through which suction is applied. This method has the advantage of being suitable for producing large preforms, although the method is largely dependent upon the skill of the operator.

(c) Aqua slurry Technique. This method has basically the same technique as that in the phenolic pulp preform process. By this method the chopped fibers are fed into a tank of water and agitated continuously with a stirrer. The preform screen is then raised slowly out of the water and the water is drained through a vent, leaving the preform behind. Resin is then poured over the preform and , finally, the mold is closed and pressure applied.

3. Spray Molding

The two methods described above both suffer from certain disadvantages. The preform method requires a high initial capital outlay and the wet lay-up technique requires a large amount of labour, which is also costly.

The spray molding technique is relatively simple and consists of mixing two systems in separate containers. The first container is filled with the resin/promoter and the second with the resin/catalyst. The glass fibers are contained separately, having been previously cut into convenient lengths. The resin system is applied by means of a twin-head spray-gun to a cutting device which cuts the glass to the required lengths. In the actual process the mold is first coated with a release agent and then a gel coat is applied by hand or spray-gun. On curing the gel coat, the resin and the glass fibers are applied simultaneously, and the final laminate is consolidated by rolling.

4. Bag Molding

The processes based on this technique are, in general, modifications of the wet-lay up methods previously described. It is possible by this method to obtain moldings with even thicknesses and high glass- fiber/resin ratios. Hot curing techniques can also be appiied, thus reducing the cycle times.

(a) *Vaccum Bag.* Basically this method consists of applying atmospheric pressure to the uncured laminated structure by exhausting the air between the lay-up and a flexible bag. This process allows for pressures up to one atmosphere (14.7 lb/in^2) to be used which, for normal work, is adequate.

(b) *Autoclave.* This process is used when higher pressures are required than are obtainable with method (a). Steam may also be used instead of air. The method is applied on only a limited scale for polyester glass reinforcement but more frequently with phenolic glass structures which require both heat and pressure for satisfactory molding.

(c) *Pressure-bag Molding.* Laminate build-up is first carried out in a female mold, which is then protected by a film of cellulose of polyvinyl alcohol and placed in a rubber bag. The rubber bag is then forced by pressure against the mold. Pressure between 20-50 lb/in^2 can be used; this enhances the mechanical strength properties of the molding. Tooling costs are low.

Premix Molding

This method is commonly referred to as 'dough molding' and consists of premixing the polyester resin, inorganic filler and fiber reinforcement into a dough or fibrous mass. The resultant product is then suitable for molding under heat and pressure in a matched mold, thus allowing rapid production. It has been said that in terms of strength these molding materials bridge the gap between conventional molding powders and the polyester/glass laminates, and as such they warrant a wide range of end uses in their own right without superseding the use of the above-mentioned types. The dough has a low glass content (5-20 per cent), is nontacky in the uncured state and retains its shape when deformed. Advantages of this molding material over other polyester molding compositions are; Articles are cheaper to produce; it allows complicated parts to be made easily and shorter press cycles (as low as 15 s have been reported as giving successful moldings); There is less waste from off-cuts, etc. The main disadvantage is that the resultant moldings have lower mechanical strength than conventional polyester laminates, although flexural strengths of the order of 20,000 lb/in^2 have been obtained.

Tube and Rod

Glass reinforced tubing may be prepared by a modification of the wet lay-up process. This is carried out either by impregnating glass rovings, mechanically wound on a heated cylindrical mandrel, or by placing glass mat inside the surface of the mold and spinning, thus impregnating by centrifugal force.

The production of glass reinforced rod is carried out by several methods of which the most popular is continuous drawing by reinforced resin through a die which is heated by a high-frequency electrical technique to give a very rapid cure.

Injection Molding

Another interesting method has been developed which consists of forcing the polyester resin into a matched mold containing the reinforcing medium. The principle is that the incoming resin forces air bubbles out of the mold, thus overcoming one of the main difficulties in producing laminates. Multiplicity of molds allows rapid production without the necessity of using hydraulic presses and associated equipment.

Casting Resin

Polyester resins can be readily cast by a variety of techniques which are fully described in Chapter 6.

FIBERS

The polymer obtained from the reaction of dimethyl terephthalate with ethylene glycol, described earlier, is in the form of chip which must first be dried. The fibers are produced by a melt spinning process which consists essentially of pumping molten polymer through a spinneret. A spinneret may briefly be described as a metal plate containing a number of fine holes. When the molten filaments emerge from the spinneret and meet cold air they solidify and are then collected together and would on bobbin. This product is termed spun yarn. It is unoriented and does not possess the required properties characteristic of textiles, therefore it is mechanically stretched or drawin to 4-5 times its original length to develop the characteristic properteis of polyester fibers. The fully drawn continuous filament yarn is then wound on a special bobbin.

Polyester fiber is also obtained in another form, viz. staple, fiber. This is produced by cominbing many hundreds of the extruded undrawn filaments together in the form of a tow, which is then stretched, crimped, and cut into suitable lengths and, finally, baled.

FILM

As will be seen later, there are normally three methods of making film used in the plastics industry; solvent casting, extrusion, and calendering. Polyethylene terephthalate has limited solubility and this, together with its sharp melting point and low viscocity above this temperature, make solvent casting and calendering impractical. However, extrusion techniques are quite suitable, and polyester film is now manufactured by this process. The normal procedure is first to render the polymer molten by heat, then filter an extrude through a long narrow slot. On emerging from the slot the film is cooled in water and then oriented to ensure the resultant film will possess good strength characteristics in all directions. The film then undergoes a drawing process which improves many of its mechanical properties. A high degree of drawing results in a decrease in elongation and, therefore, a balance must be reached. The final step in the process is termed annealing. The consists of heating the film to around 180-200°C for a given period, depending on desired and properties when the film becomes less amorphous and more heat stable.

PROPERTIES

By varying the nature and combinations of the base raw materials, filler, reinforcement, and cure time, it is possible to obtain polyester resins exhibiting a wide range of properties. The base resins may be tailored to give certain specific characteristics, for instance, resistance to solvents, alkalis, acids, or bleaching agents may be required, or possibly high heat distortion temperature flexural or compressive strengths. These are all possible by careful formulation. Certain factors should be borne in mind when formulating; for example, the heat distortion temperature is dependent on the relative amount of unsaturation in the polyester chain, whearas flexibility is dependent on the unsaturated points and on the presence of long chains of carbon atoms. Chemical resistance has been found to depend largely upon the initial choice of glycols and dibasic acids.

It is considered that a discussion of the characteristics of polyester reinforced laminates warrants most attention because, apart from casting and encapsulation, very few other applications exist for the unfilled resin. As mentioned earlier the reinforcing medium is generally a member of the glass-fiber family. A laminate prepared with these materials would exhibit many of the following properties.

High strength/weight ratio
High impact strength
Dimensional stability
Good electrical properties
Goos weather and chemical resistance
Good heat resistance
Ease of fabrication
Good light transmission
Good surface hardness

If an inorganic filler is added, a laminate becomes opaque, but shrinkage on cure is reduced, as also is the cost, as well as heat and fire resistance.

The excellent strength of a glass-fiber reinforced resin is shown in Table 5.2, which lists the properties of cured polyester resin and glass-fiber reinforced laminates.

In general, cured polyester resins will resist most organic and organic acids with the exception of strong oxidising acids. They are not attacked by weak alkalis, although they are attacked by strong alkalis, which cause hydrolysis.

Alkyd moldings are resistant to water, salt solutions, detergents and common organic solvents. In general, they are resistant to acids but have poor resistance to alkalis. They are very similar in this respect to general purpose phenolic molding material and in direct contrast with the aminoplast

Table 5.2

PROPERTIES OF CURED POLYESTER RESINS AND GLASS-FIBER REINFORCED LAMINATES

	Cast resin	*Laminate1**	*Laminate2†*
Flexural strength (lb/in.^{2})	15,000-20,000	18,000-26,000	55,000-65,000
Young's modulus in flexure (lb/in.^{2} X 10^6)	0.5-0.8	1.2-1.5	2.0-3.0
Tensile strength (lb/in.^{2})	4000-5000	15,000-25,000	35,000-50,000
Compressive strength (lb/in.^{2})	15,000-22,000	18,000-25,000	30,000-50,000
Impact strength Izod (ft lb/in notch)	0.2-0.4	10-20	20-30
Specific gravity	1.2-1.3	1.5-1.6	1.6-1.7
Heat distortion. (°C)	60-145	—	—
(°F)	140-293	—	—
Specific heat (cal/°C/g.)	0.5-0.6	—	—
Thermal conductivity (cal/sec/cm°C/cm^2)	5-6 X 10^{-4}	2-3 X 10^{-5}	3-4 X 10^{-5}
Coefficient of linear expansion (/°C X 10^{-6})	80-90	12-20	10-15
Power factor at 23°C (73°F) at 800 c/s	0.01-0.02	0.011	0.001-0.01
at 1 Mc/s	0.015-0.03	0.23	0.01-0.015
Permittivity at 23°C (73°F)			
at 700 c/s	2.8-4.0	1.48	4.0-5.5
at 1 Mc/s	3.0-4.5	1.87	3.0-5.5
Volume resistivity (ohm cm)	10^{15}-10^{16}	10^{14}-10^{15}	10^{14}-10^{15}
Surface resistivity (ohm)	1-9 X 10^{13}	1-9 X 10^{13}	1-9 X 10^{13}
Breakdown voltage (volt/mil)	–	150-200	150-200

Table by courtesy of British Resin Products Limited

* Laminate prepared from chopped strand mat glass fiber with 70 per cent resin content

† Laminate prepared from woven glass fiber satin weave with 30 per cent resin content.

moldings which resist alkalis but not acids. Some general properties of alkyd molding material are listed in Table 5.3.

The outstanding properties of polyester fibers and films include high mechanical strength combined with good electrical insulating properties over a wide temperature range. They also possess high thermal stability and low moisture absorption.

Table 5.3

GENERAL PROPERTIES OF ALKYD MOLDING MATERIALS

Molding properties	*Standard cure*	*Fast cure*
Shelf life	Good	Fair
Pelleting properties	Fair	Good
Bulk factor	3-4.3	2.0-2.2
Cup time for blister free time	60-75 s (c.f. Melamine-formaldehyde 70-100 s)	15-30 s
Hot strength	Poor	Fair
Resistance to insert cracking	Good	Poor
Specific gravity	1.6-1.8	2.0-2.2
Impact strength (ft/lb in. notch)	0.1-0.2	0.1-0.2
Electrical properties	Good	Good
Electric strength	250-350 V/mil	250-350 V/mil

The fibers and films will, in general, resist hydrocarbon solvents, chlorinated hydrocarbons, ketones, esters concentrated hydrochloric acid, and certain dilute acids. They are however, decomposed by alkalis, oxidising agents and, to an even greater extent, by alcoholic alkalis.

Thermoplastic polyester for molding applications have certain key properties; dimensional stability, extremely low moisture absorption, chemical resistance, excellent surface lubricity and resistance to wear, high fatique endurance limit, heat deflection temperatures to 420°F, excellent mechanical properties, stable electrical properties in a wide range of enviornment and outstanding rigidity.

The physical properties of a commercial range of thermoplastic polyester molding materials are given in Table 5.4.

The polyester foams used for structural applications have a high stiffness to weight ratio when compared to metals. They retain their tensile strength over a wide range of temperatures as well as high flexural modulus. They have outstanding thermal endurance and have definite advantage over many materials including metals for which they compete keenly in acoustic applications. Typical properties of a commercial structural polyester foam are illustrated in Table 5.5.

While polycaprolactone polymers are not used in any significant tonnages they are interesting materials to consider. The characteristics of

Table 5.4

TYPICAL PROPERTIES OF VALOX THERMOPLASTIC POLYESTER

Property	*Units*	*Test Method*	*"Valox" 310 (unreinforced)*	*"Valox" 310-SEO (unreinforced and UL 94 V-0 recognized)*	*"Valox" 430 (glass-reinforced)*	*"Valox" 420-SEO (glass reinforced and UL 94 V O recognized)*
Specific gravity (73°F)		D792	1.31	1.41	1.52	1.58
Specific volume	cu. in/lb		21.1	19.6	18.1	17.5
Water absorption (73OF)	%	D570				
24 h			0.08	0.08	0.06	0.07
equilibrium			0.34	0.38	0.26	0.25
Mold shrinkage	in./in/ x 10^{-3}		17-23	17-23	4-6	4-6
Tensile strength	psi	D638	8,000	8,900	17,300	17,000
Elongation at break	%	D638	300	100	5	5
Flexural strength	psi	D790	12,800	14.700	27,500	27,500
Flexural modulus	psi	D790	340,000	380,000	1,200,000	1,200,000
Compressive strength (10% def.)	psi	D695	13,000	14,500	18,000	18,000
Shear strength	psi	D732	7,700	7,700	8,900	9,000
Izod impact strength	ft lb/in	D256				
notched			1.2	0.9	2.2	1.8
unnotched			No break	No break	15	15
Gardner impact	ft lb	Falling Dart	40-45	35-40		
Chemical resistance			Excellent	Excellent	Excellent	Excellent
Deformation under load (122°F, 2000psi)	%	D621	0.17	0.15	0.12	0.15
Creep (73°)	%	D674	1.1 (1000 psi)	1.1 (1000 psi)	0.44 (4000 psi)	0.44(4000 psi)
Fatigue endurance limit (10^7 cycles)	psi	D671	2,850	3,500	5,000	5,000

Property	Units	Test method				
Coefficient of friction (self		D1894	1.17	0.16	0.16	0.16
metal)			0.13	0.14	0.14	0.14
Rockwell Hardness (R scale)		D785	117	120	120	120
Tabor abrasion (CS-17 wheel, 1000 g load)	mg/1000 cycles	D1044	6.5	10.0	9.0	11.0
Heat deflection temp.	°F	D648				
66 psi			310	325	420	420
624 psi			130	160	415	415
Coefficient of thermal expansion	in./in./°F X10-5	D696	5.3	4.7	3.3	3.5
Thermal conductivity	BTU/h/ft2/°F/in.	C177	1.1	1.2	1.3	1.3
Flammability		UL94	94 HB	94 V-0	94 HB	94 V O
	in./min.	D636	1.0	0.0	1.3	0.0
Volume resistivity	ohm. cm X 10^{16}	D257	4.0	4.0	3.2	3.4
Dielectric strength	volts/mil	D149				
short time, 1/16" thickness			590	750	750	750
short time, > 1/10" thickness						
73°F, 50% R.H.			400	375	475	425
150°F, 50% R.H.			400	375	470	420
250°F, 50% R.H.			400	340	450	415
73°F, 100% R.H.			400	375	475	425
73°F,after immersion in 130°F water			400	375	440	425
Dielectric constant		D150				
100 HZ			3.3	3.3	3.8	3.8
10^6 HZ			3.1	3.1	3.7	3.7
Dissipation factor		D150				
100 HZ			0.002	0.003	0.002	0.002
10^6 HZ			0.02	0.02	0.02	0.02
Arc resistance	s	D495	190	63	130	80
Hot wire ignition, 1/16"	s	UL55	16	20	63	34
U.L. temperature index	°C(°F) @ 30 mils	UL guide QMFZ2				
elec. & mech. properties with impact			120(248)	120(248)	140(248)	130(266)
mech. prop. w/o. impact			140(248)	140(284)	140(284)	140(284)

one particular grade of polymer are given in Table 5.6 and because the melting point of the crystalline polymer is 60°C it is possible to use lower stock temperature when processing in conjunction with high density and low density polythene as well as polypropylene. The flow properties are illustrated in Tables 5.7 and 5.8.

APPLICATIONS

The uses of glass reinforced polyester resins are now widely seen in such applications as vehicles and boats. Boat building in one of the most successful applications of reinforced polyester resins. Boats made almost entirely by the wet lay-up process are becoming widely used throughout the world, their main attraction being their resistance to salt water, sunlight, termites, and rot. While the initial cost may show no apparent saving over wood and other conventional materials, maintenance costs are lower, repairs are easier, and the boats have a longer life. Extensive use has also been made of polyester laminates in storage tanks for oil, water and certain chemicals. Pipes made from polyester/glass have been produced but no large market has yet developed. Use has been made of glass reinforced rod for fishing tackle, etc., where the high strength-to-weight ratio is fully utilised.

A widely variety of household appliances and other articles are now made from polyester laminates. Furniture, luggage, ornaments, sinks, trays and handles, washing machines, and toys are among the extensive range. In office and industry similar applications are found, including machine housing, guards, and cabinets, although many of these are now being replaced by thermoplastics.

Another use for polyester resins, one of growing importance, is roof sheeting. For such applications these laminates have the advantage of ease of handling, good strength and weathering properties, a wide range of colors and a high degree of transparency.

Typical applications of alkyd molding powders include valveholders, insulating sleeves, parts for television assemblies, capacitor and commutator parts. They have also found limited uses as oven-door housings and housings or business machines.

In general alkyd molding materials are used in applications that require good arc and track resistance, insulation resistance, nonflammability with a combination of good mechanical and thermal stability. Such applications include automotive ignition systems such as distributors caps, coil tops, rotors, motor controls, circuit breakers, and a host of other electrical components.

Table 5.5

TYPICAL PROPERTIES OF A COMMERCIAL STRUCTURAL POLYESTER FOAM

Property	*Method of testing*	*"Valox®" FV-600 resin (metric)*	*"Valox®" FV-650 resin (metric)*
Specific gravity, 73°F (22.8°C)	—	1.2	1.2
Heat deflection temperature.	ASTM-D648		
°F @ 66 psi (°C @ 45,404,6 kg/m²)		405 (207.2)	420 (215.3)
°F @ 264 psi (°C @ 185, 618.4 kg/m²)		340 (170.9)	360 (182.0)
Thermal conductivity, BTU/h/ft²/°F/in. (cal/h/cm²/°C/g-cm)	ASTM-C177	1.10 (1.36)	1.10 (1.36
UL listing **	UL Standard 94	94 V-O	94 HB
Tensile strength, psi (kg/m² X 10³) @ 73°F (22.8°C)_	ASTM-D638	9910 (6,967)	9,920 (6974)
@ 200°F (93.2°C)_	—	6350 (4465)	6,350 (4465)
Elongation at break percent @ 73°F (22.8°C)	ASTM-D638	1.3	2.3
Tensile modulus, psi (kg/m² X 10³) @ 73°F (22.8°C) [Tangent]	ASTM-D638	1,028,000 (722,790)	8,200,000 (576,540)
Flexural strength, psi (kg/m² X 10³)@ 200°F (22.8°C)	ASTM-D790	17,900 (12,585)	18,500 (13,007)
@ 200°F (93.2°C)	–	8400 (5906)	9,200 (6468)
Flexural modulus, psi (kg/m² X 10³)@ 73°F (22.8°C)	ASTM-D790	1,000,000 (703,100)	900,000 (632,790)
@ 200°F (93.2°C)	–	390,000 (27,420)	370,000 (26,014)
Flexural stiffness-to weight ratio, @ 73°F (22.8°C)	–	160	150
Compressive strength [10 percent deformation] psi (kg/m² X 10³)	ASTM-D695	11,300 (7945)	11,000 (7734)
Creep [300 h 73°F (22.8°C) @ 1000 psi] (703,100/m²) percent strain	ASTM-D674	0.12	0.12
Charpy impact,, unnotched ft./lb/in. (kg/m/cm)	ASTM-D256	5.3 (.733)	9.9 (1.37)
Gardner impact, 5/8 in. (1.58 cm) Nose : 1" (2.54 cm) Base lb/in. (g/cm)	–	11 (1964.6)	22 (3929.2)
Dielectric strength. volts/mil			
perpendicular	ASTM-D149	152	152
parallel	–	200	200
Mold shrinkage, in/in X 10⁻³ (cm/cm X 10⁻³)	ASTM-D1299	–	–
flow directions		4-6	4-6
Perpendicular flow direction		6-10	6-10

** This rating is not intended to reflect hazards presented by this or any other material under actual fire conditions.
* ¼ Nominal Wall
* All ASTM general test methods are followed, except specimen size with four sided skin is varied to accomodate Structural foam processing.
*All properties on this chart are based on the chemical foam process.

Table 5.6

SELECTED PHYSICAL PROPERTIES OF PCL-700

Chemical formula	$C_6H_{10}O_2$
Structural Formula $n > 100$ $n < 3000$	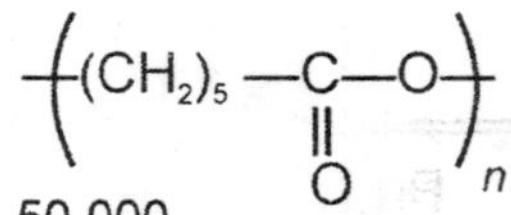
1% secant modulus, psi	50,000
Yield stress (psi)	1600
Tensile strength (psi-based on initial cross sectional area)	3000-4000
% elongation	500-1000
Melting point ($^{\circ}$C)	60
Glass transition temperature ($^{\circ}$C)	-60
Density (g/cc)	
at 0°C	1.160
at 20°C	1.149
at 40°C	1.134
Moisture content (%)	
at 50% relative humidity	0.07
at 100% relative humidity	0.43

Table 5.7

MELT FLOW OF PCL-700

Temperature, $^{\circ}$C	*Melt Flow, g/10 minutes*[1]
80	1.9
100	3.7
120	6.5
150	13.4
170	20.2
190	30.6

[1] ASTM Method D1238 at 43.25 psi., using PCL-700 dried at 40°C under vaccum for 16 hours

Table 5.8

FLOW PROPERTIES OF VARIOUS POLYMERS

Product	Melt temperature (^{o}C)	Melt flow, g/10 min Piston Load 44 psi	100 psi	220 psi
Polycaprolactone PCL-700	190	34	82	164
	140	12	32	96
8 melt index-high-density polyethylene homopolymer	190	8	26	90
3.8 melt flow polypropylene homopolymer	230	3.7	19	88

We have already mentioned the polymer of diethylene glycol bis (allyl carbonate) and this has been found to possess excellent, exceptional, optical properties. It is therefore evident that applications have been found for this material as coatings where such characteristics are required.

The uses of polyester fiber under the trade names of Terylene (I.C.I.) or Dacron (Du Pont) are probably well known to the reader and need no further mention. The industrial applications of polyester fibers include conveyor belting, vee-belting, hoses, tires (tire cord) and coated fabrics for protective clothing, and even tarpaulins.

These particular products are based on woven fabrics but over the past five years there has been a large growth in the area of polyester nonwoven fabrics. A typical material is Reemay (Du Pont) which is a spun bonded polyester. Many applications have been found for this product especially in the shoe, garment, and packaging industry.

A relatively new application which incorporates the use of metalised polyester film and nonwovens is the lamination of the film to the nonwovens to produce garments which are radar reflective. These are very useful in conjunction with life-jackets where people left in the sea by some accident can be picked up by radar scanning.

Polyester films are now used widely for electrical equipment, enabling the bulk of the insulation to be reduced and permitting the use of higher working temperatures. These films may also be metalised or laminated and are thus found in combinations of thin gauge film with certain lowcost materials. Such laminates have been used extensively for packing coffee and for boil-in-the-bag foodstuffs. Other uses for film include typewriter ribbons, recording tapes, drum linear, electronic capacitors, building insulation, and motion-picture films.

6

Epoxy Resins

The word 'epoxy' is now in everyday use although its derivation may not be obvious to everyone. It comes from the Greek prefix meaning 'over' or 'between' and the English suffix for oxygen. Thus, an epoxy material may be regarded as an 'oxygen between compound'.

Epoxy resins are thermosetting viscous liquids or brittle solids, of which the most widely used are those derived from the condensation reaction between epichlorhydrin and bisphenol A. Commercial exloitation was first initiated about the middle 1930's by I.G. Farben and this work was later followed independently by P. Castan, in Switzerland, and S.O. Greenlee, in the U.S.A., around 1938.Developments were slowed down by the Second World War and the relatively high price and scarcity of epichlorohydrin. However, at the end of the war epichlorhydrin, which was then obtained as an intermediate from the production of glycerol, became commercially available and let to wider uses for epoxy resins.

In 1962 Union Carbide Corporation announced that they would be manufacturing thermoplastic epoxide resins which could be molded by conventional thermoplastic technique. They designated these materials phenoxy and they differ from the glycidyl ether types mentioned previously only in their molecular weight which is considerably higher.

Other developments in this field include the introduction of cycloaliphatic and brominated epoxy resins. An important new family of epoxy resins is based on the nitrogen containing heterocyclic hydantoin ring.

RAW MATERIALS

Epichlorhydrin

Epichlorhydrin is a colorless liquid with the characteristics odor of many of the chlorinated hydrocarbon solvents such as chloroform. It has the following structure:

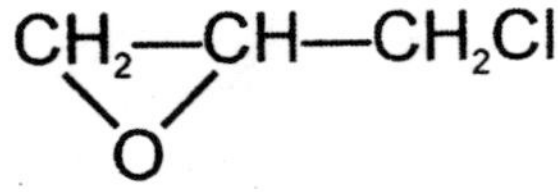

It has been known since 1854, when Berthelot reported its synthesis by saponification of the dichlorohydrins obtained by hydrogen chloride acting on glycerol. It is now produced on a chemical scale by the chlorination of propylene and is, therefore, a petroleum derivative. The resultant allyl chloride is reacted with hypochlorous acid to produce dichlorohydrin, which then undergoes what may regarded as a 'stripping' process. It is exposed to sodium hydroxide at elevated temperatures, one hydrogen and one chlorine atom being stripped off. The overall reaction is as follows :

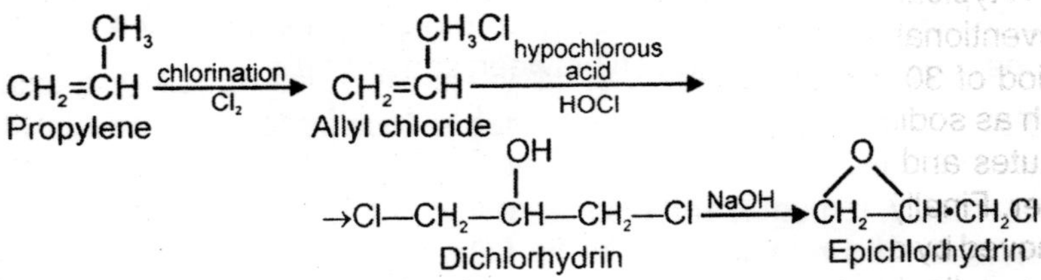

Bisphenol A

It is not uncommon to see other terminology used for this material and it is often referred to as diphenylol propane of bis (4-hydroxyphenyl) dimethylmethane.

Bisphenol A is normally prepared by combining acetone with phenol as follows :

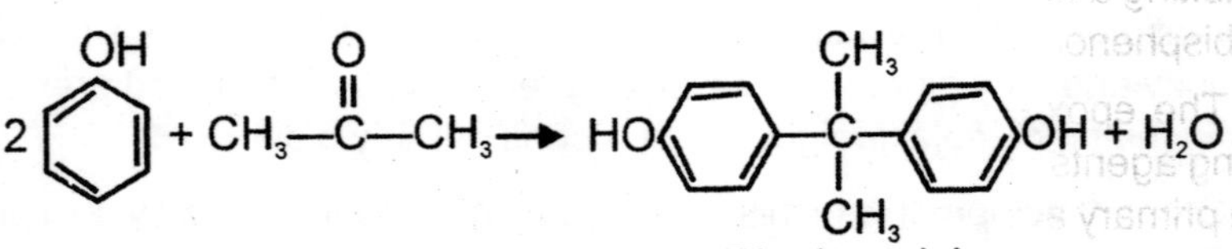

RESIN PRODUCTION

The most widely used epoxy resins at present are those based on the condensation reaction of epichlorhydrin and bisphenol A, using an alkaline catalyst such as sodium hydroxide. The general reaction may then be written as follows :

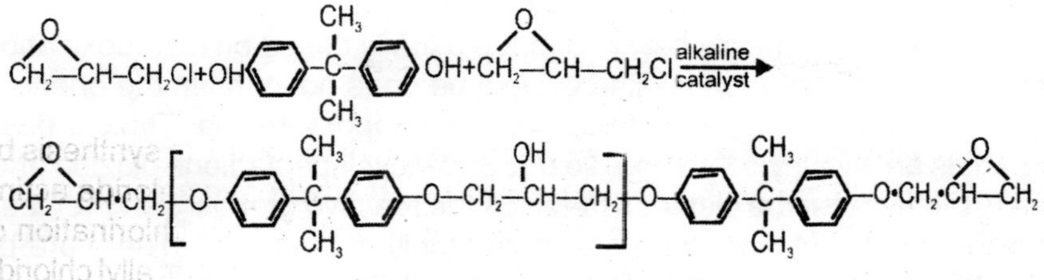

When n = 0 the molecular weight is 340 and the epoxy is in the form of a high viscosity resin but when n = 10 the molecular weight is in the region of 3000 and the resin is a high melting solid. These resins may be regarded as glycidyl ethers of bisphenol.

A typical manufacturing procedure is to mix the reactants at 50°C in a conventional resin kettle and slowly raise the temperature to 115°C over a period of 30 minutes, in the meantime slowly adding an alkaline catalyst such as sodium hydroxide. The reaction is then carried out for a further 30 minutes and the resulting product washed free of alkali and salt with hot water. Finally, the temperature is raised to 130°C and the remaining water removed by decanting or vacuum distillation. The resulting resins vary from viscous liquids to solids and the molecular weight is controlled by the epichlorhydrin/bisphenol ratios. Low ratios give high molecular weight solids, and high ratios normally produce liquid resins.

Epoxy Novolak Resins

These resins are produced by condensing the hydroxyl groups of a phenolic resin (in place of the more conventional bisphenol A) with epichlorhydrin. They have an average functionality greater than 3, thereby exhibiting a higher degree of cross-linking and superior thermal stability to the bisphenol-based epoxides.

The epoxy novolaks exhibit excellent reactively towards the normal curing agents used for epoxy resins and in practice they cure more rapidly with primary amines than do conventional epoxides.

The following structure is typical of an epoxidised novolak :

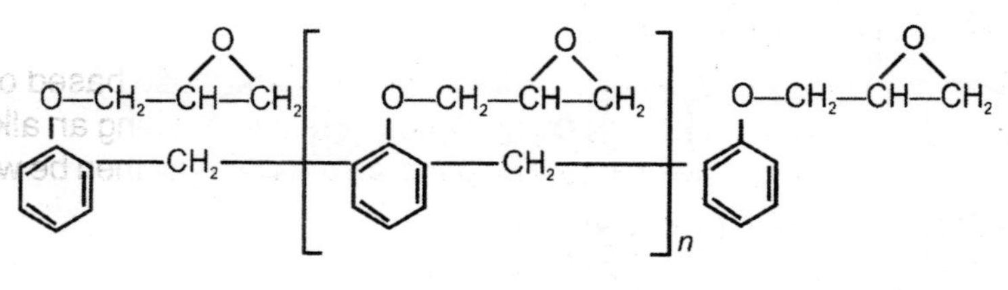

Cyclic and Acyclic Aliphatic Epoxy Resins

These comparatively new resins are usually based on the epoxidation of unsaturated compounds. The cyclo type does not contain the phenolic type structure assoicated with conventional epoxy resins. Typical base materials are vinylcyclohexene dioxide and dicyclopentadiene dioxide and, due to the fact that the distance between the reactive groups is shorter than with the bisphenol type, they are more highly cross-linked. Therefore by using the same curing agents and comparing the heat distortion temperature it is found that the temperatures for the newer types are somewhat higher

The acyclo types are similar to the cycle epoxides except that their basic structure units are long chains whereas the other resins have a ring structure. They can be broadly divided into two main types; epoxidised polyolefins and epoxidised oils. The epoxidised polyolefins can be prepared by oxidising the polyolefin with peracetic acid and/or other per acids.

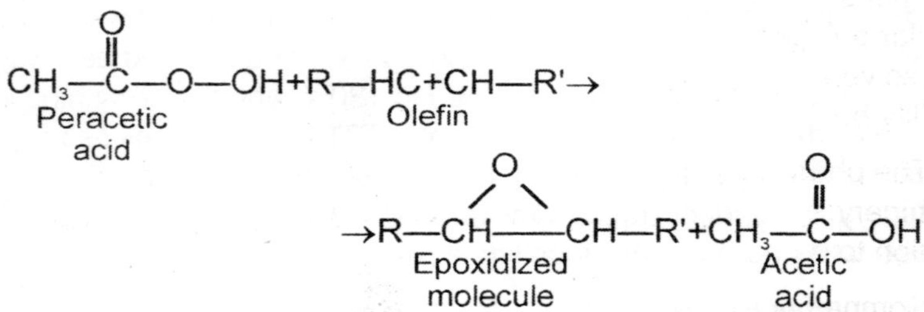

Another method of production is the condensation of an acid such as tetrahydrophthalic with epichlorhydrin followed by dehydrohalogenation. They are capable of being cured with the peroxide-type catalyst in a similar manner to polyester. However, in practice they are cured by techniques more akin to the glycidyl epoxies. Whereas these glycidyl resins are particularly reactive to bases and especially to polyamines, the cycloaliphatic ones are reactive to acidic hardeners. The anhydrides of dibasic acids such as hexahydrophthalic anhydride (HHPA) continue a very important class of anhydrides for these cyclic epoxies.

The following are some of the commercial resins available :

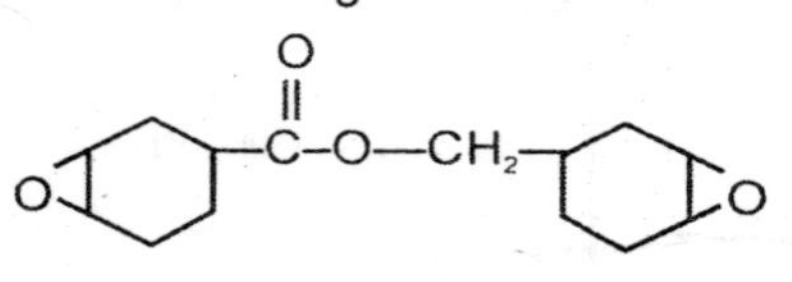

3,4-Epoxycyclohexylmethyl-
3,4-Epoxycyclohexane carboxylate

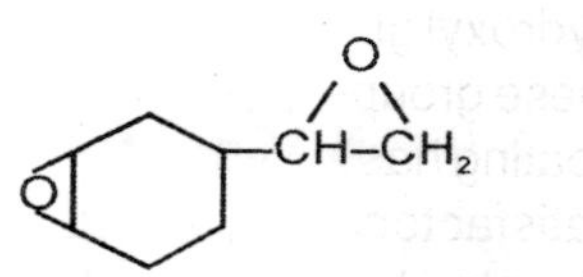

Vinyl cyclohexene dioxide

Phenoxy Resins

These resins differ from the conventional epoxies in that they are, and behave as, thermoplastic. The resins are termed phenoxies and may be classed as a polyhydroxyether.

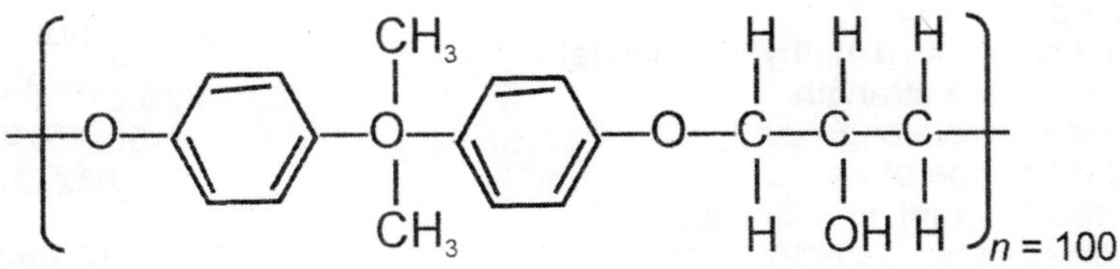

The outstanding physical characteristics of these new materials is that of ductility. The fact that their mechanical strength is not temperature dependent is also extremely attractive for many applications.

Phenoxies are strongly polar materials and as such have poor resistance to polar solvents such as ketones. Their amorphous structure also infers poor solvent resistance whereas the ether structure is indicative of chemical stability both to acids and alkalis.

The phenoxy resins may be processed on conventional thermoplastic machinery and can be injection molded, below molded, and extruded in addition to being used for adhesives and coatings, as is later illustrated.

Compared to the more conventional epoxies these materials have much higher molecular weights. A typical example, Phenoxy Resin PKHH (Union Carbide) has a molecular weight of around 30,000 as compared to 300-4000 for the uncross-linked epoxies. These resins do not have terminal reactive epoxy groups and are therefore thermally stable materials with a long shelf life as is expected of thermoplastics. The phenoxies are useful as adhesives but unlike the epoxies they do not require any further chemical conversion. No catalysts, curing agents, or hardeners are needed to make them useful although plasticisers help flexibilise the resultant adhesive film. Typical properties of the Phenoxy Resin PKHH are given in Table 6.1.

From the structure it can be seen that the phenoxy resins contain secondary hydroxyl groups (6%) and therefore these resins can be cross linked through these groups with polyisocyanates, amino and phenolic resins. The resultant coating has improved solvent and heat resistance. The polyisocyanates give satisfactory cure at room temperature whereas the other resins require elevated temperature (150-175°C) although they do not provide stable one-package systems at room temperature. Phenoxy coatings cross linked with melamine formaldehyde resins have been granted FDA approval.

Table 6.1

TYPICAL PROPERTIES OF PHENOXY RESIN PKHH

Specific gravity	1.18
Viscosity of 40% solids in MEK, Brookfield RVF, 20 rpm No. 5 spindle	5500-7700 cps
Reduced viscosity (0.2 g/100 ml. dimethylformamide)	0.4-0.6
Ultimate tensile strength	630-670 kg/cm^2
Ultimate tensile elongation	50-100%
Softening temperature	100°C
Permeability (1 mil free film at 25°C)	
water vapour (24 h/100 in.^{2})	3.5 g/mil
Oxygen (24 h/100 in.^{2})	5-8 cc/mil
carbon dioxide (24 h/100 in.^{2})	15-30 cc/mil
Bulking value	1178 g/dm^3

(Phenoxy is tradename of Union Carbide Corp.)

These resins are compatible with many amino and phenolic resins, ketone resins, rosin, and coumarone indene. They are incompatible with acrylics, rosin, esters, and vinyl resins although they can be plasticized with tri phenyl phosphite.

The hydroxyl groups on the phenoxy groups not only can be cross-linked but they are suitable of esterification.

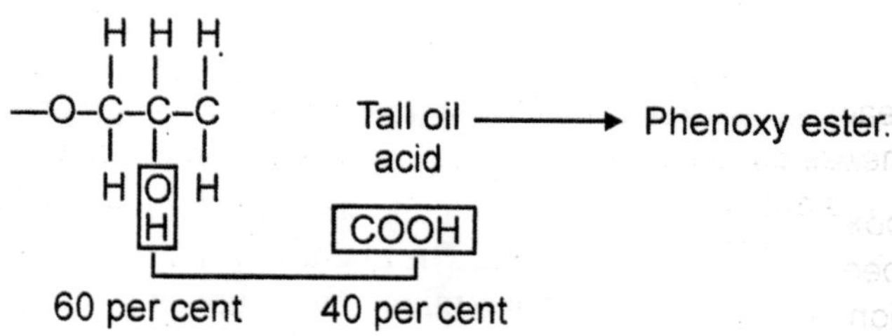

Phenoxy esters are useful materials for metal priming applications. They have better water and alkali resistance than the corresponding epoxy esters made from solid low molecular weight epoxy resins. Conventional formulating and compounding technique may be used. Typical primers include iron oxide (automotive) wash and zinc rich types. This latter type has outperformed all other primers tested in corrosive atmospheres.

To phenoxy resins when pigmented exhibit high gloss, excellent resistance to salt spray, humidity, and water. As clear coatings they are tough abrasion resistant, and either the unmodified or cross linked types are suitable for wood or floor coatings. Coatings reacted with isocyanates or catalysed melamine formaldehyde exhibit excellent resistance to cigarett burns and alcohol spotting.

CURING TECHNIQUES

A wide variety of curing agents may be used to cure epoxy resins and there are many ways in which they can be classified. They can be conveniently subdivided under room temperature of high temperature curing agents or by the grouping to which the chemical curing agent belongs. However, for simplicity it is intended to deal with the subject as follows.

1. Catalytically

(a) *Epoxy-Epoxy Reaction.* The epoxy resins are fairly reactive and because of this the group may be readily opened by tertiary amines. The actual opening is believed to take place as follows:

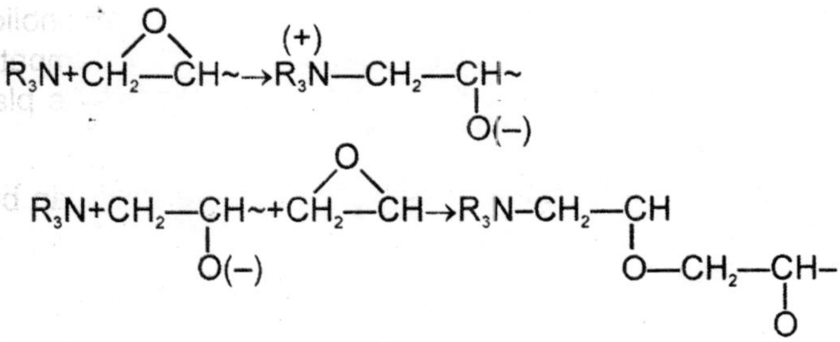

This reaction may continue and can result in a very long-chain system, although the chain may be terminated by blocking off the final activated epoxy.

(b) *Epoxy-Hydroxyl Reaction.* Epoxy rings react with hydroxyl groups that have been introduced into the resin by curing agents or certain modifiers. The reaction takes place as follows :

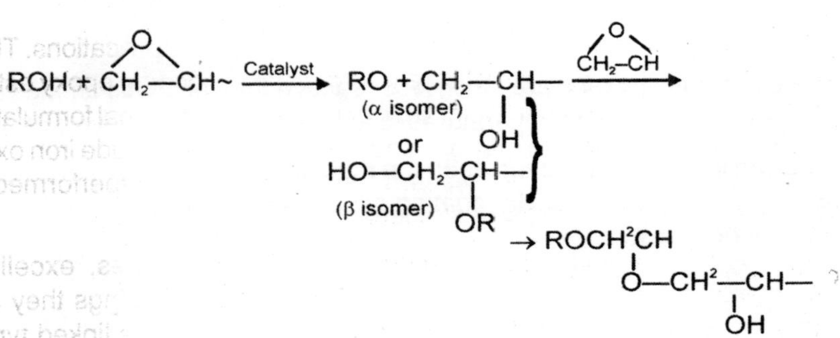

Two isomers are possible, and both provide a new hydroxyl group from which further polymerization may take place. A structure very similar to that shown for the epoxy -epoxy reaction may result and the reaction may continue until a high degree of cross linking is obtained.

2. Cross Linking Agents

Some commercial curing agents are lited in Table 6.2.

(a) *Amines.* Each amine group is difunctional and the following reactions are therefore possible.

(i)

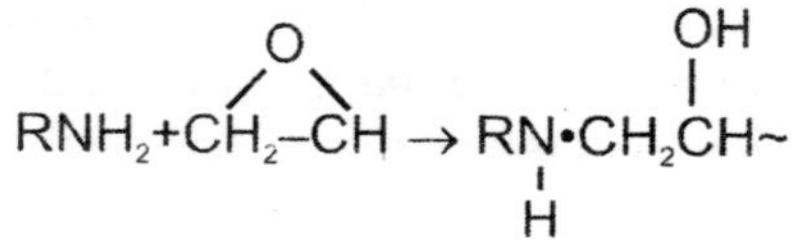

(ii)

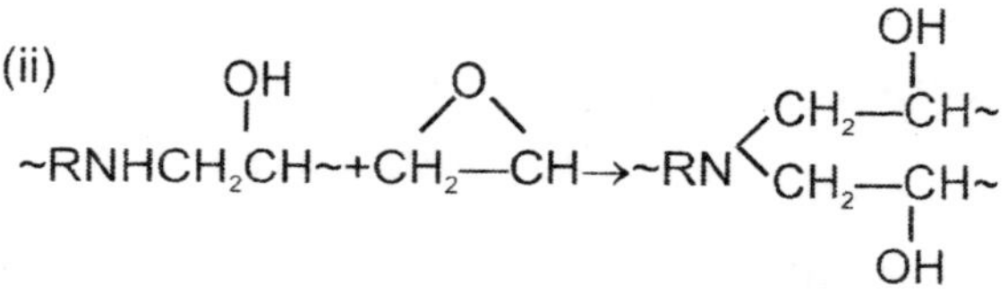

(iii) The hydroxyl groups may then start hydroxy/epoxy reactions.

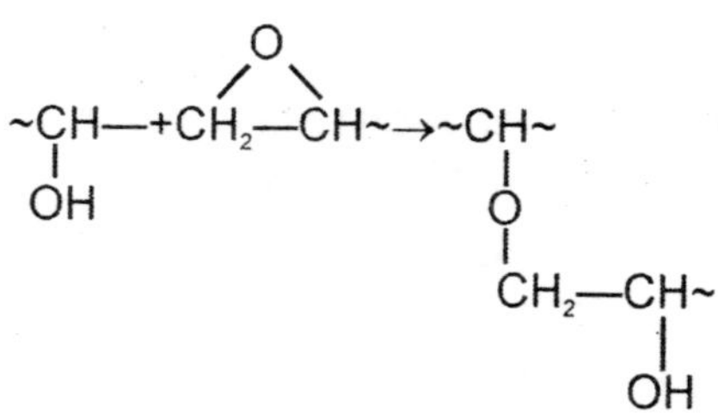

The aromatic amines are much less reactive than aliphatic amines and usually require elevated temperatures to achieve reasonable levels of cure.

Before leaving this section, mention must be made of dicyandiamide in view of its wide use in powder coating systems. The mechanism uses an amine curing agent :

Table 6.2
COMMERCIAL CURING AGENTS

Materials	*Amounts used parts per 100 resin*	*Pot life*	*Comments*	*Uses*
Diethylenetriamine (DTA)	8-11	45 min at 20°C	Liquid, volatile, and toxic. The amount used is also very critical	General-purpose room temperature curing agent
Triethylene tetramine (TETA)	Very similar to diethylenetriamine			
Pipridine	6	90 h at 40°C	Liquid, toxic, and volatile	Longer pot life and is used for casting
Triethylamine	10	7 h at 20°C	Catalytic	Adhesives
m-phenylenediamine (MPDA)	14	2½ h at 50°C	Solid with low toxicity	Chemical and heat resistant laminates
p,p' diaminodi phenyl methane (DDM)	27	8 h at 20°C	Solid toxic	General purpose laminates
p,p' diaminodi phenyl sulfone	30	2 h at 20°C	Solid	Produces a cured resin with high heat distortion, point
BF_3 monoethylamine	5	3 weeks at 20°C	Solid-has a delayed action effect	Heat resistant resins
Phthalic anhydride	30-45	14 h at 100°C	Solid-produces a low exotherm	Coatings
Hexahydrophthalic anhydride (HHPA)	80	ditto	Solid	Castings
Chlorendic anhydride (HET ACID)	100	½ h at 110°C	Flame resistant	Flame resistant laminates

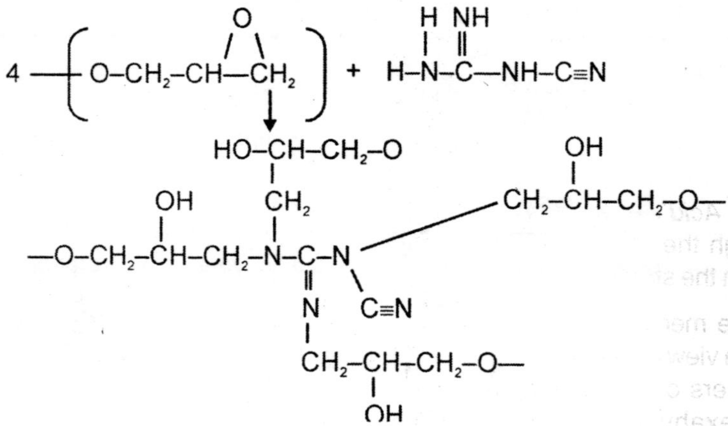

Dicyandiamide has poor solubility and a high melting point, thus it provides a poor rate of cure. Consequently the industry is moving more towards substituted derivatives which have lower melting points with improved compatibility. They have the general formula :

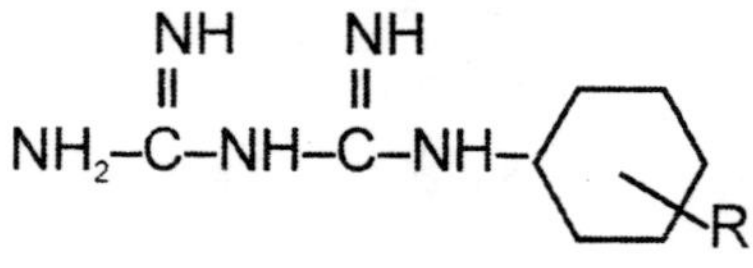

(b) *Organic Acids* : Organic acids are used mainly to esterify high-molecular weight epoxides suitable for use in surface coatings.

(i) The initital step is the esterification of the epoxy and hydroxyl groups with the liberation of water.

(ii) The next step is the etherification reaction of the epoxy with the hydroxyl group.

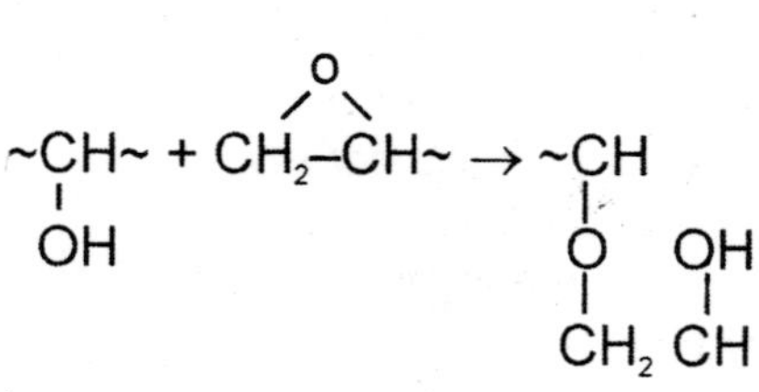

(iii) There is then a final hydration of epoxy groups by liberated H_2O.

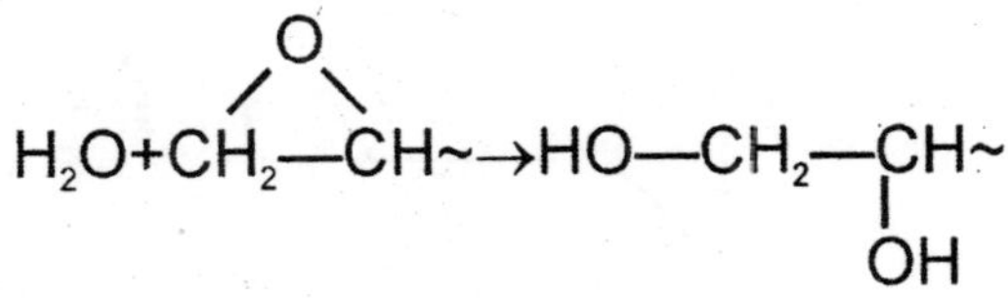

(c) *Acid Anhydrides.* Acid anhydrides react similarly to organic acids although the reaction is somewhat more complex due to the absence of water in the structure and the necessity for activating the anhydride structure.

The mechanism of curing for this group of chemicals is described in detail in view of the importance for curing cycloaliphatic epoxides. Two typical hardeners of this type are methyl tetrahydrophthalic anhydride (MTHPA) and hexahydrophthalic anhydride (HHPA). Chemically they can be represented as follows :

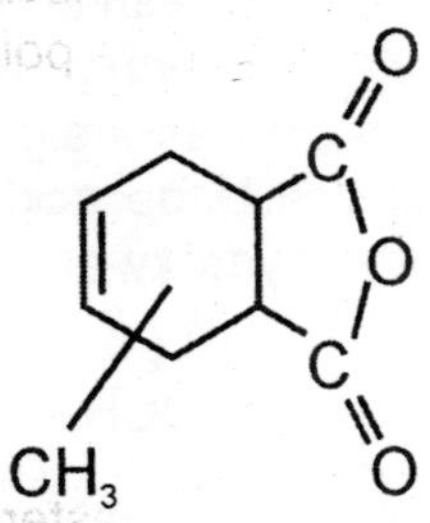

Methyltetrahydro-phthalic anhydride

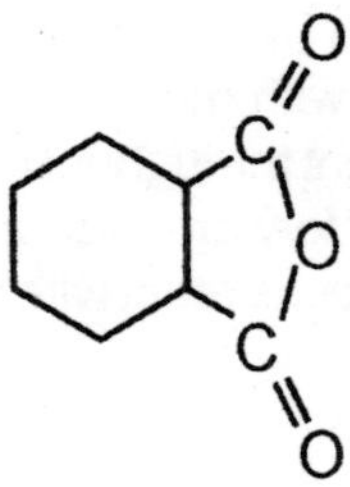

Hexahydrophthalic anhydride

It has been shown that the cycloaliphatic epoxides, made from a totally different method of manufacture than glycidyl ether types, contain very few hydroxyl groups. Therefore for the cycloaliphatic epoxide/anhydride system it is common practice to add hydroxyl rich materials. Even though it is possible to write a balanced reaction for a pure epoxide with an anhydride, in practice no reaction occurs. By adding hydroxyl rich materials the active hydrogen allows the epoxide/anhydride curing to take place in a stepwise process and adding anhydride to hydroxyl yields ester.

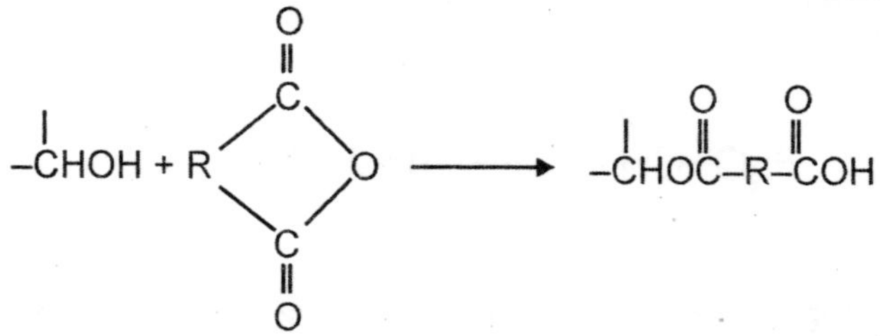

This is then reacted with epoxide groupings to form a hydroxyester.

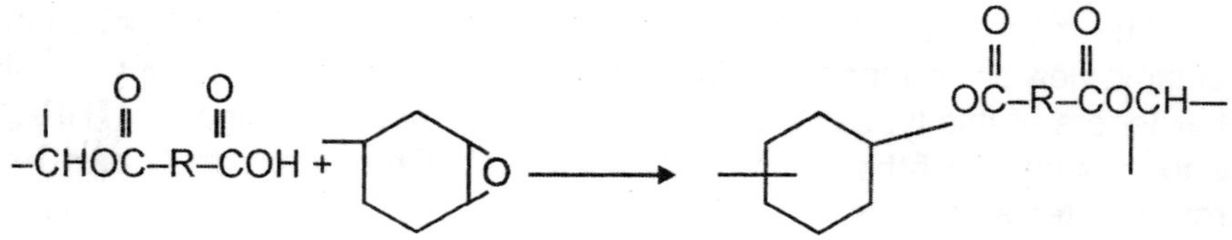

This reaction then repeats until either all the epoxide or the anhydride is consumed. The overall effect is the reaction of epoxide with anhydride to yield a diester with modification to give hydroxyls. The hydroxyls content remains constant throughout the cure. This process is not as straight forward as has been put forward because there is a complication. Under acid condition the hydroxyl groups react with epoxide to produce an hydroxy-ether.

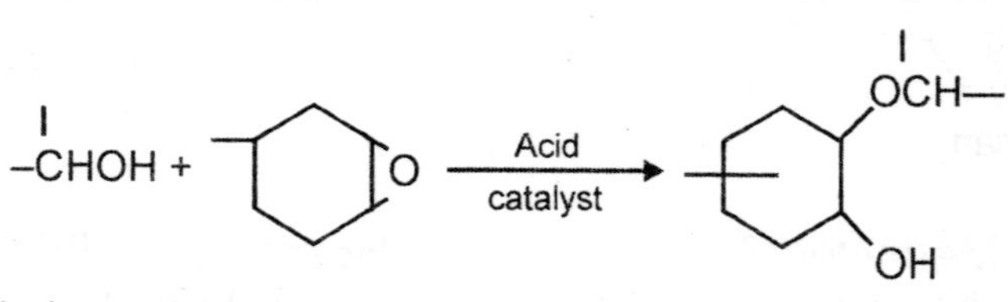

Clearly it can be seen that the important stage of the reaction of a bisphenol epoxy resin is the opening of the anhydride ring. This can be achieved in several ways :

(i) The hydroxyl group in the resin molecule used without a catalyst results in esterification and etherification processes while
(ii) tertiary amines favor esterification and
(iii) boron trifluoride complexes promote etherification.

The etherification process is generally undesirable because of the unreacted anhydride left in the cured film. Several catalysts have been suggested for use with this type of curing and benzyldimethylamine BDMA) is a commonly used tertiary amine for cycloaliphatic epoxide/anhydride system. The following are three catalysts which are finding considerable usage:

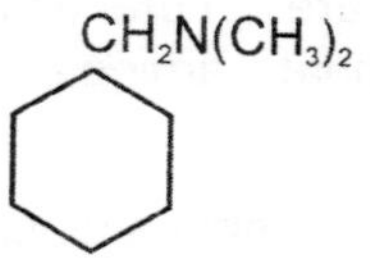

(Benzyldimethylamine)

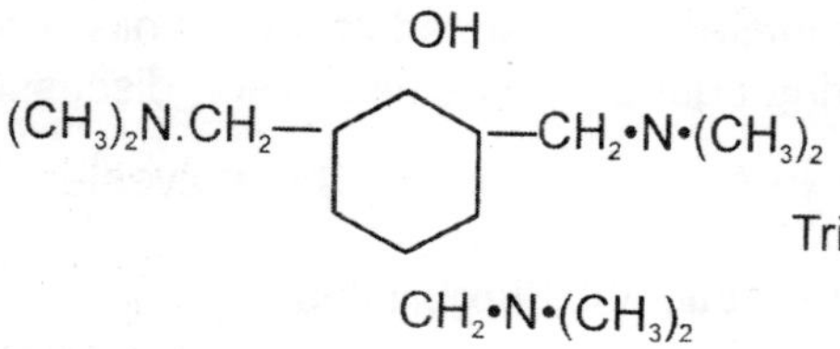

Tris(dimethylaminomethyl)phenol

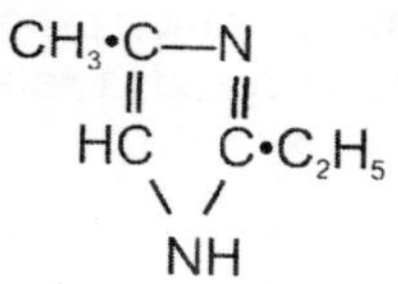

2 Ethyl 4 methylamidazole

Normally, between ½ to 2½ parts per 100 of the base resin are used.

(d) *Boron Trifluoride Complexes.* The complexes are frequently employed to delay curing and thus give the operator more time in which to work when fabricating various compounds. They are normally amines which are chemically associated with the boron trifluoride molecule such as BF_3-monoethylamine.

$$RNH : BF_3 \rightleftharpoons \overset{\oplus}{H} + R\overset{\ominus}{N} : BF_3$$

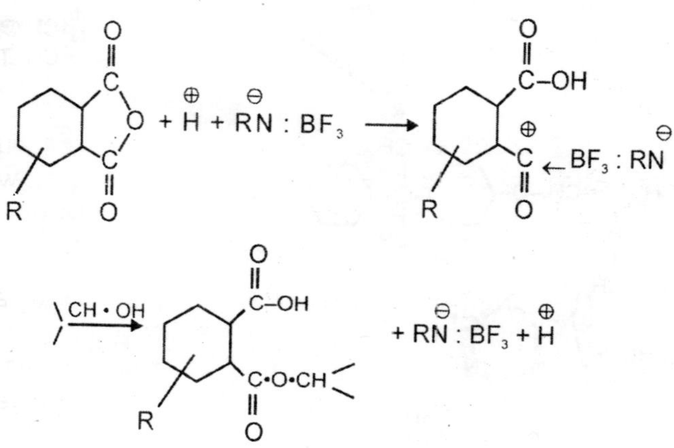

(e) *Resinous Curing Agents.* Many resins such as the polyamides, polysulfides, and phenolics react with and cure epoxides, but it must be remembered that the polysulfides are not practical curing agents and must be used in conjunction with an aliphatic amine.

(i) Polyamides

These can be regarded as polyamino amides which are produced by the reaction of polyamines with dimerised or trimerised vegetable oils. They serve a dual function both as curing agents and as flexibiliser, discussed later in the chapter.

(ii) Polysulfides

These are described under the section on Flexibilisers

(iii) Phenolics.

These resins react with epoxies by an etherification process. The cross linking occurs by the reaction with the epoxy group and the phenolic hydroxyl or the methoxy side group of the phenolic resin.

(iv) Amino Resins

It has been shown in Chapter 4 that melamine when reacted with formaldehyde in the correct proportions forms hexmethoxy melamine which in turn cross-links alkyd resins at elevated temperatures. It is also possible to cross-link epoxy resins with this modifed melamine as follows :

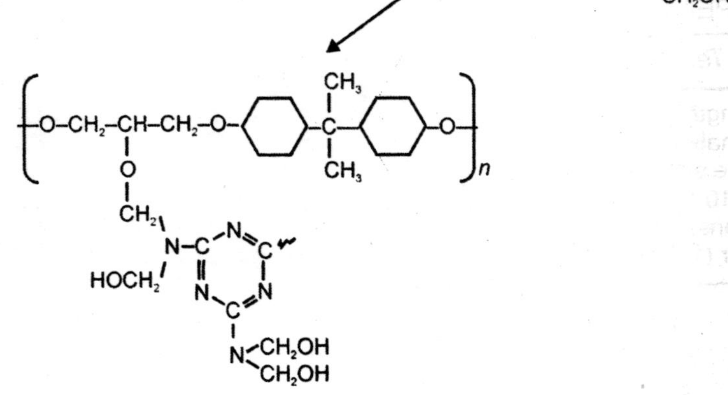

COMPOUNDING INGREDIENTS

Diluents

Diluents are normally incorporated into epoxy resins to reduce the vicosity and permit a higher loading of filler. Various types are used and they may be classified as follows :

(a) *Materials that are reactive with epoxies.* These include epichlorhydrin, allyl glycidyl ether, and pehnyl glycidyl ether.

(b) *Nonreactive diluents.* These are normally aromatic hydrocarbons such as xylene or tulene. They do not produce a permanent effect, hence the method is not popular.

(c) *Polymerisable Monomers.* Monomers such as styrene and diallyl phthalate have been used with some success.

FLEXIBILISERS

Flexibilisers, as the name implies, impart flexibility to epoxy resins and in many cases lower the viscosity of the resin. The following polymers are used for this purpose.

(a) *Polyamides.* These polyamide resins, trade name, versamid, are supplied by the Chmical Division of General Mills, and are based on vegetable diamers. They are low molecular weight polymers. They produce a two-fold effect, namely, flexibilising the resin and at the same time acting as a nontoxic cross linking agent. Table 6.3 lists the properties obtained from an epoxy resin and an epoxy/polyamide blend using 65 parts by weight epoxy resin, 35 parts polyamide, 20 parts quartz flour filler, and curing for 60 hours at 25°C.

Table 6.3
PROPERTIES OF EPOXIES AND EPOXY/POLYAMIDES

Test	*Epoxy/Polyamide*	*Epoxy resin*
Impact strength (ft lb/in notch)	1.5	0.5
Heat deformation temp (°C)	30	56
Compressive strength (lb/in^2 X 10^3)	8	15
Dielectric constant (1 Mc/s)	2.8	3
Power factor (1 Mc/s)	0.015	0.001

(b) *Polysulfides.* Polysulfides are rubber like materials and are viscous liquids. They are compatible in all proportions with epoxy resins and reduce the resin viscocity considerably. The curing reaction with epoxy resins is by addition and takes the following form :

$$R-\underset{\quad\diagdown O \diagup}{CH-CH_2} + HS-R' \rightarrow R-\overset{OH}{\overset{|}{CH}}-CH_2-S-R'$$

It must be emphasised once again that it is still necessary to add the normal amount of curing agent to complete the cure. The time for conversion varies according to the properties of the components and the temperature of cure, and may vary from a few minutes to days. Table 6.4 lists some of the properties obtainable using 100 parts by weight epoxy resin, 50 parts polysulfide resin, 20 parts curing agent, and curing for 60 hours at room temperature. Also included for comparison are the properties with out a modifying resin.

Table 6.4

PROPERTIES OF EPOXIES AND EPOXYL POLYAMIDE

Test	*Epoxy / Modifying resin*	*Epoxy*
Impact strength (ft lb/in notch)	6	1.5
Heat deformation temp. (^{o}C)	23	56
Compressive strength ($lb/in^2 \times 10^3$)	2.3	15
Dielectric constant at (Mc/s)	3.8	3.8
Dielectric strength	450	450
Power factor at (1 Mc/s)	0.006	0.004
Volume resitivity (ohm cm)	6 X 1013	8×10^{14}

(c) *Fatty Diamines.* Fatty diamines may react with epoxy resins in the same manner as do other aliphatic amines. A typical fatty diamine has the following structure :

$$R_{soya}NH(CH_2)_3NH_2$$

These materials are used in conjunction with epoxy resins required for low-temperature work. Unfortunately, they produce resins with poor thermal and chemical resistance.

(d) *Polyesters.* These act as nonreactive plasticizers similar to those used for vinyl resins and take no part in the curing reaction. The effect is not permanent and the method is not widely used.

However, a variety of polyols such as supplied by Union Carbide are very useful for formulating in the room temperature curing the cycloaliphatic epoxides. Polyacaprolactones, which were described in the previous chapter, can be used and provide the ultimate in heat distortion and toughness for hydrated aluminium field systems. A typical product is as follows :

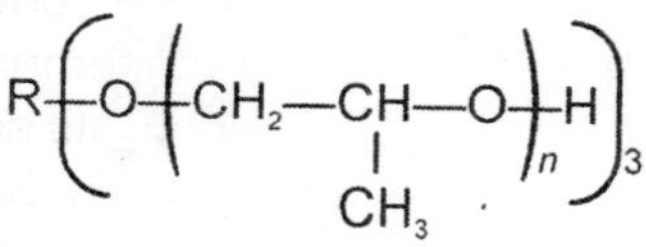

"Niax" polyol LHT 240

These materials are regarded as flexibilisers which are permanent and provide improved toughness while still maintaining a high level of electrical characteristics and heat distortion temperature.

FILLERS

Fillers are normally added to epoxy resins to reduce cost, dilute exotherm during curing, reduce shrinkage, and lower the coefficient of thermal expansion. A wide range of fillers may be used and because the uncured resin in inert the possibility of a reaction between filler and resin is remote. The following are fillers that have been suitable by experimentation for epoxy resins : mica (200 mesh), silica or quartz (120 mesh), marble flour, alumina, iron oxide, slate powder, coarse silica sand, and aerosil. The effect of using different types and amounts of fillers on the thermal properties of epoxy resins are listed in Table 6.5 and 6.6.

Table 6.5

COMPARISON OF THERMAL CONDUCTIVITYOF FILLED "EPIKOTE" 828* CURED WITH "EPIKURE" Z* AND STEEL AND ALUMINIUM

Filler	*Thermal conductivity* (Btu/h/ft^2/ft/°F)
None	0.13
Alumina (325 parts)	0.82
Silica (150 parts)	0.44
Steel	26.0
Aluminium	116.0

Table 6.6

COMPARISON OF THE THERMAL COEFFICIENT OF EXPANSION OF EPIKOTE 828*/MPD CASTINGS USING VARIOUS AMOUNTS AND TYPES OF FILLERS WITH STEEL AND ALUMINIUM

Filler		*Linear coefficient of expansion X 10^{-5} (per °C)*
None		4.5
Silica (250 parts per hundred of resin)		2.61
Silica	(30 p.h.r.)	4.5
Calcium carbonate	(200 p.h.r.)	2.3
Calcium carbonate	(35 p.h.r.)	4.6
Alumina	(150 p.h.r.)	3.0
Alumina	(50 p.h.r.)	4.1
Steel		*ca* 1.0
Aluminium		1.84
Brass		1.88
Copper		1.68

(MPD - meta phenylenediamine)

* Registered trademark of Shell Chemical Company Limited.

RELEASE AGENTS

These are normally required where the epoxy resins are being used for laminating applications. Silicone release agents, polyethylene film, cellophane, and various waxes have all proved suitable.

PROPERTIES

Epoxy resins possess many outstanding characteristics including extreme toughness, low shrinkage on cure due to the absence of volatiles, and excellent thermal, chemical, solvent, and water resistance. They do however, exhibit fairly low impact strength in the unmodified form and for certain applications, such as thin films, they have to be modified with flexibilisers. These resins also exhibit a high degree of adhesion when bonded to a wide variety of surfaces such as metal and wood. This property is correlated with their polar nature and their ability to 'wet' the surfaces of various substrates.

Other important properties include outstanding electrical insulating qualities maintained over a comparatively wide range of temperatures (Table 6.7).

Table 6.7

TYPICAL PROPERTIES OF EPOXY RESINS

Test	*Molding resin (unfilled)*	*Casting resin (unfilled)*
Specific gravity at 25°C	1.7-1.9	1.1-1.3
Tensile strength ($lb/in^2 X10^3$)	8-10	10-15
Elongation (%)	15	2.5
Compressive strength (lb/in^2 X 10^3)	12-20	14-18
Flexural strength (lb/in^2 X 10^3)	15-18	15-20
Impact strength (Izod notched ft lb/in notch)	1	0.5-2.0
Coefficient of thermal expansion X 10^{-5}	5	4-6
Heat distortion temp. (°C)	140-150	120-250
Volume resistivity (ohm cm)	1 X 10^{14}	1 X 10^{17}
Dielectric strength (V/mil)	400	400
Dielectric constant (60 c/s)	3-5	3.5-5
Power factor (60 c/s)	0.35	0.002
Water absorption (24 h immersion %)	0.05-0.1	0.1
Chemical resistance		
Effect weak acids	Resistant	Resistant
Strong acids	Attacked	Attacked
Weak alkalis	Resistant	Resistant
Strong alkalis	Resistant	Resistant
Organic solvents	Resistant	Resistant

These properties are also typical of epoxy films but they can be further upgraded by reacting with other resins (e.g. fatty acid polyamides).Molding powders can be modified by filling with glass fiber, etc., and the finished

Table 6.8

PROPERTIES OF A TYPICAL EPOXIDE MOLDING COMPOSITION (B.S. 771 Test Methods where applicable)

Property	*Units*	*Value*
Specific gravity	–	1.8-2.1
Flexural strength	10^3 lb in^{-2}	13-19
Mold shrinkage	in/in	<0.002
After shrinkage 48 h at 105°C	%	negligible
Water absorption	mg	5-10
Dielectric constant 800 c/s 10^6 c/s	–	4.5-5.5
Power factor 800 c/s 10^6 c/s	–	0.01-0.02
Volume resistivity	ohm cm	10^{14}-10^{15}

moldings have high dimensional stability, low water absorption, and good resistance to tracking. They also exhibit good heat resistance and moldings are claimed to be capable of withstanding 200°C without breakdown. Properties of a typical epoxide molding powder are illustrated in Table 6.8.

APPLICATIONS AND PROCESSING TECHNIQUES

Adhesives

On curing, epoxy resins possess excellent bonding characteristics, and the reaction takes place without the evolution of volatiles and, often, even without heat or pressure. They may be used to bond various metals, rubbers, wood and glass with satisfactory results although with certain plastics such as PVC and polyethylene and bond is usually poor.

The relatively high price of epoxy resins has limited their widespraed use for bonding processes in the wood and allied industries. Urea, melamine, and phenol-formaldehyde are normally used for plywood and the many other furniture applications, although for certain structural applications where wood laminates of high strengths are required the epoxies are generally to be preferred. Metal/metal bonding is very successful with epoxy resins which are now used extensively in the aircraft industry where, in addition to good bond requirements, good thermal resistance is also required.

Some of the epoxy resins are used not only for their good adhesive properties alone but also combined with toughness especially for floor surfacing compounds in the construction of new floors and in resurfacing old ones. These compounds in the construction of new floors and in resurfacing old ones. These compounds may be laid on concrete, metal, or wood substrates, and by suitable formulation a range of colours, surface finishes and thicknesses can be made to suit various industrial and domestic requirements. For this type of application they are normally three-components systems consisting of resin, curing agent, and aggregate.

Epoxy resins are also used as adhesives in the bonding of microscopic hollow spheres of phenol formaldehyde resin, and known as *syntactic foams*. These foams are used extensively as core sandwiches and for replacing rotten wood in old buildings. They are supplied in putty form and may be trowelled into cavities where, eventually, they set to a tough hard mass.

It has been claimed that the cycloaliphatic epoxies show distinct advantages over glycidyl ether systems particularly in their ability to yield high strength bonds on poorly-cleaned or even oily metal surfaces.

Surface Coatings

Coatings based on epoxy resins possess good flexibility, adhesion, toughness, and chemical resistance. Their many applications include primers and paints for vehicles, chemical tanks linings, and the inside coatings of beer cans. Epoxy coating resins have been blended with certain compatible phenol and urea -formaldehyde resins to give outstanding toughness as well as resistance to chemicals and solvents, and are used for coating the inside and outside of drums and tanks. They are also used in containers of beverages, meat and fish cans, and aerosols. Oil modified epoxy resins are used quite widely for collapsible tube coatings because of their ability to withstand the container being flexed and their resistance to liquid contents which might, by chemical action, corrode some substances.

Considerable work has been carried out to develop water-thinnable systems. They can be used as primers for aircraft and automobiles applications. The maintenance coating area is also important and this is served by the epoxy coal tar systems which can be cured by polyamines.

The use of epoxies is growing steadily in the field of powder coating and this is discussed in greater detail in the appropriate section later in the book.

Laminates

Epoxy resins are used in the manufacture of both low and high pressure laminates. The processing techniques are not discussed fully here as the methods used are vitually interchangeable with those used for polyesters described in the Chapter 5.

As laminating resins they are used with a variety of reinforcing agents such as glassfiber, asbestos, and certain synthetic fibers. As noted earlier, they cure without water of condensation, which makes them ideally suitable for this application. Epoxies also exhibit outstanding adhesion to glass, and on curing the laminates exhibit excellent mechanical, thermal, and electrical insulating properties. Such laminates also possess excellent chemical resistance.

The use of epoxy laminates has been somewhat restricted in all but some of the highly specialised industrial fields due to the relative high price of the base resin in comparison with some of the more common resins. Very few uses have been found in the domestic consumer field, although they are used in industry where their superior mechanical strength and good heat and chemical resistance are required. Typical applications include structural components for aircraft and missiles, chmical resistant tanks, and laminated tubes and pipes for conveying oil.

CASTING AND TOOLING

Casting techniques are now widely used with epoxy resins in the electronics industry for potting, encapsulating transformers, valves, capacitors and many other electronic components. There are variations of technique, the following being the methods most commonly used (Fig. 6.1).

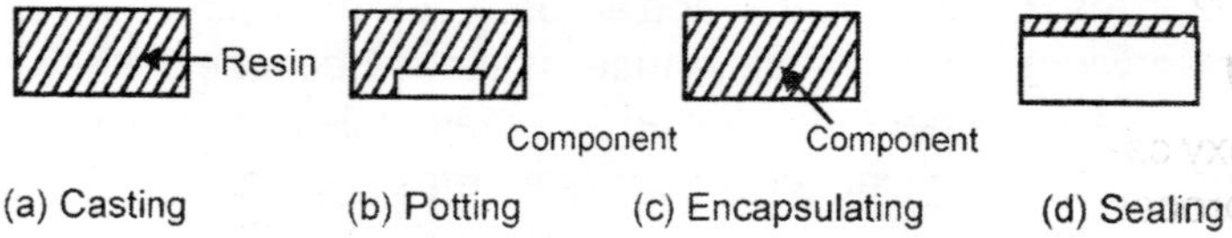

Fig. 6.1

(a) *Casting.* This process is normally carried out by simple gravity technique. The casting resin must be in the fluid, uncured state and be of sufficiently low viscosity to be conveniently poured into molds of wood, metal, plaster of paris or certain plastic and elastomers (Fig. 6.1a).

(b) *Potting.* This is a modified form of casting in which the component to be potted may be considered as a nonremovable mold. (Fig. 6.1a).

(c) *Encapsulating and Embedding.* In this method a protective shield is cast completely round the component without any impregnation being involved. Encapsulation and embedment are terms used interchangeably to describe virtually the same process (Fig. 6.1c).

(d) *Sealing and Impregnating.* A component may be sealed by placing it in a container and then completely filling the voids with a casting resin.

This method is becoming very popular with the electrical and aircraft industries (Fig. 6.1d).

Impregnating involves forcing the liquid resin into the interstices of the component. It may be a completely independent operation or can be used in conjunction with any of the other techniques mentioned above.

Before a resin is considered suitable for casting and/or tooling techniques it must possess certain of the following attributes.

Casting	*Tooling*
Good dimensional stability	High dimensional stability
Low volumetric shrinkage on cure	Low shrinkage on curing
Shock Resistant	High compressive strength

Tough and in certain applications flexible
Good electrical, chemical, and heat resistant properties
Good water resistance
Must not corrode metallic inserts or parts of components
Low coefficient of thermal expansion on curing
Sufficiently low viscocity to be purable.
Good abrasion resistance
Thermally stable
Good adhesion to material insertion
Low coefficient of thermal expansion
Must not exhibit cold flow.

Tooling

Epoxy cast tools are used mainly for making dies, jigs, foundry, patterns, plastic processing molds and Keller models. In many of these applications epoxy resins possess advantages over more conventional metal: reduction in cost and time of manufacture, reduction in weight, ease of manufacture, and modification on repair.

The idea of making epoxy tools with plastics was first considered some fifteen years ago but certain deficiencies in the materials made the idea unattractive and it was not until the epoxy resins became commercially available that interest was once more roused.

MISCELLANEOUS APPLICATIONS

Their use as a molding materials for the compression and transfer techniques was, to some extent, retarded by their high adhesive properties. Certain development have taken place which allow incorporation of a built-in release agent and these molding materials are now suitable for conventional molding techniques. They are loaded with mineral fillers, synthetic, fibers, or glassfiber. Once more, the relatively high price restricts the field applications.

Epoxy resins may be foamed by incorporating a blowing agent, such as the azo compounds which liberate nitrogen on heating. The bulk density of these foams is controlled by the amount of blowing agent; 2 per cent gives a useful balance of properties. Epoxy foams are suitable for use in encapsulation of electronic compounds where strength/weight ratio is critical. They have a fairly low coefficient of thermal conductivity and thus become a useful insulating medium.

7

Silicones

Silocones are high molecular weight semiorganic polymers built up of long chains or alternate silicon and oxygen atoms. Their history dates back to the nineteenth century, when Dumas predicted the possibility of the existence of organo-silicon compounds.

The first systematic work was carried out by Professor F.S. Kipping and co-workers at University College, Nottingham, during the first half of the twentieth century. He began his work with the preparation of asymmetric compounds of tetra-substituted silicon, and the work developed into a very full survey of the chemistry of silicon. Kipping's main interest was in the chemistry of this element and he described many of the compounds produced in the course of his studies as 'uninviting' and 'glue-like'. It is obvious from his published work that he did not foresee any technical usefulness for silicone polymers and he therefore made no attempt to develop them.

However, just prior to the outbreak of the Second World War certain industrial organisations began to show commercial interest in silicone polymers. A considerable amount of new development work was then undertaken in the U.S.A. particularly in the laboratories of the General Electric Company, the Corning Glass Works and the Dow Chemical Company. The last two companies were so convinced that there was a future for silicone polymers that they decided to join forces and form a new company, Dow Corning Corporation, to manufacture and market silicones. It was from the laboratories of this company that the first commercial silicone was produced.

NOMENCLATURE

Kipping first used the word 'silicone' to denote the organo-silicon analogues of ketones.

$$\begin{matrix} R' \\ R \end{matrix}\!\!> Si = O;$$

He quickly realised that such materials were polymeric, having the structure.

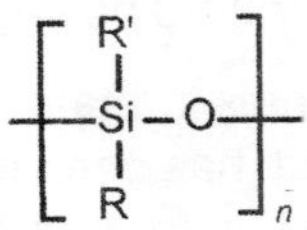

The simplest of this family is silane.

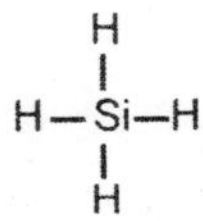

The hydrogen atoms of this material may be replaced by halogen, alkyl, or aryl groups giving compounds such as.

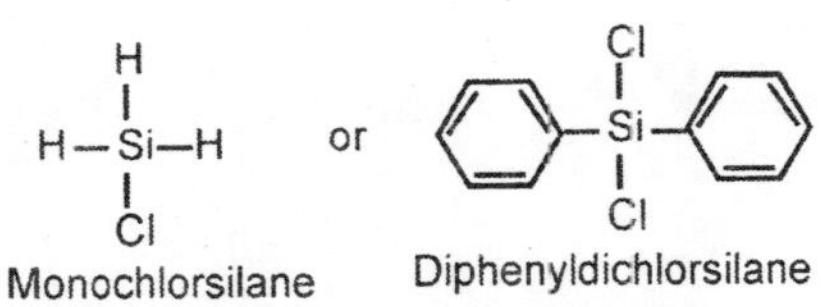

The basic structure of the building blocks from which silicone polymers are produced is

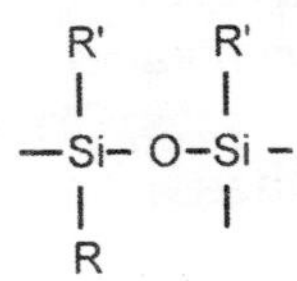

This grouping is designated as the siloxane linkage and is the characteristic structure to be found in all silicone polymers. A compound consisting of a large number of such groupings is referred to as a polysiloxane.

The pendant R groups which are attached to the silicone atoms usually are simple hydrocarbon radicals such as methyl, phenyl, or vinyl. In production many other functional groups have been introduced into the polymer structure including alkyl, cyanoethyl, fluroalkyl, and nitrile. The introduction of such functional groups has been shown to significantly modify properties as solvent resistance, high and low temperature resistance, solubility and compatibility.

This particular branch of chemistry does not only involve linear polymer structures but also branched and cyclic ones. Probably the most common cyclic material in this group is octamethyltetrapolysiloxane and unlike most of the other silicone polymers, these cyclic materials have discreet boiling and freezing points and can therefore be separated by distillation processes.

Chain stopping with materials containing such groups as $(CH_3)_3$-Si-O,-CH-CH_2 and -OH. The first group has been found suitable in the manufacture of silicone fluids and the latter two for use where cross-linking is required.

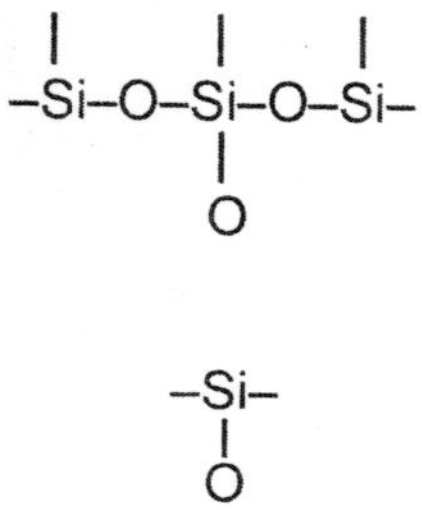

Branched structure

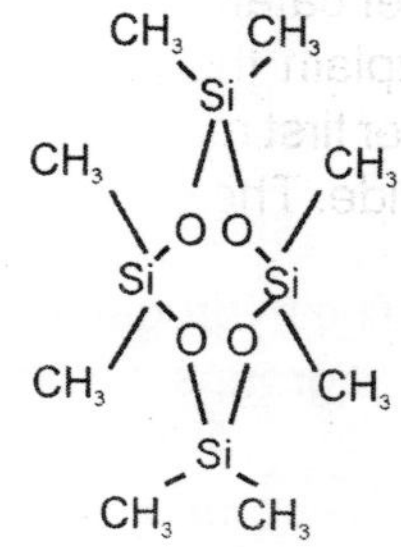

Cyclic Structure

RAW MATERIALS

The starting material for the manufacture of silicones are the substituted chlorsilanes, of general formula $R_nSiCl_{(4-n)}$. There are four methods normally used for preparing chlorsilanes suitable for commercial purposes, namely the Grignard Process, Direct Process, Olefin Addition Process, and Sodium Condensation Process. Of these, only the first two methods are of commercial imporantce.

1. Grignard Process

This process was widely used by Kipping and was first applied in 1906. The Grignard reagent is prepared by reacting magnesium metal suspended in anhydrous ether with a halide of the organic radical it is required to introduce, e.g., methyl chloride. This is then reacted with silicon tetrachloride to give a mixture of chlorsilanes.

$$\begin{aligned}
&Mg + CH_3Cl && \rightarrow CH_3MgCl \\
&CH_3MgCl + SiCl_4 && \rightarrow SiCH_3Cl_3 + MgCl_2 \\
&CH_3MgCl + SiCH_3Cl_3 && \rightarrow Si(CH_3)_2Cl_2 + MgCl_2 \\
&CH_3MgCl + Si(CH_3)_2Cl_2 && \rightarrow Si(CH_3)_3Cl + MgCl_2
\end{aligned}$$

A high yield is obtained by this process although a resultant products must be fractionally distilled to obtain single substances in a high stage of purity.

2. Direct Process

In this process the element silicon is converted into chlorsilanes, containing both an organic radical and chlorine. An organic halide such as methyl chloride is passed through a mixture of powdered silicon using a copper catalyst and heated to 250-280°C. A free radical mechanism is used to explain the reaction that occurs, but will not be discussed here. The copper first reacts with the methyl chloride to give copper methyl and cuprous chloride. The overall reaction may be written.

$$2CH_3Cl + Si \xrightarrow[\text{Catalyst}]{\text{Copper}} Si(CH_3)_2Cl_2$$

250–280°C

Methyl chloride Silicon Dimethyl dichlorsilane

The phenyl chlorsilanes may also be manufactured in a similar manner by replacing the methyl chloride with chlorobenzene. There are, however some differences in the manufacturing process and it is imperative to remember that excess chlorobenzene is passed through the reaction vessel to sweep out the high boiling phenyl chlorosilanes. The unreacted chlorobenzene may then be recovered by fractionation.

The reaction takes place as follows :

$$2C_6H_5Cl + Si \rightarrow Si(C_6H_5)_2Cl_2$$

Chlorobenzene Silicon Diphenyl dichlorsilane

3. Olefin Addition

In this process trichlorsilane is reacted under pressure with an unsaturated organic material. It can be used to prepare a wide variety of organosilicon compounds but can not be used to prepare methyl chlorsilanes.

4. Sodium Condensation Process

This process depends on the reaction between silicon tetrachloride and an organic chloride in the presence of sodium :

$$SiCl_4 + 4RCl + 8Na \longrightarrow SiR4 + 8NaCl$$

It is a tricky process to carry out and there is difficulty in disposing of the unreacted sodium. These drawbacks have to some extent limited its use on a commercial scale.

POLYMERISATION AND STRUCTURE

(a) Silicone Fluids

Silicone fluids are prepared from dimethyl dichlorsilane with a small amount of trimethyl chlorsilane used as a 'chain stopper'. The first stage in the production of these fluids is the hydrolysis of the chlorsilane:

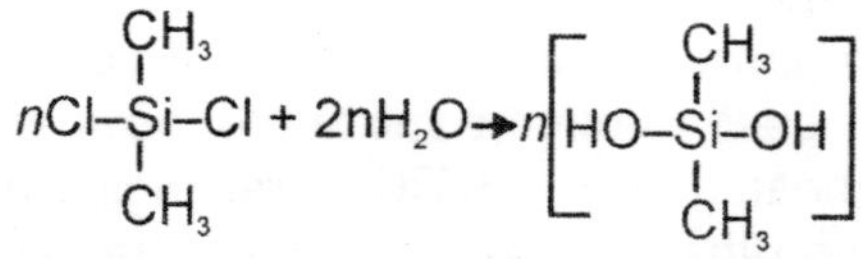

The hydroxyl groups in the silane diol formed are unstable and they therefore react with each other to form linear polymers.

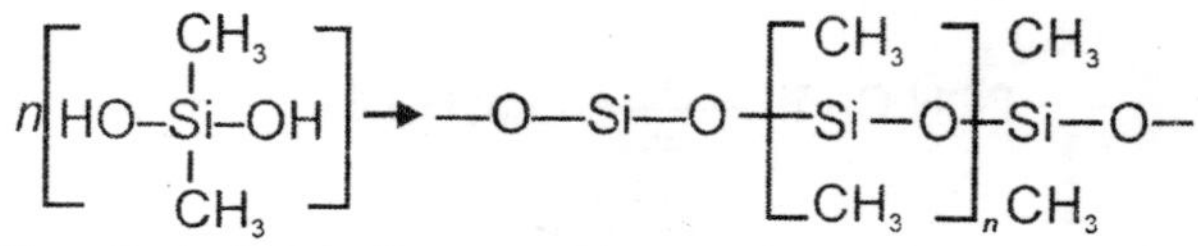

Dimethyl silane diol Polydimethyl siloxane

The molecular weight of the fluids can be varied over a wide range and may be predetermined by careful selection of chlorsilanes.

A relatively new groups of silicone polymers is desiganted silicone polycarbinols and combine the typical properties associated with the silicones plus the alcohol reactivity. Unlike the fluids the fluids described previously, these silicone polycarbinols reacted further with a variety of materials. Typical polymers which can be modified with these new silicone polymers are urethanes, polyesters, methylol melamines, acrylics and SBR.

The silicone polycarbinols take either of two basic structure (1) an ABA type Such as.

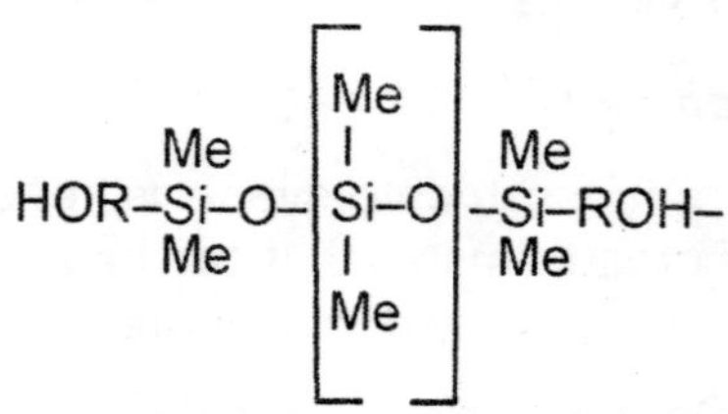

or (2) a graft copolymer, such as

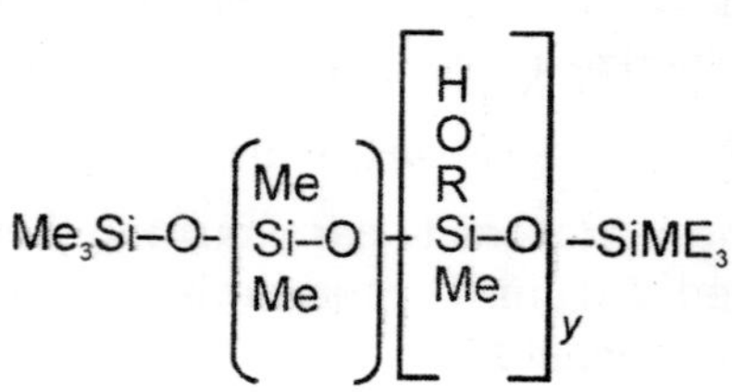

R is an organic spacer and the alcohol moiety is attached to the silicone polymer via a nonhydrolyzable Si–C bond. Dow Corning Corp. offers four materials of which Q2-8026, 1248 and Q4-3557 fluids are graft copolymers and Q4-3667 fluid is an ABA block type copolymer.

The reaction may be continued, and final curing may be effected by heating with a catalyst such as the octoates or naphthenates.

These resins can be copolymerised with certain organic resins such as the epoxides. It was seen in Chapter 6 that the epoxy resins are renowned for their outstanding strength, and by combining this characteristics with the excellent thermal stability and electrical insulating properting of silicones an excellent laminating resin is produced. Silicone resins now available are suitable for polymerising with a variety of organic resins such as the epoxy, polyester, pehnolic and polyol types. These silicones resins are low molecular weight siloxanols with a hydroxyl content of between 3-5 per cent. The hydroxyl groups act as weak acids and for this reason the intermediate can be viewed as a highly functional polybasic acid. Copolymerisation takes place as follows :

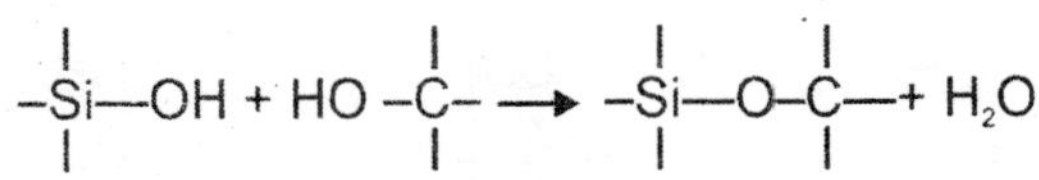

This reaction is to some exent retarded by a side reaction.

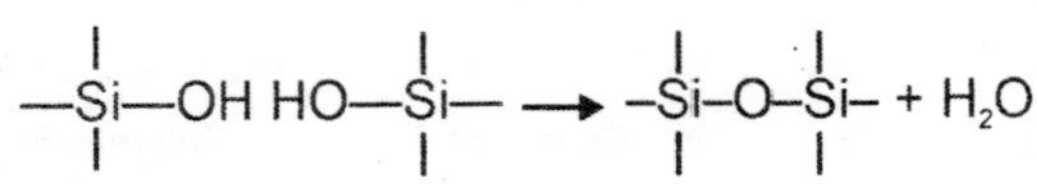

(b) Silicone Elastomers

Silicone elastomers are based upon linear polymers of very high molecular weight. The first silicone elastomers were made from polydimethyl siloxane, of the following structure.

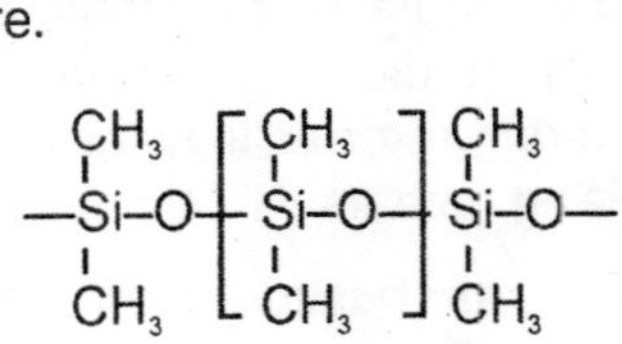

Many variations have since been developed for these elastomers including the introduction of phenyl and vinyl groups to improve certain of the physical properties of the elastomers, viz. low temperature brittle point and compression set respectively.

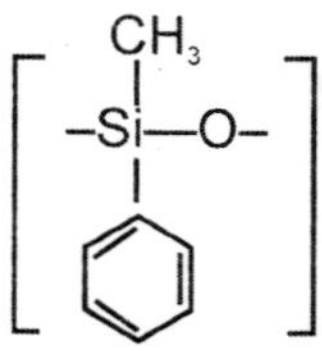

Phenyl substitution (improves low temperature brittle point)

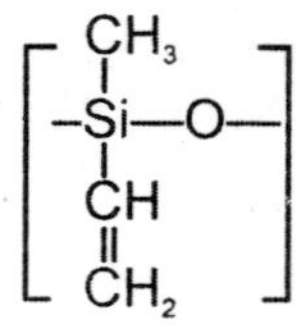

Vinyl substitution (improves compression set.)

The introduction of flourine and nitrile groups into the silicone elastomer chain structure has produced elastomers with outstanding heat stability combined with excellent petrol and oil resistance.

Fluorine substituion

Nitrile substitution

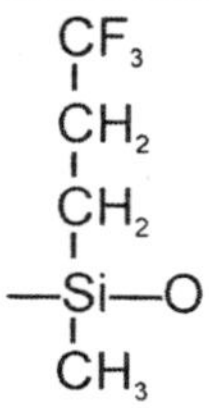

(i) Trifluoropropyl-siloxane

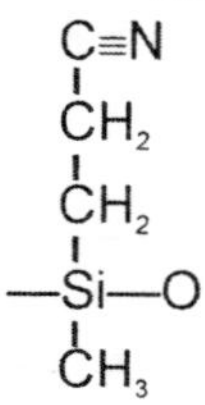

(ii) Cyanoethyl

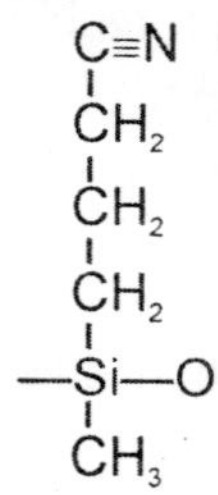

(iii) Cyanopropyl

Another variation can be obtained by introducing hydroxyl groups into thepolymer chain. This produces elastomers which are suitable for curing at room temperature. The curing reaction is normally carried out by means of an organo metallic salt such as dibutyl tin dilaurate or stannous octoate. These elastomers are generally referred to as either cold-curing rubbers or room temperature vulcanising rubbers (RTV).

In general these rubbers are based on low molecular weight silicone polymers with reactive end groups. As with the heat curing types mentioned previously, specific groups such as flourine, nitrile, and phenyl groups can be built into the polymer structure to impart desired characteristics. Generally the curing system for these RTV rubbers can be classified into two main groups and the first group which is a condensation type can be further subdivided into sections "with and without moisture".

1. Condensation

(a) *Without moisture.* With this type of reaction the reactive end group is usually a silanol (≡Si–OH) . As would be expected with the Kienle theory of functionality the curing agent must have a number of at least three or greater

$$\equiv Si\text{–}OH + OH\text{–}Si\equiv \xrightarrow[\text{base}]{\text{Organic}} \equiv Si\text{–}O + \text{–}Si\equiv + H_2O$$

Alkoxy containing cross linking agents such as ethyl o-silicate requires a tin soap as catalyst.

$$\equiv Si\text{–}OH + CH_3CH_2\,O\text{–}Si\equiv \xrightarrow[\text{Soap}]{\text{Tin}} \equiv Si\text{–}O\text{–}Si\equiv + CH_3CH_2OH$$

Catalysts can be omitted if polyfunctional aminoxy silicone compounds are used.

$$\equiv Si\text{–}OH + R_2NO\text{–}Si\equiv \longrightarrow \equiv Si\text{–}O\text{–}Si\equiv + R_2NOH$$

Industrially these types of cold curing silicone elastomers are normally sold as two-pack systems which are mixed just prior to use. The curing takes place without the presence of moisture and large thicknesses can be cured.

(b) *With moisture.* These particular types are based on a silanol terminated polymer to which a polyfunctional silicone-containing curing agent is added. Variations include using a polymer which is end-stopped with the curing agent and in general a condensation catalyst is used.

This curing takes place only in the presence of atmospheric moisture so the reaction takes place initially at the surface and the diffusion of the moisture further into the matrix ensures that complete cure takes place throughout the rubber.

A typical reaction, with X representing the reactive groups of the curing agent which terminates the polymer chain, follows :

$$\equiv Si\text{–}XH_2O\equiv \longrightarrow \equiv Si\text{–}OH\ HX$$

$$\equiv Si\text{–}OH\ X\text{–}Si\equiv \longrightarrow \equiv Si\text{–}O\text{–}Si\equiv\ HX$$

These polyfunctional, silicone-containing, curing agents can be based on alkoxy, amino, and ketoxino groups.

2. Addition Cure

This type of reaction takes place without the formation of any volatile or requirement of moisture. The curing system involves the metal ion-catalysed addition of a polyfunctional, silicone hydride, cross-linking agent to a dimethyl-vinyl siloxy terminated silane polymer.

$$\equiv Si{-}CH{=}CH_2 + H{-}S\equiv \longrightarrow \equiv Si{-}CH_2CH_2{-}Si\equiv$$

In general they are two part systems but some use has been made of a one component system using an initiator.

PROPERTIES

Certain properties are common to all silicones, of which the most important are their exceptional stability to heat, cold and oxidation.

1. Fluids

The influence of temperature on the viscocity of methyl silicone fluids is relatively small. They also exhibit unusually high resistance to mechanical shearing, particularly in hydraulic systems. They are also highly water repellent and water condenses as discrete droplets on surfaces previously treated by the fluids.

Dimethyl silicone fluids are colorless, odorless, nontoxic and physiologically inert. They are resistant to oxidation, have excellent resistance to a wide variety of chemicals, and are available in a wide range of viscosities. Some physical properties are given in Table 7.1.

The typical properties of the silicone polycarbinols are given in Table 7.2 but as such it is probably more useful to examine the properties obtained when reacting these materials with other more conventional polymers. The following are the properties which can be improved for these organic polymers by the reaction with the silicone types; release, abrasion resistance, water repellancy, water vapor transmission, low and high temperature flexibility and electrical insulative properties. Specially, in such applications as textile treatment with resins, as described in Chapter 4, the reaction with silicone polycarbinols and methylol derivatives leads to enhanced properties such as softer hand and water repellancy.

2. Resins

The physical properties of silicone resins are dependent to a large extent on the Me. Si ratio, and it has been found that a ratio between 1 : 3 and 1 : 5 gives a most useful products. Resins prepared with such ratios exhibit excellent stability at high temperature and are also resistant to moisture. The excellent thermal and electrical resistance exhibited by silicone resins has made possible the upgrading of the suitability of certain electrical equipment that has been impregnated with these resins. These resins

Table 7.1

PHYSICAL PROPERTIES OF SOME SILICONE FLUIDS

Fluid	*Viscocity at 25°C cS*	*Permittivity at 25°C (100 c/s)*	*Freezing point (°C)*		*Boiling point (°C)*	*Flash point min. (°F)*	*Thermal conductivity cal. cm. sec. cm²°C at 50°C*	*Specific gravity at 25°C/25°C*	*Refractive index at 25°C*
MS 200/3	3	2.52	—65		70-100	215	0.00027	0.90	0.39
			Pour point						
MS 200/10	10	2.65	–65		>200	325	0.00032	0.94	1.40
MS 200/20	20	2.68	–60		>200	520	0.00034	0.96	1.40
				°C	Volatility after 48 h at per cent				
MS 200/500	500	2.75	—50	200	<2	600	0.00038	0.97	1.403
MS 200/12,500	12,500	2.82	Solidification temp. –46	200	<2	600	0.00038	0.97	1.403
			Freezing point						
MS 510/50	50	2.7	-70	250	10	525	—	0.99	1.42
MS 510/550	550	2.8	-70	250	6	525	—	0.99	1.43
MS 550	100-150	2.9	-50	250	15	575	0.00035	1.06-1.08	1.49-1.50

Table 7.2

TYPICAL PROPERTIES OF SILICONE POLYCARBINOLS

	Dow Corning brand fluids			
	1248	Q4-3667	Q2-8026	Q4-3557
Structure	Graft	ABA	Graft	Graft
Alcohol functionality	Secondary	Primary	Primary	Secondary
Weight per cent OH	0.9-1.1	1.4-1.6	2.0	4.5
Average no. OH groups per molecule	3	2	3	3
Viscocity	160 cs.	320 cs.	465 cs.	40 cs.
Flash	250°F	285°F	400°F	>200°F
Refractive index	1.4110	1.44	1.45	1.43
Pour point	–130°F	65°F	60°F	–80°F
Color	Clear	Clear straw	Clear straw	Clear straw
Average hydroxyl eq. wt.	2000	1200	800	400

possess good chemical resistance especially to dilute mineral acids and alkalis. Their resistance to many organic solvents such as toluene and xylene is not good. The properties of some silicone resins are given in Table 7.3.

3. Elastomers

Silicone elastomers may now be produced with tensile strengths in the region of 1500 lb/in^2. They remain serviceable and stable over a wide temperature range from as low as –70°C to as high as 250°C. They also possess excellent electrical resistance and insulating properties. Typical properties of silicone elastomers are listed in Table 7.4.

Silicone elastomers are generally resistant to a wide variety of chemicals and, in general, will resist the attack of oxidising agents, weak acids, weak

Table 7.3

TYPICAL PROPERTIES OF SOME SILICONE RESINS

	Coating resins		*Impregnating varnish*		*Bonding resins*	
Properties of cured resin	*MS 935*	*MS 994*	*MS 997*	*MS 1360*	*MS 840*	*MS 2103*
Electric strength, film thickness 10 mil (V/mil)	>1000	>1500	>1000	>1500	>1000	>1000
Power factor at 10^2 c/s	0.003	0.001	0.006	0.005	0.003	0.002
Power factor at 10^6 c/s	0.004	0.001	0.007	0.013	—	0.002
Permittivity at 10^2 c/s	2.9	2.8	3.1	3.6	2.9	2.9
Permittivity at 10^6 c/s	2.7	2.8	3.0	3.5	—	2.8
Craze life (min, h at 250°C)	800	3000	1000	—	—	—
Flex life (min, h at 250°C)	100	1000	250	—	—	—
Property of resin solution						
Solid content (per cent)	50	50	50	50	80	60
Solvent	Xylene	Xylene	Xylene	Cresylic acid	Acetone	Toluene
Viscocity at 25°Ccs	80-150	80-125	100-200	4300-8600	350-1750	60-125
Processing	Require curing at 200-250°C			Cures at 50°C above vinyl formal wire enamels	Will rapidly air dry tack-free to form a soft film. Require curing at 250°C to form hard nonthermoplastic bond.	

Table 7.4

TYPICAL PROPERTIES OF SILICONE RUBBER

Temperature stability (°C)	–100 to + 250
Specific gravity at 25°C	1.0-2.0
Hardness (B.S. deg.)	40-85
Tensile strength (lb/in^2)	700-1500
Ultimate elongation (%)	100-400
Compression set (% at 150°C)	10-70
Brittle point (°C)	-110 to -60
Tear strength (lb)	4-5
Electric strength (V/mil)	250-600
Permittivity at Mc/s	3.0-4.0
Power factor (1 Mc/s)	0.001-0.007
Coefficient of cubic expansion/ °C	≈ 0.0007
Thermal conductivity (cal cm/cm s)	≈ 5 X 10^{-4}
Specific heat (cal/°C/g)	0.275 to 0.325

bases, salts and vegetable oils. They swell in the presence of strong acids and bases, chlorinated solvents, and reducing agent but they are not attacked chemically and normally return to the original shape on removal from the source of the chemical. Silicone elastomers are also unaffected by u/v light, ozone and many oxidising agents. These elastomers do not harden up and become brittle over a wide range of temperature as do the conventional

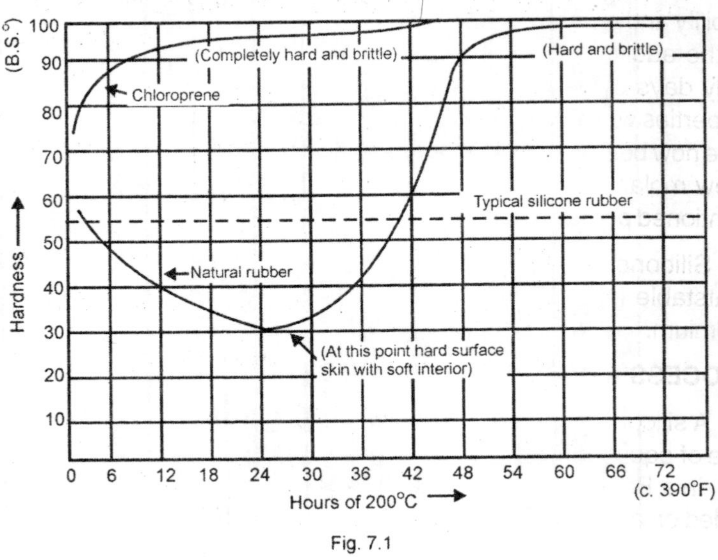

Fig. 7.1

natural and synthetic organic elastomers. This can be seen in Fig. 7.1. where the temperature aging of silicone rubber is compared with chloroprene and natural rubber.

COMPOUNDING

(a) *Fluids*, Silicone fluids are normally used without fillers or additives; therefore, very little compounding is necessary. However, in fluids for the production of greases, inert fillers such as silica and carbon black as well as metallic soaps, e.g., lithium octoate, are added.

(b) *Resins*. Relatively little compounding is required with silicone resin and they are generally supplied either solventless or in solutions of xylene and toluene. The resins may be used in conjunction with glass fibers and the processing details vary little from those described for polyesters in Chapter 5.

(c) *Elastomers*. Unfilled silicone gums have negligible mechanical strength and must therefore be reinforced by the addition of a filler. The fillers are classified as reinforcing or semireinforcing and nonreinforcing. The reinforcing fillers commonly used as precipitated and fume silicas. There are numerous semireinforcing fillers of which the following are frequently used and include diatomaceous earth, quartz, calcium, carbonate, and precipitated calcium silicate.

Special additives are frequently used in conjunction with silicone elastomers to provide certain enhanced properties including improved heat stability and reduction in compression set. Heat stability is normally improved by the addition of ferric oxide, ferric octoate, or barium zirconate. In the early days of the development of these elastomers the compression set properties were improved by adding various quinones, but these chemicals have now been generally rendered obsolete. The new technique is to introduce a few molar per cent of vinyl groups and thus tailor the polymer chain as mentioned previously.

Silicone elastomers may be readily pigmented by the addition of heatstable inorganic oxides such as iron, nickel, chromium, titanium, or cadmium.

PROCESSING TECHNIQUES FOR SILICONE ELASTOMERS

A silicone elastomer stock is compounded and processed on the same type of equipment as used for organic rubbers. It can be mixed on a two roll mill, in a Banbury or in a dough mixer. The curing agent should always be added on a mill to avoid premature setup. Unvulcanised silicone elastomers is softer and weaker than organic rubber, and a scraper blace attachment on the mill is recommended for removing the silicone compound. After compounding, the next step is to cure the rubber. The first stage of curing is carried out in a press, hot air chamber or steam vulcaniser, the process being referred to as set-cure. The second stage is carried out in an air-circulated oven and is especially necessary in order to develop the optimum physical properties required for many applications and for maximum resistance to compression set.

Fully compounded silicone stocks may be molded, extruded, laminated calendered, or applied from solvent dispersion. Conventional rubber processing machinery is used and should include a two-roll mill equipped with scraper blades, a steam or electrically heated molding press operating at temperatures between 100-150°C with provision for water cooling. A steam vulcaniser capable of operating at pressures up to 100 lb/in^2. should also be available. In addition, a forced air-draught circulating oven is essential to obtain an adequate final cure for optimum physical properties.

APPLICATIONS

1. Fluids

Because silicone fluids have small viscocity change with temperature and nonsticking properties, they are now being used where such properties are of prime importance. The silicone fluids have certain advantages over hydrocarbon oils and are therefore being used more and more in aircraft hydraulic systems. Antisticking characteristics have led to at least two large uses, namely in polishes and as mold release agent in plastics and rubber molding.

Silicone oils may be used in the form of an aqueous emulsion or solvent solution for mold release application. They offer a unique combination of properties, viz. inertness, heat resistance, low surface tension combined with good lubricating power. These materials have now replaced many of the more conventional mold release materials such as soap and talc. A typical formulation for the preparation of a mold release agent would be as follows :

Dimethyl silicone fluid - - -	35 parts
Emulsifier - - -	2 parts
Water - - -	63 parts

The above ingredients are mixed together and then diluted to a concentration of around 1 per cent.

The use of silicone fluids in car and furniture polishes has grown in popularity over the past few years. Normally about 2-4 per cent is added to either wax or waxless formulation and in the case of the wax polish the silicone fluid serves to lubricate the microcrystalline wax. The following are suitable formulations for a wax and a waxless polish.

		Waxless (%)	Wax (%)
A	MS200*	4	3
	White spirit	19	94
	Wax	-	3
	Kerosene	2	
	Oleic acid	2.5	
	Morpholine	0.75	
	28% NH_4OH	15.75	
	Water	14	
B	Silica	40	'B' is stirred
	Water	Suspension	Into 'A'

*Registered trademark of Midland Silicones Limited.

Silicone fluids are now widely used in the paint industry as antiflotation and antisilking agents. The addition of a small amount of a low viscocity dimethyl silicone fluid (1-50,000 ppm) assists in the grinding and dispersion of the pigment as well as inhibiting flotation and flow lines. It has also been established that a small addition of a silicone fluid proves effective in reducing 'foaming' in certain materials susceptible to this phenomena. They are also used in the production of polyurethane foams to control certain characteristics such as cell size. Silicone antifoams are now widely used in food manufacture and sewage disposal.

One of the earliest uses of silicone fluids was as a water-repellent treatment for a wide variety of surfaces. They are now being used extensively for treating textiles, paper, and leather. In the textile treatment the silicones not only confer excellent resistance to water but also to staining.

As stated previously, the silicone polycarbinols are also being used for treating textiles but in conjunction with other resins such as hexamethylol melamine. The demand for improving the basic performance characteristics of urethanes is increasing as the market acceptance of the urethane family grows. The suppliers of the silicone polycarbinols (Dow Corning) recommend that these polymers afford a simple unique method for upgraded the physical properties of urethanes to meet the ever increasing new demands. Benefits claimed are improved scuff resistance, wear, water repellancy, stain resistance, weatherability, low temperature flex, hydrolytic stability, and rate of water vapor transmission. Other claims are that the blocking and rustle of fabric catings are reduced.

2. Resins

The film-forming properties of silicone resins are not a good as those of the more conventional organic polymers, but they do possess greater heat stability. Paints based on silicone resins and aluminium pigments can effectively withstand direct heating to around 700°C. Their overall cost may be reduced by blending them with organic coating materials such as glyptals, urea, and phenol-formaldehyde as well as the epoxy resins. The aluminium-based silicone paints are used for coating certain parts of jet engines which are subjected to high temperatures.

The silicone resins have found extensive use in high temperature insulation for electrical equipment. Silicones are classified according to Class H insulation which has a top working temperature of 180°C. They are therefore used for high temperature resistant coatings for electrical equipment. The main advantages of Class H insulation is to permit an increased output per unit volume of meter. Such a property is very important where space and weight saving are required in traction motors, aircraft and submarines.

Other interesting applications for silicone resins include the waterproofing of masonry and utilisation as a release agent. Silicone resins containing solvent may be sprayed on brickwork, and on the subsequent evaporation of the solvent the bricks are left with a coating of silicone resin and are thus water repellent. As a mold release agent they offer an advantage over the fluids in that their effect is semipermanent. The baking industry has used silicone resins for coating bread tins and they have found that they are able to obtain many hundreds of satisfactory releases before the treatment wears off.

Silicone resins have also been used in preparing molding powders suitable for the compression and transfer molding techniques. These resins are expensive, and although the overall price may be reduced by addition of fillers such as asbestos powder or chopped glass wool, their use is still somewhat limited.

Another use for these resins is in the preparation of laminates with glass fiber, asbestos, and mica as the reinforcing material. Such laminates may be manufactured by press molding at both high and low pressures, by vaccum bag molding, or by filament winding. The resin is normally applied from a solvent solution (usually of the high-boiling aromatic type such as xylene or toluene) and is procured on the reinforcing material, although solventless silicone laminating resins are also available. The main field of application is in the aircraft industry, where heat resistance is required, or in the electrical industry where the insulating properties are of prime importance. The fact that the laminates have relatively poor strength characteristics has been overcome by the copolymerisation with epoxy resins, etc. as mentioned earlier, and this has opened a wider field of applications.

3. Elastomers

Undoubtedly the growth and popularity of the use of silicone elastomers can to a large extent be attributed to the requirements of the aircraft and electrical industries. It is often the unique combination of properties of silicone elastomers that influence branches of certain industries to utilise these high-price elastomers in preference to the conventional organic types.

The main uses of silicone elastomers in the aircraft industry are for door seals, hot air ducts, flexible sleeving, gaskets, and vibration dampers. The fluorinated silicone elastomers are now widely used for such applications where their outstanding resistance to chemicals and fuels may be used effectively.

A relatively big market for these elastomers is for the insulation sleeving used on power and control cables in ships. There are many adavantages in using silicone rubber as an insulator, namely resistance or oxidation, ozone and a variety of chemicals. One particular advantage that is gained for use with cables in ships is that in the advent of a fire on board, the silicone would burn, leaving a silica ash which would have sufficient insulating value, possible, to allow the ship to return to base.

The comparatively high price of silicone elastomers has somewhat restricted their use in domestic and industrial appliances. However, incertain instances where specialised properties are required these rubber have been used. Typical appliances include use as oven-door seals, cable insulation, belting, gaskets and caulking pastes for sealing joints (e.g., joints to be found in a domestic steam iron).

More and more uses are being found for silicone elastomers in the medical field and here the physiological inertness of silicones has been fully exploited. Applications already include tubing, vial stoppers, gaskets, teats, and heart valves. An important use is for tubing on blood transfusion

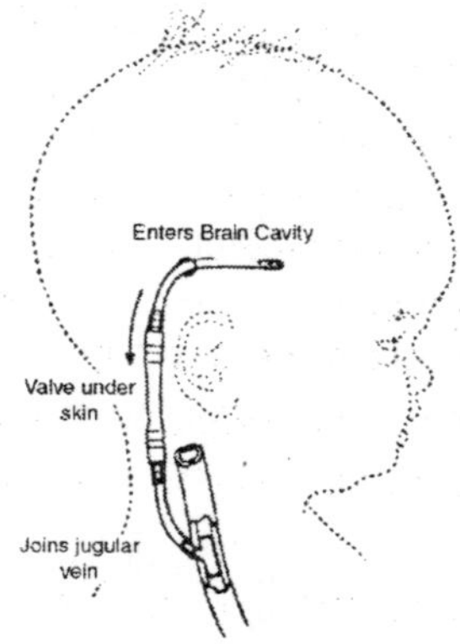

Fig. 7.2

equipment and it has been found in service that such tubing is unaffected by 30 heat sterilisations involving exposure to steam at 20 lb/in^2. pressure for thirty minutes each times. Natural rubber tubing is rendered unserviceable by comparatively few sterilisations. Other advantages for using silicone elastomers in such applications include the fact that this matetial has no effect on the quality of the blood and possesses a surface to which the blood does not adhere as readily as it does to natural rubber.

An interesting advance has occurred in the medical field, made possible only by the availability of silicone elastomers. This can be seen in Fig. 7.2, which is a diagram of a baby's head with an implanted silicone automatic brain valve, the most promising cure yet developed for hydrocephalus (water on the brain). The silicone elastomer valves have certain advantages over the conventional plastic brain valve. They can be sterilised, and their complex mechanism does not go out of adjustment. They consist of two-side slit directional nipoles accurate to 0.0003 in., inside stainless-steel cases instead of steel springs or sapphire ball-checks in an acrylic housing. Connected with a silicone rubber housing, the nipples open at the slightest input pressure, but provide a double seal against fatal backflow of blood. Thus, the system can drain into the jugular vein instead of the stomach, greatly easing installation. The double valve gives the assembly a pump action which can be checked by hand for accuracy and functioning.

A property of equal significance is that of the imcompatibility of silicone elastomers to organic bodies over a wide range of temperatures. This property has been utilised in the fabrication of silicone rubber-covered rollers for use by the plastics industry as guide and pressure rollers during the calendering and embossing of plastic films and coated fabrics.

The cold-curing silicone elastomers are also being used extensively in a variety of applications including sealing, caulking, potting, encapsulating, and impregnating. They are excellent materials for encapsulating delicate and electronic components especially where severe humidity conditions have to be met. Because they do not require a heat cure they are used for encapsulating heat-sensitive components or where temperature precludes high temperature curing. Electrical equipment such as resistors, capacitors, and transformers may also be encapsulated quite easily.

A relatively new material has been introduced to the electronic potting and encapsulating field, called silicone dielectric gel. This material is supplied as a two-component system, containing no filler, being a water-white viscous liquid. It exhibits unusual properties in that it does not exhibit cold-flow, is self-sealing and remains in place even after curing, although it still remains soft and flexible. This has the advantage that in the event of an electrical breakdown occurring with the potted component it is possible to explore into the potting medium and thereby locate the point of weakness. This material is also an excellent damping medium and has found application in dash-pots.

8

Polyurethanes

The term 'polyurethane' refers to a group of polymers which have found widespread application over the past quarter of a century. In general, they are produced as a result of the reaction between an aromatic di-socyanate and a compound rich in hydroxyl groups. The initial development work as carried out on polyurethane produced from hydroxyl enriched polyesters but over the past few years considerable interest has been given to the use of polyoxyalkylene glycols. These latter materials are commonly referred to as polyester polyols.

The foundation for the new well-known polyurethane field was the original isocyanate synthesis carried out by Wurtz in 1849

$$R_2SO_4 + 2KNCO \rightarrow 2RNCO + K_2SO_4$$

The preparation and chemical reaction of isocyanates have therefore been known for over a hundred years but it was not until the middle 1930's that interest in their industrial importance grew to any proportion. Much of the original development work was carried out in Germany in an attempt to produce polymers competitive with those being produced by Du Pont at that time, viz. polyamides. In 1937, Dr. Otto Bayer experimented with the addition products of di-socyanates. The object of this work was to produce synthetic fibers not covered by the Du Pont patents. His work quickly bore fruit when it was shortly announced that he had discovered the di-socyanate poly addition process. A German patent No. 728 981 covering all aspects of this work was obtained and today the number of patents on these polymers runs into many hundreds. Thus it is to Bayer and his coworkers that most credit must go for the development of these interesting materials.

Polyurethanes exist in various polymeric forms, of which the most important are the foams, elastomers, and coatings. They are also used as adhesives, molding compounds and fibers, although such applications are discussed in less details in this chapter.

A relatively new class of urethane polymers are those which are designated as ionomers. They are block polymers which are linear, containing ionic centers at wide intervals and may be regarded as hereto polymers having a pronounced segment structure. The main field of application for this group of products appears to be a aqueous dispersions for coating of textiles, paper, and plastic film.

RAW MATERIALS

The production of polyester resins has been described in Chapter 5, the type in general use for the production of polyurethane being the adipic acid and ethylene or propylene glycol. For polyether polyurethanes used in the manufacture of flexible foam the polyether is normally obtained by the alkali catalysed polymerisation of propylene oxide, ethylene, oxide, or tetrahydrofuran.

These reaction can be initiated by the addition of small amounts of hydroxy bearing materials, e.g.,

$$HOCH_2CHOH + n\underbrace{CH_2{-}CH_2}_{O} \rightarrow HO[(CH_2)_2O]_nCH_2CH_2OH$$

Preparation of Di-socyanates

The di-socyanates used in the production of polyurethanes are normally aromatic materials, the most common being tolylene di-socyanate, a mixture of 2 : 4 and 2 : 6 isomers (often referred to as TDI). There are many ways of making isocyanates but the following has found most commerical use and consists essentially of reacting an amine or amine salt wit phosgene in an inert medium such as *o*-dichloro benezene.

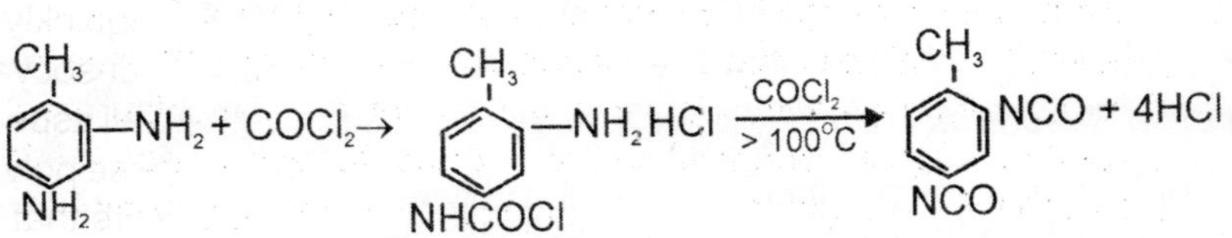

1-Tolylene diamine — Phosgene carbamyl chloride — Tolylene 2,4 di-socyanate

This di-socyanate is generally preferred although others such as diphenyl methane —4,4, di-socyanate, (MDI), *m*-phenylene di-socyanate, 1,6-hexamethylene di-socyanate are used as well as many others.

The MDI is made by the condensation of aniline with formaldehyde in the presence of hydrochloric acid followed by phosgenation.

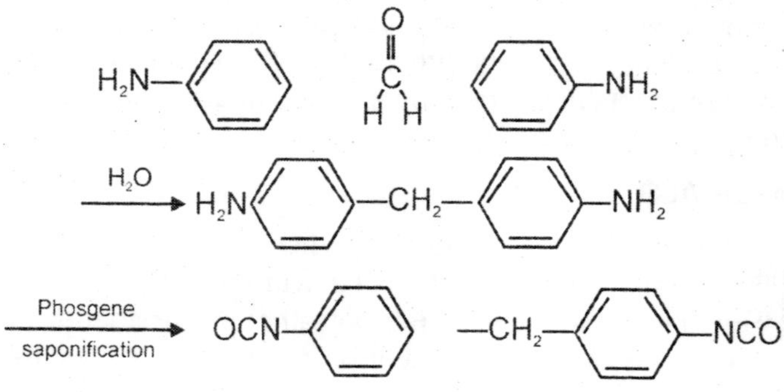

MDI

General Reaction of Isocyanates

Isocyanates can react with all compounds containing reactive hydrogen atoms, and the basic reaction may be represented as

$$\text{—N=C=O} + \underset{\text{Active hydrogen}}{\text{H}} \rightarrow \text{—NHCO—}$$

In such reaction the hydrogen normally becomes attached to the nitrogen atom and the remainder of the compound links to the carbon atom of the isocyanate group thus

$$\text{R—N=C+O} + \text{H—R} \rightarrow \text{RNHCOR}$$

The reaction products formed in this way all contain active hydrogen atoms which enable further reactions to make place. The reactivity of the urethane hydrogen is comparatively low, and this has certain advantages as will be seen later in the preparation of prepolymers.

Typical Reactions

(i) *Isocyanate and Water.* The reaction between in isocyanate and water leads to the formation of an unstable substituted carbamic acid which breaks down very quickly to give an amine and carbon dioxide.

$$\underset{\text{Isocynate}}{\text{R—N=C=O}} + \underset{\text{Water}}{H_2O} \rightarrow \underset{\text{Substituted carbamic acid}}{\text{RNHCOOH}} \rightarrow \underset{\text{Amine}}{\text{RNH}_2} + \underset{\text{Carbon}}{\text{CO2}}$$

(ii) *Isocyanate +Hydroxy compound.* This reaction leads to the formation of a urethane.

$$\underset{\text{Isocyanate}}{R\text{—}N{=}C{=}O}+\underset{\text{Hydroxy compound}}{R'OH}\rightarrow\underset{\text{Urethane (Carbamic acid ester)}}{RNHCOOR'}$$

(iii) *Isocyanate + Amine.* This reaction which would, of course, follow on from the reaction with water leads to the formation of a substituted urea.

$$\underset{\text{Isocyanate}}{R\text{—}N{=}C{=}O} + \underset{\text{Amine}}{R'NH_2} \rightarrow \underset{\text{Diisocyanate urea}}{RNHCONHR'}$$

(iv) This could be an extension of the reaction with a hydroxy compound and leads to the formation of an allophanate.

$$R\text{—}N{=}C{=}O + R'NCOOR'' \rightarrow RNHCONR'COOR''$$

(v) *Isocyanate + Di-substituted Urea.* This reaction could possibly follow from the reaction with an amine to form a substituted biuret.

$$\underset{\text{Isocyanate}}{R\text{—}N{=}C{=}O} + \underset{\text{Disubstituted urea}}{R'NHCONHR''} \rightarrow \underset{\text{Substituted biuret}}{RNHCONR'CONHR'}$$

(iv) *Isocyanate+Acid.* This reaction could lead to the formation to an amide, as follows :

$$R\text{—}N{=}C{=}O + RCOOH \rightarrow \underset{\text{Amide}}{\text{—}NHCO\text{—}}$$

It is interesting to note that reactions (i), (iii), (iv) and (v) all take place during the production of a polyurethane foam, and the production of the allphanate can be prevented by strict control of pH. Reaction (vi) is indicative of what can take place should acid impurities the present.

(vii) *Isocyanate + Oxazolidine.* The reaction takes place by the oxazolidine ring opening thereby providing active hydrogen sites to react with the isocyanate to yield urethanes. The chemistry is more fully described under section 5 on Surface Coatings.

POLYMERISATION AND STRUCTURE

We have seen in Chapter 1 that if one of the reactants taking parts in a polymerisation mechanism has a functionality greater than two ($f = 2$) and the other reactant has a functionality of two ($f = 2$) then the cross linking occurs. This assumes that one of these coreactants is not present in large excess. Polymers can therefore form from a 2, 3 system which are thermoset, infusible and highly insoluble materials and by continuing the interaction a highly cross-linked structure results. This forms a basis for preparing many of the polyurethane coatings which can be cross-linked by tri-or polyfunctional coreactants.

In the general reactions of isocyanates described earlier only monomeric materials have been represented, but it follows that plurality of reactive centers can lead to polymerisation; therefore, if several mols of a polymeric hydroxy compound and a diisocyanate are used the resultant product is not a urethane but a polyurethane. This is represented as follows by showing only functional groups.

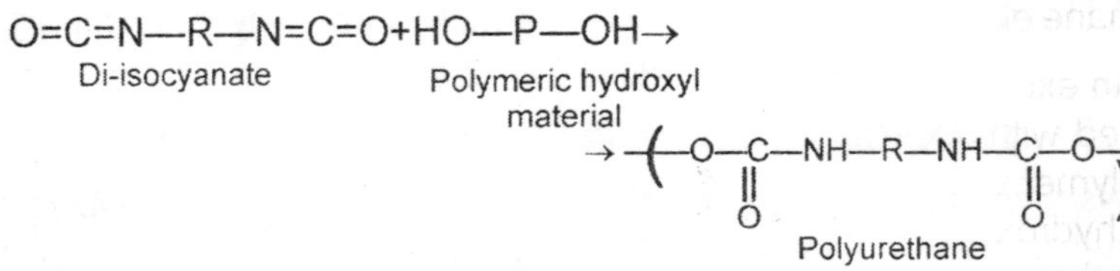

The ionomers are produced by reacting diisocyanates with ionisable nitrogen compounds. The reaction with mono-or bifunctional quatemary agents yield linear or cross linked elastomers.

MANUFACTURE

Foams

There are two main types of polyurethane foam, viz, the rigid and the flexible. At present there are two techniques used to produce foamed polyurethanes. One method consist of forming a prepolymer (mixing a polyhydroxylic compound with a polyisocyanate) and then reacting it at a later stage with water, catalyst is normally a tertiary amine and, in addition, an emulsifying agent (e.g., octyl-phenol/ethylene oxide condensate) as well as a structure regulator (e.g., silicone oil) are added. This process is sometimes referred to as the two stage process. This is in contrast to the other shot technique.' Essentially this latter process consists of mixing together a polyhydroxylic compound, a diisocyanate and an aqueous activator mixture. Water is generally necessary to produce the foaming which is effected by the liberation of carbon dioxide although foaming can also be produced by the addition of certain fluorocarbons. The water is mixed with the activator system which, in addition to the catalyst, contains small quantities of a silicone oil (stabiliser/structure regulator) and organometallic compounds to give quick gel strength. The resultant mixture may then be discharged in the liquid state into the mold, where the foaming takes place. It must be pointed out that the density of the foam is controlled largely by the ratio of the diisocyanate and water.

Rubbers

Much of the initial development work was carried out on reacting polyester containing trifunctional alcohol groups with isocyantes. Unfortunately, elastomers with poor tear resistance were obtained. Similar results were also achieved from reacting triisocyantes with linear polyesters. Further work was subsequently carried out using a short-chain polyester with terminal hydroxyl groups and a bulky diisocyanates, the resultant product being a high enough mechanical strength to warrant commercial interest.

It is interesting to look at the steps involved in the building up of a polyurethane elastomers.

(a) An excess of a polyhydroxy alcohol (e.g., glycols, glycerol, etc.) is condensed with a dibasic acid (e.g., adipic acid) to obtain a short-chain linear polymer with a degree of polymerisation around eight to ten, having terminal hydroxyl groups. If we let 'P' represent the bulk of the polyester molecule then we have :

$$\underset{\text{Ethylene glycol}}{HO{-}(CH_2)_2{-}OH} + \underset{\text{Adipic Acid}}{HOOC(CH_2)_4COOH} \rightarrow \underset{\text{Polyester}}{HO{-}P{-}OH}$$

(b) An excess of a suitable bulky diisocyanate when added to this polyester results in chain-lengthening, through the urethane linkages so formed, giving long complex chain having terminal isocyanate groups.

(c) The terminal isocyanate groups so formed are reacted with a polyhydroxy alcohol (glycol) and this result in further chain-lengthening, and active hydrogen atoms are formed which are capable of being cross lined.

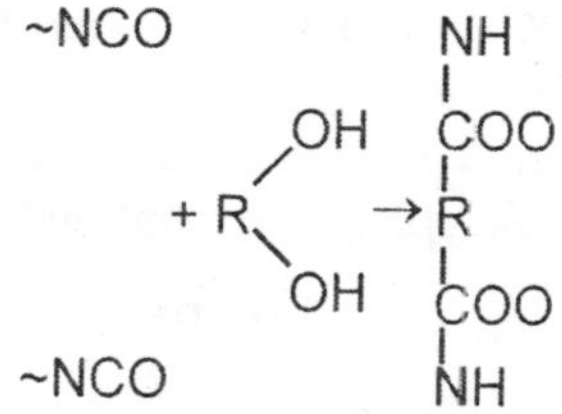

Urethane link

If water is used instead of the alcohol, carbon dioxide is formed, as we have previously from the foamed products, and it is therefore essential to remove all traces of water in the preparation of polyurethane elastomers.

In the early 1960's the textile coating industry used on component urethanes. Technically these can be considered copolymers in which every molecule oflong soft segments (polyester, polyether) is combined with short hard segments (urethane and urea groups). The hard segments from bridges between the molecular chains, resulting in an elastomers structure like vulcanised rubber. The reaction product of hexamethylene diisocyanate and 1, 4 butane diol shows strong intermolecular bonds similar to the superpolyamides described in Chapter 12. Even through they are still relatively low in molecular weight, they have great difficulty in being converted to solutions and are only soluble in such solvents as cresol and formic acid.

(d) The cross-linking mechanism which takes place takes one of the two forms; it can either be at the urethane or at the urea bridges which are formed. This latter method is effected by the addition of surplus diisocyanate. In actual practice it is usual to modify and catalyse the reaction by the addition of diamines or amino alcohols such as ethanolamine.

There are two different methods used for preparing polyurethane elastomers. One method consist of producing a prepolymer containing sufficient isocyanate to effect complete cure. These are termed cast rubbers. They have limited self-life, a defect which has been overcome in the second method by carrying out chain extension of the polyester or polyether with a diisocyanate. The proportions are calculated to give no free isocyanate end-groups and the final curing is effected by the addition of more isocyanate or by the conventional rubber-curing agents such as sulfur or certain organic peroxides.

Molding Compounds

Polyurethane molding compounds have certain elastomeric properties have could possibly have been included in the last section. They were originally based on the reaction between castor oil and a diisocyanate, used either in a one-shot or prepolymer technique. It is now obvious that in the first method on the complete reaction between the diisocyanate and the other reactants are carried out by the end-user, whereas with the prepolymer system the diisocyanate and castor oil are partly reacted before being delivered to the customer. A typical formulation found suitable is :

Anhydrous castor oil	1.66 parts
Tolylene diisocyanate	3.5–4.0 parts
2-Ethyl hexane diol	1 part
Ethyl diethanolamine	0.2 part

The anhydrous castor oil and isocyanate are simply mixed together and digassed in vacuo, the resultant mixture is then poured into a female mold and then either allowed to cure by the action of a catalyst or by heating to somewhere is the region of 100°C.

These products based on castor oil have been replaced to a large extent by polymers obtained as the reaction product of tetramethylene glycol and hexamethylene diisocyanate. It has now become possible to injection mold and extrude these polymers with the resultant finished molding being harder than the castor oil types.

Sufrace Coatings

The production of surface coatings based on polyurethanes generally takes either of the following :

(i) *Urethane Oils.* This type of isocyanate coatings is one of the earliest reported uses of such materials in the surface-coating field. The diisocyanates combine with unsaturated drying oils and then dry in the same manner as conventional drying oils, that is by air oxidation. The oils are prepared by converting a conventional drying oil into a mixture of mono-and diglycerides and then reacting the free hydroxyl groups with a diisocyanate. If we take, for example, the conventional material linseed oil diglyceride which we can represent by 'L' then the reaction proceeds as follows :

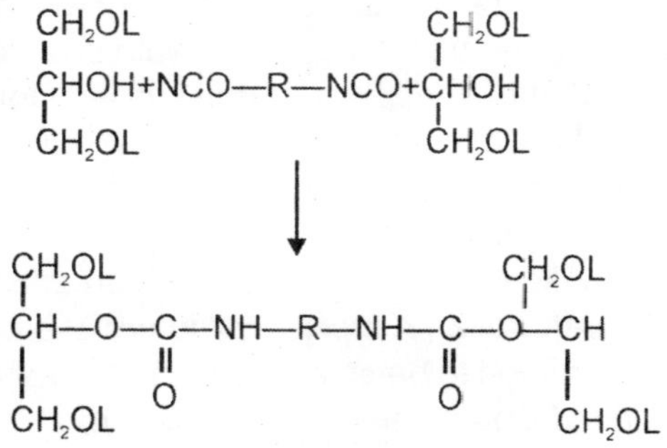

These oils so formed may be used as clear varnishes or pigmented and used as paints. As mentioned previously, the curing takes place by oxidation of the unsaturated centers in the drying oil residues, and autoxidation catalysts, usually cobalt salts (e.g., cobalt naphthenate) are used to promote oxidation and subsequently polymerisation.

(ii) *Moisture-cured Polyurethanes.* These consist of adducts of hydroxy containing resins with a large excess of polyisocyanate. They are prepared by refluxing a polyol with a polyisocyanate or, alternatively, the polyol and polyisocyanate may be simply mixed and allowed to react at room temperature over a period of days. The adduct so formed is then dissolved in water-free solvents to form a lacquer. (N.B. Water must be absent at this stage otherwise premature curing takes place.) On applying this lacqer to a surface the moisture present in the atmosphere reacts with the isocyanate groups present in the resin, and subsequent reactions lead to gelation and the formation of a cured paint film.

(iii) *Two-pot Systems.* These are systems in which the high molecular weight polyester polyether is reacted and cured with a polyisocyanate at room temperature. When the two components are mixed the subsequent coating will, of course, have a limited shelf-life. It is important to print out that at least a portion of the hydroxyl-containing material must contain three or more hydroxyl groups so that cross-linking results, as previously indicated. The degree of cross linking can therefore, of course, be controlled by the amount of trihydric materials present which, in turn, provides a means of 'tailoring' the final properties of the coating.

The chief characteristics of such coating systems are excellent gloss, hardness, good solvent and fuel resistance, and good chemical and water resistance. They may also be used in combination with two-pack epoxy primers and, as such, make ideal coatings for reinforced plastics.

A later development is the addition of a polyester with a molecular weight of 2000 to an adduct of three molecules of TDI with one mold of a trihydroxy compound. The resultant product is stable under storage and can be conveniently cross-linked for coatings as shown by a typical polyfunctional TDI based isocyanate. Other coatings for substrates such as textiles utilise amino-modified and TDI-preextended glycol adipates from solution of ethyl acetate or methyl ethyl ketone cross-linking with an addition of TDI-based NCO containing isocyanurates. A typical commercial product is desmodur TH (Bayer) which is claimed to be an adduct from 2,4 toluene diisocyanate (3.0 mols) and 3-methylol pentylene glycol -2,4 (1 mol).

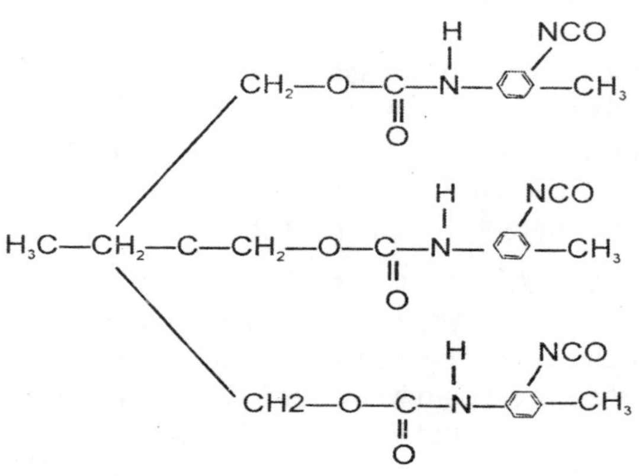

(iv) *Blocked Isocyanate Coatings.* We have seen previously that an isocyanate reacts with a monohydric alcohol or phenol to form a urethane which is not reactive with hydroxyl or other functional groups at room temperature. This is not so when heat is applied, when the urethane decomposes to make the isocyanate group available for reaction. A blocked isocyanate prepared from phenol when mixed with a polyester or polyol gives a medium which has unlimited shelf-life. On heating to around 150°C isocyanate groups are set free and films are formed which exhibit excellent hardness and chemical resistance. The cleaved blocking agent diffuses into the surrounding surface of the coating or volatilisers into the atmosphere.

The formation and thermal cleavage of blocked isocyanates is shown as follows :

$$\underset{\text{Isocyanate}}{R(NCO)n} + \underset{\text{Blocking agent}}{n\,XH} \underset{\substack{\text{Thermal}\\ \text{cleavage}\\ 100\text{-}200^\circ C}}{\overset{\text{Formation}}{\rightleftharpoons}} \underset{\text{Blocked isocyanate}}{R\,(\overset{H}{N}-\overset{O}{C}-X)n}$$

A few typical blocking agents are ethyl malonate, novolaks (PF resins), dimethyl amino methyl phenol, caprolactam, pyrocatechol, phenol and ketoximes.

Commercial materials include Hylene MP from Du Pont which is a phenol blocked MDI, Mondur S from Mobay, a phenol blocked TDI adduct, and Isonate 123P from Upjohn which is a caprolactum blocked PAPI. A relatively new groups of product are aminimides from Ashland Chemical Company and it does not have a hazardous phenol as a by product. Their chemistry is as follows :

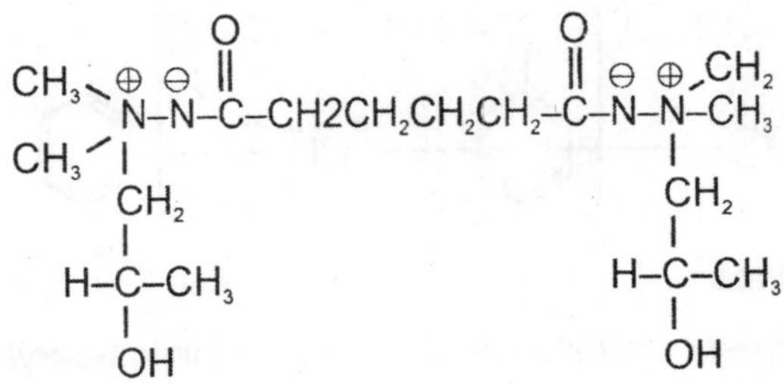

These materials are advantageous, apart from not having phenol as the by products, because they can be used in conjunction with aqueous dispersions. The above material is sold commercially under the number AL-X-300.

The following are the structures for two blocked isocyanates in common use.

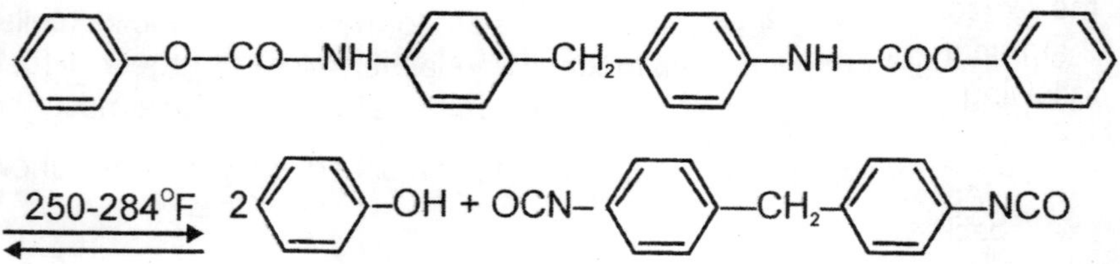

Phenol MDI

(ii) Isonate 123P (ε–caprolactam-blocked PAPI)

PAPI– polymethylene polyphenyl isocyanate

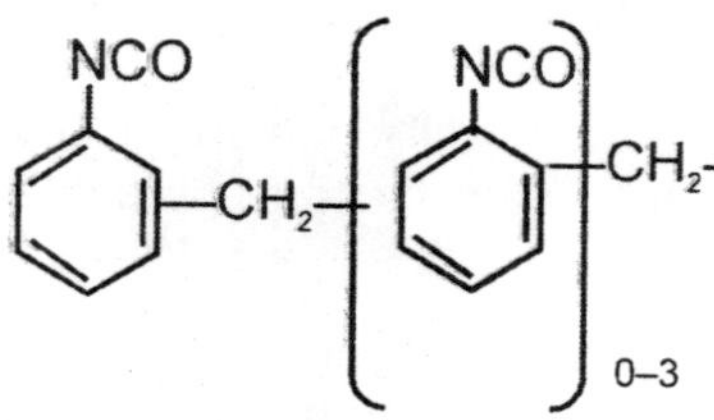

Structure of blocked PAPI

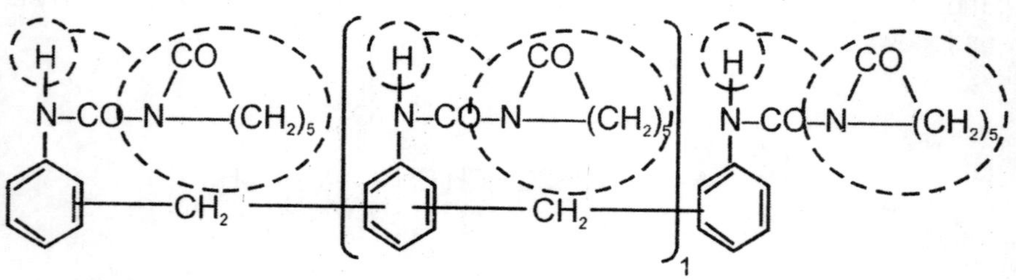

Acrylic Urethanes

These polymers may also be termed oxazolidine-acrylics.

Many polymers are now commercially available which reacts with isocyanates to form useful coatings. A new class of materials is claimed to have unique properties and offer fast cure without the addition of a catalyst. Such polymers possess a unique functionality as a site for cross-linking with isocyanate polymers. This is stated in a patent by W.D. Emmons, U.S. Patent 3,743, 626 (1973) assigned to Rohm and Hass Company.

This groupings is known as oxazolidine and reacts with isocyanates when activated by moisture. In the absence of moisture the equilibrium of the oxazolidine reaction is heavily in favour of the blocked reactive site so that minute amounts of moisture do not cause premature activation. The following reaction shows this equilibrium :

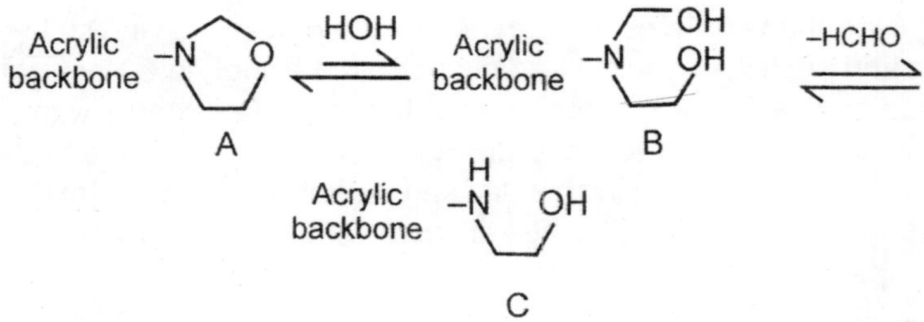

The ratio of components A, B and C is approximately 99:0.5:0.5 at equilibrium. When an isocyanate is added to the system, it has been found to react rapidly and preferentially with the amine active hydrogen, pulling the equilibrium to the right and activating more of the oxaxolidine functionality (A).

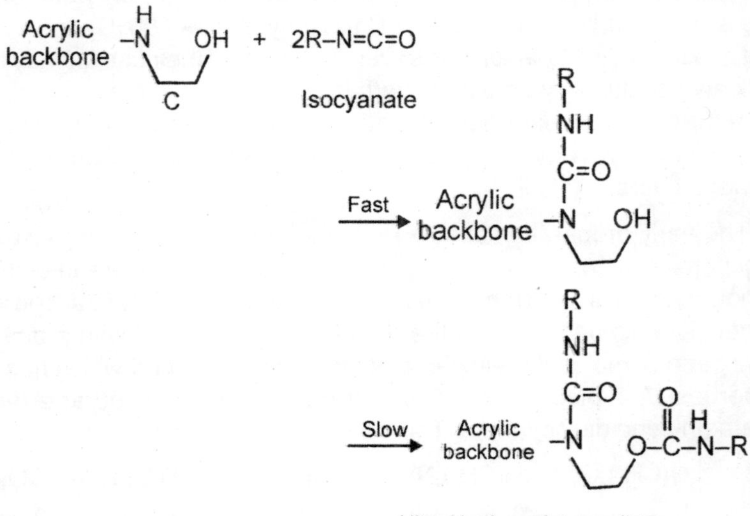

Ultra Urethane intermediate

D

This reaction has found to be much faster than a conventional bydroxyl-isocyanate reaction and proceeds without the need for a catalyst at a very fast rate. The reaction of intermediate D̄ with more intermediate C leads to cross-linking.

Water is a necessary component of the oxazolidine reaction with isocyanate. A sufficient amount for a room temperature cure is normally available in the atmosphere. With heat curing systems, it is advisable to inject steam into the oven, otherwise rapid cross-linking does not take place.

Adhesives

Polyurethane adhvesives can be prepared by dissolving by hydroxylic compound such as based on adipic acid and a triol, in 80 per cent ethyl acetage and then mixing three parts of the resultant product with one part of an isocyanate (e.g., tolylene diisocyanate). The adhesive is then first spread on the substrate being bonded and the solvent is allowed to evaporate. Final curing is carried out either at room temperature or accelerated by heat.

Fibers

It is probably true to say that polyurethane fibers have yet to reach any major degree of commercial importance. Some use has been found, however, as monofilaments which are obtained from the reaction of hexamethylene diisocyanate with tetra methylene glycol or butane diol. Polyurethane fibers have a softening point around 170°C (cf. polyamides 280°C) and a melting point as low as 183°C which has severely restricted their use for may textiles applications. But they do exhibit certain outstanding characteristics which are of interest, including good abration, oxidation and acid resistance as well as elasticity. They may be used either alone or in admixture with other synthetic fibers.

The early preparation of polyurethane fibers involved the reaction of a diisocyanate with a diamine to give a polyurea. They were infusible and strongly hydrophilic and therefore were of limited interest for fiber application. In later developments, when the diamine was replaced with a diol of the same general molecular weight, a polymer was obtained which has useful properties. A typical reaction would be between 1,4 butane diol and hexamethylene diisocyanate. This gave the following structure :

$$-[(CH_2)_4OOCNH(CH_2)_6NHCOO(CH_2)_4OOCNH(CH_2)_6NHCOO]-$$

PROCESSING

Foams

As stated earlier, rigid and flexible polyurethane foams can be prepared by acurately mixing an hydroxylic rich material with an isocyanate, catalyst, water and other additives and finally dispersing them into specific shaped areas. The actual mixing procedure can be carried out either by hand or with equipment which can be operated intermittently or continuously. A typical machine might feed the resin at the rate of 4 liters/minutes; the diisocyanate at 2 liters/minute at the rate of 9000 injections/minutes; and the activator solutions at 0.4 liters/minute at the rate of 3000 injections/minutes. The material is then thoroughly mixed in the machine and is then dispersed into the mold where it foams (see Plate 9). If the molds are for making slabs of material, which is often the case, they move past the mixing head continuously while the head transverses the width of the mold. After foaming is complete, the slabs may be allowed to either set and self-cure or they are placed in curing ovens. The slabs are then cut according to requirements. One great advantage of these materials is that they can be foamed *in situ* which enables them to be used to fill awkward voids and cavities.

Rubbers

The liquid-cast rubbers are formed in a two-stage process which does not permit the incorporation of fillers. Processing techniques are similar to those used in the casting of epoxy and polyester resins.

Certain polyurethane rubbers now available are suitable for processing on conventional rubber machinery using conventional techniques (see Chapter 19). They are cured by means of a high boiling point liquid isocyanate and they differ from the conventional natural and synthetic rubbers in that they do not require accelerators in processing. Unlike the cast rubbers, these materials may be compounded using fillers such as carbon black and silica.

Reaction Injection Molding (RIM)

This process has been developed in an attempt to combine the best features of conventional fast injection molding with the liquid casting techniques to produce large elastomeric polyurethane moldings. It has been discussed that a polyurethane is produced as a result of the reaction of a polyester or polyether (polyol) with a polyisocyanate. Cellular products are produced using a polyol of molecular weight in the region of 3000 and an isocyanate such as TDI or the more reactive MDI, with a catalyst and blowing agent. For the RIM process, precise amounts of these reactive homogenised and injected under relatively low pressure into a closed mold. Immediately the materials begin to react and foam slightly giving a micro cellular structure. Reaction times of two to three seconds are used and mold resistance times of one minute can also be achieved. As an example, a 10-pound component could be molded with a shot to shot cycle time of under two minutes.

This technique has high economic advantage in its ability to mold large parts of high surface quality at production rates competitive with injection molding, while offering lower tooling and equipment costs. Other advantages include the ability to mold-thin walled articles and the requirement for only a low energy consumption in molding.

There has been considerable work carried out in the developing new chemicals for this process and recently new materials have been introduced with a high flexural modulus of up to 300,000 psi. These materials have become contenders for sheet metal replacement, (fenders and body panels) on automobiles. The original RIM materials were only suitable for automotive facia panels and self skinning low density foams.

The ability of this new process to make large parts quickly, in high automotive production, suggests many other possible applications for production of both low and high modulus parts. It is claimed that the ultimate goal for production cycle time is two minutes but even at the four minutes which is achievable at present puts the cost about equal to injection molded parts. One big attraction of this technique is that it requires less expensive equipment than injection molding techiques, which require high torque extruders and very high tonnage clamps to process high viscocity melts and mold large parts. The molds can also be fabricated from less expensive materials such as aluminium-field epoxy toolings rather than steel.

PROPERTIES

Foams

Many of the foams produced today use polyethers for those of the flexible kind and polyester for the rigid ones. The following is a range of typical properties exhibit by polyurethane foams, although it must be emphasised that such properties have a bearing on their selection for particular end uses.

Foams can be produced with densities ranging from as low as 1.5 lb/ft^3 to as high as 40 lb/ft^3, depending on the choice of the base raw materials. For the cushioning field, however, flexible open-cell foams of density about

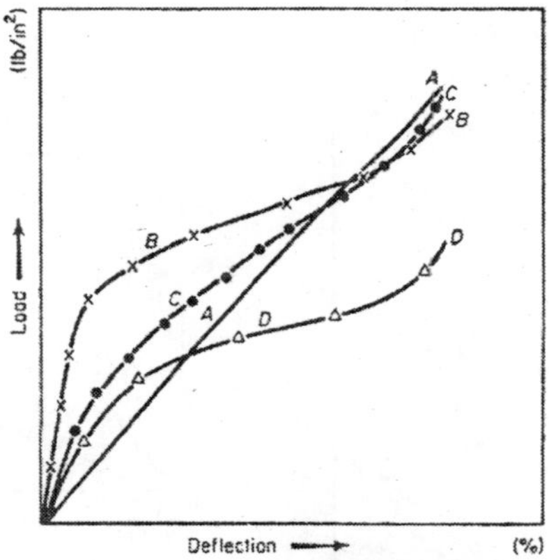

A. *Natural rubber latex foam density 5·6 lb/ft³*
B. *Polyester polyurethane foam density 2·2 lb/ft³*
C. *Polyether polyurethane foam density 2·1 lb/ft³*
D. *Vinyl foam density 6·0 lb/ft³*

Fig. 8.1 Comparison of compression/deflation curves for polyurethane foams, latex foams, and vinyl foam

2 lb/ft^3 are to be preferred. The load capacity of these foams is some four times as high as that of natural rubber latex foam of equivalent density (Fig. 8.1). Tensile strengths varying from 18 to greater than 300 lb/in^2. covering the range flexible to rigid, can be achieved. 25 lb/in^2. is a common figure for the flexible foams prepared from polyether polyols as against 18-20 lb/in^2. for polyester based foams. Foams with an elongation of 200 per cent are possible, and foams with an elongation as high as 300 per cent have been formulated for the cushioning field. Flexible polyurethane foams are claimed to have considerably higher tear strength than natural rubber foams. A property that is prime importance in the cushioning field is that of compression set. Figures as low as10 per cent are possible with polyurethanes (Fig. 8.2).

These foams have good resistance to rot, vermin, and many organic solvents. They burns only in the presence of a flame and can be made self extinguishing. The polyurethane foams have good thermal and acoustic insulating properties and also good radar, radio, and X-ray transmission properties.

Rubber

Polyurethane rubbers, if correctly compounded and cured, exhibit excellent physical characteristics, including high tensile and tear strengths. The resistance to mechanical abrasion is high and they also have excellent shock absorption properties. Their main disadvantages is the relatively poor

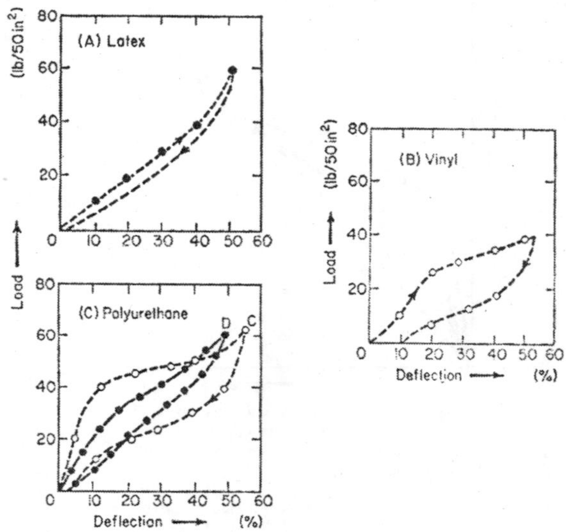

A. *Natural rubber latex foam density 6·9 lb/ft³*
B. *Vinyl foam density 6·0 lb/ft³*
C. *Polyester polyurethane foam density 2·7 lb/ft³*
D. *Polyether polyurethane foam density 2·7 lb/ft³*

Fig. 8.2 Comparison of hysteresis curves forpolyurethane foams, latex foams, and vinyl foams

resistance to hydrolytic agents (e.g., acids), steam and high temperatures. They do, however, exhibit excellent resistance to oxidation, uv light and they do not burn readily. These elastomers also have the outstanding characteristics to extreme resistance to aromatic hydrocarbons (oils, etc.). They are not, however, very resistance to chlorinated hydrocarbons such

Table 8.1

COMPARISON OF PHYSICAL PROPERTIES OF POLYURETHANE AND NATURAL RUBBER

Test	*Polyurethane rubber*	*Natural rubber*
Tensile strength (lb/in^2)	5000	2500
Elongation at break (%)	650	700
Shore hardness	65	40
Tear strength (lb/in^2)	2200	1500
Resilience at R.T. (%)	65	70
Oil and chemical resistance	Good	Fair

as methylene chloride and will show a volume increase of over 300 per cent if immersed in this solvent for only a few days. The resistance of these elastomers to ketones is better than that of natural rubber although inferior to the plychloroprenes. The physical properties of the polyurethanes are compared with those of natural rubber in Table 8.1.

MOLDINGS

Moldings obtained from polyurethane resins will absorb a considerable amount of shock and exhibit little shrinkage on curing. The typical values obtained on measurement of the physical properties of certain polyurethane molding materials are given in Table 8.2.

Reaction Injection Molding

Both the conventional and high modulus types have essentially a solid skin with a cellular core. Typical specific gravity is 1.0 (about 6.2 lb/ft^3) although development work is being carried out to produce foamed and nonfomed products with densities down to 0.6. Micro cellular RIM materials in general have density reductions of 5-10 per cent and this may be reduced even further by the addition of nitrogen on air. The hardness is generally between 65-75 Shore D. The properties can be modified by glass reinforcement as with conventional thermoplastics and the preferred reinforcement for these new cellular products is milled glass fiber. Expected improvements include higher stiffness, heat-deflection temperature, and tensile strength with lower mold shrinkage. The properties of elastomeric and high modulus RIM urethanes are given in Table 8.3 and the effect of adding glass fiber is illustrated in Table 8.4.

SURFACE COATINGS

These materials exhibit excellent adhesion to many surfaces (including leather and rubber), high gloss, and abrasion resistance. The weather resistance of polyurethane coatings is also good and they are therefore finding many uses in outdoor finishes. They have good electrical insulating properties, low permeability to gases, and good chemical resistance. They are regarded as superior to alkyds in many respects, although they are somewhat more expensive.

APPLICATIONS

Foams

The major parts of the polyurethanes flexible foams goes into cushioning materials, although certain of the polyester types foams are not used due to their high hysteresis properties (i.e. poor recovery after compression -

Table 8.2

PHYSICAL PROPERTIES OF POLYURETHANE MOLDING MATERIALS

S.G. at 25°C	1.1-1.5
Shrinkage on cure (%)	2-3
Hardness shore A	50-80
Tensile strength (lb/in²)	800-2000
Elongation at break %	200-500
Dynamic resilience	8
Working temperature range (°C)	-80-+125
Water absorption %	0.1
Volume resistivity cohm (m)	$1X10^{12}$
Dielectric strength (V/mil)	350-450
Dielectric constant	3-4
Chemical Resistance	
Concentrated acids	Resistant
Concentrated alkalis	Resistant
Oils and fuels	Resistant
Steam	Resistant
Solvents	Resistant
Chlorinated hydrocarbons	Resistant

Table 8.3

PROPERTIES COMPARISON OF ELASTOMERIC AND HIGH-MODULUS RIM URETHANES

	Elastomer (fascia type)	*High modulus (RIM 125*)*
Density (lb/ft³)	62	62
Shore D hardness	50-54	70
Tensile strength (psi)	2500-3000	4100-4500
Elongation (%)	200-300	100-120
Die C tear strength (pli)	400-500	750-850
Flexural modulus, 10^3 psi		
–20°F	60-70	220-260
75°F	19-24	120-125
158°F	8-11	37-45
Modulus multiple (–20 to 158°F)	6.8	5.8
Sag (4"OH, 1 h @ 250°F)—in	0.3-0.5	0.3-0.6
Dart impact break (°F)	–50	—
Izod impact (ft/lb/in)	–	5.5

*Union Carbide Corp. urethane system

Table 8.4

HOW GLASS FIBERS AFFECT PROPERTIES OF SF-4*

Glass level in polymer (wt %)	*0%*	*10%*	*20%*
Overall density (lb/ft^3)	66.0	72.7	76.2
Tensile strength (psi)	4300	4350	4000
M_{20}	3500	3800	
M_{50}	4100		
Elongation (%)	75	30	20
Set %	31	9	3
Shore D hardness	71	72	75
Flex mod. @ 73°F (psi)	100,000	130,000	218,000
Die C tear (pli)	360	350	280
Sag (4" oh, 1h @ 250°F)-in.	.20	19	0.9
Linear coefficient of expansion (in/in.°F)	7.11×10^{-5}	4.75×10^{-5}	2.48×10^{-5}

*Mobay Chemical Corp. experimental high modulus urethane system

see Fig. 8.2). They are now firmly established in furniture cushioning, where both slab and molded shapes are used for seating, chair backs, and arms. They are also used extensively in automobiles for car upholstery, crash pads, instrument panel trim, and for arm rests, which can also be used in conjunction with a 'Vinyl' skin. Carpet underlay also utilises these foams and the packaging industry is a big potential market. A recent development has been the lamination of the foam to textiles, giving what are commonly known as 'foam-backs'. These have become important in the clothing industry where such materials are used for interlinings or as thermal insulation against the outer cloth surface.

Most of the applications found for rigid polyurethanes have utilised their combination of good thermal insulation properties, structural strength, buoyance characteristics, and shock resistance combined with light weight. They have, therefore, been used as a lightweight reinforcement in conjunction with a skin of polyester/glass laminate in the aircraft industry. Such applications include radome and antenna housings. Sandwich construction of rigid polyurethanes with metals and certain plastics have a high potential in the building industry. Rigid foams, blown by using fluorocarbons have been used both in industrial and domestic refrigerators as insulating materials.

Rubbers

One of the largest potential markets available to polyurethane elastomers is the rubber-tire market. The consumption of both natural and synthetic rubber for tires in Great Britain is over 150,000 tons, and this presents a potentially large market. Tires have already been produced from a polyurethane is U.S.A. but have been more of a research project than a commercial proposition for cars although now they are used on the wheels of fork-trucks. Their potentialities are obvious and the high abrasion resistance exhibited by such elastomers is of course of prime importance for use as a tire material. Unfortunately, this is not sufficient to offset the high cost of this material in comparison with conventional rubbers. Others disadvantages which must be overcome for this application include the low resistance to heat built-up of this elastomer.

The shoe industry has utilised the high mechanical properties of these elastomers and it has been reported that rubber heels fabricated from a polyurethane give a life of some eight times that of conventional rubber heals. Printing rollers are also produced from the cast polyurethane elstomers and give excellent performance under severe working conditions. It has also been suggested that such rollers give nearly three times the life of the conventional 'compositions' rollers.

Miscellaneous applications include mallet heads, shock absorption pads, oil-seals, diaphragms, and a host of aircraft applications.

Surface Coatings

The four main fields of application for polyurethane coatings are as clear finishes, industrial finishes, marine finishes, and floor finishes. They can be used for coating wires, rubber, steel, reinforced plastics, and wood. They are used for coating rubber in order to improve ozone resistance and also impart chemical resistance to substances which hitherto were prone to such attack. One use of particular interest is that of polyurethane coatings to achieve a patent leather finish.

While they are not specifically surface coatings, the aqueous dispersions based on polyurethane ionomers are included under this section. As a result of interactions between chains, the properties of these materials are similar to coatings based on cross-linked elastomers. These ionomers, when placed in polar organic solvents, spontaneously from aqueous dispersions on the addition of water. The physical properties of the dried films are not satisfactory and have not gained acceptance in the coating industry. Now however, they are being used for tie coats in textile and films.

Adhesives

Urethane polymers can be used to bond metal to metal, rubber to fabric, (tire cords), porcelain to porcelain, and phenol-formaldehyde to a wide variety of other plastic substrates. Considerable use is now being made of these polymers for laminating textiles to textiles and textiles to foam. The resultant bond is both washable and dry cleanable. The process for bonding normally consists of reacting a two-component system to polymer and isocyanate in solvents such as ethyl acetate or methylene chloride. The addition and reaction of the isocyanate *in situ* leads to chemical bonding rather than the simple mechanical types that result in a high level of adhesion being obtained.

Miscellaneous

Polyurethane fibers have yet to fulfil the early promise and their uses fall far short of the polyamides. Uses recommended for these urethane fibers include filter cloths, ropes and cable insulation. Over recent years they have found use in hosiery and underwear and there is an increasing application for them as the elastic component of ladies' swim-wear and foundation garments. One such product which has made an impact on the textile field as Spandex fiber. This is a generic name for a fiber-forming substance composed of at least 85 per cent of a rubbery polyurethane.

Another use which is yet to fulfil the earlier promise is that in poromeric coatings for shoe uppers. These are thermoplastic polyurethanes which have been dissolved in a solvent such as dimethyl formamide and then coagulated to give a porous structure which enables the coating to breathe like leather which the added claim of improved abrasion and scuff resistance. Corfam was one of the earlier types of these materials introduced by Du Pont in the U.S.A. but was withdrawn later for a variety of reasons and now an English product named Porvair is being used extensively as well as in the U.S.A. by Inmont Corporation which has an arrangement with the English company.

Thermoplastic polyurethanes are used in a variety of coating applications for apparel because of the appearance and "hand". Such coatings of these polymers are claimed to provide better breathability than PVC and are more dry cleanable.

The polyurethane molding materials mentioned earlier in the chapter based on castor oil were largely used for potting and encapsulation. The latter types which are harder and have good resistance to abrasion with low coefficients of friction between them and other materials are finding uses for pinions, brushings, and high precision parts in electrical and mechanical systems. They are advantageous where humid conditions exist and are used in washing machines.

9

Polyolefins

The class of materials formed by the polymerisation of certain unsaturated hydrocarbons, known as 'olefins', is an extremely important one. The main members are low and high-density polyethylene and polypropylene together with some copolymers. They are conveniently studied under one chapter heading since, on the whole, they form a family of polymers with a particular range of properties. Technically, polyisobutylene and polyisoprene are also polyolefins, but their properties render them more suitable. Common usage has, in fact, made the term 'polyolefins' synonymous with the polymers and copolymers of ethylene and propylene, and this meaning is normally implied wherever the term polyolefins' occurs in the text.

Two distinct types of polyethylene are known and these are dealt with separately. Although there is now available a broad spectrum of polyetheylene, due to copolymerisation with small amounts of other olefins such as butene-1, or to the blending of the two types of polyethylene, the respective methods of manufacture deserve separate mention. The influence of molecular structure on physical and chemical properties is also well illustrated by the two polymers.

Since one of the basic difference in the two polyethylenes is that of density they are often referred to as low-density and high-density polyethylene. Another system of nomenclature is derived from the fact that the manufacturing conditions are very different. In particular, one is made under conditions of high pressure (15-30,000 lb/in^2), while the other uses pressures which are normally below 500 lb/in^2. Unfortunately, the high pressure process produces the low-density polymer and vice-versa, and this has often led to confusion in the past. The terms 'linear' and 'branched' polyethylene may also be encountered and these refer to the structure of the polymer molecules. The high density polyethylene (produced by the low-pressure process) is the linear type while the low-density (high-pressure) polyethylene possesses the branched molecule. The influence of these different structure on density and other properties of polyethylene is discussed later in the chapter. Future reference in the text to polyethylene uses the terminology 'low-density' and 'high-density', to describe the two main types of polymer.

POLYETHYLENE

History of Development. Low molecular weight polymers of ethylene were prepared as early as 1879, while a condensation process using diazomethane was described in 1990.

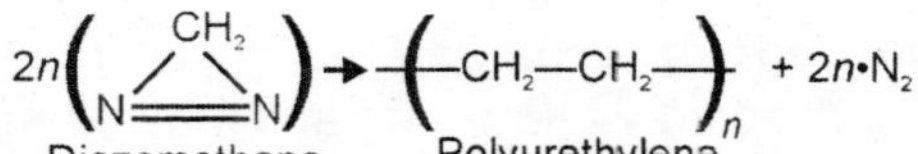

Diazomethane Polyurethylene

In 1913, Ipatieff polymerised ethylene using metallic halides as catalysts:

$$n\cdot CH_2{=}CH_2 \xrightarrow[\text{metallic halides}]{400^{\circ}C\ 70\ atm.} \left(-CH_2-CH_2-\right)_n$$

Ethylene Polyethylene

Again, only low molecular weight products were obtained.

The first high molecular weight product was obtained by Imperial Chemical Industries Ltd., in 1933, during a pure research program devoted to the effects of very high pressures on chemical reactions. Pressures of the order of thousands of atmospheres were used and special equipment had to be developed to withstand these pressures. During the course of experiments on the reaction between ethylene and benzaldehyde, a white powder was discoered in the reaction vessel and this was later found to be a polymer of ethylene.

Repetition of the experiment using ethylene alone led to the explosive decomposition of the ethylene and damage to the apparatus. Two years later, work was again initiated on the project using improved apparatus which had been developed in the meantime. It was here that chance intervened, as so often happens in even the best planned research. A fall in pressure occurred during the reaction and fresh supplies of ethylene were added to restore the pressure to its original value. When the experiment was completed, about 8 grams of a white powdery solid (polyethylene) was obtained. The success of this experiment was eventually traced to the fact that the replacement ethylene had contained, by chance, the right amount of oxygen to catalyse the formation of the polyethylene. The real element of chance in this whole affair was the occurrence of the pressure drop, which was greater than could be accounted for by polymerisation and which must, therefore, have been due to a leak at one of the joints in the apparatus.

It was not until 1935 that sufficient materials was obtained for extensive evaluation of the polymer but it was soon realised that the material had a great many properties of interest to the electrical industry, particularly as in insulating material for underwater cables. The first full-scale manufacturing unit came into use in September 1939 and its output was used almost exclusively for radar equipment, thereby making a vital contribution to the war effect.

After the war the search for new uses for polyethyelen led to the development of extruded film (for packaging, agriculture and building), bottles toys, household goods, cold-water pining and may other uses.

The next major step came in the early 1950's when Professor Ziegler, in the course of work on organo-metallic copounds, discovered catalysts that made possible the polymerisation of ethylene at near atmospheric pressures. At about the same time, two other low-pressure methods were developed in the U.S.A. One of these was associated with the name of Phillips Petroleum Co. and the other with Standard Oil of Indiana. Apart from the natural interest attaching to a completely novel method of producing polyethylene, the discovery was of immense importance because the resultant product was found to differ in several important respects from the conventional polymer. As already mentioned, one difference was in density, and this has become the commonest means of distinguishing between the two polymers.

PREPARATION OF MONOMER

Ethylene has the formula $CH_2 = CH_2$. The double bond has a functionality of two so that the ethylene forms predominantly linear molecules. It is a gas, boiling at -140^oC at atmospheric pressure, and can be prepared by several methods, some of which are given below :

(a) In the laboratory, ethylene can be prepared by the dehydration of alcohol.

$$\underset{\text{Ethyl alcohol}}{C_2H_5OH} \xrightarrow[\text{acid.}]{\text{Conc. sulfuric}} \underset{\text{Ethylene}}{CH_2{=}CH_2} + H_2O$$

Recovery of the sulfuric acid is difficult and phosphoric acid is sometimes used instead. Even better is the use of toluene *p*-sulfonic acid which, with alcohol vapor and steam, is passed over aluminium oxide at a temperature of 350°C. The acid can be recovered by crystallisation.

(b) Industrially, ethylene can be obtained by the cracking of natural gases, For example

$$\underset{\text{Propane}}{CH_3{\bullet}CH_2{\bullet}CH_3} \longrightarrow \underset{\text{Ethylene}}{CH_2{=}CH_2} + \underset{\text{Methane}}{CH_4}$$

(c) Ethylene is also obtained by the thermal cracking of light oil fractions from oil refineries.

The later process is the one in common use in the U.K. In all cases very careful purification of the ethylene is necessary since purities of atleast 99.8 per cent are required for polymerisation. Oxygen is removed by passage over a reduced copper catalyst or by treatment under pressure with molten sodium at 150°C. Acetylene (which is a cross-linking agent) is removed by catalytic hydrogenation.

POLYMERISATION

As already mentioned, there are two fundamentally different processes for the production of polyethylene and example of each of these are described below :

High Pressure Process

The polymerisation of ethylene can occur under a wide range of pressures and temperatures. Most commercial high-pressure processes, however, utilise pressures between 1000° and 3000° atmospheres and temperatures between 100 and 300°C. Temperature above 300°C are not normally used as the polymer tends to degrade. Various catalysts have been used, oxygen being the first. The concentration of oxygen is critical and optimum yields are obtained with about 0.05-0.06 per cent oxygen. Other catalysts used are organic peroxides (such as benzoyl peroxide and ditertiary butyl peroxide), metal alkyls and azo compounds. The reaction is highly exothermic and one of the early difficulties in this process was the removal of excess heat from the contents of the reaction vessels.

The highly purified ethylene is first led over a reduced copper catalyst to remove oxygen. The precise amount of oxygen necessary to act as an initiator is then added and the gases are compressed in multistage compressors. They are then pumped into the reaction vessel by compressors of special design. Two main types of reaction vessel are used, the autoclave and tubular. In both cases provision must be made for the close control of catalyst concentration, temperature, and pressure. Unconverted ethylene

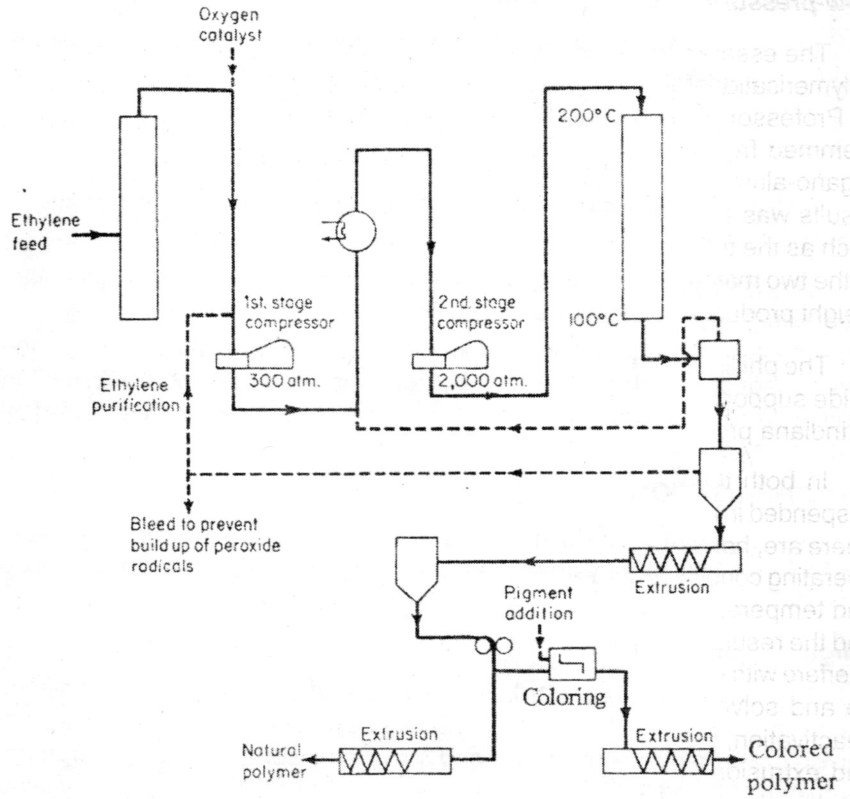

Fig. 9.1 Simplified flow scheme for the high-pressure polymerization of polyethylene

is separated from the molten polymer and is recycled. The polymer is extruded as a continuous band or ribbon, solidified by cooling and cut into granules. Where further homogenisation is needed as, for instance, in film and certain other grades, the product may undergo further processing in refiners, Banburys or screw extruders. A simplified flow-sheet of the high pressure process is given in Fig. 9.1. the vigorous nature of the reaction at high pressure leads to a great deal of chain branching and this has an important bearing on the properties of the product.

Low-pressure Processes

The essential difference between the low-pressure and high-pressure polymerisation of ethylene lies in the catalyst used. The catalysts discovered by Professor Ziegler to give polymerisation at near atmospheric pressures stemmed from his work on organo-metallic compounds, particularly the organo-aluminium compounds. The first catalyst system to give satisfactory results was a combination of aluminium triethyl and a titanium derivative such as the tetrachloride. The active catalyst is actually a reaction product of the two materials since neither will polymerise ethylene to high molecular weight products if used alone.

The phillips process utilises such catalysts as partly reduced chromium oxide supported on steam activated silica/alumina, while the Standard Oil of Indiana process makes use of nickel oxide on charcoal.

In both the Ziegler and the Phillips process, the catalyst system is suspended in a liquid hydrocarbon through which the ethylene gas is passed. There are, however, some differences the subsequent procedure and in the operating conditions. In the Ziegler process, pressures are near atmospheric and temperature are of the order of 50-70°C. Polymer granules settle out and the resultant slurry is stirred until the viscosity becomes high enough to interfere with efficient dispersion. The mixture is then passed through working-up and solvent recovery stages. In general, the sequence is chatalyst deactivation, catalyst decomposition and removal, solvent recovery, drying and extrusion, and granulation (Fig. 9.2). Complete removal of catalyst residues is extremely important as the electrical properties of the polymer may be seriously affected by their presence. One method of the polymer may be seriously affected by their presence. One method used for Ziegler polymers is to add dry hydrochloric acid gas which forms alcohol soluble complexes with the titanium (the titanium being the more difficult metal to remove). After preliminary washing with alcohol, the polymer is well washed with water. The resultant slurry is filtered or centrifuged and then dried.

The phillips process operates at higher pressures (400-500 lb/in^2) and higher temperature (100-175°C). The liquid medium is usually cyclohexane and at the temperature used, the polyethylene dissolves, and is removed as an approximately 10 per cent solution in cyclohexane. The catalyst is removed quite simply by hot sentrifuging. The polymer is obtained by cooling, to affect precipitation, filteration and drying (Fig. 9.3). Alternatively, the solvent is removed by water and steam stripping and the polymer air-dried.

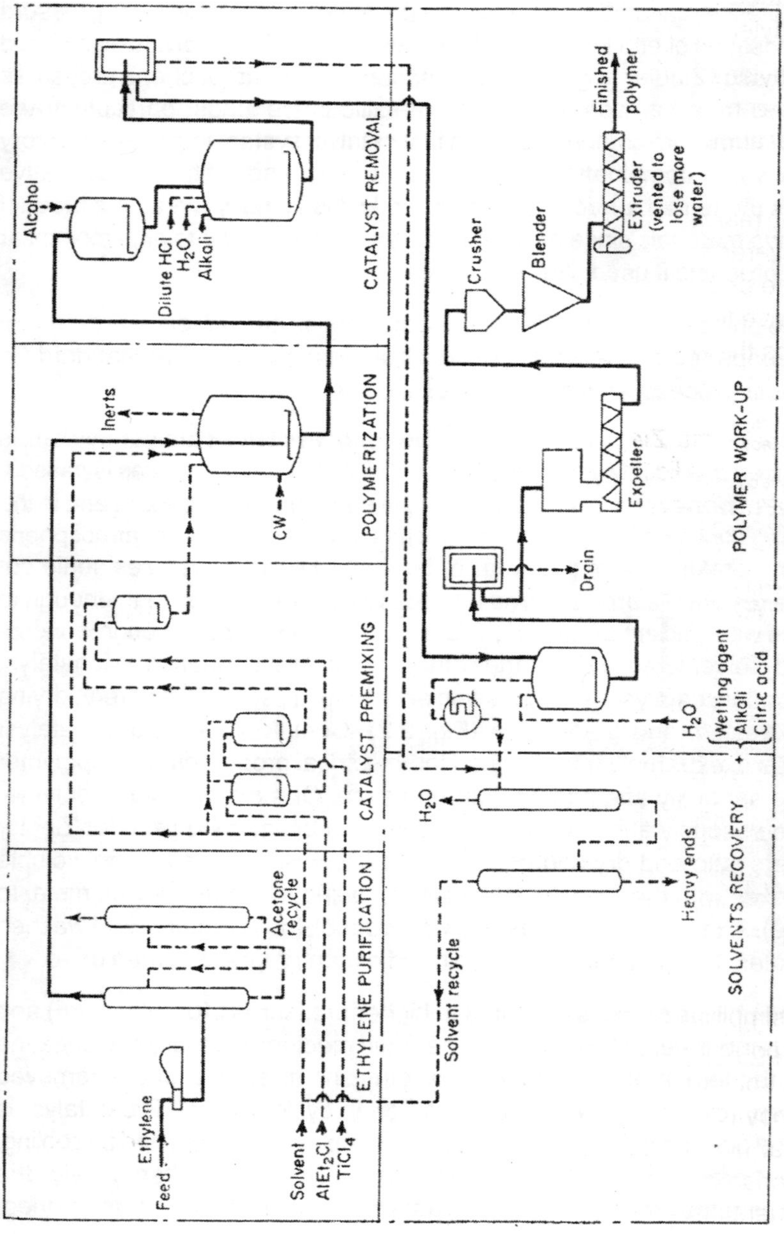

Fig. 9.2 Simplified flow scheme for polyethylene manufacure by Ziegler process

More recently (during the late 1960's) Union Carbide Corporation has introduced a gas phase process for the manufacture of high density polyethylene based on a catalyst of thier own development.

Ethylene a small quantity of hydrogen, catalyst and comonomer (if used) are fed continuously to a gas phase reactor where a polymerisation takes place at about 285 lb/in^2. pressure and at a temperature within the range 85-100°C.

The reactor is discharged to a product receiver where unreacted ethylene is recovered and recycled to the reactor. The polymer product is transferred from the product receiver to a product purge tank and then through a gas lock valve to a conveying system which takes it to the storage silos. From the silos the product is withdrawn for mixing, extrusion, granulation, etc.

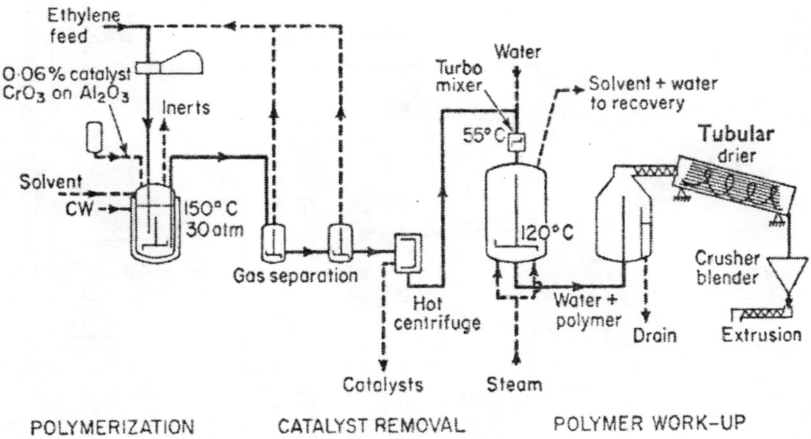

Fig. 9.3 Simplified flow scheme for polyethylene manufacture by Phillips process

A simplified process block diagram is shown in Fig. 9.4. Because gas phase polymerisation requires no solvent there is no need for the separation of the solvent from the polymer, or for solvent recovery. The catalyst efficiency is also said to be sufficiently high as to render residual catalyst removal unnecessary. Thus there is no necessity to wash and dry the polymerisation product and so there is no recovery of washing solvent and no effluent.

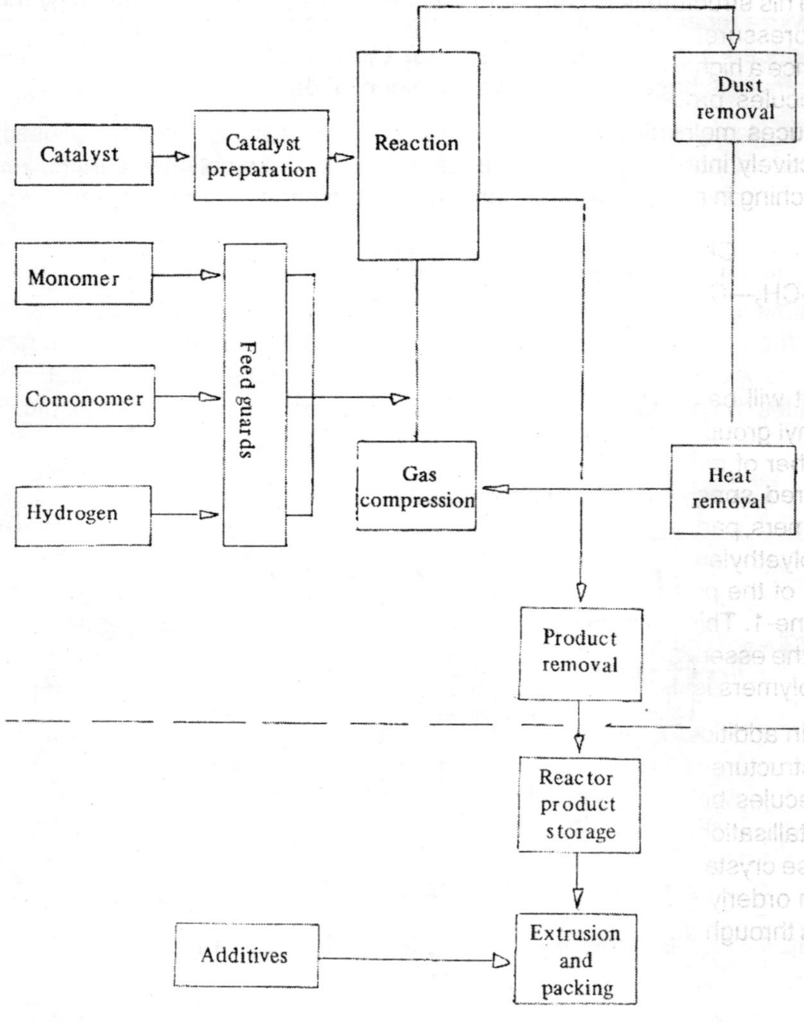

Fig. 9.4 High density polyethylene gas phase process (Union Carbide Corp.)

STRUCTURE

The simplest structure for polyethylene would be a completely unbranched chain of —CH_2 units as shown :

$$-\left(CH_2—CH_2\right)_n-$$

This structure is closely approached by the polymers produced by the low-pressure. Such a structure allows close packing by the molecules, and a hence a higher density and greater rigidity than is possible with the branched molecules produced by the high pressure process. The latter process produces molecules which contain long and short branch-chains which effectively interfere with a close approach by the molecules. Example of branching in a low-density polyethylene molecules are shown below :

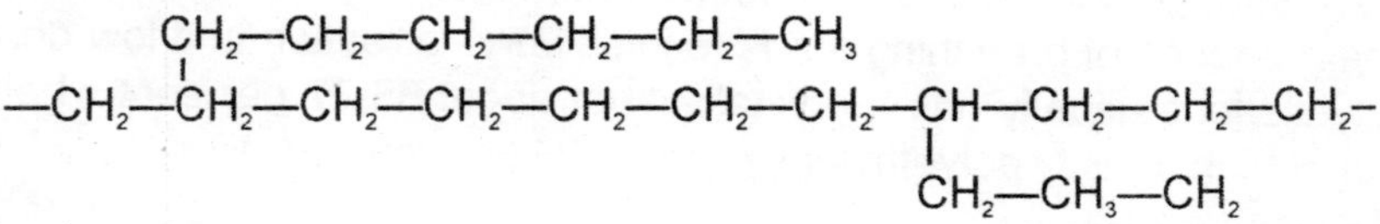

It will be noticed that each of the branch chains contains a terminal methyl group (—CH_3). A conveninet way of measuring branching is by the number of methyl groups per 100 carbon atoms and this can be done by infrared spectroscopy. Some short branches occur in the high density polymers, particularly in those having densities around 0.95 but the molecules in polyethylene of 0.96 are very largely linear. Mention must also be made here of the production of copolymers of ehtylene with about one per cent butene-1. This is a method of introducing controlled amounts of branching into the essentially linear polymers normally produced. The density of these copolymers is usually about 0.95.

In addition of density, one other important property that is affected by the structure of the molecule is crystallinity. Because of their length, polymer molecules become entangled with each other. This prevents completely crystallisation and there are thus disordered areas between the crystallites. These crystallites are areas where the linear molecules are closely packed in an orderly arrangement. One theory stated that a single molecules can pass through both ordered and disordered states and can, therefore, be part

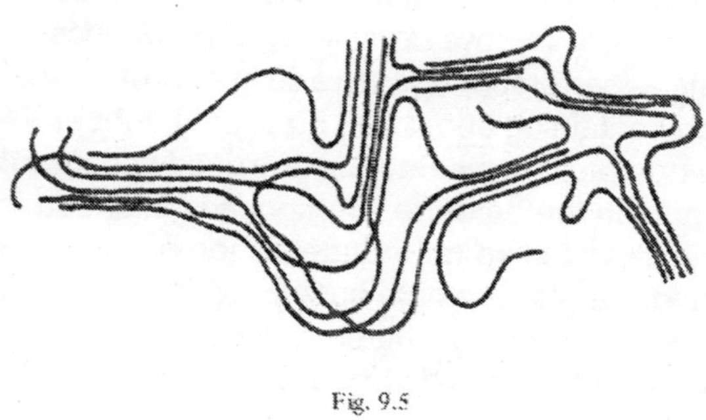

Fig. 9.5

of more than one crystallite (see Fig. 9.5). More recent work seems to point to molecules folding on themselves in a parallel arrangement to form lamellae. Crystallisation spreads as other molecules align themselves into position and also start to fold. Irregularities in molecular structure cause this crystalline growth to occur in more than one direction with the consequent formation of larger structures, known as spherulites. In either case, the close approach of the molecule chains in the crystalline areas leads to the formation of much stronger intermolecular forces in them than in the amorphous ones. The presence of branching tends to inhibit crystallisation and low density polyethylene usually has a crystallinity of about 55-77 per cent whereas that of high density polyethylene from 75-95 per cent.

COMPOUNDING

For certain applications, it may be necessary to incorporate pigments, carbon black, antioxidants, slip additives etc. with the polymer and further processing is therefore carried out. Such compounding is done one a variety of equipment the choice of which is governed by the scale of operations and the quality of end-product desired. In some cases the components of the compound are thoroughly premixed in a tumble or ribbon blender before being fed to the compounding equipment where the polyethylene is melted and then subjected to high shear stresses.

For large scale operations the most popular equipment is the Benbury mixer, but compounding may also be carried out in an extruder, provided that most ot the heating is supplied by the mechanical work done on the polyethylene in the extruder. If too much external heat is supplied then extrusion is facilitated and can occur before complete mixing has been achieved.

Carbon black is incorporated in cases where resistance to weathering is required, and about two per cent is usually sufficient. It should be well dispersed and the particle size should preferably be under 25 μ. The use of polyisobutylene or butyl rubber blends to improve stress-cracking resistance is another example of compounding. When preparing such a compound it is usualy first to prepare a master batch containing about 50 : 50 of butyl rubber and polyethylene. Higher final temperature in the Banbury are used because the melt remains very viscous at high temperature. Compounds intended for film extrusion usually contain slip additive (to reduce friction between filk surfaces) and antiblocking additives (to promote ease in opening of bags, for example). Antistatic compounds (usually long-chain amines) may also be added to film and bottle blowing grades to reduce static dust attraction.

PROPERTIES

The properties of polyethylene depend not only on chemical constitution and molecular weight but on degree of crystallinity (and, hence, density). In most cases, therefore, there is a range of properties corresponding to the range of densities now available. The molecular weight distribution can also effect polymer properties. In particular, polyethylenes with a narrow molecular weight distribution have better resistance to low temperature brittleness and enviornmental stress cracking.

General

For any particular density of polyethylene there is a range of polymer of different molecular weights. These materials vary, particularly in processability and in a mechanical properties and it is, therefore, essential that the converter should have some measure of the molecular weight of the particular polyethylene in which he is interested. A simple method which depends on measurement of the melt visocity of the polymer was evolved by I.C.I. The apparatus is basically on extrusion plastometer with a standard orifice. The weight, in grams, of material extruded in ten minutes under a constant dead-weight load, at a temperature of 190°C, is called the 'Melt Flow Index'. A low melt flow index corresponds to a high melt viscosity. Since melt viscosity is related to the molecular weight of the polymer a low MFI corresponds to a high molecular weight. A strict relationship applies only to polymers of similar density. For polyethylene of a higher density, a particular melt flow index will correspond to a slightly smaller molecular weight. More details of the measurement of melt flow index are given in Chapter 27.

The relationship betwen melt viscocity and melt index is logarithmic. Thus, for a melt flow index of 0.2 the melt viscosity of a 0.92 density polyethylene would be 300,000 poises, while for a melt flow index of two, it would be 30,000 poises. Similarly, a melt flow index of 20 corresponds to a melt viscosity of 3000 poises. The melt flow index is effectively used as a method of grading polyethylenes and together with density, is a good guide (though not a complete one) to the type of polyethylene under consideration.

Physical Properties

Low-density polyethylene is a tough, slightly translucent, waxy solid. Increasing the density has the effect of raising the softening point, increasing the rigidity and surface hardness, and decreasing the impact strength. The higher density materials are also less waxy in appearance and feel. One of the most significant differences between low- and high-density polyethylene is that of softening point since one is below the boiling point of water while the other is above. Articles manufactured from the high density material can thus be steam-sterilized, thereby opening up many applications previously closed to polyethylene.

The increased rigidity of high-density polyethylene means that equivalent rigidity can be attained with lower wall thickness and consequent savings in raw material costs. In many cases now, materials of densities intermediate between those of low-and high-density polyethylene are used. These are produced either by modified high-pressure processes (giving polymers with densities up to about 0.935) or by blending low-and high-density materials.

The range of physical properties available with polyethylene is shown in the Table 9.1.

Chemical Properties

In general, polyethylene are resistant to most chemicals except oxidising acids, free halogens, and certain ketones. At room temperature polyethylene

Table 9.1

PHYSICAL PROPERTIES OF POLYTHYLENE

Property	*Test method*	*Units*	*Value* Low density	High density
Specific gravity			0.915-0.925	0.945-0.965
Yield stress	B.S. 2782 : 301. E.	lb/in^2	1250-2000	3000-4600
Yield elongation	B.S. 2782 : 301. E.	%	16-20	11-16
Ultimate stress	B.S. 2782 : 301. E.	lb/in^2	1000-2300	3100-5500
Ultimate elongation	B.S. 2782 : 301. E.	%	200-600	50-600
Impact strenth (Izod)	B.S. 2782 : Pt. 3.	ft. lb/in. notch	Does not break	2-12
Low temperature brittleness point		°C	<-70	<-70
Hardness (Shore)	A.S.T.M. D.955-51	D Sclae	41-46	60-70
Softening point (Vicat)		°C	85-87	127
Power factor 10^6 c/s	B.S. 2782 : Pt. 2.		<0.0002	0.0003-0.0005
Dielectric constant 10^6 c/s	B.S. 2782 : Pt. 2.		2.25-2.35	2.25-2.35
Volume resistivity	B.S. 2782: Pt. 2.	ohm/cm	$>10^{18}$	$>10^{16}$

is insoluble in all solvents. At elevated temperature the solubility of polyethylene in hydrocarbons and chlorinated and hydrocarbons increases quite sharply. The solubility in any particular solvent is dependent on the density of the polymer, the high-density polyethylene having the lower solubility. Although insoluble at room temperature, polyethylenes slowly absorb hydrocarbons and halogenated hydrocarbons with subsequent swelling. Here again, the effect is less for the high density materials. Table 9.2 shows the resistance of low and high density polyethylene to certain common chemicals.

Owing to the paraffinic nature of the polyethylene molecule, it is extremely resistant to water, the water absorption at room temperature being so low as to be negligible. In this respect, there is very little difference between the low and high density polymers. The water vapor permeability is also low but in this case the high density material is a better barrier than is the low density, by a factor of about seven times. Water vapor permeability is closely

Table 9.2

EFFECT OF VARIOUS CHEMICALS ON POLYETHYLENE (AS NORMAL TEMPERATURE)

Chemical	*% Weight increase (30 days immersion*		*Remarks*	
	Low density	*High density*	*Low density*	*High density*
Acetic acid (glacial)	0.85	0.75	Some attack	Some attack
Acetone	1.25	0.65	Some loss of strength	Some loss of strength
Alcohol (ethyl)	0.20	0.15	Some loss of strength	Some loss of strength
Ammonium hydroxide	Negligible	Negligible	Unaffected	Unaffected
Carbon tetrachloride	36.0	14.5	Swelling and loss of strength	Swelling and loss of strength
Ethyl acetate	3.1	2.3	Slight attack	Slight attack
Motor oil	3.4	0.7	Slight attack	Satisfactory
Nitric acid (conc.)	0.35	0.3	Some attack (yellowing)	Some attack (yellowing)
Pertoleum	13	6	Swelling and loss of strength	Slight Swell-ing and loss of strength
Sulfuric acid (conc.)	Negligible	Negligible	Some attack	Some attack

affected by crystallinity and this is primarily a matter of molecular structure, although it can be modified by extrusion conditions. The higher the crystallinity, the lower the permeability although the relation is not linear. Permeabilities of low and high density polyethylene to water vapor and certain gases are shown in Table 9.3.

Table 9.3

PERMEABILITY OF POLYETHYLENES CM^3 (N.T.P.)/CM^2/S/CM HG/MIL X 10^8 AT 25°C

Gas or vapor	*Permeability*	
	Low density	*High density*
Oxygen	15	3
Carbon dioxide	55	13
Nitrogen	5	1
Water Vapor	420	60

An important phenomenon which must be taken into account when considering the chemical resistance of polyethylene under conditions of stress is that of 'environmental stress cracking.' When polyethylene is stressed multiaxially, in contract which cause this 'stress cracking', may not be solvents for, or even be more than slightly absorbed by, the polyethylene and if the polyethylene sample is unstressed no cracking occurs in contact with these very same substances. The probability of stress - cracking occurring decreases with decreasing melt flow index (increasing molecular weight), while the addition of 5-10 percent of polyisobutylene also confers protection. The influence of density is more difficult to assess.

Table 9.4

CLASSIFICATION OF MATERIALS AS ENVIRONMENTAL STRESS CRACKING AGENTS FOR POLYETHYLENE

Active	*Inactive*
Metallic soaps	Water
Sulfonated and sulfated alcohols	Sugars
Polyglycol esters	Inorganic salts (acid and neutral)
Liquid hydrocarbons	Polyhydric alcohols
Silicone fluids	Rosin
Organic esters	

Figures may be encountered which appear to prove that high-density polyethylene are more liable to stress crak, but these are largely due to the fact that the tests were carried out under constant deformation conditions. The greater rigidity of the high-density polymer means that the test sample is under conditions of higher stress concentrations than a similarly deformed low-density sample. (A brief account of a test for stress craking resistance is given in Chapter 27.) Table 9.4 gives a classification of certain materials as stress cracking agents for polyethylene.

The resistance of low-density polyethylene to oils and greases is rather poor but, again, improvement is noted with increases in molecular weight and density.

Polyethylene is susceptible to oxidation, particularly in the presence of uv light. Prolonged exposure to heat also accelerates oxidation with consequent deterioration of electrical and mechanical properties and appearance. The addition of antioxidants (such as substituted phenols, aromatic amines, etc.) overcomes oxidation due to high temperatures but photo-oxidation degradation is best combated by the incorporation of about 2 per cent of carbon black which screens out the uv light. For outdoor use in tropical countries, further protection is obtained by the addition of 0.1 to 0.2 per cent of an antioxidants. Reports have been published of polyethylene protected in this way, being serviceable after six or more years in the tropics.

APPLICATIONS

Polyethylene is an extremely versatile polymer and has a very wide range of applications. Among the fabrication techniques which can be used for polyethylene are extrusion (into pipe, sheet, cable covering, or film). Injection molding, blow molding extrusion coating, vacuum forming, sintering, and flame spraying, and it is this ease of processing, coupled with its toughness and good chemical and electrical properties which have led to its position as one of the foremost plastics in the world today.

Film

The largest single oulet for polyethylene is film and most of this is consumed by the packaging industry. One very large use for low density polyethylene film is the manufacture of heavy duty sacks. The first products to be packed in these sacks were compound fertilisers which were previously sold in multiwall paper sacks with an inner ply of 0.001 inch thick, low density polyethylene. The main advantage claimed for the all plastic sack was that the filled sack could be stored in the open air, thereby freeing valuable storage space for the farmer. In addition, the fact that the plastics sacks of fertiliser could be kept in the fields where they would later be required, would save labour in distributing sacks from a central storage point. Although this market now consumes many thousands of tons of polymer per annum, many difficulties were encountered in the early days of development. One of the first was that of handling. When the open mouth sack was filled and sealed it assumed a pillow-like shape that was difficult to stack. The stack instability was often wrongly attributed to a lower coefficient of friction for low density polyethylene but in fact polyethylene on polyetheylene has a higher coefficient than paper on paper and it was soon recognised that the main trouble was the small area of contract between the pillow shaped sacks as opposed to the large area between block-shaped paper sacks. A solution was found to be the provision of a few microperforations along the top of the bag. These allowed the air inside the sack to escape and the contents of the bag were consolidated under the influence of imparts received during handling. The holes were small enough to exclude moisture except during heavy rainfall. This meant that the sacks could not be stored in completely unprotected conditions but a light tarpaulin or sheet of polyethylene film over a stack was found to be sufficient protection. This was still better than for paper sacks that loss strength under conditions of high humidity.

There are also many situations where the available filling equipment demands valved sacks so that these had to be developed for polyethylene sacks in order to complete fully with paper. Today, polyethylene valved sacks are commercially available, with a block bottom construction so that neither filling nor stacking is a problem. Low density polyethylene sacks are also used for the packaging of peat, plastics granules and even coal.

Another large outlet for low-density polyethylene film is shrink wrapping. Shrink wrapping is based on the fact that a plastics film that has been stretched under heat during its manufacture reverts to its original dimensions when reheated. The technique was first applied to the packaging of oven-ready turkeys for deep freeze storage using vinylidene chloride/ vinyl chloride copolymer as the film and hot water as the shrinkage medium. Nowadays, low density polyethylene is the most popular film for shrink wrapping and the heating is usually carried out by means of hot air tunnels. The applications for shrink wrapping have also greatly increased in numbers. One popular field of use is that of transit packaging, where a shrink wrapped package of , say, one or two dozen tins or jars, collated on one or two trays, is used instead of a fiberboard ease. The mechanical protection given by the shrink wrap is not as great as that given by a well designed fiberboard case but is usually completely adequate. In addition, a shrink wrapped package can be seen to be fragile and is usually handled more carefully as a result. Advantages to the retailer are :

(1) There is less packaging material to be disposed of, after use.

(2) The package takes up progressively less space on the warehouse shelf as the goods are sold, whereas a fiberboard case takes up the same amount of room whether it contains one can or twenty.

Low density polyethylene film is also used for the shrink wrapping of whole pallet loads, giving stable loads with good weather-proofing. Miscellaneous applications include the wrapping of awkwardly shaped objects such as cucumbers, rolls of wallpaper and central heating radiators. Low density polyethylene is used for these applications because it is cheap, tough and waterproof. Where a clearer or more sparkling film is required, then polypropylene or PVC are the more likely choice.

One of the earliest uses for low density polyethylene film was the packaging of fresh fruit and vegetables. In the general trend towards the packaging of foodstuffs, fresh products had tended to lag behind out the adevent of a cheap, tough film made the packaging of fresh produce an economic and technical feasibility. The good water-vapor barriers characteristics of polyethylene made it eminently suitable for preventing the drying out of green vegetables while still enabling the housewife to clearly see the contents of the package. However, although, polyethylene is comparatively permeable to oxygen and carbon dioxide, it was found that the permeability was insufficient to maintain free interchange of the carbon dioxide developed inside the bag with atmospheric oxygen outside the bag. In the absence of such interchange, necessary for the respiration of the produce, off-odors were developed although the produce might still look green and fresh. Ventilation of the polyethylene bags by means of a few small holes, about ¼ drying out of the produce.

Ventilation is also employed in bags used for the packaging of potatoes, although for a different reason. the potatoes are washed before packaging and are usually still damp when packed. Since polyethylene is an efficient water-vapor barriers, condensation of moisture occurs on the inner surface of the film unless ventilation is provided and such condensation would look unsightly and reduce the sales appeal of the package. Excess moisture in the bag could also lead to rotting of the produce.

The toughness of low density polyethylene at low temperature and the fact that it can be formed into bags on a form/fill/seal basis has led to extensive uses in the packaging of frozen foods. The first outlet was the packaging of frozen peas. Frozen peas were originally packed in cartons, the catron being filled and then frozen between plates. The peas were received by the housewife as a solid block. In the case of form/fill/seal bags, the peas are frozen in the blast of air and remain loose enough to be filled into a polyethylene bag formed from flat film round the filling mandrel. The use of polyethylene film has spread to frozen soft fruits, brussels sprouts, and other produce able to be handled by this type of filling operation.

The general inertness of low density polyethylene film has led to a widespread use in many areas of food packaging including made up bags for use in the home for the storage of food in the refrigerator or deepfreeze.

Another market is for the pacakging for sliced bread. Initial progress was slow because the traditional wrapping material-waxed paper— was cheap and difficulties were experienced in handling a limp, totally fusible film as opposed to the stiffer waxed paper in which only the wax melts during heat sealing. Low-density polyethylene's success came when equipment was developed for packaging sliced loaves into ready made-up bags. These are closed with wire ties or plastics clips thereby overcoming the problems of heat sealing. Easy reclosure is another advantage from the housewife's point of view.

The use of high density polyethylene film in packaging was restricted for many years to areas where its higher softening point was necessary, i.e., in boil-in-the-bag food packaging. The development of ultra-thin high density polyethylene film (down to about seven microns) opened up many new markets. Such film, in the range of seven to ten microns, is similar to tissue paper in feel and appearance and also has the property of greaseproofness. It is produced using blow-up ratios of from 4 : 1 to 7 : 1 and draw ratios of around 10 : 1. Among the advantages that it has over paper are waterproofness, low gas and water vapor permeability, and good aroma retention. It is heat sealable, can be printed and is readily self colored. It can be made into bags either by heat sealing or by the use of adhesives. High density polyethylene tissue has been used as a wrapping material for a number of food-stuffs, including meat, wet fish, meat pies, and dried fruits. There are also a number of nonfood packaging uses, one good example being the wrapping of cut flowers. The flowers are less prone to wilting through loss of moisture and the wrap itself does not wilt or drip water even after a big journey. It is also used for the wrapping of delicate instruments to keep them dust-free and to prevent corrosion and staining which can occur with paper, unless expensive chloride and sulfur-free grades are used.

The slightly thicker film (20-30 microns) is also used as a wrapping material. Its barrier properties are even better by virtue of its increased thickness and it is particularly suitable for the packaging of frozen meat. In Greece, it has been attractively printed and sold as a gift wrap while in Belgium it is sold in packs of twelve sheets for household wrapping uses. More generally, it is replacing paper bags for retail use. Finally, even thicker film (around 100 microns) is beginning to find use as a free-standing supermarket carrier bag.

Nonpackaging uses for polyethylene film include applications in building agriculture, and horticulture. In building for instance, low density polyethylene film is used as a cover for wet concrete to promote more even curing as a damp-proof course and for the protection of building and workers so that work can continue under cover during bad weather.

Agricultural and horticultural uses are extremely varied and include silage covers, linings for temporary reservoirs, seed-bed covers, and green houses. The latter is an interesting application since it makes use of the fact that the light transmission characteristics of polyethylene are similar to those of glass in the visible region while having an absorption band in the ultravoilet. It is necessary to enclose an air space between two layers of polyethylene if heat losses at night are to be eliminated, since polyethylene is more transparent than glass to infrared radiation; therefore, the ground loses heat through the film by radiation. Black low density polyethylene film makes an excellent mulch for plants such as strawberries. The ground is covered and the seedling planted out in prepared holes in the film. The black film absorbs heat and encourages earlier growth of the seedlings but inhibits weed growth in surrounding soil by excluding the light. Rain water percolates through in holes in the film but general evaporation is retarded. Low density polyethylene film has also been used as an impermeable cover for soil that has to be fumigated with poisonous fumigants such as methyl bromide.

Film Tapes and Fibers

Film tapes are widely used in the manufacture of woven sacks. Polypropylene is the most popular polymer but high density polyethylene is often used and a range of sacks is marketed in the U.K. based on high density polyethylene coated with low-density polyethylene. One application is for the packaging of expensive grass seeds of export. The woven polyethylene sacks are 50 per cent more expensive than the film sacks previously used but elimination of burst sacks more than compensates for this in product savings.

Coatings

The use of polyethyelene for the coating of various substrates is notable for the many new applications available for such traditional materials as paper, fiberboard, aluminium foil, and regenerated cellulose film. Practically by coating with plyethyelene is done by extrusion coating techniques and low-density resins are used almost exclusively. Apart from the higher temperatures which have to be employed with high-density polyethyelene, which present no insuperable difficulties, it is not always possible to make economic use of high-density polyethylene's better barrier properties. This is especially the case with paper where there is a danger of individual fibers penetrating very thin coatings and thus vitiating the moisture vapor resistance by 'wicking'. This can be obviated to some extent by using papers with glazed finishes. It is some times necessary to have a minimum thickness of coating in order to give adequate heat seal strength thereby not utilising high-density polyethyelene's superior barrier properties to the fullest. This is not to say that high density polyethylene has no future as a coating material but only to suggest that its main uses are where low-density polyethylene cannot do the job except at heavy coating weight.

In the U.S.A. one of the largest outlets for polyethyelene coated board is the packaging of milk. In a land where doorstep delivery of milk has largely given way to collection from the local supermarket, cartons very soon replaced the glass bottle. At first, wax-coated board was used but the advent of polyethylene-coated cartons are used for milk in the U.K. but the different pattern of distribution favors returnable glass bottles. In the U.S.A. and Canada there has since since heen a further change towards high-density polyethylene bottles. In the U.K. there are also some high-density polyethylene bottles together with some form/fill/seal low-density ones.

Polyethylene coated regnerated cellulose film is used in many cases where a vacuum-pack is requried, for example, with bacon, cheese and coffee, especially if transparency is also desired. In this type of coated material, the gas barrier properties of the cellulose film are added to the flexibility, water-vapor resistance, and heat-sealing properties of polyethylene. In addition, the cellulose film can be reverse printed on its inner surface. The printing is thus sandwiched between the cellulose and polyethylene, giving it protection against scuffing.

Injection Molding

In the injection-molding field both low-and high-density polyethylenes have found extensive use in household articles such as buckets, bowls, laundry baskets, baby baths, and many other items including such large moldings as dustbins. The laboratories and hospital also benefit from polyethylene's toughness and chemical inertness and a whole range of equipment has been molded, including breakers, funnels, measuring cylinders, jugs, and petrie dishes.

Polyethylene has also made extensive inroads into the toy market because of its relative unbreakability and its possibilities for colour. The flexibility of the lower-density polymers also makes them excellent materials for manufacturing construction kits where parts fit into each other by means of the 'snap-in' principle.

In the packaging field, both low-and high-density polyethylene are used for closures, spouts, and dispensers. Low density polyethylene is used for snap on caps or plug fittings where its resiliency ensures a good seal, while high density polyethylene is used for screw caps where rigidity is needed.

Blow Molding

Blow-molding articles provide a very large market for polyethylene. Bottles, jerricans, drums, and containers of all shapes and sizes are manufactured by this process and the polyethyelene bottle has almost become the symbol of the plastics age.

The high density polymer is favored when a high softening point, better berriers properties, or greater rigidity are required. Its better barrier properties are utilised in the bleach bottle (where a low permeability to chlorine is required) and for the manufacture of jerricans for paraffins (kerosene). Other applications for high density polyethylene bottles include household and car polishes, lubricating oils, and ethylene glycol antifreezers. In addition to packaging applications, the blow molding technique has also opened up many other outlets for low-and high-density polyethylene. Toys, in particular, show cost savings when blow-molded in one piece as against injection molding of component parts with subsequent assembly. Dolls, too, are often molded in polyethylene instead of being slush-molded in PVC. Other miscellaneous applications for blow-molded polyethylene include coat hangers, rolling pins, mooring buoys, and pipe fittings.

Pipe

Both low-and high density polymers have been used for the extrusion of pipe. In agriculture, low-density polyethylene pipe is often used for water supply and for irrigation where its flexibility makes it easy to install and handle. Low density polyethylene pipe has been also used for domestic cold-water services, one big advantage being that it is not damaged should the water freeze. Polyethylene pipe is also used in chemical plants, the high density material being preferred because of its regidity and superior chemical resistance.

Monofilament

High density polyethylene can be extruded and cold drawn to give monofilament suitable for many applications. In particular, it has been used for filter cloths, woven material for deck-chairs, ropes, tennis-nets, fishing-nets and in thicker strands, pot-scourers. Polyethylene ropes have the advantage of being water resistant, and hence they do not become water logged and, in fact, float on water since they have a density less than unity.

A remarkable extension of the monofilament extrusion technique is extruded plastic netting. One method of producing this is to use a circular die in which the inner core and outer portion of the die can be counter rotated while the molten polymer is extruded through notches cut in the outer surface of the inner core and the inside of the outer die component. Polyethylene was the first polymer used and the resultant netting is widely used for the packaging of oranges, lemons, apples, nuts, onions, etc., as welll as for decorative overwrapping of cosmetics, for multipacks and as protective sleeving.

Electrical Applications

The first major use of polyethyelene was as an electrical insulator, replacing gutta-percha in the manufacture of submarine cables. In addition to its good electrical properties it possesses the virtues of water impermeability and chemical inertness and is thus an excellent material to replace paper insulation in telephone cables. The use of polyethylene in radar and other high-frequency equipment has already been mentioned and is part of history. The experience thus gained has enabled polyethylene to find many other uses in the electrical industry, a familiar example being that of transatlantic and Commonwealth-linking submarine telephone cables.

Miscellaneous Applications

Polyethylene powder can be used in fluidised bed coating and gives coatings of good gloss, chemical resistance, and abrasion resistance. Polyethylene powder is also used for the dispersion coating of irregularity shaped objects by means of spraying with subsequent heating.

Polyethylene may also be used for the powder coating of cloths or carpet backs. The powder is spread on the surface by a doctor blade, then passed through an oven to melt the polyethylene. On leaving the oven, the coated material is nipped between two rollers. That in contact with the molten polyethylene being water-cooled and polished.

An increasingly large outlet for polyethylene is in the sinter molding of large containers, tanks etc. In the U.K. low-density polyethylene is the most popular, while on the Continent high-density polyethylene is more often used. Among the objects produced by this method are small boats, milk churns,and tote-bins.

ETHYLENE COPOLYMERS

It was briefly noted under 'Structure', that controlled amounts of chain branching could be introduced into the substantially linear 0.96 density polymers by means of copolymerisation with small amounts of butene-1. One property which is improved by the introduction of a certain amount of branching is that of creep resistance. With a linear molecule such as high-density polyethylene there is only a small resistance to creep under static loads but the introduction of even a small percentage of branching has an appreciable effect by interfering with the free movement of the molecules relative to each other. The introduction of branching also improves the resistance to stress cracking. Other copolymers are dealt with in the following sections.

Polyallomers

Polyallomers are high crystalline block copolymer of ethylene and propylene and were introduced in 1962 by Eastman Chemical Products. These copolymers exhibit a degree of crystallinity usually found only in homopolymers yet they differ in many physical properties from polyethylene, polypropylene, and blends of the two. They are also different from copolymers of ethylene and propylene produced by other processes. These block copolymers are, in fact, examples of allomerism which is defined as a variation in chemical composition without change in crystalline form. The term polyallomer was coined, therefore, to identify this new class of copolymers and distinguish it from the previously known homopolymer and copolymer variations.

The highly crystalline nature of polyallomers is confirmed by their in solubility in hexane and heptane, while infrared spectra indicate that they are block and not random copolymers. Propylene/ethylene polyallomer exhibits many of the properties of both high-density polyethylene and crystalline polypropylene but has a specific gravity lower than both (0.896)

The surface hardness of polyallomer is slightly less than that of a polypropylene but its abrasion resistance is greater. Polyallomer is superior to high density polyethylene in flow characteristics, moldability, softening point, and hardness. Like polypropylene it gives excellent molded-in hinges and has an even better resistance to flex fatigue. Polyallomer also offers better color and lower susceptibility to blush marks than polypropylene. Polyallomer tends to crystallise slowly, even after solidification from the melt. From a practical standpoint this means that tough parts can be produced from polyallomer without the necessity for rapid cooling that is essential for manufacturing tough parts from either of the two homopolymers.

Applications include finishes tackle boxes, bowling ball bags, and type writer cases which utilise its integral hinge property, its toughness and its good modability. Polyallomer is also used for luggage shells, loose leaf binders, etc., made from pre-embossed sheet.

Ethylene/Vinyl Acetate Copolymers (EVA)

The proportion of vinyl acetate in EVA copolymers can vary, the oretically, from 1-99 per cent but commercially available products normally contain less than 50 per cent. Of these, the ones with 21-50 per cent vinyl acetate are used as additives for waxes and adhesives, to give increased strength, improved barrier properties, and better processing characteristics.

EVA copolymers containing seven to eight per cent of vinyl acetate may be considered as modified low-density polyethylene whereas those with around 15-28 per cent of vinyl acetate behave more like flexible PVC. One advantage that EVA has over flexible PVC is that its flexibility is inherent and does not depend on the presence of plasticisers, which could be leached out.

In general, the properties of EVA compare with those of low-density polyethylene as follows :

(1) It has a higher impact strength.
(2) It has a greater elasticity.
(3) It has a higher permeability to water vapor and gases.
(4) It has better low temperature properties.
(5) It has a greater resistance to environmental stress cracking.
(6) It has a higher filler retention.
(7) It has a lower heat seal temperature.
(8) It has a greater flexural life.

Properties to be noted in the case of films are the tackiness of high vinyl acetate content copolymers and a greater coefficient of friction. This means that EVA films have a greater tendency to blocking and lower slip characteristics than low density polyethylene films.

Applications include snap-on caps, the lining of bag-in-box containers and stretch wrapping. In the U.S.A. a copolymer with a fairly high vinyl acetate content has been chill roll cast to give a flexible, high-clarity film which competes with flexible PVC as a meat wrap.

Ionomers

The term 'ionomers' was coined to describe a family of polymer in which there are ionic forces between the polymer chains, as well as the usual covalent bonds between the atoms making up each chains. Basically they are ethylene/methacrylic acid copolymers with some of the acid groups present as a metal salt. The metal ions provide the cationic part of the link while carboxyl groups, located along the polymer chain, constitute the anionic portion. Sodium, potassium, magnesium, and zinc are all suitable metal ions.

A typcial ionomer has been found to contain 2.8 per cent sodium which is equivalent to 17 sodium ions per 1000 carbon atoms. There were also 9 COO and 5 COOH groups per 1000 carbon atoms.

The ionic interchain links strengthen and stiffen the polymer but, unlike the covalent cross-links per cent in thermosets, they do not destroy its melt processability. Ionomers do have greater melt strength than plyethylen itself, however, and they are, therefore, very suitable for extrusion coating, skin packaging and vacuum forming. The ionic interchain forces also have an appreciable effect on crystalline morphology. Low-density polyethylene itself is a semicrystalline polymer and can only be given good clarity by rapid quenching and a consequent inhibition of spherulite growth. The ionic forces in ionomers eliminate all traces of visible spherulites thus giving excellent clarity.

Ionomers have a greater resistance to oils and greases than low density polyethylene at room temperature although the differences are not so marked at elevated temperature. Chemically they are resistant to weak and strong alkalis but they are slowly attacked by acids. Environmental stress crack resistance is good and is claimed to be higher than that of low density polyethylene of equivalent melt flow index. Other chemical properties of ionomers are similar to those of low-density polyethylene, being resistant to alcohols, ketones, and esters but swelling slightly in hydrocarbon solvents.

The use of carbon black as an antioxidant is also necessary for applications involving outdoor exposure.

Get permeability of ionomers is similar to that of low-density polyethylene but water vapor permeability is somewhat higher as is water absorption. The polar nature of ionomers means that printing is easier than on low-density polyethylene but some pretreatment is still necessary.

Electrical properties are similar to those of low-density polyethylene but the polar nature again has an effect and the volume resistivity is lower (10^{17} ohm cm as against 10^{17}-10^{19} ohm cm for low density polyethylene). The dielectric strength is higher than that of low-density polyethylene, however, while the dielectric constant is the same.

Transparent vials with integrally hinged snap caps have been molded from ionomer but the majority of uses lie in the realms of films and coatings. It has been used in skin packaging, for example, because of its high resistance to puncturing and its good adhesion to porous board surfaces. Its high melt strength means that it can be drawn down to very thin coatings (down to 12 microns) without pinholing in extrusion coatings. Finally, its grease resistance has led to its use in form/fill/seal pouches for a range of convenience foods with a high added fat content.

Irradiated Polyethylene

Work by Charlesby and others has shown that many long chain polymers undergo cross-linking when subjected to high energy radiation. Polyethylene has received particular attention in this respect and several improvement in the properties of this polymer have been noted. When polyethylene is irridiated, hydrogen (and smaller amounts of methane, ethane and propane) is liberated and the polymer becomes increasingly insoluble due to cross - linking of the molecules by C—C bonds. Increasing irradiation leads to yellowing and, eventually, the polyethylene becomes a dark ruby red in color. At first the polyethylene becomes more flexible but later it turns harder and harder, eventually becoming quite brittle.

In the U.S.A. irradiated polyethylene film has been produced by passing ordinary low-density polyethylene film continously through a high energy electron field. This converts it to an infusible film which, with appropriate stabilisers, withstands prolonged aging at 150°C or short-term exposure to 230°C. Pipe can also be irradiated with similar results. It is obvious that this idea of converting a thermoplastic polymer to a thermosetting one, after forming, opens up many new possibilities.

Modified Polyethylene

It is possible to modify polyethylene chemically by a number of means including oxidation, halogenation, and chlorsulfonation. Of these the most important, commercially is chlorsulfonation.

Oxidation. Controlled oxidation of polyethylene can be carried out by heating the molten polyethylene at 160-200°C for some hours on a mixing mill in contact with air or by heating the polyethylene with an oxidising agent, such as nitric acid, in the liquid phase. The first process yields carboxylic acid derivatives with molecular weights of the same order as the unmodified polymer. The higher molecular weight products are partially cross-linked. The second process yields dicarboxylic acid derivatives, the molecular weights of which very between about 250-1000. A further process of oxidation is by treating a solution of polyethylene in carbon tetrachloride at 71-78OC with ozone and oxygen. A mixture of products is obtained but the chief ones are partially esterified hydroxydicarboxylic acids. Molecular weights very between 100-2000. Polyethylenes which contain carboxyl groups can be easily dispersed in water, giving stable emulsions, and are of commercial interest on this account.

Halogenation. The reactions of chlorine, bromine and fluorine have all been investigated but chlorination has received the most attention. Many process have been described, including solution and suspension chlorination with photo or chemical catalysis. A wide range of chlorinated polyethylenes has been produced, from soft, pliable, rubber-like materials to rigid, transparent plastics similar in some respects to unplasticised polyvinyl chloride. The patent literature contains, references, to the use of chlorinated polyethylenes for electrical insulation, sheet and flooring.

Chlorinated polyethylens are also used as impact modifiers for rigid PVC. Resins with a chlorine content of around 36 per cent offer the best balance between compatibility with PVC and the greatest favourable effect on impact strength.

Chlorsulfonation. The chlorination of polyethylene in the presence of sulfur dioxide effects the introduction of chlorine and sulfonyl chloride groups to the molecule and produces a vulcanizable rubber with good chemical and abrasion resistance.

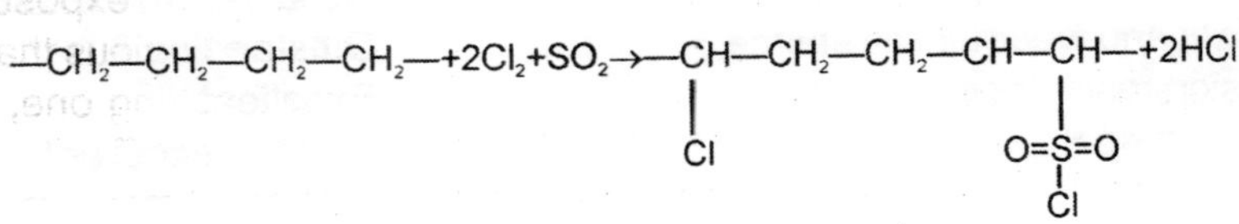

The chlorine confers oil resistance on the polymer while the highly reactive sulfonyl chloride groups enable easy cross linking (or vulcanisation) by zinc and other metal oxides. The presence of water is necessary for cross linking and the reaction may be visualised as shown below.

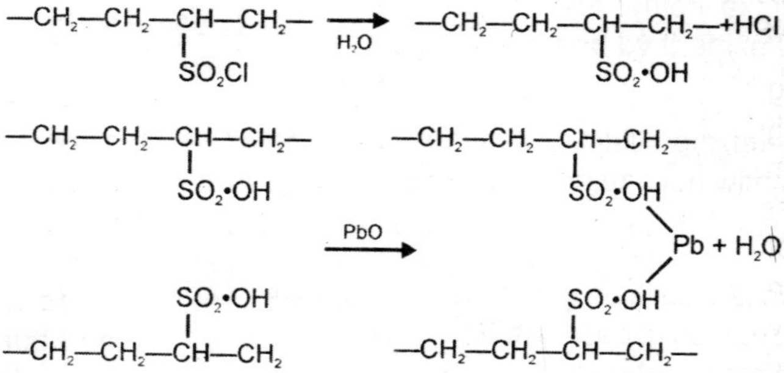

Chlorsulfonated polyethylene has excellent resistance to abrasion coupled with resistance to a wide ragne of chemicals. It also possesses good weatherability, even in coloured grades. This latter property (and the abrasion resistance) has been utilized in the manufacture of white sidewall tires. It is extremely resistant to oils, and strong oxidizing chemicals such as chlorine bleaches.

Table 9.5

PROPERTIES OF HYPALON
CHLORSULFONATED POLYETHYLENE

Hardness range	40-95 (Shore A)
Temperature range (in use)	—62°-182°C
Tensile strength	over 3000 lb/in²
Adhesion to fabrics	good
Adhesion to metal	Excellent
Chemical resistance	Good to excellent
Compression set resistance	Fair
Ozone Resistance	Outstanding
Flame resistance	Good
Sunlight and weather resistance	Outstanding
Abrasion resistance	Excellent
Oil resistance	Good to excellent

Among the applications of chlorsulfonated polyethylene are ventilator strips, spark-plug covers. jacketing of iginition wire, industrial hose for corrosive chemicals such as bleaches and sulfuric acid, and the lining of chemical tanks. The following table of properties (Table 9.5.) refers to Hypalon, marketed by E.I. Du Pont de Nemours & Co. Inc.

VERY HIGH MOLECULAR WEIGHT HIGH DENSITY POLYETHYLENE

During the past few years, very high molecular weight grades of high density polyethylene has been developed. Such grades are also known as ultra-high molecular weight polyethylene, or UHMWPE. Increased molecular weight gives products with high abrasion resistance, low coefficient of friction, high impact strength and self lubrication properties. However, as molecular weight increases, processability becomes correspondingly more difficult. Molecular weights range from one to five million. The resin is supplied as a powder and is compression molded into sheets and plates or ram-extruded into bars, profiles, rods, and tubes. In Europe, rods, pipes and profiles are being produced on twin-screw extruders, using special lubricants and extrusion aids or blends of UHMWPE with lower molecular weight grades.

Applications include starwheels, guide rails, and bushings on packaging machinery and chute and bin liners, wiper blades, and skirt boards in materials handling equipment. The excellent impact and abrasion resistance also makes it suitable for wear and bearing surfaces in prosthetic devices for hip, knee and finger repair.

POLYPROPYLENE

History of Development. Early attempts to polymerise propylene using high-pressure processes gave only oily liquids or rubbery solids of no commercial value. Meanwhile, Professor Natta, in Italy had been investigating the use of Ziegler type catalysts. He found, for instance, that if in the Ziegler catalyst system, $Al(C_2H_5)_3$ + $TiCl_4$, the $TiCl_4$ was replaced by TiC_3, a stereospecific catalyst was formed which yielded crystalline high molecular weight polymers of propylene. A stereospecific catalyst is one which controls the position of each monomer units as it is added to the polymer chain, thus allowing the formation of a polymer of regular structure from asymmetric monomer units such as propylene. The announcement of Professor Natta's stereospecific polymerization of propylene was greeted as a major breakthrough in polymer technology since this was the first time that polymers with a regular spatial structure had been produced synthetically.

Preparation of Monomer

Propylene, $CH_3 \cdot CH{=}CH_2$, is a gas, boiling at —48°C at atmospheric pressure. It is obtained commercially from refinery gases by distillation from propane/propylene mixtures. Propylene required for polymerisation has to be very pure. Water must be absent since this destroys the catalyst, while methyl acetylene. $CH_3C{=}CH$, should be removed as it acts as a cross-linking agent.

Polymerisation

Basically, the polymerisation of propylene is similar to the ziegler process for the preparation of high-density polyethylene. A typical process is described below.

Propylene at a pressure of about 100 atm is led into a reaction vessel in which is a well-stirred dispersion of catalyst in a liquid hydrocarbon. The temperature is kept low enough to ensure precipitation of the polymer as it is formed. Stirring is continued until the polymer content is between 35 and 40 per cent, when the slurry is pumped to a flash drum where the unreacted propylene is removed the recycled. The slurry is then centrifuged to remove the liquid hydrocarbon. The liquid hydrocarbon and the temperature conditions are chosen so that most of any 'atactic' polymer formed remains is solution and is removed in the liquid phase. (The definition of 'atactic' is given below).

Catalyst removal from the polymer is carried out by extracting with a weak solution of hydrochloric acid gas in methyl alcohol. After removal of the extractant, the polymer is washed with water to remove the acid, steam distilled to remove solvent traces, dried, extruded, and pelletised.

More recently it has been announced that a new catalyst has been developed jointly by Montedison in Italy and Mitsui Petrochemical Industries in Japan. The new catalyst is said to give a polymer needing no catalyst removal and with a high isotactic index, thus eliminating extraction of the amorphous 'atactic' material almost entirely. The new system means simpler and less expensive plants while plant running costs are also reduced.

Structure

The basic structure unit of polypropylene is

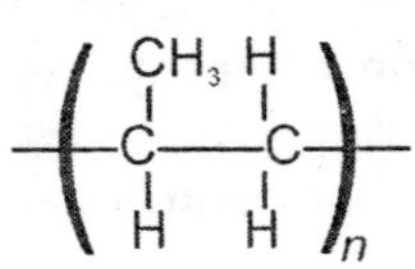

and is thus similar to that of polyethylene with a methyl group substituted for one of the hydrogens. The polymerisation of propylene without the use of stereospecific catalysts produced hapharzard linkages of monomer units to give a rubbery polymer with what is known as an 'atactic' structure, shown diagramatically in Fig. 9.6. Such chains could obviously not group together

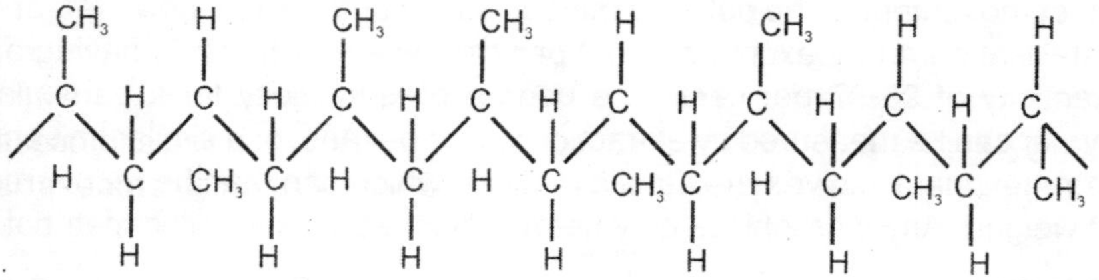

Fig. 9.6 'Atactic' polypropylene

to form a crystallisable structure. The name 'isotactic' was given to the regular structure of the polypropylene produced by stereospecific catalysts because it was though that the methyl groups were always along one side of the polymer chain (see fig. 9.7).

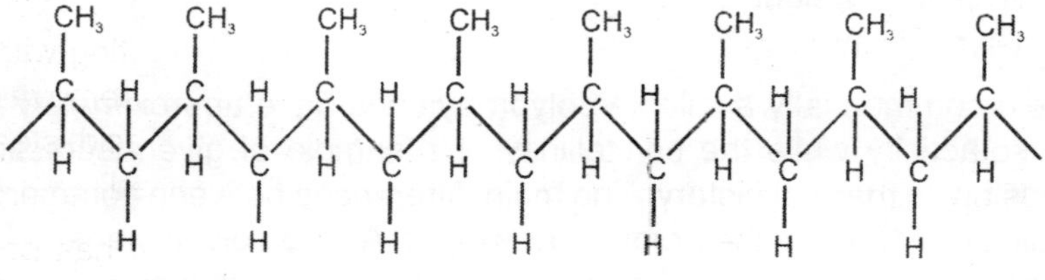

Fig. 9.7 'Isotactic' polypropylene

Later work has shown the existence of a form in which the methyl groups occur on alternate sides of the carbon chain ('syndiotactic') while it is also possible to obtain what is known as a 'stereoblock' polymer, in which short-chain lengths of isotactic configuration occur alternatively (Fig. 9.8.).

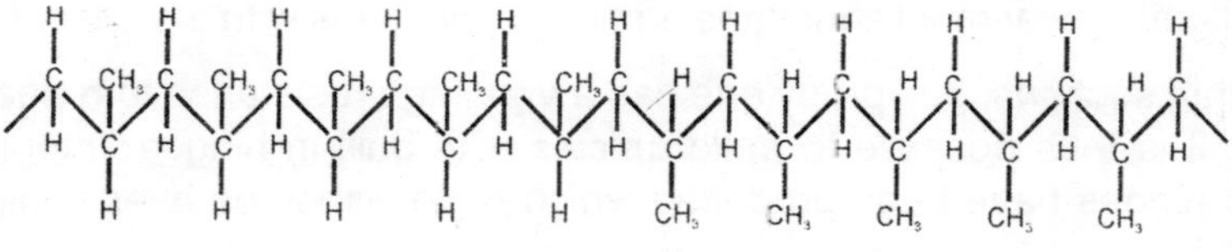

Fig. 9.8. 'Stereoblock' polymer

In general, a stereoblock polymer with infrequent inversion in a longchain possesses properties only slightly different from a high molecular weight isotactic polymer.

The regular structure of isotactic polypropylene allows close approach of the polymer molecules, and crystallisation can then occur in a similar manner to that of polyethylene. The presence of the methyl group does restrict movement of the polymer molecules to some extent, however, and crystallisation rarely exceeds 65-70 per cent even for material having an isotacticity of 95-97 per cent. The degree of isotacticity for a particular polymer can be measured by extraction with *n*-hexane, or a similar solvent. The *n*-hexane dissolves the atactic material which can then be recovered and weiged. Any stereoblock polymer remains with the isotactic material.

Properties

Polypropylene is colorless, odorless and is the lightest plastic so far produced (with the exception of course, of foamed or expanded plastics), having a specific gravity of 0.90.

Physical Properties. The physical properties of polypropylene depend mainly on :

(a) Percentage of isotactic material present.
(b) Molecular weight
(c) Crystallinity

Most commercially available polypropylenes have approximately the same isotacticity while the crystallinity of a sample of given isotacticity depends on its thermal history. The main differences between commercial gradeslie, therefore, in their molecular weight. As the polyethylene, this is commonly denoted by the melt flow index. In the case of polypropylene the determination is carried out at 230°C instead of 190°C in order to allow for the higher melting point of polypropylene.

General physical properties are similar to those of high density polyethylene. Properties which are significantly better are hardness (high density polyethylene, 65-70; polypropylene, 75-shore D), and softening point (high density polyethylene, 122-130°C; polypropylene, 140-150°C), while it has a slightly lower mold shrinkage and gives moldings with a higher gloss.

In thin sections, polypropylene has a very high resistance to repeated flexing. It is thus possible to mold articles with built-in hinges. Integrally molded hinges have been produced which have withstood over a million flexes without failure and even at temperature down to -70°C, correctly designed and molded hinges survive over 50,000 flexes while at -30°C the figure would be over 200,000.

The impact strength of polypropylene is lower than that of high-density polyethylene although still adequate for most purposes. The impact strength is affected by temperature and there is some reduction in that of polypropylene at temperature below about 10°C. This reduction in impact strength is much less in the case of rapidly quenched film because of the very find crystalline structure obtained by such treatment. The impact strength at low temperature can be improved by the addition of small quantities of butyl rubber or polyisobutylene although this entails some sacrifise in rigidity and in resistance to high temperature. Another method of achieving higher impact strength at low temperatures is by copolymerisation of polypropylene with other olefins.

The presence of the bulky methyl groups along the polypropylene chain leads to an increased resistance to creep over that displayed by low or high -density polyethylenes. This is particularly noticeable at temperature above 100°C and under high dead weight conditions.

Polypropylene has excellent electrical properties, due to its nonpolar nature, and is similar in this respect to the polyethylenes. The electrical properties are unaffected by isotacticity or molecular weight but may, of course, be influenced by the presence of catalyst residues. The particular advantage of polypropylene for electrical uses lies in the fact that in addition to its excellent electrical properties it has superior thermal and mechanical properties.

Polypropylene is subjected to oxidative degradation at the elevated temperature necessary for processing but the addition of small amounts of an antioxidant is able to stabilize it during processing and at elevated service temperatures. For photo-oxidative degradation, the incorporation of about 2 per cent of finely divided carbon black is satisfactory. Table 9.6. shows the physical properties of a typical polypropylene.

Chemical Properties. The chemical resistance of polypropylene is similar to that of polyethylene although here again it possesses the additional advantage of being usable at higher operating temperature. It has better resistance to oils and greases than has polyethylene and is not subject to environmental stress cracking. The permeability to oxygen, carbon dioxide and water vapor lies somewhare between those of low density and high-

Table 9.6

TYPICAL PROPERTIES OF POLYPROPYLENE

Property	*Test method*	*Units*	*Value*
Specific gravity	–		0.90-0.91
Tensile strength	BS. 2782, Pt.3	lb/in2	4000-5200
Elongation at break	BS. 2782, Pt. 3	%	400-900
Impact strength (Izod) injection molded bar	BS. 2782, Pt. 3	ft lb/in notch	2.5-4.0
Hardness (Shore)	ASTM. D. 1484-57T	D scale	71-75
Softening point (Vicat)	Bs. 2782,Pt.1	°C	150
Power factor (10^6 c/s)	ASTM.D. 150-54.T		2.3×10^{-4}
Dielectric constant (10^6 c/s)	ASTM.D.150-54.T		2.0-2.15
Volume resististvity	ASTM.D.257-54.T	ohm/cm	$0.7\text{-}1.0 \times 10^{16}$

density polyethylene, but it should be noted that biaxial orientation of polypropylene film reduces its permeability.

APPLICATIONS

Polypropylene's interesting combination of properties has led to its use in a wide variety of products. In the field of injection molding it has been used for domestic holloware, chair shells, crates and tote boxes, domestic appliances parts such as washing machine tops, and a wide range of automotive applications. The latter include distributor caps, radiator fans, glove boxes, and accelerator pedals utilising integral hinges. Luggage and a wide range of containers have also been molded with integral hinges.

Talc-filled grades of polypropylene have also found a wide range of uses. In injection molding, talc contents of about 40 per cent give high stiffness moldings for use in industrial and automotive fields. A talc-filled sheet grade has also been developed which reduces heat sag during thermoforming, giving faster cycles with reduced mold shrinkage. Because rigidity is also improved it allows the use of thinner sheet. Talc-filled polypropylene sheet also has attractions as a material from which to make cartons. It can be folded to give a good dead fold and can be handled by high speed carton making machinery. Its advantages over fiberboard include the fact that it is sterilisable, crush-resistant, and stands up to deep freeze conditions and to heating in microwave ovens. As it is waterproof it competes with plastics coated boards but it has the additional advantage that the edge of the material are also completely non-absorbent to liquids. Cartons made from this material can be fitted with tear tapes and can be printed by gravure, litho, and flexographic processes.

Polypropylene is emerging as a competitor in the thin-wall injection molding market to polystyrene. The price gap between the two plastics has narrowed since the large increases in crude oil prices because polypropylene is less vulnerable to increase in feed-stock prices. In addition, polypropylene has performance advantages such as a much higher softening point. Another packaging application is screw on bottle closures where polypropylene's resiliency allows it to be used for linerless closures (with molded in sealing features Fig. 9.9) or closures with snap-in decorative inserts.

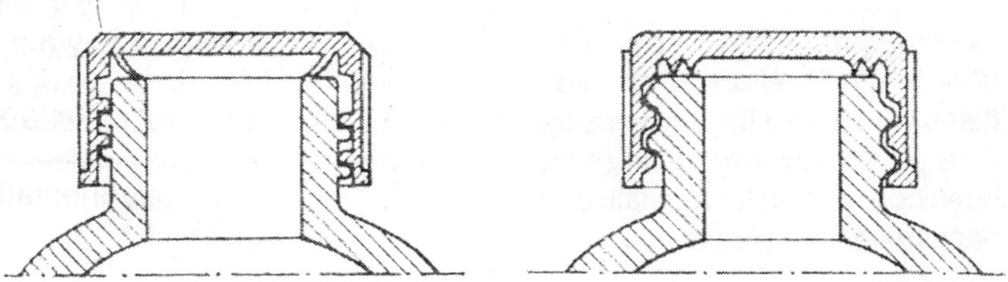

Fig. 9.9 Examples of Polypropylene Linerless Closures

A rather newer and extremely interesting use for polypropylene is an extruded 'corrugated board'. It is not really a competitor with normal corrugated fiberboard but rather with wooden cases and in the development of new packaging systems needing a reusable, high duty medium with easy 'knock-down' properties. It also offers scope in horticulture for the packaing of wet produce straight from the fields.

Polypropylene can be slit-die extruded on to a chilled roller to give film of good clarity, gloss and strength. Its permeability in this from to gases and water vapor is a little higher than that of high density polyethylene acteristics and its impact strength at low temperature.

Cast polypropylene films find their main outlets in textile packaging. These outlets are not major ones and these require the superior properties of oriented polypropylene film (OPP). One of the problems of using OPP as a packaging film is that of heat sealing which causes the film to shrink at the heat seal. One solution to this problem is multi-point heat sealing which uses seal bars having a large number of raised points. The area of heat seal contract is thus extremely small at any point and cooling is rapid. However, the heat seal area is not completely gas or vapor proof. A more widespread solution is to coat the polypropylene film with another polymer of lower melting point and then utilise this coating as the heal seal medium. The polypropylene substrate is not heated sufficiently to cause shrinkage. One advantage of this solution is that the coating can be one which also contributes to the barrier properties of the film. Vinlyidene chloride/vinyl chloride copolymers are widely used for this purpose in the same way that they are used as coatings for regenerated cellulose films (MXXT grades.)

These coated OPP grades are used for wrapping biscuits, where extremely good barrier properties, to water vapor and to oxygen, are necessary. They are also used for the packaging of a wide range of snack items which are similarly sensitive to the pick-up of water vapor and oxygen. One potentially large field of use is cigarette packaging but success has been confined so far to relatively minor brands, running on fairly slow running packaging machinery.

OPP films have been used for shrink wrapping where extra sales appeal is required. They are more expensive than low-density polyethylene films and their use is only justified where greater clarity and sparkle are considered essential. One such field is in the shrink wrapping of collations of cosmetics and toiletry items.

Polypropylene is also used for the overwrapping of single cartons in order to confer protection against water vapor pickup. One of the advantages of OPP film in such applications (compared with regenerated cellulose film) is that the water vapor barrier properties do not depend only on the coating. With moisture proof grades of regenerated cellulose film the barrier properties are often reduced because of damage to the coating at the edges and corners of the carton.

Polypropylene's high softening point and chemical inertness has promoted its use for ducting, tank linings, and piping for chemical plant, especially where these items may be used at elevated temperatures. Extruded sheet can be thermoformed, using suitable equipment. In general, doublesided heating is necessary and the heaters should be of high capacity. Where more complicated structures are required they can be fabricated from sheet by hot gas welding techniques.

Rather more novel markets are likely to develop in thin wall moldings via the solid phase forming techniques, such as stretch forming and solid phase pressure forming, described in Chapter 26. Cycle times are lower than for thermoforming and the clarity is greatly improved. Because of polypropylene is not heated to very high temperatures in these processes the containers so formed are free from odor and taint.

The blow-molding technique is also applicable to polypropylene and bottles with freedom and stress cracking and with good resilience (for squeeze action) have been obtained. Tonnages are unlikely to be large because processing speeds are lower than for other polymers. The use of special copolymer grades and specially developed production techniques can give bottles with good clarity and general performance but they will probably remain more expensive than PVC and the polyethylene.

Polypropylene is used in large quantities in the fields of film tapes and fibers (see Chapter 26.) Woven polypropylene sacks, for example, are used for the packaging of horticultural produce, grain and animal feeding stuffs. Ventilation is important in the case of grain because condensation inside the sack would lead to fermentation of the grain. A woven sack is also necessary because of the practice of sampling the grain, with a probe, through the wall of the sack. Additional applications in tropical countries include the packaging of coffee and sugar, fish, cotton and groundnuts.

Because of the trends towards bulk delivery in countries such as the U.S.A. and the U.K. the market for sacks may remain static but in the developing countries demand is increasing because of new and expensive agricultural products needing efficient protection.

Tufted carpet backing is another large market for polypropylene woven film tapes and a high degree of penetration has been achieved in the American and European tufted carpet industries. This is because woven polypropylene fabrics are much lighter, are not roof and moisture proof and give a higher pile than can be achieved with jute backings. A similar backing is used for needle-punched 'indoor-outdoor' carpeting where the carpet pile is itself made from polypropylene. For this application the polypropylene tapes are fibrillated, then chopped into staple lengths.

Film fibers have been used as a replacement for sisal in agricultural baler twine, packaging twine, and ropes. Polypropylene baler twine is rotproof and waterproof and (when ultra-violet stabilisers are added) has a longer life than sisal twine. Sisal has a slightly greater breaking load than polypropylene but the latter has a much higher strength to weight ratio.

Polypropylene can be extruded and 'cold drawn' to give monofilaments of low density, high tenacity, and good abrasion resistance. Ropes made from polypropylene monofilament have a advantage of floating on water even after prolonged immersion, and they are, of course, rot proof. Polypropylene in fiber from has also found outlets in the field of textiles.

POLY (BUTENE-1)

Butene-1 (butylene) is the next step up from propylene in the olefin family and is polymerised with the aid of Ziegler-type catalysts to give a stereoregular polymer with the basic structure shown below :

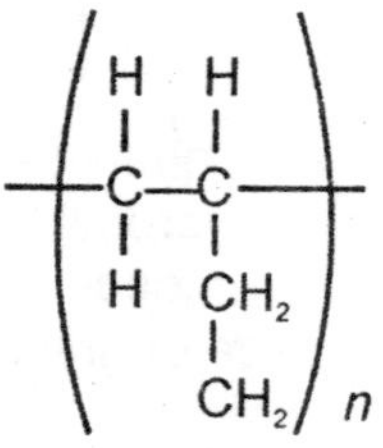

Poly (butene-1) crystallis es from the melt as the tetragonal crystalline Form II and this changes over a period of three to six days to the more stable hexagonal Form I. The change is accompanied by an increase in density, hardness, rigidity, and strength. Crystallinity also increases from around 30 per cent to about 50 per cent.

Poly (butene-1) possesses the flexibility of low-density polyethylene coupled with very low creep properties more characteristics of the engineering thermoplastics. Its tensile yield strength is about 2300 lb/in^2. At stress levels of around 1150 lb/in2., (50 per cent tensile yield stress) the 1000 hour creep figures are only about one per cent at 23°C. At 75 per cent yield stress the 1000 hour creep figure is still only about 6 per cent. AIn some cases poly (butene-1) could be more useful than a higher strength material with poor creep properties. This is particularly true at elevated temperatures where the creep properties of many common thermoplastics fall off rapidly. For example, long term stress tests at 82°C have shown poly (butene-1) pipe to have approximately the same strength at that temperature as low-density polyethylene has at room temperature. The resistance to creep allied with a high resistance to environmental stress cracking makes it a very suitable material for pipes.

Poly (butene-1) can be made into film by blow extrusion or by chill roll casting. The resultant film is tough, with good tear resistance, puncture resistance and impact strength. Its retention of strength at elevated temperatures makes it suitable for hot-fill packaging applications. It is a good water vapor barrier but is not a particularly good barrier to gases. It has been used in the U.S.A. for milk pouches.

POLY (METHYL PENTENE) (TPX)

Methyl pentene polymers are based on 4-methyl pentene-1 as the principal monomer. This is copolymerised with other monomers, using Ziegler type catalysts at atmospheric pressure. Properties distinguishing this polymer from the other polyolefins are transparency (light transmission 90 per cent), high crystalline melting point (240°C) and a low specific gravity (0.83). It also retains useful mechanical properties up to about 205°C. Chemical properties are broadly similar to those of the other polyolefins. Like them it is resistant to acids and alkalis as well as to many solvents. It is softened and swells in contact with hydrocarbons and is subject to environmental stress cracking (like the polyethylenes but unlike polypropylene). Electrical properties are good, in line with other polyolefins, but its permeability to gases and water vapor is much higher.

Polymethylpentene has a wide range of uses, from laboratory and medical ware (syringes, halloware, and connector pieces), lighting diffusers, lenses and reflectors, and packaging (closures and cook-in food container).

10

Polyvinyls

These polymers are members of the very large family generally referred to as vinyls. This name is also used to refer to a broad range of thermoplastics such as polystyrene, but is now normally used, although somewhat loosely, to describe polymers described in this chapter. The vinyl polymer series can be divided into three main groups :

1. Polyvinyl chloride (homopolymer)
2. Vinyl chloride copolymer e.g., with vinyl acetate, vinlyidene chloride, ethylene, and propylene as the comonomers.
3. Polyvinylidene chloride, polyvinyl acetate, polyvinyl alcohol, polyvinyl acetals, and polyvinyl ethers.

Of these polyvinyl chloride, vinyl chloride/vinyl acetate and vinyl chloride/vinylidene chloride copolymers are the most important and are described in more detail than any of the others.

The existence of the monomer vinyl chloride was reported as early as 1838 when it was presumbly first synthesised by a French chemist, Reganault, from ethylene dichloride. The ability of this monomer to polymerise was not known at that time although Regnault did report that a white substance was formed when the monomer was sealed in a tube and exposed to sunlight. This effect of sunlight on vinyl chloride was later investigated by Baumann, in 1872, who observed that a tough white substance formed as a result. Very little significant advance was then made in this field until 1912 when the Russian chemist, Ostromislensky, reported that sunlight catalysed the polymerisation of vinyl halides to yield resinous products. About the same period a patent was granted in Germany for the manufacture of vinyl chloride by reacting hydrogen chloride gas with acetylene at 180°C in the presence of metal chloride as the catalysts. This period is regarded by many as being the birth of polyvinyl chloride although its beginnings as a technically useful product stemmed from the patent disclosures of Semon of the B.F. Goodrich Company in 1933 and Ried of Carbide and Carbon Chemicals in 1934.

Considerable development work was carried out on the preparation of the chemistry for vinyl derivatives and the decade preceding World War II brought about a technological break through. This was achieved in Germany by the I.G. Farben Company, who developed a process for the handling of high pressure acetylene. The work was directed by Dr. J.w. Reppe and his work was recognised as leading to the development of many new vinyl polymers. Many of the major vinyl polymers can be classified as originating from acetylene, including poly vinyl chloride, poly vinyl acetate, poly vinyl acetals, and the poly vinyl ethers. The latter materials were developed in the U.S.A. in 1948, although they have not reached the major tonnages consumed as some of the other vinyl polymers.

The main disadvantages of these polymers prior to the 1930's were their insolubility in common solvents, but when it was later discovered that it was possible to dissolve them in high boiling solvents such as tritolyl phosphate (then known as tricresyl phosphate) many new applications were opened up. By the start of WW II, the significance of plasticising PVC was fully realised, as well as the need for considerably more development work if the polymer was to become commercially important. It was during the war that the real importance of this polymer became obvious when, due to the acute shortage of rubber, many companies began to look for a substitute. They found that plasticised PVC was suitable for many of the applications that hitherto had been restricted to rubber, including cable insulation and sheathing. After the war many countries returned to using rubbers but may still continued to use PVC and today this polymer is one of the leading thermoplastics.

RAW MATERIALS

Vinyl Chloride

There are basically two sources of vinyl chloride monomer depending on whether acetylene or natural gas is readily available. The PVC produced in Europe has been largely on acetylene obtained from calcium carbide, and in the U.S.A. from ethylene. At the present time, however, the ethylene route is becoming increasingly important due to the widespread growth of the petrochemical industry. The basic ethylene is, of course, obtained by cracking oil, and the two main routes being represented as follows :

(i) *Direct Addition.* The first method is the direct addition of hydrogen chloride to acetylene using a catalyst such as mercuric chloride.

$$CH{\equiv}CH + HCl \rightarrow CH_2{=}CHCl$$

(ii) *Chlorination of Ethylene.* This method involves the chlorination of ethylene which is then followed by abstraction of hydrogen chloride as follows.

$$CH_2{=}CH_2 + Cl_2 \rightarrow \underset{\text{Dichloroethane}}{CH_2Cl{-}CH_2Cl} \xrightarrow{HCl} CH_2{=}CHCl{+}HCl$$

The dichloroethane is first purified and dried, then it is led through the tubes of a pyrolysis furnace where it is cracked to give hydrogen chloride and vinyl chloride. The reaction mixture at this stage also contains some unconverted dichloroethane, which is therefore led to an absorber where the vinyl chloride and dichloroethane are separated from the hydrogen chloride and the vinyl chloride is separated from the dichloroethane by distillation.

Vinylidene Chloride. This monomer may be prepared by chlorinating ethylene to give 1,1,2, trichloroethane which is, in turn, pyrolysed to dichloroethane. The required monomer 1,1 dichloroethane ($CH_2{=}CCl_2$ boiling point 31.7OC) is separated from the cis and trans 1,2 isomers.

$$CH_2{=}CH_2 + Cl_2 \rightarrow \underset{+\,HCl}{CH_2Cl{-}CHCl_2} \xrightarrow{CaO} CH_2{=}CCl_2{+}CaCl_2{+}H_2O$$

Vinyl Acetate. The monomer is normally prepared commercially by the liquid or gaseous state reaction of acetic acid and acetylene. Mercuric sulfate is used as a catalyst in conjunction with lot dilute sulfuric acid, which hydrates acetylene to form acetaldehyde. The intermediate in this reaction is the unstable vinyl alcohol which readily isomerizes to the aldehyde.

$$CH_3COOH + CH \equiv CH \rightarrow CH_2 = CHOCOCH_3$$

VINYL ALCOHOL

This monomer does not exist as such and is tautomer of acetaldehyde with the equilibrium in favour of the acetaldehyde. Therefore polyvinyl alcohol is prepared by the hydrolysis of polyvinyl acetate. Polymers prepared by such techniques are high molecular weight resins containing varying percentage of hydroxyl and acetate groups.

$$-CH_2-\underset{OH}{\underset{|}{CH}}-CH_2-\underset{OH}{\underset{|}{CH}}-CH_2-\underset{OHC}{\underset{|}{CH}}-$$

Process used involve alcoholysis in methanol or ethanol using an acid (e.g. sulfuric acid) or alkaline (e.g. sodium methoxide) catalyst.

Poly vinyl alcohols are usually classified as partially hydrolysed (15-30 per cent poly vinyl acetate groups) and completely hydrolyzed (0-5 per cent acetate groups).

Vinyl Acetals

Acetals are formed by the well known classical reaction between aldehydes and alcohols. The addition reaction of one molecules of an alcohols with one molecules of an aldehyde produces what can be regarded as a 'half acetal'. These are rarely isolated because of their inherent instability. They are therefore reacted with another molecule of alcohol to form a stable acetal.

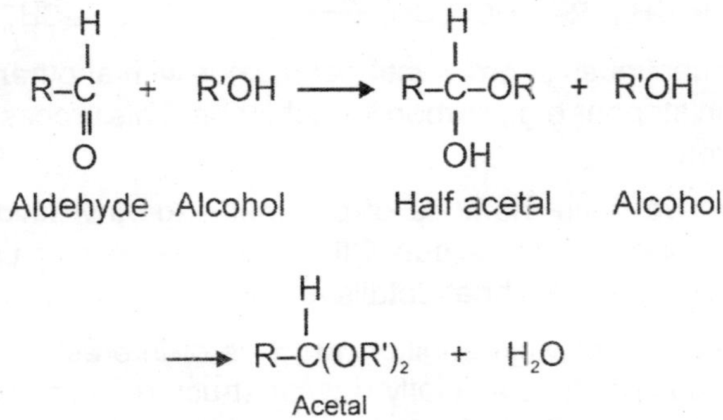

The overall reaction of one molecule of aldehyde and two molecules of alcohol can be illustrated as follows :

$$\underset{\text{Aldehyde}}{RCHO} + \underset{\text{Alcohol}}{2R'OH} \longrightarrow \underset{\text{Acetal}}{R\text{–}CH\text{–}(OR')_2} + H_2O$$

Vinyl Ethers

Two methods have been used for the commercial synthesis of vinyl ethers.

(1) The pyrolysis of the corresponding acetal.

$$CH_3\text{–}CH(OR)_2 \longrightarrow CH2{=}CHOR + ROH$$

(2) Direct vinylation of the alcohol with acetylene.

$$HC{\equiv}CH + ROH \xrightarrow{KOH} CH{=}CHOR$$

The latter process which can be regarded as a vinylation process probably offers what must be regarded as the easiest the most economical approach.

Typical and reaction conditions are

Temperature : 130-170°C
Catalyst : 1-3 per cent potassium hydroxide (the potassium alcoholate is thus formed *in situ*)

Acetylation Pressure : 100-150 psi (reduced with nitrogen)
Yield : 90-98 per cent

Polymerisation: The polymerisation of vinyl chloride monomer is carried out by a free radical process, the free redicals being provided by the decomposition of an initiator.

$$R + CH_2Cl{=}CH_2 \rightarrow \underset{R—R' \rightarrow}{R—CHCl—CH_2} \xrightarrow{VC} \underset{R—R'}{R—CHCl—CH_2–CHCl—CH_2}$$

The chain continues to grow until it combines with another free radical such as a chain stopper,e.g., carbon tetrachloride. This process is referred to as termination.

There are two main methods of polymerising vinyl chloride; by an emulsion or a suspension technique. Other methods are also used but only on a very small scale. Only brief details are given.

Another process of vinyl addition which is of interest is that of ionic catalysis. This can produce spatially regular structures in polymer chains. In this technique the vinyl bond is activated either as a carbonium ion, i.e. by cationic Friedel Crafts acid catalyst or as a carbonium ion , i.e., ionic basic catalysts. Both Professors Ziegler and Natta found that certain heterogenous catalyst system e.g., titanium tetrachloride plus aluminium triethyl are particularly useful for the production of stereo regular polymers.

Suspension Polymerisation. This method is undoubtedly the predominant process for the preparation of PVC in the world today. It consists essentially of suspending the monomer in water to form droplets, this state being maintained by a suspension agent such as gelatin, ethyl, or methyl cellulose and polyvinyl alcohol. The suspending medium of water helps in controlling the heat formed during the polymerisation reaction. A wetting agent such as sulfonated castor oil is also used and the free radical polymerisation is initiated by an oil soluble/water insoluble type catalyst such as benzoyl or leuroyl peroxide. Strong agitation is necessary to keep the reactants in suspension, and polymerisation occurs in each individual monomer droplet. The speed of stirring is a very important factor and controls the size of the particles; the greater the speed of stirring the smaller the particle size and vice versa. The polymerisation is carried out by a predetermined time, normally between 12 and 24 hours, and on completion of the reaction the polymer is in the form of a slurry. The slurry is then passed to a stripping tank to remove any unreacted vinyl chloride, filtered, and finally dried. Normal methods of drying are to pass and material through a heated continuous rotary drier and then finally flash-dried.

Emulsion Polymerisation. As with the suspension process this technique uses water as a suspending medium to control the heat produced during the polymerisation reaction. The actual mechanism is different and produces polymers with completely different properties. The monomer is first emulsified with a fatty acid or a cationic soap and the initiation is carried out with inorganic materials such as potassium and ammonium persulfate or hydrogen peroxide. In contrast to the previous suspension methods these initiators are soluble in the water phase. The vinyl chloride diffuses through the water layer to the emulsifier micelles, thereby acting as the muclei for polymerisation. This process also requires the use of protective colloids such as carboxyl methyl cellulose. On completion of the polymerisation the emulsion is either spray-dried or coagulated by adding an electrolyte, then filtered and finally flash dried. Various washing process are necessary for the removal of the soap if polymers of high purity are to be obtained.

Bulk Polymerisation. This is not very satisfactory method of polymerisation and produced polymers of low molecular weight. A commercial method, however, involves the liquifying of the monomer, then dissolving the initiator into the monomer and finally polymerising. The polymer so formed in insoluble in the monomer and is therefore precipitated as it is formed, to give low molecular weight polymers. The final stage therefore the monomer phase. The polymers produced by this method have excellent purity with good clarity although they have poor mechanical strength. This, coupled with the problem of heat dissipation makes the method unattractive.

Solution Polymerisation. Modification have been made to the bulk polymerisation technique, one method being to add solvents, such as acetone, during the polymerisation. This gives the finished polymer a higher molecular weight. The process requires the use of chain stoppers which somewhat limits the choice of the solvent, and since the process is a hazardous one it is seldom used.

Vinyl Acetate

The polymerisation of this monomer also takes place by the free-radical addition reaction described previously. The free radicals are generated by the decomposition of organic peoxides such as benzoyl peroxide or inorganic salts such as potassium or amonium persulfate. Conventional methods of suspension, emulsion, bulk, and solution are used. This monomer also copolymerises with vinyl chloride, vinylidene chloride, alkyl maleates, and fumarates. There are many other comonomers too numerous to name. A relatively new development has been in the copolymerisation of vinyl acetate with ethylene. These are either emulsions or solid polymers and are described in Chapter 9.

Vinyl Acetals

Polyvinyl acetals are prepared from aldehydes and polyvinyl alcohols. It has been stated that there are two basic types of oplyvinyl alcohols, (15-30 per cent and 0-5 per cent acetate groups) and both types in various molecular weights are used in preducing commercial polyvinyl acetals.

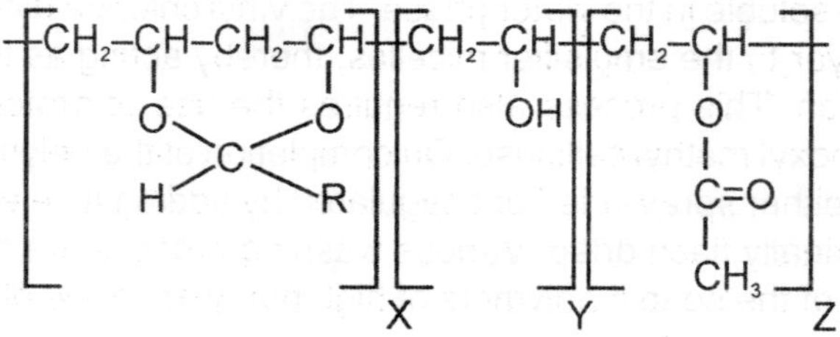

PV Acetal PV Alcohol PV Acetate

The conditions for the acetal reaction and the concentration of the particular aldehyde and polyvinyl alcohol used are closely controlled to yield polymers containing predetermined proportions of hydroxyl acetate and acetal groups. The end product may be shown by the following schematic structure.

The X, Y and Z segments are distributed randomly along the molecule backbone. The polyvinyl acetal is a cyclic acetal because the hydroxyl groups are attached to the same chain. It may also be cross-linded by heating or with a trace of mineral acid. It seems in general, that cross-linking takes place by transcetalisation but it may involve more complex reactions such as that between the acetate or hydroxyl groups on adjacent chains.

Vinyl Ethers

Vinly Ethers polymers can be produced from this monomer by free radical processes, however, only very low molecular weight products are obtained. Acid type catalysts have been found to yield low to high molecular weight polymers, the low temperatures tending to favour higher molecular weights. Catalysts which have been reported as being suitable are BF3 (hydrate or etherate) Sn Cl_4, Fe Cl_3, Al Cl_3, SO_2, and iodine.

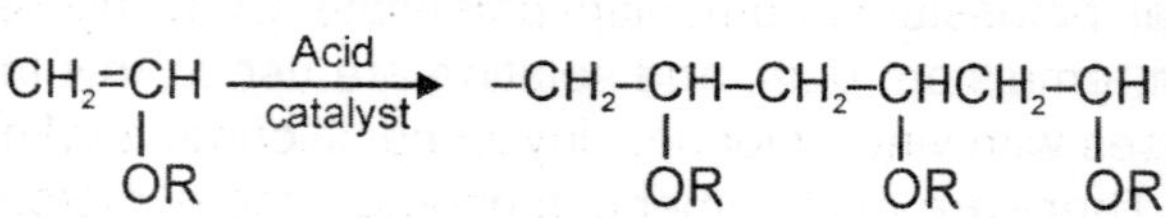

Low and medium viscosity polyuvinyl ethers are obtained by a bulk technique at 0°-10°C by dropwise addition of the monomer and catalyst to a brine cooled, stirred reactor. The reaction is rapid and exothermic and therefore the rate of monomer addition must be carefully controlled.

High viscosity grades have been prepared of polyvinyl isobutyl ether at much lower temperatures, e.g., -50°C . A low bonding solvent such as propane can be used to control the exotherm.

Propylene-Vinyl Chloride

Compositions containing two to ten per cent by weight of propylene are made by copolymerisation of propylene with vinly chloride. The structure of this copolymer is

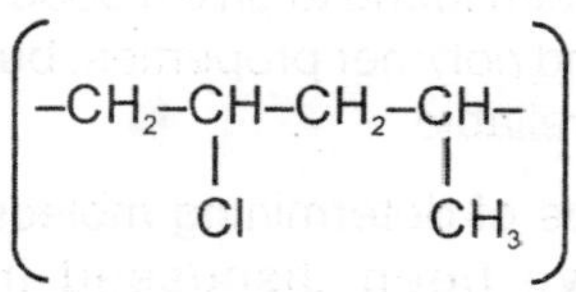

The introduction of stable hydrocarbon structure into the vinyl chloride chain results in an increased resistance to thermal degradation and reduction in dehydrochlorination.

MANUFACTURE OF VINYL CHLORIDE/VINYL ACETATE AND VINYLIDENE CHLORIDE COPOLYMERS

These copolymers are usually manufactured with a vinyl acetate content between 3-30 per cent, using solution techniques. The correct choice of solvent for the monomer and catalyst allows the copolymer to precipitate as soon as the required molecular weight is reached. Polymerisation is normally carried out between 30-40°C wigh vegorous stirring for about 48 hours or more. For paint applications these copolymers may be further modified by the addition of maleic anhydride and /or by partial hydrolysis of some of the acetate groups. It has been established that both these additional processes improve adhesion and reactivity and at the same time also give an increase in water resistance. The copolymerisation with vinyl acetate or other such similar comonomer serves to reduce the fusion temperature and can be regarded as internal plasticising.

Vinylidene chloride polymerises more readily than vinyl chloride, which makes it somewhat more difficult to obtain homogenous polymers. Strict control is therefore essential during polymerisation, by the addition of further vinylidene chloride and-or the removal of vinyl chloride.

CLASSIFICATION OF PVC POLYMERS

Various methods are used in classfying thermoplastics and with those containing a high proportion of crystallinity such as polyethylene; it has been relatively simple to carry out such a classification by molten viscosity measurements (MFI). This is, of course, related to the molecular weight and density of the polyolefin. PVC and its copolymers are almost amorphous, therefore density does not have the same significance, hence molecular weight measurements have been used to classify the polymers. The viscosity of PVC at high temperatures is considerably higher than that of the polyolefins and therefore measurement is somewhat more difficult. Other alternative methods of measurement have been investigated and those based on solvent solution techniques have been found the most reliable. Such results have also been found to give a good indication of the molecular weight and of ultimate end polymer properties, but unfortunately processing properties tend to be unreliable.

The various methods of determining molecular weights on a solution viscosity method have been discussed in Chapter 1. Viscosity measurements are used to classify PVC by what is termed the 'K' value, which is obtained directly from viscosity measurements of a solution of the polymer in a solvent such as cyclohexanone or ethylene dichloride (concentration normally 1g/100 ml of solvent). The K value can then be calculated from the equation developed by Fikentscher (Ref: Cellulose Chem. 13.60.(1932)) as follows:

$$\frac{\log n_r}{c} = \frac{75k}{1 + 1.5kc} + k \qquad (1)$$

where N_r is the relative viscosity and C the concentration (g/100ml).

From equation (1) we obtain

$$K=1000k \qquad (2)$$

The actual K value is not dependent on concentration but on the solvent, and the measurement in cyclohexanone is some 4 units higher than if measured in ethylene dichloride.

STRUCTURE OF PVC

The structure of the vinyl chloride polymers is different from that of the polyolefins in that it is substantially amorphous and does not readily crystallise, a fact which is confirmed by X-rays. The basic structure is as follows:

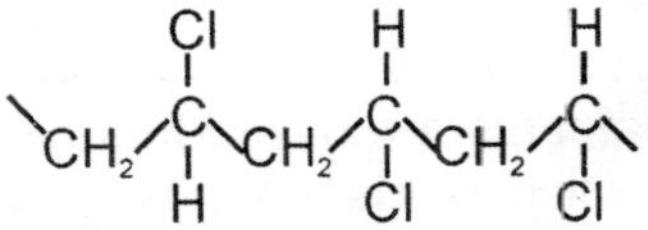

It can be seen that the bulky chlorine atoms are on alternate sides of the chains and the units are repeated in a head-to-tail arrangement. There are strong cohesive forces present in PVC due largely to strong dipole moments caused by the chlorine atoms. Such polarity causes incompatibility with nonpolar hydrocarbons and thus PVC is resistant to petrol and mineral oils although it has the effect of making the polymer suloble in strong polar solvents (e.g. ketones and chlorinated hydrocarbons).

It is also interesting to consider the structure of PVC when heated to 80°C and above. Heating not only produces a structural change but also a series of color changes, from light yellow, through dark yellow, orange and, ultimately, to reddish brown and even black. The release of HCl during this reaction suggests that defradation has resulted, yielding the following possible polynene structure:

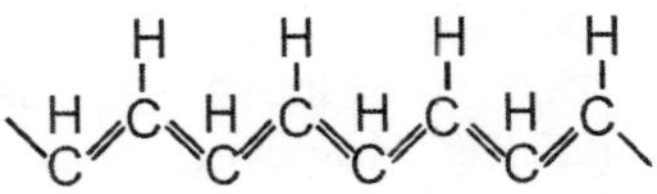

The presence of this unsaturated structure has been confirmed by absorption studies and is indicative of color formation.

PROCESSING

In view of the scope of this book and the wider variations of processing for PVC, only this homopolymer and its related copolymers are discussed in any detail.

In general, most thermoplastics are delivered in a form suitable for processing by the many techniques described later in the book. This is not so with PVC which is in a form which usually requires compounding by the processor. Compounding is necessary because of the relatively low thermal stability and high melt viscosity of this material. By correct choice of compounding additives it is found that processing is made easier and, in some instances, the cost of the compound can be reduced. In general, the compounding techniques can be classified according to whether the polymer is plasticised or not. Polyvinyl compounds mormally contain the base polymer together with stabiliser, lubricant, filler, and pigments and in the plasticised type, plasticiser is, of course, added.

METHODS OF COMPOUNDING

The fact that it is necessary to add such additives makes it imperative to ensure that these materials are mixed thoroughly. The initial mixing is done in a simple mixer which exerts a low friction action opn the mass. the most homogenous compounds is obtained if the dry materials, e.g., base polymer, stabiliser, lubricant are mixed first and the liquid ingredients added as required, e.g., plasticisers. Extenders may be added when all the dry materials are fully despersed, and at this stage the compound is referred to as a premix and may also be prepared on machinery which exerts a high friction action on the mass. The next stage is to flux the PVC either in a two-roll mill or by an internal mixer technique (e.g., Banbury). This process serves to gel and homogenise the compound which is then either charged on to a mill where it is sheeted, cooled and chipped ready for feeding into conventional fabricating equipment, or fed directly to a mill and transferred as a hot strip to the calender.

The premix may also be fed directly into a continuous mixer/extruder, and such machines are suitable where long runs of specific compounds are required. The extruders used for this purpose are single or double screw although the extruding action is usually modified to improve missing efficiency. Temperatures required for these methods depend to a large extent on the compound formulations. However, for most purposes a Banbury temperature of 130-150°C and a mill temperature of 125-150°C suffice.

In contrast to these compunding methods, which depend upon dispersion and gelation of the various compounding ingredients, there is another method based on mixing the compounding ingredients to yields a free-flowing powder.

The process consists of blending the dry ingredients, i.e. polymer, stabiliser, and lubricant in the cold for a few minutes, then adding the liquid components by spraying them on the agitated dry blend in a jacketed, steam-heated mixer. Heating is applied until the temperature reaches 1100°C, at which its maintained for a few minutes, then the mass is cooled to 50°C, discharged from the mix, and finally sieved to remove any agglomerated particles that may have occurred. This final compound is then referred to as a dry-blend powder.

The use of compounding extruders is now generally preferred for pounding riged vinyl formulations. The absence of plasticiser also leads to the absence of difficulties in the feeding of the extruders. The process of compounding PVC is regarded as an art in itself and many tailor-made formulations can complicate the choice of a particular compound for a specific application. Table 10.1 gives formulations that can be used to give a

Table 10.1

TYPICAL PVC FORMULATIONS

End-use	*Designed properties*	*Polymer (parts)*	*Plasticiser (parts)*	*Stabiliser (parts)*	*Lubricant (parts)*	*Filler (parts)*	*Pigment (parts)*
Wire insulation	Flame resistant, flexible, insulator with good aging properties	100 (suspension) electrical grade	40 dioctylphthalate 20 tritolyphosphate	6 lead carbonate or tribasic sulfate	1 calcium stearate	15 china clay	1-2 as required
Floor tile	Good abrasion resistance, low creep, low cost	Copolymer v.c./v.a. 100	20 dialphanol phthalate 5 polymeric plasticiser	2 lead carbonate 6 lead salicylate	1 lead stearate	100 asbestos 250 calcium carbonate also 10 chlorinated paraffin wax	10 titanium dioxised
Calendering	Rapid gelling	100 (emulsion)	45 dialphanol phthalate	1 organo tin stabliser	1 lead stearate	–	1 as required
Rigid transparent sheet	Easy processing polymer	100	–	2 dibutyl tin mercaptide	1 calcium stearate	–	–
Gramophone records		Copolymer 100 v.c./v.a.	–	–	1½ lead stearate	–	1½ carbon black
Extruded hose	Stable, fairly stiff mix	100	45 dialphanol phthalate	7 lead carbonate	1 calcium stearate	30 china clay, 20 chlorinated paraffin wax	
Mine belting	(Flame resistant-antiomony compounds added to improve this characteristic)	100 (suspension)	35 tritolyphosphate 20 dioctylphthalate 5 dioctyl sebacate	9 barium ricinoleate, 1 cadmium laurate, 1 calcium stearate		10 calcium carbonate 5 antimony oxide	5 carbon black
Nontoxic application		100	40 dioctyl phthalate	2 diphenyl urea	2 calcium stearate		

(N.B. These formulations are given only as a guide and it does not follow that they are used on a commercial basis.)

suggested end-product; two main factors to be borne in mind when making a choice are desired properties and cost. It must be noted than when processing the copolymers, lower temperatures are generally used.

CALENDERING

Of all the processing methods associated with PVC, calendering is probably the most widely used. Products obtained from calendering include unsupported film and sheet, coated fabric and paper, and flooring. This process is described in detail elsewhere in the book: it consists basically of passing the material between two or more pairs of rotation rolls, each pair of rolls forming a nip through which the material is drawn or extruded.

The calendering process may be considered as a combined forming and finishing operation, the physical properties of the finished product depending on the processing temperature, which can vary considerably, depending upon the nature of the base polymer, and may range from 130-200°C. A final press polishing at higher temperatures than these would improve the clarity of the sheet and the gloss, and increase the tensile strength.

The calender generally used for PVC is invariably a four-roll machine, the rollers, or bowl as they are more often called, arranged in the form of an inverted L or having a Z-type arrangement. Calenders used for producing floor tiles, etc., normally consist of two rolls in a I shape, used either singly or in series. The actual thickness of the end-product is largely governed by the gap between the bowls, which is referred to as the nip.

Plasticised film formulations are normally based on PVC grades of medium to high K values. For thicker plasticised sheeting and even for rigid sheet it is normal to use lower K values or even vinly choloride/vinyl acetate copolymers. Another point to note is that with rigid sheet, higher calendering temperatures are required than used for plasticised polymers. Mass temperatures above 200°C have been reported. The thickness of the sheet obtained by calendering is from 4-24 mil (0.1 to 0.6mm). Sheet with thickness of over 40 mil (1 mm) is obtained by laminating the calendered sheet. By the extrusion method, either flat sheet is extruded directly from sheet. A schematic diagram of the producation of riged PVC is given in Fig. 10.1.

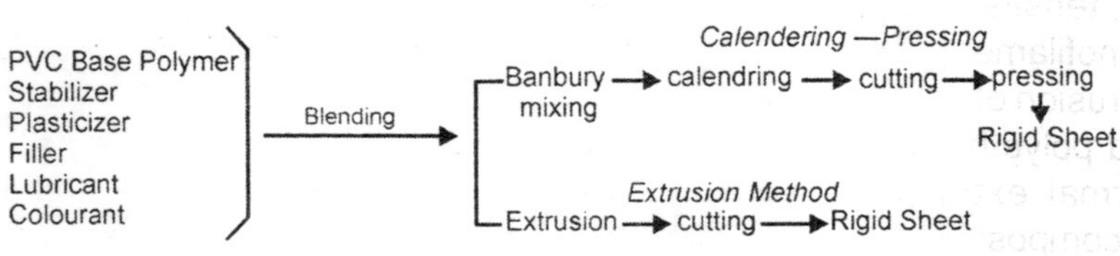

Fig. 10.1 Production of rigid PVC sheet

For coating fabrics it is first necessary to preheat the fabric immediately before it enters the nip to ensure that it is approximately the same temperature as the stock of the calender. The actual coating process can be carried out by one of two methods: the fabric can either be fed through the final nip of a four-roll calender or post-calendered by passing the calendered film and fabric through a further pair of rolls for subsequent lamination. A precaution that must be observed with paper coating is that of drying the paper stock 24 hours befere coating.

For the production of PVC flooring, the following sequence of processes is used: internal mixing, milling on a two-roll mill, calendering, and finally pressing to give a product which can be sold either in continuous form or as individual tiles.

EXTRUSION

This proces is second in importance to calendering and consists of forcing the uniformly heated and softened compound through a die and then cooling it. Both rigid and flexible sections can be extruded to give the following applications: pipe, tube (hose), rod, and profile extrusion; cable and wire covering; film and bottle blowing; sheet and filament.

Suitably plasticised PVC compounds can be processed readily on single or double-screw extruders using either the granulate or dry-blend materials discussed earlier. The actual extrudate is normally cooled by passing through a water trough, when it is finally wound on to rollers. Plasticised extrusion is used to produce garden hose, certain profiles and cable covering.

PVC film and sheet are uusally manufactured by the calendering process, therefore the film-blowing technique is used only when a seamless bag is requered for such applications as packaging. As yet the process is not often used for processing the homopolymer but it is used extensively for producing film from polyvinyl chloride/vinylidene chloride copolymers. Film in tubular form is obtained from the extruder, quenched below 20°C to an amorphous condition, and then biaxially stretched by air inflation at 20-25°C. During this orientation process crystallinity is induced and as a result the tensile strength and solvent resistance of the film is increased. Monofilament can also be produced by similar extrusion techniques. The extrusion of rigid PVC is somewhat more difficult than with plasticised PVC and polyethylene. This is due largely to the high viscosities obtained at normal extrusion speeds, leading to difficulties in homogenisation. Decomposition tends to take place and it therefore is essential to use a powerful stabilising system. Despite such difficulties unplasticised polymer is extruded to form rigid pipes suitable for use in electrical conduit, chemical plant, and for the transportation or disposal of water, gas, and sewage. Formulations suitable for extrusion of these pipes are as follows:

1.	PVC Polymer	100 parts
	Dibasic lead stearate	2 parts
	Dibasic lead phosphite	1/2 part
	Stearic acid	1/2-1 part
2.	PVC polymer	100 parts
	Tribasic lead sulfate	5 parts
	Lead stearate	2 parts
	Steraric acid	1/2-1 part

It is generally recommended that the exact amount of lubricant, i.e., stearic acid in these formulations should be determined experimentally for the particular equipment to be used.

There are two general methods of processing open to the manufacturers of rigid PVC pipe: direct extrusion from a powder premix, or a two-stage process whereby partial precompounding and pregelling precedes extrusion. The above formulations can be used as powder premix, or a two-stage process whereby partial precompounding and pregelling precedes extrusion. The above formulations can be used as powder premix for the production of pipe for nincritical applications such as electrical conduit, in a twin or single-screw extrudcer with a high length/diameter ratio, preferably 20:1. However, in order to obtain higher thrughout of pipes with optimum physical properties, the two-stage process involving partial precom pounding and pregelling is preferred by many processors. It must be poined out, however, that it is now also possible to use powder premixes to produce pipes. The extrusion of rigid vinyl sheet is complicated still further by difficulties in die design, which, however, have been largely overcome by using fishtail dies. For best results it has been found necessary to use screws of the long compression type, i.e., about two-thirds of the total effective length. This is in contrast to the polylefins which require screws of the short compression type.

The blow-extrusion of rigid PVC to form bottles and similar containers is becoming increasingly important. With the plasticised compounds very little difficulty is experienced and nearly all compounds can be blown into containers of one form or another. Higher temperatures are, of course, essential with rigid PVC and articles can be blown by either extrusion/blowing or injection blowing techniques; another technique which has certain advantages is the preformed parsion.

INJECTION MOLDING

Plasticised compounds can be injection molded without any difficulty on conventional ram-type machines. Temperatures in a range of 150-170°C are normally employed and, provided the compound is adequately stabilised, good quality moldings can be obtained. Difficulties are experienced with rigid PVC due to the base polymer softening over this very wide temperature range, and it does not obtain a very flowable state until heated to a temperature somewhere in the region of 190°C. Even at this temperature it is stable only for a short time and decomposes rapidly if heated to too high a temperature for too tong a period. These conditions must be avoided if production runs are to be successful . Injection machines providing pressures around 20,000 lb/in.^{2} are normally quite adequate for most thermoplastics but due to the high melt viscosity of the rigid PVC, machines capable of providing pressures of 30,000 lb/in^2. are necessary. Suspension polymers with a lower K value are usually preferred for injection molding because they can be processed at slightly lower temperatures, whereas emulsion polymers stabilised with conventional materials degrade far too early. By using injection machines with a screw preplasticiser instead of the ram, it is possible to obtain more uniform frictional heat. Lower injection pressures can then be used with polymers of normal K value. High plasticised PVC compounds suitable for footwear can be procesed by extrusion-injection molding techniques in which injection pressure is developed by rotation of a screw rather than by a reciprocating action. This permits low injection pressures and the use of light alloy molds which are cheap in comparison to converntional molds.

COMPRESSION MOLDING

This process, although more commonly associated with thermosetting polymers can be used also for PVC. The process, of course suffers from the fact that the mold requires cooling to a temperature that allows the molding to be rigid enough to remove. The technique, nevertheless, is of great importance in the production of gramophone records from vinlyl chloride/ vinyl acetate copolymers. It is also used to a small extent in the production of floor tiles but the extrusion process is generally preferred.

PROPERTIES

The base polymer is a white granular material with a denisty of 1.4 containing approximately 56 per cent chlorine. The range of physical properties for the homoplymers and copolymers are given in Table 10.2. Its properties depend on molecular weight, the lower molecular weight polymers being soluble in a wide range of solvents, while the higher molecular weight

Table 10.2

TYPICAL PROPERTIES OF PVC AND COPOLYMERS

Property	*Flexible*		*Rigid*	
	General purpose	*Electrical*	*Normal impact*	*High impact*
Physical				
Specific gravity	1.2–1.6	1.2-1.6	1.4-1.6	1.3-1.4
Tensile strength (lb/in^2)	1500-3000	1500-3000	6500	9000
Elongation at break (%)	100-500	100-500	25	35
Compression strength (lb/in.^{2})	1250	1250	10,000	5-9000
Shore hardness	A50-95	A60-95	D75-85	D75-80
Specific heat (cal/cm)	0.3	0.4	0.25	0.25
Coefficient of linear expansion (°C X 10^{-5})	1	1	5	5
Maximum operating temperature (°C)	54-80	80-104	70	65-70
Water absorption (24 h%)	0.25	0.5-1	0.1-0.4	0.05-0.2
Flammability	← Self-extinguishing →			
Electrical				
Volume resistivity ohm/cm	10^{11}-10^{13}	10^{11}-10^{14}	10^{12}-10^{16}	10^{12}-10^{14}
Power factor (60 c/s)	0.08-0.15	0.08-0.15	0.02	0.03
Chemical				
Effect of weak acids	← Resistant →			
strong acids	← Resistant →			
weak alkalis	← Resistant →			
strong alkalis	← Resistant →			
solvents	Resistant to alcohols, aliphatic hydrocarbons, and mineral oils, soluble in ketones, esters, and to a certain degree automatic hydrocarbons and chlorinated hydrocarbons			

materials are insolube. The following indicates the effect of molecular wieght on end-uses.

Molecular weight	*End uses*
9,000	Surface Coatings
10,000	Calendering, coatings
12,500	Compression molding
21,000	Cable sheathing
22,000	Textile fibers

The high chlorine content of the base polymer accounts for the polar nature of PVC which makes it resistant to petrol and mineral oils, and on the other hand, soluble in solvents such as acetone and chlorinated hydrocarbon. PVC is also resistant to most acids and alkalis, and the high cholorine content also confers on it a high degee of flame-resistance.

Polyvinyl acetate

These resins are normally supplied as thermoplastic solids or aqueous emulsions at solids content around 50 per cent. The solid resins are odorless, tasteless, nontoxic, essentiallly clear, and colorless. The emulsions have a tendency to smell of the characteristic odor of the free unpolymerised monomer. Most grades of these resins have a somewhat broad molecular weight distribution. They do not possess a sharp melting point and soften over a relatively wide temperature range. These resins are neutral and non-corrosive, unaffected by sunlight, ultraviolet, and air. The various grades have good heat stability up to 100°C but at 150°C slight discoloration occurs and at 200-250°C decomposition takes place. It will burn slowly and soften at 50°C. They can be dissolved in acetone, methyl ethyl ketone, ethyl acetate, etc. and may be plasticised with a wide variety of plasticisers including the phthalates.

The chemical properties and reaction of polyvinyl acetate are those typical of stable esters. Some of the properties of polyninyl acetate are listed in Table 10.3.

Table 10.3

PHYSICAL PROPERTIES OF POLYVINYL ACETATE

Density, at 20°C	1.19 g/ml
Refractive index, at 20°C	1.466
Water absorption	2%
Thermal coefficient of linear expansion	8.6 X 10^{-5} per °C
Thermal conductivity	38 X 10^{-5}
Specific heat	0.39 cal/g/°C
Dipole moment	1.85 Debye units
Dielectric strength at 30°C	1000 v/mil

Polyninyl Alcohol

The properties iof aqueous solutions of this polymer vary with the per cent hydrolysis and the molecular weight of the intermediate polyvinyl acetate resin. Low molecular weight, low (70-80) per cent hydrolysed grades dissolve rapidly in water at room temperature. High molecular weight, high (95-100) per cent hydrolysed grades are best dissolved by dispersing in cold water and heating to 85-90°C in the stirring.

The arrangement of hydroxyl groups is predominantly 1,3 glycol units and the possibilities for hydrogen bonding in solution and film form leads to a high degree of versatility. It has been seen that one of the most useful reactions of polyvinly alcohol is the condensation with aldehydes to form acetal resins. They may be unsolubilised by reacting with formalehyde, forfural and certain amino resins. Plasticisation is pollibel by adding glycerol, glycols, and sorbitol.

Table 10.4 lists some typical properties of polyvinyl alcohol.

Table 10.4

PHYSICAL PROPERTIES OF POLYVINYL ALCOHOL

Physical form	Write to light straw granular powder
Specific gravity	1.19-1.27
Bulk density	30-40 lb/ft^3
Refractive index, ^{n}D, 25°C	1.51
Tensile strength, 50% relative humidity	to 22,000 psi
Elongation, 50% relative humidity	to 300% unplasticised; to 600 plasticised
Thermal coefficient of linear expansion	1 X 10-4/°C, at 0-50°C plasticised
I.C.I. Sward hardness	27-57% vs glass at 50% relative humidity
Heat sealing temperature	110-150°C
Heat stability	Darkening, slow degradation >100°C, Rapid degradation, decomposition >200°C
Effect of light	Negligible
Burning rate	Slow
Gas impermeability	High
Mold resistance	Good
Organic solvents	Generally insoluble

Polyvinly Acetal

The properties of polyvinyl acetal resins depend chiefly on the types and amounts of functional groups present and on the resin molecular weight. As a general rule, the substitution of butyral or formal group for acetate groups results in a more hydrophobic polymer with a high heat distribution polymer. Coupled with this is an increase in the polymer's toughness and adhesion to a wide variety of surfaces. The outstanding specific adhesive of the acetal resins is believed to be a result of their multifunctional constitution, because each molecule presents the choice of three different functional groups to a surface. This increase the probability of adhesion to a wide variety of substrates.

These resins are thermoplastic and soluble in a range of solvents. They may also be cross-linked by heating in the presence of a mineral acid. The mechanism of cross-linking has been discussed previously. The various reactions are shown as follows :

(1) Reaction with Isocyanates

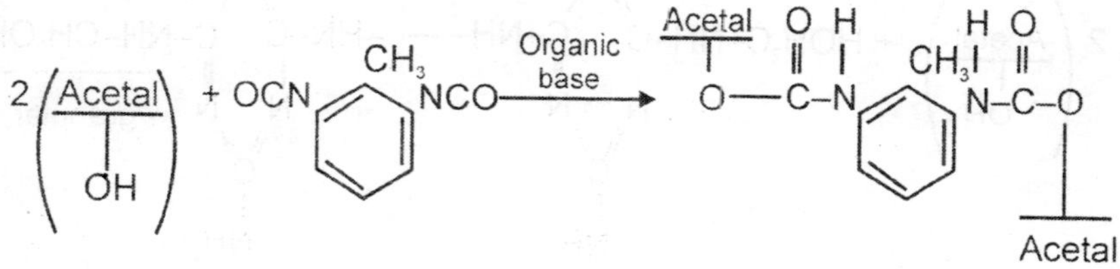

(2) Reaction with Phenolics

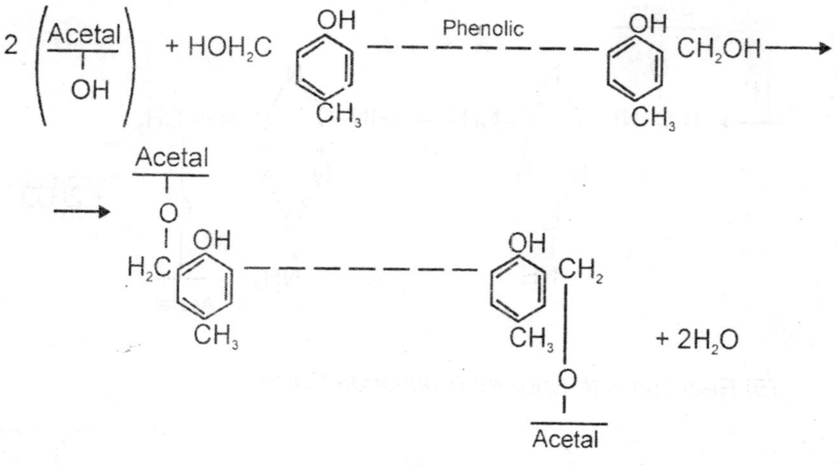

(3) Reaction with Dialdehydes

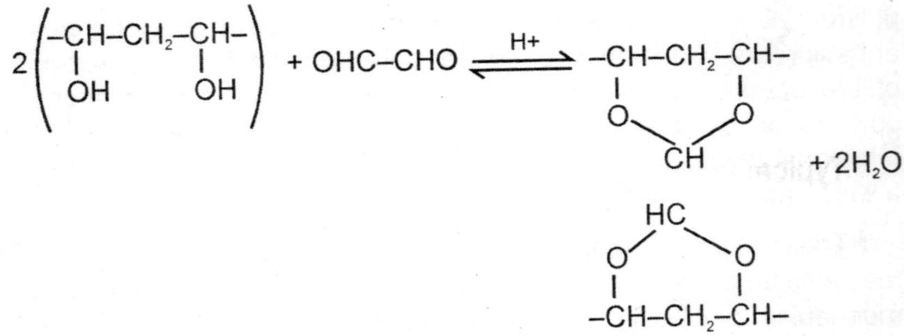

(4) *Reaction with Melamines*

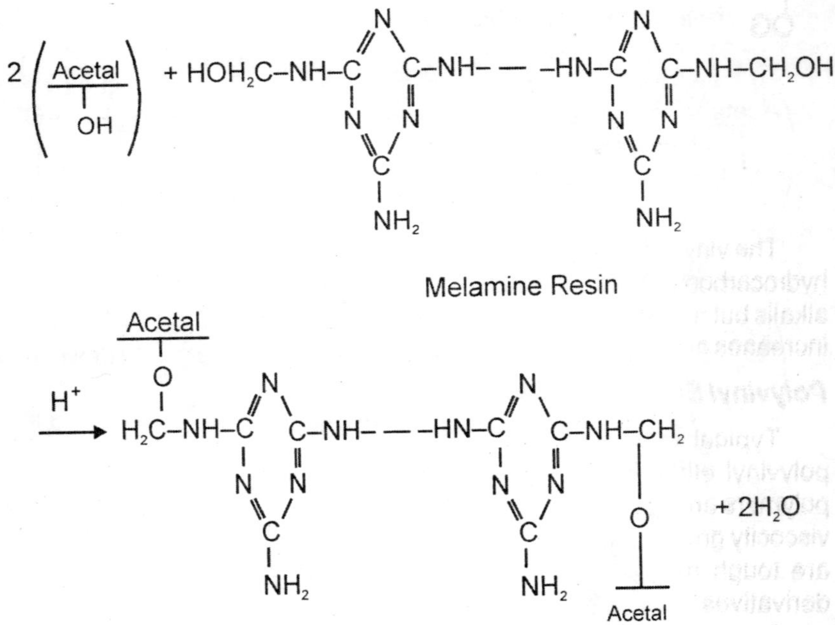

(5) *Reaction with Epoxies (Anhydride Cure)*

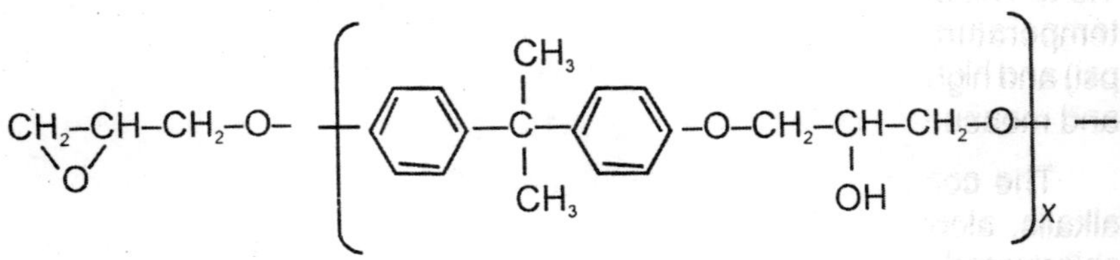

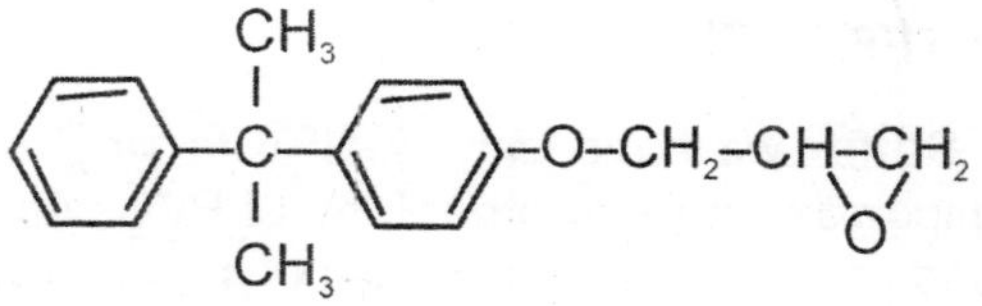

Typical Epoxy Resin

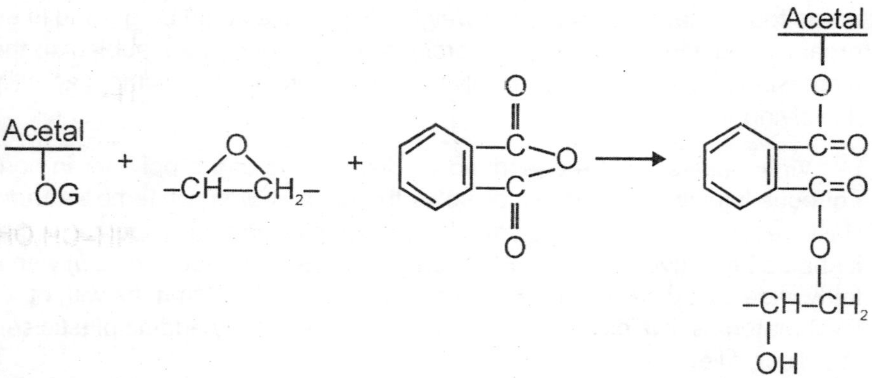

The vinyl acetal coatings are characterised by high resistance to aliphatic hydrocarbons, mineral, animal, and some vegetable oils. They withstand strong alkalis but are attacked by strong acids. By cross-linking the stability to acids increases and they can withstand heating up to 200°F for prolonged periods.

Polyvinyl Ethers

Typical materials in this group are polyvinyl methyl ether (PVM), polyvinyl ethyl ether (PVE), and polyvinyl isobutyl ether (PVI). All these polymers are essentially of the atactic noncrystalline type. The low or midium viscocity grades are sticky, viscous gums. The high molecular weight grades are tough rubber solids. They are compatible with phenolics and rosin derivatives.

Propylene-Vinyl Chloride

Most of the copolymers used are compounded and densities range from 1.3 to 1.4. Molded parts can be used up to temperatures of 60°C with room temperature tensile strengths of 7000 psi, high flexural modules (340,000 psi) and high impact strength (14 ft lb/in). They also have low water absorption and measured figures report less than 1 per cent after 30 days at 24°C.

The compounds have good chemical resistance especially to acids, alkalis, alcohols, aliphatic hydrocarbons, greases and oils. Exposure to chlorinated solvents has little effect on stress cracking properties.

PASTES

So far we have only dealt with vinyl compounds in the powder or semipowder form. Another form of PVC which is used quite extensively is based on the dispersion of the polymer in a volatile liquid and is referred to as a paste. Its development goes back over 100 days ago when, in Germany, it was found that high molecular weight vinyl resins could be ground in an organic media to give stable dispersions. This is, of course, subject to the dispersing phase having some solvating action on the resin without actually dissolving it.

Vinyl pastes can be described as dispersions of the polymer in non-aqueous liquids which do not dissolve the resin at ordinary tempeıatures. Basic requirements of the polymer for good paste-forming properties is that it should be derived from small spherical particles (averae size, 2*u*) with a fairly wide size distribution. It must also be emphasised that, as with other PVC materials, it is essential to compound the paste by adding plasticiser, stabiliser, fillers, etc.

When the paste is heated to between 145-175°C, fusion takes place and this can be regarded as a mutual solubilisation of resin and plasticiser. On cooling to 50°C it becomes a tough vinyl material exhibiting all the usual characteristics associated with the normal vinyl molded compounds.

These pastes can be divided into two main categories; plastisols, which are based on 100 per cent solid mixtures of polymer, plasticiser, and compounding ingredients; and organosols, which are low viscocity mixtures of paste polymer and compounding ingredients dispersed in a mixture of plasticiser, and an organic diluent having a solids content varying between 60 to 80 per cent. The volatile solvents are removed during the fusion process. Other types of paste are used but only to a small extent. These include the plastigel, which is a based on a polymer dispersed in a plasticizer but with the addition of a thickening agent. The thickening agent increases the viscocity of the compound and produces a paste with butter to putty like consistency. Rigisols are another form of paste; they have a reduced plasticiser content and can be used in slush molding.

The viscocity of the paste does not remain constant as varying rates of shear and therefore, does not behave like a Newtonian fluid. It exhibits either dilatant or pseudoplastic properties, and for such fluids the rate of shear, dv/dr, is directly proportional to the shear force.

$$F = n \frac{dv}{dr}$$

where F = applied shear force per unit area (dynes/cm^2)

$$\frac{dv}{dr} = \text{shear rate } (s^{-1})$$

$$n = \text{viscosity (dyne /s/ cm}^2 = \text{poise)}$$

A dilatant liquid exhibits the phenomenon that with increasing shear force the increase of shear rate is less proportional. Therefore, at high shear rates the flow of the liquid becomes relatively more difficult. This is often referred to as shear thickening, and some vinyl pastes are prone to this. However, in general, the majority of these pastes can be formulated to become shear thinning, particularly so if phthalate plasticiser are used. Such pastes are then termed pseudoplastics, their viscocity decreasing as the shear rate is increased. The types of flow illustrating shear-rate dependence, the effect of temperature and storage time on plastisol viscocity, and aging are shown respectively in Figs. 10.2, 10.3 and 10.4.

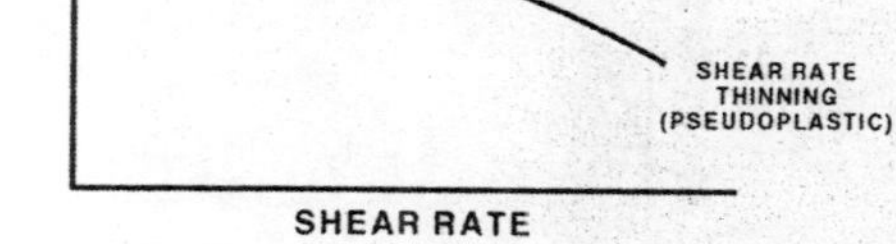

Fig. 10.2 Types of flow illustrating shear-rate dependence

Processing

The vinyl pastes are first prepared by thorough mixing in a dough or paddle-type mixer and sufficient plasticiser to form a thick paste. This will allow the maximum shearing effect from the mixing action to be obtained.

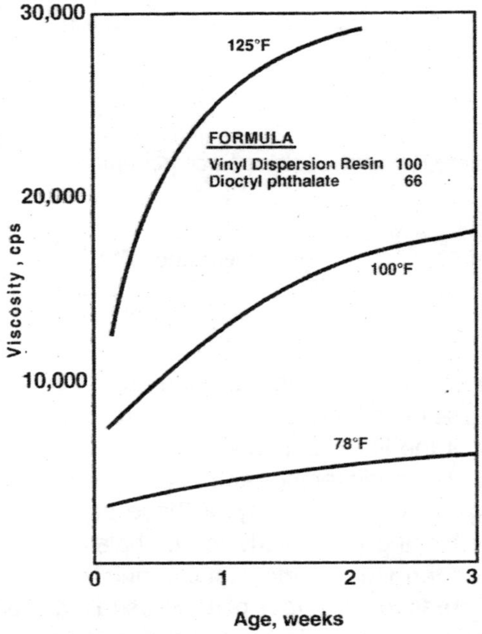

Fig. 10.2 Effect of temperature and storage time on plastisol viscosity

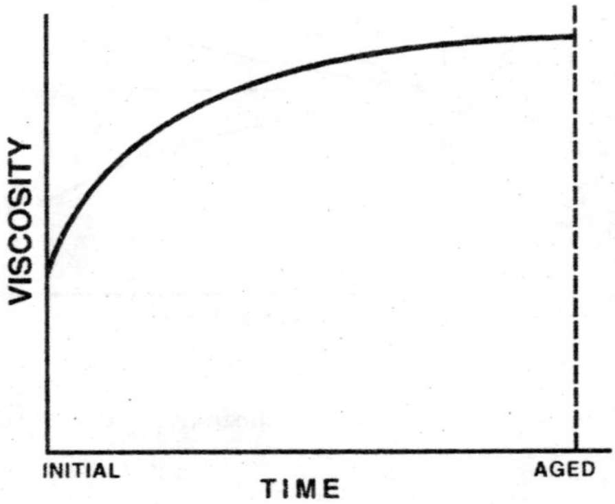

Fig. 10.4 Viscosity aging of vinyl dispersions

Other compounding ingredients are then added and the remainder of the plasticiser is finally added when all the other ingredients are well dispersed. Unfortunately, during the mixing process, air bubbles are entrapped in the paste, and these must be removed either by allowing to stand for 5-10 hours or by mixing under vaccum. One very important aspect to bear in mind with such pastes is that of storage. Due to the mutual interaction between the polymer and the plasticiser, the viscocity tends to increase, and the higher the storage temperature the more rapidly the viscosity increases, emphasising the need for the paste to be stored in a cool place (see fig. 10.3). The methods of processing vinyl paste are relatively simple and easy to carry out; they include spreading, dipping, slush molding and rotational casting, and the production of foams. These are nearly all described in Chapter 24 and no further elaboration is needed here. Table 10.5, however, gives the specific requirements of the paste for each particular processing method, with an indication of the end-use.

The fusion temperature is an important characteristics of vinyl pastes and depends on the molecular weight, amount and type of comonomer, plasticiser level, and polymer-plasticiser interaction parameter. Fusion of pastes is accomplished normally by heat alone and the particle size, shape, and distribution of the vinyl polymer particle affect this characteristic.

APPLICATIONS

Many of the initial applications for PVC were merely direct replacements for cellulose nitrate, because the high degree of inflammability of this latter polymer made certain applications hazardous. This introduction of PVC meant that a polymer was available with a high degree of flame resistance and the opportunity was taken quickly to replace these older materials in such applications where flame resistance was required. It is by its high chlorine content that PVC and its copolymers are distinguished, and this is reflected in various important properties shown in applications.

The excellent chemical resistance of PVC enables tubes, rods, and sheets to be used by constructional engineers in designing chemical plant with corrosion problems in mind. Rigid PVC sheet is used extensively for the fabrication of covers, ducts, tank linings, and many other items of chemical plant equipment. Because such sheet is dimensionally stable it also lends itself to precision engineering. In the actual fabricating process the sheet is softened by heat, shaped on formers, cooled, and then joined by welding. It can readily be built up into large units which, incidentally, need no painting. Pipe and fittings made from rigid PVC have many industrial

Table 10.5

PVC PASTE PROCESSES- REQUIREMENTS AND END-USES

Method	Type	Requirement	End-use
1. Spreading Coating	Plastisol and/ or	Medium viscosity No dilatency - thixotropic	Leather cloth Convey or belting
(Knife and roll coating)	Organosols	Pastes are preferred because they are more mobile at	Coated paper Unsupported film
Dipping		high shear rates Gel temperature 180° C	Wire goods, gloves
2. Casting			
(a) Normal	Plastisol	Low-medium shear with good pourability	Shoe soles
(b) Slush molding			
Conven-tional	Plastisol	Low-medium viscosity	Hollow articles, e.g., toys (dolls)
Rota-tional	Plastisols/ Rigisols	as above but must exhibit special temperature/ viscosity behavior	Playballs
3. Foams	Plastisols	Low-medium viscosity can be chemically or mechanically blown	Flotation, cushioning

uses, including the transportation of chemicals and in effluent disposal systems. It is also attractive for the transportation of water and gas because of its noncorrodability in acids soils and freedom from scale formation.

The weather resistance of PVC is good if the correct polymer/stabiliser system has been chosen. It is useful for garden hoses, likely to be left lying around in the open. Another application that has made use of the good weather resistance of PVC is corrugated roofing. The sheets developed over the past few years are now competitive with acrylic and reinforced polyester sheets.

By far the largest use of PVC at present consists of film and thin flexible sheet, which has already been discussed. Both film and sheeting can be made in all colors or with excellent clarity, they can be embossed or printed to give many different kinds of finish, and an added attraction is their relative ease of heat sealing. Uses of these films are growing quite extensively and already include the packaging of shampoos, collapsible containers and drum linears. It is likely that PVC sacks for fertilizers and many other such materials will become more and more popular and that PVC will take a large share of the ever-growing packaging market.

Laminates of PVC cloth, made from cotton, nylon, jute, terylene, and other synthetic fibers by spreading, dipping, or calendering techniques, provide a product suitable for use in a wide range of applications. PVC leathercloth is being extensively used for upholstery fabrics and interior decoration in all types of passenger transportation such as buses, coaches, ships, boats, and aircraft. Its use for upholstery, interior trim, car hoods, and covers in automobiles is now firmly established. Other uses for coated fabrics include substitutes for leather, such as document cases and wallets, and for protective and foul-weather clothing. Coatings can also be applied by dipping techniques to form end-products such as industrial gloves and wire goods for industrial and domestic use.

The replacement of rubber coal conveyor belting non-flammable belting made from PVC has been one of the most important developments in the coal-mining industry in recent years. Unlike natural and certain synthetic rubbers this polymer does not propagate flame and therefore fire risk in the mine in reduced.

Cable coatings and sheathing form the biggest outlet for PVC after the film and sheet applications. It is because of this polymer's excellent electrical properties, good aging chracteristics, and toughness that it is used widely, mainly in domestic and industrial cables and wires. Diverse uses range from bell-flex to large cable sheathings and the fact that PVC can be produced in many contrasting colors is an added advantage in that it aids the identification of complex circuits. Its specific uses include industrial and domestic wiring, telephone exchange wiring and telephone installations, radio and television sets.

The fact that PVC does not rot or perish and that it is relatively tough makes it a suitable material for soft flexible toys. These may be produced by rotational casting, and include dolls and play balls.

The use of PVC for domestic applications such as furnishing and interior decorations has grown quite considerably; it is by no means unusual to find

PVC floor tiles in practically any new building. PVC curtaining is available in an unlimited range of patterns and colors, and because it does not shrink in steamy conditions it can be used in the bathroom and in the kitchen. Other domestic uses include resilient carpet backing, wall covering, gay shelf and table covers in a wide range of attractive styles and designs. The low-flammability chracteristics of PVC are particularly attractive to architects when specifying components to be used in public buildings; PVC floors-covering and wall tiles are now used extensively in building shops, and factories in addition to stair treads and covers for handrails.

In 1950 the gramophone industry was revolutionised by the advent of unbreakable long playing records, which could be played for anything up to half-an-hour per side. The shellac record was found inadequate for long playing use and was therefore superseded by a vinyl chloride/vinyl acetate polymer. This copoylmer has the required combination of molding properties when hot, together with good acoustical and mechanical properties when cold. The material can be precision molded to produce records with hundreds of grooves per inch.

As a foam material PVC has relatively few end-uses due to its somewhat high cost and its dependence of flexibility on temperature changes. Uses include cushioning material in cars and furniture upholstery, carpet underlays, matteresses and shop mountings. Foamed PVC is now raising considerable interest as a buoyancy and insulation material and the market is expected to grow quite considerably in the next few years. These foams have excellent heat-sealing qualities and are therefore used where they have an advantage over rubber latex and polyurethanes, viz., abrasion and chemical resistance coupled with fire resistance.

Various developments have taken place in the past few years in the technology of PVC, particularly in injection and injection/extrusion molding. Moldings as widely different as vaccum-cleaner components and raincoat buttons can now be produced at high speeds, while other applications include electrical components such as flexible terminal blocks and hand grips for cycles and tools. Molded footwear, formerly, produced by casting techniques, can now generally be made by low-pressure injection/extrusion techniques. This allows wider possibilities in design, and inner linings can be applied during the actual molding operation. PVC compounds can also be extrusion blow-molded to produce containers which have the advantage of excellent clarity, good rigidity, high resistance to a wide variety of chemicals and also a few permeability to gases. In addition, printing on these articles can be accomplished without the necessity for post treating the surface. Typical applications include packaging of inorganic chemicals and solutions, petrol, motor oil, paraffin and white spirit based materials, lotions, perfumes, and food flavouring and essential oils.

Very little has been said of the uses of vinyl/chloride acetate copolymers but as emulsion paints they are well known and need no further elaboration. However, before closing the chapter mention must be made of the use of polyvinyl chloride/vinylidene chloride copolymers. The most important applications of these copolymers are in the filament and sheet industry. The filament and stable fibers are normally prepared by solution spinning, and their main use is in carpets, uphostery, and industrial filter cloths, although wider use has been restricted by the growth of the polyamides, polyester and polyolefin fibers. The processing of the films may be made easier by the addition of plasticisers such as diphenyl diethyl ether. Films with good tear resistance, water and chemical resistance can be produced; they are an excellent water vapor barrier, much better than polyethylene films in this respect. The polymer also possesses a very low permeability to oxygen and most other gases, protective qualities which make it an important component of some laminates. Unfortunately, it is not very heat-stable, either physically or chemically, small quantities of HCl being driven off when it is heated above 60°C for any length of time. Soluble copolymers have also been used for improving the moisture and oxygen resistance by coating cellophane film.

Polyvinyl acetate is used extensively as an adhesive for paper, wood, leather, tiles and many other porous substrates. It is also used in surface coatings for painting wood, plaster, and other similar surfaces. A limited use has been found in the textile industry for finishing nonwovens.

The main applications for polyvinyl alcohol is in adhesives, textile sizing, emulsifiers and protective colloids. Miscellaneous uses include cosmetics, pharmaceuticals, photosensitive coatings, plastics film and release agents.

The first and most important use of polyvinyl butyral is as the interlayer for automotive safety glass. In this application the excellent adhesion, impact strength and light stability of this polymer has been put to full use. Increasing applications include structural adhesives, textile coatings, surface coatings (wood and metal), washed primers, and lately as an additive in the compounding of polymers for powder coatings. The most important use of polyvinyl formal is as a wire enamel to provide electrical insulation on magnetic wire.

The main use for the polyvinyl ethers are as adhesives and surface coatings. The adhesives are essentially pressure sensitive, hot metals, and remoistenable types.

11

Polyamides

The synthetic thermoplastic polymers characterised as polyamides are better known under the name of nylons. The discovery of the first nylons arose out of the classic researches of W.H. Carothers in the U.S.A. in 1928. He and his coworkers were searching for new synthetic fibers, and in the course of their work, investigated a large number of chemical reactions. These researches culminated in the discovery that the condensation products of diacids with diamines gave long-chain polymers with the desired properties. The first nylon to be developed commercially was the condensation product of hexamethylene diamine. $NH_2(CH_2)_6NH_2$, and adipic acid, $COOH(CH_2)_4COOH$. It was called type 6,6 (six-six) nylon, the name being derived from the number of carbon atoms in the parent diamine and diacid. A further type to be developed was Type 6,10 (six-ten) this being made from hexamethylene diamine and sebacic acid, $COOH(CH_2)_8COOH$.

Later particularly in Europe, a different method of making nylon polymers was discovered, namely, by the condensation of certain ω–amino acids. Nylons prepared by this method are described by a single number, which is derived from the number of carbon atoms in the parent amino acid. Commercial examples of this type are Nylon 6 prepared from ω-amino-caproic acid, Nylon 11, prepared from ω-amino-undecanoic acid, and Nylon 12 prepared from dodecyl lactam (laurilactam).

Although the polyamides were originally developed as fiber-forming polymers, they have since attained a growing importance in other fields, notably, injection molding and extraction. To a smaller extent, nylons have also been used for the production of bottles by the blow-molding process.

Over recent years considerable use has been made of Nylon 11 and 12 in powder form for coating metals and the copolymers of Nylon 6/66/12 for textiles.

PREPARATION OF RAW MATERIALS

Adipic Acid

As was mentioned above, adipic acid is one of the starting materials for Nylon 6,6 and is derived from phenol by the following sequences of operations. The phenol is first hydrogenated to cyclohexanol, which is then catalytically dehydrogenated to cyclohexanone. The cyclohexanone is then reacted with nitric acid in the presence of a vanadium or copper catalyst, the result being a splitting of the ring and oxidation of both ends to a carboxylic acid grouping.

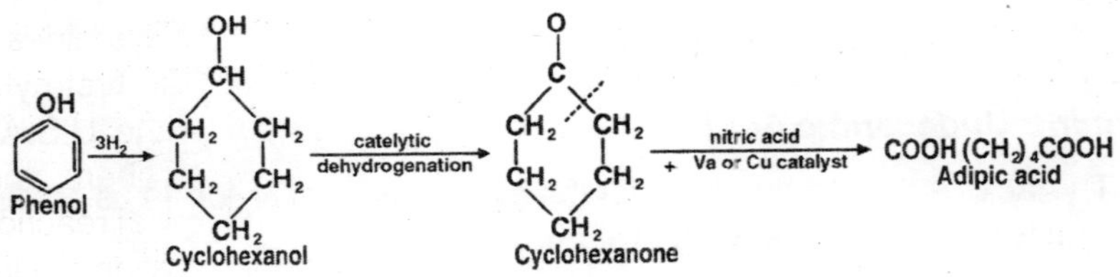

Hexamethylene Diamine

Hexamethylene diamine is the other starting material for Nylon 6,6 and is prepared from adipic acid (see above). The sequence of operations is shown by the equations below :

$$\underset{\text{Adipic acid}}{COOH(CH_2)_4COOH} \xrightarrow[350^\circ C]{NH_3} \underset{\text{Adipamide}}{CONH_2(CH_2)_4CONH_2} \xrightarrow[\text{125°C 600 atm Pressure}]{\text{Co/Cu catalyst}} \underset{\text{Hexamethylene diamine}}{NH_2(CH_2)_6NH_2}$$

Sebacic Acid

Sebacic acid has the formula $COOH(CH_2)_8COOH$, and is the dibasic acid from which 6,10 nylon is prepared. It is obtained by the alkaline extraction of castor oil. The details of the preparation are described in Chapter 5.

ω-Amino-Caproic Acid

Since the acid is normally used in the form of its anhydride (ε–caprolactam) it is more convenient to describe the method of manufacturing the latter. The starting point is again phenol, and this is successively reacted to give cyclohexanol and cyclohexanone as in the preparation of adipic acid described earlier. After purification by distillation, the cyclohexanone is reacted with hydroxylamine sulfate and the cyclohexanone oxime, so formed, is then heated with sulfuric acid containing free sulfur trioxide, followed by the addition of ammonia. This causes a molecular rearrangement to give ε-caprolactum.

The relationship between an ω-amino acid and its anhydride to exemplified by ω-amino-caproic acid and ε-caprolactam.

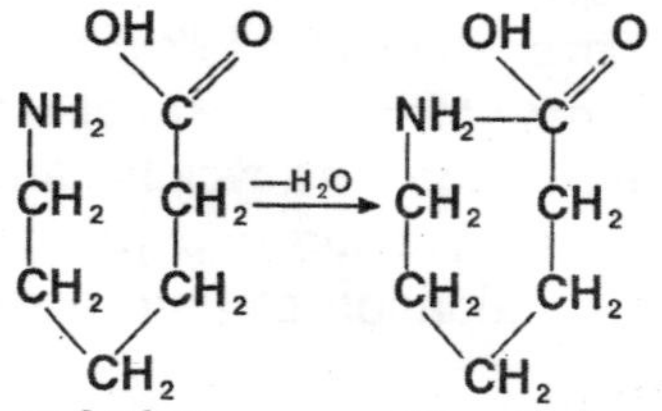

ω-Amino-caproic acid ε-Caprolactam

ω-Amino-Undecanoic Acid

This acid, is the starting point for the manufacture of Nylon 11, is obtained from castor oil by the following procedure.

Castor oil is first treated with methyl alcohol to give methyl ricinoleate. Pyrolysis of this gives methyl undecylenate, which is then hydrolysed to give the acid. This in turn is reacted with hydrogen bromide to yield the 11-bromo and not the 10-bromo compound. Finally it is reacted with ammonia to give the 11-amino undecanoic acid. This acid is obtained after recrystallisation as an aqueous paste which is suitable for charging directly into a continuous polymerisation unit. Phosphoric acid has been found as a suitable catalyst for this reaction.

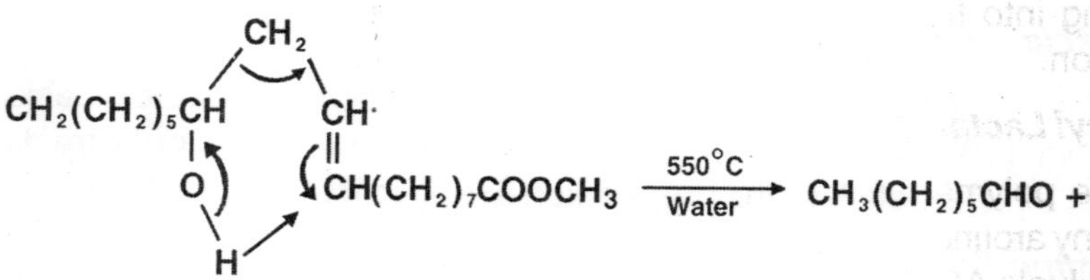

Methyl ricinoleate

$$CH_2=CH(CH_2)_8COOCH_3 \xrightarrow{\text{Hydrolysis}} CH_2=CH(CH_2)_8COOCH$$

Undecylenic acid

$$\xrightarrow{\text{HBr, air}} Br(CH_2)_{10}COOH \xrightarrow[\text{Water}]{NH_3} H_2N(CH_2)_{10}COOH$$

11-Aminoundecanoic acid

MANUFACTURE OF POLYMERS

Nylon 6,6

The reaction of adipic and hexamethylene diamine to form Nylon 6,6 is carried out in two stage. Both materials are dissolved in boiling methanol, whereupon a 'salt' is precipitated. This 'nylon salt' is then recrystallised

(i) $\underset{\text{Hexamethylene diamine}}{NH_2(CH_2)_6NH_2} + \underset{\text{Adipic acid}}{COOH(CH_2)_4COOH} \rightarrow$

$\rightarrow \underset{\text{Nylon salt}}{NH_2(CH_2)_6NH.CO(CH_2)_4COOH} + H_2O$

(ii) $n\underset{\text{Nylon salt}}{[NH_2(CH_2)_6NH.CO(CH_2)_4COOH} \xrightarrow{\text{heat}}$

$\rightarrow \underset{\text{Nylon 6,6 polymer chain}}{\left[NH(CH_2)_6NH.CO(CH_2)_4CO \right]_n} + n \cdot H_2O$

from water and charged into a glass or stainless-steel lined vessel. The vessel is purged with nitrogen and the contents heated to 280°C. The reaction may be followed by viscocity measurements, by electrical conductivity, or by checking on the ability of the material to 'cold draw'. The reaction can be stopped at any point by the addition of a monofunctional acid or amine. When the reaction is complete, the water formed during the reaction must be removed by refluxing under a vaccum. The reaction product is then pressure-filtered while still hot, and is then in a suitable form for spinning into fibers, for conversion into pellets for injection molding or extrusion.

Dodecyl Lactam (laurilactam)

The polymer Nylon 12 was first produced on a commercial scale in Germany around the middle of 1965. The monomer is prepared by Chemische Weke Huels AG as follows :

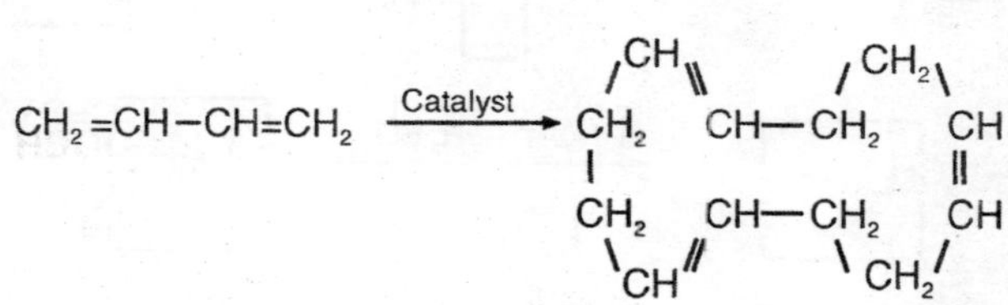

Butadiene Cyclodecatriene

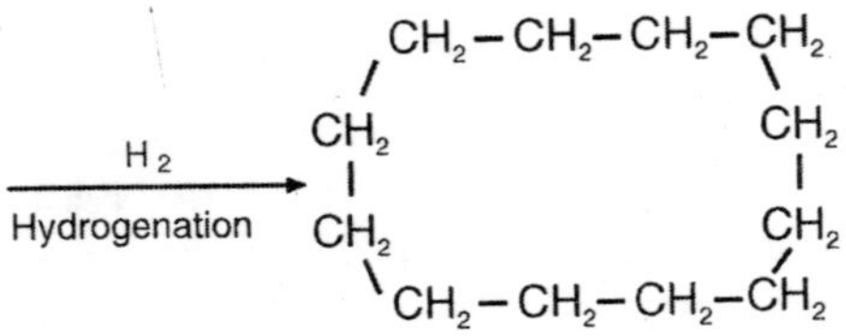

Cyclodecane

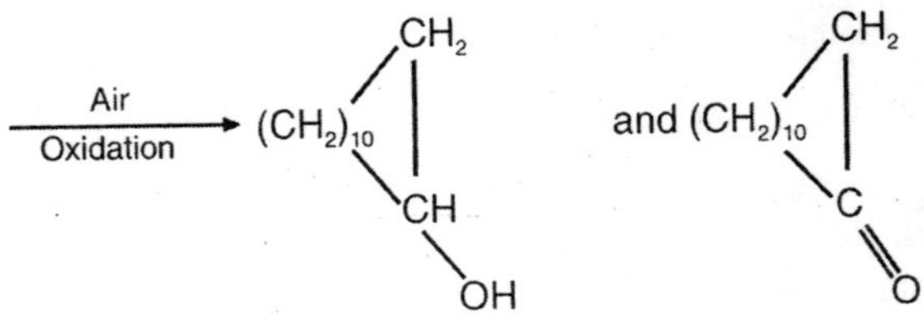

Cyclodecanol Cyclodecanone

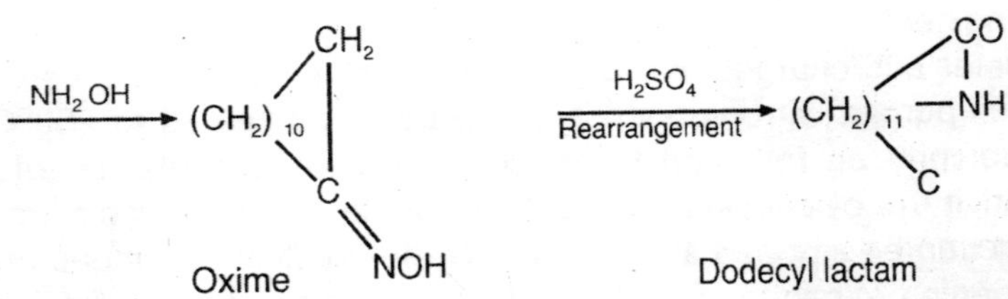

Oxime Dodecyl lactam

Several other routes to the lactam have been announced including those attributed to Badische Anilin- and Soda -Fabric (Germany), Aquitaine Organico (France) and Mitsubishi Toray (Japan).

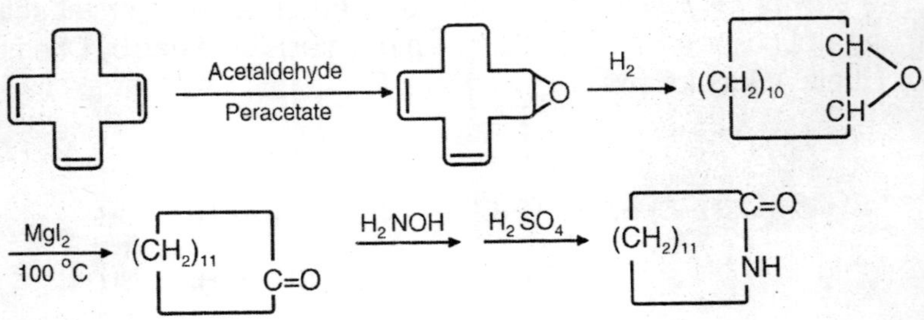

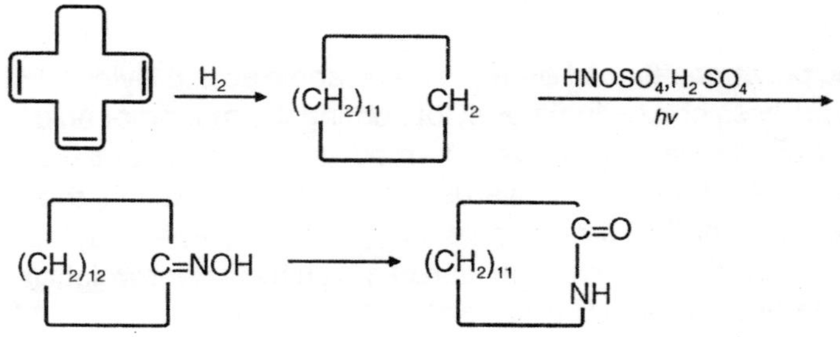

Nylon 6

The condensation of ε-caprolactam to give nylon 6 can be carried out either batch-wise or continuously. In the batch process, jacketed reaction vessles fitted with spade stirrers can be used. The reaction vessel is charged with the caprolactam, water (as a catalyst) and a stabiliser to limit the molecular weight. The mixture is kept under a blanket of oxygen-free nitrogen gas and heated for 12 hours at a temperature of about 250°C. An equilibrium mixture is eventually obtained which consists of about 90 per cent polymer and ten per cent low molecular weight products, and this is forced out by nitrogen pressure through an exit cock at the base of the reaction vessel. It is then in the form of a thick monofilament but, on cooling, it is broken up into the more conveninet form of small chips about 1/12 in square. If colored material is desired, the color is introduced at this stage by dry blending, followed by extrusion and chipping. The low molecular weight constituents mentioned earlier are then washed out and the chips dried and packed into air-tight tins.

In the continuous process, a stream of caprolactam, water and a stabiliser is maintained to the reaction columns which are kept at 250°C. A continuous stream of polymer leaves the column, is cooled, cut into chips, washed, dried, extruded, chipped and packed. The low molecular weight contents referred to earlier, consist mainly of the monomer which is fed back to the distillation plant employed for the purification of the caprolactam.

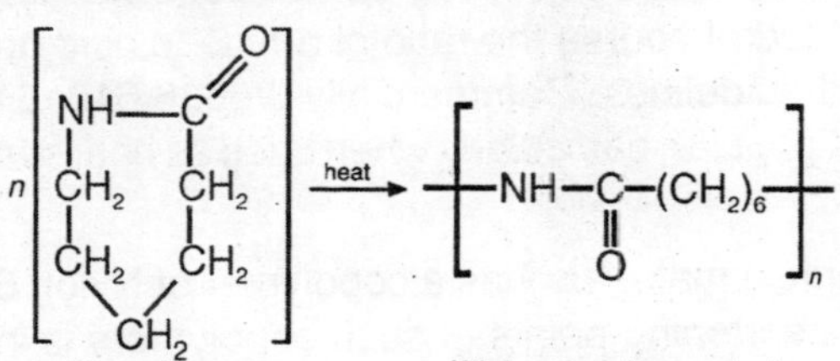

ε-Caprolactam Nylon 6 polymer chain

Nylon 11

The polymerisation of ω-amino undecanoic acid to Nylon 11 is relatively simple process consisting merely of heating the monomer acid to just over 200°C, while distilling off the water formed as a reaction by product. Catalysts may be added if desired. Towards the end of the reaction, the pressure is reduced in order that a high molecular weight polymer may be produced. Another essential for the production of a high molecular weight is the use of a pure starting material (French Patent No. 885, 694).

The molten polymer can either be spun directly into fibers or extruded into a ribbon, which is cut into chips and packed into air-tight tins.

Nylon 12

The polymerisation of dodecyl lactam (laurilactam) to Nylon 12 is a relatively simple process akin to that of the Nylon 11. However, because of the high degree of stability of the ring the polymerisation is much slower. Acid catalysts are used to speed up the reaction but even so temperature of 300-350°C are required to achieve an acceptable molecular weight. If, for example, laurilactam is heated in the presence of water or small amounts of acid, such as acetic acid, at the usual polymerisation temperature of 260°C, 50 per cent of the lactam remains unconverted even after a polymerisation time of 30 hours. A french Patent specification No. 1,261,286 states that the polymerisation of laurilactam can be carried out between 315 and 320°C in the presence of aliphatic mono-or dicarboxylic acid. This lactam has a low polymerisation of heat -1.4 k cal/mol and as stated previously, the ring has a high degree of stability which accounts for the high temperatures required to obtain acceptable degree of conversion.

Copolymers

These materials are finding extensive use as adhesive coatings for fusible interlinings. Suffice it to say that the manufacture of polyamide copolymers simply requires the desired ingredients to the charged to a reaction vessel and simply polymerised. All the diamines, diacids, amino acids, and lactam mentioned previously can be used in virtually any kind of combination provided of course the ratio of amine to acid grouping is kept with in the desired guidelines. Commercially 6/66, 6/610, 6/66/610 and 6/66/12 are the most popular, particularly when used as heat sealable coatings for textiles.

One of the earliest materials was a copolymer of Nylon 6 and 66 in the ratio of 70/30. The softening points of such copolymers is in the region of

170°C which was too high for this particular application. Therefore it was found necessary to dry blend up to equal parts of ortho-para toluene solfonamide to this copolymer in order to reduce the softening point to a satisfactory level. The following is a list of softening points of a wide range of polyamides. The difference between external plasticisation and internal plasticisation by copolymerizing with different monomers is illustrated.

Material	*Softening Point °C*
Nylon 6/6	265
6/10	220
6	215
11	185
6/66	170
6/66/610	120
6/66/12	120
6/66 (plasticised with equal amounts of o-p toluene sulfonamide)	105

Other satisfactory plasticisers are n-ethyl sulfonamide, butyl benzene sulfonamide, urea, and proprietory esters of hydroxy benzoic acid.

The formation of intermolecular hydrogen bonds is controlled by selection of the basic monomers and the respective ratio, which in turn controls the degree of crystallinity. The triangular coordinates of Fig. 11.1 (representing

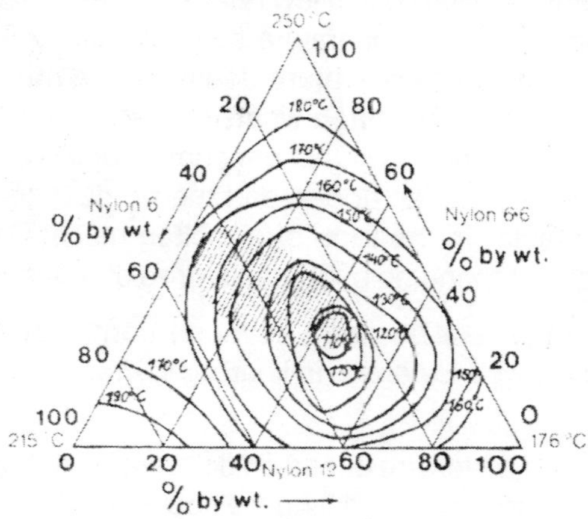

Fig. 12.1 Fusion temperature (°C) triangular coordinates of copolyamide 6,6-6,12. All polymers of the same melting temperature are joined by isotherms. Shaded areas are compositions soluble in 85 : 15 alcohol : water solutions.

the fusing temperature of various ratios of Nylon 6,66 and 12) show the correlation between the ratio of monomer components and the resulting softening temperatures. The shaded area covers these terpolymers which are soluble in an 85/15 alcohol and water solution. The greater the proportion of Nylon 12, the lower the water absorption but the greater the degree of resistance to chlorinated hydrocarbon solvents such as perchlorethylene and trichlorethylene. The melt viscosities can be lowered by controlled techniques but this leads to a determination of other characteristics.

Versamids

Versamids are condensation products of dimerised vegetable oil acids and polyamino compounds such as polyalkylene polyamines. General Mills Inc. in the U.S.A. has produced these type of polyamides of many years under U.S. Patent No. 2,379,413. A cross licensing agreement covering resin research, manufacture, and sales has been in operation between General Mills and Cray Valley Products Ltd., in the U.K. They are marketed under the General Mills reference Versamid, Versalon, and Milvex;

$$n\,\text{HOOC–R–COOH} + n\,\text{H}_2\text{NR'–NH}_2 \rightarrow \text{HO(–OC–R–CONHR'–NH–)}_n\text{H}$$

R is a hydrocarbon group of an indeterminate configuration containing 34 carbon atoms. The polyamine used in the manufacture of Versamid polymaide resins 900, 930, 940 and 950 is ethylene diamine, and R' is —CH_2CH_2—

The ingredients are blended at low temperatures in an autoclave fitted with an efficient agitator. The temperature is raised until water is being distilled off at such a rate that the temperature does not rise much above 100°C. When distillation reaches the stage where it is so slow as to be negligibe (reaction temperature 150-250°C) a vaccum is applied to complete the reaction. An intert gas is then added and the product cooled slightly and drawn from the reactor in the form of a molten mass. The resin may be either liquid or solid, depending upon the degree of reaction.

Liquid versamids are package in metal containers while the solid products may be allowed to harden in fiberboard drums, or may be flaked or chipped.

Milvex type polyamides are based on different feedstock and are higher molecular weight materials resembling the copolyamides in characteristics.

STRUCTURE

The general structure of the nylons (polyamides) is an alteration of hydrocarbon groups (in this case methylene groups) and imido (–NHCO–) groups. This is typified by Nylon 6,6 (see below).

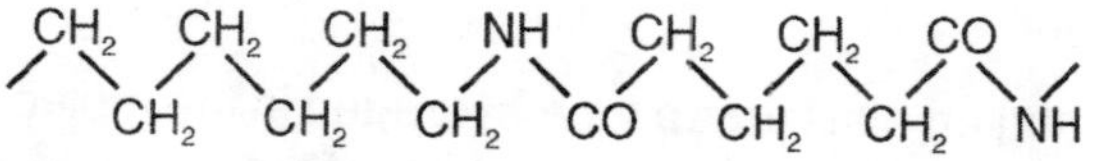

The presence of the polar imido groups leads to a strong attraction between the molecules, due to hydrogen bonding, thus conferring a high melting point on the polymer. The hydrogen bonding also tends to make the chains lie parallel to each other, especially after cold drawing. The consequent increase in crystallinity is shown up practically by X-ray diffraction photographs.

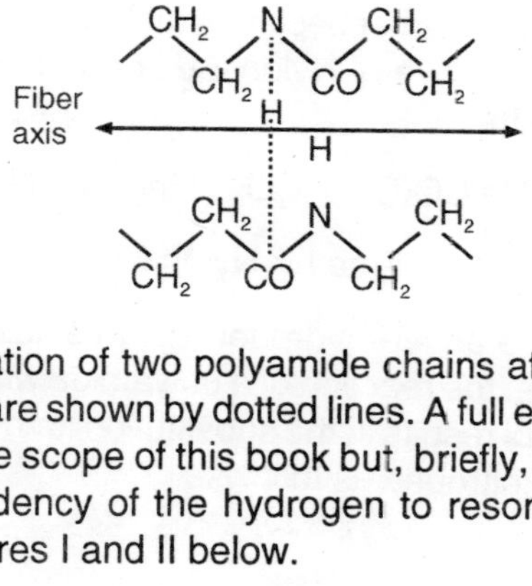

In the representation of two polyamide chains after cold drawing, the hydrogen bond links are shown by dotted lines. A full exposition of hydrogen bonding is beyond the scope of this book but, briefly, it may be considered to be due to the tendency of the hydrogen to resonate between (in this case) the two structures I and II below.

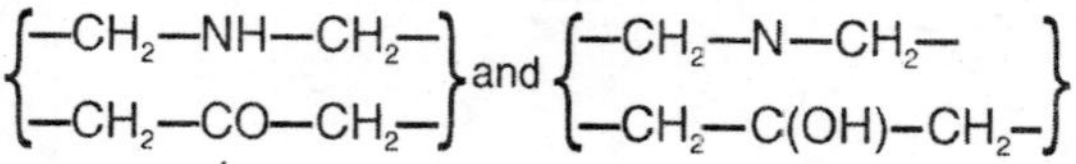

I and II

An alternate link is thus formed between the CO and N groups as shown by dotted lines in the preceding diagram.

With the picture in mind it is possible to visualise the way in which the properties of the polyamides can be altered. The longer the hydrocarbon part of the chain, for instance, the less the attraction between the chains and, therefore, the lower the softening point because the hydrogen bonding is, in effect, 'diluted' along the chain. Thus, Nylon 6,10 has a lower softening point than Nylon 6,6.

cf.–$(CH_2)_6NH{\cdot}CO(CH_2)_4CO{\cdot}NH{\cdot}(CH_2)_6{\cdot}NH{\cdot}CO$–Nylon 6,6 S.Pt. 265°C

–$(CH_2)_6{\cdot}NH{\cdot}CO(CH_2)_6CO{\cdot}NH(CH_2)_6{\cdot}NH{\cdot}CO$–Nylon 6,10 S. Pt. 220°C

Longer hydrocarbon groups also lead to a reduction in water absorption and, for this reason, Nylon 6,10 is often preferred for the manufacture of tooth-brush bristles.

Substituting an alkyl group for a hydrogen in the molecule chain lowers the melting point and increase the solubility of the molecue. The explanation for this effect lies in the fact that the bulky alkyl groups prevent close approach of the molecules, thus reducing the hydrogen bonding between adjacent chains.

The properties of the polyamide may also be altered by substituting the hydrogen in the –NH groups by some other grouping. This can be done either in the polymer or in the intermediate 'nylon salt'. The hydrogen bonding in thus removed and the polymer becomes rubbery, elastic, and amorphous. Thus the *N*-methyl derivative of Nylon 6,6 is a viscous syrup, setting to a 'glass' at low temperature.

$$-(CH_2)_6{\cdot}Me{\cdot}CO(CH_2)_s{\cdot}CO{\cdot}N{\cdot}Me(CH_2)_6{\cdot}N{\cdot}Me{\cdot}CO-$$

N-methyl Nylon 6,6

Substitution of the amide hydrogen by an alkoxyl group can also be achieved; for instance, the reaction of a polyamide with formaldehyde in the presence of an alcohol results in the substitution for methoxy methyl groups groups on the amide nitrogen as follows :

$$\begin{matrix} \backslash \\ NH \\ / \\ CO \\ \backslash \end{matrix} + CH_2O + ROH_2 \xrightarrow[\text{catalyst}]{\text{Acid}} \begin{matrix} \backslash \\ N-CH_2OR \\ / \\ CO \\ \backslash \end{matrix} \text{ or } \begin{matrix} \backslash \\ N(CH_2O)_2R \\ / \\ CO \\ \backslash \end{matrix}$$

Methyl methoxy nylons have been commercially available for some time and about one third of the –NH groups have been substituted. These materials are soluble in lower aliphatic alcohols such as ethanol and absorb up to 21 per cent of moisture when immersed in water. On heating this product with 2 per cent citric acid at elevated temperature cross-linking takes place. Typical conditions are 20 minutes at 120°C with the following reaction taking place.

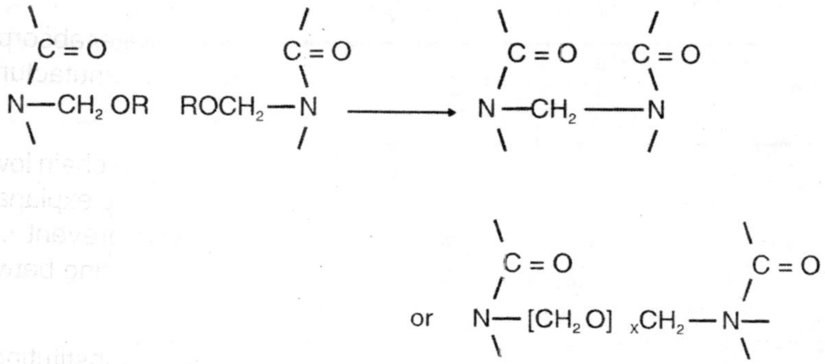

PROPERTIES

Nylons, generally, are produced in the form of hard, horny chips, creamy in color and slightly translucent. As was explained in the section on structure, the various types of nylon can vary in their properties, but the following generalisation can be made for Nylons 6,11, 6,6, and 6,10.

Physical Properties

Nylons are tough materials with high tensile strengths and a marked resistance to abrasion. Because of their high crystallinity, they prossess sharp melting points which are appreciably higher than most other thermoplastics. However, destruction of the cyrstallinity by substitution in the –N group alters the behaviour of the polymer completely. In contrast to the majority of thermoplastics, nylons exhibit very little cold flow.

Nylons are slightly hygroscopic and the material must be dried by heating before use. The amount of moisture absorbed is a function of the relative humidity of the atmosphere. The mechanical properties of nylons are reduced somewhat by the absorption of water but the effect is not permanent and the full mechanical properties are restored when the nylon is dried.

The electrical properties are also effected by the ambient relative humidity. For instance, at low humidities nylons have reasonably good electrical insulation properteis but these deteriorate as the humidity increases. As with the mechanical properties, the electrical properties are restored to their full value when the nylon is redried. In spite of this disadvantage, nylon moldings find many uses in electrical applications because of the additional advantages of toughness and high temperature resistance. Some typical values for the physical properties of various nylons are given Table 11.1.

Table 11.1
PROPERTIES OF A RANGE OF POLYAMIDES

Property	*Units*	*Type* 6,6	6,10	6	11
Specific gravity	–	1.14	1.09	1.13	1.05
Tensile strength	lb/in.^{2}	11,000	8,000	12,000	8500
Elongation	%	90	100	300	120
Hardness (Rockwell)	R scale	118	111	118	101
Dielectric Constant	V/mill	385	470	420	430
(at 10^3 cycles)	–	4.0	4.5	4.0	3.5
Volume resistivity (at 23°C and 50% R.H.)	Ohm/cm	4.5×10^{13}	4.5×10^{14}	4.5×10^{13}	4.5×10^{14}
Power factor (at 10^3 cycles)	–	0.02	0.04	0.06	0.03
Water absorption	%	1.5	0.4	1.6	0.4
Modulus of elasticity	lb/in.^{2}	400,000	260,000	300,000	180,000
Melting point	°C	265	220	215	185

It may be worth reiterating at this point that some copolymers have also found commercial use and have somewhat different properties. In general, they are more soluble, less stiff and softer than the homopolymers. They also have lower melting points and tensile strengths. This is due to the irregularity set up in the molecules, with consequent interference with the intermolecular forces of hydrogen bonding. The irregular spacing of the amide groups in the molecule also reduces the tendency to crystallise. The effect on polymer melting point brought about by using substituted diamines or dibasic acids is shown in Table 11.2.

Table 11.2
EFFECT OF SUBSTITUTION IN THE PARENT DIACID OR DIAMINE ON THE MELTING POINT OF NYLON 6,6

Dibasic acid	*Diamine*	*m.p.°C*
Adipic acid	Hexamethylene diamine	265
α–Methyl adipic acid	Hexamethylene diamine	166
Adipic acid	3-Methyl Hexamethyl diamine	180

Amide groups react with formaldehyde and, in the presence of an alcohol, formation of an alkoxy methyl group occurs on the N-atom. The effect of this substitution on the melting point of Nylon 6,6 is shown in Table 11.3.

Table 11.3

EFFECT OF N-ALKOXY METHYL SUBSTITUTION ON THE MELTING POINT OF NYLON 6,6

Polymer	*m.p.°C*
Nylon 6,6	265
20% N-alkoxy methyl substituted nylon 6,6	190
30% N-alkoxy methyl substituted nylon 6,6	135

The versamids have sharp melting points and the characteristics of these hard polyamides are little affected by temperature until very near their melting points and at room temperature they are nonblocking. They exhibit excellent flexibility which is due to the long fatty chains spaced between the functional groups which are in integral part of the resin chain. Adhesion of these resins to a wide variety of difficult substrates is excellent. The typical properties of a range of different type Versamids is given in Table 11.4

Chemical Properties

In general, nylons are inert to inorganic reagents, including liquid ammonia and liquid sulfur dioxide, although they are attacked by oxidising agents such as hydrogen peroxide and chlorine bleaches. Aqueous solutions of inert inorganic chemicals still exert some effect on the physical properties of molded nylon specimens, however, because of the plasticising effect of the water itself. Nylons are attacked by concentrated mineral acids at room temperature but dilute acids have little effect except when hot.

Organic acids have little or no effect (especially in low concentration), notable exceptions being 90 per cent formic acid and glacial acetic acid, which cause swelling and solution.

Nylons are resistance to caustic alkalis, even to concentrations up to 20 per cent, while they are even more stable towards other alkaline solutions such as trisodium phosphate, sodium carbonate, and potassium carbonate.

It is in their resistance to organic solvents that the nylons are of particular interest, however. In general, they are inert to alcohols, ether, acetone, petroleum ether, carbon tetrachloride, benzene, xylene, hydraulic fluid, and aviation oil. They are, however, attacked by phenols, hot formamide,

Table 11.4

PROPERTIES OF A RANGE OF VERSAMID RESINS

Resin	100 (1)	920	930 (1)	950 (1)	1117	1124	1138 (1)	1139	1140	1160	1200	SR21	1235 (1)
Ball & Ring Softening Point (°C)	semi-solid	147	110	95	117	124	140	138	140	160	200	160	200
Suggested Application Temperature °C	–	–	150-160	105-115	150-160	170-180	205-215	245-255	245-255	200-210	240-250	215-225	–
Specific Gravity	0.98	0.97	0.97	0.95	0.98	1.00	0.99	0.98	0.99	0.97	0.99	0.97	1.00
Viscosity at 205°C (poise)	–	–	–	–	8	13	62	140	100	43	136	58	1g6g (4)
Viscosity at 150°C (poise)	12	24 (2)	55	21 (3)	54	90	–	–	–	–	–	–	–
Elongation at 25°C (%)	–	–	20	10	120	520	560	680	890	370	400	430	400
Tensile Yield at 25°C (psi)	–	–	1800	870	310	260	460	410	340	1900	2100	2000	2800
Tensile Break at 25°C (psi)	–	–	1800	870	180	130	450	730	450	1650	3400	2000	6000
Tensile Shear-Steel (psi)	–	–	750	480	300	300	950	1200	1700	1650	1800	1600	3200
Tensile Button-Steel (psi)	–	–	725	1100	1560	1410	1840	2200	2100	1100	1700	960	–

(1) Can meet the statutory requirements under paragraph 121.2520, Subpart F, of the Federal Food, Drug and Cosmetic Act for adhesives
(2) Viscosity at 160° C (3) Viscosity at 130° C (4) Melt Index Range

formaldehyde, hot benzyl alcohol, and hot nitrobenzene. It should be realised, however, that certain copolymers or plasticised grades may be less resistant to certain chemicals. A copolymer of 6, 6,6 and 6,10 nylons, for instance, is attacked by alcohols. Nylons are relatively unaffected by prolonged service indoors at room temperature but at elevated temperatures oxidation occurs with consequent yellowing and embrittlement, while strong sunlight also has in adverse effect on their mechanical properties.

The versamid polyamide resins have excellent resistance to alkalis, aliphatic hydrocarbons, mineral and vegetables oils; good resistance to acids reasonable resistance to esters and ketones; only fair resistance to alcohols due to their alcohols solubility.

APPLICATIONS

Film

Blown nylon film has been used for the packaging of oils, fats, greases, and oil-based products such as putty. It has also been used for food packages such as boil-in-the-bag foods (where nylon's high softening point is useful) and vaccum packed cheese, bacon, etc. where low gas permeability is essential. Blown nylon film has also been used for tapes and cable insulation.

Coatings

The Versamids, particularly, are used in alcohol or alcohol/hydrocarbon solvents as coatings for paper, aluminium foil, regenerated cellulose, etc. These coatings are used to give heat sealability and to improve the grease and water barrier properties of the substrate. Versamids are particularly useful for coatings because of their flexibility, elongation, and adhesion. Versamids with reactive amine groups can be combined with epoxy resins to give thermosetting materials, and these have found application as drum linings, wire coatings, and coatings for all sorts of industrial articles.

Nylon 11 and more recently Nylon 12 have become widely used in the powder coating of metals. The reduction of these polymers to the powder form is very difficult and industrially it is carried out by cryogenic techniques. These coatings impart to the object all the chemical resistance and other excellent characteristics associated with this family of polymers. Further details of these powdered polymers are given later in the book.

Fibers and Monofilaments

The first commercial application of polyamides was for toothbrush bristles. This was in 1938 and was followed, in 1939, by the appearance of nylon stockings. Other fiber uses quickly followed, including such diverse items as parachute cords, safety belts, and monofilament for rackets.

The success of nylon filaments of toothbrush bristles has been followed by their use for tufting brushes of all sorts from toilet brushes to heavy industrial brushes. For paint and distemper brusher, taper monofilaments are available. The main advantages of nylon for this application lies in its durability, and nylon paint brushes are said to last three to five items as long as those made from natural bristles.

Uses for continuous monofilament are also extremely numerous and include fishing lines, surgical sutures (which can be sterilised by boiling or by treatment with steam under pressure), pot scourers, bead stringing, spectable manufacture, corrosion-resistant screens or sieves, tire cords and various types of rope. Tow ropes for gliders are a particularly good example of the use of nylon's special advantages; nylon low ropes are capable of absorbing the stock during glider pick-up, owing to the fact that they are capable of stretching upto 40 per cent of thier length.

Textile uses of nylon are well-known. Apart from women's hosiery, where it has displaced silk, nylon is used extensively (either alone or blended with other fibers) in the manufacture of parachute cloth, under wear, night attire, negligees, gloves, corsetry and men's ties, hose and shirts. In addition, waterproofed nylon is used for umbrellas, raincoats, lightweight tents, and shower curtains.

Nylon has also found many uses as a staple fiber for making into yarn for swim-suits, coats and sweaters. Nylon 'fur', in particular, makes an attractive and relatively inexpensive substitute for many natural furs.

The types of nylon particularly useful for fiber forming are 6,11 and 6,6 for textile fibers (although 6,10 is also used) and 6,11, 6,6 and 6,10 for filaments and bristles. Types 6,10 and 11 are preferred for the manufacture of bristles, sutures, and fishing lines because of their lower water absorption. Another factor leading to the preferred use of Nylons 6,10, and 11 for brushes is their high rigidity. High molecular weight polymers are necessary for fiber-forming properties, together with a tendency to orientation on cold drawing. The latter property is closely related to the polymer's potentially for hydrogen bonding, as explained in the sction on 'Structure'. For textile fibers it is also important that the polymer should have a relatively high softening point in order that the fabric should be melt with ironed.

Nylon fibers can be coated with various materials to give certain properties not otherwise available. Melamine formaldehyde resins, for instance, confer a crisper finish, and nylon taffetas are produced with degrees of stiffness ranging from very slight to the perchment like finish required for petticoats.

Adhesives

Polyamide based adhesives may be of the hot-melt or the solution type. The resins most frequently encountered in adhesive compositions are vegetable oil polyamides (Versamids), copolymers (such as the 6, 6,6,6,10 interpolymers) or modified nylons such as the *N*-alkoxy nylons produced by the reaction of nylon with formaldehyde in the presence of alcohol. It will be noticed that all the resins have low melting points (thus giving ease of application as hot-melt adhesives) and ready solubility in alcohol, alcohol/ hydrocarbon mixtures, etc. (for solvent based adhesives).

For hot melting adhesives, various modifying agents are added. The basic polymers are solid thermoplastics which, when heated at temperature above their softening points, quickly from low viscocity liquids which can be applied with ease to a variety of substrates. If a second surface is brought into contact with the molten adhesive a simple, yet highly effective bond is rapidly formed as the resin cools. Plasticisers are necessary to give low temperature flexibility while waxy materials are sometimes added to prevent blocking or sealing of the adhesives at room temperatures. Other polymers or resins may also be added in certain instance to improve moisture vapor resistance, initial tack, and adhesion to particular surfaces or to reduce costs without decreasing performance. Solution-type adhesives may also contain modifying agents.

Polyamide-based adhesives have a wide range of application including heat-seal adhesives for bread wrappers, dried soup packets, cigarette packages, and laminating adhesives for many flexible packaging materials such as glassine, aluminium foil, regenerated cellulose, paper and cellulose acetate. Polyamide adhesive have also been used as side-seam cements in tin cans, as pressure-sensitive adhesives, shoe cements, and bookbinding adhesives.

Polyamide based thermosetting adhesives have also been prepared from highly branched amino-polyamide resins such as certain of the Versamids. These contain amine end groups so that reaction can take place with epoxy or phenolic resins. In use, a blend of the polyamide resin and epoxy resin is applied to the surfaces to be joined together. These are held in position until cured. Such curing may be at room or elevated temperature.

Polyamide/phenolic adhesive compositions differ from the epoxy ones in as much as pressure is necessary during the bonding operation due to the fact that water is produced as a by-product of the curing reaction. In addition, high curing temperatures are necessary (150-205°C).

Uses for the polyamide thermoset adhesive include wood bonding, bonding of aluminium honeycomb structures for aircraft, bonding copper foil to epoxy/glass or paper-reinforced phenolic laminates, as in printed circuit bases, and as adhesives for steel.

The polyamide copolymers have found widespread use over the last ten years in the heat sealing of textiles. The adhesive bonding of textiles has grown into a very large industry since its early beginning in the U.K. in the middle 1950's.

Printing Inks

When Versamid polyamide resins are combined with suitable pigment and other modifying agents they can be used with great success in flexogrphic inks. Gloss, adhesion, and pigment-wetting properties are among the factors making polyamide resins suitable for these inks, coupled with high alcohol solubility. The latter property is of importance in flexographic ink formulations because alcohols do not attack the rubber rollers which are normally used in such printing processes. Solvents such as aromatic hydrocarbons and ketones used in some other printing ink compositions do attack rubber and are not, therefore, suitable.

Polyamide-based inks can be used for the printing of paper, polyethylene, regenerated cellulose, etc. giving good adhesion and resistance to abrasion.

Moldings

High tensile strength and moderately high melting point are usually demanded in molded applications for nylon; thus high molecular weight resins of the 6, 6,6, 6,10 and 11 types are normally used. Applications where nylon's great mechanical strength and toughness and its high melting point are particularly useful are more often found in the field of engineering. A particularly useful property of nylon is its self lubrication. Thus, it is widely used for grears, bushes and bearings, came, etc., especially in the food and textile industries where contamination by lubricants is a problem. In addition, nylon mechanical components are quiet-running and are light in weight, the density of nylon being less than half that of even light metals such as aluminium. Examples of engineering uses of nylon are almost too numerous to mention but include speedometer gears, connecting rods in electric shavers, pump impellers, cams and ratchets on calculating machines, timing gears, camera parts, lock-nut inserts, meter wheels, sound projector gears and conveyor chains.

Nylon has also found many outlets in the domestic fields, outstanding among which are nylon combs, curtain runners, slide fasteners, soda siphon tops, furniture castors, door catches, for refrigerators (and cars), and brush backs.

Nylon's high heat resistance has lead to its use in surgical and clinical moldings such as hypodermic syringes, which can be sterilised by boiling water or steam. However, it should be noted that nylon is more sensitive to dry heat than to wet and continuous exposure to dry heat in excess of 120°C could lead to embrittlement.

Extrusions (other than film)

Nylon has been used for the extrusion of abrasion-resistant sheathing of communication cables and for heat and oil resistant sheathing on cables in aircraft and similar motors.

Tubing and extrusion blow-molded bottles have also been used for a wide range of chemicals and pharmaceuticals because of their chemical inertness. Other useful properties include strength, flexibility, and sterilisability, the latter property being utilised particularly in babies' feeding bottles. Fine-bore nylon tubing has also been found very suitable for blood transfusion equipment and for the draining of wounds.

Finally, an interesting application demonstrating the successful marriage of traditional and new materials, is the manufacture of heavy duty driving belts by laminating leather to oriented nylon strip.

Glass Reinforced Nylon

The useful range of nylon moldings can be increased by the addition of chopped glass fiber to the molding powder. This increases the elastic modulus, tensile strength and heat distortion temperature and reduces thermal expansion and dimensional changes due to water absorption. Creep is also improved (particularly at elevated temperature). Such compounds can produce moldings which are often capable of replacing light metals and, in particular, zinc alloys in die casting. Applications include door handles, rollers for sliding doors, and hinges on domestic equipment. The oil resistance of such moldings has been made use of for the manufacture of oil dip-stick tubes while strength and rigidity are utilised in window fasteners and door fittings.

A relatively new member to the family of polyamides is the amorphous types which has been introduced by Emser Werke Ag in Switzerland and now being offered by Union Carbide Corp. in the U.S.A. under the trade name Amidel. Other similar materials are Trogamid T supplied by Dynamit Nobel AG and PACP 9/6 supplied by Phillips Petroleum.

Most polyamides are crystalline and opaque but this particular type is transparent and has been developed for applications where this property is essential. Such a plastic is more economical than glass because it is possible to mold complex parts at low costs and at the same time cut weight and the hazard of breakage.

The exact nature of the chemistry of these new polyamides is obscure because of the scant information offered by the manufacturers but certain claims are made for their properties. Like all other polyamides these materials have a high degree of resistance to most solvents and are better than other clear thermoplastics such as the polycarbonates. in particular, they are resistant to fuel, oil, grease, with the added advantage of having a low humidity absorption. They also have outstanding resistance to stress cracking.

The claims for the applications for these new materials are numerous and include sight glasses for measuring instruments, caps and covers for fuse and junction boxes in the electrical industries, valves, filter and flow meters. At the moment these polymers are under test by many large consumers of plastics and it is anticipated that the field of application will widen in the not too distant future.

Casting

Where large parts are required, the processes of extrusion of injection molding are not suitable and in situ polymerisation, or monomer casting, is utilised. This process offers the advantage of lower cost and is effective for parts ranging in weight from one to several hundred pounds. Where smaller parts are required they can be machined from rod or sheet.

Lactam type monomers are used in the casting process, the polymerisation being effected with anionic co-catalysts. Lactam flakes are melted under conditions of controlled temperature and atmospheric humidity. The melt is divided into two portions to which are added the catalyst and co-catalyst (or activator) respectively. The solutions are then thoroughly mixed and poured into the molds. Additives, such as colorants, must be thoroughly dried prior to use in order to prevent incomplete polymerisation. Cooling of the cast part is allowed to proceed very slowly in order to prevent the development of internal stresses. Packing in insulating material for up to 24 hours, cooling in an oven or annealing in a bath of highly refined mineral oil have all been used, the last-mentioned giving the best results.

Cast nylon has a higher molecular weight than molded or extruded nylon and has a greater crystallinity. It has, therefore, a higher modulus, higher heat deflection temperature, lower moisture absorption, and better dimensional stability.

Applications for nylon castings include gears, slide, bearing, and heavy duty rotational bearing where the material's lubricity, strength and wear resistance are important. Nylon's chemical resistance has been utilised in pulleys for overhead gates in dilute chlorine environments and for chain wear strips in contact with caustic soda. Other factors influencing cast nylon parts, such as gears, are reduced noise levels and reduced use of oils, greases, and other lubricants.

12

Acrylic Polymers

POLYACRYLATES AND POLYMETHACRYLATES

The laboratory history of acrylic monomers began as early as 1843 when acrylic acid was first synthesised.

This was followed in 1865 by the preparation of ethyl methacrylate by Frankland and Duppa, while in 1877 Fitting and Paul noted that it had a tendency to polymerise. By 1900, most of the common acrylates had been prepared in the laboratory and some work had also been done in their polymerisation. In 1901, Dr. Rohm, in Germany, started systematic work in the acrylic field and later took an active part in the industrial development of the acrylic ester polymers in the country. Polymethyl acrylate was the first acrylic polymer to be produced industrially. It was marketed as a solution of the polymer in an organic solvent and was used mainly in lacquers and surface coatings. Later, Rowland Hill (of I.C.I.) studied methyl methacrylate and its polymerisation in detail, while Crawford (also of I.C.I.) development an economic method of manufacturing the monomer.

Preparation of Monomers

In order to avoid possible confusion between acrylic and methacrylic esters and acids, the basic acrylic formula should be noted. This is :

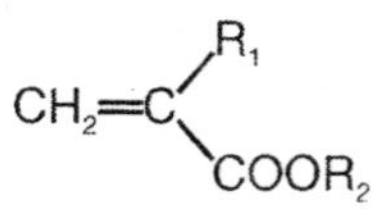

Replacement of R_1 or R_2, or both, by hydrogen, or an aliphatic group such as methyl (CH_3) or ethyl (C_2H_5) yields as wide range of acrylic monomers. Replacement of R_1 and R_2 by hydrogen, for instance, gives acrylic acid, while if R_1 is replaced instead by a methyl group, we have methacrylic acid.

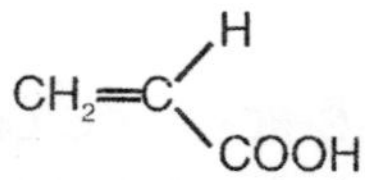
Acrylic acid

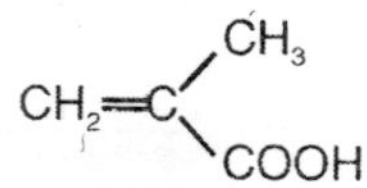
Methacrylic acid

All the monomers dealt with in the next two sections are esters of one or the other of these two acids. The formulas of the methyl esters, for example, are given below :

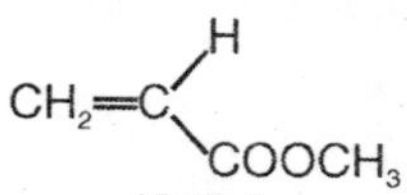
Methyl acrylate

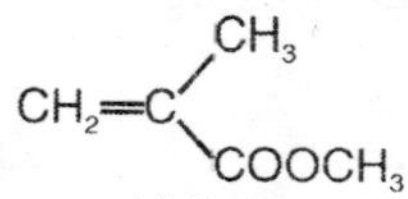
Methyl methacrylate

Preparation of Acrylates

Methyl acrylate is a liquid, boiling at about 90°C, which can be prepared as follows :

(a) One commercial synthesis is based on the reaction of ethylene oxide with hydrogen cyanide which yields ethylene cyanohydrin. Further reaction with methyl alcohol and sulfuric acid then gives methyl acetate.

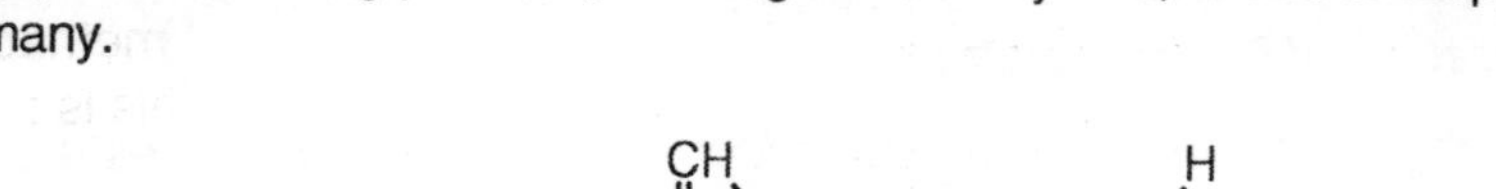
Ethylene oxide — Hydrogen cyanide — Ethylene cyanohydrin — Methyl acrylate — Ammonium bisulfate

(b) The following process, starting from acetylene, is due to Reppe in Germany.

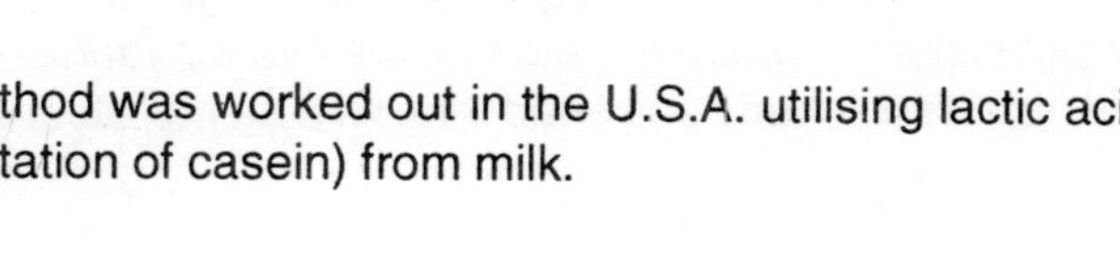
Acetylene — Nickel carbonyl — Methyl acrylate

(c) A method was worked out in the U.S.A. utilising lactic acid wastes (after precipitation of casein) from milk.

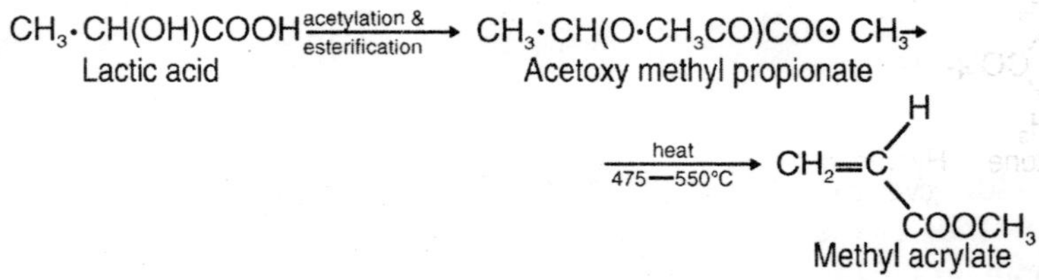

(d) A more recent process is based on the oxidation of propylene.

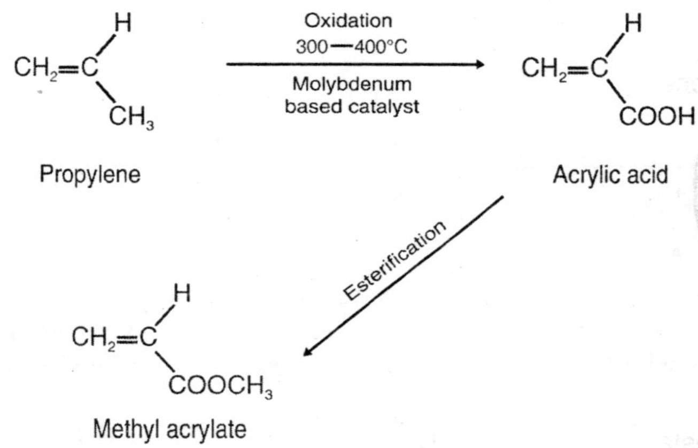

The higher acrylic esters, such as ethyl acrylate, may be produced by process (a) and (b) abcve, by substitution of the appropriate higher alcohol for methyl alcohol.

Preparation of Methacrylates

Methyl methacrylate, the most important of the methacrylic esters, is a liquid boiling at about 101°C. Methods of preparation are given below.

(a) The first commercial preparation of methyl methacrylate was as follows :

Acetone was reacted with hydrogen cyanide, or sodium cyanide, in the presence of potassium hydroxide. The acetone cyanohydrin so formed was then reacted, first with sulfuric acid, and then with methyl alcohol and water.

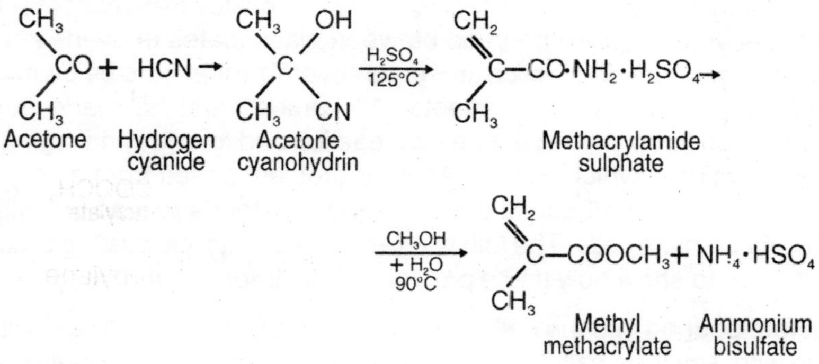

(b) A process utilising acetylene is the following.

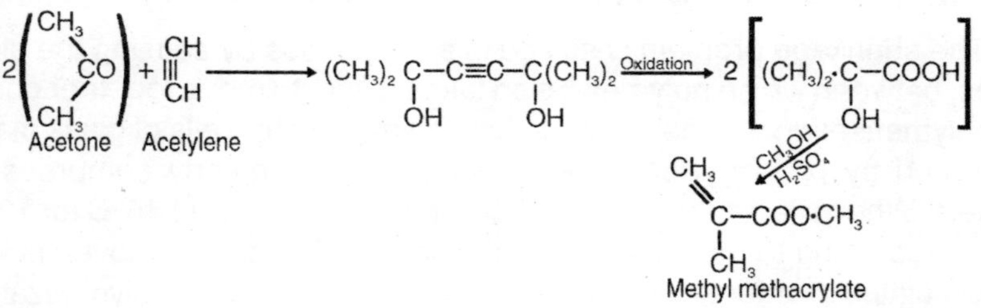

Higher esters may again by prepared by substitution of the appropriate higher alcohol for methyl alcohol.

Polymerisation

Five basic methods can be used for the polymerization of the acrylates and methacrylates. These are :

(a) Bulk polymerisation
(b) Solution polymerisation
(c) Emulsion polymerisation
(d) Suspension polymerisation
(e) Granulation polymerisation

(a) *Bulk Polymerisation.* This process is the one used for the manufacture of cast sheet, rods, and tubes and can be illustrated by the method of making methyl methacrylate sheet. Since the monomer usually contains an inhibitor (such as hydroquinone) to prevent polymerisation during handling and storage, this must first be removed by washing with alkali or by distillation under reduced pressure. A monomer suoluble catalyst, such as benzoyl peroxide or azoisobutyronitrile, is added to the inhibitor-free monomer and polymerisation allowed to proceed between glass plates in ovens kept at medium temperature. In practice, there are several problems to be overcome in order to produce flawless sheets. Allowance must be made during polymerisation for removing the heat of reaction and for the shrinkage of 20 per cent in volume which occurs. Another problem arises from a very low viscocity of methyl methacrylate monomer which tends to lead to leakage from the glass-plate cells. The following account of a typical casting process should serve to show how these problems have been overcome.

Before pouring into the cells, the monomer is thickened into a syrup by heating with, say, one half per cent benozyl peroxide for a few minutes, with stirring. It is then cooled to room temperature and deaerated by vaccumisation. After filtering through a cloth, it is ready for use. If the syrup is not to be used immediately, it can safely be stored under refrigeration.

The shrinkage problem is solved in an ingenious by causing the glass plates, between which polymerisation takes place, to move together during the polymerisation process. This is done by making up cells of glass plates separated by polyvinyl chloride, or some other similarly compressible gaskets. When filled, the cells are placed in an oven at about 45°C for 12-40 hours (according to the thickness of the sheet). The air in the oven is kept well circulated in order to dissipate the heat generated during polymerization. Towards the end of polymerisation, the viscocity becomes extremely high thus preventing free circulation of the small amount of monomer still remaining. The temperature is raised, therefore to about 90°C for a short time in order to cure and sheet completely. After removal from the cell, the sheets are annealed to remove residual stresses, by hanging vertically in an oven, and heating to about 140°C for a period of time (depending on the thickness of the sheet), following this by show cooling.

(b) *Solution Polymerisation.* This method is of particular value where the residual product is desired for use in solution form, as in adhesives or lacquers. The molecular weight is usually lower than is attainable by the bulk process. The monomer is added to an organic solvent in which both the monomer and polymer are soluble. Typical solvents which have been used for acrylic esters are toluene, acetone, and ethyl acetate. The catalyst used must also be soluble in the solvent, and organic peroxides such as benzoyl peroxide and lauryl peroxide have been found suitable. Solution polymerisation is carried out in stainless steel or glass-linked reaction vessels fitted with agitators and cooling jackets.

(c) *Emulsion Polymerisation.* The emulsifier and a water soluble catalyst are first added to the water, followed by the monomer which is dispersed by agitation. Polymerisation is then carried out by heating. Typical water soluble catalysts suitable for this reaction include hydrogen peroxide, ammonium persulfate, and potassium persulfate. Emulsifiers may be anionic or nonionic surface active agents but the nonionics are favoured because of their greater stability. Acrylic emulsions so formed are used for leather-coatings and in the manufacture of water-based paints.

(d) *Suspension Polymerisation.* This method is very similar to emulsion polymerisation described above and utilises similar equipment. The monomer is added to water and broken into small droplets by agitation. A protective colloid is also added in order to prevent the possible coalescence of these droplets when polymerisation is partially completed. Typical protective colloids include polyvinyl alcohol and sodium polyacrylate. In suspension polymerisation, the reaction takes place in the monomer phase so that monomer-soluble catalysts must be used, the most common being benzoyl peroxide. The water acts as a heat transfer medium and the temperature of the bath remains constant. The product is obtained in the from the small beads which are screened, washed and dried.

(e) *Granulation Polymerisation.* This process is one often used for the production of molding powders and is a variant of the suspension technique. Only a small amount of water is used, together with some lubricant and either a water or monomer-soluble catalyst. Polymerisation is carried out in a heavy duty mixer with a sigma blade agitator. Continual kneading of the material during polymerisation results in the formation of fluffy, granular particles. No emulsifiers or protective colloids, are added and the product is thus extremely pure.

Properties

A wide range of properties exists, depending on the type of monomer or monomers used. In general, for both polyacrylates and polymethacylates, the lower esters are tougher, harder, and have higher softening points than the higher esters. For example, polymethyl methacrylate has softening point of about 125°C and a tensile strength of 9000 lb/in_2, while polybutyl methacrylate softens at 33°C and has a tensile strength of 1000 lb/in^2.

Polymethyl methacrylate is soluble in most ketones, esters, and aromatic and chlorinated hydrocarbons, and is swollen by contact with ether. It is resistant, however to attack by alkalis, most dilute acids and aqueous solutions of inorganic salts.

Electrical properties are excellent, a particular virtue of polymethyl methacrylate being its nontracking properties.

Some of the physical and chemical properties of polymethyl methacrylate are shown in Table 12.1.

Table 12.1

PHYSICAL AND CHEMICAL PROPERTIES OF POLYMETHYL METHACRYLATE

Property	*Units*	*Cast*	*Molded*
Specific gravity		1.17-1.20	1.17-1.20
Refractive inde		1.48-1.50	1.49
Tensile strength	lb/in.^{2}	8000-11,600	7000-11,000
Elongation at break	%	3-7	3-10
Modulus of elasticity	lb/in.^{2}	3.5-4.5 X 10^5	4.5 X 10^5
Impact strength	ft lb/in notch	0.4-0.5	0.3-0.5
Hardness	Rockwell Scale M	80-100	85-105
Water absorption	% in 24 h	0.3-0.4	0.3-0.4
Vol. resistivity	ohm/cm	$>10^{15}$	$>10^{14}$
Power factor (10^6cycles)		0.02-0.03	0.02-0.03
Effect of weak acids		Negligible	Negligible
Effect of weak alkalis		Negligible	Negligible
Effect of strong acids		Attacked by oxidising acids and sulfuric acid	
Effect of strong alkalis		Attacked	Attacked
Effect of organic solver		Resistant to alcohols at room temperature, Soluble in esters, ketones, and aromatic chloric-nated hydrocarbons	

The most important differences between polymethyl methacrylate and polymethyl acrylate are as follows :

(a) The methacrylate is more stable to aging and to discoloration than the acrylate.

(b) The methacrylate has the lower water absorption of the two.

(c) The acidity of the methacrylate is nil whereas the acrylate has a slight acidity.

(d) The methacrylate is resistant to alkaline hydrolysis whereas the acrylate hydrolyses to give the sodium salt of polyacrylic acid, which is water soluble.

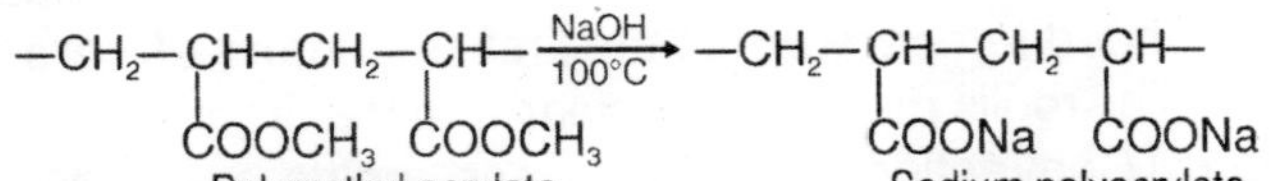

Polymethyl acrylate   Sodium polyacrylate

Many other esters are knwon and a wide variety of material has been obtained by copolymerisation but these are outside the scope of this book. However, mention may be made of polyethoxyethyl methacrylate which is obtainable as a soft, flexible film, and polybutyl methacrylate which is intermediate in properties between the polyethoxyethyl methacrylate and polymethyl methacrylate (which is hard and brittle).

Processing techniques

Polymethyl methacrylate can be machined with conventional wood or metal working machinery provided the tools are sharp and cleanly ground. Fractional overheating must be avoided in order to prevent gumming up of the tools. One method of cooling is to blow compressed air on the work; this has the additional advantage of removing swarf,etc. After machining operations have been completed, the work can be polished by means of a rotating head fitted with chamois or flannel. If the finish is too rough after machining, it will be necessary to sand and buff the work before final polishing can be carried out. It is also desirable to finish with an annealing operation to relieve any stresses induced by the machining or by the heating and cooling undergone during the finishing operation.

Polymethyl methacrylate sheet can readily be formed when heated to 150-170°C when it is soft and pliable. If no stretching is required, the material is simply draped over the required from and allowed to cool. If stretching is necessary, matched molds are used or else the sheet is made to conform to the surface of a single mold by means of air pressure or vaccum. Only simple molds are required as a rule, and these may be made from wood, metal, plaster etc. Vaccum-forming of polymethyl methacrylate and other plastic sheets is considered in some details in Chapter 24.

Polymethyl methacrylate molding powders can be injection molded extruded or compression molded. The extrusion process obviously offers another means of manufacturing sheet, especially where very large sizes are concerned. Widths of up to five or six feet are available with, of course a practically unlimited choice of lengths. Much developmental work has been carried out on the extrusion of acrylics and it is now possible to produce sheet with uniform thickness, freedom from residual stresses, an even gloss, and freedom from surface defects. Air quenching is used, and the cooling should not be too rapid otherwise freeze-off lines appear across the sheet. The recommended temperature of the first set of take-off rolls is between 38 and 55°C. The roolls must also be clean and free from any sort of surface imperfections. Conventional machines and molds are used in injection molding but it should be noted that the molding powder has a tendency to pick up moisture, and predrying for two to three hours in tray ovens at about 85-95°C is recommended just prior to molding.

Articles can be fabricated in polymethyl methacrylate by means of cements. The three main methods of joining polymethyl methacylate to itself are by straight solvents (chloroform, ehtylene chloride etc.) or by solutions of the polymers in either the monomer or a solvent.

Emulsions and solutions of acrylate and methacrylate can be made up into paints and adhesives, or used for the coating of textiles, paper, leather, etc. Among the desirable properties which can be imparted to textiles by acrylic emulsions are also fast to washing and do not yellow grease and oil. Acrylic emulsions are also fast to washing and do not yellow with age. Acrylic emulsion paint exhibit good scrub resistance, are resistant to freezing and, again, do not yellow with age.

Applications

One of the best-known uses for polymethyl methacrylate sheeting in glazing. During WW II it was extensively used on aircraft for wind-shields, cockpit covers, gunners' blisters, etc. Similar applications have also been found in the motor-boat industry, namely, wind shields and canopies. The use of acrylic sheeting in buildings is also growing. In addition to the replacement of glass in conventional glazing, polymethyl methacrylate sheet lends itself to the use of molded skylight domes, which are less liable to breakage, are airtight and rain-proof. Another form of roof glazing in creasing in popularity is corrugated polymethyl methacrylate sheet. Indoor building uses include room dividers, doors, and shower cubicles.

A further large market for polymethyl methacryalte sheet includes outdoor signs and other display materials where its opitcal properties lend themselves to some interesting lighting effects.

In the domestic field, the development of sanitary were and baths manufactured from acrylic sheet provides color at no extra cost. It has greatly increased the market for colored baths compared with that which existed when only expensive enameled cast-iron baths were available. The injection molding field, too, has benefited from the color possibilities of acrylics a good example being telephones.

Industrial uses of polymethyl methacrylate are also numerous and include instrument panels, safety shields, inspection windows, protective goggles, and water baths. It has also been used to construct various demonstration models or equipment, the clarity of the material allowing complete visibility of all working parts.

Medical uses of the acrylics are many, the most interesting being the manufacture of artificial eyes, contact lenses, and artificial dentures. The latter utilises a slurry of a polymer in a monomer. The polymer powder is mixed with the monomer and made into a dough with a catalyst and an activator. The dough is pressed into a plaster mold which has been coated with a release agent, and plymerisation is carried out at low temperature.

The resistance of breaking of polymethyl methacrylate is also used to advantage in the manufacture of so-called unbreakable is also used to the faces of delicate instruments. Similarly, it is extensively used for lenses (torches, magnifying lenses, etc.) and bulkhead covers for lighting units.

Acrylic polymers in the form of emulsions and solutions are used extensively in the treatment of textiles, paper, and leather. In the treatment of textiles, for instance, acrylic, resins, are added to improve abrasion and flex resistance. They are also added to give improved crease resistance to fabrics already treated with the thermosetting resin. Upto about 5 per cent of the acrylic polymer is usually recommended. In leather, acrylic emulsions are used for the base coating, the emulsion serving as a binder for the pigment and forming a strong bond with a surface of the tanned hide.

Paints based on acrylic emulsions are now available in the U.S.A. as well as the better known polyvinyl acetate and butadiene/styrene based products. The acrylic emulsion paints are claimed to possess better scrub resistance and to be applicable over damp surfaces. Another advantage is their resistance to yellowing on aging.

A wide range of adhesives is available using various acrylate monomers and polymers. One extremely important property in certain application is their clarity. Adhesives based on monomers alone are usually polymerised in situ to form excellent bonds. Polymer based adhesives on the other hand can be solvent based (air drying) hot melt, or pressure sensitive types.

The versatility of acrylic emulsions is also shown by their use in floor waxes. The polymers normally used for this purpose are based on methyl methacrylate, methyl and ethyl acrylates, and methacylic acid. The acrylic emulsions are usually added to the wax or wax/polyethylene emulsion and are said to give clear, hard, and glossy and films with excellent toughness and rigidity.

Reference may also be made here to the use of methacrylate monomer as a cross-linking agent for polyesters (see chapter 5).

MISCELLANEOUS ACRYLICS

Acrylic Rubbers

The main class of acrylic rubbers is formed by the copolymerisation of acrylonitrile and butadiene. The production of both of these monomers has already been described in Chapter 11. The normal method used for copolymerising butadiene and acrylonitrile is based on emulsion techniques. The latex so produced can be used directly for coating or impregnation or it can be coagulated by precipitation with a salt solution, followed by washing and drying. This produces a dry crumb which is then compounded and milled into slab form.

Basically acrylonitrile/butadiene rubbers are resistant to solvents and oils but the extent of this is development on the acrylonitrile content of the rubber. This, of course, also holds true for other properties. An increase in the acrylonitrile content produces an increase in oil and solvent resistance, tensile, strength, and hardness, together with a corresponding decrease in solubility, resilience and low temperature impact strength. Acrylonitrile/butadiene rubbers have low permeability to gases and a better resistance to chemicals than that of natural rubber. Resistance to heat, abrasion, and creep is also good.

Acrylonitrile/butadiene rubber latics are used for coating industrial gloves, various metal items, tarpaulins, and electrical tapes. They also find outlets in caulking and gasketing materials.

Acrylic rubbers based on ethyl acrylate, have also been produced. One example of this type is lactoprene EV, which was originally developed by the U.S. Department of Agriculture. It is produced by the emulsion polymerisation of ethyl acrylate (95 per cent) and α-chloroethyl vinyl ether (five per cent). It possess good oil resistance, flex life, and resistance to degradation by heat and aging. Lactoprene, and other rubbers based on ethyl acylate are easily cross-linked (vulcanised) using such systems as amines, metal oxides, dioximes, and sulfur, plus accelerators.

Fluoroacrylic elastomers are also known but are best treated in relation to the other fluorocarbon polymers.

Acrylic Fibers

These are based on acrylonitrile and have made an important contribution to the science of man-made fibers. Research was first started on the possible use of polyacrylonitrile as a fiber by Du pont, in the early years of WW II and considerable success has since been achieved. High molecular weight polymers of acrylonitrile are necessary for the production of fibers. There are two possible routes for fiber formation, depending on whether the polymer is melted or dissolved in a suitable solvent. Whichever method is used, the resultant viscous liquid is extruded through a die with very fine holes. At this stage, therefore, is to stretch the fiber in order to orient the molecules along the exis of the fiber and produce a degree of crystallisation. This is accompanied by great increase in tensile strength, the fiber then being ready for normal processes such as spinning and felting. It can also be used in monofilament form.

Dyeing 100 per cent acrylonitrile presents problems because of its chemical inertness. This had led to the production of various copolymers in order to improve dye reception. Other methods used to improve dyeability include opening the fiber to facilitate diffusion of the dyestuff, and the use fo anionic dye receptors.

In general, polyacrylonitrile fibers have good resistance to chemicals, heat and moisture, while their resistance to aging and sunlight is outstanding. In addition to the extensive use of acrylic fibers in the field of clothing, they are used for filter cloths, blankets, awnings, and ropes. Acrylic fibers have also been used in the manufacture of excellent imitation furs.

MISCELLANEOUS COPOLYMERS

Styrene-Methyl Methacrylic Copolymer

This was developed to improve the ease of molding of polymethyl methacrylate while still retaining its good resistance to outdoor weathering, its light stability and its heat resistance. An example of the type of molding possible with this copolymer is a street-lamp globe developed in the U.S.A. The globe was injection molded in two halves and solvent cemented with toluene. The diameter of the larger part was 16 inches and it was16½ inches high. Shatter resistance was found to be much greater than that of similar glass globe and the total efficiency, in terms of lighting performance, was similar. The diffusion properties, however, were significantly better in the plastic globe.

Ethylene-Methyl Acrylate Copolymer

This material has a very high degree of flexibility, coupled with good low-temperature characteristics (usable down to-100°C). Typical application include flexible conduit for industrial use. This tubing is constructed by extruding a continuous strip, roughtly, S-shaped in cross section, which is then spirally wound and heat sealed.

Lopac

Lopac is the trade name for a material by Monsanto Chemical Company Limited and is a terpolymer. The basic monomer is methacrylonitrile and this is copolymerised with about 5 per cent styrene and 5 per cent methyl styrene. It is a hard and rather brittle polymer but it has a high resistance to creep and is an excellent barrier to gases, especially carbon dioxide. It also possesses good clarity. The terpolymer was developed mainly as a brittle blowing material for the carbonated drinks market where these properties are important.

Chemical resistance to aqueous liquids is good but the material is soluble, in acetone, methyl ethyl ketone, and methylene chloride.

Barex

Barex is the trade name for a material made by Vistron Division of Standard Oil of Ohio. It is made by copolymerising a 75:25 mixture of acrylonitrile and methyl acrylate in the presence of a small amount of a butadiene/acrylonitrile elastomer. This material was also originally developed as a brittle blowing material for carbonated drinks. It has good clarity, excellent gas barrier properties, and high resistance to creep. In addition, it has good impact strength and is insoluble in most organic solvents.

It is also produced in the form of film and sheet and when laminated with other materials such as low density polyethylene it is suitable for thermoforming containers for cheese and meat. In such applications it competes with nylon/polyvinylidene chloride laminates by virtue of its low gas permeability, its resistance to uv light and its toughness.

13

High Performance Thermoplastics

In recent years, the light and non ferrous metal industries have met with keen competition from plastics, particularly in the building and automobile industries. Some of the advantages of plastics, as compared with some of the better known metals, are their excellent resistance to corrosion, non-requirement of highly skilled methods of finishing, and comparatively low price per unit volume. Aluminium, in particular, has been rivaled by polyethylene, the modified polystyrenes and polyvinyl chloride. The introduction and development of other thermoplastics, dealt with in this chapter, has made available materials which are suitable for high performance application that hitherto have been restricted to metals.

CHLORINATED POLYETHERS

Chlorinated polyethers first became commercially available in the U.S.A. around 1959, although initial investigations were carrried out in the early 1950's. They were made by the Hercules powder Co. Inc. and sold under the trade name of Penton. The base polymer was produced from pentaerythritol by initital preparing a chlorinated oxetane and then opening the ring structure and polymerising to a high molecular weight polyether using a Lewis acid, the indicated number average range being 250-350,000.

Unfortunately, about four yeas ago the manufacturers of the chlorinated polyether decided that they could no longer make this polymer as a commercial proposition and withdraw if from the market. However, it is still included in the book because the chemistry of manufacture is interesting and some very novel uses were found for it.

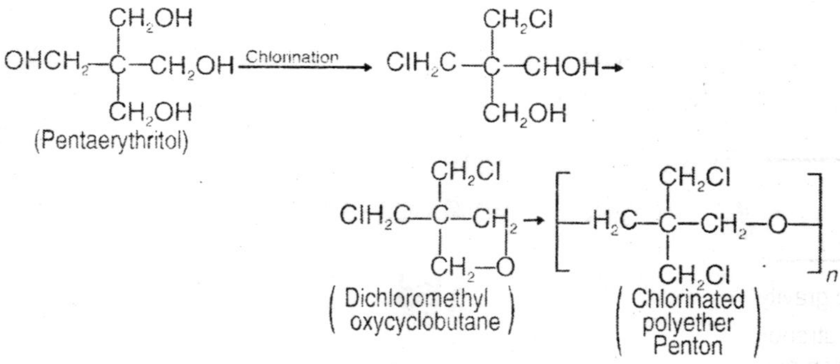

A commercial chlorinated polyether contains approximately 46 per cent by weight of chlorine and the position of each chlorine atom in a chloromethyl group attached to the central carbon atom makes for excellent chemical stability. The polymer so formed is a linear high molecular weight material possessing a high degree of crystallinity and, unlike most halogenated polymers, it is extremely resistant to thermal degradation. Due to its highly crystalline nature, the polymer has a fairly low melt viscocity which, of course, is an aid to the easy filling to molds; thus a molding with low shrinkage on cooling is obtained (usually 0.005 in./in.). This low volume change from the liquid to the solid state also facilitates the manufacture of molds from which moldings can be produced with a high degree of precision. Unlike some thermoplastics which, on solidifying, set up with internal stresses, the chlorinated polyethers rêturn from the amorphous to the crystalline state at a rate which produces stress-free moldings that can be machanised very easily; thus, components with exceptional dimensional stability are obtained.

Properties

The properties of Penton are fully listed in Table 13.1 The normal maximum surface temperature (120°C) of this material is above that of conventional thermopastics, and this factor, coupled with a lower water absorption value, makes it suitable for components which require sterilising repeatedly. The chlorinated polyethers possess excellent electrical properties as well as a high degree of chemical resistance. Like most materials containing chlorine in the polymer chain they are inherently self-extinguishing.

The chlorinated polyether resins were characterised by a very high degree of chemical resistance to alkalis, solvents, and mineral acids. They are attacked by fuming nitric acid and sulfuric acid as well as chlorinated solvents.

Table 13.1

PROPERTIES OF CHLORINATED POLYETHERS, POLYACETALS AND POLYCARBONATES

Test	*Method A.S.T.M.*	*Chlorinated polyether*	*Polycarbonate*	*Polyacetal homopolymer*
Specific gravity	D 792	1.4	1.2	1.425
Tensile strength (lb/in.^{2})	D 638	6000	9000	10,000
Elongation at break (%)	D 638	50-150	60-100	15-75
Flexural strength (lb/in.^{2})	D 790	5000	11,000	14,000
Impact strength (ft lb/in. of notch)	D 256	0.4	12-16	1-2
Thermal expansion (10^{-5} per °C)	D 696	8	7	8
Heat distortion temp. °F (66 lb/in.^{2})	D 648	285	280-290	338
Volume resistivity (ohm-cm)	D 257	1×10^{16}	2×10^{16}	6×10^{14}
Dielectric Strength (V/mil)	D 149	400	400	450
Dielectric constant (10^6 c/s)	D 150	3	3	3.7
	D150	0.011	0.01	0.004
Inflammability	D 635	self-extin-guishing	self-extin-guishing	burns very slowly
Water absorption % (24h)	D 570	0.1	0.3	0.12
Mold shrikage in./in.		0.005	0.006	0.0256
Chemical Resistance				
Ketones		R *	A **	R
Water		R	R	R
Aldehvdes		R	A	R
Esters		R	A	R
Aromatic hydrocarbons		R	A	R
Weak organic bases (aniline)		R	A	R
Ammonia		R	A	A
Weak acids		R	R	R
Strong acids		A	A	A
Weak alkalis		R	R	R
Strong alkalis		R	A	A

* R = resistant

** A = attackee

Processing

These polymers may be injection molded in standard machines, using ordinary chromed or polished hard steel dies. Components with wall thicknesses of up to 1/16 in. can be molded in 20 s or less. It may also be extruded, using screw designs similar to those used for nylon or polyethylene, with extrusion barrel and die temperatures in the range 182-230°C. Preheating is recommended where increased rates of extrusion are required and in this respect it is, of course, similar to conventional thermoplastics. However, predrying the molding material is not necessary before use for injection or extrusion as with some thermoplastics. This material can be readily formed into rods, tubes, shapes, sheet, films, and wire coatings. Sheet and film can be extruded by conventional means using a three stack calender for sheet, or a single casting roll for film. Coatings with a homogeneous void-free finish up to 40 mil thick are used for coated valves, pumps and meters, and they may be applied to various substrates such as steel, glass or paper, by water or solvent dispersion systems or by using the fluidised-bed technique of coating.

Applications

The chlorinated polyethers were high price, high performance materials, the price restricting their wider usage. The present markets are mainly in the field of chemical processing and precision injection molded industrial parts, and include solid, lined, and coated metal pipes, pipe fittings, valves, pumps and lines tanks. As a lining material this polymer readily converts carbon steel tanks into vessels capable of handling highly corrosive fluids at elevated temperature. The precision injection-molded parts may take the place of some of the more conventional materials used in the metal casting industry. The growth of the market undoubtedly lies in the excellent combination of high strength, heat resistance, and excellent electrical properties and chemical resistance exhibited by these materials.

POLYACETALS

Polymers based on formaldehyde have been known since 1859 when they were first described by Butlerow. Formaldehyde is a very reactive material yet the initial polymers obtained from it were of low molecular weight and melted with rapid decomposition at about 150°C. Until recently, therefore, these polymers have been of little commercial use and were originally largely regarded as mere research curiosities. It has been suggested earlier that thermoplastics polymers produced from aldehydes are of no importance for such applications as fibers, surface coatings, plastics of rubber due to their tendency to depolymerise rapidly. The polymerising, this material may take one of the following forms :

(i) Polyoxymethylene or polymethylene glycols

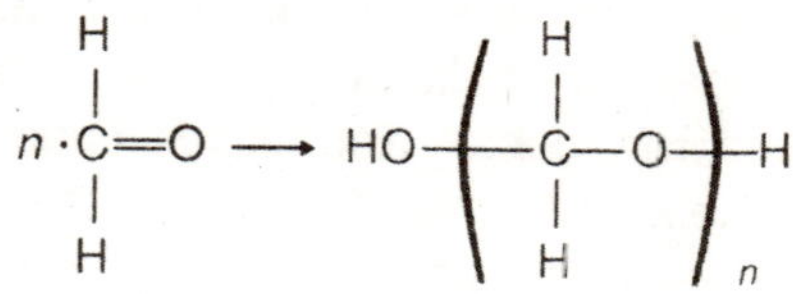

(ii) Sugar-type polymers

If formaldehyde is polymerized under midly alkaline conditions, polyhydroxy compounds are formed.

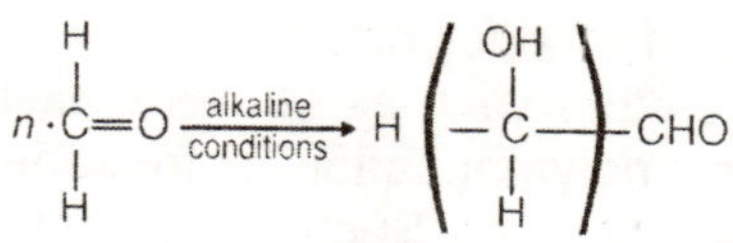

Most of the oxygen atoms are lateral to the main backbone in sugar type polymers; they are low molecular weight and are thought to have little or no industrial applications.

A great deal of research work has been carried out on these polymers throughout the past years, and early as 1920 Staudinger and coworkers produced formaldehyde polymers which exhibited plastic-like properties. It was established that these polymers were not of the sugar-type but consisted essentially of molecular chains with repeating oxymethylene groups. Unfortunately, although insoluble in cold solvents, they decomposed on heating. The fault of decomposition on exposure to heat has now been overcome and during the last twenty years a large chemical company, E.I. Du Pont de Nemours, has been trying to correct this drawback. Methods have now been devised for polymerising formaldehyde to give high molecular weight polymer possessing high thermal stability. Either nucleophilic or electrophilic agents are used as initiators in forming industrial polymers.

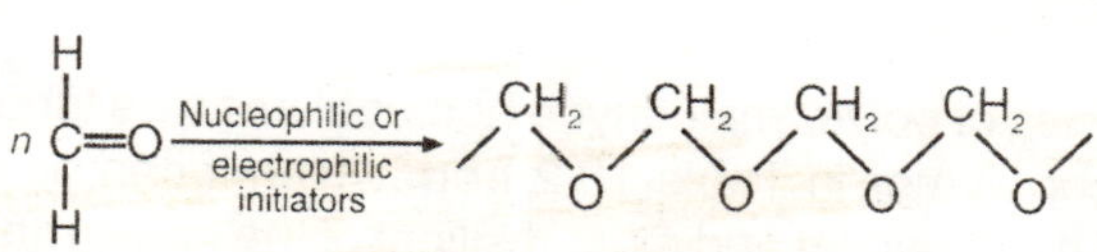

Polyformaldehyde
(mol. wt approx 20 000)

These are high molecular weight stable polymers with good mechanical strength. This letter property results from the ability of the oxymethylene (—CH_2O) chains to pack together into a highly ordered cyrstalline configuration as the polymer moves from the molten to the solid state.

The types of initiators used are: simple acids and bases, organic, acids, Lewis acids, amines, organo-metallic components, phosphines, arsines, stibenes, or carbonyls of iron, cobalt, and nickel. These polymers may be regarded basically as linear, with molecular weights in excess of 20,000. The end hydroxyl group may be esterified to give a polymer with acetate and group, which give it greater thermal and hydrolytic stability. For a typical polymerisation method for formaldehyde, the reaction medium can be hexane and the inititator may be triphenyl phosphine.

A later development in this field was the introduction by the Celanese Corporation of America of a copolymer having formaldehyde as a major constituent and a cyclic ether such as ethylene oxide as the minor one. Another variation is the polymerisation of trioxane,, a cyclic trimer of formaldehyde, to give acetal resins. Such a polymer has a highly crystalline structure and the C—C double bonds which are randomly distributed in the polymer chain from the comonomer help to stabilise the polymer against thermal oxidative and acidic attack. If these copolymers are heated to high temperatures, oxidation occurs and the depolymerisation which generally results in such a reaction is cut short at the —C—C— bond which both accounts for the high level of resistance of these polymers to attack by strong alkalis..

These polymers are known as acetal resins and are manufactured in the U.S.A. under the trade names of Delrin for the homopolymer and Celcon for the copolymer. Their unique properties are regarded as a bridge betwc en plastics and metals, having, in fact, replaced metals in a large number of important mechanical structural applications. The metal like properties exhibited by these polymers make them high performance materials, with high strength and rigidity, excellent dimensional stability, resilience and toughness.

Properties

The properties of polyformaldehyde homopolymer are tubulated in Table 13.1 and the copolymer in Table 13.2 from which it can be seen that the family is one of the toughest and most resilient of the known thermoplastics. The load-bearing characteristics of the acetal polymers, in both compression and tension, are impressive compared with conventional thermoplastics.

Table 13.2

PROPERTIES OF HIGH PERFORMANCE THERMOPLASTICS

Property	ASTM Method	UNREINFORCED RESINS: Acetal Copolymer	Acetal Homopolymer	Styrene Modified PPO	Polycarbonate	G.P. and H.S. Nylon 66	Thermoplastic Polyester
Specific gravity (g/cm^3)	D 792	1.410	1.425	1.06	1.20	1.14	1.31
Tensile strength : @ yield (psi)	D 638	8800	10,000	9600	9000	8500*	8000
Elongation : @ break (%)	D 638	60	25	25	110	300*	300
Tensile modulus (psi X 10^{-5})	D 638	4.10	5.20	3.55	3.45	-	-
Flexural strength (psi)	D 790	13,000	14,100	13,500	13,500	6000*	12,000
Flexural strength (psi X 10^{-5})	D 790	3.75	4.10	3.60	3.40	1.85*	3.30
Fatigue endurance limit (psi/no. of cycles)	D 671	4200/ 10 MM	5000/ 1 MM	2500/ 2 MM	1000/ 2.5 MM	-	2850/ 10 MM
Compressive stress, psi : @10% Def.	D 695	16,000	18,000	16,400	12,500	-	13,000
Rockwell Hardness (M)	D 785	80	94	78	70	61*	78
Notched Izod Impact (ft-lb/in. of notch)	D 256	1.3	1.4	5.0	14	2.0*	1.0
Tensile Impact (ft-lb/in.^{2})	D 1822	70	100	120	-	475*	-
Shear strength (psi)	D 732	7700	9500	10,500	10,000	8200*	7700
Water absorption: 24 h Immersion (%)	D 570	0.22	0.26		0.15	1.50	0.09
Tabor abrasion: 1000 g load, Cs-17 wheel (mg/1000 cycles)	D 1044	14	20	20	10	5*	6.5
Coefficient of dynamic friction against :	D 1894						
Steel		0.15	0.10-0.30	0.35-0.40	-	0.15	0.13
Brass		0.15	-	0.38-0.49	-	0.11	0.13
Aluminum		0.15	-		-	0.12	0.13
Self		0.35	-	0.24-0.30	-	0.24	0.17
Mold shrinkage :							
Average (mils/in.)		20	20	5-7	6	16	20
Flow Dir. (mills/in.)		22	22	-	-	-	23
Transverse.Dir. (mills/in.)		18	18	-	-	-	17

* Value obtained on specimens containing equilibrium moisture content at 50 percent R.H. (73°F).

Other outstanding properteis are their resistance to repeated impact and high abrasion resistance. The physical properties are virtually unaffected by continuous service at 80°C or intermittent use at 120°C and it remains dimensionally stable over a wide range of operating temperature. These characteristics make the polyacetals attractive for a wide variety of industrial applications.

They are excellent dielectric materials and retain their electrical characteristics under conditions of high humidity, factors which, in combination with their high mechanical properties, make them of particular value for electrical applications where high strength, resistance to abrasion, dimensional stability and good high temperature performances are required. The polyacetals also exhibit excellent resistance to organic solvents, although resistance to strong acids, bases, and oxidising agents is somewhat limited for the homopolymer. They are also unaffected by ultraviolet light and are nontoxic.

The Celcon resins are self-lubricating with good resistance to abrasion and hot water exposure. They are highly resistant to gasolene, motor oils, and greases even at elevated temperature. Specimens of this copolymers can be immersed in boiling 50 per cent sodium hydroxide solution and other such bases for many months and show no change. However, with strong acids prolonged contact should be avoided to prevent breakdown.

The polyacetals offer a combination of properties which make them important as engineering plastics. These include :

1. High rigidity combined with good short-term and long-term mechanical strength.

2. Good performance in mechanical applications combined with stability of properties and dimensions under changing ambient conditions.

3. Excellent resistance to organic chemicals and water combined with a wide operating temperature.

Processing

The acetal polymers may be fabricated with the same ease as is normally excepted with the conventional thermoplastics, with consequent cost advantages over metals. The normal molding range is between 200-230°C and the best performance is achieved on machines with fast ram speeds and high available pressure. It has been reported that one-piece integral shapes produced on injection molding do not normally require finishing and this, of course minimises the number of rejects. Rod, tube, and sheeting can be extruded from the polyacetals on conventional equipment. Extruders with a high length to diameter ratio (20 : 1) are recommended, along with a metering screw with a constant-pitch feed section. Other methods of forming, such as blow molding, may be used and both thin-walled and thick-walled containers may be produced. Thick-walled containers as required for aerosols are now manufactured from these polymers, and many are already on the market, replacing the traditional metal ones. Molded components can be machined quite simply and they may also be welded, painted, metallised, and printed on.

Applications

Typical uses that have already been found for this versatile family of plastic include ring bearings and cams, venturi-tubes, automobile instrument housings, door-knobs, pump and air impellors, hinges, shoe heals, mechanical toys, and window catches. Their use as aerosol containers is now established and other miscellaneous uses include pen and pencil parts, bottle closures, and business machine housings.

These polymers are sold in the medium price range and because of the exceptional resistance to hot water exposure they are being widely used for plumbing fittings. Added to this characteristics is a high level of corrosion resistance with a smooth self-lubricating surface which obviously resists the build-up of scale and thus makes it eminently more suitable than metals for plumbing. Further still, this family of polymers costs less than brass on a cents per cubic inch basis and can be processed into finished parts by injection molding. There has been a continued expansion of applications for these polymers over the last few years. As started previously, much of the market for these materials have been the replacement of metals of both the ferrous and the nonferrous types. Particularly die-cast zinc, aluminium, and brass have been replaced because of improved properties of reduced costs. Many other uses have been established as well as in the plumbing industry, particularly in the all-consuming automotive industry. The plumbing applications include such items as ball-cocks, shower heads, valves, pumps, and faucets.

POLYCARBONATES

These polymers may be regarded as linear polyesters of carbonic acid. As early in 1898 attempts were made by A. Einhorn to prepare cyclic carbonates from the reaction of hydroquinone with phosgene in an alkaline medium, but his work was not particularly successful in this respect since he obtained a product which was insoluble, and infusible. This material was probably a polycarbonate and the forerunner of the polymers now known today. He also reacted phosgene with resorcinol and obtained a polymer with a melting point around 200°C.

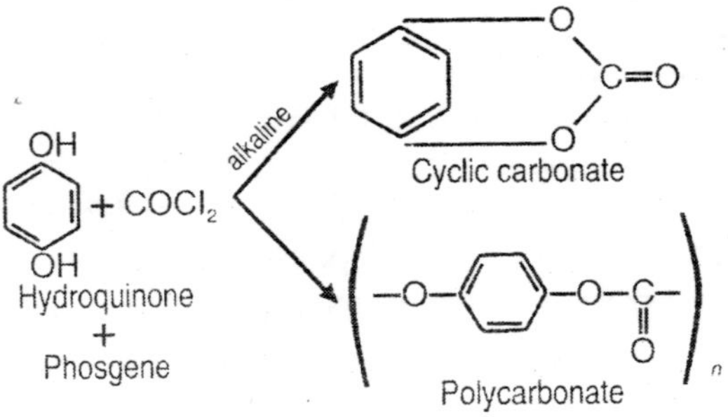

Bischoft and von hedenstorm repeated Einhorn's work early in the twentieth century, preparing the same materials by means of an ester exchange reaction. Further reserch was carried out both in Germany and the U.S.A. but it was not until 1956 that the polycarbonates were first reported as useful plastic materials. The polymers of commercial importance now manufactured are produced from bisphenol a and a diphenyl carbonate. The preparation of bisphenol A has been described in Chapter 6.

Commercially available materials include Makrolon (Bayer-Germany), Lexan (General Electric-U.S.A.) and Merlon (Mobay-U.S.A.).

Structure

H. Schnell in his 1976 Swinburne award address to the Plastic and Rubber Institute in the U.K. discussed and described the structure of a bisphenol a Polycarbonate. He found that this polymer is capable of crystallisation but it is greatly impeded. Moldings can be produced from this polymer which are either (a) x-ray amorphous, (b) x-ray amorphous and oriented (c) crystalline, or (d) oriented and crystalline.

Manufacture

There are at present three possible process and used in manufacturing polycarbonates :

(i) *Ester-interchange.* This process involves the heating of an aromatic dihydroxy compound such as bisphenol A with a metacarbonate such as diphenyl carbonate. The reaction is carried out by heating the reactants to 200-230°C, at the same time reducing the pressure to 20-30 mm Hg to remove the phenol, and finally raising the temperature to 290-300°C. The process is a simple ester interchange which may be catalysed by a basic material such as sodium hydroxide. On completion of polymerisation the resultant polymer is extruded from the reaction kettle under an inert gas.

The reaction must be stopped when the polymer is sufficiently liquid to be extruded from the resin kettle.

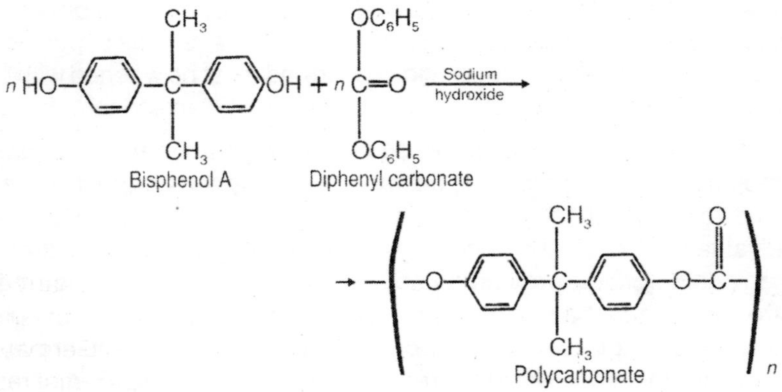

(ii) *Phosgenation Process.* This process resembles the original method used by Einhonr in preparing the first known polycarbonate. Basically, it consists of reacting the disodium salt of bisphenol A with phosgene, when a condensation reaction takes place. The bisphenol A is suspended or dissolved in sodium hydroxide and the reaction is carried out in the presence of a solvent such as methylene chloride or pyridine which is capable of dissolving the phosgene as well as the polycarbonate which is formed. This is followed by an addition of an equimolar quantity of phosgene at 20-30°C. The resultant product is a solution of low molecular weight polycarbonate which may then be converted to a higher molecular weight by continual stirring or by the addition of catalysts such as tertiary amines or quatemary ammonium bases.

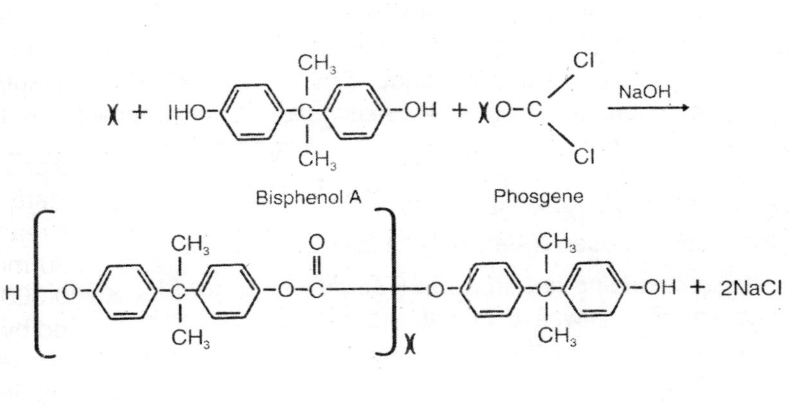

There is at least two mols of pyridine per mol of bisphenol A.

(iii) *Interfacial Polycondensation Process.* This method has achieved great significance but only recently became a practical propositions when it was discovered that the reaction could be catalysed by the addition of tertiary amines. This reaction must be kept to a minium to prevent the saponification of the phosgene. The viscous solution so formed must be washed with water and a good recovery of the solvent must be made to be an economic process.

Of the methods of polymer production it would appear by comparison that the phosgenation process is the more advantageous in that the reaction proceeds quickly with the possibility of obtaining very high molecular weight. Disadvantages include the necessity to recover solvents, and separation of inorganic salts from the polycarbonate solution. The ester interchange method has the advantage that the inorganic salts at this stage can be completely and easily separated, and it also produces an easily formed granular polymer. The main disadvantage is that the reaction is carried out at high temperatures and in vaccum, which leads to the formation of unwanted side reactions. It is difficult to choose between the two methods of production but all commercial processes known today apart from bisphenol A.

Properties

The properties of the polycarbonates are listed in Table 13.1.

A polycarbonate does not have a sharp melting point but begins to soften above the glass-transition temperature of 149°C. It then goes into a rubbery state until between 200-220°C. When it passes into the truly thermoplastic state. These materials have fairly high molecular weights and this coupled with high melt viscocity imposes a limitation as to what molecular weight types can be commercially exploited. Their excellent mechanical properties make it possible to mold high-precision structural articles with a combination of hard, rigid, and resilient characteristics, they have good thermal properties, and they have excellent electrical insulating properties, as well as transparency. Other useful properties include low water absorption, the ability to self-extinguish and fair chemical resistance to aqueous solutions. Their resistance to organic bases such as ammonia, however, is limited. The polymers are readily soluble in chlorinated hydrocarbons, are partially soluble in aromatic hydrocarbons and ketones, and are decomposed by strongly alkaline substances.

the outstanding features of these polymers are their clarity and high impact strength as well as high thermal stability, which is an important fact in processing; this is, of course, only true if moisture is absent.

Processing

Before processing polycarbonates it is essential for the base polymers to be absolutely dry. Although they possess relatively high melt viscocity they can still be processed on all conventional types of molding machines and may be injection molded at temperatures between 240-300°C. Extrusion can also be carried out satisfactorily at this temperature and good results have been obtained with single, flighted screws of hardened steel with equal pitch and increasing core diameter. Rod, pipe sheeting, and film can be easily processed by extrusion. Coatings may be cast from solution or applied by fludised bed techniques. Molded parts are easily finished by such operations as drilling, turning, milling, planning, and sawing, punching and polishing. It can be also metallised, printed, and heat sealed.

Applications

This material has found many uses as a film and molding material, and the potential industries include electrical, building, automobile, and lighting. Applications include tail lights for cars, parts for x-ray equipment, holders for fluorscent tubes, bowls and measuring cups, to mention but a few, and household utensils which are unbreakable and easy to clean. In the medium price range the polycarbonates compete with better known thermoplastics and with some metals and glass.

Unlike many thermoplastics of parts made from a polycarbonate resin are 100 per cent dishwasher-proof. In the kitchen and transparency of glass is a very important feature but the hazards make it potentially dangerous. The impact strength of polycarbonates in fifty times greater than glass which means a dramatic reduction in breakages with the added advantage of safety. Comparing identical parts made of glass and polycarbonate, it can be seen that the plastic weighs one-third of its counterpart. Processing is also easier with the plastic although the transparency of light transmission is better (91 per cent) the polycarbonate has a figure of 89 per cent and this difference is of very little significance.

A typical vaccum cleaner made of polycarbonate is 50 per cent lighter than its metal counterpart. It offers strength to weight ratios equal to die cast aluminium, twice that of zinc with four times greater impact strength than either metal. Whereas metals are conductors the polycarbonates have high dielectric strength.

Polysulfones

Another thermoplastic which saw its introduction onto the market in the 1960's is the family of resins based on polysulone. These polymer were developed as a result of the work carried out by the Union Carbide Corporation in the preparation of new aromatic polyethers by nucleophilic aromatic substitution. The synthesis involves the condensation of a dialkali metal salt of a dihydric phenol with an 'activated' or negatively substituted dihalide or anhydrous dipolar aprotic solvent at elevated temperatures. The most commercially successful of these materials from Union Carbide can be prepared by this method and is based on the reaction of the disodium salt of bisphenol A [sodium salt of 2,2 bis (4-hydroxyphenyl) propane] with 4,4'-dichlorodiphenyl sulfone in dimethyl sulfoxide. The sodium phenoxide end groups react with methyl chloride to terminate the polymerisation. This enables are molecular weight of the polymer to be controlled and at the same time assisting in thermal stability.

From the following reaction it can be seen that the diaryl sulfone grouping in a feature of the molecular chain structure.

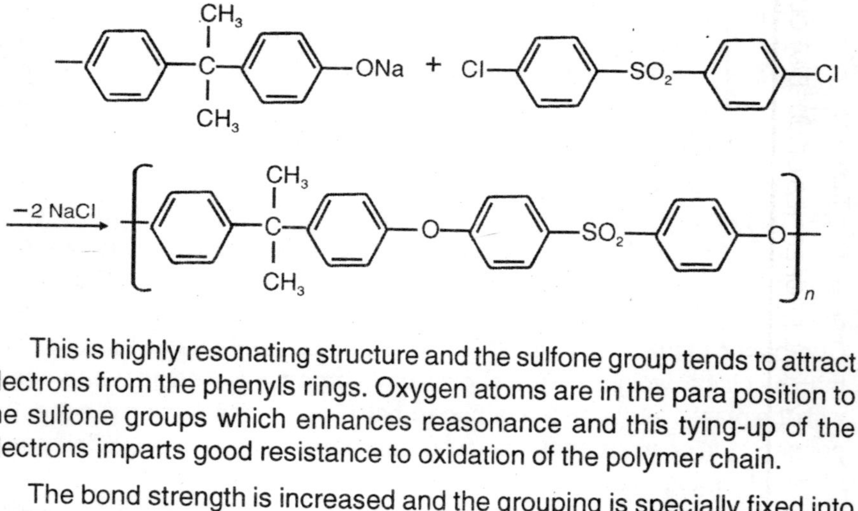

This is highly resonating structure and the sulfone group tends to attract electrons from the phenyls rings. Oxygen atoms are in the para position to the sulfone groups which enhances reasonance and this tying-up of the electrons imparts good resistance to oxidation of the polymer chain.

The bond strength is increased and the grouping is specially fixed into a planer configuration which is due to the high degree of resonance. This leads to good thermal stability and the chain exhibits rigidity even at relatively high temperature.

Properties

Currently this family of polymers have been given the trade name of Udel by Union Carbide. They are a family of tough, rigid, high strength thermoplastics which maintain their properties over a wide temperature range from —60°C to above 150°C. The deflection temperature of this resin is

Table 13.3

TYPICAL PROPERTIES OF UDEL ® POLYSULFONE

Property	ASTM Methods	Value				
		P-1780	P-1710	P-1720	P-3500	P-6050
Appearance in Natural Form		Natural 11 or transparent light amber. Available in opaque and transparent colors.	Natural 15 or light beige opaque.	Natural 13 or light beige translucent.	Natural 11 or transparent light amber. Available in opaque and transparent colors.	Natural 15 or opaque off-white.
General						
Melt flow, at 650°F (343.3°C), 44 psi, g/10 min	D 1238	6.5	6.5	6.5	3.5	3.0-7.0 [a]
Density (g/cm^3)	D1505	1.24	1.25	1.25	1.24	1.40
Mold shrinkage (in./in,)	D 955	0.007	0.007	0.007	0.007	0.005
Water absorption (% in 24 h)	D 570	0.3	0.3	0.3	0.3	0.26
Mechnical						
Tensile strength at yield (psi)	D 638	10,200	10,200	10,000	10,000	13,000
Tensile modulus (psi)	D 638	360,000	360,000	360,000	360,000	720,000
Tensile elongation at break (%)	D 638	50-100	50-100	50-100	50-100	4.0
Flexural strength (psi)	D 790	15,400	15,400	15,400	15,400	20,400
Flexural modulus (psi)	D 790	390,000	390,000	390,000	390,000	750,000
Izod impact (at 72°F, 18-in. specimen, ft-lb/in.notch)	D 256	1.3	1.3	1.3	1.3	1.5
Izod impact, at-40°F, (1/8-in. specimen, ft-lb/in.notch)	D 256	1.2	1.2	1.2	1.2	-
Tensile impact, ft-lb/in^2	D 1822	200	200	160	200	43
Rockwell hardness	D 785	M6 9 (R120)	M6 9 (R120)	M6 9 (R120)	M6 9 (R120)	M6 9 (R120)

Property	Method					
Thermal						
Heat deflection temp., at 264 psi (°F)	D 648	345	345	345	345	345
Coefficient of linear thermal expansion, in./in./°F	D 696	3.1×10^{-5}	3.1×10^{-5}	3.1×10^{-5}	3.1×10^{-5}	2.5×10^{-5}
Flammability (*) average time of burning (ATB), seconds	D 635	5	5	< 5	5	10
average extent of burning (AEB)	D 635	0.0 in. (10 mm.)	0.4 in. (10 mm.)	< 0.2 in. (< 5 mm.)	0.4 in. (10 mm.)	<0.2 in. (5 mm.)
	UL (File No. E-36098A	← 1/16-in. thickness: 94V-2 → ← 1/8-in. thickness: 94V-2 → ← 1/4-in. thickness: 94V-0 →		0.040-in. thickness; 94 V-1 1-16-in.and thicker: 94 V-O	-	-
Oxygen index rating	D 2863T	30	30	32	30	
Thermal conductivity Btu/h/ft²/°F/in.	C177	1.8	1.8	1.8	1.8	1.85
Electrical						
Dielectric strength, 1/8-in. specimen, S/T, v/mil	D 149	425	425	370	425	425
Arc resistance, s (tungsten electrodes)	D 495	122	122	60	122	-
Volume resistivity (at 72°F, ohm-cm)	D 257	5×10^{16}	5×10^{16}	5×10^{16}	5×10^{16}	5×10^{15}
Dielectric constant (at 72°F, 60 Hz-1 MHZ)	D 150	3.07-3.03	3.07-3.03	3.15-3.06	3.07-3.03	3.43-3.34
Dissipation factor (at 72°F, 60 Hz-1 MHZ)	D 150	0.008-0.0034	0.008-0.0034	0.008-0.0056	0.008-0.0034	0.011-0.005

(a) at 707°F (375°C).

* NOTE : This numerical flame spread rating is not intended to reflect hazards presented by this or any other material under actual fire conditions.

175°C at 264 psi and 180°C at 66 psi. Aging these resins for long periods at 150-200°C has little or no effect on their electrical or physical properties. Even down to temperature as low as –65°C there is little deterioration in the properties of these resins. The electrical properties of polysulfones are good and are maintained over a wide temperature and fequency range. Added to these excellent characteristics is the fact that such resins also have low creep and cold flow properties. These materials differ from other amorphous thermoplastics in that their rheology is Newtonain and is not particularly shear sensitive. The glass transition temperature is 175°C.

Polysulfone resins exhibit a high degree of resistance to mineral acids, alkalis, and salt solutions. They are also resistant to detergents and hydrocarbon oils even at high temperatures under moderate stress. Polar organic solvents such as ketones, chlorinated hydrocarbons, and aromatic hydrocarbons attack these polymers.

Table 13.4

EFFECT OF COMMON CHEMICALS ON UDEL© POLYSULFONE

Property	P-1700	P-1710	P-1720	P-3500	P-6050
Inorganic acids			No effect		
Alkalies			No effect		
Alcohols			No effect		
Esters			Partly soluble, swells		
Ketones			Partly soluble, Swells		
Aliphatic hydrocarbons			No Effect		
Aromatic hydrocarbons			Partly soluble, swells		
Chlorinated hydrocarbons			Dissolves		

Processing

These resins must be thoroughly dried before any melt processing is attempted. While the presence of water has no direct effect on the the over all characteristics, it causes bubbling in the finishing molding.

These materials are moldable in most commercial injection molding machines. Mold temperatures are about 95°C for the moldings and 160°C for thicker components with stock temperatures around 340-400°C. They have been extruded as sheet and thin film, pipe, tubing and other profiles as well as wire insulation. The temperature of extrusion is higher than normal for most thermoplastics and typically within the range of 300-360°C which is the extrusion melt temperature. Typical properties are given in Tables 13.3 and 13.4.

Applications

The Udel polysulfones can be used in a wide variety of applications because of its good balance of mechanical, electrical and thermal properties. It has good dimensional stability and offers the user many opportunities. These include; electrical-electronic (circuit carriers, terminal blocks, brush holders), domestic appliances (coffee markers, parts for cameras), automotive and aircraft (cabin interior products).

Polyphenylene oxide

This polymer was introduced to the market in the middle 1960's by General Electrical Company, U.S.A. under the trade name Noryl. It was made from a patented process from the oxidative coupling of phenolic monomers and currently the manufacture consists of the oxidation of 2,6-xylenol using a copper catalyst. The basic phenylene oxide structure is as shown:

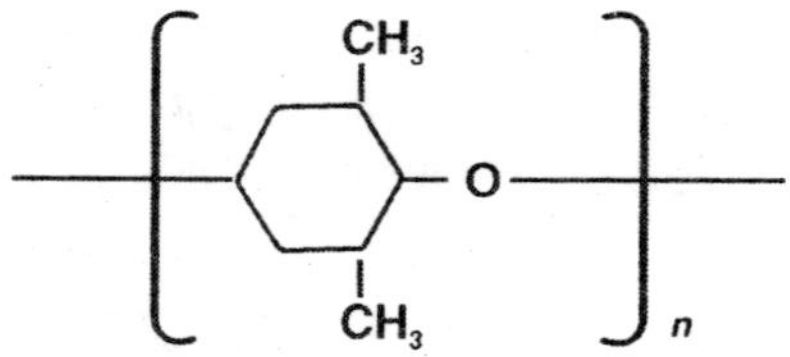

It is claimed that these resins have filled a performance gap between commodity plastics and higher price materials in many major markets.

Properties

This family of engineering materials, which is made up of at least eight different grades, is characterised by outstanding dimensional stability at elevated temperature with a broad temperature range for use (—5° to above 150°C). It has a low coefficient of expansion with a low creep figure, a high hydrolytic stability, and excellent dielectric properties ove a wide range of frequencies and temperatures.

Unlike may other thermoplastics, repeated autoclave cycling of hot and cold water or prolonged exposure to steam have little effect on the properties of these resins. They are an ideal choice for applications under load at elevated temperatures because of the heat resistance under high levels of stress. The properties of an unfilled polymer N300 and a filled RN300 are given in Table 13.5 and a range of properties of a modified polymer can be found in Table 13.2.

Table 13.5

PHYSICAL PROPERTIES OF POLYPHENYLENE RESINS

Properties		*N 300*	*RN 300*
Specific gravity	73°F	1.06	1.26
Water absorption	24 h; 73°F %	0.006	0.005
Heat deflecton	°F@264 psi	300	300
temperature	°F@264 psi	315	315
Thermal conductivity	Btu/h/ft^2 °F/in.	1.10	1.15
Flammability	1/16"	UL 94 V-0	UL 94 V-0; V-5
Tensile strength (psi)	73°F	11,000	12,000
	150°F	8,600	10,000
	200°F	7,500	8,700
	250°F	5,400	7,500
Elongation at break	%	20	15
Flexural strength (psi)	73°F	15,000	17,500
	150°F	12,200	14,700
	200°F	9,900	12,700
	250°F	7,300	10,500
Flexural modulus (psi)	73°F	350,000	575,000
	150°F	325,000	540,000
	200°F	305,000	520,000
	250°F	275,000	500,000
Izod impact			
Notched-ft lb/in.	73°F	10.0	3.0
1/8" Specimen	-40°F	3.2	1.5
Unnotched- ft lb/in.	73°F	No Break	45.0
Gardner impact in.-lb	73°F	300 +	250 +
Mold shrinkage in./in . y 10^3		.005-.007	.002-.004

Polyethylene oxide resins dissolve or soften in many halogenated or aromatic hydrocarbons. They are resistant to hot and cold water, detergents, and weak and strong acids and bases.

Processing

All types of injection molding machines can be used with these resins although screw types are preferred over the plunger or combination presses because of the rapid uniform heating of the resin. General purpose screws with L/D ratios up to 24/1 and compression ratios 2/1 to 3/1 are satisfactory although vinyl screws and tips are not recommended.

Typical mold temperatures range from 85-105°C and the cylinder temperatures, 255-300°C. These resins can be painted with a variety of attractive finishes such as alkyd, acrylic, vinyl or epoxy base paint. Both dry offset and silk screen printing can be used to achieve exact durable image reproduction on these resins. Other processing techniques which can be used successfully are metallising and electroplating.

Applications

These resins have found increasing use in several major areas; these include appliances (parts for cameras and projectors), electrical-electronic compounds (switches and terminals), furniture (institutional, such as nurseries or hospitals where stringent) conditions are required), automobile, business machines, and components for the handling of liquids such as valves and pumps.

14

Natural and Modified Rubbers

The birth of natural rubber dates back to the fifteenth century when Columbus first reported that he had been intrigued on his journey through the New World to see native playing with a ball that actually bounced.

The Hevea brasiliensis tree is the main source of natural rubber and its existance in the Amazon basin was first reported by Charles de la Condamine to the French Academy in 1736. He described to them the native methods of obtaining rubber from this tree and also methods that were used to convert it into useful products. La Condamine named this material 'cahutchu' the word being of Indian origin, and from this has come the more common word 'cauoatchouc'. The actual derivation of the word 'rubber' is attributed to John Prisley, the chemist who discovered oxygen in 1774, who successfully used this material for rubbing out unwanted pencil marks.

In 1876, Sir Henry Wickham collected many thousands of seeds used for growing rubber trees in South America, and shipped them to Kew Gardents. Many of these rubber-tree seeds grew into healthy young plants some of which were sent to Ceylon. A few years later, Henry Ridley, who was at that time a director of Singapore Gardens, against strong opposition planted rubber trees in Malaya. Today, thanks to his action, this country is the leading producer of raw natural rubber.

The uses of natural rubber for certain applications were limited for some time owing to the fact that it deteriorated badly in the presence of oxygen. Fortunately, chemicals were developed for inhibiting this action, and in 1924 the first commercial antioxidant became available, since when many other similar materials have been used successfully.

Raw Materials

Raw natural rubbers are obtainable from a wide variety of trees and plants founds in tropical surroundings. The Hevea tree is by far most important source, due largely to its high yield. The rubber is obtained as a milky latex which comes not from the sap, as many people believe, but from the latex capillary vessels are cut by making an incision in the bark of a tree and allowing the latex to drip out slowly, the process being commonly known as 'tapping' and can be seen in Plate 21. The actual process consists of tapping the tree, allowing the latex to collect in an aluminium cup, then staining and diluting followed by coagulation with formic or acetic acid. The coagulated material is then washed and thoroughly dried. It may then be converted into any one of the following forms :

(a) *Pale Crepe.* In this process the coagulated material is first wash and pressed between tightly closed rolls until a thin crepe is obtained. This is then allowed to dry in the air, a light-colored rubber with a slow cure rate being obtained.

(b) *Smoked Sheet.* Smoked sheet is obtained by pressing the coagulated rubber between rolls, washing and finally drying in an atmosphere of smoke and hot air. A brown rubber results which cures faster then crepe rubber.

(c) *Blankets.* The coagulated rubber may be kept for some weeks on plantation where it undergoes a maturing cycle. This essentially is decomposition of the nonrubber substances by bacterial attack. The natural rubber is subsequently passed through rolls to form a thick crepe which is then air dried. The rubber is a dark color and cures fairly quickly.

(d) *Concentrated Latex.* The latex may be concentrated by centrifuging and then stabilised by adding ammonia as a preservative.

Structure

Chemically natural rubber is largely cis, 1,4 polyisoprene and the hydrocarbon has the empirical formula C_5H_8. It is a linear high molecular weight polymer of the general formula

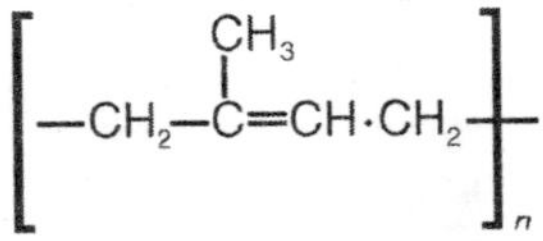

The naturally occurring polyisoprene are in the predominantly cis from the natural rubber of the trans from of gutta percha. The geomatric isomers are as follows :

(a) cis-isomer (natural rubber)

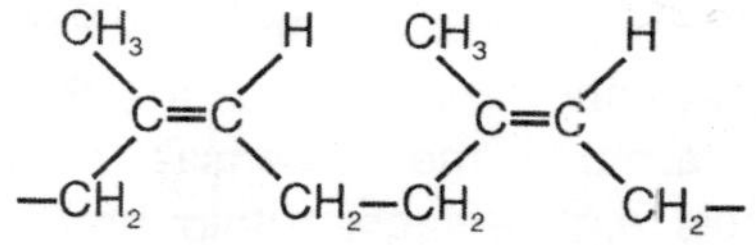

(b) trans-isomer (gutta percha, balata and chicle)

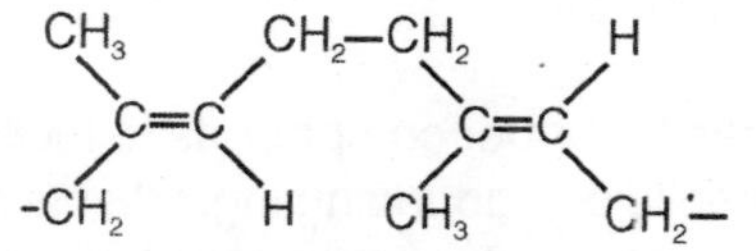

Compounding Processes and Ingredients

Before the raw natural rubber is processed, it is essential to compound it because in the raw state it is technically and economically unsuitable for direct use. To make the natural rubber suitable for compounding it must undergo a process known as 'mastication', which consists of kneading the rubber between warm rolls until it becomes thermoplastic by breaking down the polymer chains. The rubber is then soft enough to enable the compounding ingredients to be added.

Mastication

Raw natural rubber consists of long chains as follows :

Fig. 14.1

There are basically two forms of mastication.

(a) *Physical Chain Scission.* This effect is achieved by the high shearing forces obtained by passing rubber through a two-roll mill.

(b) *Oxidative Chain Scission.* This method can best be accomplished by masticating the rubber in an internal mixer such as the banbury.

The resultant masticated rubber consists of short chains and the rubber also develop greater optical homogeniety.

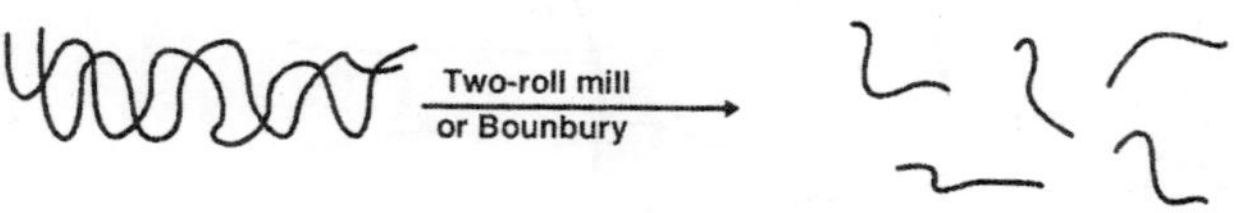

Fig. 14.2

Peptisers

These speed up the break-down in the process of mastication. They are chemicals, the most important of which are the aromatic hydrazines (e.g. phenylhydrazine), aromatic mercaptans (e.g. β-naphthyl mercaptan), and aromatic thiophenols (e.g. pentachlorothiophenol). There main function is to block off the broken ends of the polymer chain, thereby preventing the short chains from recombining.

Softeners

Softeners are added to rubber compounds to facilitate the addition and dispersion of the other solid compounding ingredients as well as to enhance the processing properties for extrusion, calendering, etc. Tack is another property achieved by adding softeners, and is essential for many applications such as tire building.

Numerous materials are used as softeners in the rubber industry, including, vegetable and petroleum oils, waxes, bitumens, pine tars, and various resins. Coumarone-indene is one such resin; it improves the adhesive tackiness of the rubber, thus making it suitable of such applications as adhesive plasters and tapes.

Softeners used as processing acids for the uncured rubber have also been referred to as lubricants, plasticisers, tackfiers, and dispersing agents.

Another important softener is known as 'factice' which may be prepared by heating drying oils with sulfur or sulfur monochloride. The product varies from a soft to a hard rubbery material, depending upon conditions used. It is now used not only as a low density resilient filler but also as a processing aid and softener for rubber. Factice has also been shown to have some curing action when added to rubber compounds.

Vulcanisation

The process of vulcanisation improves the rubber's mechanical strength and elasticity and reduces its sensitivity to changes of temperature. The discovery and development of the process of vulcanisation is discussed in the section on 'Hard Rubber'; it can be briefly defined as the treatment of a raw rubber which decreases its plasticity but retains its elasticity. The process is schematically represented in Fig. 14.3.

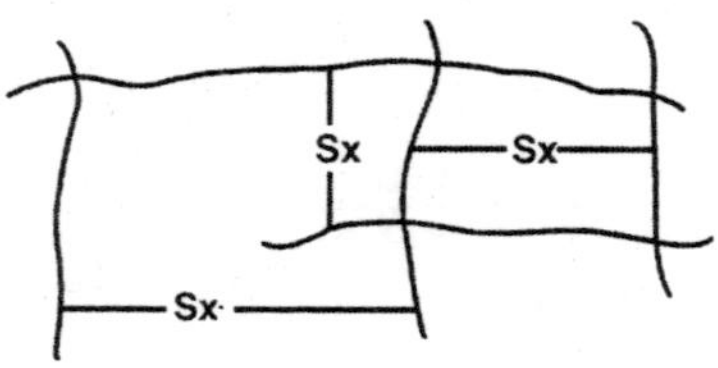

Fig. 14.3

There are various theories of vulcanisation but most authoritative bodies agree that it is a cross-linking process. A three dimensional structure is obtained by cross-linking the individual polymer molecules at those points of the molecules which react with the vulcanizing agent.

The vulcanising process with sulfur alone takes some time to carry out and, therefore, to speed up the reaction, accelerators and activators are mixed with the rubber compound. The accelerator and activators are chemicals whose main functions are to reduce the time and temperature necessary to obtain a rubber possessing the desired physical properties.

The most popular and widely used vulcanising agent is sulfur, although many other materials such as selenium, tellurium, sulfur monochloride, thiuram disulfide, or some alkyd phenol sulfides may be used. As little as 0.2 per cent of sulfur causes vulcanisation, although it is normal to use 2-3 per cent to give a flexible rubber, and as much as 30 percent for a hard rubber.

Accelerators

These materials are chemicals and , as the name implies, serve to accelerate the rate of vulcanisation. The original accelerators were inorganic oxides and salt such as lead carbonate, lime, magnesia, zinc oxide and litharge. Lead carbonate was mentioned in the original patent of Goodyear of vulcanisation.

The work carried out on the inorganic accelerators was followed by the discovery, by George Oenslager, in 1906, that antiline and other organic materials such as hexamethylene tetramine speeded up the rate of vulcanisation. Aniline, however, is toxic and after a few years it was replaced by *p*-aminodiphenylaniline and and diphenylguanidine. These developments were then followed by the introduction in 1925, of the theazoles, of which mercaptobenzthiazole (MBT) has become one of the most well-known and probably the most widely used. New classes that have found use since are the thiurims, their derivatives the carbamates, and the xanthates.

Accelerators can therefore be conveniently classified in the following general chemical groups :

(a) Aldehyde-amine reaction products (e.g., aniline and hexamethylene tetramine)

(b) Guanidine derivatives (e.g., diphenylguandine and diortho-dolyl guanidine)

(c) Thiazoles and their derivatives (e.g., mercaptobenzthiazole)

(d) Thiurams and dithiocarbamates (e.g., tetramethylthiuram disulfide and zinc dimethylthiocarbamate)

(e) Xanthates (e.g., Zinc isobutyl xanthate and sodium isopropyl xanthate)

(f) Sulfonamides (e.g., N-cyclohexyl benzothiazole-2-sulfonamide and N-tert-burvl benzothiazole-2-sulfonamide)

(g) Thioureas (e.g., thiocarbanilide).

Activators

Both organic and inorganic types may be used to activate the accelerators mentioned above without any apparent effect on the final properties. The majority of accelerators require both zinc oxide and a fatty acid such as stearic acid to develop optimum final physical properties. The amount may vary between 2-5 parts by weight per hundred parts of rubber (p.h.r.) zinc oxide, and 1-3 p.h.r. stearic acid. The activators should always be added at the beginning of the compounding process because of the dificulty in dispersing them evenly throughout the rubber mix.

Antioxidants

The main functions of an antioxidant is to protect the rubber against decomposition by oxidation and thereby improve the resistance to aging. Antioxidants therefore maitain the physical properties of the rubber while in service and constant use. The types used for rubbers are normally oxidisable derivates of aromatic amines and certain phenols. However, in this particular chapter mention is given to the general classification into three main groups: (i) Nonstaining- these are also non discoloring for use in white or light colored stocks. Typical materials are 2,2' methylene-bis (4 methyl-6 tertiary butyl phenol), fortified alkylated mixed phenols, alkylated bis phenol and straight alkylated phenols. (ii) Semistaining-these are used for light colored applications but not where minimum discoloration is a requisite. Typical materials are octylated diphenylamine and polymerized 1,2 dehydro-2,2,3 trimethylquinoline. (iii) Staining- these are not used for critical applications and find use in tire stocks and other black furnace compounds. A typical material is the reaction product of diphenylamine and acetone.

Retarders can also be used with thazoles or activated thiazole type accelerators to prevent scorching during processing. One of the more common materials is a modified phthalic anhydride.

Ozone attacks rubber, but antiozonants can be added to improve its resistance; antiozonants are alkyl substituted amines. A typical product is N,N' bis (1,4 dimethylpentyl- *p* -phenylene diamine) and these materials also offer fair protection against oxidative degradation.

Fillers

Raw, uncompounded rubber is deficient in mechanical strength but certain inorganic compounds improve its physical properties. The requirements of a suitable filler are discussed later in the book, but they may be classified in two broad grups :

(a) *Reinforcing Fillers.* This group include carbon black, furnace and channel black, magnesium carbonate, china clay, hard clay, hydrated silica, and aluminium and calcium silicates.

(b) *Nonreinforcing Fillers.* Fillers of this group impart little or no improvement to the physical properties of a rubber. They do, however, perform a useful function in improving processing properties, hardness and chemical resistance. They may also act merely as diluents, and as such reduce the cost of the final molding. Known also as inert fillers, they include whiting, barytes, talc, kieselguhr, and state dust.

Processes and Processing Techniques

Natural rubber and compounded latex are processed and farbicated by many of the techniques used for plastics, which are, in fact, basically modifications of those developed originally for rubber. such processes include compression and transfer molding, extrusion, calendering, and even injection molding, and these are described fully elsewhere in the book no further elaboration is made here. It must be pointed out, however, that processing conditions used for plastics cannot, without discretion, simply be transposed to rubbers. The schematic representation in Fig. 14.4 gives a general picture of the processes natural rubber undergoes before becoming a sound useful technical and commercial product.

Properties

Physical. The properties of natural rubber are largely dependent on the degree of cure and type of additives and filler reinforcement used. To list properties of all the possible different natural rubber mixes is beyond the scope of this book but as a general guide some of the typical physical properties of natural rubber in comparison with synthetic rubbers are listed in Table 14.1.

Chemical. Natural rubber, in general, has good resistance to alkalis as well as to dilute acids. The resistance to most concentrated acids is not good and resistance to aromatic and aliphatic hydrocarbons solvents is poor Natural rubber is unaffected by concentrated hydrocholic acid, although it is decomposed by oxidising acids such as concentrated nitric acid.

Applications

The uses to which natural rubber, both in a solid form or as a latex, has been put are so numerous and widespread that enumeration would be difficult. Briefly, the uses for solid rubber may be summarised as follows: rubber types, gaskets, seals, o-rings, footwear, cable, covering, adhesives, belting, hose, proofing, flooring etc. The use for the latex form includes seating (cushioning), coatings, paints, and adhesives.

Before leaving this section, mention must be made of reclaim rubber. This name is used to describe scrap vulcanised rubber that has been subjected to chemical and mechanical breakdown. These processes make the rubber soft and plastic and thereby capable of further processing. The advantages of incorporating such a material in rubber compound are obvious, since the reclaim rubber contains nearly all the ingredients of the original rubber compound plus the added factor that it is cheaper than the raw rubber. This makes it an extremely valuable extender, and a large industry has grown around this material.

MODIFIED RUBBERS

Hard Rubber

The terms hard rubber, ebonite, and vulcanite are all used to describe the product obtained by heating a mixture of rubber with up to 30 per cent by weight of sulfur to a temperature of 120-160°C until the reaction is virtually complete.

It has been stated previously that rubber in the raw uncompounded state tends to lose its strength on continuous use and is adversely affected by temperature changes, and this is presumably why no large-scale use was made of rubber until 1839. Fortunately, at this time two pioneers of the rubber industry, Thomas Tancock (Britain) and Charles Goodyear (U.S.A.), both discovered that raw rubber could be hardened by heating with sulfur, thereby improving the physical properties of the rubber. Hancock termed this process 'vulcanisation', derived from Vulcan (Roman God of fire and Volcanoes). He based the name on the fact that both heat and sulfur are present in volcanoes. In the strictest sense, the term vulcanisation is not correct as it may be affected without heat or the addition of sulfur.

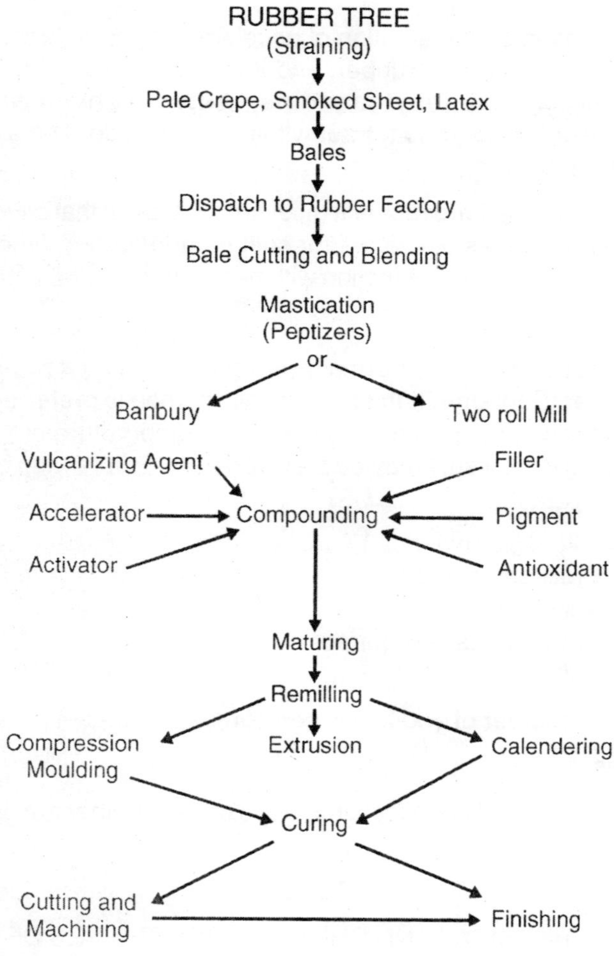

Fig. 14.4 Processes involved in converting raw rubber into finished molded articles.

General

The methods of processing and compounding hard rubbers are essentially the same as those used for natural rubbers. The most popular filler is ebonite dust, which is obtained from scrap ebonite or by grinding specially prepared blocks, although coal dust, certain clays, whitings, and even carbon black have been used for this purpose. It has already been mentioned that the speed of chemical reaction between natural rubber and a vulcanising agent can be increased by the addition of accelerators and activators. This is,of course, also true for hard rubber, and the most effective ones have been established as diphenylguandine, butyraldehyde-aniline, zinc dimethylthiocarbonate, and tetraethylthiuram disulfide. The amount varies between 1-3 p.h.r.

In compounding hard rubber it must be pointed out that although metallic oxides are suitable as activators for solft natural rubber, other effects are obtained when used in conjunction with hard rubber.

Mixing

Hard rubber mixes are normally prepared by suing a two-roll mill or an internal mixer (Banbury). If the two roll mill method is preferred it is normal to band the raw rubber on the front roll at a temperature of 40-60°C. The compounding ingredients may be then added in the following order.

(i) Peptizers
(ii) Fillers (ebonite dust)
(iii) Processing aids
(iv) Accelerators
(v) Antioxidants (if required)
(iv) Sulfur

The actual order of addition is sometimes a matter of personal choice.

Properties

The physical and chemical properties of hard rubber are given in Table 14.1.

Table 14.1

PHYSICAL AND CHEMICAL PROPERTIES OF HARD RUBBER (ACCORDING TO B.S. 903)

Test	*Property*
S.G.	1.13-1.18
Tensile strength (lb/in_2)	7000-9000
Elongation at break (%)	3-10
Cross-breaking strength (lb/in^2)	12-16,000
Impact strength (ft lb/inch notch)	0.5
Dielectric constant ($f=10^6$ c/s)	3
Power factor (10^6 c/s)	0.5-0.8

Volume resistivity (ohm-cm)	2-3 X 10^{16}
Chemical Resistance	
Hydrochloric acid	Resistant
Dilute sulfuric acid	Resistant
Concentrated sulfuric acid	Attacked
Organic acids	Resistant
Sodium hydroxide	Resistant
Aromatic hydrocarbons	Attacked
Aliphatic hydrocabrons	Attacked
Easters	Resistant
Ketones	Resistant

Limitation and Applications

Unfortunately, hard rubber has poor light stability and degrades on prolonged exposure to light. The relatively long cure times necessary are not attractive to industry and other materials are now preferred for certain specific applications. Hard rubber has a high shrinkage volue and the better the grade the more prone it is to shrink, which limits its use for precision requirements.

Uses found for hard rubber include; battery boxes, although in this application hard rubber is losing ground to certain other polymers such as styrene/butadiene and PVC. There is still, however, some use for hard rubber as battery separators. It has also found some use in general chemical plant equipment and as linings for industrial chemical plant such as containers and structural units. Expanded ebonite has been used extensively for thermal insulation especially at very low temperature although this material is now receiving severe competition from cork, expanded polystyrene, and plyurethane foams. Miscellaneous uses include combs, mouthpieces for musical instruments, and barrels for pipes.

Cyclised Rubber

In the latter part of the eighteenth century Leonhardi (1791) treated rubber with sulfuric acid and observed that the material became hard and brittle. It was not until some time later, when many of the classical theories of organic chemistry had been developed, that Harries (1910-1919) suggested cyclising rubber by treating it in a solution of benzene with sulfuric acid. The mechanism of isomerising rubber has been examined by many scientists, and the structure shown below has been supported by M. Gordon (1951).

Structure

Natural rubber may be modified by heating with sulfuric acid, chlorostannic acids, metallic halides, or phenols. A reduction in unsaturation occurs and is attributed to cyclisation.

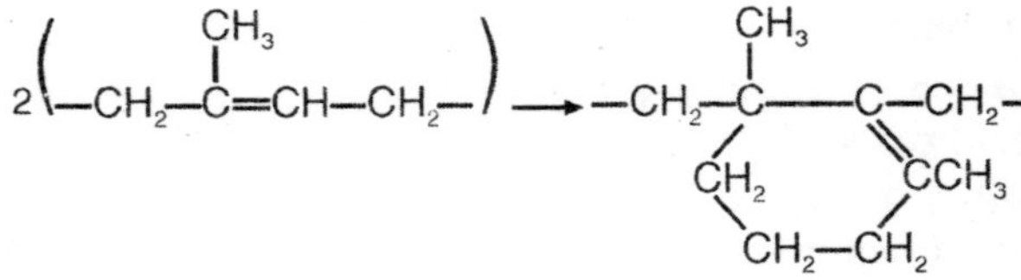

Properties

The properties of cyclised rubber are given in Table 14.2

Table 14.2

PHYSICAL PROPERTIES OF CYCLISED AND CHLORINATED RUBBER

Test	*Cyclized rubber*	*Chlorinated rubber (properties dependent upon chlorine content)*
	Typical	*Typical*
S.G.	1.0-1.05	1.06-1.07
Hardness-Shore	85-90	70-80
Tensile strength (lb/in.^{2})	3000-4000	4000-4500
Elongation at break (%)	low	2-10
Flexural strength (lb/in.^{2})	6000-8000	10,000-14,000
Impact strength Izod (ft lb/in. notch)	3	1-2
Water absorption (%)	< 1.0	< 1.0
Water permeability	Highly impermeable	Highly impermeable
Dielectric constant	2.5	2.5-3.5
Power factor (1 Mc/s)	0.002	0.006
Volume resistivity (ohm-cm)	10^{16}	10^{13}-10^{14}

Applications

Cyclised rubber originally found use as a compounding ingredient in shoe-soling but has now been displaced by the more popular styrene resins. It is also used as an adhesive for rubber to metal bonding, and as a moisture proof coating for paper and for paints and varnishes.

Chlorinated rubber

The action of chlorine on rubber was investigated in 1880 by W. Rox burgh. Industrial applications were first suggested for derivatives in 1881 but it was not until 1930 that the excellent oil-moisture of these rubbers was utilised.

Preparation and Structure

(a) *Chlorination.* Chlorination is carried out by substitution and addition of the halogen to a latex solution. The percentage of chlorine can be as high as 72 but to obtain maximum stability of polymers should not contain more than 68 per cent of chlorine. Commercial polymers usually contain between 64-66 per cent chlorine. Alloprene, which is manufactured by Imperial Chemical Industries Ltd. contains approximately 65 per cent chlorine in its combined state and has the empirical formula $C_{10}H_{11}C_{l7}$. The molecular weight varies according to the different grades and is from 5000 upwards.

The structure may be represented as follows :

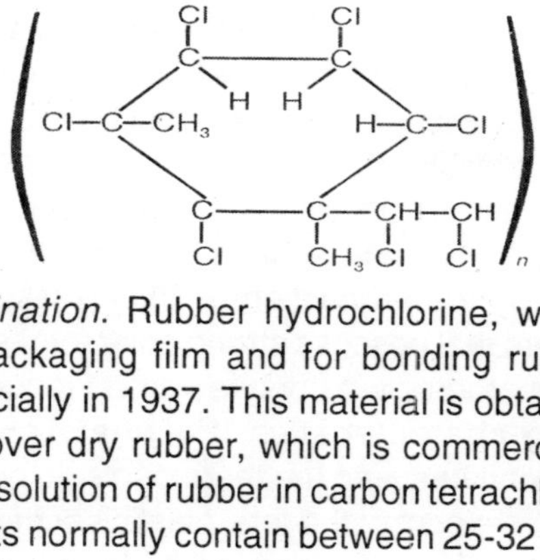

(b) *Hydrochlorination.* Rubber hydrochlorine, which is being used extensively as a packaging film and for bonding rubber of metal, was introduced commercially in 1937. This material is obtained by passing dry hydrogen chloride over dry rubber, which is commercially impractical, or better still through a solution of rubber in carbon tetrachloride or in benzene. Commercial products normally contain between 25-32 per cent of chlorine.

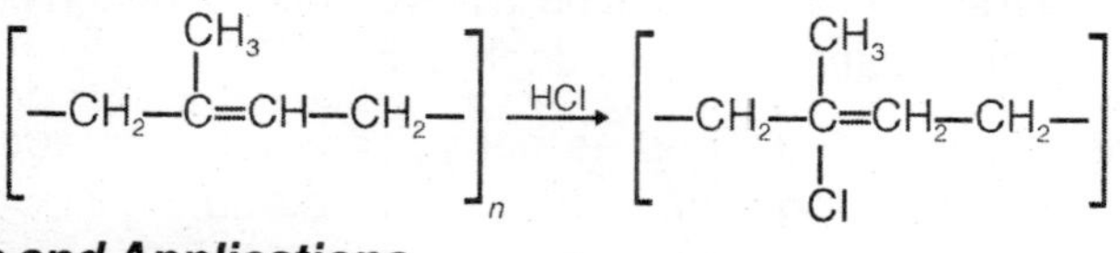

Properties and Applications

The physical properties of chlorinated rubber are given in Table 14.2.

Rubber hydrochloride has found wide use as a protective film (grease resistant) both alone and as a laminate to paper and aluminium foil, etc. Chlorinated rubber has been successfully used for bonding rubber to metal and in formulating electrical insulating lacquers.

15

Plasticisers, Stabilisers, and Related Additives

Plasticisers are regarded by many people in the polymer industry as relatively new materials but they have been known for some hundreds of years although probably not specifically recognised as such. Early reports of the uses of plasticisers can be traced back to the Red Indians who used a mixture of bear's grease and spruce gum to seal the joints in their birch bark canoes. Other early uses include the plasticising of pitch with certain oils for caulking ships to render them waterproof.

Probably the earliest use of a plasticiser of plastics was initiated by Parkes who in 1868, added camphor to cellulose nitrate. This latter material, until this innovation, was a tough inflexible substance, but an adding camphor it became the more flexible material commonly known as celluloid. The family of cellulosics were the major consumers of plasticisers until WW II, when the necessity to find substitutes for natural added led to many developments, notably the production of PVC. Plasticisation is normally adopted with polymers that possess strong polar forces which tend to make them horny, brittle materials with only a limited range of application and difficult processing characteristics. Polymers such as polyolefins, polystyrenes,, polyacrylates, and the thermosets do not, in general require plasticisers. Over 80 per cent of the total plasticiser market is used for PVC which is the main subject for discussion in this chapter although brief aspects of the other thermoplastics are also dealt with.

Plasticisers may be defined as nonvolatile solvents added to high polymers to soften and render them plastic or flexible during processing, or to impart permanent flexibility and rubber-like extensibility. The mechanism by which inclusion of plasticisers with PVC results in increased flexibility is attributed to a reduction of the intermolecular forces, i.e. the plasticiser act as a lubricating agent to allow the macromolecules to slide over one another freely, or by the solvation of the polymer. Unplasticised PVC can be regarded as a three dimensional gel formed by the attachments between molecules at active centres, i.e., at points of high polarity. Plasticisation can be looked upon as a reduction of polymer-polymer unions by creating polymer-plasticizer unions in their places. One important criterion for a material to be considered as a suitable plasticiser is that it should possess a fair degree of polarity in order to effectively solvate the polymer dipoles. This statement can be somewhat contradicted if we look at dimethyl oxalate, which is composed entirely of polar groups but, in practice, is a poor plasticiser for PVC. It has been concluded that as PVC contains both polar aliphatic groups the plasticiser must bear some relation to the base polymer. It has also been established in practice that a good plasticiser should possess, in addition to a polar group, one of the following; a polar izable nonpolar group (e.g. triphenyl phosphate), a nonpolarisable group (e.g. dialkyl sebacate) or both (e.g. dialkyl phthalate). Therefore, to sum up it can be said that the kind of chemical groups present are of fundamental importance in determining the suitability of a material as a plasticiser. Polar group are essential but other groups must also be present to modify their effect and to provide overall polar characteristics similar to those of PVC itself. The amounts of the various groups present are also of fundamental importance in order to achieve the desired balance of polar forces. Certain disadvantages are unfortunately exhibited to many plasticisers and this had led to another approach which helps to overcome such shortcomings as exudation, exactability, and loss through evaporation of the plasticiser. We have now seen that plasticisation consists essentially of the separation of the macromolecules so that the polar forces cannot come into action. This effect can also be achieved by synthesising a polymer structure with appropriate side chains spaced at intervals along the polymer chain. The side chains so formed would then keep the macromolecules apart, and this is achieved in practice by copolymerisation of the monomeric vinyl chloride with vinyl acetate or vinlydene chloride. The copolymerisation results in a less regular structure, a reduction in close packing, and attraction of the polar groups.

FUNCTIONS OF A PLASTICISER

Plasticiser serve three basic functions:

(i) to lower the processing temperature of the polymer to below the decomposition temperature;

(ii) to modify the properties of the finished product (i.e., flexibility or extensibility);

(iii) to modify the processing properties.

GENERAL CLASSIFICATION

The plasticiser field for PVC can be devided into two basic categories;

1. True Plasticisers

These can be further subdivided into

(a) *Primary Plasticisers.* These are materials which exhibit good compatability with PVC and can, and often are, used by themselves. they may be regarded as true plasticisers for the polymer.

(b) *Secondary Plasticisers.* These usually exhibit from fair to good compatability with PVC but are normally used in conjunction with (a)

2. Extenders

Also referred to as softeners, or even secondary plasticisers, extenders exhibit only limited compatibility with PVC and are used in conjunction with primary plasticisers. They may be regarded as aggregates of molecules in the form of droplets which soften the mix mechanically and, as such, they can be likened to liquid fillers analogous to diluents in sufrace-coating technology. One basic requirement of these materials is that they must, of course, of reasonably compatible with the polymer.

REQUIREMENTS OF AN IDEAL PLASTICISERS

The properties to be looked for in a plasticiser may be classed under two headings; those that are essential and those that are desirable. Essential properties include free availability, permanency, low volatility and compatibility. Desired properties include low cost, low odor, absence of color, nontoxicity, nonmigratory, nonbleeding, nonflammable, heat and light resistance, and good processing characteristics (e.g., ease of dispersing in resin). One main property which is highly desirable for a plasticiser is its ability to impart to the polymer, and to maintain, the characteristics of an elastomer over the widest possible temperature range. Unfortunately, no single plasticiser embodies all the desired properties mentioned above. Therefore, for any specific application it is necessary to choose the correct plasticiser or combination to suit the requirement by using a general-purpose plasticizer as the basis and building-in other specific requirements with specialised plasticisers.

PLASTICISATION OF RUBBERS

Rubbers can be plasticized with the variety of materials such as plasticisers, softeners, and processing acids.

These may be classified as follows :

(a) *Pure softeners or plasticisers.* It must be noted here that, as with the polar thermoplastics, the usefulness of a material as a plasticiser of a material suitable as a plasticiser for one polymer may be unsuitable for another. These materials include the mineral oils with the ester plasticisers, the latter type being used primarily with polar rubbers.

(b) Materials which aid processing but have no permanent softening action, e.g., coumarone-indene resins, mineral rubber, and phenolic resins.

(c) Miscellaneous materials of varying compatability which are analogous to the extenders and lubricants used in thermoplastics.

TYPES OF PLASTICISERS

Phthalates

These are probably the most important single group of plasticisers, of which probably, the most significant are dioctyl, disooctyl, and mixed (C_7 to C_9) octyl (alphanol) types. This type of plasticiser offers a good balance of all round properties within a medium price structure and therefore is probably the most widely used type. In general, such plasticisers have medium volatility, extraction, migration, moisture, resistance, chemical stability, and low temperature flexibility.

The phthalates are prepared mainly from *o*-phthalic anhydride, obtained by air oxidation of naphthalene, though some isophthalates have recently become available. The preparation is effected by esterifying the alcohol with the dibasic acid, using acid catalysts, commonly sulfuric or *p*-toluene sulfonic acid, in an inert atmosphere to minimise coluor formation. The esterification is carried out in the temperature range 130-200°C for a period between 4-10 hours. Solid plasticisers can also be manufactured by using cyclic alcohols are the esterifying alcohol and a typical plasticiser of this type is dicyclohexyl phthalate.

Phosphates

Tricresyl phosphate (TTP) was the earliest commercial plasticiser for PVC but unfortunately it has rather poor-low temperature characteristics and has been replaced in many application. This advantage can be overcome to some extent by mixing it with certain other phosphate plasticisers such as crysyl diphenyl phosphate.

The phosphates are commonly prepared by reacting coal tar or cresylic acid derived from petroleum and the corresponding alcohol with phosphorus oxychloride or phosphorous pentachloride.

The most widely used of this family are of two general types; triaryl phosphates and alkyl phosphates. The former materials have low volatility and excellent flame retarding efficiency but are relatively poor with respect to low temperature flexibility. The alkyl aryl phosphates are good on low temperature flexibility but at some sacrifice to other properties. The phospate family is a group of highly compatible plasticisers which are aggresive solvators for most commonly used resins.

Diesters

This group includes the sebacates, azelates, and adipates, of which di (2 ethyl-hexyl) sebacate (DOS), di (2 ethyl-hexyl) azelate (DOZ) and di (2 ethyl-hexyl) adipate (DOA) are typical. These materials are used mainly for their extremely good low temperature properties but normally only in role of secondary plasticisers due to thier limited compatability with PVC. They are produced by methods similar to those used for the phthlates. The adipates impart excellent low temperature flexibility somewhat better than the phthalates. They are relatively volatile and do not process easily.

Polyesters

This group together with the epoxidised oils are commonly referred to as polymeric plasticisers, although the term is somewhat of a misnomer and 'high molecular weight plasticiser' is to be preferred. There are two major types of polyester plasticisers used. The first have molecular weights in the range of 3000-8000 and are produced as a result of the polycondensation reaction between a dicarboxylic acid, i.e., adipic, azelic, or sebacic and a dihydric alcohol, i.e. propylene or butylene glycol. The end groups of such a material (i.e. OH and COOH) are not modified whereas in the second type the groups are primarily to lower the molecular weight. Monocarboxylic acids or monohydric alcohols can be used, when molecular weights in the range of 850-2000 can be obtained.

In general, these types of plasticisers are incorporated along with primary plasticisers as their compatability with PVC is often not very good. They are used in compounds primarily to decrease the danger of migration and oil extraction.

Another group of polymeric plasticiser is based on polyurethane chemistry and the resultant plasticisers are colorless and odorless. One commercial product is Ultramoll PU, which is made by Bayer in Germany and contains have five percent of PVC and also designed especially for use in plasticising PVC. This plasticiser has excellent compatibility with the polymer and thus it can be processed in high concentrations. The resultant compound has permanent flexibility and the plasticiser is very resistant to extraction by a wide variety of solvents.

Epoxies

Conventional vegetable oils and alkyl esters of their fatty acids are not sufficiently polar to be compatible with PVC. Epoxidising the double bonds of the unsaturated acids, as with the triglycerides and certain esters of the fatty acids, remedies this. Thus, with the epoxy plasticisers we have two main types, namely the epoxidised triglycerides produced from soyabean and other oils, and epoxidysed alkyl esters derived from fatty acids such as steric and oleic. Such epoxidised materials, in addition to this plasticizing action, also exhibit marked stabilising action against both heat and light.

One method of epoxidising the double bonds is to add hydrogen peroxide to an ecetic acid solution of the unsaturated ester in the presence of a calyst between 60-70°C.

The most common and best understood method of preparing such materials is the esterification of the epoxy resins with drying oil fatty acids and the subsequent oxidative polymerisation of the fatty acid radicals. Coarboxylic acids, which may be fact be of almost any origin, first attack the oxirane ring in preference to the secondary hydroxyls. In this reaction another secondary alcohol grouping is formed.

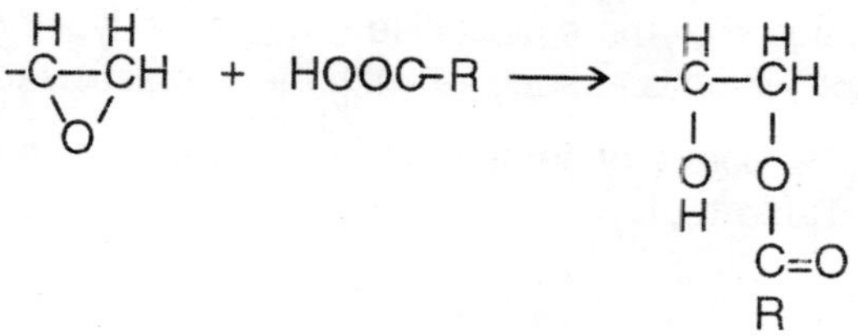

This sequence consisting of the attack on the oxirane ring followed by the generation of an adjacent secondary hydroxyl group may be regarded as another unifying principle for most of the epoxy resins.

Theoretically a complete esterification of all epoxy and alcohol groups is possible :

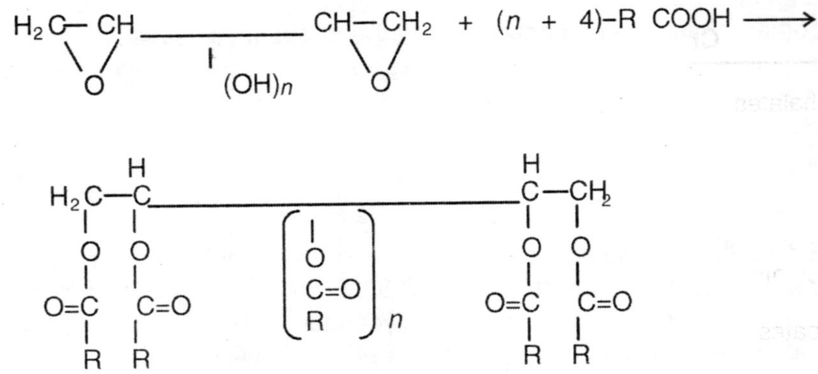

In practice a minimum of 10 per cent excess epoxy resin is necessary and usually the excess is much greater.

Nitrile Rubbers

These are used only on a limited scale for applications where specific resistance to petrols and oils combined with low volatility are necessary. They can be vulcanised in situ are compatible in all proportions with PVC.

SULFONAMIDES

This type of plasticiser is generally compatible with resins other than polyvinyl chloride. They are uniquely comptible with some hard to plasticise polymers such as the nylon family. Their high polarity and molecular configuration make them readily adhere to a wide variety of substrates, suggesting they are eminently suitable for such applications as adhesives and surface coatings. Polymers plasticised with these types usually retain a tack free surface which is associated with the unplasticised resin.

The chemical structure of some of the main groups of plasticisers are demonstrated in Table 15.1.

EXTENDERS

These are commonly referred to by other names such as secondary plasticisers or softeners. They are not true plasticisers for the base polymer and as such cannot be used alone. They are used invirably to effect a cost reduction and are normally the cheapest component of a PVC compound apart from the filler. Among the well-known extenders are classed the aromatic hydrocarbons, alkyl-aryl hydrocarbons, hydrogenated alkyl-aryl hydrocarons,

Table 15.1

CHEMICAL STRUCTURE OF PLASTICISERS

Phthalates

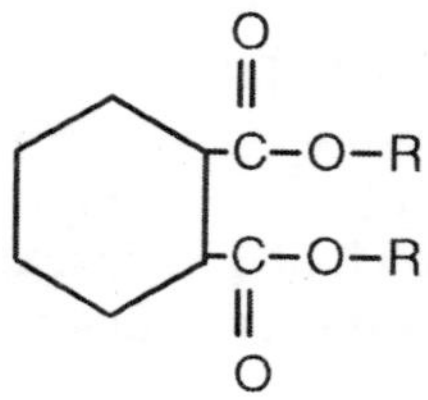

Adipates

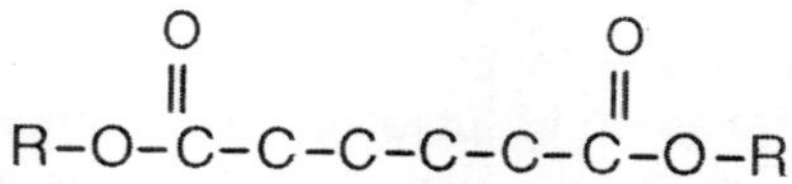

Phosphates

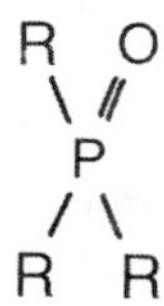

Sulfonamides

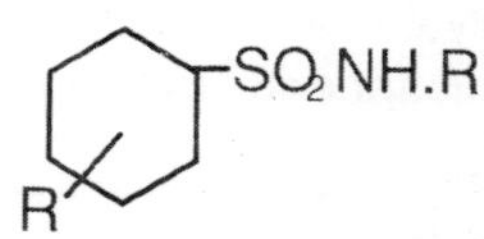

chlorinated paraffins, and special petroleum fractions. Certain of these materials also impart certain improved characteristics, such as chlorinated paraffins which improve flame resistance. Generally, the use of extenders results in a poor smell and colour in the final compound. It is quite usual, therefore, to use conventional fillers rather than extenders to cheapen formulation.

Before leaving this section mention should be made of plasticisers used for thermoplastics other than PVC. Dibutyl phthalate is quite suitable for use with polyvinyl acetate, although with PVC it has been found to somewhat too volatile. Butyl benzyl phthalate, tricresyl (or tolyl) phosphate (TTP), and diethyl phthalate have all been used satisfactorily with polyvinyl acetate. Cellulose nitrate the 'mother' of thermoplastics has been satisfactorily plasticised and camphor for molding compositions, and for coating applications the following have been used; dibutyl phthalate, dioctyl phthalate, and butyl-benzyl phthalate. For cellulose acetate polymers it is necessary to used polar plasticisers and diethyl, dimethyl phthalate as well as triphenyl phosphate have all been used satisfactorily. In general, it is unnecessary to use plasticisers with polyamides although the flexibility can increased by incorporating a mixture of *o*-and *p*-ethyl-toluene sulfonamide Acrylics for molding applications are not, in general, plasticised although for coating applications it has been found necessary and butyl benzyl and dichlohexyl phthalate have been employed satisfactorily.

STABILISERS

The majority of polymers known at present suffer some physical or chemical deterioration when subjected to the atmosphere unless previously protected by the discrete use of certain compounding ingredients. This fact is apparent in loss of strength, surface erosion, warping, cracking, loss of transparency, in addition of other phenomena. Certain physical changes are not necessarily inherent disadvantages of the base polymers and such effects as warping, shrinking, and embrittlement may be brought about solely by the loss of plasticizer due to migration. Exposure to alternate high and low humidity may cause swelling and/ or shrinkage with hydrophylic materials such as nylon or cellulose acetate. Deteriorative chemical changes in thepolymer structure depend largely in the basic design of the polymer. The degradation process which can effect polymers are as follows; shelf-aging, oxidation (i.e. by metallic catalysts), effect of heat and light, flex cracking (accelerated by ozone) and atmospheric cracking.

Certain specific polymers which are adversely affected by some of the above-mentioned processes follow. It is now well known that when PVC and certain copolymers are heated to high temperature (above 170°C) they tend to decompose and become discolored. This is largely due to the fact that hydrochlorine acid is split off, when the material tends to become brittle and is unsaturated; in addition, it loses many of its electrical properties. The decomposition is believed to begin with the abstraction of a hydrogen atom, by a free radical which can be generated by light, heat, or even shearing. this results in the chain being left in a form of a radical which immediately stabilizes itself by expelling a chlorine atom and forming a double bond. This highly reactive chlorine atom immediately reacts with the nearest hydrogen atom (probably the one adjoining the chain), and the process repeats itself, generating a conjugated polyene structure as follows :

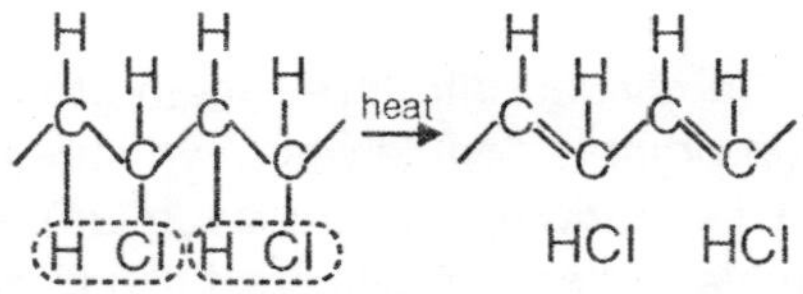

The progress of this 'zipper' reaction is believed to be halted by the branching points and other imperfections in the chain, or by intervention of antioxidants which from a most important part of modern stabilizer systems.

The polyene structure so formed is 'chromophoric' and the organe colour formed is partly explained by the fact that the structure so formed resembles that of carotene, the colouring matter of carrots. The colour range which occurs when heating PVC at elevated temperatures is yellow, orange, red brown, and finally black, the last colour being typical of degraded polymers.

Light stabilization can be distinguished from heat stabilization in that the former provides protection against oxidation whereas the latter effect provides protection solely against heat. Light aging, in comparison to heat, does not cause such severe discolouration but still results in brittleness, loss of rigidity, and decomposition.

It is now evident that with PVC and copolymers in order to obtain useful products it is essential to add materials that prevent degradation. Such materials are common referred to as stabilizers and they may be classified in five main groups; (i) acid acceptors, which combine and fix the HCl as it is liberated from the polymer; (ii) antioxidants which prevent any further decomposition of oxygen; (iii) ultraviolet absorbers which filter out uv light and thus reduce that total energy available to activate the polymer; (iv) materials which react with double bonds, to break up the polyene structure and destroy the color formation; (v) free radical acceptors which terminate or destroy the free radicals which otherwise would initiate and propagate degradation. The five groups may be regarded as requirements of an ideal stabilizer; in addition, the material should also be permanent, compatible, nonleaching, free from odor and taste, nontoxic, and should neither bleed or sweat out of the compound nor be stained by sulfur.

Despite extensive research work to find the ideal stabilizer, as yet no such material has been found. However, many materials now available impart a remarkably high degree of stability of PVC compounds and these are discussed. Before doing, so however, a description must be given of phenomenon can be said to occur when the efficiency of a stabilizing compound is greater than the sum of the efficiencies of each of the constituents which make up the compound.

Types of Stabilizers

Stabilizers may be divided into three main groups; (i) inorganic and organic lead salts; (ii) organic derivatives of various metals of Group II of the Periodic System, i.e. barium, calcium, cadmium, and zinc; (iii) organic derivatives of tetravalent zinc. Stabilizers falling into these groups are normally added in varying amounts from 1-3 parts per hundred parts of polymer. Specialised types of the purely organic stabilizers such as diphenyl urea, which gives nontoxic compounds, can be used.

Group I. Lead compounds were the first really satisfactory materials to be used for vinyl stabilization. They are excellent heat stabilizers and some types also provide light stability. Resins stabilized with these lead compounds have good electrical insulation characteristics, but the following disadvantages limit their general applicability; sulfur staining (black discoloration), inability to obtain a high degree of clarity unless at the expense of heat stability, toxic hazards and poor results given with phosphate plasticisers. However, they are comparatively cheap, and the majority of the previous drawbacks are relatively unimportant in many applications. They therefore account for nearly 70 per cent of the total vinyl stabilizer market.

The basic lead content of a lead stabilizer is often taken as a measure of its reactivity and general heat stabilizing efficiency.

The cheapest and most widely used lead stabilizer is basic lead carbonate (white lead). It is normally used in excess but still provides no light stabilizing action at even such high concentration. Other lead stabilizers used include tribasic lead sulfate, dibasic lead phosphite, dibasic lead phthalate, and tribasic lead maleate. The maleates are dienophils and break up the conjugation of the vinyl system, thereby reducing colour formation. Thus tribasic lead maleate gives excellent long term colour stability to the vinyl compound during processing.

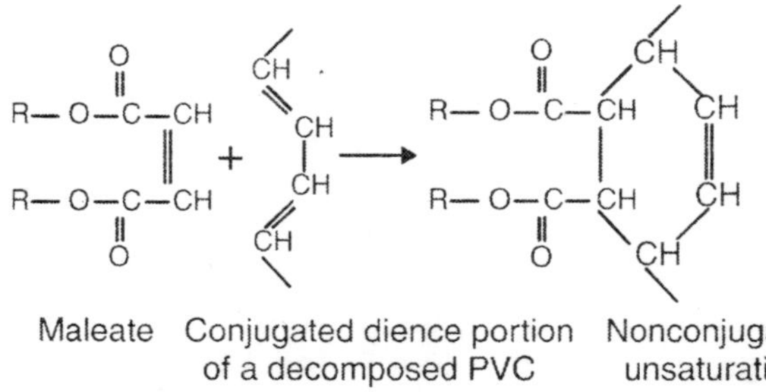

Maleate — Conjugated dience portion of a decomposed PVC chain — Nonconjugated unsaturation in this product

Some stabilizers serve a dual roll, and these include lead stearate and dibasic lead stearate which are moderate stabilizers but good lubricants. Lead salicylate exhibits uv light screening properties and is frequently used in combination with basic lead stabilizers to improve light stability.

Group 2. We have seen earlier by the definition of synergism, that when certain metallic stabilizers are combined it is often possible to obtain a much higher heat stability for a vinyl compound than by using a single stabilizer type. This effect is of particular value with derivatives of the metals barium, cadamium, zinc and calcium. An important derivative of these metals are the 'soaps'. The most popular solid soap system is obtained by coprecipitating, barium cadimium laurate, which gives a good general purpose heat stabilizer when combined with some secondary stabilizers such as the epoxides and chelating agents. Other derivatives include barium nonylphenate, barium, decanoate, cadimum octoate, zinc laurate, and octoate.

Group 3. The organotins have been claimed to be the best vinyl stabilizers as yet discovered. Their most important advantage is that they products with high clarity. They have no effect on paste viscocity and are therefore used for stabilizing plastisol and organosol systems. Unfortunately, they are expensive, which restricts their wider use, and they are therefore limited to certain small specialised applications. Typical materials are dibutyl tin dilaurate, dibutyl tin maleate, dibutyl tin mercaptides, and certain dioctyl tin compounds.

Before leaving this classification it is important to mention the secondary stabilizers of which the epoxy materials are the most important. They haver very little influence alone but when used in conjunction with groups 2 and 3 they have a pronounced effect inimproving the heat stability. We have seen in the previous section that there are two main types of epoxides used for plasticizers and these are also used as stabilizers, therefore, we can say that the epoxide or internal group is prone to accept HCl as follows :

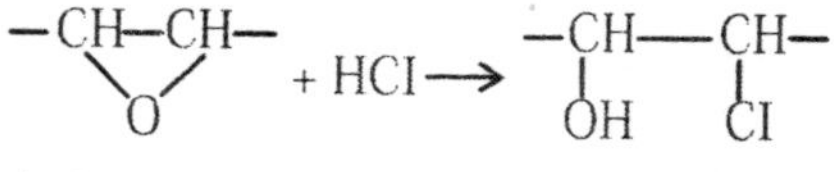

Polyhydric alcohols have also been used in stabilization systems with PVC, especially in conjunction with lead stabilizers.

CHELATING AGENTS

They are used in certain stabilizing systems since they improve the clarity by the fact that they 'chelate' the metal chlorides formed during the reaction of the stabilizer with hydrochloric acid. They are frequently included in barium /cadmium stabilizer system in a concentration of 1-2 p.h.r. Probably the most common chelating agents used in PVC compounds are the alkyl or aryl phosphites such as triphenyl and trioctyl phsphite.

Polyolefins

The problems of stabilization is also necessary with the polyolefins for certain specific applications. It has been shown, with certain members of this family, that if exposed to light and air for 2-3 years they become brittle and useless products; if however, they are stored in the absence of light at room temperature they remain perfectly satisfactory. Specific experiments carried out on polyethyelene which had previously been subjected to such aging conditons showed the following polar groups to be present

$$—CO, —COOH, —OH \text{ and } RCH{+}CH_2R$$

Protection against such degradative effects can be achieved by adding two per cent carbon black or other antioxidants of the nonstaining types which are originally developed for natural rubber, i.e. substituted or hindered phenols or the organic phosphites. It has been reported that an addition of two per cent of finely dispersed carbon gives a thirty fold improvement in the resistance of polyethylene and it is probably for this reason that polyethylene pipes are invariably black. Since carbon black is a pigment, it is also used, aside from its stabilizing qualities, to colour the polymer black.

We have seen earlier that there are basically two major types of polyethylenes, low and high density, and both these polymers exhibit a difference in their suceptibility to oxidation. The high density materials have higher amounts of crystallinity and, consequently, less amorphous regions that the low density and, therefore, they have somewhat better resistance to oxidation. The use of organic metallic catalyst for the preparation of a high density polymers necessitates the use of a stabilizer or a chelator to inactivate the metallic salts which could possibly act as a catalyst and speed up oxidation. It would also appear that the amorphous region of the polyethylenes, which have more side chains, are primarily attacked by oxygen.

Polypropylene is more prone to oxidation that the 'polyethylenes' therefore the overall picture is somewhat more complicated, and polypropylene must also be stabilized against heat degradation during processing a synergistic mixture of alkylated phenol with certain sulfides has been shown to impart a high degree of stability.

Polystyrene

This polymer has quite good ozone and oxygen resistance although poor weathering properties. When this material is exposed to heat or uv radiation in the presence of oxygen, carbonyl, and hydroxyl groups are formed; further, the uv light attack results in discoloration. Infrared studies and mass spectrometric analysis of the gaseous product obtained or degradation of the base polymer by heat and uv degradation indicated that the degradation involved two different processes, first, a breakdown of thermolabile groups by heat at temperature above 110°C; second, an oxidation of the polymer by exposure to uv radiation in the presence of oxygen.

ANTIOXIDANTS

We have seen earlier that when a polymer is aged by beat, light chemical attack, exposure to bacteria or even storage, its properties change, resulting in a loss of certain physical characteristics. This degradative process cannot unfortunately be entirely eliminated, but it can be retarded, and it is presumed obvious that the addition of materials termed antioxidants helps in this respect. It may also help to make the subject clearer if the requirements of an ideal antioxidants are summarised. They must; (i) be permanent; (ii) be capable of inhibiting oxidation under all conditions of storage, processing and service; (iii) be nonblooming; (iv) not discolour during processing, or later, when the product is exposed to light; (v) not adversely effect any of the characteristics properties of the base polymer; (vi) be nontoxic and odorless.

The properties of a polymer can be seriously affected without the addition of antioxidants. This is deleterious and the following properties can be influenced; melt viscocity, discoloration, clarity, tensile and impact strength.

The oxidation of a polymer is a chain process which is initiated and propagated by a free radical mechanism. This mechanism is basically the same as previously by Bolland and coworkers, which can be illustrated as follows;

Polymer oxidation

1.1 Initiation

$$P \longrightarrow P.$$

1.2 Propagation

$$P. + O_2 \longrightarrow POO.$$

$$POO. + PH \longrightarrow POOH + P.$$

1.3 Chain branching (autocatalysis)

POOH → PO. + .OH

PO.(.OH) + PH → POP (H_2O) + P.

1.4 Termination/crosslinking

2P.
2PO.
2POO.
P. + POO.
P. + PO.
PO. + POO.

→ Nonradical products

Inhibition by antioxidant

2.1 By radical termination

POO. + AH → POOH + A.

PO. + AH → POH + A.

OH. + AH → H_2O + A.

2.2 By peroxide decomposer

POOH + PD → Stable, nonradical products

Polymer chain scission

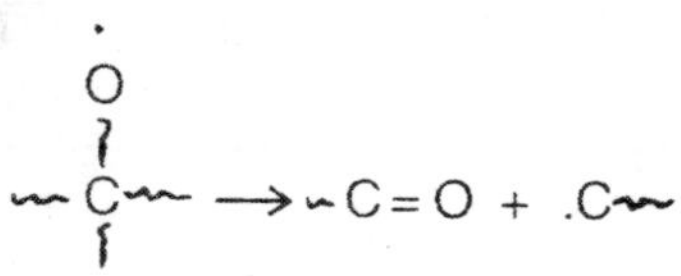

Antioxidants are normally used in commercial liquid stabilized systems to reduce plasticizer oxidation in the plasticized formulations. The organic phosphites have certain antioxidative properties but, as yet, they are not used to any large extent. The most popular types are certain amines and hindered phenols, e.g., 2,4 dioctyl phenol. Other materials are also used including the condensation products of the previous materials with ketones and aldehydes.

16

Fillers, Colorants, and Special Additives

The science of enhancing the properties and characteristics of a polymer by use of special additives has been known and practiced for many years. The origin of two of the, probably, most important additives, fillers, and colorants, can be traced back to times when polymers were unknown. Industries based on paint and printing ink, for example, were quick to realize improvement that should be achieved by incorporating of such additives.

During the past 50 years, more and more has come to be expected to polymers as regards performance, and many improvements have been achieved solely by the addition of special purpose additives, among these flame-retarders, which have been in use since the early days of cellulosic plastics and other which by chemical means after the actual polymer structure. The change in structure, of course, is not a chemical change but, rather, a physical one. The polymer is no longer solid but contains minute, discrete cells which give the polymer a cellular structure. Many changes have taken place in the types of blowing agents used to produce these, and they are discussed later.

It is well known that if rubber is exposed to the weather it loses its elasticity and is said to have 'perished'. This action is accelerated if the rubber is held in tension, the cause probably being due to oxidation and ultraviolet attack. The actual mechanism of the degradation has been the subject of much debate in the past and considerable work has been carried out in trying to find the correct answer.

Space does not permit the exhaustive treatment necessary for describing all these special additives but it is hoped that the reader will consult the reading list at the end of the chapter for further information on each individual additive. These additives are of great importance to the polymer industry, and it must be stressed that to obtain optimum effect it is essential that the correct choice and amount of additive is made.

FILLERS

The use of fillers is recorded in the Bible where reference are made to the use of straw in brick making. Fillers are, of course, not essential for every polymeric compound, but some are vitally necessary for specific end-uses and, many are added solely to reduce costs. They are widely in availability, cost, composition, and physical and chemical characteristics, and the choice of a filler in the formulation of a molding compound is usually governed by end-use application.

Effects and Requirements of a Filler

Unfortunately, no single known meats all the requirements necessary to be classed as the complete filler. The following are some requirements of a potential filler for polymer modification:

(a) Low cost.
(b) Low specific gravity.
(c) Heat stability.
(d) Easily and readily obtainable.
(e) Neutral– should not be acidic or alkaline.
(f) Easy to handle.
(g) Low water and oil absorption
(h) Suitable for wetting by the polymer binder.
(i) Must not absorb the polymer.
(j) Must not prevent flow of the polymer.

In addition to possessing certain of these above properties, the fillers must also confer certain advantages on the final product. These include enhancement of :

(a) Heat resistance and thermal stability.
(b) Dimensional stability
(c) Mechanical strength, e.g., impact and tensile.
(d) Processing techniques
(e) Mold shrinkage and after crazing tendencies
(f) Surface finish of the molding.
(g) Thermal expansion
(h) Electrical properties
(i) Chemical resistance
(j) Flow.
(k) Special effects such as making the polymer magnetic, conductive or flame-retardant.
(l) Dilution of exotherm as necessary.

Classification

Fillers may be broadly classified as (1) inorganic or (2) organic. The main fillers are listed in Table 16.1.

1. Inorganic Fillers

These fillers have certain advantages over the organic types but in many respects their uses are complementary to one another. The inorganic fillers are not widely used for modifying thermosetting molding materials but are now used much more in reinforced plastics. The main advantages in comparison with the organic fillers are that they impart better heat, water, and electrical resistance. They also have better dimensional stability and, in some cases, better chemical resistance. The main inorganic fillers are :

(a) *Asbestos.* Asbestos consists of hydrated metal silicates and is partly related in chemical composition to glass. It is a natural occurring mineral product and may be found in South Africa, Canda, and Russia. The base material is readily separated into more or less flexible fibers of staple length, varying between 1/16 inch to two inches, although it is not unusual for greater lengths to be used. there are four main types of asbestos occurring in nature of which chrysotile, crocidolite, and amosite are the most important. The first two are used extensively in the polymer industry. Little use has been made of amosite because of the brittleness of the molding obtained from it. It is, however, used in specialised cases for its acid resistant characteristics. Chrysotile fibers are long and, thus ideal for use in laminating plastics, but chrocidolite fibers are preferred for general moldings because of the high tensile strength they impart. The moldings produced with asbestos are the filler have excellent heat resistance and low water absorption but they have a high density.

(b) *Glass.* Glass is an inorganic product of fusion which is cooled to a rigid state without crystallisation. It is transparent, hard, at heat-resistant and has a theoretically high strength as compared with plastics. Fibers produced in glass are of immense importance as a reinforcement for synthetic resins such as epoxies and polyesters. Various forms of fibers are used although it is probably correct to say that terms describe the use of glass fibers in conjunction with resin is reinforcing agent rather than a filler. The fibers are generally used in a cloth or mat form for laminate although use is now made of the fibers for a technique known as dough molding. The various forms of glass fiber are :

1. Continuous filaments-rovings, etc.
2. Staple yarn cloth.
3. Glass mats, needle mat, diamond mat, and coil mat.

Table 16.1

PRINCIPAL FILLERS FOR POLYMERS

Type	*Fibrous*	*Nonfibrous*
(1) *Inorganic*	Asbestos Glass fiber Mica	Aluminum powder Iron oxide Titanium dioxide Zinc oxide Antimony oxide Slate powder Barytes Marble dust China clay Calcium carbonate Talc Carbon black (various types) Graphite Silicas Ebonite dust (hard rubber)
(2) *Organic*		
(i) Cellulosic	Cotton fabric, flock, and powder Woodflour, sawdust, and wood shavings Paper and wood pulp Linen fabric and fiber Lignin, sisal	'Microballoons', e.g., P/F and U/F Microspheres
(ii) Noncellulosic	Cork dust Wool and wool felt Cotton seed hulls	
(3) *Miscellaneous*	Walnut shell flour Coconut shell flour	

(c) *Mica*. Mica occurs in nature mainly in India and the U.S.A. and, like asbestos, it is a silicate. When used as a filler it imparts excellent electrical properties although, unfortunately, it is not wetted by resins, and homogenous moldings are therefore difficult to obtain. Use of mica as a filler for polymers is somewhat limited because the base material is fairly costly.

(d) *Diatomaceous Silica.* The material when used as a filler improves heat resistance and the electrical properties of the polymer without increasing its specific gravity. However, it is an abrasive and will effect the surface of the mold, which is then likely to cause the molding to stick.

2. Organic Fillers

(a) *Wood flour.* One of the most common and cheapest fillers, wood flour is used mainly for pheno and aminoplasts. The type of wood used is most important, the best wood flour fillers being obtained from soft woods such as deal and spruce. The wood flour is normally ground to a particle size of a 100 mesh with a moisture content of 6-8 per cent. This filler produces moldings with fair strength properties and good moisture resistance, but its electrical properties could be better.

(b) *Cotton Flock.* This is a short staple cotton fiber which is of little use for spinning due to its relatively small fiber length. It is a pure fiber and is normally light in color with a high bulk factor. It provides moldings with improved impact strength and mold shrinkage. It is more costly, however, than wood flour.

(c) *Paper (α-Cellulose).* Very important as a filler with the amino plastics and paper is normally used in the form of bleached sulfite pulp. It is practically colourless, with a short fiber and is, therefore, fairly expensive. The use of α-cellulose as a filler, apart from the amino plastics, is somewhat limited.

(d) *Chopped Fabric.* This type of filler is obtained from cuttings from the garment and related industries. It is, therefore, relatively cheap, but it is difficult to reproduce moldings with it. Moldings of outstanding impact strength are obtained although their water absorption is high.

(e) *Walnut-Shell Flour* : Moldings with smooth surfaces and medium gloss are obtained with the filler and their properties are comparable with those obtained from wood flour. The cost however, is higher:

(f) *Carbon Black.* Channel black has been replaced to a large extent by a furnace black which is a more coarse variety. This latter black consists of rod-like clusters of spherical particles, which can be up to 800 angstrom unit.

Carbon blacks have low surface energy and they highlight shielding capacity which makes them very useful for retarding to photo oxidation of polythene. This type of filler also increase the modulus of elastomers but may decrease the tensile strength and increase the embrittlement temperature of some plastics.

Another use of carbon as a filler is in a fibrous form. Both rayon and polyacrylonitrile can be pyrolyzed to produce carbon fibers. These fibers have found an interesting use as a reinforcing material in conjunction with certain resins in processing technology methods akin to the better known technology associated with polyester glass fiber. The composition so formed have already found uses in the aircraft industry and one particular example is the use in the Lockheead Tristar as fan blades in the engines produced by

Properties and Choice of Filler

The choice of a filler plays a very important part in determining the final physical properties of the molding. This is illustrated in Table 16.2, which shows the effect of adding different types of fillers to phenol and urea-formaldehyde resins. This effect is further emphasised in Table 16.3, which lists the physical properties of polyester and epoxy casting resins resulting from using various fillers. In this table it is seen that the calcium carbonate-filled resins give the best general characteristics and the micafilled the best electrical properties.

Table 16.2

SOME TYPICAL PROPERTIES OF THERMOSETS WITH VARIOUS FILLERS

	Unfilled P/F	*Wood flour P/F*	*Asbestos P/F*	*Wood flour U/F*	*α-Cellulose U/F*
Specific gravity 15°C	1.3	1.33	1.7	1.4	1.45
Tensile strength (lb/in.^{2})	5000	7000	5000	7000	7500
Impact strength (ft/lb)	0.1	0.2	1	0.16	0.2
Plastic yield B.S. 771 at 100°C	3	2	2	3	3
Coefficient of linear expansion X 10^{-6}/°C	25	40	25	30	30
Water absorption (168 h) mg B.S. 771	30	90	50	300	300
Volume resistivity (ohm/cm)	$1X10^{8}$	$1X10^{11}$	$1X10^{9}$	$1X10^{11}$	$1X10^{12}$
Power factor 1 Mc/s	0.2	0.15	0.1	0.3	0.3
Permittivity at 1 Mc/s	6	7	7	6	6

Previous mention (see chapter 5) has been made of a process known 'as dough or gunk' molding, which was originally developed to use waste material obtained from the conventional lay-up technique for fiber-glass reinforcement. It consists essentially of mixing the glass fiber with polyester resins, catalysts,, and initiators, pigments, and additional fillers such as calcium carbonate, to form a material with a dough-like consistency. The material is then suitable for molding into a variety of shapes. The term 'gunk' is a American origin and means waste or scrap and this process now consumes a considerable amount of glass fiber as a filler.

Many developments have taken place with fillers for use with polymers, one such being employed for casting resins. These fillers are either now density aggregates or hollow spheres, the actual density of the final product being determined by the amount of low-density filler added. Two types are available, inorganic and organic. The organic low-density fillers are hollow spheres in the form of 'microballons' and they are used for filling epoxy and polyester resins. The microballons are tiny nitrogen-filled polymeric spheres, usually produced from urea or phenol-formaldehyde, with a diameter from 0.0002 inch to 0.0035 inch. This inorganic type is based on glass, a material typical of this group being the 'Eccospheres'.

COLORANTS

It has been suggested that one of the reasons for the tremendous growth in the use of polymeric materials is that they can be supplied in almost any color. Extensive experience in color matching is required, for colorants can play a dual role in many polymer formulations, particularly with PVC. The pigments used in PVC paste are added primarily by impart the decorative effect but they may also act as stabilizers. Many pigments produce an adverse effect on some polymers; for example with PVC the volume resistivity is affected. The correct choice of colour for individual polymers is essential, Table 16.4 listing the various colorants suitable for different polymers.

Three basic colorants are used for polymers. These are inorganic pigments, organic pigments, and dyes. The inorganic pigments are generally metallic oxides which have been calcined to around 2000°C. Typical examples are titanium dioxide, zinc oxide, and antimony trioxide. These pigments have certain advantages over their counterparts in that they possess superior light stability. Pigments are also used extensively in paint formulations to impart colour, covering powder, weather resistance, and to give strength to the film. A wide variety of materials are used in paints

Table 16.3

EFFECT OF VARYING TYPE OF FILLER IN CASTING RESINS

Property	*Epoxy*			*Polyester*		
	Unfilled	*Calcium carbonate*	*Mica*	*Unfilled*	*Calcium carbonate*	*Mica*
Specific gravity 15°C	1.2	1.5	1.4	1.25	1.5	1.35
Tensile strength ($lb/in.^2$)	9500	6000	5500	7000	4000	5000
Compressive strength (lb/in^2)	16,000	7500	5500	18,000	18,500	19,500
Coefficient of linear expn.$X10^{-6}/°C$	70	55	40	95	84	64
Water absorption (mg)	22	22	22	50	50	50
Dielectric strength (V/mil)	300	350	400	300	270	400
Power factor 1 Mc/s	0.030	0.035	0.035	0.018	0.017	0.02
Dielectric constant 1 Mc/s	4	4.5	4	3	4.75	3.5

including white lead, titanium, zinc, iron, and chromium oxide. The inorganic pigments are normally characterized by their high specific gravity and low oil and plasticized absorption. They are generally resistant to most chemicals although they produce opaque polymers, but in some a certain degree of transparency can be obtained. This group of pigments is very popular due largely to the fact that the higher molding temperatures now required are obtainable only with these pigments, which are stable at elevated temperatures.

Organic pigments have lower heat stability than the inorganic types and they can conveniently be subdivided into toners and lakes which are characterized by limited solubility, low specific gravity, and high oil and plasticizer absorption. Organic pigments also imparts greater luster and brightness to finished components than the obtainable with other types. They also provide better transparency and covering powder than inorganic pigments.

Dyes may be defined as synthetic or natural organic chemicals which are soluble in most common solvents such as alcohol and water. They possess very good color strength and are available in a wide range of colors. The specific gravity of dyes is normally low and they are also normally

Table 16.4

COLORANTS FOR POLYMERS

Polymer	*Suitable colorants*
Thermosets	
1. Aminoplastics	Inorganic pigments, organic pigments, or phthalocyanines.
2. Phenoplastics	Spirit and hydrocarbon soluble dyes, inorganic and organic pigments
3. Epoxies	Inorganic and organic pigments, also phthalocyanines
4. Polyesters	Inorganic and organic pigments as pastes, also selected hydrocarbon soluble dyes
5. Silicones	Inorganic pigments
Thermoplastics	
1. Polyvinyl chloride and copolymers	Spirit and hydrocarbon soluble dyes. Inorganic pigments (except those with the tendency to bloom and migrate)
2. Cellulosics	Spirit, hydrocarbon soluble dyes, and basic dyes
3. Polyolefins	Organic pigments, phthalocyanine pigments
4. Polymethylmethacrylate	Hydrocarbon soluble dyes, pththalocyanine products
5. Polystyrene	Hydrocarbon soluble dyes, inorganic and organic
6. Polyamides	Inorganic pigments, phthalocyanine, and some anthra-quinone pigments
7. Fluorcarbons	Inorganic pigments

disadvantages including poor heat stability and light resistance. Dyes also tend to bleed out from the polymer and rub off from the surface.

The requirements of a colorant can be summarized as follows :

(a) Low specific gravity.

(b) Relatively inexpensive.

(c) Heat and light stable.

(d) Weather resistant.

(e) Low plasticizer and oil absorption.

(f) Chemically resistant.

(g) Bright and high strength of color.

(h) Disperse easily.

(i) Resistant to migration.

(j) Soluble and suitable solvents.

Methods of Color Addition

Colorants are normally supplied in one of two forms, as a dried base or as concentration of pigment dispersed in a paste or solid. The thermoplastic polymers may be colored by dry coloring techniques and this is normally carried out in a tumbling machine. The premix thus obtained is sent straight to the injection molding machine. This is relatively cheap process and has been used successfully of polystyrene, polyolefins, and polyamides. Another method used for thermoplastics quite successfully is the 'masterbatch' technique. In this method the pigment is supplied at a high concentration mixed into a solid polymer, such as PVC, and the technique is to dilute the 'masterbatch' with further polymer. This has a advantage of being clean and easy to handle although more expensive than dry coloring. Another method that has become extremely popular with some thermosetting resins is that of using high concentrations of prepared colored paste. This technique has been established as the easiest for the fabricator incorporating colorants in polymers. It has been widely adopted for use with epoxy resins, the procedure being to mill the pigment into the resin, the end-product obtained being a reactive part of the overall system.

SPECIAL ADDITIVES

Flame-retarders

In general, the flame-resistance of polymers is good in comparison with such materials as wood, cotton, and other cellulosic derivatives. However, even from the early days of the cellulosic plastics the need to improve the flame-or fire resistance of polymers has been very much in the minds of the polymer manufactures. The present-day uses of plastics, rubbers, paints, and fibers for many applications that were hitherto considered impossible has only served further to highlight the limited flame-resistance of many polymers. Typical applications where the problem is of considerable importance include the building and clothing industries.

There are at present many terms used interchangeably to describe the degree of flame resistance and it is hoped that the following suggested definitions help in clarifying this subject.

(a) *Fire-resistance.* This is the ability of a material to stop the penetration of flame.

(b) *Flame-retardant.* This is the ability of a material to retard the penetration of flame.

(c) *Self-extinguishing.* The ability of a material to cease burning immediately on removal of the source of the flame.

(d) *Nonburning.* The ability of a material to resist combustion.

(e) *Flame-spread.* The spreading of a flame over the surface of a material due to its characteristic properties when in contract with a flame.

Unfortunately, at the present time there is not one polymeric material available that meets all the requirements for complete flame resistance. Fortunately, in many cases certain improvement can be obtained by the addition of flame-retardant chemicals and modification of the polymer chain, although there may be an effective increase in the cost.

Until recent years the most common method of imparting flame resistance to polymers was by chemical additives such as antimony trioxide or phosphorous-containing compounds. Antimony trioxide has successfully been used with polyvinyl chloride and polyethylene. It has, however, been suggested that antimony trioxide does not impart flame-retarding properties unless the polymer to which it is added contains chlorine in the polymer chain or unless a chlorine-containing substance is also added. There are some drawbacks in using antimony trioxide one of which is that the final color of the molded article is affected and may possess a light or dark shade, depending on the grade used. This material can also be used with phosphate plasticizers, and satisfactory results have been obtained with such combinations in PVC mixes. They phosphate plasticizer alone imparts a certain degree of flame-retardancy although it is preferable to mix between two to five parts of antimony trioxide in the compound.

The flammability characteristics of the more common polymers are given in the Table 16.5. The main attempts to improve the flame-retardant properties of polymers can be summarised thus:

(a) By adding antimony compounds such as antimony oxide and triphenyl stibene used in conjunction with chlorine releasing agents.

(b) By adding monomeric phosphorus containing plasticizers.

(c) By treating the polymer with halogen-containing derivatives such as 2,3-dibromopropyl phosphate.

(d) By tailoring the polymer chain by such processes as chlorination or bromination.

(e) By adding flame-proof low molecular weight inorganic polymers such as phosphonitrilic chloride.

Table 16.5

INFLAMMABILITY CHARACTERISTICS OF POLYMERS

	Material	Burning rate	Contact with a flame
(a)	Rubber		
	Natural rubber	Burns readily	Melts and decomposes at 200°C
	Chlorinated rubber	Burns only on continuous contact with flame	Does not melt fully
	Polybutadiene	Burns readily	Decomposes
	Polychloroprene	Nonflammable	Decomposes only at elevated temperatures
	Polysulfides	Burns readily	Hardens at high temperatures
	Polyisobutylene	Burns readily	Decomposes at 200°C
(b)	Plastics		
(i)	Thermosets		
	Urea-formaldehyde	Does not burn readily	Decomposes at high temps.
	Melamine-formaldehyde	Does not burn readily	Decomposes at high temps.
	Phenol-formaldehyde	Does not burn readily	Melt and decompose above 150°C
	Silicones	Burns slowly	Do not melt
	Polyester (cross-linked type)	Burns slowly	Do not melt
	Epoxy resins	Burns	Do not melt
(ii)	Thermoplastics		
	Cellulose nitrate	Burns very quickly	Ignites in air at 160°C
	Cellulose acetate	Does not burn readily	Melts above 200°C
	Polyamides	Does not burn readily	Decomposes
	Polyethylene	Burns readily	Melts between 110-115°C
	P.T.F.E.	Burns	Does not melt
	Polystyrene	Burns readily	Decomposes around 150°C
	Polyvinyl acetate	Burns readily	Decomposes above 200°C
	Polyvinyl alcohal	Burns	Decomposes without melting
	Polyvinyl acetals	Burns readily	Rapid combustion
	Polyvinyl chloride	Does not burn unless continued assistance is given	Decomposes above 150°C
	Polyvinyl chloride	Does not burn readily	Melts about 140°C
	Polymethacrylate	Flame may be rapidly extinguished	Decomposes around 230-300°C

Blowing Agents

A blowing agent my be defined as a compound, organic or inorganic, that releases a gas when heated to a definite minimum temperature. It is , in fact, the decomposition temperature which determines the usefulness of a blowing agent. Many different and diverse materials have been used for blowing agents, ranging from the domestic product baking powder to materials which can be classed as mild explosives. The ideal blowing agent, however, has yet to be marketed. This statement may be better understood if we look at the requirements suggested for an ideal blowing agent.

(a) Gas must be released over a definite and short temperature range.
(b) The release rate must be controllable, although at a reasonable rate.
(c) Gas evolved should be noncorrosive. Nitrogen is normally preferred although carbon dioxide is used for certain applications.
(d) The compounds should disperse readily in the polymer stock and, preferably, dissolve.
(e) It should be cheap.
(f) Stable in storage.
(g) Should not have an unpleasant or obnoxious smell.
(h) Nontoxic.
(i) Colorless and nonstaining.
(j) The compound should not give rise to a large exotherm or decomposition.
(k) Should not effect the rate of cure when added to thermosetting polymers.
(l) Should work equally well in closed molds and, therefore, not be affected by pressure.

Blowing agents are incorporated in polymer matrices in order to alter the structure of the polymer from that of the solid to the cellular state. Simple inorganic and organic salts such as alkali carbonates (e.g., sodium bicarbonate) have been used but due to their poor dispersability have found limited use. the main materials may be compounds of the following groups (1) azo compounds, e.g., azodis isobutyronitrile (AZDN); (2) N-Nitroso compounds, e.g., *N,N'*-dimethyl-*N,N'*-dinitroso terephthalimide; (3) sulfonyl hydrazides, e.g., benzene sulfonyl hydrazide.

Many patents for blowing agents have been taken out and the reader should consult the bibliography for further information.

Ultraviolet Absorbers

It has been established that the breakdown of polymeric materials under exposure to ultraviolet rays involves a light-catalyzed free radical mechanism.

This results in rupture of the bond along the polymer chain with the subsequent discoloration and degradation of the physical properties of the polymer. In practice, one or more of the following effects can result from exposure of unstabilised polymers to ultraviolet energy sources; (i) discoloration from the formation of conjugated structures or complex radicals, (ii) reduction in tensile and impact strength, (iii) distortion of initial flexibility, (iv) dimensional change, (v) surface crazing and cracking, (vi) powdering, and (vii) increase in electrical conductivity.

The addition of antioxidants gives some protection already discussed in Chapter 15. The various polymers, of course, differentiate in their sensitivity or uv light; polymers such as cellulose nitrate deteriorate quite rapidly whereas polymethyl methacrylate is more resistant. This deleterious effect can be overcome by adding compounds which themselves absorb uv light and at the same time resist decomposition. The uv stabilizer addition is incorporating normally at 0.1-0.5 per cent of the polymer weight at the point of fabrication or during polymerization.

The requirements of a material used for uv solution purposes are :

(a) Material must absorb uv light in the desired region.
(b) Stable to uv light.
(c) Stable to processing conditions.
(d) Compatible with polymer.
(e) Chemically inert.
(f) Neutral in color.
(g) Nontoxic.

The principal groups of materials successfully used as a uv light absorbers are

(i) *Metallic Complexes.* These include complexed nickel or cobalt salts of substituted pheols, thiobisphenol, alkyphenones, dithiophosphinates and phosponates, e.g., dicyclohexyl dithiophosphinate.

(ii) *Substituted 2-hydroxybenzophenones.* This is probably the most common and widely used type of which the most popular is 2-hydroxy-4-oxtoxybenzophenone.

(iii) *Benzotriazoles.* Most of this family are derivatives of 2-(2'-hydroxyphenyl) benzotriazole and the 5'-t-oxtyphenyl) analog. They are very popular with strong intensity, and broad uv absorption.

(iv) *Substituted Acrylonitriles*. These give good protection to a wide variety of polymers and absorb uv radiation in the range most damaging to the bulk of common polymers. A popular material in this family is ethyl-2 cyano-3,3'-diphenyl acrylate.

(v) *Aryl Esters*. Aryl salicylates, e.g., *P*-octyl phenyl salicylate and benzoate are weakly uv absorbing compounds. They are photochemically unstable and rearrange under uv radiation to from more stable products such as 2-hydroxybenzophenones.

(vi) *Inorganic Pigments*. Most inorganic pigments absorb uv radiation and act as screening agents. Carbon black is probably the most effective of this group but cannot be used in many applications because of its objectionable color. Other types are titanium dioxide and zinc oxide but have limited use although they have found some application where translucency and opaqueness is of prime importance.

17

Extrusion

The basic extrusion process is designed to continuously convert a thermoplastics material into a particular form. Extrusion is an extremely versatile process and the final shapes or forms which can be produced include pipes, films or sheets, fibers, profiles, coatings for paper and other substrates, and covering for wires and cables. Extruders are also used to feed blow molding machines which produce bottles and other hollow articles. The basic sequence of events is as follows :

(a) Plasticisation of the granular raw material.
(b) Metering of the plasticised product through a die which forms it to the desired shape.
(c) Solidification into the desired shape and size.
(d) Winding into reels or cutting into units.

Processes (a) and (b) are carried out in the extruder, while (c) and (d) are ancillary processes.

The extruder itself (Fig. 17.1) consists fundamentally of an archimedian screw which revolves inside a close fitting, heated cylinder or barrel. The thermoplastic granules are fed through a hopper at one end, and carried forward along the cylinder by the action of the screw. As the granules move along the screw, they are melted by contact with the heated walls of the barrel and by the generation of frictional heat in the viscous melt. The final action of the screw is to force the melted polymer through a die which determines its final form.

This apparently simple process is, in fact, far more complicated than it sounds, and highly developed machines and techniques are necessary to achieve the best results. For an understanding of some of the problems involved, a more detailed examination of the various components of an extruder, and of their function, is necessary.

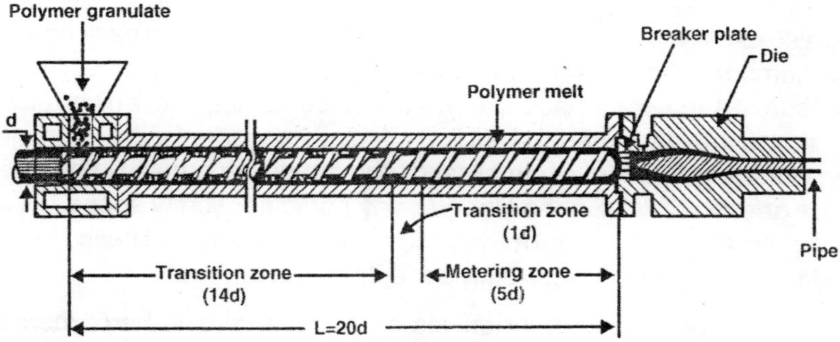

Fig. 17.1 Scheme for a typical single-screw extruder (1/d=20) shown extruding pipe.

The most important component of any extruder is the screw and it is often found impossible to extrude one material satisfactorily using a screw designed for some other material. Screws are characterised by their length/ diameter ratios (common written as 1/d ratios) and their compression ratios, namely, the ratio of the volume of one flight of the screw at the hopper end to the volume of one fight at the die end. L/d ratios most normally used for single screw extruders vary from 15 : 1 to 30 : 1 while compression ratios are usually in the range 2 : 1 to 4 : 1. The screw is usually divided into three sections, namely, feed, compression, and metering. The feed section merely conveys the material from under the hopper mouth along to the compression section where the gradually diminishing depth of thread causes volume compression of the melting granules and consequent removal of trapped air which is forced back through the feed section. This ensures an extrudate free from porosity, while another consequence of the volume compression is an increase in the shearing action on the melt, due volume compression is an increase in the shearing action on the melt, due to relative motion of the screw surfaces with respect to the barrel wall. Improved mixing results, together with the generation of frictional heat, which leads to a more uniform temperature distribution in the molten extrudate. The function of the final section of the screw is to meter the molten polymer through the die at a steady rate and to iron out pulsations. The screw is usually cored for steam heating or water cooling.

Thus far, we have talked about the build-up of back pressures due to the compression ratio of the screw, but, in fact, there would be very little back pressure at normal speeds if the extruder were operating with an open head so that the extrudate could pass through without restriction. The presence of the die alone, of course, sets up an appreciable restriction but it is also usually to have a breaker plate supporting a screen pack consisting of a number of find or coarse mesh gauzes. In addition to increasing back pressures, the screenpack filters out any contamination which might be present in the few material. This is particularly important in the extrusion of thin films, where even the smallest of contaminating particles could cause holes or even breaks in the film. For any particular screw speed, a higher back pressure improves the mixing and homogenisation (and hence extrusion quality) but slightly reduces extruder output.

The motor employed for driving an extruder should be of more than adequate power for its normal needs. The question of screw speeds is also an important one and variable screw speeds are now considered to be essential. Either variable speed motors or constant speed motors with variable speed equipment such as hydraulic systems, infinitely variable speed gearboxes, step-change gearboxes, etc., are available. Because of the very high back pressures generated in an extruder, it is important to have thurst bearings of robust construction, and the trend towards higher screws speeds makes this even more essential. Overload protection in the form of an automatic cut-out should be fitted. One circumstances which could arise is the failure of a heater at the tip of the extruder when extruding nylon. Since nylon has a sharp melting point, solidification could occur and a blockage arise.

An important piece of euipment at a feed end of the extruder is the feed hopper. It is obviously essential that the flow of granules to the screw of the extruder material is 'bridging', which can be avoided by fitting a vibrator or, better still, a screw feed. Another possible cause of blockage at the feed opening of the hopper is melted granules but this is easily avoided by water cooling at the hopper end of the barrel. Special hopper driers are sometimes fitted, especially when extruding hygroscopic materials such as nylon or polyethylene containing carbon black. A typical method of accomplishing predrying is to pass hot pass air through the granules in the hopper.

We have dealt with some of the requirements for an extruder drive and for feeding the thermoplastic granules and we come now to one of the most important factors govering the quality of the extrudate, namely, temperature control. Heat is supplied to the granules in two ways-by external heaters (which may be oil, steam, or electric heaters) or by fractional heat generated internally by the shearing and compressing action of the screw. The frictional, or adiabatic, heating, appreciable, and in modern high-speed machines can supply the whole of the heating required for steady running, external heating being required only to prevent the machine from stalling at the start of the run when the material is cold.

The most popular type of external heating is electrical because of its compactness, cleanliness and accuracy of control. Electric resistance heaters are popular because they present few maintenance problems, but induction beating is also widely used is claimed to give quicker heating with less variation and, also, to facilitate efficient cooling. In extruders running at low or medium speeds (except large machines with screw diameters of about 6-8 inches where frictional heat is again large), external heaters supply a larger proportion of the total heating but it either case temperature controllers are essential and heating and cooling must be carefully balanced. Either air or water cooling may be used, but in their case it should operate automatically. The barrel is usually divided into three or four heating zones, the temperature being lowest at the feed end of the barrel and highest at the head end.

As already mentioned, the screw is also cored for heating or cooling, where the maximum amount of compounding is required a screw is cooled. This improves the quality of the extrudate but slightly reduces the output.

Correct design of the head is important and should promote streamline flow of the material with no 'dead spots' where material could stagnate and thus decompose due to overheating. This is particularly important in the case of PVC where the degradation point of the material is close to the temperature necessary for adequate flow.

Die design, too, must take account for these factors but to an even more marked degree. Steamlining of the die and die entry is important not only because of polymer degradation but also because tubelent flow can lead to defects in the extrudate. Such defects may surface effects as, for instance, a roughness or mattress, or a total distortion leading to an effect variously described as knobbly, wavy, or bamboo-like.

A fairly recent development in extruder design has been the use of venting or degrassing zones in order to remove any volatile constituents from the extrudate before it emerges from the die. This is achieved by releasing the plastic melt from the state of compression to which it has been subjected, whereupon the water or other volatiles will vaporise and cause the melt to froth. In effect, two screws are used, in series, and separated by the degassing zone. The first has three sections, namely, feed , compression, and discharge, the latter having a shallow thread and normally running full. The second screw has a degassing section, fed by the discharge section of the first screw, followed by a discharge section of its own. The degassing section has a deeper thread than the final section of the first screw and, thus the polymer suddenly finds itself in an increased volume and hence is at a lower pressure. Frothing occurs as the volatiles are released from the melted polymer, which is again compressed and them fed to the die. The volatile vapors are released either through a vent-hole in the top of the extruder barrel, or through the hollow core of the screw via a hole drilled in the trailing edge of one of the flights in the degassing section. In either case, a vaccum is sometimes applied to assist in extraction of the vapor. Vaccum hoppers are also sometimes used, particularly for dry-blend powders to reduce porosity, in which case the screw must be sealed at the thrust bearing in order to prevent rearward polymer leakage.

Multiscrew extruders, particularly twin screw extruders are also available and have their own advantages and limitations. In general, multiple screws machines are more expensive and, because of their more complicated construction, are likely to be less sturdy. A more positive transport of the molten polymer is possible, however, and better mixing is obtained. By virtue of their positive pumping action multiple-screw extruders produce less shear heat and this makes them very suitable for materials that are heat sensitive, have low coefficients of friction or must leave the die at low extrusion temperatures. They find their main application in the extrusion of unplasticised PVC, particularly for large diameter piping produced from powder. Multiple -screw extruders are also used for compounding all sorts of additives into polymers. Multiscrew systems may be intermeshing (either counterrotating or corotating) or nonintermeshing, counterrotating.

FILM EXTRUSION

Film is usually defined as material having a thickness of up to ten thousandths of an inch (10 mil), thickness above this being referred to as sheet. There are fundamentally two different methods of extruding film, namely, blow-extrusion and slit die extrusion. The former method produces tubular film, which may be gussetted or lay-flat, while the latter results in flat film.

Blown Film Extrusion

A typical setup for blown film extrusion is shown in Fig. 17.2. In this case the molten polymer from the extruder head enters the die from the side, but entry can also be effected from the bottom of the die. In the die, the melt is made to flow round a mandrel and emerges through a ringshaped die openign in the form of a tube. The tube is expanded into a bubble of the required diameter (with consequent reduction in thickness) by blowing air

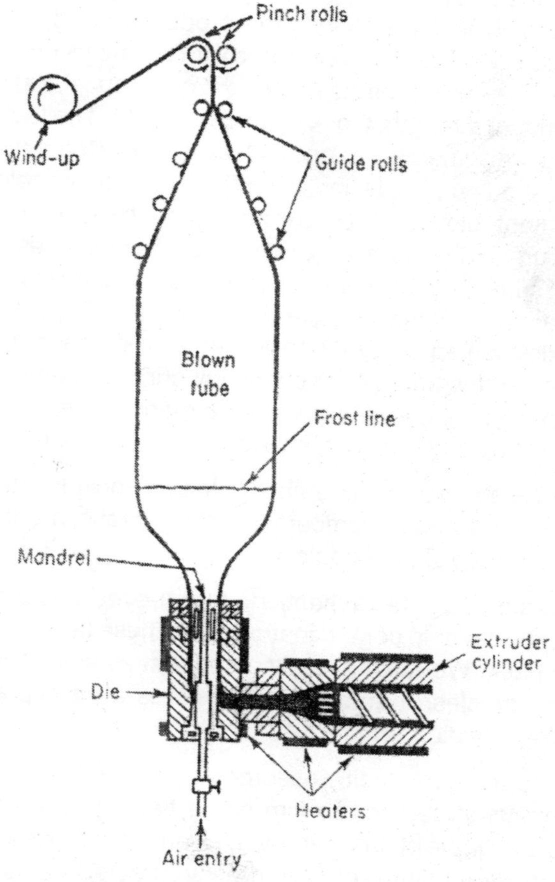

Fig. 17.2 Blown Film extrusion

through the center of the mandrel. The tubing is usually extruded upwards but can be extruded downwards or even horizontally. The air is contained in the bubble by the pinch rolls at one end and the die at the other, and it is important that an even pressure of air is maintained in order to ensure uniform thickness and width of film.

The film bubble is cooled by blowing air on to it from a cooling ring placed round the die. The 'frost' line shown in Fig. 17.2 is more correctly a 'frost' ring, and is the zone where the bubble first appear 'frosty' because the temperature has fallen below the softening point of the polymer.

Blown film extrusion is an extremely complex subject and there are numerous problems associated with the production of good quality film. Among the defects likely to be encountered with variations in gauge, surface defects such as 'fish-eyes', 'orange peel', or 'applesauce', haze, low tensile strength, low impact strength, blocking and wrinkling. The factors effecting film properties are also numerous and include extruder temperatures (barrel and die), extruder output, die design, takeoff speed, rate of cooling of bubble, die ring adjustment, blowup ratio (diameter of bubble/diameter of die) and pinch-roll pressure. With such a large number of film properties and extrusion factors, it is not surprising that it is often necessary to effect the compromise between the various requirements, and it is the balancing of film properties that makes extrusion still very much an art. For instance, good slip and antiblocking properties are obtainable by lowering the temperature of the molten polymer and using a fairly low blowup ratio, whereas toughness and transparency require higher melt temperature and blow ratios.

Film gauge is affected by a number of factors including takeoff speed, extruder output, barrel and die temperature, blowup ratio, die ring adjustment and the rate of cooling of the bubble.

Among the surface defects mentioned, 'fish-eyes' are due to imperfect mixing in the extruder or to contamination. Both these factors are controlled by the screen pack. We have already noted that as well as screening out contaminating particles, a screen pack creates a back pressure which improves homogenisation.

It has of course, been tacitly assumed above that when talking of the influence of extrusion factors on film properties, we were referring to a particular type and grade of polymer. Even when considering a sing polymer, such as polyethylene, film quality is greatly affected by such factors as density and molecular weight. High molecular weight polymers give tougher films as will lower density polymers, while high density also means increased stiffness which leads to greater susceptibility to wrinkling during windup

The advantages of blown film extrusion over flat extrusion include the ability to produce film with a more uniform strength in both the machine and transverse directions. In fat film extrusion (particularly at high take off rates), there is a relatively high orientation of the film in the machine direction and a very low one in the transverse direction. In the blown film extrusion process it is possible, by balancing blow-up ratios against takeoff rate, to achieve physical properties which are very nearly equal in both directions, and this gives a film of minimum toughness. Another advantages of blown film is in bag making, where the only seal necessary is one across the bottom of the bag, whereas with flat film either one or two longitudinal seals are also necessary. The main disadvantages is the lower clarity of the blown film but this can be improved by more efficient cooling. Blown film is often slit, after extrusion, and is then wound up as flat film. Blown diameters of 7 feet or more have been produced, giving flat film width of up to 24 feet. This is much wider than anything so far produced by slitdie extrusion. Such large width of polyethylene film find extensive uses in agriculture, horticulture and building.

Flat Film Extrusion

In flat film extrusion, the melt is extruded through a slit-die and then either into a water bath or on to a chilled roller. In both cases, the essence of the process is rapid cooling of the extruded film and the cooling is applied within a very short distance of the die lips. Figure 17.3 shows an arrangement using water quenching.

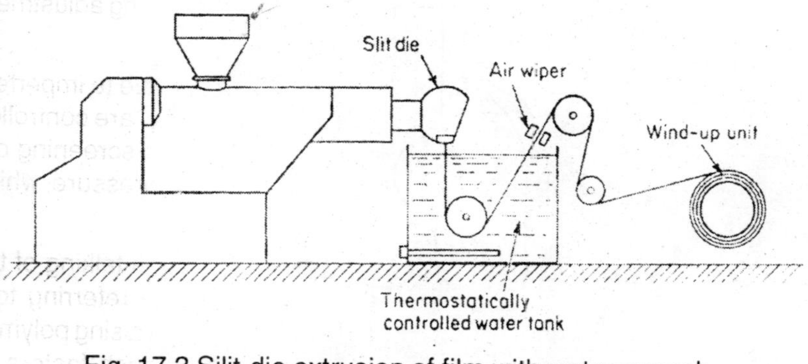

Fig. 17.3 Silit-die extrusion of film with water quench.

In the chill roll 'casting' method, the quenching is replaced by two or more chromium-plated rollers which have been cored for water cooling. The chill roll method of producing flat film gives a product with extremely high gloss and clarity. Since the width of the slit-die for flat film is large compared with the diameter of the extruder head, the flow path to the extreme edges of the die is longer than to the center (Fig. 17.4).

Flow compensation is usually obtained, in the case of thin film, by a manifold die, a cross section of which is shown in Fig. 17.5. It consists of a lateral channel (or manifold) of a diameter such that its flow resistance is small compared with that offered by the die lips. The inside surface of the die

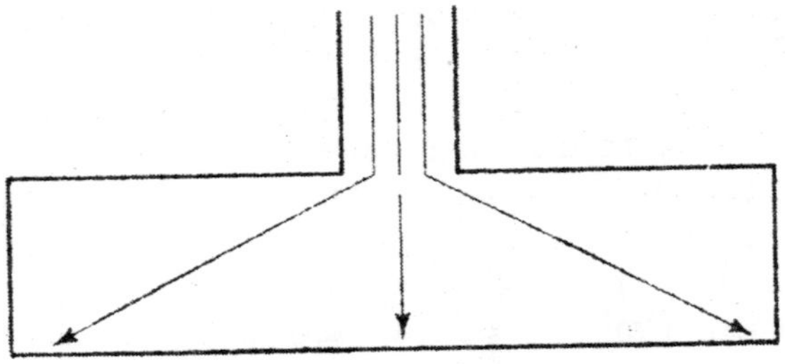

Fig. 17.4 Varying flow paths in simple slit-die

should be precision machined and well polished since the slightest is efficient in its task of flow compensation only if the viscocity of the melt is fairly low, so that higher temperature are necessary for flat film extrusion. This, in turn, limits the use of the manifold die to materials of good thermal stability. Another consequence of the higher extrusion temperature is that a heavier screen pack is necessary in order to maintain satisfactory back pressure.

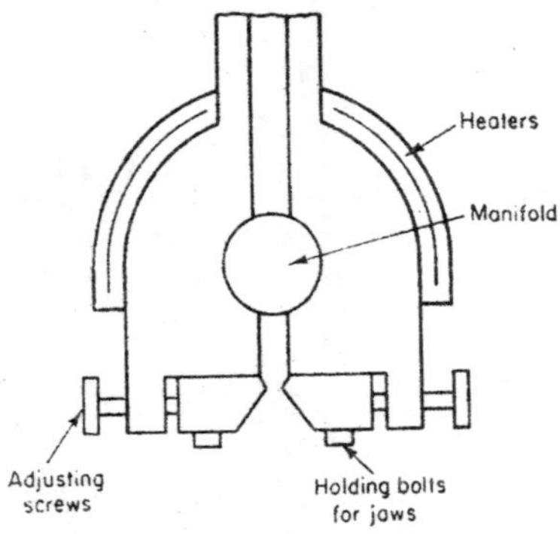

Fig. 17.5 Cross Section of manifold type dor for film

SHEET EXTRUSION

Sheet can be extruded in a manner analogous to that outlined for large width film, namely, by extrusion of a tube, which is then split, continuously, opened out until flat, then passed through polishing rolls. This method, which is usually referred to as the 'indirect' extrusion method has the advantage that it utilise a simple and cheap die system with good flow characteristics and is therefore suitable for use with thermally unstable polymers such as PVC and polymethyl methacrylate. There is, however, bound to be a residual strain in this sheet and the direct extrusion method is now almost universally used for those polymers which are more thermally stable. As with flat film extrusion, dies giving flow compensation are necessary. The fish-tail die, illustrated in Fig. 17.6 shows one type which was once widely used for sheet extrusion. The fish-tail cavity is so shaped internally as to offer more resistance to flow at the center of the die than at the edge.

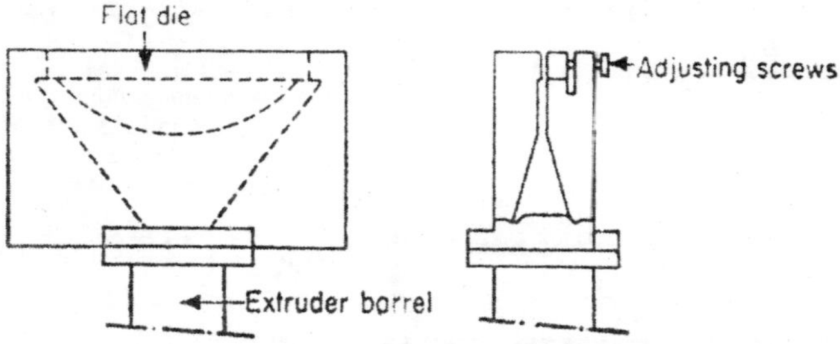

Fig. 17.6 Diagram of fish-tail die for sheet

The fish tail die is extremely bulky, especially for wide-sheet requirements and the heating of such a large surface becomes a very difficult matter. On the other hand, the simple type of manifold die described for film extrusion is limited, as was mentioned, to low viscocity materials. Greater homogeneity of flow can be obtained by introducing a throttle, as shown in Fig. 17.7.

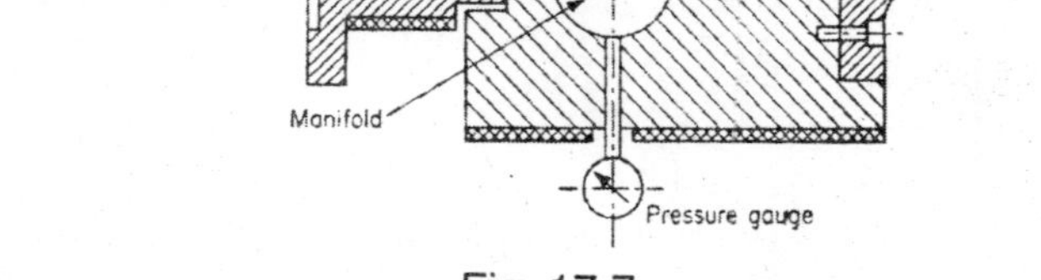

Fig. 17.7

Typical takeoff arrangements for handling extruded sheet are shown in Fig. 17.8. The heated rollers shown are highly polished to give a good surface to the semimolten sheet. The final polishing process can not be used to cover up defects in the sheet caused by faulty extrusion, and great attention must be paid to eliminating surface effects before the sheet leaves the die. A brief note on sheet faults and their probably causes is given below.

Defect	*Probable Cause*
Continuous lines in direct of extrusion	Die contamination or scored rollers or mioisture in the polymer
Continuous lines across the sheet	Jerky operation; may be too low a temperature
Curved lines across a colored sheet	Color not well enough mixed
Discoloration	Too high a mass temperature or too high a percentage of reground material added
Bad gloss	Roll temperature too low or defective rolls
Dull strip	Die set too narrow at this point

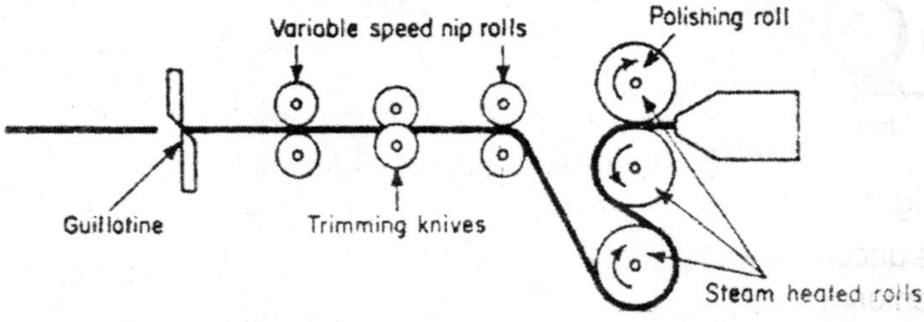

Fig. 17.8 Scheme of process for extruded sheet.

WIRE AND CABLE COVERING

The demand for covered wire and cable in the ratio and electrical industries is already very large and steadily increasing, so that this extrusion process is a very important one. A cross-head die is used for the job, a typical design being shown in Fig. 17.9.

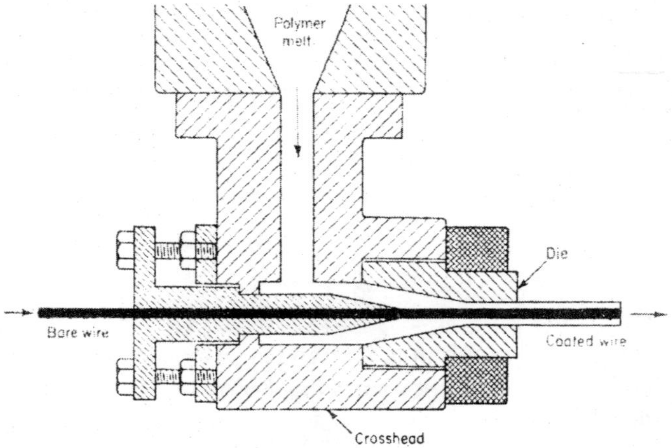

Fig. 17.9 Wire coating cross head

The polymer melt is forced through the extruder breaker plate and screen pack assembly and then over and round the wire guide carrying the wire, and then out through the die which forms the coating round the wire. This in essence, deals with the actual covering of the wire but the complete operation requires a complex array of equipment in addition to the extruder, as can be seen from a glace at Fig. 17.10.

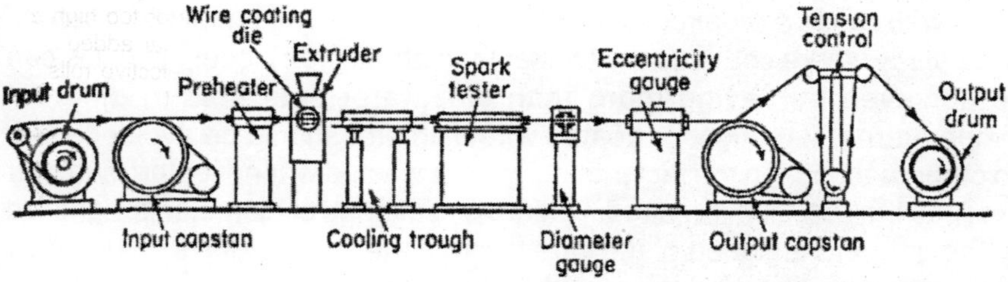

Fig. 17.10 Diagrammatic representation of wire coating layout.

The uncoated wire is paid out from a drum and passed through a preheater prior to entering the covering crosshead mounted on the extruder. The preheating is carried out in order to remove any moisture or drawing die lubricant which may possibly be left on the wire, and which could adversely affect adhesion. In addition to this, the coating adheres more readily to a hot wire.

On leaving the crosshead die, the coated wire is cooled by passing through a water tourgh. Damage to the insulating coating has to be avoided at all costs, and a neat arrangement for ensuring that the wire travels through the water bath without touching anything solid is shown in Fig. 17.11.

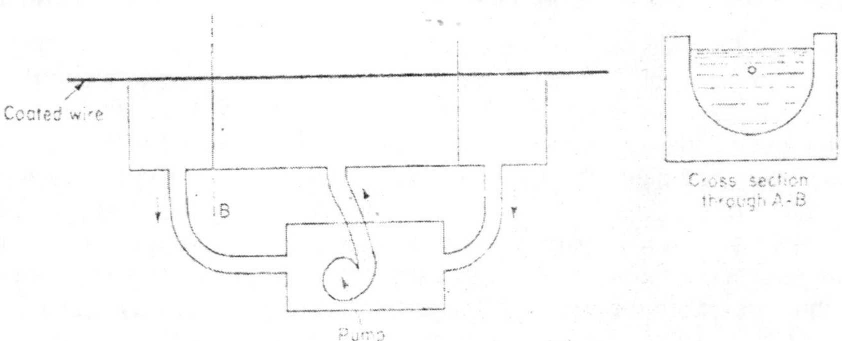

Fig. 17.11 Cooling of coated wire

Various items of equipment for testing the quality of the coating are usually inserted in the setup at this point and may include a spark-tester (to discover the presence of pin-holes or other faults in the insulation), and diameter and eccentricity gauges. The wire is pulled through the coating system by a driven capstan and then passed through a tension controller on to the wind-up drum. The cooling operation is particularly critical in the case of wire and cable covering because the existence of voids or bubbles might well cause a breakdown in the insulation. Cooling should be gradual, particularly where coatings are thicker than about 0.02 inches, and this can be achieved by having more than one water bath held at different temperatures. Variations is coated wire diameter should be avoided, if for no other reason than the fact that polymer is wasted whenever the diameter exceeds the minimum required. whenever a change of diameter is signalled by the gauge, the speed of the wire through the coating die is adjusted by altering the wind-up capstan speed.

PIPE EXTRUSION

The die used for the extrusion of pipe consists of a die body with a die mandrel and an outer die ring which control the dimensions of the inner and outer diameters respectively. A die mandrel is positioned in the die by a three or four-spoked piece known as a 'spider', while the outer die ring is held is four adjusting screws which allow centering to be carried out during extrusion. An air channel passes through one of the 'spider' legs, connecting with an air-hole drilled up the center of the mandrel. By sealing the end of the extruded tube with a plug, and supplying compressed air through the air channel described above, the pipe can be pressurised to any required extent.

After the pipe leave the die, the procedure is calibration (or sizing), cooling and takeoff. The actual passage of the molten polymer through the pipe die causes a certain amount of molecular orientation. Loss of orientation after leaving the die causes the material to swell. Attached to the die is a water-jacketed pipe which has an inside diameter equal to the outside diameter of the finished pipe. The internal pressure maintained the pipe causes a slight circumferential stretching. Contact is made with the cooled inner surface of the water-jacketed calibrator. The outer surface of the pipe is thus cooled and set sufficiently to enable it to retain its size while passing through the cooling bath. An interesting variation on the method of calibration described above is to apply a vaccum to the cooled calibrator, so that the molten material is forced against the inner surface by atmospheric air pressure. Takeoff is achieved by means of reeling drums in the case of flexible tubing such as plasticized PVC or low density polyethylene but for the more rigid pipes, a caterpiller type of takeoff is often used.

PROFILE EXTRUSION

Profile extrusion is similar to pipe extrusion except that the mandrel and 'spider' are obviously not necessary. A die plate, in which an orifice has been cut, is bolted to the face of the normal die assembly so that it is then possible to change from one profile to another without the necessity of a major die change. To maintain a smooth flow, the die plate orifice is blended to match the bore of the die body.

There is a surface drag on the molten polymer as it passes through the die and this has the effect of lessening the flow through the thinner sections of the orifice. To counteract this tendency, it is necessary to alter the shape of the orifice, and there is often a wide difference in the orifice shape and that of the desired extrusion profile. Some examples of sections and the die orifices necessary to produce them are shown in Fig. 17.12

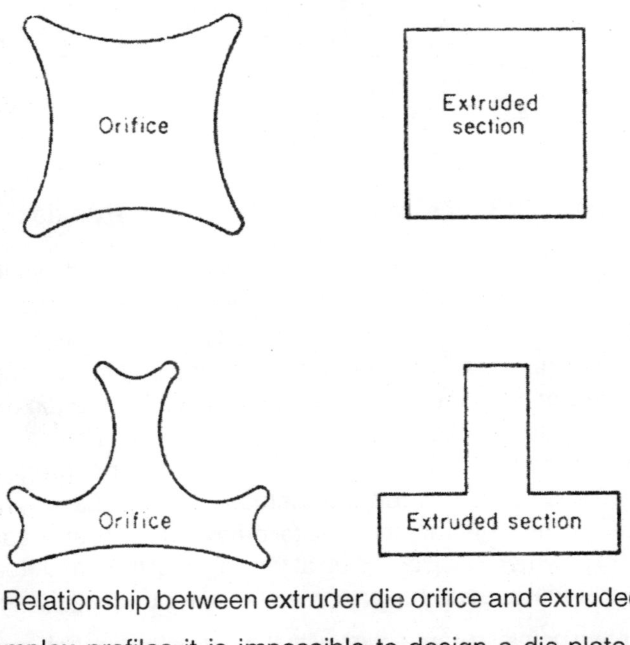

Fig. 17.12 Relationship between extruder die orifice and extruded section.

For complex profiles it is impossible to design a die-plate from first principles. It is usual to produce a first approximation in an unfinished form and then to arrive at the correct orifice form by trial and error on the extruder.

EXTRUSION COATING

Many substrates, including paper, fiberboard, cellulose film, aluminium foil, and hessian are today being coated with polymers by the direct extrusion process. By far the commonest polymer used for this process, at present, is low-density polyethylene, the basic process consisting of extruding a thin film of molten polyethylene and pressing it on to the substrate without the use of an adhesive. The equipment used is similar to that employed for the extrusion of fat film, Fig. 17.13 showing a typical extrusion coating setup.

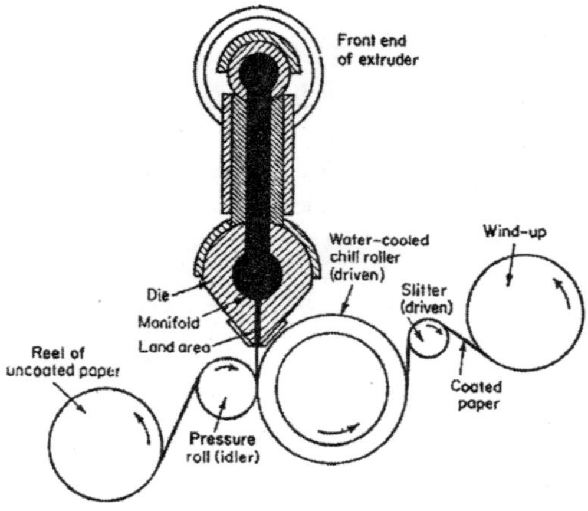

Fig. 17.13 Cross section of paper coating extruder.

As it leaves the die lips, the thin molten film is pulled down into the nip between two rolls situated directly below the die. The substrate, which is moving at a speed faster than the extruded film, draws the hot film to the required thickness, while the pressure between the chill-roll and the pressure roll forces the film on to the substrate. Meanwhile, the molten film is being cooled by the water cooled, chromium-plated chill roll. The pressure roll is also metal but is covered with a rubber sleeve, usually, neoprene or silicone rubber. After leaving the chill-roll, the coated material is drawn over a driven slitter-roll where the edges are trimmed to remove the uncoated edge and the small bead of polymer which builds up at the edges of the film. After trimming, the coated material is wound up on conventional wind-up equipment.

One or two points in connection with the extrusion coating process may be mentioned here since thay have a bearing on the type of equipment used. In the first place, it is not economical to coat narrow substrate width, since the cost of equipment is high, so that die width are large with a consequent need for large extruders. Higher temperatures are required for extrusion coating than for unsupported film extrusion, and oil heating is not sufficient in this case. The usual form of heating employed in coating extruders and dies is high capacity electrical heaters.

The weight of the coating deposited on the substrate is governed by the speed of the chill-roll. For any given extrusion rate, the higher the chilroll speed, the greater draw down and, hence, the lower the coating weight. The chill-roll has two other functions, one of which is, of course, to cool the coating to a temperature low enough to enable it to be stripped from the roll. This cooling has to be accomplished in about half a revolution of the roll thus necessitating very efficient water-cooling of the roll. The chill-rolls also determines the surface finish of the film. For high gloss, the chill-roll surface must be very highly polished but where dull film sufaces are required, the chill-roll may be etched or sand-blasted.

Adehsion of the coating to the substrate is a matter of prime importance and is affected by several factors. High-melt temperatures are essential while other factors include coating thickness (thick coatings adhere better than thin ones) and draw down rate (high draw-down rates have an adverse effect on adhesion). Different substrates also have their own individual problems as in the case of paper and board, where a low moisture content is required for good adhesion. Adhesion of polyethylene to aluminium foil is not an easy matter to achieve and the problems are sometimes overcome by an etching treatment of the aluminium foil surface. To coating of regenerated cellulose film also presents a problems. If a moisture-proof cellulose film is required, then a single-sided film is used and the coating is carried out on the uncoated side of the cellulose film, the reason being that stripping of the cellulose film's original coating would otherwise occur.

One of the problems encountered is extrusion coating is that of 'beading' at the edges of the hot film where 'necking in' occurs. This local thickening of the film has to be removed during the trimming operation otherwise, when the roll is wound up, the beads at the either end support the weight of the roll, leaving a loosely wound and sagging roll in the middle. The extra trimming required means a reduction in the usable web widths, thus increasing the coating costs. In the case of polyethylene the indicence of 'neck in' can be reduced by decreasing the melt index or the density out the risk of voids in the hot film at low coating speeds increases because of imperfect melt flow, so that an optimum combination of these two factors has to be found. The distance between the die lips and the chill-roll should also be at a minimum for minimum 'neck in' while increasing the screw speed also reduces 'neck in'. It can be seen that the balancing of requirements such as minimum 'neck in', high coating speeds, absence of voids, etc., is a matter of experience.

EXTRUSION OF EXPANDED POLYSTYRENE SHEET

Initial work on the extrusion of expanded polystyrene sheet showed that the normal blowing agents used tended to form solutions in the polystyrene at extrusion temperatures. This led to the formation of large pubbles and hence a coarse cell size. This is undesirable so a nucleating agent, such as a mixture of citric acid and sodium bicarbonate, is used. As mentioned earlier, in Chapter 11, there are two main methods for production of expanded polystyrene sheet. The first starts with expandable polystyrene beads, i.e., beads that have been impregnated under pressure with a liquefiable gas, such as pentane. The sheet is blow extruded, using a twin-screw extruder, the nucleating agents having been mixed with the beads just prior to extrusion. To avoid premature decomposition of the nucleating agents it is essential that the expandable beads be predried just before the mixing. One suitable method is to blow dried air through the beads for two to three hours. This method of sheet production of sheet production is particularly suited to low tonnage production of the order of 300-350 tons per annum.

The other method is direct gassing in the extruder. Ordinary crystal polystyrene is premixed with the nucleating agents and loaded into the feed hopper of the extruder. The granules are melted during the first 20D length of the extruder barrel, the melt temperature being then about 240°C. A liquid blowing agent (one of the fluorinated hydrocarbons) is then injected into the melt, using a high pressure diaphragm metering pump. A mixing section of the extruder screw ensures good dispersion of the blowing agent. The temperature of the melt is then reduced to about 130°C and the melt is forced through the annular die of the blowing head. This method is the most economical for large tonnage sheet manufacture and has the added advantage that the use of fluorinated hydrocarbons as blowing agents eliminates the risk of fire during manufacture and storage.

Whichever method of extrusion is used it will be appreciated that the material leaving the extruder expands considerably with a consequent drop in density from 65 lb/ft^3 to about 5 lb/ft^3 (1040g/ℓ to about 80 g/ℓ). Thus, a thirteen fold increase in volume occurs. The sideways compound of this expansion would cause corrugation to occur if a slit die were used. Using an annular die the corrugations can be eliminated by blowing the tubular extrudate into a bubble, as with lay-flat polyethylene film. After the bubble has been collapsed during the haul-off operation the lay-flat tube is trimmed on each side to produce two flat sheets that can be reeled up together or separately. This is necessary because of the folded edges of the tube are a source of weakness due to the rigidity of polystyrene. Control of sheet orientation is achieved in the usual way by adjusting the blow-up ratio and the haul-off speed. Orientation should be as balanced as possible to avoid splitting of the seet during any subsequent thermoforming operations.

Although the density of the sheet as it leaves the extruder is about 5 ponds per cubic foot (80g/ℓ), subsequent operations such as blowing-up, and stretching during haul-off, tend to compress the sheet and so increase the density. In addition, the collapsing of the bubble and subsequent passage of the sheet through nip rollers also increase the density. Normally, therefore, the density of the finished sheet will be of the order of 8-10 lb/ft^3 (128-160 g/ℓ). The density can be reduced by passing the sheet under an infrared heater, at the same time supporting the sheet across its width by a roller. If the expanded sheet is reeled and allowed to stand for a few horus prior to the thermoforming process the cells absorb air and a further reduction in density is obtained when exposed to the thermoforming heaters. This thickening effect is useful in countering the tendency for a thermoformed article to become thin at the corner.

COEXTRUSION

An important development in the extrusion of film is coextrusion where two or more layers of film are extruded simultaneously to produce a laminate with improved barrier or mechanical properties. Basically the process the consists in coupling two or more extruders to a single die head. Tighter control in necessary of extrusion process variables such as melt pressures, screw speeds, melt temperatures and power capacity of the extruder drives. For example, the temperature of each polymer must be closely controlled in order to maintain the proper level of viscocity in the die. The success of the technique lies very largely in the design of the die and the way in which the individually extruded melts are brought together, prior to their extrusion as a multilayer film.

There are three basic methods of carrying out this operation. The fact is the multislit die system where the various polymers are each fed to separate manifolds in the die, then pass through separate slits and are combined after they leave the die. In the blow extrusion process the separate films are brought together below the 'freeze line' of both bubbles, i.e. while still molten (Fig. 17.14). Provision can be made in the die for the space between the films to be saturated with a reactive gas, such as ozone, which 'treats' the adhering surfaces and improves the bond strength. This method is particularly useful when combining unlike materials, e.g. nylon and polyehtylene.

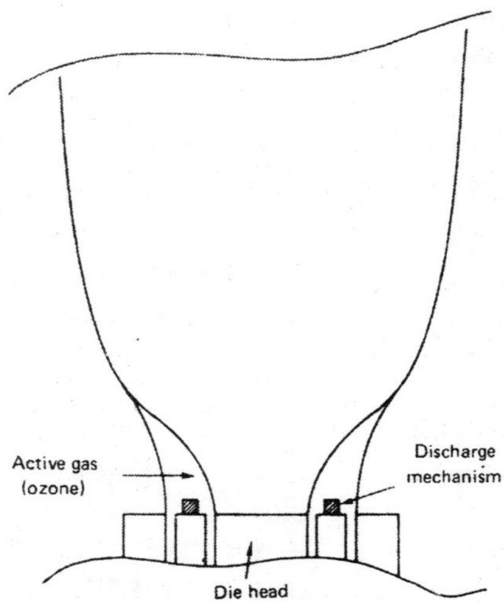

Fig. 17.14 Coaxial extrusion with provision for treating with active gas to improve adhesion.

The second method is the multimanifold die. The various polymers are again fed to separate manifolds in the die but here they are combined in the final land prior to leaving the die. Figure 17.15 shows typical setups for two and three film processes.

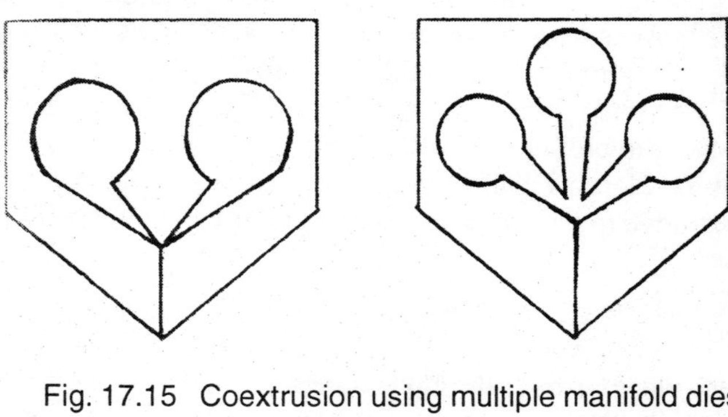

Fig. 17.15 Coextrusion using multiple manifold dies

The third method is the combining adaptor and this is probably the most common method for the coextrusion of flat films. The separate melts are brought together in a common manifold (Fig. 17.16). The flow passages are so designed as to minimise turbulence and avoid mixing of the separate streams. In general, the viscocities of the various polymers should be closely matched when using a combining adaptor. It is also desirable that the viscocities match at about the same temperature to eliminate problems associated with maintaining different melt temperatures in the die.

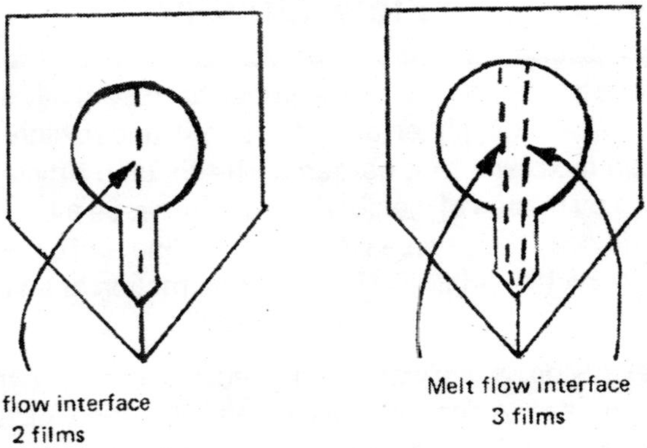

Fig. 17.16 Coextrusion by Laminar Flow Process using single manifold dies

The combining adaptor allows great flexibility in operation. It can be extrude two or more layers relativeiy easily and it can extrude a polymer in a much thinner layer than would be possible if it were extruded as a single film. However, it is not possible to maintain a large temperature difference between layers (which is possible in the multislit process). There are also many combinations of materials that do not flow together and produce a uniform product.

Whichever method is used, coextrusion is an important addition to the various techniques used for producing composite films. One important difference is the fact that coextrusion makes it possible to produce a multilayer tubular film, with consequent savings in bag making. It is also possible to produce laminates with very thin component plies. This enables expansive polymers with specialised properties to the utilised economically.

Disadvantages of coextrusion include the difficulty of utilising the scrap produced during extrusion and the fact that laminates with sandwith printing cannot be produced.

18

Injection Molding and Blow Molding

The injection molding process consists essentially in softening the material in a heated cylinder and injecting it under high pressure into a relatively cold mold where it hardens. The molded article is then ejected from the mold by means of ejector pins, compressed air, a stripper plate, or some other device. The process is a versatile one and can be applied to the production of articles ranging in weight from fraction of an ounce to several pounds.

Unlike extrusion, which was considered in Chapter 17, injection molding is a cyclical process. A complete cycle consists of the following operations which can be followed by reference to Fig. 18.1.

1. The mold is closed and a lacking force is applied.
2. The plunger moves forward, carrying a fresh charge of material into the heating zone of the cylinder and displacing previously heated material through the nozzle, which is in intimate contact with the mold. This heated material flows through the sprue opening in the die into runners which terminate in 'gates' leading to the mold cavity itself.
3. Pressure is maintained on the plunger for the period during which the material in the mold cools and contracts.
4. The plunger is retracted.
5. The mold is opened and the molding is removed.

It should be noted that the feed mechanism is actuated by the plunger stroke, and a fresh charge of material is deposited during the plunger return stroke, ready for the next cycle. The function of the torpedo in the heating cylinder is to force the polymer melt into closer contact with the heated cylinder walls. The fins which keep the torpedoes centered also serve to conduct heat from the hot cylinder walls to the torpedo, although it some machines the torpedo is heated separately.

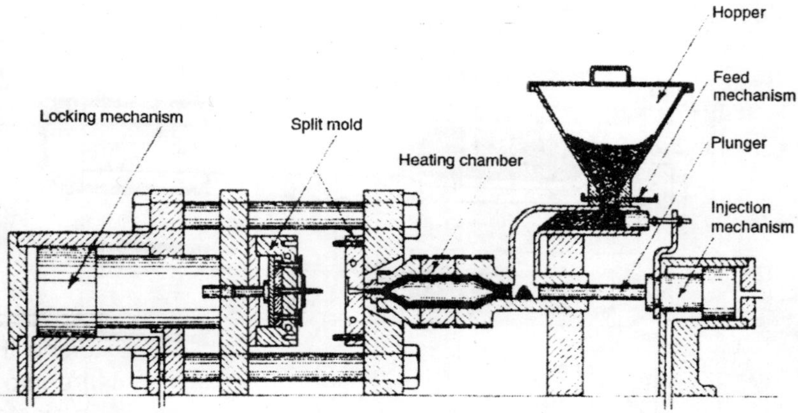

Fig. 18.1 Diagrammatic representation of an injection molding machine.

Machine Characteristics

Injection molding machines are characterised by their shot capacity plasticizing capacity, rate of injection, injection pressure, and clamp pressure (or mold locking force).

Short capacity may be given in terms of the maximum weight which can be injected per shot, in which case it is usually quoted in terms of ounces of polystyrene or cellulose acetate. This has the disadvantage that since the figure is dependent on swept volume of the cylinder during one stroke of the plunger and on the volumetric capacity of the feed mechanism, it is necessary to correct for bulk density and specific gravity when dealing with other materials. A better way of expressing shot capacity is in terms of the volume of material which can be injected by the plunger to a mold at a specific pressure.

One of the factors affecting the output of an injection molding machine is the plasticising capacity, which is usually defined as the number of pounds per hours of a particular material which can be brought to the temperature required for molding. In addition to the provision of a torpedo (or spreader) many of the larger machines are fitted with preplasticising units to increase the plasticising capacity. Preplasticisation may be achieved by screw extrusion of by plunger injection into a preheating chamber. In the latter case, the preplasticised material is usually transferred to a second cylinder, when it is injected in the normal manner, although in-line systems also

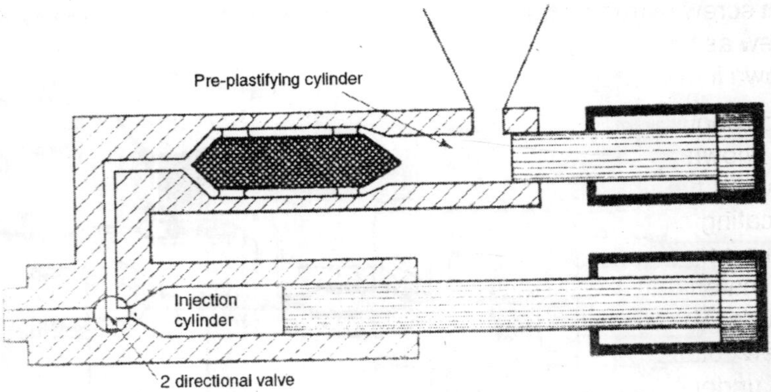

Fig. 18.2 Plunger preplastifier ('piggy-back' type)

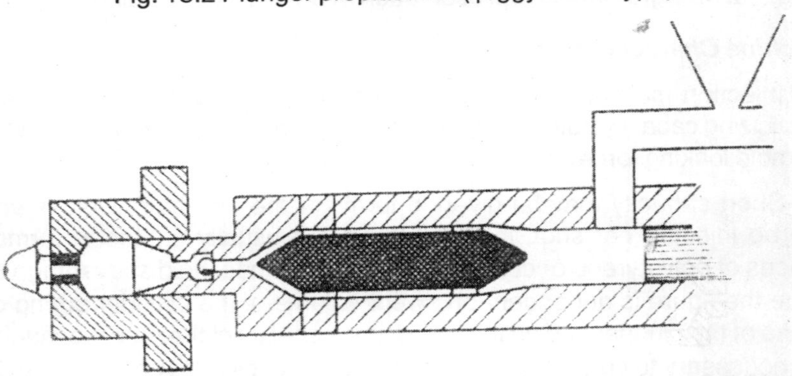

Fig. 18.3 Plunger preplastifier (in-line type). The whole plastifying cylinder moves back as the injection chamber is filled. During the injection stroke the whole plastifying cylinder then moves forward, pressure being exerted by the ball valve on the molten polymer in front of if.

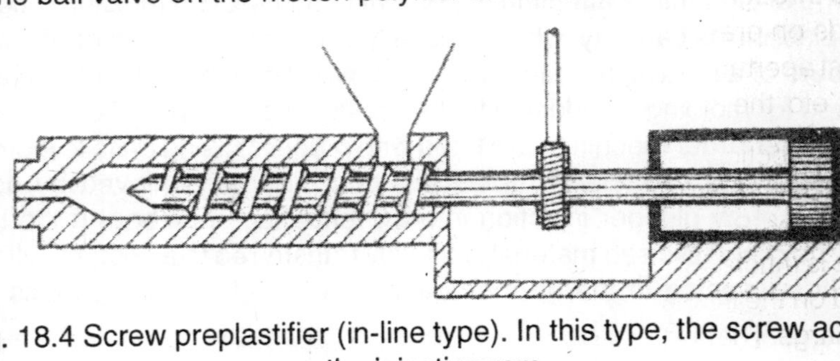

Fig. 18.4 Screw preplastifier (in-line type). In this type, the screw acts as the injection ram

exist. In screw extrusion there is a further possibility, namely, that of using the screw as the injection ram. Examples of these preplasticizing methods are shown in Figs. 18.2, 18.3, 18.4 and 18.5.

Type shown in Fig. 18.4 where the screw also acts as the injection ram is also known as the reciprocating screw machine and is now the most widely used type of unit, with the exception of very small machines. In a reciprocating screw unit the molten plastic passes from the screw fights through a screw tip nonreturn valve as the screw rotates. The build-up of molten material in front of the screw causes the screw to move axially backwards. The size of shot can easily by controlled, therefore, by stopping the screw rotation at a predetermined position. The screw is then moved forward under pressure, thus forcing the melt into the mold. Advantages of the reciprocating screw system include reduced residence time in the cylinder prior to injection and less chance to material hang-up in the cylinder.

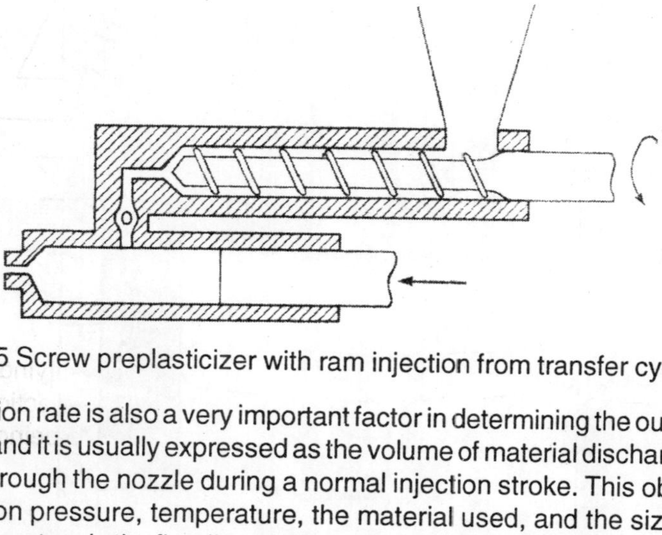

Fig. 18.5 Screw preplasticizer with ram injection from transfer cylinder.

Injection rate is also a very important factor in determining the output of a machine and it is usually expressed as the volume of material discharged per second through the nozzle during a normal injection stroke. This obviously depends on pressure, temperature, the material used, and the size of the smallest aperture in the flow line. With low viscosity materials and fairly large 'gates', etc. the injection plunger speed may be a limiting factor.

The injection pressure of an injection molding machine is the pressure exerted by the face of the plunger and can vary from about 2000 lb/in^2 to 25,000 lb/in^2. Pressure loses in the system mean that pressure in the mold cavities is much less than the plunger pressure. Neverthless the actual force exerted on the inside surface of the mold is large if the projected area of the mold is large. The clamp pressure is, therfore, an important factor in determining the maximum projected area that can be molded on particular machine. On large machines, the molds are normally closed by means of large, direct-acting hydraulic rams while on the smaller models a 'toggle' action is usually preferred (Fig. 18.6). Direct acting rams are more easily adjustable for different-sized molds but are slower and need greater pumping capacity. The 'toggle' system has the disadvantage of introducing multiple joints.

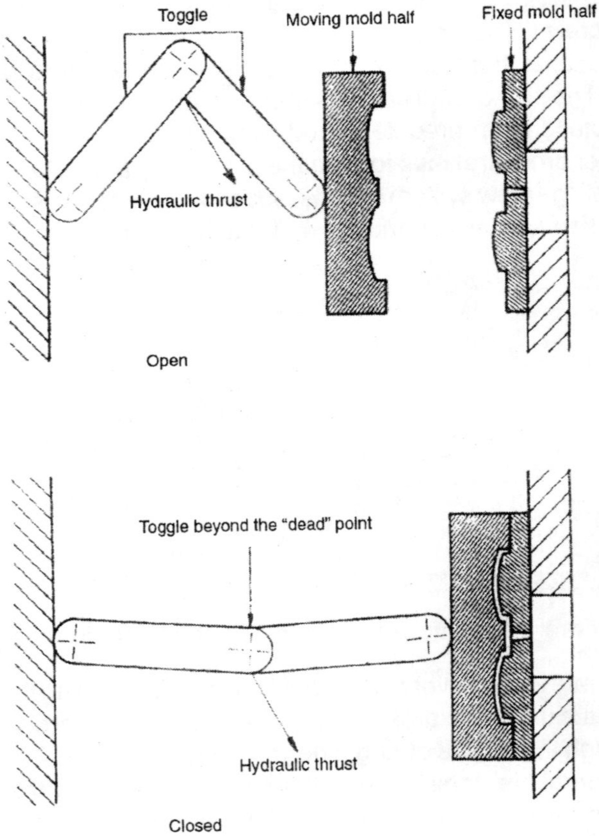

Fig. 18.6 Toggle action mold closing.

Machine Types

Enough has been said to indicate that the range of injection molding machines is an extremely wide one. Apart from the different sizes, ranging from those with the shot capacity of a fraction of an ounce to the giants capable of delivering several pounds in one operation, there are machines with or without preplasticization, automatic and semiautomatic types, and fixed or rotary machines. In addition, as we have seen, preplasticizer machines can be further subdivided into plunger or screw plasticizers, still further subdivisions being 'in-line' or 'piggy-back' designs.

Development of the larger type of injection molding machine has not been due solely to the demand for larger single moldings. Since, for example, a four ounce machine is slightly lower in cost than two, two-ounce machines, there is a tendency to use larger machines with multicavity molds. However, flexibility of operation is a point in favour is where several different colored moldings are called for, and here again it is obviously better to run several smaller machines rather than one large machine using multicavity molds.

A different approach to the problem of speeding molding cycle times is the development of the rotary mold machine. In essence, such machines consist of a single, high-plasticizing capacity injection unit which feeds a number of molds mounted on a rotating table. Much controversy exists as to the economics of such machines and there is no doubts that any problems still exists. One of the disadvantages lies in the high cost of molds required for a rotating system, and these can be justified only where large numbers of moldings are required. The saving in time has also been questioned in the case of large machines with heavy mold assemblies, a valid argument being that the speed of opening and closing a single mold in a reciprocating system is probably comparable with that of indexing, from one position to another, a mold assembly of high moment of inertia.

Although not strictly a different machine, it may be worth marking at this point the existence of special nozzle for the injection molding of very fluid polymers such as nylon. These are designed to prevent the polymer flowing out the nozzle between cycle. Mechanical nozzles, which only open when an appreciable pressure is exerted on them, have been used, but a more elegant method is the nozzle designed to freeze when in contact with the mold. The slug of nylon, so formed, is thawed by a specially controlled heater just in time for the next injection stroke.

Machine Variable

For any particular material, successful molding is determined by mold design and the correct setting of the following injection molding machine variables.

Injection Pressure. Injection can vary quite widely and are dependent on mold design and on the size of machine. In general, the aim is use of minimum pressure to produce full shot moldings, free from such defects as surface sink marks or voids. Excess pressure should be avoided as this could lead to 'flashing' i.e. escape of material from the mold joints.

Cylinder Temperature. The object of heating the molding material is to bring it to a suitably plasticized condition by the time it is ready for injection to the mold cavity. The temperature of the material depends not only on the temperature of the cylinder but also on the rate at which the material passes through it. Uniform heating of the material is, therefore, dependent on accurate temperature control of the heating cylinder and on strict control of the time cycle. Heating is usually carried out by band heaters on the outside walls of the heated cylinder, and these band heaters are arranged in two or three zones, each of which is controlled separately, Thin-wall moldings require higher cylinder temperatures than those with thick sections. This is because the thin-wall moldings require less time to 'freeze' in the mold, thus reducing the overall time cycle and, consequently, the residence time of the molding material in the heating cylinder.

Cycle Time. From the standpoint of economics, the aim should be the minimum time for each part of the molding cycle consistent with good quality molding. The question of the injection stroke has already been discussed when it was pointed out that the speed was mainly governed by the viscocity of the material (and hence material temperature), the ram pressure and the minimum aperture size in the flow line. The minimum ram forward time is governed by the fact that if pressure is removed too early from the molding, then surface 'sinking' or internal 'voiding' can occur and it is, therefore, essential that the gate should freeze-off completely before the ram is retracted.

Mold Temperature. Constant mold temperature, below the softening point of the material, is the aim, and this is normally carried out by circulation of a constant temperature fluid through channels in the mold.

Mold Design

Good mold design is a prerequisite for the production of good quality moldings and no amount of juggling with machine controls can compensate for a badly designed mold. The subject of mold design is highly complex but some of the more general points are briefly considered in the next few paragraphs.

Number of Mold Cavities. There can be no clear cut answer to the question of the optimum number of mold cavities, since it depends on the complexity of the molding, the size and type of machine availabe, the cycle times likely from each possible number of cavities, and the number of molding required. With the remarkable decrease in cycle times possible with the latest fast-cycling machines, coupled with the development of superflow molding materials, there is a marked tendency towards the use of single-cavity molds. This is especially so with thin wall moldings because of the difficulty of accurately centering multicavity cores when dealing with clearances of the order of 0.015-0.020 inches. The question of the number of moldings required is also important when considering the number of cavities. If a fairly accurate estimate of the various mold costs and cycle times can be made and a cost of running the machine (without material) is assumed, a break-even quantity can be calculated which can be compared with the total production required. An example will slow the general idea, although it is emphasized that the problem is rather more complicated than is shown here. If we assume that the mold costs for one, two, and three cavities are $3,500, $5,500 and $7,500 respectively and cycles times are 10, 15 and 22½ seconds, then the number of moldings per hour is 360 (single cavity), 480 (2-cavity) and 480 (3-cavity) and there is thus no economic advantage to be gained from using a three cavity mold. It will be noted that cycle times are not increased pro rata with the number of cavities. This is because in a single-cavity mold the limiting factor is the cooling time of the molding, whereas with higher numbers the plasticizing capacity of the machine tends to be the controlling factor.

From the number of moldings per hour, we can calculate the piece price of the moldings, if the cost of running machine is known. This again is a complicated factor but we will assume here a cost of $3.60 per hour. The piece price for a single-cavity mold is therefore, one cent, while that for the two-cavity mold is 0.75 cents, a saving of 0.25 cents. The extra mold cost of $2000 has therefore, to be justified on the numbers to be molded, mulitiplied by a piece cost saving of 0.25 cents, i.e.

$$\text{number of moldings} \times 0.25 = 2000 \times 100$$

$$\text{number} = \frac{2000 \times 100}{0.25} = 800{,}000$$

This represents a minimum number since other factors tends to add to the extra cost of multicavity moldings.

Mold Heating or Cooling

The control of mold temperature is usually achieved by circulating a constant temperature fluid through strategically placed channels. Initial mold design should make provision for these channels, bearing in mind such factors as symmetry of cooling and the effect of the temperature gradient across the mold on the flow of material. Cooling should be more intensive at the mold gate, as the plastic which reaches the furthest extremities has more time to become cooled. This evens up the cooling times and lessens the possibilities of warpage.

Mold Venting. If no provision is made in the mold for venting, then the air in the world is trapped in some corner and is then highly compressed. If the compression is rapid enough, the resultant rise in temperature may be sufficient to cause scroching at this particular point of the molding. With fairly simple shapes it may be possible to arrange the mold so that the point of venting is along the mold parting line. If this is not possible, then trial shots are made and the plastic flow observed. Vents can then be placed in the mold where they will provide for the most efficient release of air. A suitable venting can be achieved by a slot about ¼ inch wide and two thousands of an inch deep. This allows the escape of air, but not the plastic material because of its great viscocity.

Removal of Molding. This is essentially a problem of design of the molded piece, together with provision of means of ejection in the mold. It is advisable, for instance, to avoid undercuts which may prevent separation of the molding from the cavity, while for deep moldings it is necessary to provide a slight taper on the walls.

Ejection is carried out by ejector pins, stripper plates, or compressed air. If ejector pins are used, care must be taken that their cross-sectional area is large enough not to push through the molding, and they should be a perfect filt so that so flash is formed. Stripper plates are preferred for flexible moldings such as those from polyethylene.

Shrinkage. When designing a mold, allowance has to be made for the shrinkage of the plastic. This varies with the material, being between 0.002 and 0.008 inch/inch for polystyrene and between 0.015 and 0.025 inches for Nylon 66, and polypropylene. A particular problem arises in the case of polyethylene since the shrinkage rate is different in the direction of flow and across the flow of the material. This can lead to warpage, and if a large, flat area has to be molded it is best to have several gates in order to equialise the flow.

Gating of the Mold. Gating of the mold has a very big effect on the type of molding obtained, one example being briefly mentioned above. In general, the aim is to produce the best possible flow conditions consistent with ease of finishing, while interfering as little as possible with the final appearance of the molding. The type of gate will depend on the type of molding and on the material being molded. The size of gate can also be varied. Small gets are used for preference in order to leave as small a blemish as possible and to provide a smooth flow, but in general, the thicker the section of the molding, the larger is the size of the gate.

The positioning of gates is important, and it is usually advisable for ease of cavity filling and evenness of flow to feed into the thickest section of the cavity and in such a way that the material impinges on the core or cavity wall. Some typical gates are illustrated in Fig. 18.7.

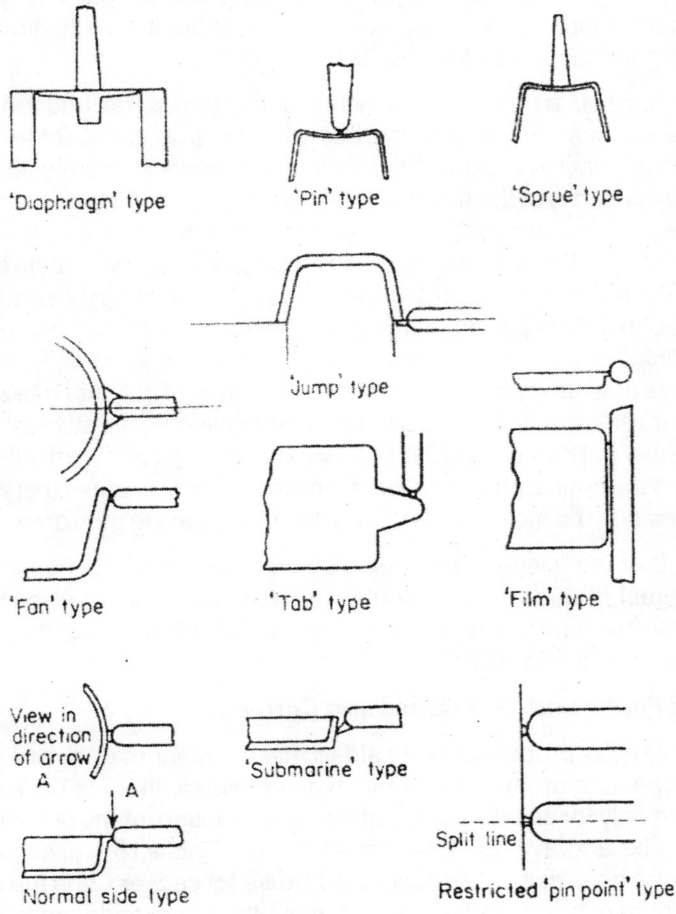

Fig. 18.7 Gating systems

The sprue gate is normally used where the cavity is difficult to fill or when feeding the runners of multiple cavities. Disadvantages of this gate are the expense of trimming, the length of time taken to 'freeze,' and the liability of surface sink marks to form opposite the sprue. On the other hand, there is a low pressure loss across the gate it is possible to utilise 'after pressure'.

The pin gate is preferable when cavities are easy to fill or when easy molding materials are used. Disadvantages of this sort of gate are, as one might expect, a high pressure loss and an inability to utilise 'after pressure'. It possesses several advantages, however, including ease of trimming, freedom from sink marks opposite the gate, a short 'freeze' time, and a tendency to homogenise the melt by frictional heat.

Hot runners. In normal multicavity molding the sprues and runners are cooled and removed at each cycle, being later reground and remolded. The amount of material needed to fill the sprue and runners at each cycle is all part of the shot capacity of the machine and, hence, reduces the possible size of the molding. For short cycle molding or for articles of thin section, the hot-runner technique has become popular. Strictly speaking, hot runners are those in which the runners are heated in the mold while insulating the runners from the cooled mold. This is expensive and is technically difficult. More usual is the technique of insulated runners, widely used with polyolefins. The provides for runners of large diameter so that the outer layer of polymer freezes while the center remains fluid, the frozen polymer acting as an efficient insulant between the 'hot runner' and the cooled mold. In both cases, the effect is the same, and the temperature gradient along the runners ensures that when the mold is opened the moldings part from the runners at the gate area.

A further technique is the 'hog slug' system where the heated nozzle makes direct (though limited) contact with the mold. A hot slug is formed and is insulated from the mold by a frozen layer of polymer, as in the insulated runner techinque (Fig. 18.8).

Molding Faults and their Cause and Correction

Enough has probably been said to make it clear that, because of the interdependence of the various machine variables, there is unlikely to be one cause only for any defect in a molding. In addition, many of the possible faults can be aggravated by bad mold design. Table 18.1 gives the most common molding faults, their suggested cause (or causes), and the possible ways of remedying them but, as with most things, experience is the best teacher of all.

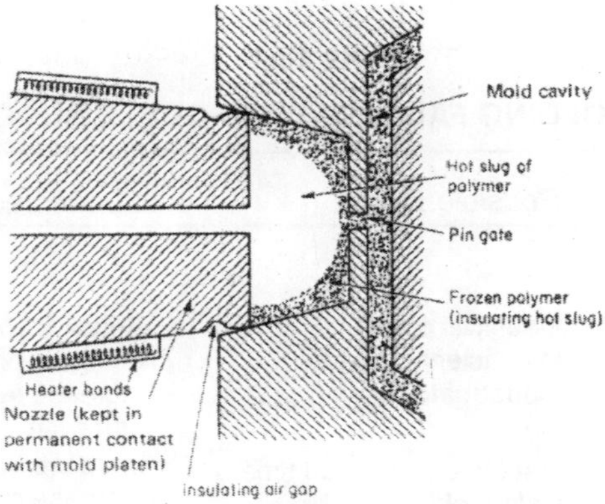

Fig. 18.8 Hot slug injection molding

Safety

The pressure and temperature involved in injection molding make safety an important factor in machine design. Front and rear gates interlock mechanically, electrically, and hydraulically to prevent clamp movement should the gates be left open, or be opened during the operating cycle. In most machines a low pressure saftey condition operates during clamp closing. During this part of the cycle, if any obstruction is encountered the slight increase in force above that needed to close the mold signals the clamp to stop,.

Injection Molding of Thermosets

Although thermosets are usually processed by compression or transfer molding they can also be injection molded provided great care is taken to ensure proper heating of the molding powder without premature setting up the passage of the mold or even in the cylinder. A screw-injection molding machine is used. Accurate control of heat input is essential. Too much heat causes premature curing of the material with consequent short shots or curing in the cylinder while too little heat makes it difficult to fill the mold (through high viscosity) and this leads to unecomonically long cycle times.

In one process, known as 'jet molding', the nozzle is heated only while the material is actually flowing. When flow ceases the nozzle is rapidly cooled so that any material remaining in the nozzle does not harden.

Structural Foam Molding

In structural foam molding the injection molding process is modified to produce an article with a foamed interior, integral with substantially unfoamed inner and outer skins.

Table 18.1

INJECTION MOLDING FAULTS AND TROUBLE SHOOTING GUIDE

Defect	*Possible Cause*	*Suggested Remedy*
Short molding	Insufficient feed	Adjust feed setting
	Insufficient pressure	Increase pressure
	Inadequate heating	Increase temperature or lengthen cycle
	Insufficient injection time	Increase injection time
	Cold mold	Increase mold temperature
	Back pressure due to entrapped air	Improve venting of mold
	Unbalanced cavity in a multicavity mold	Check sizes of cavities
Flashing at mold parting lines	Insufficient locking force	Increase locking force
	Injection pressure too high	Reduce injection pressure
	Material too hot	Reduce cylinder temperature
	Mold faces out of line	Re-bed mold faces
	Mold faces contaminated	Clean mold faces
	Flow restricted to one or more cavities (in multicavity mold)	Check and remove restriction
Surface sink marks	Material too hot when gate freezes	Reduce cylinder temperature or enlarge gate
	Insufficient dwell plunger forward time	Increase dwell time
	Insufficient material shot into cavity	Increase feed. Increase cylinder temp. Increase mold temp.
	Insufficient pressure	Increase pressure
	Piece ejected too hot	Increase cooling time in the mold
Voids	Material too hot (Gas formation)	Reduce cylinder temp.
	Condensation of moisture on polymer granules	Predry granules
	Condensation of moisture on the mold surface	Increase mold temp.
	Internal shrinkage after case-hardening of outer layer	Increase pressure Increase mold temp. Enlarge size of gates Lengthen dwell time

Table 18.1 *(Cont'd)*

Defect	*Possible Cause*	*Suggested Remedy*
Weld Lines	Material too cold	Increase cylinder temp.
	Mold too cold	Increase mold temp.
	Injection pressure too low	Increase injection pressure
	Gates wrongly located (including too big a distance from gate to weld joint) or designted	Relocate gates and/or redesign
Distortion of moldings	Ejection of molding at too high a temperature	Increase mold cooling time
	Ejection pin working unevenly	Correct or adjust ejection pins
	Existance of molded-in stresses due to :	
	(1) Material too cold	Increase cylinder temp.
	(2) Bad design	Redesign molding
	(3) Cavity overpacked in vicinity of gates	Check feed setting. Reduce injection pressure and cylinder temperature. Reduce injection time
Crazing and blistering	Excessive surface strain because of cold mold	Increase mold temperature
Surface streaks	Overheating of material	Reduce cylinder temperature
	Moisture in granules	Predry granules
Burn marks	Air trapped in mold cavities	Improve mold venting
Brittleness	Material too cold	Increase cylinder temp.
	Material has degraded	Decrease cylinder temp.
	Contamination with other material	Check the material for contamination

An inert gas is dispersed throughout the polymer melt, either by introducing the gas directly into the melt or by premixing the polymer with a chemical blowing agent. When the blowing agent is heated during processing it decomposes and releases an inert gas. The pressure within the injection molding machine barrel is sufficiently high to prevent foaming at that stage. A measured quantity of the polymer/gas mixture is then discharged under pressure into the mold cavity whereupon expansion takes place and the material fills the mold. The foam tends to collapse at the comparatively cold walls of the mold and a tough skin is formed. Because the mold is filled by expansion of the polymer melt, external pressures can be low so that mold costs are lower and platen areas and molds can be large.

The advantages of structural foams include the following :

(1) High stiffness to weight ratio, due to the foam-sandwich structure.

(2) Lower mold costs which means that smaller runs become economical.

(3) Molded parts exhibit lower warping and are essentially stress-free because filling of the mold is achieved by foaming of the polymer melt and not by high pressure injection.

(4) Sink-marks or depressions are greatly reduced thus allowing the molding of ribs, bosses, and intersecting walls. This, together with the possibility of large platen areas allows the injection molding of large parts.

One limitation is the fact that the minimum wall thickness attainable is fairly high (around 5 mm). This is because below about 5 mm the wall consists mainly of the two solid skins with a ngligible foam content.

The structural foam technique has been applied to high-density polyethylene, polypropylene, polystyrne, and especially to the high performance thermoplastics such as polycarbonate, polyphenylene oxide, and thermoplastic polyesters.

Applications for structural foams include business machine housings

BLOW MOLDING

The blow molding process is a versatile one, which is not confined to the production of bottles and other containers. Toys, automobile parts and accessories, and engineering components have all been manufactured by blow molding techniques, and many design problems have been solved by their use.

The principles employed in blow molding are essentially the same as those used in the production of glass bottles. Air under pressure is forced into a sealed molten body, surrounded by a cold mold. The air causes the molten material to expand and take up the shape of the mold, being cooled at the same time, by contact with the cold surface of the mold. The mold is then opened and the bottle ejected.

Most of the blowing processes in commercial use today fall into one or other of the two main classes described below :

1. Injection Blowing

This process resembles, very nearly, that used for blowing glassware. The material from which is object is formed is molded round a blowing stick, in a conventional injection molding machine, as a thick-walled tube called a parison. The parison is transferred to a second, or blowing, mold in which the final shape is obtained by passing compressed air down the blowing stick into the injection molded shape, which is thus blown out to desired form. The sequence is shown in Fig. 18.9.

2. Blow Extrusion

The blow extrusion process, which accounts for by far the largest percentage of blow-molded objects produced today, consists basically of the extrusion of a predetermined length of a hollow plastic tube into a split die, which is then closed, sealing both ends of the tube. The trapped portion of the tube is inflated to fit the internal contours of the mold by compressed air, introduced via a blowing tube. The blowing tube may be concentric with the extrudate, or may be introduced at the side, either in the neck or in an extension above the neck. The molding is again cooled by contact with the cold mold, the mold is opened and the object ejected. The sequence can be followed by reference to Fig. 18.10.

Mention may be made here of a variation of the blow extrusion process which is particularly suitable for materials subjects to thermal degradation as, for instance, PVC. Tubing is produced by normal extrusion and stored until needed. The required length of tubing is then reheated and blown to shape as before, in a cold mold. Since the extruder is no longer coupled directly to the blow-molding machine, there is less chance of a stoppage occurring, with consequent risk of degradation of the polymer remaining in the extruder barrel. The risk of polymer degradation is also reduced since the tubing can be extruded on a straight-through die rather than the usual cross-head, which is necessary when used in conjunction with the usual type of blow-molding machine. There is, therefore, less chance of 'dead' pockets of material forming in the die and becoming thermally degraded.

Some advantages and disadvantages of the injection blowing and blow extrusion methods are shown in the Table 18.2.

Machine Developments

Injection Blowing. The sequence of operations shown in Fig. 18.9. depicts the early hand-operated type of process. Later development aimed at automatic production have included the provision of blow molds either side

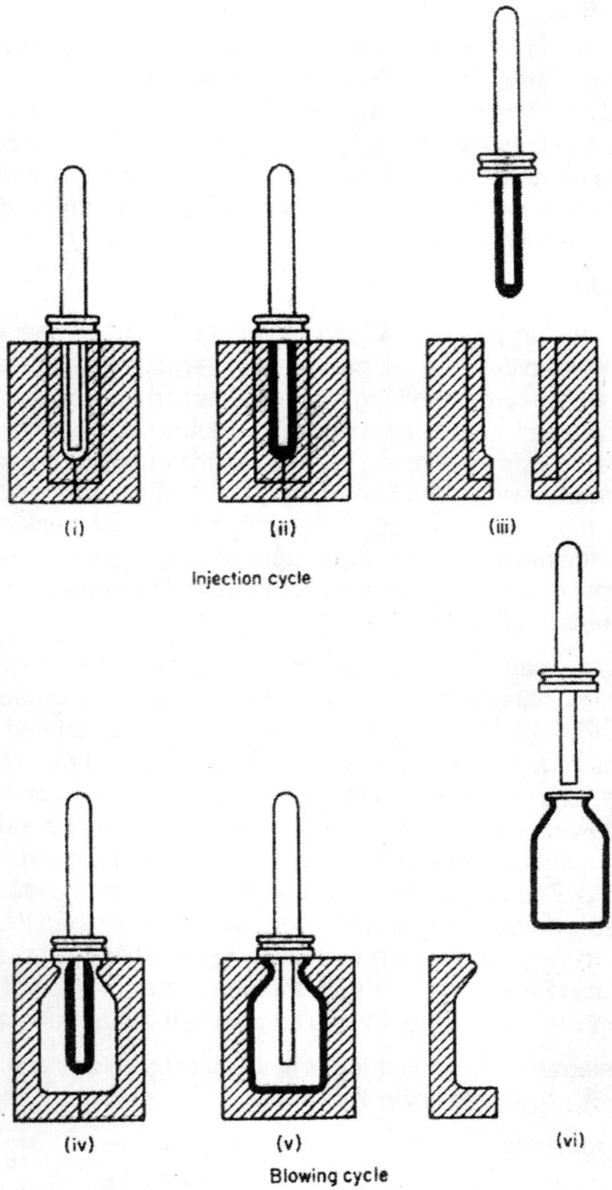

Fig. 18.9 Diagrammatic representation of injection blowing process

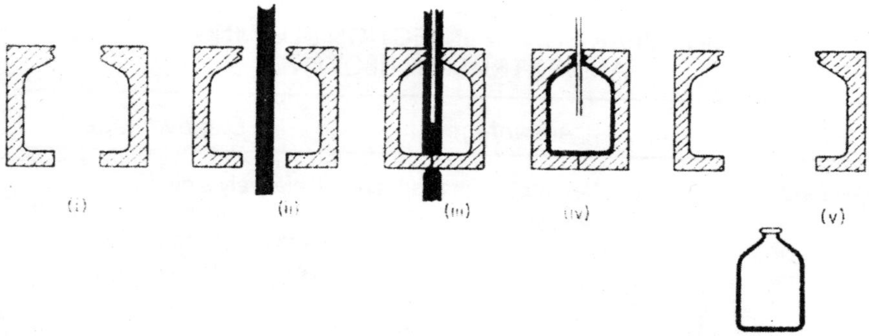

Fig. 18.10 Diagrammatic representation of extrusion blowing process.

of the injection mold, with automatic transference of the parison into each of the blowing molds alternately. A further development is the use of multiple mold cavities, which thus permits even greater increases in output speeds.

Extrusion Blowing. From the basic idea of extruding a single tube into a single mold, extrusion blowing has developed in many directions. One obvious developments is to use more than one mold, moving the filled mold away to cool while another is ready to receive the next section of extruded tube. This basic idea can be carried out in more than way, either with reciprocating molds or with a series of molds mounted on a rotary table. Either of these two methods can be further adapted by having multiple die heads attached to the extruder, and feeding these of multiple cavity dies.

The provision of large blow moldings has been made possible,in extrusion blowing, by the development of extruders feeding into an accumulator from which the large parison necessary can be expelled very quickly. If the parison necessary to produce say, a 50-gallon container, was extruded in the normal manner, it would sag and deform under its own weight long before extrusion was complete and it would be impossible to produce anything like an even wall thickness.

Another development in extrusion blowing is the conception of parison thickness control by means of a variable mandrel at the die head. It thus becomes possible to increase the thickness of the parison wall at those points where it is most needed in the final molding.

Machine Design

1. *The Extruder.* Since the time taken for the blow molding to cool is the major factor controlling cycle time, the mass temperature is usually kept as

Table 18.2

COMPARISON OF INJECTION BLOWING AND EXTRUSION BLOWING

	Advantage	Disadvantage
Injection Blowing	Strain-free moldings produced Good congrol of neck and wall thickness Easier to produce unsymmetrical moldings. No post-finishing necessary	Relatively slow More restricted in choide of moldings materials Two molds required
Blow Extrusion	Strain-free moldings produced	More difficult to control wall thickness (but modern technique *can* produce excellent results)
	High production rates obtainable More versatile with respect to materials handled	Necessary to have trimming operation

low as possible, subject to the production of bottles having good appearance and performance. Good homogeniety of the melt can, therefore, be attained only by the use of high back pressures and high shearing forces, which necessitates the employment of robust extruders with good thrust bearings.

Screws with high L/D ratios (around 20 : 1) are preferred with a short compression stage and a fairly long metering stage (5 to 6D for an L/D ratio of 20 : 1).

2. *Blow Heads.* A typical blowing head is shown in Fig. 18.11. In the early heads, the mandrel was supported by a perforated plate or a webbed 'spider' and the material flowed over the mandrel from above. This system gave rise to 'spider' memory effects (flow lines caused by imperfect fusion after flowing past the webbed supports or the perforated plate.) Later designs employed the system shown in Fig. 18.12 of a ring-type mandrel which is side fed. Even in this design there tends to be a weld line beyond the mandrel, opposite the point of entry, but this is largely eliminated by restrictions further down the head, causing appreciable back pressures, and the long land length.

Mention was made earlier of parison thickness control by means of a variable mandrel. Briefly, this consists of an inner mandrel with vertical freedom of movement. The mandrel tip forms a variable die gap, and by up

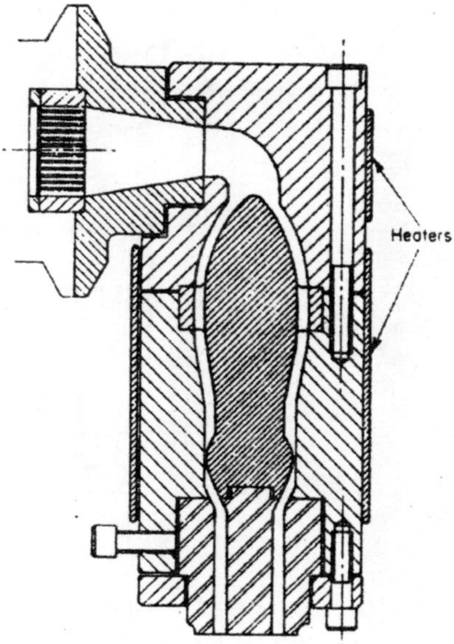

Fig. 18.11 Typical blowing head having a spider supported type mandrel

and down movements of the inner mandrel the vertical distribution of material in the blow molding can be controlled.

3. *Molds.* Materials in common use for blow molds include aluminium and aluminium alloys, steel, zinc allosys such as Kirksite, cast bronze, and beryllium-copper. For experimental purposes and short runs it is also possible to use metal filled epoxy resin castings and glass reinforced thermosetting resins. Steel is expensive and is usually economic only where long production runs are possible. Its use is also dictated, however, where the pinch-off area is large because of its excellent hardness and wear resistance. The heat transfer steel is lower than those of the other metals mentioned so that the design and location of cooling channels in steel molds is rather more critical.

Design of the pinch-off points of the mold particularly important because of possible weaknesses in the bottle at these points due to poor welding. If the pinch off is too thick another difficulty is encountered, namely, that of removal of excess material from base and necks due to too thick a connecting web. Where cast aluminium or zinc alloys molds are used, pinch offs are made of steel inserted in the casting.

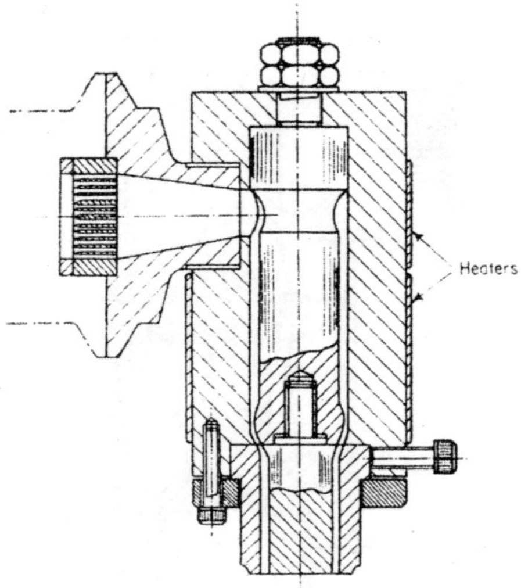

Fig. 18.12 Typical blowing head having an axially supported or ring-type mandrel.

In general, the pinch off section has a land length of between 0.020 and 0.100 inch. A typical pinch off-area off high density polyethylene is shown in Fig. 18.13. Vapor honing or fine sand blasting gives a matte finish to the mold, which is preferable to a polished surface as the latter can lead to air being trapped between the hot plastic material and the mold. Where a matte finish on the molded product is unacceptable, other methods of mold venting must be used. These may take the form of very fine holes or shallow slits. Vents are required where projections occur on the molding, since entrapped air cannot otherwise escape from the corresponding depressions in the mold cavity.

Operating Variable

Mass Temperature. When discussing extruder design, we mentioned that mass temperature were kept as low as possible in order to reduce cooling time. Too low a temperature prevents complete plasticisation which can be lead to residual strain in the molding as well as bad surface defects, such as 'melt fracture'. Too high a temperature on the other hand, increases the cycle time and can also give rise to thinning of the parison, especially where a long parison is required. The latter fault depends too, of course, on extrusion rates and on the melt viscocity of the polymer. The effect of parison thinning can be corrected to some extant by using the adjustable mandrel system described earlier. Mass temperature also affects the

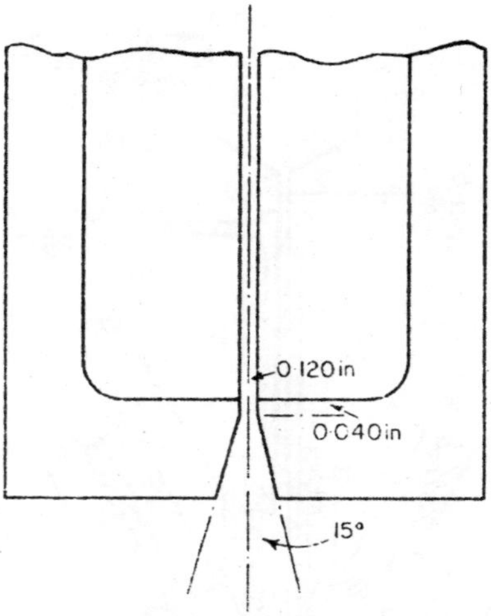

Fig. 18.13 Typical pinch-off for high-density polyethylene

phenomenon known as 'die swell' (also known as diameter swell). This is measured by the actual relaxed outside diameter of the parison after leaving the extruder die minus the die ring bore diamter, expressed as a percentage of the extruder die diameter. It is caused by the fact that when the molten polymer is extruded through an orifice under pressure alignment of the molecules occurs along the line of flow. When the extrudate emerges from the orifice, the pressure conditions are relaxed and the molecules tend to resume original random distribution with the consequent shrinkage in length and swelling in diameter. An increase in mass temperature generally reduces die swell. A reduced rate of extrusion also reduces the amount of swelling. Die swell is affected by material properties such as melt tensile strength and melt viscosity. Increasing melt viscosity tends to increase die swell while a lower melt tensile strength increases sag and draw-down and thus reduces die swell.

Air Pressure. Good reproduction of mold detail and good surface contact with the mold (to increase cooling rate) are both factors which require high blowing pressures, and in practice pressures up to about 80 lb/in^2 are used. Other factors of importance include preventing incoming air from jetting, which could lead to local cooling, and providing air free from moisture and oil from the compressor.

Mold Temperature. Mold temperature are always low because of the importance of rapid cooling of the molding.

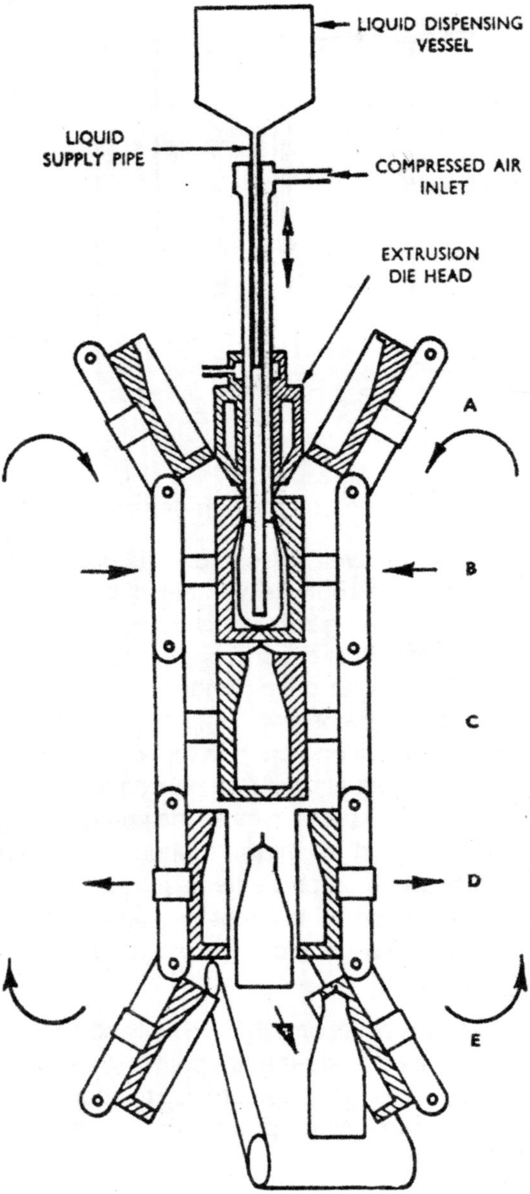

Fig. 18.14 Schematic drawing of the series 4000 Bottlepack Machine

Mold Closing Rate. Too high a rate of mold closing can cause of container of split on the inside of the neck or shoulder, and it is becoming usual to incorporate damping devices in the machine design.

Form/Fill/Seal Bottling

Machines are now available that will blow or bottle, fill it, and seal it while it is still in the mold. One advantage is that aseptic filling is possible (provided sterile air is used) and this is particularly valuable in the ease of pharmaceuticals and foods. It is also possible to make very thin wall (and hence cheaper) bottles because they do not have a separate existance while empty but are supported by the mold until filled and sealed. In normal bottle blowing the minimum bottle weight is often determined more by performance requirements in filling than by its performance in use. The principle of operation can be seen by reference to Fig. 18.14 which shows a high speed machine (3000 X ½ liter bottles X 2 liter bottles per hour). It consists of a series of rotary molds mounted vertically on an endless conveyor. The two halves of the mold enter the cycle at A and engage the parison. At B, the parison is blown into shape and the liquid product is injected. At C, the mold cut-off closes to seal the container, which is ejected at D when the mold opens onto a belt conveyor.

Ornamentation, including instruction for use, etc., is often carried out by embossing in the mold, or by subsequent labelling. Silk screen printing of the filled bottles is possible but the rejection rate is high and may also involve loss of product as well as the bottle.

Applications to date include the packaging of milk and transfusion liquids.

19

Thermoforming

In thermoforming, a heat softened plastic sheet is formed either into or around a mold. The simplest example of this technique is 'bubble-blowing' polymethymethacrylate sheet to form aircraft canopies,but there are now many variations both in basic technique and in their degree of automation. In general, thermoforming techniques are best suited for producing moldings of large area, for very thin-walled moldings or where only short runs (including the production of prototypes) are required.

METHODS OF FORMING

Thermoforming may be divided into three main types.

(a) *Vaccum Forming.* In its simplest form, the method consists of clamping the sheet in a frame attached to the mold box. The sheet is heated until rubbery and a vaccum the drawn between the sheet and the mold Atmospheric pressure above the sheet forces the sheet on to the mold where it is cooled sufficiently to retain its shape.

(b) *Pressure Forming.* This is the same as vaccum forming with the exception that a positive pressure is applied to the sheet from above, which again has the effect of forcing the softened sheet on to the mold. The pressure which can be applied to the sheet on to the mold. The pressure which can be applied to the sheet is not limited to atmospheric pressure which is, of course, the case with vaccum forming.

(c) *Matched Molds Forming.* As the name implies, the heated sheet is pressed into shape by trapping it between matched male and female molds.

POLYMERS USED IN THERMOFORMING

Polystyrene

Toughened polystyrene sheet is one of the most widely used materials for thermoforming being cheap and easy to manipulate. It is fairly rigid and gives good depths of draw. Outdoor weathering is poor, as is surface gloss. One of the largest outlets is for vending and other disposable drinking cups. The material is also used for forming a wide range of tubs, trays and box inserts. The cigarette pack is a good example of the material's versatility. The wall thickness is around 15 thousandths of an inch (375 microns) with a large depth of draw. Using a 24 impression mold, outputs of 20,000 packages an hours are claimed.

Toughened polystyrene is translucent and cannot be used where good clarity is required. Normally, general purpose (crystal) polystyrene gives too brittle a sheet but if it is biaxially oriented it produces a much superior sheet that can be transformed to give crystal clear packages. The strain per cent in the oriented sheet causes difficulties in thermoforming but it can be pressure formed using special equipment.

Expanded polystyrene sheet can also be thermoformed, matched molds being preferred for deep and complicated draws. The main problem is that the foam structure gives the sheet a very low heat conductivity and it is difficult, therefore, to heat the sheet right through without overheating the surface. Double-sided heating is usually necessary, therefore. Typical applications include trays for repackaging meat, fruit, and vegetables, and for the transport of delicate electronic components.

Cellulose Acetate

Cellulose acetate is readily thermoformed and has excellent clarity. It gives rigid moldings that are particularly good for blister packaging. It is more expansive than polystyrene but is used where high class formings are required. One disadvantage of cellulose acetate is its dimensional instability under conditions of changing humidity, due to moisture pick-up from the atmosphere. This makes it unsuitable for outdoor applications.

Temperature control during forming is critical because too high a termperature causes surface defects like blistering, while too low a temperature leads to 'molkiness' in the finished forming. Formings from cellulose acetate are easily fabricated either by adhesives or by solvent welding.

Cellulose Acetate/Butyrate

Cellulose acetate/butyrate (CAB) is more expensive than cellulose acetate take but has better water resistance which makes it suitable for advertising signs and other outdoor applications. Like cellulose acetate it possesses good rigidity and clarity and it easily fabricated by adhesives and by solvent welding.

PVC

PVC sheet has good clarity and is often used where good chemical resistance is required. Good forming, with good mold detail can be obtained even from very thin gauges of sheet. It is self extinguishing which makes it particularly useful in applications such as aircraft food trays. Other uses include blister packs and a wide range of food packaging applications, including margarine tubs and chocolate and biscuit box inserts.

Acrylonitrile/Butadiene/Styrene (ABS)

The thermoforming properties of this material are similar to those of toughened polystyrene (which is resembles chemically) but it is more expensive. It is also tougher so that the price differential can often be reduced by the use of thinner guages.

Polymethylmethacrylate

This material has excellent opitcal qualities and resistance to outdoor conditions but it is expensive. Sheet may be prepared by polymerisation casting or by extrusion (see Chapter 12) and it has found extensive use in the forming of advertising signs and in lighting applications.

Polyolefins

Low and high-density polyethylene and polypropylene are all available as extruded sheet but are difficult to form becaue of their combination of high specific heat (leading to low heating) and low thermal conductivity, with leads to trouble when heating thick sheets. Heating both sides of the sheet at once (sandwich heating) is recommended for the polyolefins in order to overcome these difficulties. Another snag is that because of their crystallinity, the temperatures at which the polyolefins become formable are not far below their softening points, and the sheets have tendency to sag. High molecular weight grades are recommended, therefore, and molds should be heated slightly to prevent the sheet setting as soon as it contact the mold.

Thermoforming is easier with high-density polyethylene than with the low-density material but fast heating and accurate control of temperature are still essential. The finished moldings have good rigidity and hardness.

Polypropylene has been greater stiffness and is not subject to environmental stress cracking (as are the polyethylene). It is also more resistant to high temperatures. The forming properties of polypropylene are similar to those of high-density polyethylene and, in general, the same methods can be used for both.

Polycarbonate

Polycarbonate can be thermoformed but higher forming temperatures are necessary because of its high softening point. It has very good clarity and a very high impact strength. It is particularly useful for the manufacture of blisters for hard, sharp articles such as hardware.

MACHINE VARIABLES

Heating

Radiant heat form infrared heaters is the useful from of heating employed. Many of the larger machines have heating panels consisting of a large number of separate elements wired up in 'chessboard' fashion, thus allowing differential heating, when required, in different parts of the sheet. The heaters are positioned fairly closely to the sheet, about 4-6 inches in order to give efficient utilisation of the heating capacity. Too close an approach has to be avoided, however, otherwise a heater pattern may be impressed on the sheet.

Greater speed and uniformity of heating is obtainable, if double sides heating is employed, especially with the polyolefins or expanded polystyrene, for the reasons discussed earlier.

Cooling

If cooling is unassisted a very long molding cycle results since all plastics are poor conductors of heat. The molding cycle is made as short as possible by removing the molded sheet from the mold as soon as it is dimensionally stable but the actual cooling time is also reduced, in many cases, by air blasts or water-mist sprays directed onto the sheet. Cooling is also affected by the choice of mold material (see below).

Molds

One of the big advantages of thermoforming is that molds are relatively inexpensive. In fact, for prototype work and other short runs, the molds can often be extremely cheap. Thermoforming molds have been made from wood, plaster, steel, aluminium, and filled epoxide resins, perhaps the most common of these being aluminium. It is easily worked be cored for temperature control.

One thing to be avoided in designing thermoforming molds is the existence of deep and sharply angular corners, as they cause severe thinning of the sheet.

Printing

Printing of the sheet can be carried out before forming, the design being distored in such a way as to give the required appearance after forming. One way of determining the distortion necessary is to form a sheet with a number of small squares marked out on it. A less satisfactory method is to paint a formed article and then shrink it flat again by reheating.

Trimming

Trimming may be carried by a variety of equipment ranging from a simple knife to a complicated cutting press. Roller presses, for example, are widely used in combination with a cutting board.

THERMOFORMING METHODS

Some of the many methods of thermoforming now available are mentioned below and are illustrated in Figs. 19.1 to 19.7.

Vacuum Forming

Either male or female molds may be used (Fig. 19.1 illustrates the process being a male mold). Vacuum forming into a female mold is probably the simplest of the mold but only simple designs are possible because of excessive thinning at bottom and corners of the cavity. With a male mold the thickest section is on top instead of at the side walls.

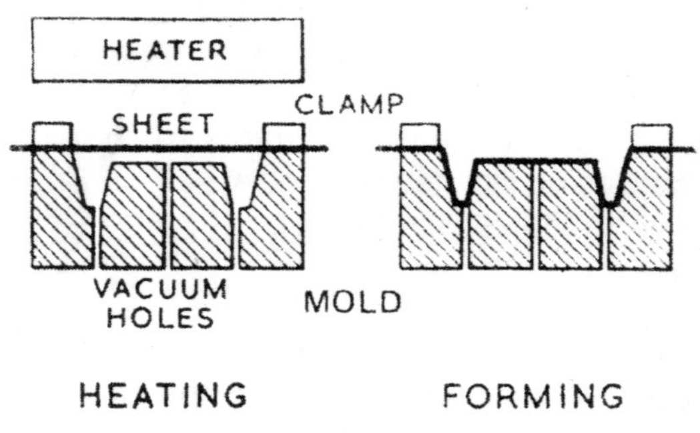

Fig. 19.1 Vacuum forming into male mold

Drap Forming. Drape forming with a male mold is illustrated in Fig. 19.2. The mold moves up into the sheet and the vacuum is then applied. High draw ratios are possible with drape forming but more complex equipment is necessary.

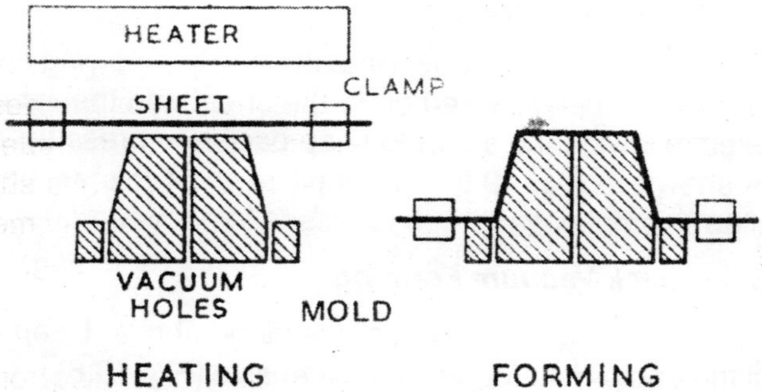

Fig. 19.2 Drape forming into male mold

Plug-assist Vacuum Forming

This method allows even deeper drawing, more even wall thickness and lower cooling cycles. Very close temperature control of the plug and the sheet material is required, however, and complex equipment is necessary (see fig. 19.3). A heated 'air slip' around the plug is often employed to avoid marking the sheet and to give a more even stretch.

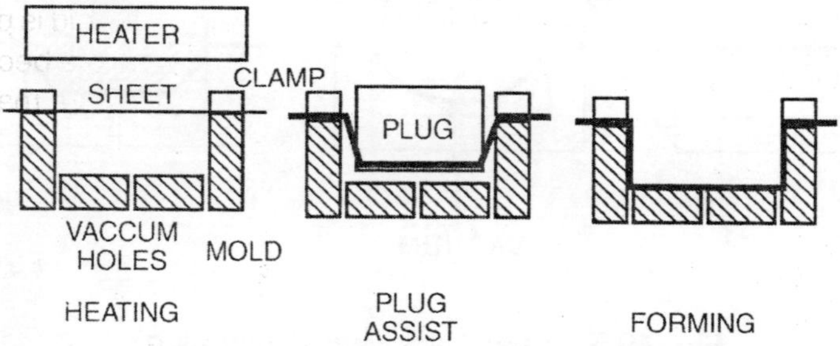

Fig. 19.3 Plug-assist vacuum forming

Plug and Ring Vacuum Forming

This method uses only simple equipment and is especially suitable for shallow drawing of tough sheets (see Fig. 19.4).

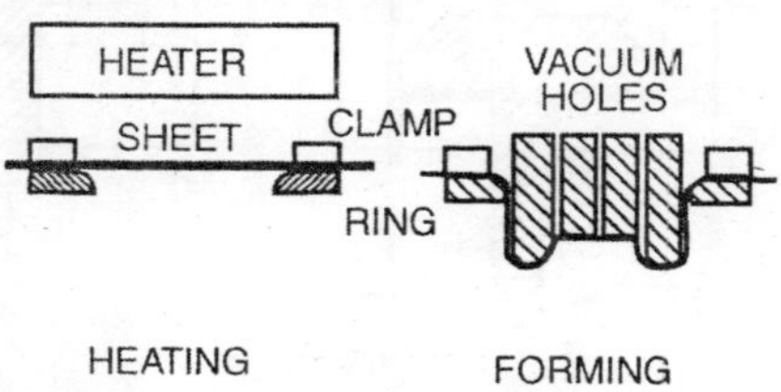

Fig. 19.4 Plug and ring vacuum forming

Snap-back Vacuum Forming

The heated sheet is drawn down into the box by applying a vacuum to the box. The mold is then lowered on to the sheet and the vacuum in the box is released, allowing the sheet to snap back and press tightly against the mold as shown in Fig. 19.5. The application of this second vacuum operation allows complex parts with recesses to be formed.

Pressure Snap-back Vacuum Forming

This is the reverse of the process described above. Deep drawing is possible but the equipment required is expensive (Fig. 19.6).

Blow-back Forming

This method is illustrated in Fig. 19.7. and is used for producing deep drawn parts from heavy, tough sheeting not normally formable by ordinary vacuum forming, since pressure greater than atmospheric can be used.

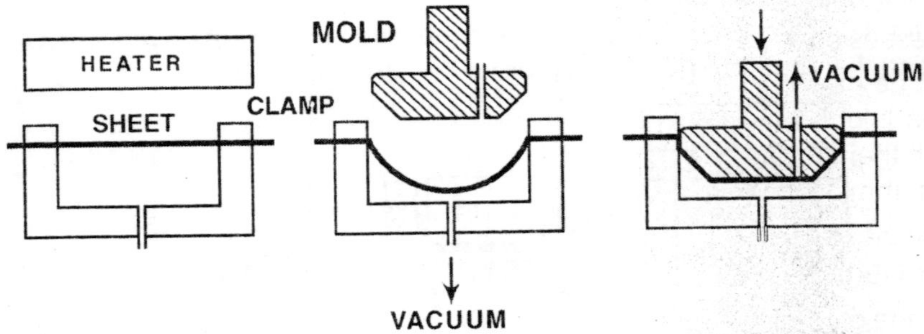

Fig. 19.5 Snap back vacuum forming

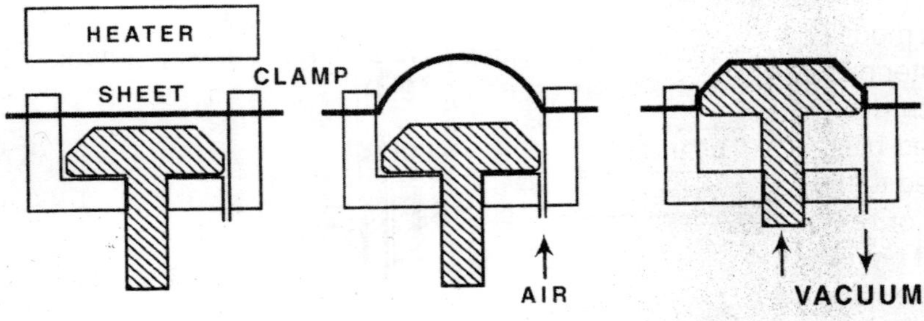

Fig. 19.6 Reverse Process of Fig. 19.5 for pressure snap back forming

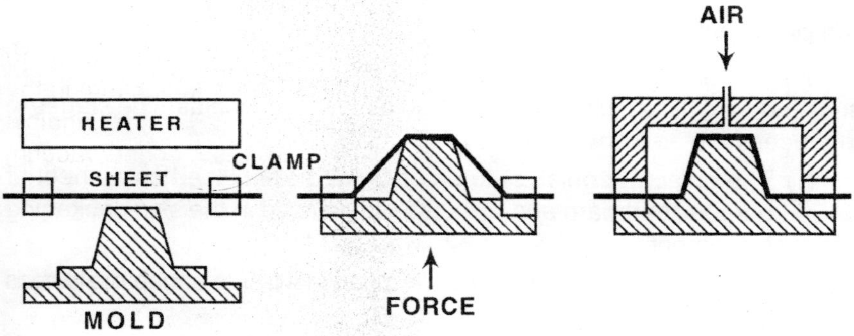

Fig. 19.7 Blow back molding

The above notes give some idea of the different techniques available but much work has also been carried out to increase the usefulness of thermoforming methods by speeding up the forming process and associated processes such as trimming and, in the case of packages, filling and sealing.

One method of speeding up operations is to use multistation machine of the linear or rotary type. The sheet is mounted on a clamping frame which then moves from a heating station, on to a molding station and then to a trimming station.

In the case of small to medium size moldings, operations can be speeded up still further by the use of multicavity molds.

One of the major recent developments has been the increasing size of articles manufactured by thermo-forming techniques. Examples in the U.S.A. include small car bodies and a caravan body, the latter being formed from sheet 87 inches wide by 192 inches long (2210 mm X 4877 mm).

Blister Packaging

A modification of normal thermoforming techniques that is widely used in blister packaging. In a blister pack the product to be packed is supported on a card or plastics backing and then completely covered by a transparent, flanged blister formed from PVC, cellulose acetate, etc. This is glued or stapled to the backing card. The blister may be a simple shape, such as a circle or rectangle, or it may be specially shaped to fit the contours of the object being packaged. An example of the latter is the blister packaging of sponge flan cases. Blister packaging suppliers an effective display pack that also gives protection against dust, grease, and mechanical damage. Fig. 19.8 shows the stages in producing a typical blister pack.

Skin packaging

This interesting variant of vacuum forming utilises thin film rather than sheet and the articles to be packaged act as their own molds. The stages in the process are as follows :

(1) The object (or objects) to be packaged are placed on a sheet of porous fiberboard and the assembly placed in the skin packaging equipment.

(2) Film is drawn from a reel and clamped in a frame above the loaded board.

(3) A cutter severs the film from the reel and a radiant heater moves over the film.

(4) The film is heated for a set period.

(5) The heater retracts and the hot film is drawn down over the board and contents.

(6) A vacuum is drawn through the porous board causing the film to be drawn round the articles to be packaged and into intimate contact with the board, forming a permanent bond.

(7) The assembly is moved away and the film is allowed to cool.

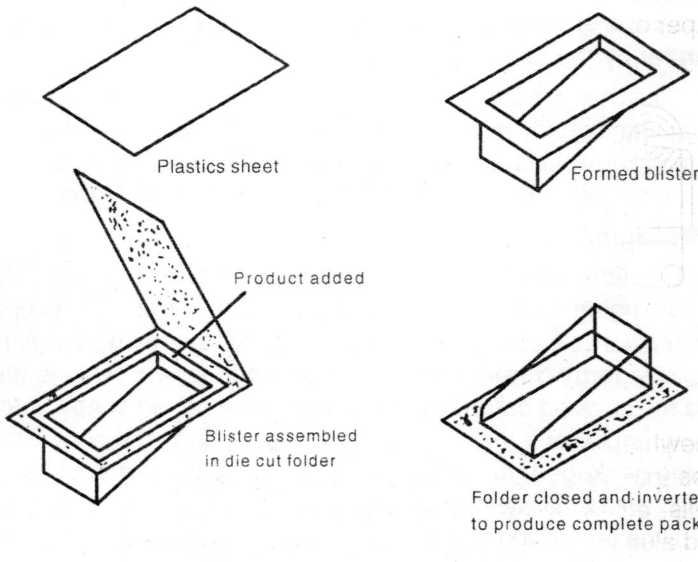

Fig. 19.8 Production stages of a typical blister pack

Films used for skin packaging should be flexible enough to provide a good contour wrap and have a high melt strength. The latter is essential if pinholing and puncturing at sharp corners is to be avoided. Low density polyethylene and ionomer films are among those that have proved suitable for skin packaging.

FORM / FILL / SEAL

The thermoforming process is well adapted to form/fill/seal operations. In one type of machine, for example, blisters are formed to a profile roughly similar to the article to be packaged. Articles are fed continously into the blisters and a reel of fiberboard is sealed over them. The individual packages are then trimmed and separated. This type of operation is used for the packaging of high sales volume items such as razor blades, reels of cotton, etc.

The other main area of thermoform/fill/seal is the packaging of a wide range of foodstuffs, including jam, crea, sauces, and cheese. This type of operation is shown schematically in Fig. 19.9. Two reel-fed plastics webs are used, the first being formed into a series of tray-like depressions by heating and drawing a vacuum through the base of appropriately shaped molds. The formed sheet is then indexed under a filling head and the filled compartments are lidded containers is then cut and the individual packs separated. The web used for lidding is often preprinted. A thermoplastics coated paper or aluminium foil may also be used for the lidding operation.

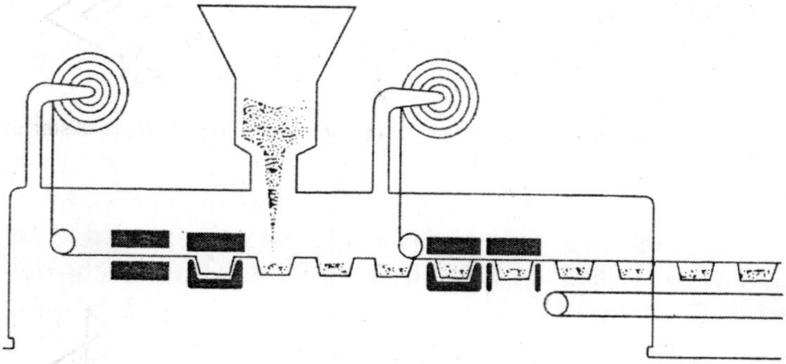

Fig. 19.9 Form/fill/seal thermoforming

A somewhat similar technique is used for the packaging of tablets, pills or capsules into 'push-through' blister packs. A multicavity mold is used and the pills, etc., are fed automatically into the thermoformed cavities. The coated aluminium foil lidding web is then brought down over the filled plastics web and heat sealed to it. When required, the individual pills, etc are dispensed by pushing them from the plastics side through the relatively brittle aluminium foil.

20

Powder Coating

Plastic coatings are applied to substrates for a variety of reasons including corrosion protection, electrical insulation, decoration and prevention of damage to delicate components. The two main original applications were dipping and spraying either from solution, dispersion, plastisol and now today we have the emergence of powder techniques. The powder coating process was developed to permit the application of plastic coatings without the necessity to dissolve the polymer in a liquid carrier. This process is akin to the technology of hot melt adhesives but instead of applying the coating is molten form, powder is used.

The conception of this technology can be traced back to the early 1940's when the precipitation of low-density polythene was developed. The main substrates which have utilised powder coating technology are metals and textiles. The development for metals was basically for ecological reasons but for textiles the development arose to fulfil a requirement which was otherwise not obtainable with more conventional materials.

The early developments of the low-density polythene powder by chemical precipitation provided a base material which could be used to produce coatings by preheating an article and immersing it in a bath of static powder. This coating method was very crude and little interest was aroused. It was not until some ten years later, in 1953, that the fluidized bed technique was developed in Germany (Knapsack Griesheim). The introduction of this technique was quickly followed by the development of the other thermoplastic powders such as nylon and PVC. In the 1950's the thermosetting type of powders were introduced in the U.S.A. and another stone was laid in the foundation of the development of powder coating technology. The basic chemical developed in this country was the epoxide-type resin compound. During the period and electrostatic coating technique was developed for those types of resinous compounds.

Clearly the early developments in this technology were based on thermoplastics which utilised the fluidized bed techniques and later the thermoplastics technology. Advances in grinding technology such as freeze and cryongenic processes for thermoplastics led to their wider uses. The superpolyamide, nylon 11, is a difficult material to grind and must be cryogenically ground using liquid nitrogen and temperatures below — 130°F. This also applies to nylon 12 and because of high basic polymer price and cost of grinding, the development of markets for this family of polymers has been somewhat restricted.

Coating of textiles with powders provides finished products which are termed by the garment industry in fusible interlinings. The history of such materials dates back to the early 1950's, when a company in the U.K. named Staflex Limited, then still small, developed a coated textile which could be heat fused into garments. These interlinings exert a dimensional control or can even be used to impart controlled stiffness/bulk to a garment part. The early product developed by this company was continuously coated, i.e., an all over coating. This gave a disadvantage to the resultant laminate in that it imparted in undesirable, a uncontrolled stiffness. The next development came in 1955 when the random scattering of predetermined size particles of low-density polythene powder were used by this company for coating fabrics. This produced a laminate which still had limitations in that the polymer used was not completely resistant to the solvents used in the dry cleaning operation. Such a limitation resulted in the interlining only being suitable for use in small area applications. The next breakthrough came in 1964 when once more, through the innovation of staflex, a product was introduced with equidistant dots based on plasticized vinyl chloride/acetate copolymer. Copolyamides as described in Chapter 11 were made available in 1967, followed by the terpolyamides some two years later with the introduction in 1969 of the nylon 6/66/12 types in Germany and Switzerland. Since that time little basic process or polymer development has occurred apart from the powder calender printing and limited use of thermoplastic polyesters. There have been considerable improvement made in the printing of powders and aqueous pastes. It is very feasible that one day thermosetting polymers analogous to those used to metal coating will be realised for textile coating and the garment producer will no longer require fusible interlinings but will coat his own garment lining immediately prior to attaching it into a particular area of his garment.

Processing of Powders

The technologies used to produce powders for metals and textiles are very similar although the amount of compounding for metal coatings is considerably more.

Compounding

Before this process is carried out, it is generally premixed in order to ensure good homogeneity. It has been found advisable to premix particles of comparable size wherever possible. The main type of premixing machines are tumbler, horizontal, conical, high speed blenders, and air jet mixers.

Once all the components are dry blended and homogenous, they are ready for hot melt compounding. The components for powders in metal coating technology include pigments, extenders, hardeners, flow-aids, and flexibilizers (plasticizers). The two main factors which govern the temperature of compounding are the viscosity of the polymer melt and the reaction temperature of the hardeners.

The main compounding techniques used for this powder technology are all well established procedures in the polymer industry. They are : (i) batch process as typified by the Z-blade mixer, (ii) semicontinous process which uses heated rolls or Banbury mixers, and (iii) extrusion which is a fully continous process.

These compounding processes are not necessary for the production of powder for use in textile coating, although some compounding is necessary to make certain basic polymers suitable for use under specified conditons. This compounding is largely required to incorporate the plasticizer into the polymer matrix and both cellulose acetae and copolyamide powders, for example, can be made by incorporating solid plasticizers either by the more preferable extrusion techniques or simply dry blending.

Grinding

As mentioned in the previous section, it is necessary to compound polymers for use with metals and obviously the resultant compound must first be granulated to ensure it is in an acceptable condition to be fed into the grinding equipment. The granulating equipment can be a Kibbler or a machine operating on the Masson cutter principle.

The basic principle of grinding solids into powders is a process of attribution in which the size reduction is carried out by impacting the solid lamps of resin against a grinding surface or by reducing the size of the particles simply by impacting themselves with each other. The resins associated with thermosetting powders have low molecular weights and as such, in general are bottle and friable, thus making them relatively easy to grind. However, they must be controlled closely in order to avoid overheating which can lead to premature curing. The thermoplastics have considerably higher molecular weights which lead to them being tough and resilient. In general, they are therefore ground by either freeze or cryogenic methods.

The temperature at which polymers can be ground efficiently vary widely as can be seen from Table 20.1

Table 20.1
GRINDING RANGE FOR RESINS

Material	Grinding Range °F
Cellulose acetate butyrate	0 to -50
Epoxy	+110 to +50
Nylon	0 to -130
Polyethylene	+14 to -180
Polypropylene	+10 to -80
PVC	20 to -50

Obviously the temperature of grinding, depends to a large extent upon the size of particle required. For example, low-density polythene can be ground at ambient temperature if a mesh size of 35 (500 microns) to 50 (300 microns) is required. To achieve smaller particles it is often necessary to use freezing conditions or some form of chemical precipitation technique.

There are three main types of refrigerants used with thermoplastics: solid carbon dioxide or dryice, liquid carbon dioxide, and liquid nitrogen (LIN). The conditions of refrigeration available from these materials are given in Table 20.2.

Dry ice is relatively inefficient and requires large amounts of solid carbon dioxide. Even, so it is difficult to maintain thermostatic control and the large amounts of refrigerants can cause irritation to the eyes of the operators as well as affecting their breathing. Liquid nitrogen is the most favored method because like CO_2 it is essentially nontoxic and may be added in relative small quantities. The resultant system responds readily to thermostatic control and at the same time provides in inert gas atmosphere within the grinding chamber, thus reducing the hazards of explosion. The liquid nitrogen is introduced through the spray header (see Fig. 20.1) directly into the feed hopper of the mill. The LIN is stored under normal atmospheric pressure and does not go through a solid state in changing to a gas and so can be metered into the header. There is a greater driving force with the LIN at 320°F then the dry ice at -109°F. Embrittlement of the polymer particles

Table 20.2

CONDITIONS FOR FREEZING THERMOPLASTICS

Refrigerant	*Initial condition*	*Heat absorption*[1]
Dry ice	Solid at - 109°F	268
Liquid CO_2	Liquid at 0 °F (300 p.s.i.g.)	140
LIN	Liquid at - 320°F	166

[1] **From initial condition to final gas temperatures of 0°F.**

occurs very quickly and this results in the particle size distribution being more uniform. However, LIN is relatively expensive and the cost of the refrigerant can add to 10 per cent to the total manufacturing cost.

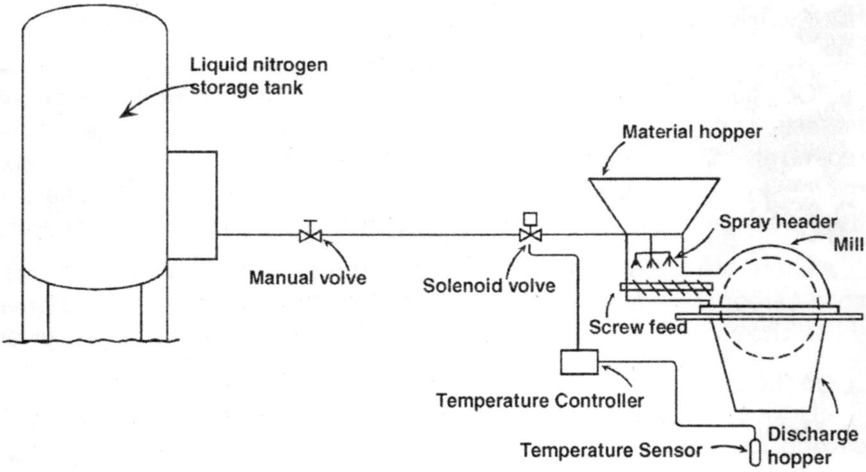

Fig. 20.1 Liquid nitrogen grinding of thermoplastics

Certain other techniques are used to produce fine powders i.e. particles below 100 microns. The main process is a solvent precipitation which involves dissolving the thermoplastic polymer granules in a solvent either in the cold or hot and then by cooling with stirring, a powder is precipitated out. This produces a particle with a relatively spherical shape and can be as small as 10 microns than the crygenic grinding. This process was first introduced in Europe by Technoplast Spindler (now Plast Labor, Switzerland) and in the U.S.A. by USI Chemicals. Both these companies utilise such proceses on a commercial scale and powders are available that are spherical in shape and are below 100 microns. In Fig. 20.2 and 20.3 it is possible to see the difference of particle shape for powders obtained by mechanical and chemical techniques.

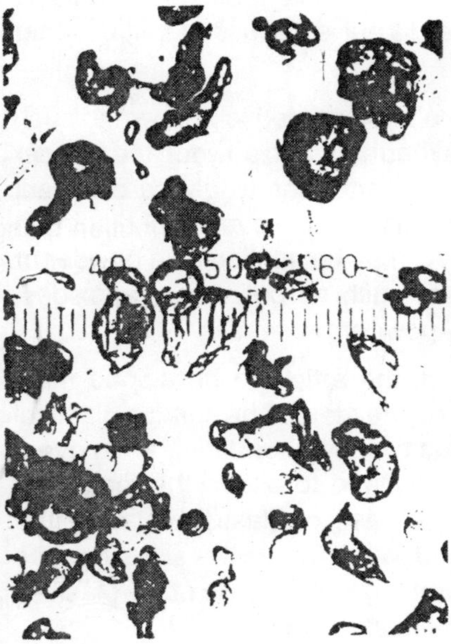

Fig. 20.2 Mechanical grinding

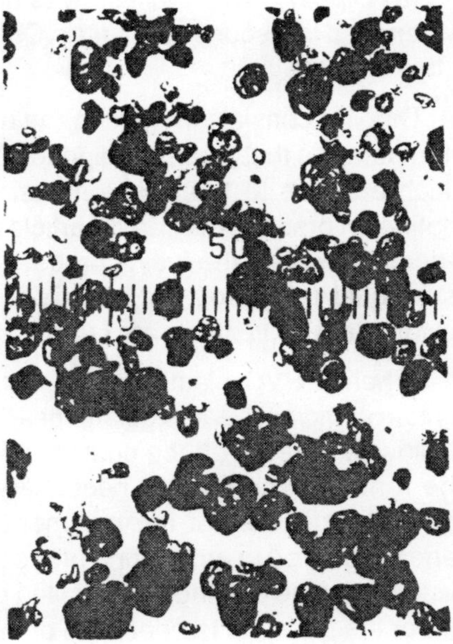

Fig. 20.3 Mechanical grinding

COATING PROCESSES

1. Metal

Before any coating process can be carried out it is essential to remove all forms of oxidation. Descaling is sometimes first necessary and this is usually carried out with acid pickling or mechanical abrasion. The acid pickling can be done using a dilute acid solution and then removing by washing with water. The mechanical method can be carried out by sand blasting, wire brushing, or grinding.

The next step is a degreasing operation which is essential if good adhesion is required between the coating and the substrate. A well established method is a chemical wash with caustic soda, phosphate soaps, synthetic detergents, etc. Solvents can also be used in baths or vapor phase systems and for this purpose trichlorethylene, toluenne, acetone, and isopropyl alcohol have all been found to be satisfactory. The final stage is the primping of the cleaned article and adhesive and the powder costing. The primers in general require heating after applying to be effect and since it is necessary to heat the metal objects in order to pick up the powder for coating the operation also serves to cure the primer.

(a) *Dipping*. This process was developed to coat metals from a liquid system and is discussed briefly in Chapter 19 but is discussed a little further in this chapter.

Dipping consists in heating the article to be coated in an oven to such a temperature that when it is dipped into a thermoplastic powder, the powder which adheres to the article melts, flows, and fuses to give a coherent coating. In practice the coated article is replaced in the oven after dipping in order to complete the fusing process. PVC may be applied as a powder or as a liquid (plastisol) but other polymers such as polythene, epoxides, polyamides, polyesters, etc., utilize only powder processes.

When a PVC plastisol is to be used, the article to be dipped must contain sufficient heat to gelate the PVC on the metal. The surplus plastisol is allowed to drain off the coated object is cured by reheating in an oven. The reheating process is necessary to dry and to obtain the maximum physical properties of the polymer. In the case of plastisol coating it is general referred to as a curing process and with powders it is sintering. The thickness of the coating is controlled by varying the viscosity of the plastisol and/or the time and temperature of the preheating process.

Dripping from use of the plastisol technique can be a distinct disadvantage and for this reason many processors prefer to use powders. However, dip coating using powdered polymers is not a straightforward matter of dipping a hot metal article into a box powder. After a few articles are dipped into a powder reservoir, a number of holes would appear in the powder and subsequent articles would pick up very little, If any, powder. This limitation is overcome by the fluidized bed technique which is described next and illustrated in Fig. 20.4.

This process is a device which enables fine powders to be used as if they were liquids. Essentially as can be seen from the illustration, the equipment consist of two chambers which are separated by a porous ceramic plate. The upper chamber contains the powder and the lower is a plenum chamber fed by an air supply. If sufficient pressure is provided by the air supply each particle bubbles up and falls back in different places. The overall effect in the fludized bed is to make it appear like simmering water. As in

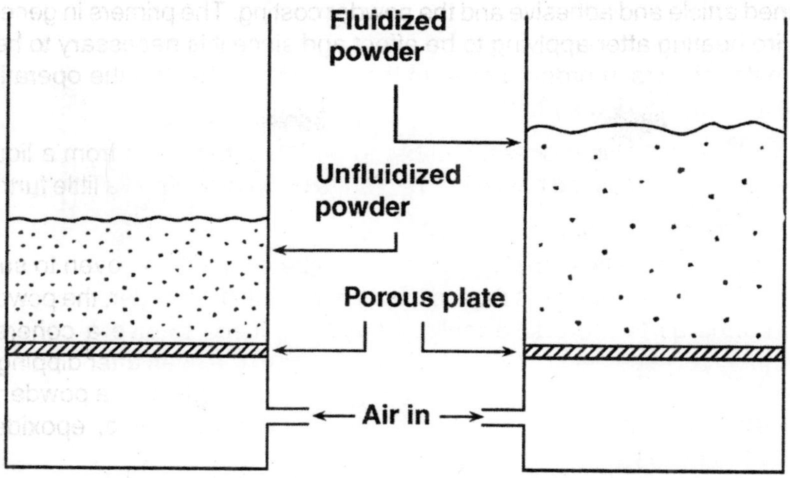

Fig. 20.4 Fluidized bed technique

the other process, the resultant coated product must be reheated in order to sinter the coating and render it homogenous.

The particle size of powder should be in region 50-250 microns (0.002-0.010 in.) and the shape should beas spherical as possible.

(b) *Electrostatic Powder Spray Coating.* Powder coatings may also be applied by electrostatic spraying or in an electrostatic fluidized bed. This technique does not require the prior preheating of the metal object since the powder clings to the part to be coated by electrostatic attraction. The powder is therefore fed by air through a gun (see Fig. 20.5) and at this stage a high voltage, low amperage charge is applied to the nozzle of the powder spray gun. The powder is sprayed at a low velocity and acquires a strong negative charge and this in turn is attached to the object to be coated which is earthed. When the powder builds up to a certain thickness, usually about 8 mils, a dielectric barrier is created and further powder is rejected. The particle size of the powder is normally between 10-80 microns (0.0004-0.0032 in.).

It is clear that in electrostatic powder coating techniques there are four processes involved, each of which has in influence on the resultant products. These are : powder charging, transfer of powder from charging region to object, adhesion, and limiting process, and the fusion of the dry powder layer.

Details are given in Table 20.3 which lists details as to the faults occurring with this technique in production and suggested remedies to overcome such defects.

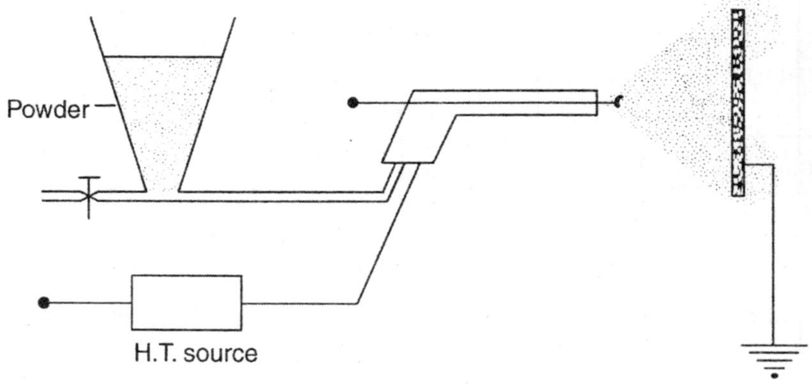

Fig. 20.5 Electrostatic powder coating

Mention must also be made here of the electrostatic fluidized bed process which is a combination of the electrostatic spray technique and the more conventional fludized bed process. This is also referred to as a cloud chamber technique and the apparatus can consist of a batch of electrostatic elements on the bottom of a shallow bed with a number of auxillary air jets. The small amount of powder is fluidized by the normal method of the element imparts a ngative charge to the powder with the result that a cloud of charged powder is formed. Any earthed object placed in this cloud is attracted by a layer of electrostatically charged particles rather than the fludized ones. The big advantage of this process is that it requires only small amounts of powder but offset against this is the fact that the density of the cloud so formed varies considerably from the top of the bottom of the chamber.

(c) *Flame Spraying.* This method of coating is especially useful for articles that are too large for dip coating. It consists of blowing out finely divided polymer powders through a specially designed burner nozzle, using compressed air as the propelling force. The nozzle is usually flame-heated by means of acetylene or some similar gas, or else it can be electrically heated. The molten polymer particles impinge on the article to be coated where they fuse together and cool. Subsequent sintering is unnecessary. It is difficult to obtain a uniform and homogenous coating and a great deal depends on the skill of the operator. On other problem is that at the temperature necessary to melt the polymers used, degradation is likely to occur.

Before leaving this section mention must be made of another technique of spray coating which is based on a dispersion of the polymer either in

Table 20.3

TROUBLESHOOTING FOR ELECTROSTATIC SPRAY COATING (information supplied by Rilsan Corp. U.S.A.)

Nature of defect	*Origin*	*Remedy*
Bubbles in coating	Any excessive deposit of powder in one spot creating poor air release.	Even out spray pattern or output of gun.
	Overheating.	Reduce fusion temperature.
	Presence of significant water either in the powder or in the compressed air.	Vacuum dry powder. Correct air dehumidifier.
	Release of gas from the object as porous casting.	Preheat to a temperature above fusion to remove occluded gas prior to coating.
	Poor drying of primer.	Assure that all solvent is removed from primer coat prior to fusion.
Yellowing	Overheating of coating during fusion.	Reduce fusion temperature or time. Sometimes film thickness is too thin, allow-ing primer to show through.
Uneven thickness or over thickness	Wet powder.	Vacuum dry powder and correct air supply.
	Poor spray technique.	Even out spray pattern and projection dwell times.
Orange peel	Powder underfused causing poor flow-out.	Remelt using an additional 20° F fusion temperature.
	Distance between the nozzle and object too short.	Regulate distance from the gun to nozzle and insure uniform and fine powder output.
	Primer too concentrated.	Cut back to normal viscosity and assure smooth and even coat.
Pinholes	Shortage of powder, low coverage.	Increase coverage.
	Poor substrate wetting.	Insure proper removal of grease and /or oil.
Craters	Contamination by surface-active agents.	Reduce fusion temperature to increase melt viscosity. Remove source of contam-ination through clean up.

Table 20.3 *(cont'd)*

Nature of defect	*Origin*	*Remedy*
Poor adhesion	Object not properly degreased and primed.	Assure adequate surface preparation.
Edge-pull	Poor wetting. Fusion temperature too high.	Assure adequate surface preparation and priming. Reduce fusion temperature.

aqueous or solvent media. The polymer to be applied is dispersed in an aqueous or solvent base and then sprayed in a manner similar to that of conventional paint spraying. Sintering is necessary and it is usual to apply one or two subsequent costs with intermediate sintering in order to build up a reasonable coating thickness. This technique of coating is particularly useful with polymers such as PTFE and PTFCE which can only be applied from dispersion.

2. Textiles

There are numerous basic methods of applying a polymer onto a base fabric to produce what are termed fusible interlinings. These include (i) sintering (random scatter or spray), (ii) paste printing, (iii) powder printing (engraved roll or rotary screen technique), (iv) preformed plastic net, (v) hot melt printing, (vi) extrusion, and (vii) spraying from solution.

Only the first three techniques are used widely and these are dealt with in detail although brief mention is made of certain of the other techniques.

Only the first three techniques are used widely and these are dealt with in detail although brief mention is made of applying of certain of the other techniques.

(a) *Sintering*. This is method of applying powders by sprinkle coating in a random pattern using vibratory screens or brush rollers. The range of powder particles is from 100-800 microns. The finer powders are used mainly for coating fabrics with a fairly tight construction (close weave), e.g., nonwoven, cotton shirt, and blouse fabrics. In practice it would be usual to use powders in the range of 100-300 microns. Heavier interlinings such as canvasses, made from horse hair, etc., used in the construction of men's jackets and top costs would require 300-800 microns. The disadvantage of this method is the irregular application of particles provided by the random technique. Another disadvantage is that if there is a considerable proportion of small particles they tend to fall into the interstes of the interlining, provided no contribution to adhesion but at the same time giving a disadvantage of a stiff hand. A schematic diagram of this technique is given in Fig. 20.6.

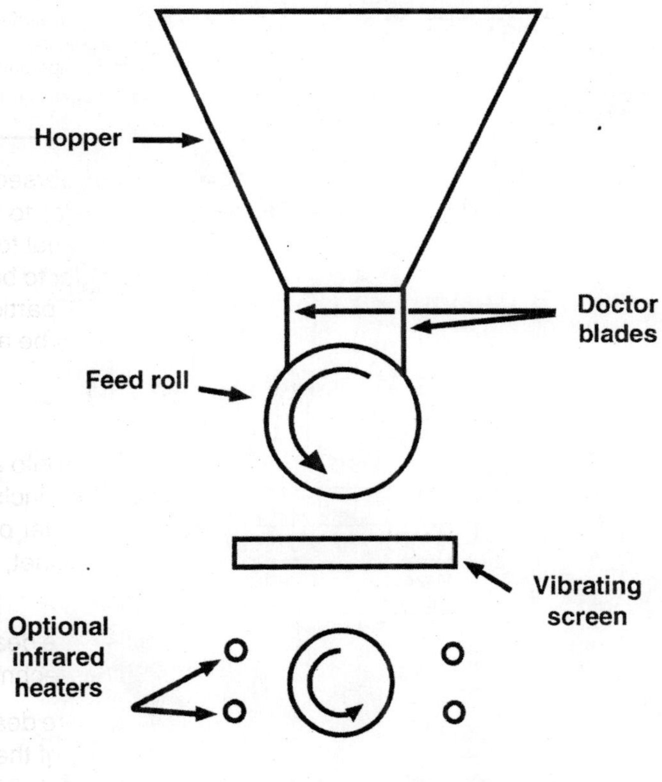

Fig. 20.6 Sinter coating equipment

On sprinkle coating the powder onto the substrate it is then essential heat the powder particles in order that they may become molten and thereby adhere to the fabric interlining. The coated fabric can then be calendered to modify the hand of the fabric or can be simply passed over chill rolls for subsequent rolling up and inspection (this is illustrated in Fig. 20.7).

This method of applying powder to a substrate has been widely used to coat other substrate such as wood and metal. One interesting use for this

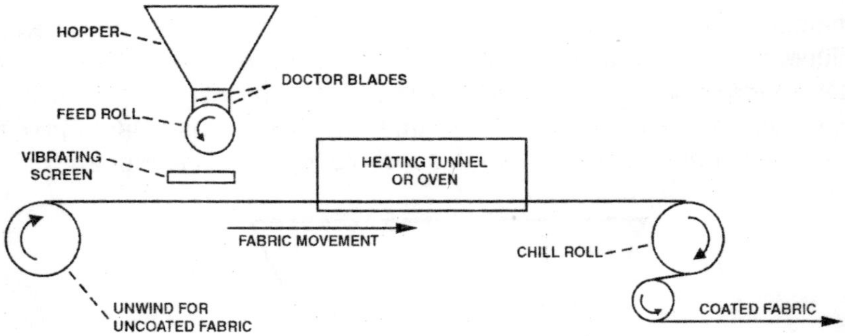

Fig. 28.7 Sinter coating process

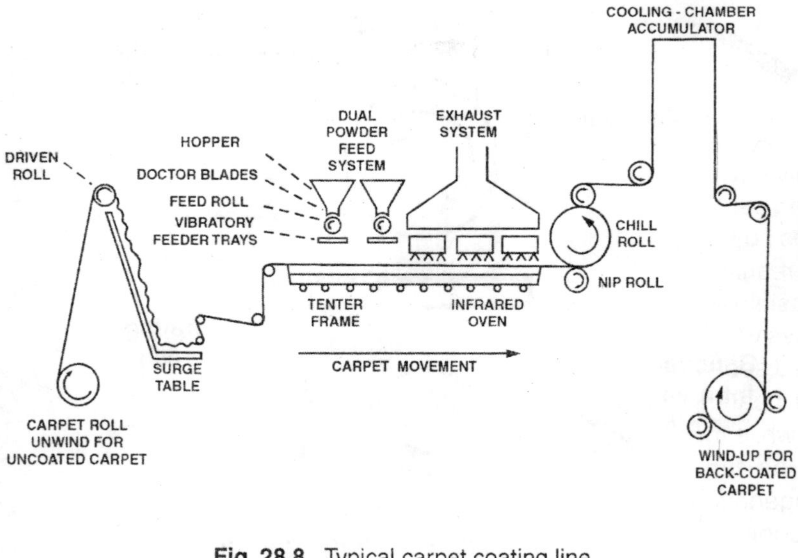

Fig. 28.8 Typical carpet coating line

coating process has been found in the carpet industry where the sinter coating of polyethylene powder has been used to apply backing material or for tuft retention. Coatings of this nature have meant that the carpet so formed could be molded and thus have found extensive use in the automobile industry (see Fig. 20.8).

(b) *Paste printing.* In this technique, powder below 80 microns is first converted into an aqueous or solvent dispersion. A suitable thickener such

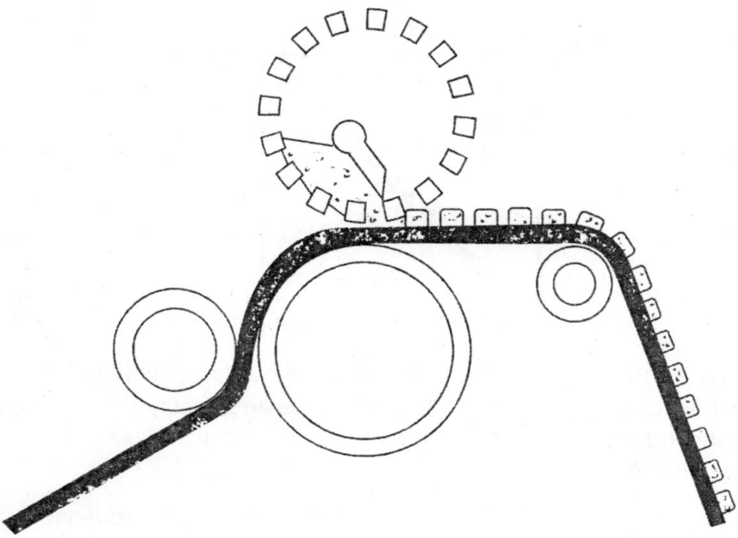

Fig. 20.9 Printing head for paste and powder techniques

as polyvinyl alcohol and a dispersing agent are used and a solids content of 50 per cent is recommended in order to achieve the best results. The pastes so formed may be printed by means of a gravure roller, silk screen, or if a regular pattern of dots is required then a perforated screen is necessary. For fusible interlinings, the last method is the preferred one and provides a process which has the distinct advantage of placing the adhesive in precisely located spots. After the screen printing process, the coated fabric is passed under heaters in order to drive off the volatile materials. At this stage the dots, while they are loosely attached to the fabric, are little friable dots and must be further heated in order to coalesce them and render them homogenous. The fabric can then either be calendered or simply passed over cooling rolls in order to solidify the molten dots (see Fig. 20.9).

The geometry of the pattern of the dots available is normally 9 up to 30 mesh. For example, a 14 mesh screen infers that there are 13-14 dots per inch measured on the diagonal of a square one inch in measurement, as indicated below.

(c) *Powder Printing.* There are two methods of printing directly from powder, one is based on an engraved roll and the other uses virtually the same equipment as for paste except powder is used. The former technique

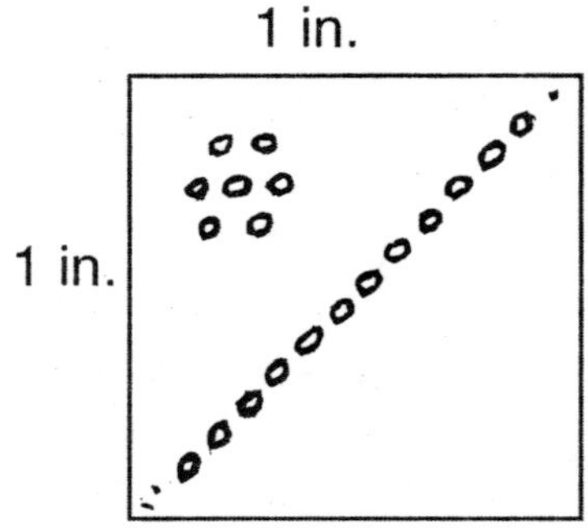

of using the engraved roll is more widely used by the textile industry and combines the advantages of the high quality of paste printing with the relative ease of handling which has become associated with the sintering technique previously described.

In this process, thermoplastic powders are filled into the recesses of a rotating engraved roll by means of a doctor knife system (see Fig. 20.10).

The engravings are generally in the range of 9 up to 30 mesh and the application of the doctor blade ensures that powder collects only in the depressions. The engraved coating roll is heated to the point where the powder in the depressions is just beginning to agglomerate. At this stage the powder is evacuated from the depressions by transferring it to the heated moving web. The hot roll is heating the moving web at the widest possible angle of contact to temperatures will above the melting point of the powders. It is obvious that the powder dot must be pulled out at the right moment and therefore the machine operators must have a certain amount of skills. If the powder flows too freely it trickles out of the gravure holes before touching the web but if it is agglomerated too much it simply clogs up the printing roller. Once the powder has agglomerated, the hot web is pressed against the engraved, roll by means of heating rolls. The agglomerated powder dots then adhere to the web and are then pulled out of the depressions in the form of loosely sintered particles. The coated web is then passed under a sintering zone where the dots melt and all the separate particles fuse together to form nicely rounded spheres which are sitting proudly on the surface of the web. The coated web is then calendered, if required, or simply cooled ready for batching.

The powder size for this process, as well as the powder technique using a rotary screen, is either 0-200 microns or 50-200 microns. It is apparent

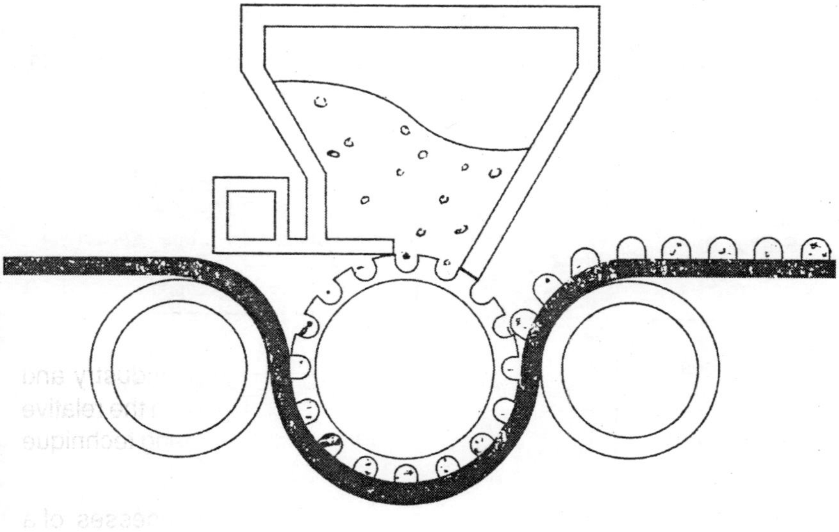

Fig. 20.10 Powder dot printing by means of engraved roll

that the particle size distribution not only plays an important part in determining the ability of the powder dot to be pulled from the engraved roll but it is very important for controlling the amount of adhesive which is applied to the web. In practice, during the coating operation,it is possible to add additional fine particles, say 0-80 microns which can modify the coating weight.

For garment fusible, an engraving size of 9-17 mesh is generally used and for shirt collars, 25 and 28 mesh are preferred.

In certain areas, the powder printing technique using a rotary screen is used largely because of the relative cheapness of the equipment. However, limitations have been established with this process in that it is not commercially possible to produce coated fabrics with mesh sizes above 17. Another disadvantage with this technique is that there is a tendency for debris to be found between individual dots. Machines are available which can be used both the paste and powder all on one machine. Reports have been made of recent work in which the screen powder printing process has been modified by electrostatic technique.

(d) *Preformed Net.* This net was developed largely as a result of a joint effort by Staflex Limited and Smith and Nephew Limited in the U.K. Essentially the process consists of embossing high-density polythene film and stretching the film in two directions, which leaves the structure of bosses

Table 20.4

POWDER REQUIREMENTS FOR FUSIBLE COATING PROCESSES

	Process	Powder size Microns	Polymers	Manufacturers
(1)	Sprinkle (also termed Scatter, spray Sintering)	100-800	Polythene Polyamides Polyesters E.V.A.	Caratsch AG Saladin AG Eugen Knobel AG Schaetti & Co. Zappa
(2)	Paste (a) Aqueous (b) Plastisol	 0-30 0-80	 Polythene Polyamides PVC	Caratsch AG Saladin AG Eugen Knobel AG Schaetti & Co. Zappa Zimmer Stork Brabant Schaetti
(3)	Powder (a) Calender Intaglio (b) Screen Printing (c) Electrostatic	 0-200 50-200 0-200 0-200	 as in (1) as in (1) as in (1)	Caratsch Saladin Eugen Knoble AG Schaetti & Co. No commercial suppliers - under development.
(4)	Preformed Net		High - density Polythene	Patented process Staflex Ltd. Smith & Nephew Hercules Corp.

connected by filaments. This net, in turn, is laminated to a web and on heating the coated web the filaments shrink back into the bosses. This leaves a web coated with equidistant spaced dots which are thermofusible. The big disadvantage with this process spaced is that there is a limiting factor as to which polymers are capable of being embossed and stretched. Only high density polyethylene with very specific physical characteristics have proved suitable and so far there are no commercial polyamides produced by these techniques.

A table listing the processes available, particle sizes of powder, polymers most widely used and manufactures of coating machines are given in Table 20.4.

Miscellaneous Coating Techniques

Extrusion coating of fusible was one of the original processes used to produce fusible interlinings but it suffers from the severe limitation in that it provides an overall coating which makes the hand very stiff and boardy. However, low-density polyethylene film is still used today to laminate to certain cotton basic interlinings is order to produce fusibles for shirts.

The coating of fabrics by spraying the adhesive from solutions was used in the early development of these materials but suffers from severe limitations, especially from the ecological standpoint. The early polyamides were alcohol soluble and were coated by a spray technique and added to disadvantages mentioned previously the resultant coating had poor wash fastness and these polymers were quickly replaced by the coterpolyamides.

In recent years considerable interest has been given to the possibility of using polymer granules rather than powders. Obviously to avoid a grinding on cost of 10-20 per cent would be a big saving in the cost of the final fusible interlining. Melting the polymer granules and directly printing the molten adhesive onto the fabric would not only save the cost of grinding but theoretically it could lead to higher speeds in the coating operation. Unfortunately, processes which have been demonstrated so far, suffer from two main disadvantages; (i) poor print difinition and smearing and (ii) excessive polymer degradation. These disadvantages are pertinent to the polyamides which have to be cryogenically ground and would realise the biggest cost saving if they could be hot melt printed. Polythene and ethylene -vinyl acetate do not present such problems in printing but interest in their use for this technique is not so great presumably because of the relatively low cost of grinding.

Principle Polymers for Powder Technology

(a) *Metals*. The main materials used for metal coating include low and high density polythene. PVC, nylon, epoxy, polyester, PTFE and PTFCE. These are all well covered in the relevant chapters so no further elaboration is given. However, for interest two formulations are provided as a guide as to what is required in order to produce a satisfactory powder coating compound.

A typical decorative compound would be

Material	Parts by Weight
Epikote 1004[1]	6.0
Titanium dioxide	27.5

Cadmium red	3.0
Polyvinyl butyral[2] (Butvar D510)	5.0
Aerosil 2941/380[3]	0.5
Dicyanidiamide	3.0

A typical polyester powder coating compound would be :

Material	Parts by Weight
Crylcoat 311[4]	100.0
Araldite GT 7004[5]	100.0
Modaflow	1.0
Titanium dioxide	200.0
Coloring dioxide	Trace
Irganox 1010[5] (antioxidant)	0.10

Key

1.	Epikote 1004	Shell Chemical Company, U.K.
2.	Butvar D510	Monsanto Chemicals
3.	Aerosil	De Gussa AG
4.	Crylcoat 311	UCB, Belgium
5.	Araldite GT 7004	
	Irganox 1010	CIBA Geigy

(b) *Textiles.* The polymers used for fusible interlinings at present are all thermoplastics and include low-and high density polythene, plasticized PVC, copolyamides, plasticized cellulose acetate, ethylene-vinyl acetate copolymers, and hydrolyzed ethylene-vinyl acetate. Like the metal coating polymers, these are all discussed in greater detail but Table 20.5 lists some of the main characteristics of some of the fusible polymer systems.

Uses for Powder Coated Articles

In Europe much of the uses for powder coating has been in the field of decorative finishes. It was soon established that single coatings of powder could provide tough decorative finishes without the hazards associated with solvent based systems. One of the major fields for powder coating is in the use of coating garden furniture. Powder coated furniture has many attractions and the fact that it provides a very smooth surface, which is both dirt free and detergent resistant, makes such a method eminently suitable for this particular application. Markets are also growing steadily in the appliance, building, and electrical industries.

Table 20.5

CHARACTERISTICS OF MAIN FUSIBLE POLYMER SYSTEMS

Polymer	Melting range °C	Melt Index 19°C	Fusing temperature °C	Resistance to	
				Washing	Drycleaning
L.D. polythene	100-120	2-200	120-150	Fair	Fair
H.D. polythene	125-136	6-50	155-175	Excellent	Good
Hydrolyzed ethylene-vinyl acetate	95-110	50-100	120-150	Good/fair	Good
PVC plastisol	100-120	Med.	140-160	Good/fair	Good
Polyestor	110-135	20-80	140-160	Good	
Copolyamide	110-135	50-100	Steam and / or 130-160	Good/fair	Very good
Terpolyamide	90-120	20-50	Steam and / or 130-160	Good/fair	Very good
Plasticized copolyamide	90-120	Mid.	Steam and / or	Fair	Good

Economically, powder coatings can be compared with the cost of two costs normally required with conventional solvent systems. The application of powder to substrates is also cheaper and provides a lower reject rate although in general the initial outlay on capital expenditure is higher.

It would appear that at present, the uses of powders for coating applications is more widespread in Euorpe than in the U.S.A. However, we are seeing increasing uses of powders in this country for more technical applications. Particular ones already reported are the coatings obtained with epoxide powders for large diameter pipes for gas and oil transmission. The huge potential of powders for coating car bodies has yet to be realised, however, material and process technologies are still evolving and the automobile industry has already shown some directions.

Fusible interlinings offer several advantages over conventional interlinings which are placed into a garment by the conventional technique of sewing. Apart from easier, higher production rate and less expensive manufacture, it is possible to impart special qualities of controlled stiffness, shape retention, stability, or resilience into selective areas of a garment in order to improve its fit, aesthetics, or performance. Other advantages include the stabilisation of the outer fabric with improved hand retention in wear. Disadvantages include the fat that once the interlining has been positioned and fused any error is extremely difficult to rectify. Very few problems occur in manufacture providing the correct fusing conditions are used in conjunction with modern presses.

The uses of fusible interlinings are too numerous to mention here but suffice it to say that a fusible can be found in almost any garment where sewing can be involved apart from seaming. Major uses are in the chest area of ladies and mens jackets, shirt, and blouse collars, cuffs and the hemming of garment parts, and household draperies.

21

Miscellaneous Processing Techniques

CALENDERING

Calendering is the process by which continous sheet (either rubber or thermoplastics) is made by passing the heat softened material between two or more rolls. Calenders were originally developed for processing rubber, but they are now widely employed for producing thermoplastics (mainly flexible PVC) sheet and coatings. Although the subject of calendering is included here under miscellaneous processes, its importance should not be underestimated.

In essence, the calendering process consists of feeding a plastics mass into the nip between two rolls where it is squeezed into a film which passes round the remaining rolls. It then emerges as continous film the thickness of which is governed by the gap between the last pair of rolls. The surface of the sheet is determined on the last roll and may be glossy, matt or embossed. After leaving the calender, the sheet is cooled by passing it over cooling rolls and then through a β-ray thickness gauge before being wound up. If fabric or paper is fed through the last two rolls, the film can be pressed into the surface of the web and the calender thus becomes a coating machine. A four roll calender coater is shown in Fig. 21.1. This method of coating is generally restricted to heavy coating weights and is often used for applying high viscocity vinyls to paper or fabrics. The thickness of coating is controlled by the gap between the last two rolls.

The plastics mix fed to the calnder may be a simple hot melt as in the case of, say, polyethylene, but in the case of PVC a great deal of effort is put into the precalendering processes such as blending, mixing, gelling, and straining. In addition to the polymer there may be inert mineral fillers (added to reduce the cost and modify the physical properties), pigments lubricants (to assist in processing), stabilizers and plasticizers. The dry components (with the exception of the pigment) are loaded into a ribbon blender and agitated sufficiently to produce an even dispersion. If plasticizers are to be added, they are sprayed into the powder mix during the initial period of blending. When correct dispersion has been achieved the blend is removed via a valve at the base of the mixing chamber and weighted-out into batch tins. If a pigment is required it is added at this stage to each separate batch. The batch tins are then emptied into a primary mixer, such as a Banbury, for about five to ten minutes at 120-160°C. The combination of heat and the 'kneading' action of the Banbury causes partial gelation of the mix. This partly galled material is then passed to a two roll mill and made to form a sheet round the front roll. This may be fed directly to the calender, but for good quality sheet or for thin sheet (say about 0.1 mm) a straining process is added to remove any coarse particles. A typical strainer consists of a single screw extruder with a filter screen immediately in front of the screw. The screen consists of a fine stainless steel woven wire mesh backed up by a medium and coarse mesh for mechanical support, together with a thick perforated stainer plate.

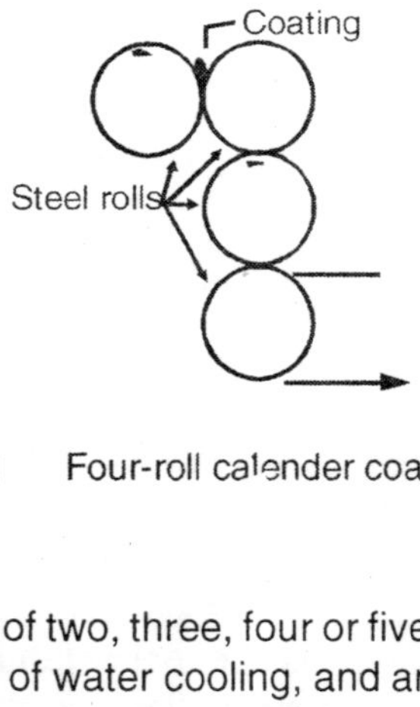

Fig. 21.1 Four-roll calender coater

Types of Calenders

Calenders may consist of two, three, four or five hollow rolls (or bowls) arranged for steam heating of water cooling, and are characterised by the number of rolls and their arrangement as, for example I, Z or inverted L types. Four roll inverted L and Z types are the most actual usual, the Z types having the advantages of lower loss of heat in the sheet (because of shorter travel) and of being easier to construct. The latter factor arises from the fact that less attention has to be paid to compensation for roll-bending since there are no more than two rolls in any vertical line (as opposed to three in a four roll inverted L.)

Other variations in calender design are dictated by the fact that very high forces have to be exerted on the rolls in order to squeeze the plastic material to a thin film. These high forces cause the rolls to bend, thus giving sheet which is thicker in the middle than at the edges. This can be counteracted in a number of ways, three of which have been used commercially :

(a) The use of 'crowned' rolls, i.e. rolls having a greater diameter at the middle than at the edges.

(b) Crossing the rolls slightly, thus increasing the nip opening at either end of the rolls.

(c) Roll blending. In this method, a bending moment is applied to the end of each roll by having a second bearing or each roll neck, which is then loaded by a hydraulic cylinder.

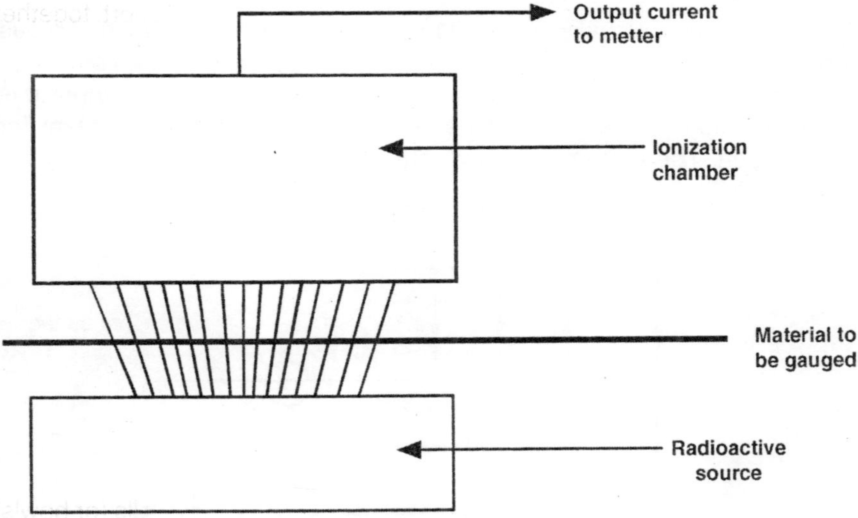

Fig. 21.2 Beta-ray gauge

As mentioned earlier, thickness of the sheet leaving the calender is measured using a β-ray gauge (Fig. 21.2). This gives an average reading of thickness over an area of sheet. Radiation from an isotope such as Thallium 204 is passed through the sheet and then collected in an ionization chamber. The radiation received by the chamber is inversely proportional to the weight per unit area of the material being measured.

Calender Requirements

As will be seen by a glance at the illustration of a typical machine, calenders are of massive construction. They call for high temperatures, with little variation across the rolls, and high pressures, again with low tolerances.

The required uniformity in temperature can be achieved by leading steam through concentrically drilled holes beneath the surface of the rolls and by circulating hot oil through the bearings in order to prevent heat losses at the end of the rolls through transfer to the bearings.

The high forces are necessary to squeeze the plastic mass into a very thin film and any unevenness in the forces along the roll is reflected in variations in the film thickness. One cause of pressure fluctuations is too much clearance in the bearing, which can be solved either by pulling back the rolls against one side of the bearing or by using tapered roll bearings.

Lubrication is usually of the 'flood' type, a system in which copious supplies of oil are circulated by gravity or pressure through sealed bearings. After passage through the bearings the oil passes to a sump where it is cooled and then pumped through filters on its way back to a header tank for recirculation. The system is shown schematically in Fig. 21.3.

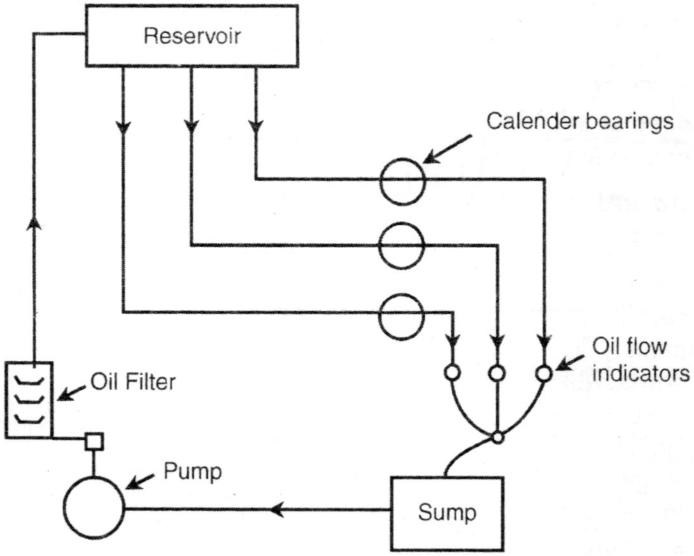

Fig. 21.3 Flood lubrication of calender

Calendering Faults

1. Bank marks : shiny patches on the surface of the sheet.
2. Cold marks (crow's feet) : these are marks, thus, caused by the stock being too cold.
3. Blistering. This is due too high a temperature or too large a bank of rolls and is prone to occur mainly in thicker sheet.
4. Pin-holes; these are caused by foreign matter or by the presence of unplasticized polymer particles.
5. Water marking; usually due to lubrication contamination.

Luvitherm Process

Because calendering is a capital intensive process, calenders tend to cater for wide width film (around 1.8 meters wide) because the running costs per unit width are proportionately less. However, such large machines tend to be used only for plasticized PVC because unplasticized PVC has a much higher melt viscocity, which makes it harder to handle on rolls of this width.

A special calendering process known as the Luvitherm process was developed, therefore, to produce unplasticized PVC films. The PVC is flash heated to a temperature of 220°C while in contact with a specially designed aluminium roll. The hot film so produced is normally oriented immediately rower than the large units described earlier (usually less than one meter) and the output is significantly lower. Special grades of PVC are used with special stabilizers, and the compounding stage can be an extruder compounder feeding directly to the calender.

Advantages of Calendering

Calendering usually produces film having a better guage (thickness) uniformity than that obtained by extrusion. One reason for this is the great care that is paid to the engineering of the calender bowls (as mentioned earlier). The final gauge is dependent on the gap between the final two bowls, whereas the extrusion the gauge is dependent more an draw-down speeds (in the case of slit-die film) or blowup ratios (in the case of tubular film). In addition, in an extruder cross head die there may be a range of path lengths which lead to preferential flow with consequent variations in gauge. In the tubular die process there are complicating factors such as the structures supporting the mandrel in the die. This also affects the melt flow, leading to gauge variations.

Another advantage of calendering is that better mixing is obtained. Because the amount of energy expended in a calendering line is so much greater than in an extrusion line, calendering film is less dependent on feed stock uniformity.

The main advantage of extrusion methods where PVC is concerned is that shorter runs are possible at economic rates.

COATING (WEBS)

One of the principle methods of coating substrates with a polymer namely, extrusion coating has already been dealt with in the chapter on Extrusion while another method was briefly described above under Calendering. The coating process is important, not only as a means of modifying film properties but also as a means of applying adhesive in the adhesive lamination of two substrates.

Coating processes can be divided into two main classes. In the first, an excess of the coating material is applied to the web and the surplus is removed by means of a rigid knife, smoothing bar or air-jet knife (air doctor). In the second class of processes, a predetermined amount is applied to the web by means of a calender, rollers, brushes, or by curtain coating. Extrusion coating also falls into the class.

Excess Application Systems

In knife coating, the thickness of the coating is controlled by a sharply profiled bar (or knife), the coating having previously been applied either by passing the web over a roll running partly immersed in the coating material or by running the coating material on to the face of the web, just in front of the knife. This technique is used extensively for coating fabrics with PVC, where it is often referred to as spreading. The PVC is prepared in the form of a paste and this is applied to the fabric by means of a knife. In general more than one layer is applied, each layer being gelated by means of heat before the next layer is added.

Three methods of providing a base, over which the knife can spread the paste, are generally used. In the floating knife system, the fabric alone provides the required base while in other systems a rubber blanket or a backing roll may also be present (Fig. 21.4).

Gelation of the applied film is usually carried out by radiation on convection in a tunnel-type oven, followed by treatment with an embossing or polishing roll to give the required finish.

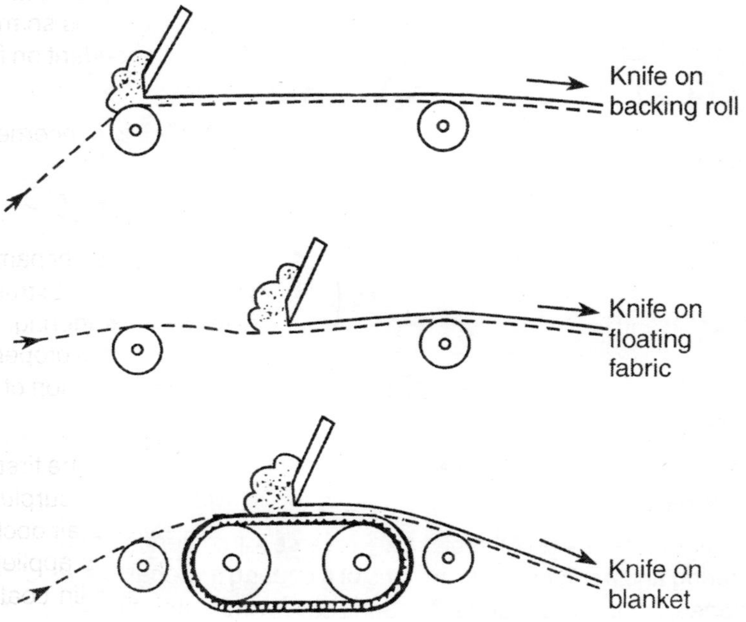

Fig. 21.4 Spreading

Where low to medium viscosity coatings are to be applied, the use of an air knife is to be preferred. The excess of coating material applied is comparatively small (about 1 : 1 to 1.6 : 1), and the main determining factor for coating weight is the air knife pressure. Other factors include air stream angle, web speed, and the physical properties of the coating. The air knife method is widely used for coating a variety of webs, including plastics films. In the past its use has been more or less restricted to the application of water based coatings because of the difficulties in handling large volumes of air mixed with flammable solvent vapors, and surface drying of the coating by the air knife. New equipment and techniques are leading to improvement in this respect. An air knife coating system is shown in Fig. 21.5.

The smoothing bar coating process employs either a smooth or a wire wound bar, which is usually rotated slowly against the direction of web travel. The smooth bar is normally used for the china clay coating of fiberboard but the wire wound one can be used for hot melt coatings. It is difficult to achieve an even coating weight with this method and it is liable to produce occasional scratch marks on the coating.

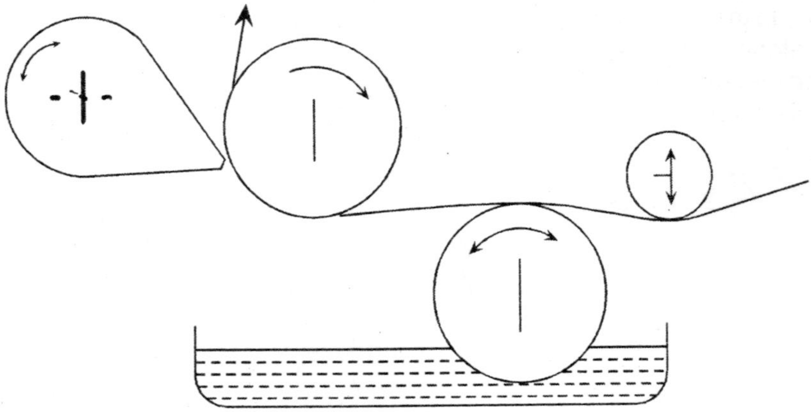

Fig. 21.5 Air doctor coating

Predetermined Systems

Common members of this class are reverse roll coaters. They are capable of metering and applying uniform films of a coating material to a wide variety of surfaces, using a wide range of coating solids and viscosities. The simplest forms of roll coaters, such as the single roll and two roll reverse coaters, have only a limited metering action, however, and are not recommended when precise coating control is required. In a one-roll reverse coater, the roll rotates in a bath containing the coating and the web passes over the top of the roll in the opposite direction to the rotation of the roll. The two roll coater merely adds a rubber backing roll run at the line speed (Fig. 21.6).

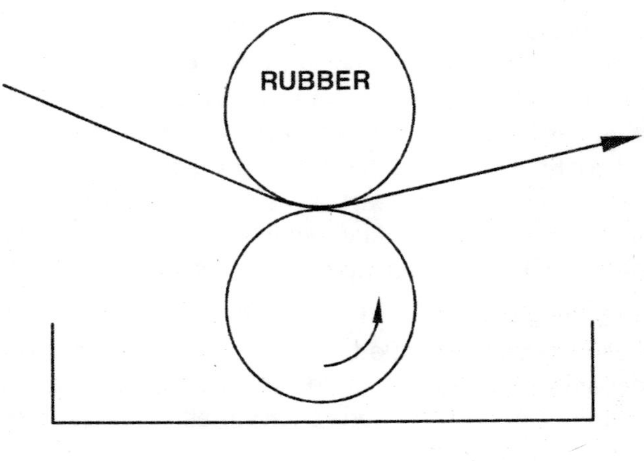

Fig. 21.6 Two-roll reverse-roll coater

In three or four roll coaters the extra rolls are used to give more precise metering of the coating (Fig. 21.7.) Coating weight is controlled primarily by the metering roll gap and the rate of rotation of the applicator and metering rolls in relation to the web speed. In systems where the web passes over

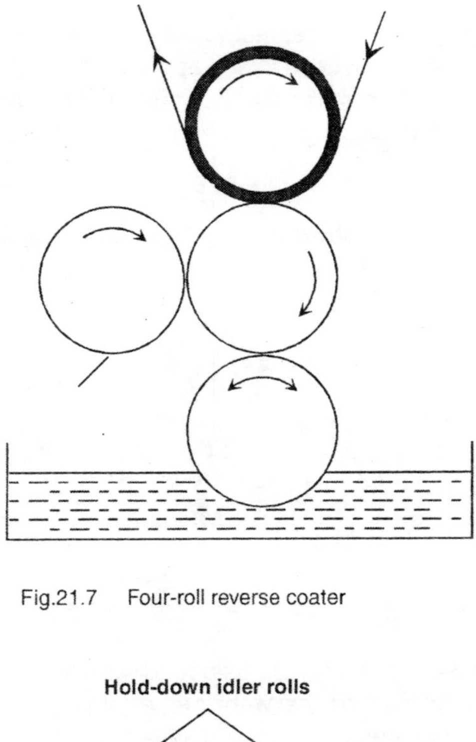

Fig.21.7 Four-roll reverse coater

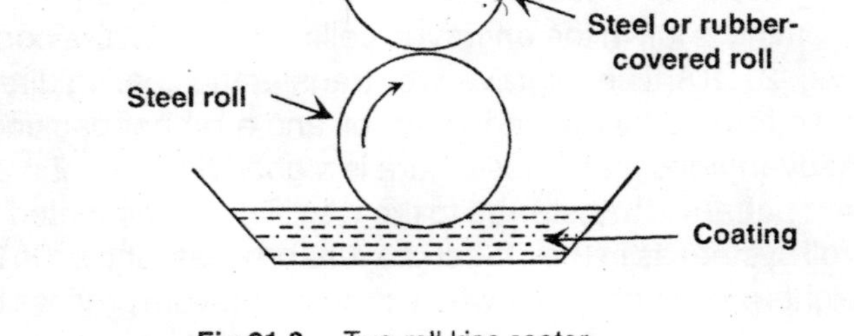

Fig.21.8 Two-roll kiss coater

the applicator roll without the assistance of a backing roll, the process is referred to as 'kiss' coating. Uniform then depends on maintaining complete contact of the web with the applicator roll and good control of web tension. These are usually achieved by the use of holddown idler rolls on either use of the applicator roll (Fig. 21.8).

Nip roll coaters are another method of applying a predetermined amount of coating. They are often used for the application of thin coatings, difficult to apply by normal reverse-roll methods. The coating is applied to the web as it passes between two coating rolls, one of which is usually rubber covered (Fig. 21.9.)

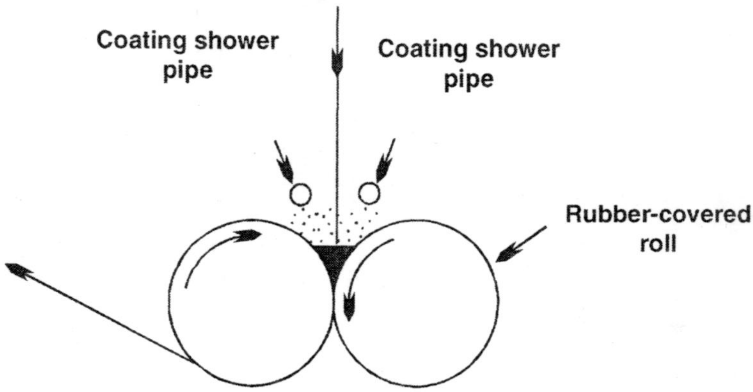

Fig. 21.9 Two-roll nip coater

The nip between the two rolls is flooded with the coating and the amount that is actually applied to the web is controlled by the hardness of the rubber rolls, the nip pressure, the web speed, the coating viscocity, and the characteristics of the web material.

Next, there are gravure coaters which employ on engraved cylinder, running in a tough of coating material, to meter the transfer of coating to the web. The engraved roll is doctored with a thin blade to ensure that an even amount of coating is left in the engraved cells. Direct gravure consist of two rolls only (Fig. 21.10). The engraved roll transfer the coating directly to the web at the nip formed by the engraved roll and a rubber backing roll. This has the disadvantages that unless there is a good flow-out of the coatings, the engraved pattern is transferred to the web. This is eliminated by the use of a three-roll system as in the off-set gravure process, shown in Fig. 21.11. Coating weights are generally low when using the gravure process but precise control is possible. One disadvantage is that the engraved cylinder must be changed when a change in coating weight is required.

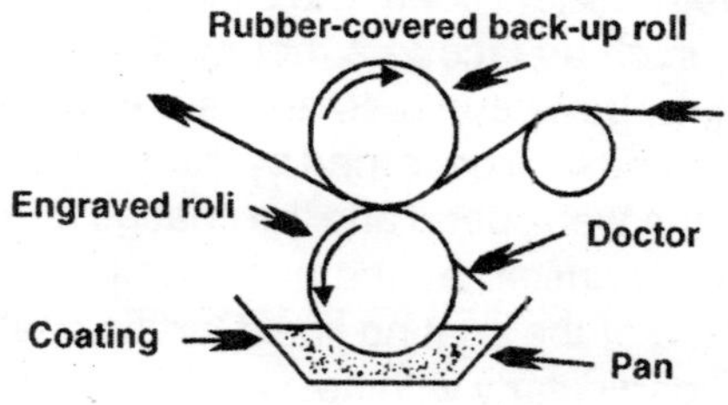

Fig. 21.10 Direct gravure coater

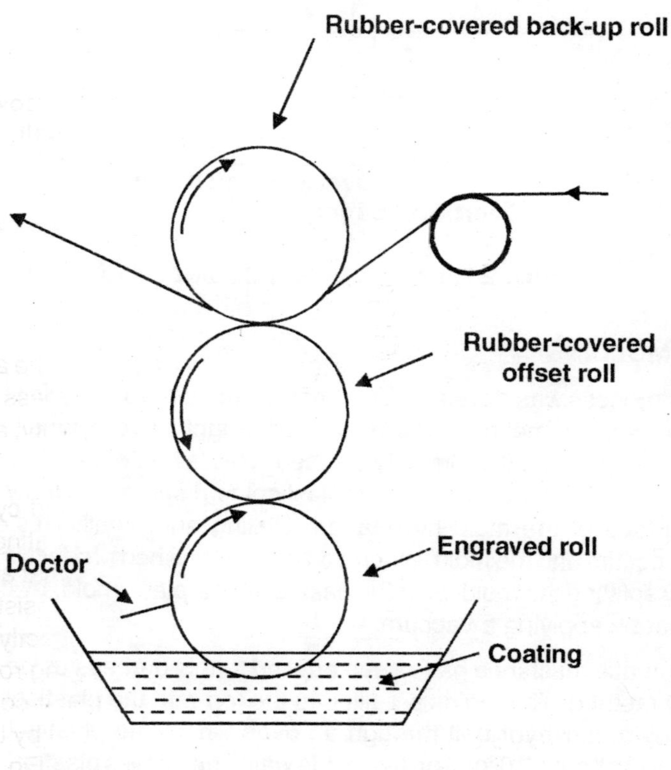

Fig. 21.11 Offset Gravure coater

Finally, there is curtain coating, a typical example being shown in Fig. 21.12. A laminar film of the coating material is extruded through a slotted orifice or over a weir. Curtain coating is suitable for moderately thin, evenly flowing materials, such as lacquers, hot melts, and some latices. It gives good coverage of irregular surfaces and is particularly suitable for carton blanks. Coating thickness is governed by the orifice dimensions or the flow rate over the weir, the web speed and the coating formulation. The thinness of the filling curtain is limited by the need for it to be continuous and this also limits the speed of the coating line. Curtain coating is widely used for hot melt coatings, particularly with hot wax blends, many of which are now specially formulated for this process.

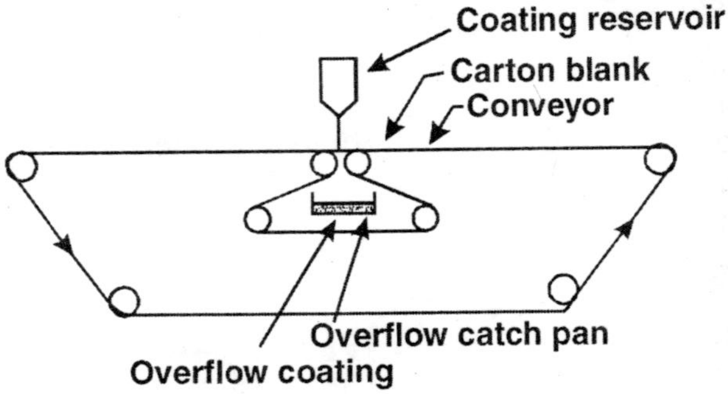

Fig. 21.12 Curtain cooler

SLUSH MOLDING

This process was developed for manufacturing hollow articles from PVC plastisols (and, sometimes, low molecular weight polyethylenes). Either a split or one-piece metal mold may be used. This is heated, and a measured amount of plastisol poured in. The plastisol is dispersed evenly over the inner surface of the mold by rotation. Gelling and, finally, fusion of the plastisol occurs and the mold is then cooled. The finished product is removed either by splitting the mold, or in the case of a one-piece mold, by collapsing the object by applying a vaccum.

Automatic machines have been applied to this process using a slightly different method. The molds are filled to the top with the plastisol and then carried by a conveyor belt through an oven where the plastisol gels to a thickness of about 1/16 inch on the inside wall. The excess plastisol is poured out and the molds are transferred to another oven where curing is completed.

Slush molding has been extensively for making dolls, balls and flexible toys of all sorts.

MELT SPINNING OF FIBERS

In this process the polymer is heated and the resultant viscous melt is pumped through a plate containing a large number of fine holes, known as a spinnerette. Solidification of the extruded fibers is carried out by passing them through a transverse current of air. Special pumps have been developed to operate in the temperature range necessary to produce a manageable melt (230-315°C). Another practical detail is the provision of an inert atmosphere in the melting chamber, prior to the pump. A schematic diagram of a typical set-up is shown in Fig. 21.13.

Fibers produced by the melt spinning process are oriented by cold drawing from two to six times their original length. This brings the linear molecules close together and increase the attractive forces between them, Cold-drawing is most important since it increases the tensile strength to many times its initial value.

FILM FIBERS AND TAPES

The production of fibers by melt spinning is relatively expensive and finds outlets mainly in the field of textiles. A much more varied field of applications is opening up for film fibers and tapes. The earliest outlets were for course fibrillated yarns used in the making of ropes and twines. This was quickly followed by the manufacture of woven sacks from stretched film tapes. Later applications include primary carpet backing, sail cloth, artificial grass, and artificial seaweed.

Before studying in subject in more detail it is helpful to define some of the terms used so that they can be referred to again without further explanation.

Film Tape

Water bath, chill roll cast, or blown film is split into narrow tapes (usually 2 to 3.5 mm wide and 50 or 25 mm thick, respectively) and stretched under heat. Stretched ratios are of the order of 7 : 1. Stretched film tape or film yarn are equivalent terms.

Twisted Film fibers

Water bath, chill roll cast, or blown film is split into wider tapes than the film tapes and again stretched under heat. Additionally, the tapes are then split by mechanical means into a coarse, fiber-like form. Stretch ratios are

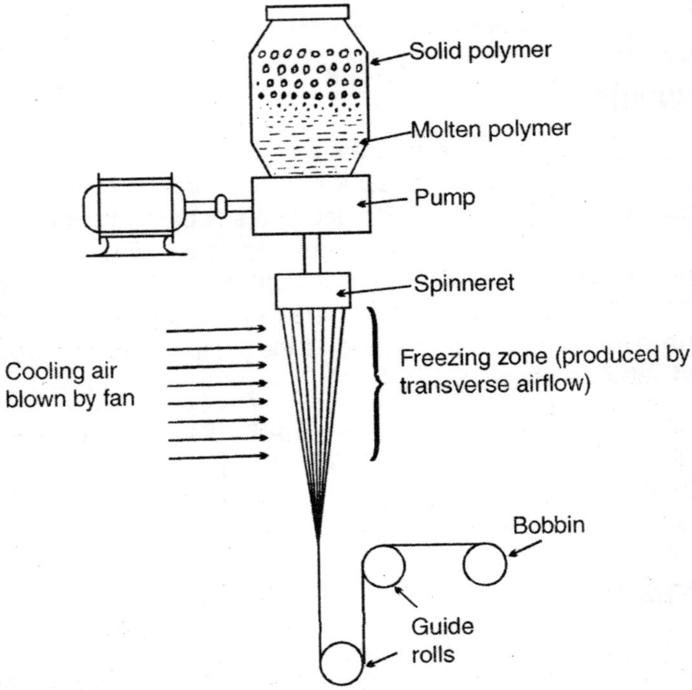

Fig. 21.13 Melt spinning of fibers

somewhat higher, being of the order of 10 : 1. Fibrillated film is an equivalent term.

Fine Denier Fibers

These result when the above process is taken still further, until a fine, soft, wool-like mass of fibers is obtained. Super fibrillated film is an equivant term.

Denier

This is the weight, in grams, of 9000 m of the fiber in the form of a continuous filament. The SI unit is the tex, which is the weight in grams of 1000 m of the fiber.

Tenacity

This is a measure of tensile strength and in SI units is measured in mN/tex.

Process and Equipment

The complete process for producing stretched film tape consists of the following stages :

(a) Production of the film.
(b) Slitting of the film to tape of predetermined widths.
(c) Heating and orientation of the tapes.
(d) Winding of the stretched tapes on to a suitable spool.

The process may be made continous or it may be split into two stages such that the film is wound on to a roll after extrusion. The roll is subsequently unwound, slit, stretched, and wound on to spools. Running the process in two stages has the advantage that the ultimate line speed isnot governed by the extruder speed so that both extruder and stretcher can be run at their optimum speeds. There is a wide range of equipment commercially available for each step but the make-up of an optimum complete line depends on a number of factors including size of plant, equipment available, cost of equipment, previous technology, and the precise products to be produced.

Film Extrusion

Blow extrusion and both slit die extrusion methods can all be used satisfactorily for the production of the basic film. There are, however, advantages and disadvantages to each of the three methods.

Slit die film systems are generally reckoned to give higher line speeds since the film can be more efficiently cooled. Better control of film thickness is also possible. One disadvantage is the greater amount of scrap generated, due to the edge thickening that occurs in flat film extrusion. When the film tapes are to be used for the manufacture of ropes, however, this is not so important since the thicker tapes can be used as part of the rope's central core. Chill roll casting has a tighter control of film thickness than has water -bath quenching but it is less efficient for thick film extrusion because of differential cooling of the two sides of the film. Apart from the higher variation in film thickness, the water quench method has one other disadvantage, namely, water carry-over. This means that devices for the removal of excess water have to be incorporated. One possible method is to include vaccum/ heat driers in the line.

Blow extrusion has the advantage of lower cost but it is important to realize that blowing of film always produces some lateral orientation of the film and this is never completely eliminated during the subsequent longitudinal orientation. The final film tapes have, therefore, a reduced tendency toward self-slitting. The strength is also somewhat less and the film has a softer hand than cast film. This softer feel is desirable in tapes intended for weaving and fibrillation, and especially for fabrics from fibrillated film because of the enhanced consumer appeal. The reduced self splitting characteristics are also an advantage in weaving and for fibrillation, the latter is because reduced splittability leads to a more controlled splitting, at least when a pin roller unit is used, and to less post fibrillation.

Other advantages of blow extrusion include lower extrusion temperature (giving higher tensile strength) and the elimination of edge trimming.

Slitting and Stretching

The film is slit into tapes of the desired width, either by rotary knives or by a slitter bar in which are set razor-like blades. During the slitting operation the film should be kept under controlled tension in order to give accurate cutting. This is best achieved by placing the slitter bar close to a roll or drag bar. After slitting, the tapes are led into a pull-roll stand (or godet unit) and through a stretching oven. The godet unit may consist of three, five, or seven power driven rolls, together with a nip roll covered with neoprene or urethane rubber to prevent slippage. The stretching oven is usually about 9 to 12 feet long and is fitted with accurate temperature control (with special attention to uniformity of heating). Circulating hot air ovens are the most usual but infrared heaters are also used for hotplates, which heat by contact, have been developed. At the other end of whatever heating unit is employed there is a second godet unit operating at a higher speed than the first. The ratio of the speed of the second godet unit to that of the first is the draw ratio (7 : 1 for weaving tapes and 10 : 1 for tapes for fibrillating). Where tapes are to be used for woven carpet backing the weaving process may generate enough heat to cause tape shrinkage, unless the tapes are previously heat set. The process of relaxation and heat setting is carried out by running the tapes through a second oven followed by a third godet unit.

In later developments the film is stretched first and slit afterwards. The blown or cast film is stretched on a unit consisting of preheated rolls, stretching rolls, and annealing rolls. It is then wound up as wide stretched film which can later be slit into tapes. In this process the stretching is controlled over a very short distance so that only a slight reduction in the film width occurs. It is possible, therefore, to produce a larger number of tapes from a given film width than with conventional methods based on slitting before stretching. Advantages of hot-roll stretched polypropylene film include :

(a) High output,
(b) High tenacity, and
(c) Low splitting tendency.

A disadvantage of this process is that output is limited by the high initial film thickness required. This is because the film thickness after stretching is directly proportional to the stretch ratio used. With a stretch ratio of 10 : 1 for example, the initial film thickness would be approximately 400-500 mm and adequate cooling and preheating of such films is difficult.

Winding

The winding of film tapes is more difficult process than the winding of monofilaments, whether natural or synthetic. This is because of the added complication of possible twisting which can reduce the tensile strength by 15-20 per cent. Another critical factor is tension which must be kept constant. Constant tension winders are available but are expensive. A cheaper alternative is the use of constant torque winders but these require manual adjustment by the machine operator as the diameter of the wound bobbin increases.

Fibrillation

Film tapes can be fibrillated by mechanical splitting in a controlled manner to give a range of fine denier fibers. The three basic systems for fibrillating stretched film tapes are :

(a) Pin-roller system,
(b) Castellated die sysetm, and
(c) Embossed roller system

Pin-Roller System

The equipment consists of a roller which revolves at a peripheral speed higher than the linear speed of the film and which can incorporate up to approximately 30,000 needles on a series of bars: an assembly of rollers for adjusting the contact area of the tapes : and draw off rollers for adjusting the tension. As they revolve the needles split the tapes, forming a regular or irregular network pattern. The size of this network can be adjusted by altering the roller speed and the contact arc. This fibrous material produced by this method is hairy and bulky, and comes nearest in appearance to a natural fiber. The fibers have a rectangular cross section which gives good coverage in, for example, carpet applications.

The tow, as it comes from the fibrillator, can be either tufted or woven directly into a carpet, or it can be collected, cut, carded, and spun into a yarn. The particular use to which it is put depends on the nature of the network structure which can be varied by altering the fibrillation conditions.

Castellated Die System

In this system the film is extruded, not through the usual flat film die but three flat dies, each having 35 profiled, castellated slots through which a total of 105 tapes are extruded. The profiles of each separate slot are such as to produce 25 ribs in each tape. Stretching of these ribbed tapes causes them to shear, so forming 25 strand fibers.

Roll Embossed Film Process

This process is similar to the castellated die system in as much as it gives a profiled film. On stretching this produces continuous multifilaments as before. The method by which the embossing is produced differs, however. A flat film is fed into the nip of two rolls, on of which is profiled with a fine pattern of grooves around the circumstances. The other roll is plain and serves as a pressure roll. The film may be either above or below its crystalline melting point; in other words it can be run through the embossing system straight from the extruder, or after if has been reeled and stored.

It will be seen that the main difference between the two embossed film systems is that the castellated die system profiles the film which it is in the die, whereas the roll embossed film process profiles it outside the die. The former is subject to die blocking when powdered additives to the polymer are used. This includes color masterbatches.

Texturization

Texturized yarns are often required because of the higher bulk they offer, compared with that obtained with conventional polypropylene film fibers. A relatively new technique is now available, however, based on the use of laminates instead of single-layer film. Bicomponent films can be made into highly crimped yarns provided that the two layers in the laminate film are chosen from materials with a sufficiently great difference in their stress-strain behavior.

When yarns are textured in this way they can have an elongation of between 100 and 400 per cent depending on the grades and on the processing conditions used. Crimping can be carried out immediately after stretching and fibrillation, or it can be applied to previously wound uncrimped yarns, after heating.

WELDING

In spite of the various techniques available for producing complicated moldings, it is often necessary to join two or more components to produce the particular setup required. One common method of achieving this union is by welding and several processes are available, some examples of which are described below. The heat sealing of film to form large sheets or to close plastic bags and sacks, is also a welding operation and is discussed here.

Hot Gas Welding

This process, which bears a superficial resemblance to acetylene torch welding of metals, is particularly useful for producing items of chemical plant, such as tanks and ducting, from thermoplastic sheets. The sheets to be joined are first bevelled and cleaned. A welding rod of the same composition as the sheets is obtained. Sheets are placed side by side so that the two bevelled edges from a V-shaped channel. The tip of the filler rod is placed in the channel and both it and the adjacent area of sheet are heated with a stream of hot gas produced by a flame or electrically heated welding-gun. Compressed air is suitable for PVC but for polyethylene an inert gas such as nitrogen must be used. Welding guns are also available which incorporate a welding rod feed (Fig. 21.14).

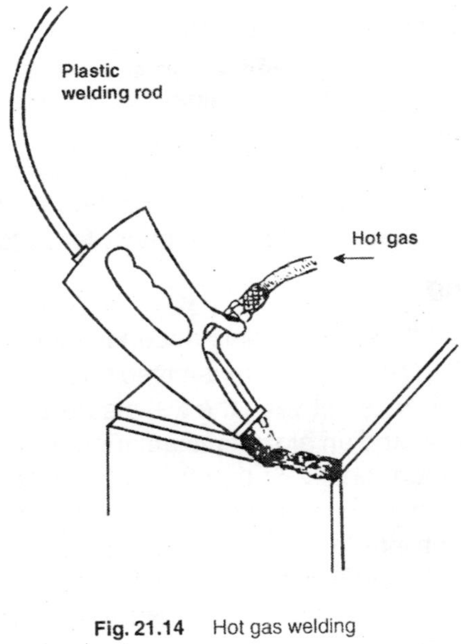

Fig. 21.14 Hot gas welding

Heated Tool Welding

In this process, a heated tool (usually of metal) is used to bring the plastic surfaces to the required temperature. An example of this type of welding is the polyfusion process for joining plastic pipes by means of injection molded couplings. The polyfusion tool is shaped so that one side of it fits into the coupling while the other fits over the pipe. The tool is heated in a flame and then used to soften the inside wall of the coupling and the outside wall of the pipe. The pipe and couplings are fitted together and allowed to cool.

Friction Welding

A particularly good example of friction welding is spin-welding which may be used for joining two rods or two injection molded halves of a bottle. One piece is fixed in a chuck which is then rotated at high speed. The matching piece is held against it until frictional heat causes the polymer to flow. The chuck is stopped, and the two pieced allowed to cool under pressure. There are limitations to this method in as much as the cross sections of the two pieces to be welded must be either circular or ring-shaped. The advantage of spin-welding when making a bottle is that the two portions can be injection molded and thus have completely even wall thickness. The technique has been used for aerosol bottles where an even wall thickness is important because of the high internal pressures when filled.

In spin-welding, any excess melt is forced from between the two mating surfaces in the form of a thin flash. This should be kept to a minimum especially in the case of hollow containers where internal flash cannot be trimmed. If necessary, the joint can be designed so that the flash is retained within pockets or undercuts, or is forced to the outside diameter where it can be trimmed. Spin-welding is usually confined to the joining of similar materials as using dissimilar materials normally leads to low strength joints.

Ultrasonic Welding

The process of ultrasonic welding depends on the vibratory energy of an ultrasonic head, or horn, being transmitted through two pieces of plastic in contact. At the interface between the two pieces this mechanical energy is converted into heat and an almost instantaneous weld is produced. The principle of the method, briefly, is that the vibratory energy from the horn radiates outward from the horn tip and is transmitted through the plastic as a wave motion. At the interface of the two components there may possibly be some reflection of energy but this should be small because of the joint is under pressure due to the force applied at the horn. Most of the energy, therefore, passes through to the lower piece of plastic. The energy is then reflected by the anvil on which the plastic is resting and sets the mating plastics surfaces vibrating against each other. Because of the high frequencies involved, the two surfaces are literally hammered together and the mechanical energy of motion is transformed into heat which melts the mating surfaces of the plastics. The frequency of vibration is around 20,000 cycles/second (cps). A power supply is used to convert the standard 60 cps current into the 20,000 cps current required and this is then fed into a transducer which transforms electrical energy into mechanical vibration. A diagrammatic representation of the process is shown in Fig. 21.15.

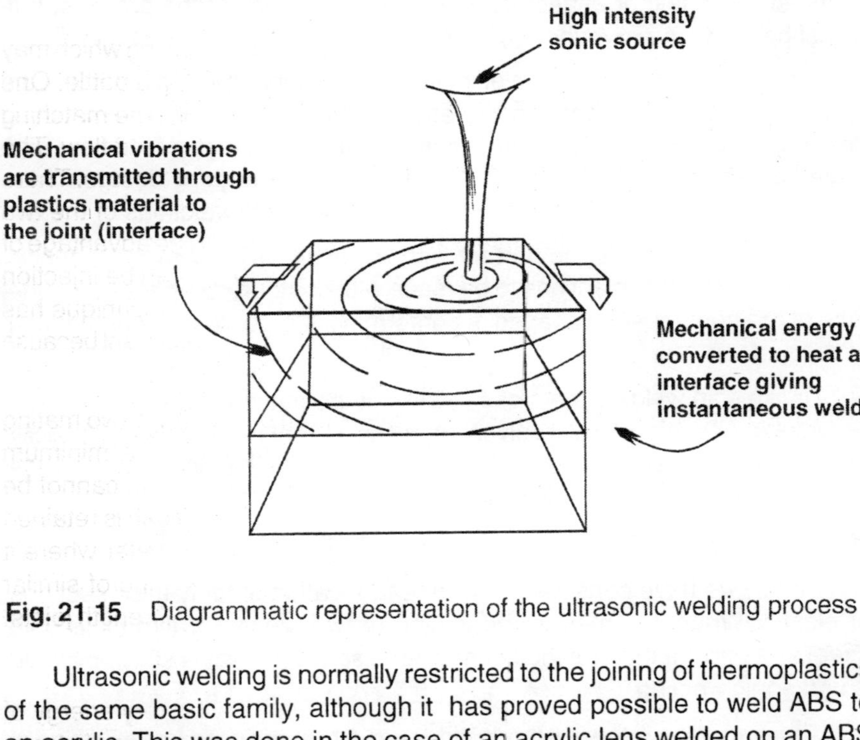

Fig. 21.15 Diagrammatic representation of the ultrasonic welding process

Ultrasonic welding is normally restricted to the joining of thermoplastics of the same basic family, although it has proved possible to weld ABS to an acrylic. This was done in the case of an acrylic lens welded on an ABS retaining ring in a car headlight reflector. Members of the styrene family of thermoplastics, such as basic and high impact polystyrenes, styrene acrylonitrile, and ABS give particularly good results with ultrasonic welding, as does polycarbonate. In general, rigid thermoplastics having a high modulus of elasticity and a low melting point are the ones which respond best of ultrasonic welding. The high modulus of elasticity is required to transmit the impressed vibrations while low melting points give rapid fusion of the surfaces. Materials with these characteristics give good welds even when the melting surfaces are remote from the horn tip. This is known as 'far field' sealing. Welds of up to 8 inches away from the horn have been made in polystyrene. Less rigid materials, such as polypropylene and high density polyethylene are unable to transmit the impressed vibrations over very large areas and good seals are made only in immediate vicinity of the horn tip. Such seals are known as 'near field' seals. Table 21.1 shows the results obtained by ultrasonic sealing with a range of plastic materials.

The presence of fillers of reinforcements also affects the weld. Some fillers, such as talc or asbestos, reduce the efficiency of the process, but glassfibers can improve the ability of the material to weld ultrasonically.

Another factor affecting the efficiency of ultrasonic welding is the design of the joint. The important consideration is that a small area of contact is desirable in order to concentrate the impressed energy and so allow rapid development of a melt. Fig. 21.16 shows various joint designs with comments on their likely performance using ultrasonic welding.

Horn design is also important and must be tailored to the specific application. When contact has to be made with contoured surfaces then the face of the horn must be shaped in conformity, in order to prevent marking of the surface.

Unlike spin welding the cross section of the mating surfaces need not be circular. Advantages over solvent or adhesive joints include lack of toxicity of flammable solvents, cleanliness, and speed. Joining times usually range from 0.5-4 s but can be as low as 0.1 s.

Heat Sealing of Film

So far, we have considered only the fabrication of fairly thick sections of plastic. When it comes to the joining of two pieces of film or flexible sheet, the only method (of the ones so far discussed) that is still applicable is ultrasonic welding.

There are many other methods, however, which are used for the joining of film and the choice is dictated by the chemical nature of the plastic, the type of seal required, and economics. By far the largest proportion of the flexible sheet and film market is held by two plastics, namely, PVC and low-density polyethylene, so it is convenient to consider methods of sealing those. On the whole, completely different methods are used for polyethylene and PVC. PVC is difficult to heat seal by direct application of heat because it tends to degrade thermally at temperatures fairs close to its melting point although

Tabel 21.1

ULTRASONIC WELDING CHARACTERISTICS OF SOME THERMOPLASTICS

	Ultrasonic Welding Characteristics	
Material	Near Field	Far Field
ABS	Excellent	Good
Cellulose Acetate	Poor	Poor
Nylons	Good	Good
Polyacetals	Good	Good
Polycarbonates	Excellent	Excellent
Polyethylene		
Low-density	Good/Poor	Poor
High-density	Good	Good/Fair
Polypropylene	Fair	Poor
Polysulfone	Good	Good
Polystyrene		
General Purpose	Excellent	Excellent
High Impact	Excellent	Good/Poor
PVC		
Rigid	Fair	Poor
Flexible	Poor	Poor

stabilizers have been developed which help in this respect. On the other hand, PVC is a material with a relatively high power factor so that appreciable heat is generated when a high frequency current is passed through it. PVC sheet, then, is generally welded by high frequency current heating. In general, frequencies of around 50-80 Mc/s are used with outputs of up to about 25 KW. For very thin materials it is essential to use the higher end of the frequency range and to lower voltage is high enough to break down the insulation resistance of the material. In other words, since a given current produces a given amount of heat, it is safer to obtain this current by using a high frequency but a low voltage in order to operate below the flashpoint.

One advantage of high frequency welding is that shaped welds are easily produced by using appropriately shaped electodes. A typical application is the encapsulation of expensive and delicate parts for automobile and aero engines. These are placed in a vacuum formed sheet of transparent, rigid PVC and a corrosion inhibitor added. A similar molded sheet is added on top and a weld made which is shaped to the component, thus giving a transparent, rigid, hermetically sealed pack which provides perfect protection.

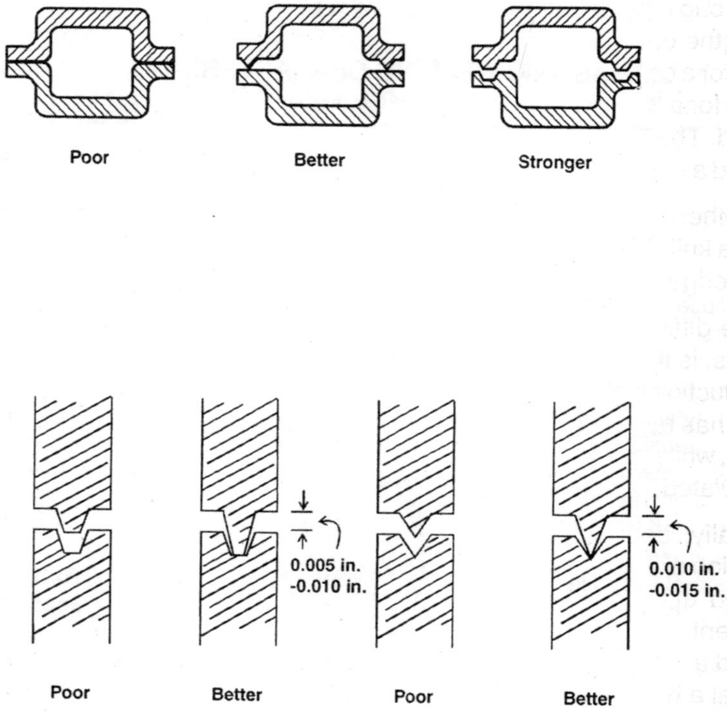

Fig. 21.16 Ultrasonic weld designs

Another advantage of high frequency welding is the ease with which the weld can be be made through a liquid. This is made use of in the manufacture of shampoo sachets where a completely filled cushion-type sachet is required.

The power factor of low-density polyethylene is much lower and high frequency welding cannot be used. The application of heated metal jaws to two layers of film is not suitble, either, because polyethylene sticks to hot metal surfaces. The heated jaws have to be coated, therefore, and PTFE or a silicone rubber are commonly used. Another snag with the straightforward use of heated jaws is that the seals are obviously weak until the polyethylene has cooled and if the seal is removed from the jaws in a molten condition, then there is a danger of rupturing the seal. One method of overcoming , this is the 'impulse sealer'. The sealing jaws are of very light construction. Usually of resistance wire covered with PTFE, and are electrically heated. Because of their small heat capacity, they cool quickly when the current is switched off. The sequence in, say, sealing a polythene bag, is as follows.

The bag is placed between the jaws and the jaws are closed. The jaws are heated (the current is usually activated by the pressure of the jaws when closed) for a certain time, the current is switched off but the bag is retained by the jaws for a few seconds, to cool. The jaws are opened and the bag is then removed. The heating and cooling time are usually preset with a sequence timer and a lamp lights when the heating cycle is in operation.

Another method, widely used in automatic bag making, is to use a hot wire as a knife so that a seal is made on the trailing edge of one bag and the leading edge of the next bag, while at the same time separating them.

One difficulty when sealing heavy duty polyethylene sacks for, say fertilizers, is the contamination of the mating surfaces by dust. This makes the production of strong seals by conventional methods rather difficult and a method has been developed which utilises a blast of hot air along the top of the sack, while the edges are held firmly together. Dust particles are completely encapsulated by molten polyethylene and do not effect the heat seat strength.

Finally, both polyethylene and PVC films can be welded with the application of infrared radiation. The efficiency depends on the temperature achieved at the junction of the two pieces of film and this is, in turn, dependent, on the amount of radiation absorbed by the material part being reflected and part passing through. Maximum absorption for most plastics occurs at a wavelength of three microns and this corresponds to a surface temperature of 700°C.

In the case of thin films, the rate of temperature rise and the final temperature are dependent on the backing material on which lies the welding area. An appreciable amount of the incident radiation passes through the film and heats the backing pad with consequent heating of the plastic film thus giving a better weld. Best results are obtained with compressed lamp black.

Heat Sealing of Closures

Although the power factor of polyethylene is too low to enable the method of high frequency heating to be used directly for heat sealing, an adaptation has been used for welding a disc-type closure onto a blown polyethylene bottle. The aperture to the bottle is circular and has ridge which fits into an annular space in the closure. Inside this annular space a metal ring is fitted. The completed assembly is then passed through a high frequency field, the metal ring heats up and melts the plastic in the vicinity, thus forming a completely tamper-proof seal.

SINTER CASTING

Sinter casting processes utilise powdered plastics rather than granules. There are basically two main methods.

Engel Process

In this process an open-ended mold is completely filled with powder and is then placed in an oven for a predetermined time. The heat from the oven causes the powder to melt, from the mold wall inwards. The mold is removed from the oven and the excess powder discharged after which the mold is replaced in the oven to complete the fusion. The wall thickness and final weight of the molding are determined by the length of the heating cycle and this is determined by experiment.

The process is simple and cheap (both capital and mold costs are low) but only open articles can be manufactured. Applications include rowing dinghies, tanks, and open end drums.

Rotational Casting

In this process the mold is loaded with a measured quantity of powder and is then rotated about two different axes inside an oven. The powder melts and flows over the inside of the mold. When all the powder has melted and is adhering to the inside surface of the mold the cooling cycle is commenced. Rotation of the mold is continued until the molding can be removed without distortion occurring. A multistation machine is shown in Fig. 21.17.

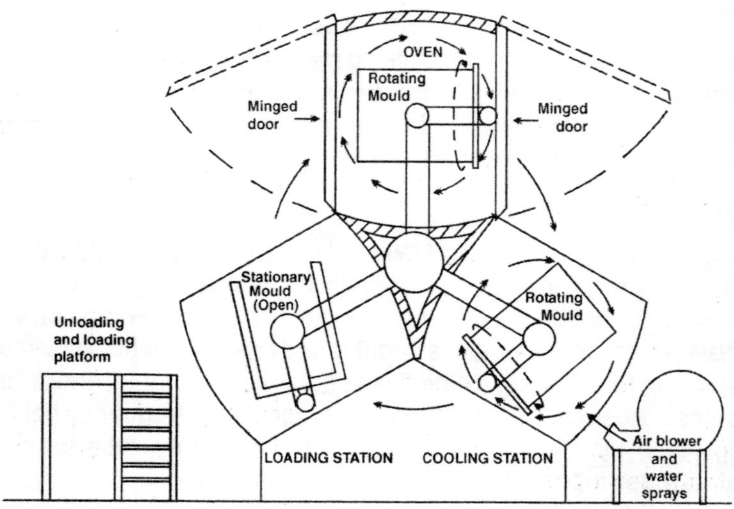

Fig. 21.17 Rotational casting

Molds for rorational casting can be light construction as high pressure are not used. The molds are rotated at fairly low speeds, just sufficient to ensure good flow of the molten polymer. Both open and closed hollow products can be made by this process and because of the low pressures used, molded-in stresses are absent.

SOLID PHASE FORMING

This heading refers to a group of thermoplastic processing techniques where the material is shaped while it is in the solid, rather than the melt phase. The phrase 'solid phase forming' is a more accurate description of these processes than 'cold forming', which is often used, because the plastic is heated, albeit to a temperature below its melting point.

One of the advantages of solid phase forming, in general, is a reduction in molding cycle times. With injection molding or thermoforming, for example, the plastic is heated to well above its melting point in order that it held until sufficiently cool to be removed from the mold without distortion. Plastic are poor conductors of heat so that this part of the cycle is often time consuming, especially where thick sections are involved. In solid phase forming the heat content of the molding is much less and cooling times are greatly reduced. Equipment costs may also be less.

Physical properties of the finished molding can also be improved using solid phase forming technique. The inherent strength of the molding may be increased because of the relatively cold working involved, while there are also less strain in the molding because of the absence of orientation, which is always present in melt forming techniques due to material flow.

Another factor is that higher molecular weight materials can be used because molecular weight choice is not constrained by the need for low viscosities to aid flow through the mold. Many physical properties are improved with increasing molecular weight, so that solid phase forming can produce stronger moldings.

The four main processes are Press forging, Rubber Pad Forming, Stretch Forming, and Solid Phase Pressure Forming.

Press Forging

In pressure forging a solid billet is squeezed between a pair of mated molds. One variation on this technique is shown in Fig. 21.18 where two shaped punches mate within a common die ring, rather than directly with each other. Advantages of press forging include simply-made, inexpensive tools and ease of removed of the finished molding.

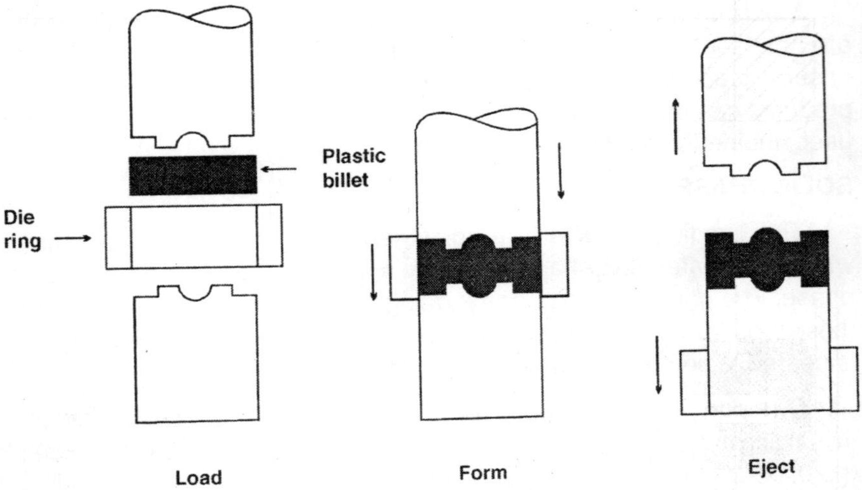

Fig. 21.18 The press forging process

In the system shown, the die ring is placed round the lower punch and the preheated billet placed inside the ring. The upper punch is brought down into the ring and pressure is then applied via simple compression press. The time taken to deform the billet varies from about ten to twenty seconds and the upper punch is then raised and the die ring is pulled down over the lower punch. The forged part is then easily removed.

The pressure required for forging rises rapidly as the part thickness decreases and too high a pressure produces poor quality moldings. Optimum pressures are of the order of two to four tons per square inch of projected area and this more or less limits the minimum thickness of press forging to about 0.125 in.

The technique of press forging is particularly suitable for the production of pump impellers, gear wheels, large diameter valve handwheels, industrial trolley wheels, and pipe flanges,

Rubber Pad Forming

Matched die stamping, as practiced with metal is one of the fastest of all forming operation but when tried with plastics spring-back usually occurs thus preventing good mold reproduction. However, a similar technique known as rubber pad forming can be adapted to plastics with excellent results. In this process a solid block of rubber is substituted for one half of the matched die sets (Fig. 21.19).

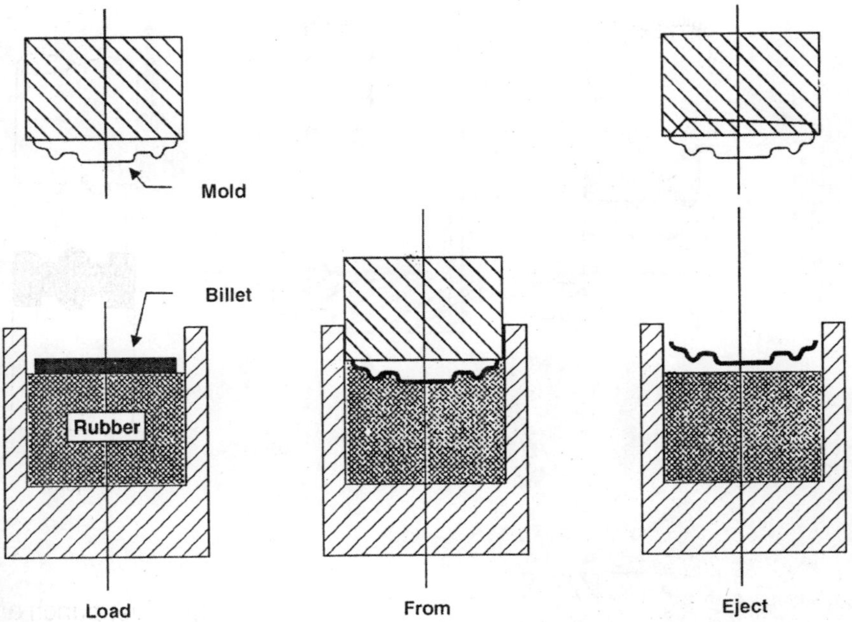

Fig. 21.19 The rubber pad forming process

The rubber block is placed within a metal cylinder, closed at the bottom end, and placed on the lower platen of the press. To the upper platen is mounted and steel plate which can be in the form of either a male or female mold. Plastics sheet is then placed on the rubber and the press closed using pressures of around 1000 pounds per square inch of rubber surface. The mold pushes the sheet into the rubber which, being easily deformed, wraps the plastics sheet around the mold. Dwell times are of the order of 10 to 15 seconds (to eliminate spring back) as compared with practically zero in the case of metals. Best results are obtained by preheating the sheet to within about 10°C of its melting point. Parts already made commercially by this process include a snow shovel, trays, and display items such as enables. In general, wall sections are fairly thick (above 0.1 inch) and draws are shallow (about two inches maximum).

Stretch Forming

In this process a preheated disc of plastic is placed in a split mold, the disc fitting into a recess at the top of the mold. The disc is then champed into position and a punch descends, stretching the plastics disc into the

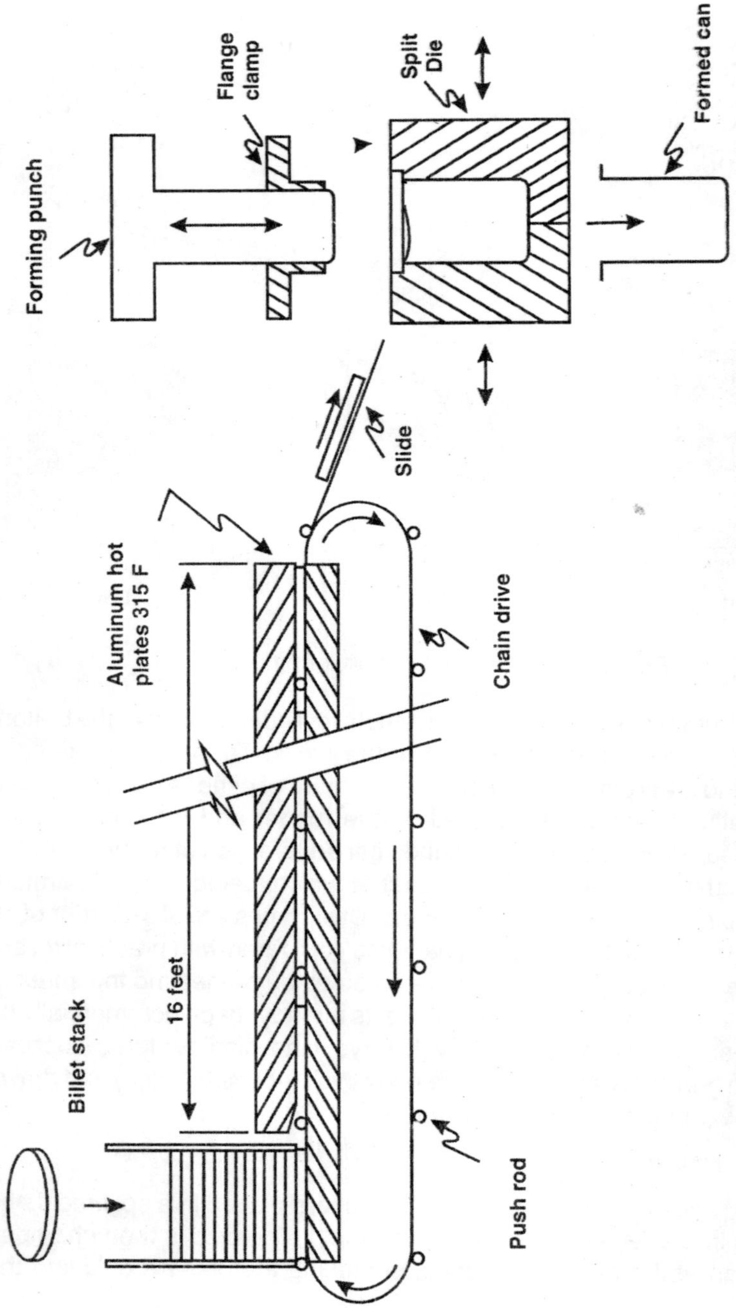

Fig. 21.20 Stretch-forming machine-design rate is 900 quart cans per hour

shape of the mold. Although the disc is heated the temperature is kept below the crystalline melting point of the plastic, so that the cooling cycle is low. Forming under these conditions also improves the clarity of the finished article, in the cae of polypropylene, giving results superior of those obtained by injection molding. The proces is particularly suited to open and containers such as quart oil cans and is shown diagrammatically in Fig. 21.20.

Solid Phase Pressure Forming (SPPF)

This process was developed mainly for polypropylne. Normal pressure forming (see Chapter 19) is a well established process for polystyrene, PVC, etc. but propylene is at a disadvantage in this area because polypropylene sheet is difficult to control at conventional pressure forming temperatures and cooling times are longer than for polystyrene and PVC. The SPPF process effectively overcomes these processing difficulties by carrying out the forming at temperature below the crystalline melting point of polypropylene. At such temperature cooling times are reduced and overall cycle times similar to those of PVC and high impact polystyrene can be attained. An additional advantage of the process is that, as with stretch forming, the clarity of the resultant moldings is significantly improved. The main field of application is expected to be packaging because other low cost polymers capable of giving clear containers (e.g. PVC and basic polystyrene) have appreciably lower softening points than that of polypropylene and cannot be used for products requiring hot filling. Also, because the polypropylene is not heated to very high temperatures in the SPPF process the containers so formed are free from odor and taint thus making them very suitable for food containers.

Only minor modifications to standard pressure forming equipment are required. Tool design is slightly more complex than for polystyrene and hence tools are more expensive but are still much cheaper than for injection molding.

22

Physical and Chemical Testing of Plastics

The testing of plastics is generally carried out for the same reasons as apply to the testing of other materials, namely, to determine their suitability for a particular application, for quality control purposes or to obtain a better understanding of their behaviour under various conditions. It is also necessary for the manufacturer of a new material to be able to measure its performance with relation to other materials and thus be in a position to assess the market likely to be available to him.

Physical Testing

The physical testing of plastics must be standarized if the comparison of physical data from two or more different sources is to have any meaning. The results of physical tests carried out on a material often depend on the ambient conditions of temperature and humidity, the size, shape and method of preparation of the test pieces, and the technique of measurement employed. Much of the early measurement of plastics properties utilised methods of test which had been developed for testing metals, textiles or wood. These were often unsatisfactory because of the difference in behaviour of the newer materials and it was not until some understanding has been obtained of the nature of plastics, and of their behaviour under conditions of stress at various temperature, that real progress was made in standarizing test methods.

The main organisations dealing with the standardization of test methods for plastics are, in Great Britain, the British Standards Institutions (B.S.I.) : In America, the American Society for Testing Materials (A.S.T.M.) and in Germany, The Deutsche Normenausschuss (D.N.A.). The latter organisation issues its standards under the initials D.I.N. (Deutsche Industrie Normen).

Reference to some of the most important of the standard methods evolved by the above organisations will made in the text out it cannot be emphasised too strongly that for information on any particular test method, the appropriate publication should be consulted.

Unfortunately, the provision of a standard test method does not mean that there is likely to be univeral agreement on the interpretation of the test results, and there are still many controversial points connected with physical testing. In addition to the interpretation of the results of various test methods, difficulties are often encountered when the results of tests are used to assess the likely performance of a molded or extruded article in practice.

In general, in physical testing of plastics can be classified as follows :

(a) Dimmensional
(b) Thermal
(c) Mechanical
(d) Electrical
(e) Optical

Before discussing the physical testing of plastics in more detail, however, the following points, which affect testing results, should be noted.

1. CONDITIONING

Many of the properties of plastics vary according to the ambient temperature of humidity or both it is essential, therefore, to condition samples before testing and carry out tests under standard conditions. The effect of temperature is obvious in the case of thermoplastics, properties such as yield stress, for example, decreasing as the temperature rises towards the softening point of the plastic.

The effect of humidity can be a factor with certain plastics such as nylon and cellulose acetate. In conditions of high humidity, water is absorbed, with consequent impairment of physical and electrical properties, although these are restored to thier original values when excess moisture is removed. Conditioning procedures are laid down in ASTM. D.618-61.

2. RATE OF TESTING

Because of long-chain structure of thermoplastics, their mechanical properties are time dependent. This is well illustrated by their behaviour under tensile stress. At very slow speeds the molecules can readily disentangle, and the measured tensile strength depends mainly on the magnitude of the weakest intermolecular. At faster speeds there is little time for disentanglement or slipping and the breaking point does not occur until the strongest intermolecular forces have been overcome. It is difficult, therefore, to compare tensile test data from different sources unless the rate of clamp separation is standardised.

3. METHOD OF FABRICATION OF TEST SPECIMEN

The method of fabricating test specimens can sometimes have an effect on the magnitude of the test properties. Orientation during fabrication and rate of cooling (affecting spherulite size in crystalline polymers) can both vary according to the type of fabrication used and both can effect the test results. In connection with the above factors, and where relevant, a standard specification for testing a particular material usually lays down the method of preparing and conditioning a sample before test. The number of test specimens is also stated in the relevant material specification but it may sometimes be desirable to alter this if a statistical approach is to be made.

(a) Dimensional Tests

One of the commonest dimensional test is the measurement of density or specific gravity, and it is usually based on archimedes principle, i.e., the apparent loss in weight on immersion in water. Though basically simple, the preparation of the sample, in the case of thermoplastics, has to be carefully controlled because the density of a polymer depends on its thermal history. An annealing process is, therefore, carried out in order that all specimens undergo the same heat treatment.

Density is usually quoted in grams per cubic centimeter and is thus numerically the same as specific gravity, which is defined as the weight of a given sample of material compared with the weight of an equal volume of water at the same temperature.

For film samples a different approach is necessary. One method utilises a density gradient column as described in ASTM D. 1505-60T or BS 2782 Part 5: 1970. A density gradient column consists of a mixture of two fluids of different densities, the proportions of which change uniformly from the top to the bottom of the column.

The liquids are chosen for their densities but must also be without any effect on the film samples. Ethanol-water and methanol water mixtures are often used, especially for measuring the density of polyethylene films. A density gradient column is prepared as follows. Both component liquids are degassed by boiling and are then mixed in the proportions required to give compositions with the densities desired for the two extremes of the column. These are then placed in separate flasks. The flask containing the lighter mixture is fitted with a capillary tube outlet which runs to bottom of the column. This flask is then stirred and connected to the flask with the heavier mixtures. The density of the liquid in the first flask thus increases linearly with time and so the flask is gradually filled with a liquid having a linear change of density.

A series of calibrated glass floats covering the range of densities required is then placed in the column. Film samples are cut and then immersed for half a minute in e.g. ethanol of methanol, and then placed in the column by means of tweezers, taking care not to introduce air bubbles. After three hours measurements are taken of the heights of the floating samples and the calibrated markers against their respective densities. The heights of the markers are then plotted against their respective densities and the best fitting curve is drawn through the points. The densities of the film samples are then read off against this curve. Finished samples are removed in intervals using a slowly moving wire gauze basket.

BS.2782 : Part 5 : 1970 gives an alternative method, using a series of liquids of different densities made up in stoppered glass vessels, kept at a constant temperature of 23°C. Film samples, prepared as before, are placed in each of the vessel and observations made as to whether the sample sinks or floats. The denest material in which the film sinks and the least dense in which it floats is observed. The density of the film then lies between the densities of the two liquids.

Other dimensional tests include Bulk Density (of granular molding material) ASTM. D. 792-50, and Apparent Powder Density, B.S. 771: 1959.

(b) Thermal Tests

The important thermal properties of plastics are thermal conductivity coefficient of linear expansion, specific heat, softening point, heat distortion temperature, and mold shrinkage.

Both softening-point tests and heat distortion tests are designed to give the plastic user some idea of safe temperature in use but care must be taken when using the results of such tests because of the possibility of creep under continuous loads, and in the case of some polymers, an accelerated breakdown of the material due to heat. When the latter possibility exists, stabilisers are added by the plastics manufacturer and the efficiency of various stabilising systems is usually measured in terms of 'oven life'. The test is a simple one which involves placing samples of the plastic material in an air oven at 135°C and examining them at intervals.

Some of the more important softening-point or heat-distortion tests are given below:

Vicat Softening Point. This test is defined in BS. 2782: Pt 1:1956 and DIN. 57302. Basically, it is a penetration type test, and results are expressed as the temperature at which an indentation of one mm occurs when the sepcimen is subjected to pressure by a standard needle (1 mm^2 surface area) under a standard load (usually 1 kg). The temperature is raised steadily during the test at a rate of 50°C/H.

Deflection Softening Point. This test is also described in B.S. 2782 : Pt. 1. The test specimen is clamped at one end and loaded at the other with a 20 kilogram weight. The assembly is then placed in an oil-bath and the temperature raised at a rate of 1°C C/min. The temperatures at which angular deflections of 30°C and 60°C occur are noted and reported.

Heat-Distortion Temperature. This is an American standard method (ASTM. D 648-56) that gives some idea of the immediate tendency of deform under very low conditions of stress. Samples 5 in long, ½ in wide and 1/8 in. and ½ in. thick are supported ½ in. from each end and loaded at the center to give fiber stresses of either 66 or 264 lb/in^2. The temperature is then slowly increased (2°C/min) until the center of the sample is deflected to the extent of 0.01 in. The temperature at which this deflection occurs at the two different loadings is then reported.

This test has certain limitations and the data obtained may be used to predict the behaviour of plastics at elevated temperatures only in applications in which the factors of fiber stress, temperature, method of loading, and duration of stress are similar to those used to this test.

Cold-Bend and Cold-Flex Temperature. Amont the tests concerned with the effects of temperature on the behaviour of plastics, B.S. 2782: Pt 1: 1956 describes the two mentioned above. The former consists of winding a standard test piece round a mandrel 5 mm in diameter at a rate of winding min. Tests are carried out at various temperature differing by 5°C. The Cold -Bend Temperature is defined as the lowest temperature at which all the samples pass the test.

The Cold-Flex temperature (also known as the Clash and Berg test) measures the temperature at which a standard angular deflection (200°) to obtained when subjected to a standard torque.

Flammability

Any assessment of the burning characteristics of a plastics involves the measurement of two distinct properties, namely, the temperature at which it ignition. The flame resistance of plastics is general is good and a large quantity of heat is usually necessary for ingnition. On an average, their rate of burning is also slow. However, there is still a wide range of behaviour from that of cellulose nitrate, which ignites readily and burns with a fierce flame, so that of some of the thermosets which are very difficult to ignite and which char rather than burn.

As with other materials the presence of oxygen is necessary for combustion to occur but this may be present in the molecules, as is the case with cellulose nitrate. Generally, however, the rate of burning depends on the amount of ambient oxygen. Experiments show that polypropylene, for example, ceases to burn when the oxygen content drops to 16 per cents, unless the temperature of the flame is very high.

With the ever-increasing use of plastics in high temperature environments or where there is the occasional risk of flame, the question of flammability of plastics has become extremely important.

The various degrees of resistance to flame can be classified as follows :

(i) Nonburning - the ability of a material to resist combustion.

(ii) Fire resistance - the ability of a material to stop the penetration of flame.

(iii) Flame retardancy - the ability of a material to retard the penetration of flame.

(iv) Self extinguishing - this means that the material ceases to burn as soon as the source of the flame is removed.

One of the application for plastics where the degree of fire resistance is important is in constructional work. In the U.S.A. a flame spread rating system has been developed on the basis of Underwriters' Laboratory Inc., Steiner 'Tunnel Test'. This test was designed to measure the speed of fire along materials exposed in the interiors of buildings. The burning chamber is a long, ventilated, horizontal tunnel in which there are controlled gas flames. The test is carried out on specimens of the material 20 in. wide. and 25 feet long. The rate of flame spread is based on a scale in which asbestos board is zero and red oak is 100. Based on this scale, the ASTM. E. 84 standard considers any material with a flame spread of 0 to 25, to be noncumbustible; from 25-50, fire retardnt; from 50-75, slow burning, and from 75-200, cumbustible. anything over 200 is highly combustible.

Another standard is ASTM. D.635-63 which uses specimens measuring ½ in X 5 in. X 'thickness as normally supplied'. For thermoplastics this thickness is usually in the range of 0.05 in to 0.25 in. Each specimen has a line scribed one inch from each end. It is then clamped at one end on a ring stand so that the lingitudial axis is horizontal, and the transverse axis is inclined 45° to the horizontal. A piece of 20-mesh Bunsen burner gauze is clamped horizontally 3/8 in. below the specimen. A bunsen, burner, placed so that the flame contacts the end of the specimen, is hend there for 30 s and then removed. If the specimen fails to ignite, the burner is replaced for another 30 s. The extent of burning is measured along the lower edge of the specimen.

A specimen that doesn't ignite is classed as 'nonburning by this test'. If it does burn, it is times until it stops or until the four inch mark is reached. A specimen which burns up to the four-inch marks is classed as 'burning by this test' and the rate of burning reported as in./min.

If the specimen does not continue burning to the four-inch mark, it is classed as 'self-extinguished by this test', and the length of the burned portion is reported as the material's as the material's 'extent of burning'.

(c) Mechanical Tests

The mechanical properties of plastics vary over a wide range from soft and flexible to hard and brittle, with many intermediate combinations. It is, therefore, difficult in some cases to lay down standard tests for the measurement of a particular property which is suitable for all plastics. Some of the more important tests are described below.

Tensile Properties. Two figures may be quoted for the tensile strength, namely, ultimate tensile strength and yield strength. The relation between these two, and their relative importance, can best be seen by reference to a stress-strain curve. Other properties which can be measured from a stress strain curve are elongation (at yield and break) and the modulus of elasticity. The latter is given by the ratio of stress divided by strain and is a measure of the stiffness. It should be noted that the term 'strain' is used here in the strict sense of the increase in length per unit length or , more usually, as a percentage. Stress/strain curves of polymers have been divided into five classes by T.S. Carswell and H.K. as on (Modern Plastics, Juen 1944) and an example of each is shown below in Fig. 22.1.

The curves shown in Fig. 30.1 represent the following types of polymer properties.

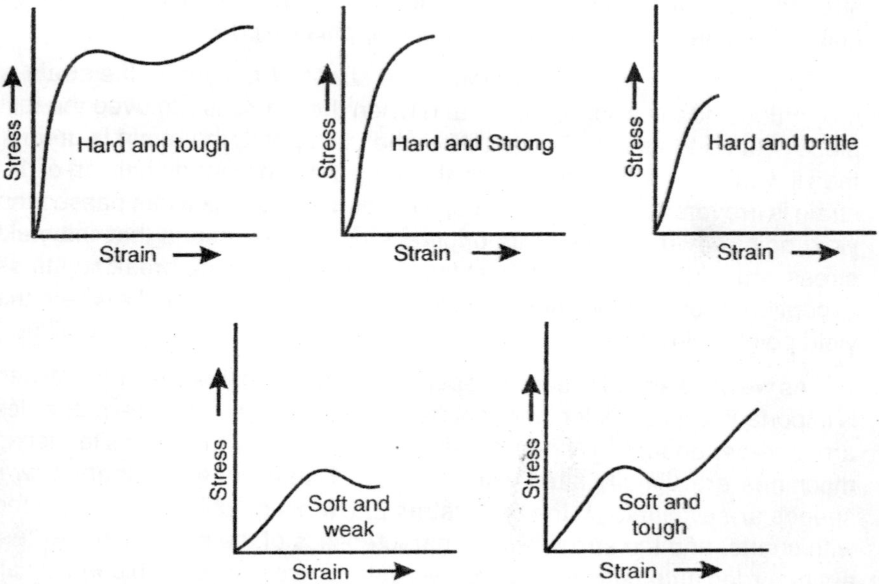

Fig. 22.1 Typical stress/strain curves obtained with polymers

(1) *Hard and Tough.* Such materials have a high modulus of elasticity, yield stress, ultimate tensile strength and elongation at break. Typical materials showing such a curve are cellulose acetate and certain of the polyamides.

(ii) *Hard and strong.* The type of material has a high modulus of elasticity, yield stress, and ultimate tensile strength and a moderate elongation at break. Typical polymers giving this type of curve are rigid PVC formulations and polystyrene copolymers.

(iii) *Hard and Brittle.* The hard, brittle type of material is characterised by a high modulus of elasticity and ultimate tensile strength. There is no well-defined yield point and the elongation at break is low. Typical example are polystyrene, polymethyl methacrylate and certain phenol formaldehyde polymers.

(iv) *Soft and weak.* Such materials have a low modulus of elasticity yield stress, and ultimate tensile strength. The elongation at break is moderate. This type of behaviour is characteristics of soft polymer gels.

(v) *Soft and tough.* These materials have a low modulus of elasticity and yield point. The elongation at break is high and the ultimate tensile strength is usually much higher than the yield stress. Examples of materials giving the type of curve include rubber and plasticized PVC.

During the straight line portion of the stress/strain curve, the strain is proportional to the applied stress and when the stress is removed the test piece returns to its initial length. After the yield point, the strain is greater than it would be for a linear relationship, and the nonproportional part of the strain is irreversible. In other words, a molded article which has passed the yield point never returns to its original shape. This means that the yield stress is usually a more practical figure than the ultimate breaking stress except in cases such as those classed above as hard and brittle where the yield point is ill-defined.

As we have already seen, the speed at which the test-pieces are stressed is important, especially for thermoplastics, since there mechanical properties are time-dependent by virtue of their long-chain structure. Tensile testing machines are usually fitted with multispeed gear boxes so that several speeds are available on the one instrument. Most machines are also fitted with charts, and the stress/strain characteristics of the material under test are recorded automatically. Computer systems are also available which can be used in conjunction with tensile testers to give printouts and visual display unit read-outs.

One effect of the dependence of mechanical properties is that where long term stresses are concerned a plastics article may rupture or deform by an unacceptable amount at a constant stress well below its short term yield stress. This continuous deformation with time, under constant load, is known as creep. It is also encountered with metal though to a lesser extent. Creep can be studied by applying a constant load to a standard test specimen and measuring the srain at intervals over long period of time. The resultant figures for strain are plotted against time when a curve of the type shown in Fig. 22.2 is obtained. When the load is first applied there is an immediate elastic deformation, OA, which can be calculated from Young's Modulus for the material.

During the initial stage the strain increases at a diminishing rate (section A-B on the curve) and this is followed by secondary screep (from B-C) where the strain increases at a constant rate. The final stage is known as tertiary creep and here the strain increases at an accelerating rate. This stage is often accompanied by crazing or cracking of the test specimen.

In general, thermosets have lower creep values than have thermoplastics, because of their network structure. Thermoplastics exhibits

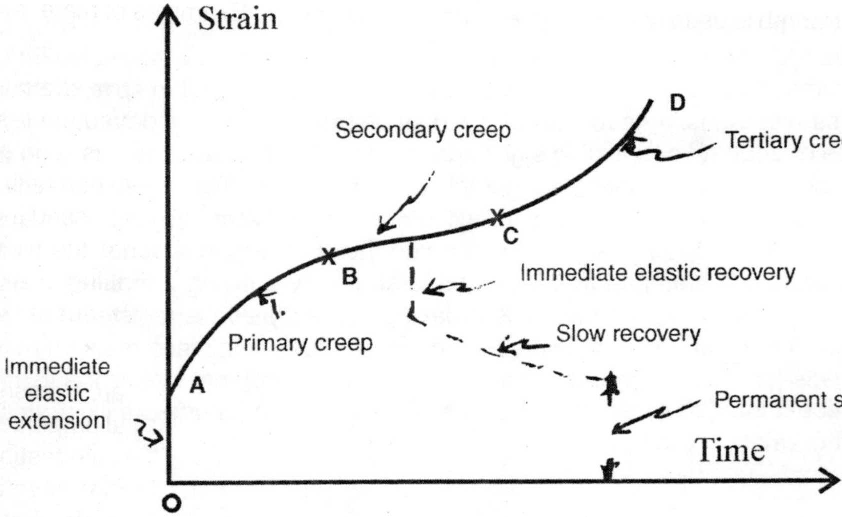

Fig. 22.2 Typical creep curve for thermoplastics

varying resistance to creep. Those materials with high intermolecular forces (e.g., hydrogen bonding) exhibit low creep, as do those thermoplastics that the below their glass transition points under the conditions to test.

In practice, it often happens that the load is applied intermittently and for limited periods. When the load is removed there is an immediate elastic recovery followed by a further slow recovery. The test specimen does not return to its original dimensions, there being is residual strain or permanent set (Fig. 22.2).

For meaningful results which can be used in practice it is necessary to obtain a series of curves at different stress levels and at different test temperatures. Any increase in temperature increases the mangitude of the creep because of the reduction in the attractive forces between molecules.

Flexural Strength. Flexural strength is sometimes referred to as cross breaking strength or the modulus of rupture. It is the maximum stress developed in the surface of a prescribed shaped test-piece when supported near the end loaded at the center until failure occurs. Flexural strength is quoted as lb/in^2. or kg/cm^2. Fuller details of the test are given in ASTM. D. 790-63or B.S. 2782: Pt. 3.

Impact strength. The measurement of impact strength is probably the most controversial topic in the subject of plastics testing and many criticism have been levelled against the methods used for its measurement. Unfortunately, no one has yet put forward a universally accepted substitute, so that tests such as Izod or Charpy continue to be used in spite of their disadvantages. Indeed, although it may be true that the test data obtained are of doubtful quantiative significance, they are still useful as providing a basis of estimating the relative shock resistance (or, perhaps more correctly, the relative resistance to stress concentration) of the various plastics. Impact testing has become standardised round the Izod test, in which a notched specimen is clamped in a vice and is struck by a swing pendulum. The energy lost by the pendulum is breaking the test-piece is registered on a dial. A popular variation is the Charpy in which the test piece rests on two anvils (one on either side of the notch) and the pendulum strikes the test - piece immediately behind the notch. The different methods are illustrated diagramatically in Fig. 22.3.

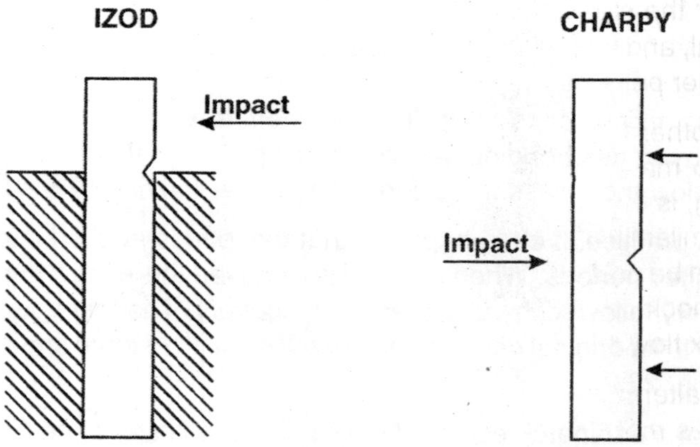

Fig. 33.3 Diagrammatic representation of Izod and Charpy impact tests

For thermosetting materials, the test specimens are compression molded, while thermoplastic materials may be either injection molded or compression molded. The method of preparing thermoplastic specimens must be started when test results are published, since this has effect on the magnitude of the result.

One fault of the Izod test is that the energy lost by the pendulum consists, not of the energy needed to break the specimen, but of a complex figure consisting of the energy necessary to produce the first crack, the energy necessary to shear off the top half of the specimen, and the kinetic energy in the broken-off piece which is manifested in its flight through the air after impact. Only the first figure represents the true impact strength and it has been maintained by some researches that the remaining two factors can contribute to errors as high as 100 per cent of the true impact strength.

Another criticism of the Izod test is that the results are influenced by the 'notch sensitivity' of the material under test. It will be seen that, although the Charpy test overcomes the first objections to some extent, it is still liable to errors due to 'notch sensitivity.'

A low Izod value may indicate notch sensitivity but may straightforwardly by due to an intrinsically low impact strength. One way of determining whether a material is indeed notch sensitive is to carry out a series of impact tests with pieces having different notch tip radii. The Izod values are than plotted on a logarithmic scale against the notch tip radius on a linear scale. The steeper the slope of the curve, the greater is the notch sensitivity of the material, and this gives a clear warning to the designer to avoid sharp radii and other points of the stress concentration in the molding.

Another factor to be considered when looking at Izod test figures for any two materials, with a view of assessing their relative usefulness for molding, is the question of stresses in the final article. Two polymers may have similar Izod impact strength and yet behave very differently in practice. This can be due to differences in flow. The one with the highest flow gives a more shock-resistant article, especially if the molding has thin walls or has complex flow paths.

An alternative method of measuring impact strength, and one which simulates more closely the knocks likely to be encountered in practice,is the Falling Weight Impact test (BS 2782). There are many variations in respect of the test pieces used but basically the test consists of dropping a known weight from a known height on to the rest piece. The estimated level at which 50 per cent of the samples are likely to fall is normally reported in this test.

Test pieces which have often been used for this test include compression molded sheets and injection molded shallow dishes. The sheets are usually mounted on a circular support and the point of impact in applied at the center. Injection molded dishes (having their 'gate' at the center of the dish) are inverted and located so that the point of impact is 20 millimeters away from the center, the area near the gate being one of the recognised weak spots of an injection molding.

Finally, mention should be made of the impact strength of film. This is usually measured by the 'falling dart' method, in which a dart with a hemispherical end-piece is dropped from a known height onto a center of a circular piece of film. Adjustment of the weight of the dart can be made by means of detachable weights which fit over the shaft of the dart. The weight which causes fracture of 50 per cent of the specimens is determined, and this, multiplied by the height from which the dart is dropped, is known as the impact strength.

Hardness. This is complex property to measure and expresses the resistance to deformation. It is usually measured by some modification of the methods used in the testing of metals, the relevant standards being ASTM.D.785-62: ASTM.D. 676-55T: and B.S. 903 (for rubber). The basis of these tests in measurement of the indentation caused by the application of a steel ball or diamond cone under a standard load. Different sizes of penetrators are used for the different ranges of hardness, and there are given letters which are quoted at the same time as the hardness number. Standard methods are Rockwell Hardness and Shore D for rigid materials; B.S. softness number and Shore A for plasticised materials, rubber, and rubber like materials.

(d) Electrical Tests

Several electrical tests are in use, the properties measured being related to the particular end-uses in view but the most important are described briefly below. Full details of British Standard electrical tests are to be found in B.S. 2782: Pt 2: 1957. When American tests are also of interest, they are mentioned below.

Arc Resistance. This is a sometimes known as resistance to tracking and is defined as the ability of the material to withstand the discharge, across its surface, of a specified voltage. Details of the American test are given in ASTM.D. 495-61.

Volume Resistivity. In this test a potential gradient is applied to two electrodes separated by the material under test. The volume resistivity is then defined as the ratio of the potential gradient applied to the electrode, to the current flowing in this material. The electrical resistance, R, along the length l, of a conductor having cross sectional area, a, (normal to land the direction of the current) can be expressed as $R=\frac{xl}{a}$, where x is the volume resistivity, i.e., $x=\frac{aR}{l}$.

If *l* and *a* are made equal to unity then the volume resistivity may be regarded as the electrical resistance between the opposite faces of a cube of unit dimensions (see ASTM. D257-61).

Power Factor. When an alternating current is applied to two conductors separated by a dielectric (in this case a plastics material) the dielectric undergoes alternating disturbances and energy is dissipated as heat. The power factor of a material used as the dielectric is the ratio of the energy losses in the capacitor to the total energy passing through the material.

A high power factor, therefore, means that a great deal of heat is liberated and the material is a poor insulator for high-frequency conductors.

Thermosetting materials usually have high power factors, as have highly polar thermoplastics such as PVC. The heat generated in PVC by the application of a high-frequency alternating current is sufficient to melt the PVC and this is the basis of high-frequency welding techniques for PVC sheeting. Polyethylene and polystyrene, on the other hand, have very low power factors and are, therefore, used in radio-frequency insulation. The American tests are covered in ASTM.D. 150-64T.

Dielectric Constant. This property is sometimes referred to as 'permittivity' and is the ratio of the capacity of a condencer using the material under test to that of a similar condenser with air as dielectric. This test is also covered by ASTM.D. 150-64T.

Dielectric Strength. This is a measure of the applied voltage necessary to cause breakdown of the material under test and is specified as the maximum voltage which the material specimen can withstand for one minute, divided by the thickness of the specimen (measured in thousandths of an inch). Details of the American test are given in ASTM.D. 149-64.

(e) Optical Tests.

These include measurements of gloss (important for film and especially for surface coatings), haze, light transmission, 'see-through' clarity (all of which are important for film), and refractive index (important for plastics used for lenses or light diffusers).

Gloss. The property of a film or coating which we know as 'gloss' is a measure of a ability of the film or reflect light as a mirror and it is determined by measuring the percentage of light, incident at an angle to the surface of the specimen, but is reflected from the surface of the specimen at the same angle.

Haze. The term 'haze' when applied to film is a measure of the 'milkiness' of a film and may be caused by imperfections within the film or on its surface. It is measured by first passing a beam of light through the film on to the highly reflecting inner surface of a sphere, all the transmitted light being gathered into a photoelectric cell. The sphere is then shifted sligtly in such a manner that the beam of light now falls on an extension of the sphere consisting of a matte black surface that thus absorbs all light travelling along the path of the beam. Light which is scattered in a forward directions by more than a small angle is still collected by the highly reflecting internal surface of the sphere into the photoelectric cell. The ratio of the second reading of the photoelectric cell to the first reading is a measure of the haze.

Light Transmission. This is an indication of the proportion of incident light passed by the film, whether or not the light is scattered on passing through. It is measured by determining the intensity of a light source, with and without the sample of film in between are light source and the measuring apparatus (a photoelectric cell), and is expressed as a percentage.

'See-through' Clarity. This property is a measure of the amount of distortion of a distant object when looking as it through a sample film. A standard wire mesh grid is illuminated and viewed through the film under test. The result is compared with a standard set of photographs taken through film with a range of clarities normally encountered in the material under test.

Refractive Index. This can be measured by any of the standard methods used for determining the refractive index of glass.

Measurement of Flow

The flow properties of any plastics material, whether thermosetting or thermoplastic, are of extremely great importance to the manipulator. They are, unfortunately, also difficult to measure. In the case of thermosets, the Cup Flow Test (B.S. 771) is probably the best known. This is carried out in a thimble-shaped and enough molding powder is introduced to produce a complete molding plus a flash of 2 to 2½g. The powder is placed into the mold (which is kept at a temperature of 163°C±1°C) by means of a scoop, and a pressure of 10 ± 0.5 tons applied to the mold. The number of seconds which elapse between the first indication of pressure on the gage and the moment that the flash ceases to move is taken as the 'time of flow'. A great deal of experience is necessary in assessing the results of the test and relating them to the flow properties of the molding powder used.

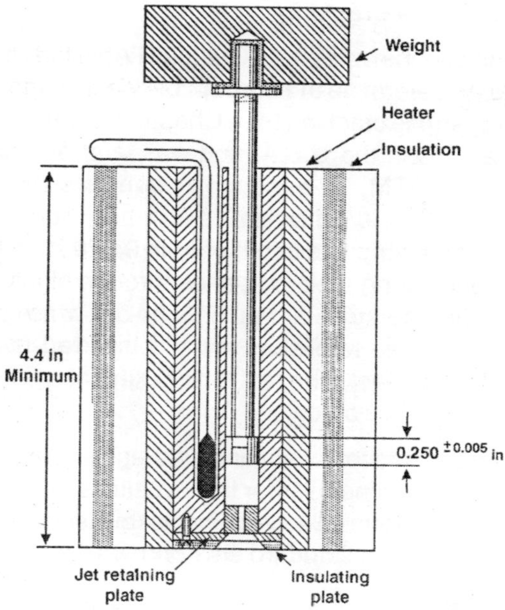

Fig.22.4 Apparatus for determining Melt Flow Index

When dealing with thermoplastics, the point of interest is usually the behaviour of the molten polymer when caused to pass through an orifice under pressure. The Melt flow indexer has already been mentioned (Chapter 9). This was developed by Imperial Chemical Industries Limited and has since been modified and accpeted as a British Standard (B.S. 2782: Pt 1) while a similar method has also been adopted as an ASTM procedure. A schematic diagram of the Melt Indexer is shown in Fig. 22.4.

The apparatus is operated at 19°C for low and high density polyethylene, and 230°C for polypropylene. The extruder piston operates under dead-weight conditions and the pressure is quite low (43.2 lb/in^2). The Melt flow index is the weight of material (in grams) extruded in ten minutes. Although the results are very useful as a method of grading, there are limitations due to the fact that the flow of molten polymers is non-Newtonian. In consequence, it is impossible to forecast the flow behaviour under the high shear conditions obtained in commercial injection molding machines and extruders from the results of tests using the very much lower shear forces in the Melt Indexer. Other equipment is available, however, which can simulate the conditions existing in an extruder or injection molding machine (see photograph).

Environmental Stress Cracking

Before turning to the section on Chemical Analysis, mention should be made of the test to determine the susceptibility of a sample of polyethylene to environmental stress cracking (see Chapter 9). The test was devised by the Bell Laboratories in the U.S.A. and was later adopted as a tentative standard by the ASTM. In essence it consists of taking a strip fo polyethylene, 1½ in long X ½ in. wide X 1/8 in. thick and scoring a line along the central ¾ in of the strip to a depth of from 0.020 in. to 0.025 in. The test strips are then bent along their long axes through 180°C, with the scored line on the outside. The strips are put in a holder which maintains them in the bent position and the whole assembly is inserted into a test tube filled with the product under test. The test tube is kept at a temperature of 50°C and the time to failure is noted.

The test can be used for evaluating different grades of polyethylene (by using a standard enviornment) or for the investigation of the stress cracking properties of different chemical environments (by using a polyethylene grade with a known reaction to a standard environment).

Chemical Analysis

Polymer materials are complex in nature, and the commercial material often contain various additive such as stabilisers, plasticisers, and fillers which sometimes appareciably alter the physical properties of the product. All this makes it very difficult to device some simple scheme for their identification. The general chemical inertness of most plastics, which makes them so attractive to the user, also presents difficulties when attempting to analyse them.

Using the fairly simple tests described in this chapter it should be possible to obtain a reasonably accurate idea of the nature of the plastic under examination, although conclusive results can be obtained in very instance. It is found that experience plays very important part in this kind of investigation and a careful note should be made of any relevant information available, such as the method of fabrication employed and the enduse to which the material was put.

Only a few years ago it used to be possible for an expert to determine not only the nature but often the previous history of a polymer merely by the use of a penknife and a match. The extremely wide range of materials now on the market means that the kind of examintion is no longer a substitute for chemical analysis, but as a preliminary exercise, it is, nevertheless, valuable, and some of these nonchemical tests are described.

A preliminary visual examination should always be made and a note taken off the color of the material. This can, in some instances, act as an initial 'sorting-out' operation. Most plastics can be obtained in a wide range of color effects excepts for polytetrafluorethylene which has as blueywhite mottled appearance. Among the thermosets, a light pastal shade rules out the possibility of its being phenol-formaldehyde, as moldings in this material are invariable dark in color. A completely transparent molding might be polystyrene or styrene copolymer, an acrylic such as polymethylmethacrylate or a polycarbonate. A visual examination will usually tell which method of processing has been employed, i.e., compression molding, injection molding, vacuum-forming, etc. and certain deductions might also be made from this observation. An injection-molded article, for instance, would not be cellulose nitrate since the material is not amenable to injection molding because of fire risk. The vacuum-formed article is very likely to be cellulose acetate, PVC, or high impact polystyrene.

In addition to their obviously different behaviour towards heat, thermosets and thermoplastics also differ in their behaviour when cut with a sharp knife. A thermoplastic cuts cleanly and may have quite a 'soft' cut, while a thermosetting material tends to chip when cut. Certain plastics have other distinctive properties which give a very good guide in subsequent testing. Polystyrene, for instance, has a characteristics metallic 'ring' when dropped on a hard surface, polyvinyl alcohol is water-soluble, polypropylene and the polyethylenes have a density less than unity and hence float on water, and PTFE and the polyethylenes have a waxy fee.

As an illustration of how even the little information geaned from the above tests can prove informative, we can take the case of a screw- top bottle closure. If this is black brown in color it is most likely made from phenol formaldehyde (especially if it is of simple design, i.e. designed for a cheap product) but an examination could be made for a 'gate' mark to check that it is not an injection molding. This can also be checked by the application of heat and observing the behaviour when cut. If white or colored and a thermoset, it is most likely urea-formaldehyde, as there is very little advantage to be gained from using thermoplastic material, it can be checked to see if it is polystyrene by dropping on a hard surface. If there is no metallic ring, it could be cellulose acetate, polypropylene, or polyethylene and the behaviour when dropped in water divides cellulose acetate from the other two. A further subdivision may be attempted by noting the reaction when the material is scratched with fingemail. Polypropylene normally has a high gloss and does not scratch, high-density polyethylene is also glossy but scratches to a certain degree, while low-density polyethylene is not usually glossy and scratches easily. Rigidity also acts as a guide between high-density and low-density polyethylenes. It is thus possible to obtain a fairly close, idea, in this particular case, from a knowledge of the materials normally used for various end-uses, plus a few simple tests. It must be admitted that the case taken was simpler then many, nevertheless a knowledge of the plastics used for particular is a help and can be gained by experience.

Certain polymers, such as PVC, PTFE and polychloroprene can be recognised by the results of a simple technique, well-known to chemists as the Beilstein Test. A freshly cleaned piece of copper wire is heated in a bunsen flame and placed in contact with the material under test, some of which will then adhere to the wire. The wire is returned to the flame, where the production of a green-colored flame is an indication that a halogen (i.e. fluorine, chlorine, bromine, or iodine) is present. The test should be taken only as an initial guide, since many compounding ingredients also contain halogens so that misleading results can sometimes be obtained.

Much information can be obtained by heating the material on a clean spatula or penknife. The following information should be noted: ease of ignition, whether self-extinguishing or not, the nature and color of the flame and the odor of any volatiles. These may all be an indication of the nature of the polymer. Some results of flame tests are given in Table 22.1.

A simple method for identifying the more common plastics is given in Table 22.2, although it is again emphasised that experience is often needed before a definite interpretation of some of these tests can be given. Once an indication has been obtained, confirmatory tests can be carried out. Some common confirmatory tests are given below :

CONFIRMATORY TESTS (20 MILLIGRAM SAMPLES ARE SUITABLE FOR THE FOLLOWING TESTS)

(a) Casein

The sample is dissolved in concentrated nitric acid by boiling for about five minutes. After cooling, excess ammonium hydroxide is added. Development of an orange coloration usually indicates a protein containing a phenyl group, but this reaction may also occur with phenolics.

(b) Cellulose, Cellulose Esters and Ethers

The sample is shaken with 1 cm^3 of water contanining two drops of B-haphthol in chloroform (10 per cent w/v). At least 2 cm^3 concentrated sulfuric acid is then carefully added down the side of the test tube so as to form a lower layer. A violet ring is obtained at the interface and, on shaking, a purple solution is obtained. Cellulose nitrate does not give a positive reaction.

(c) Cellulose Nitrate

The sample is first dessolved in 1 cm^3 of acetone, and a solution of diphenylamine in concentrated sulfuric acid (5 per cent w/v) is then added a drop at a time. A dark blue coloration is first produced but the addition of excess diphenylamine solution destroys this to give a brown coloration.

Table 22.1

CHARACTERISTIC FLAMES PRODUCED BY BURNING POLYMERS

(i) No Flame is produced	*A.* Sample deforms slowly	1. CAUTION-FUMES MAY BE TOXIC Sample not attacked by nitric acid/hydrochloric acid mixture FLUOROCARBON 2. Hydrochloric acid odor POLY-VINYLIDENE CHLORIDE or PVC or COPOLYMER
	B. Retains shape odor of formaldehyde	1. No after-odor UREA FORMALDEHYDE 2. Strong fish-like odor MELAMINE FORMALDEHYDE 3. Odor of phenol only PHENOL FORMALDEHYDE (Inorganic Filler)
(ii) Burns but extinguishes itself when flame is removed	A. Yellow flame ignites with difficulty	1. Acid odor, green spurts PVC 2. Odor of phenol mixed with that of burning wool PHENOL-FORMALDEHYDE (Organic Filler) 3. Sparks from flame. Acetic acid odor resembling vinegar CELLULOSE ACETATE (Flame Resistent Grade)
	B. Blue flame with yellow tip. Melts and drips. Odor of burn-ing wool o r hair. Slowly	

Table 22.1

(iii) Continues to burn after removal from flame. Note color of flame during first second of burning	*A.* Burns slowly and self-extin-guishing. Black smoke and sharp acrid odor similar to P/F. Sample may be light colored EPOXY	
	B. Burns rapidly, intense white flame CELLULOSE NITRATE	
	C. Slow burning. Clear smokeless blue flame. Odor of formal-dehyde ACETAL	
	D. Blue flame, yel-low at top	1. Fruit odor. ACRYLIC 2. Melts and drips. Drippings may burn. (a) Odor of rancid butter CELLULOSE ACETATE/ BUTYRATE (b) Pungent odor CELLULOSE PROPIONATE 3. Melts and drops. Drippings burn. Paraffin odor similar to burning candle. Floats on water (a) POLYETHYLENE (Low-density flex-ible, high-density more rigid) (b) POLYPROPYLENE (Rigidity similar to HD/Pe but more difficult to scratch with fingernail)
	E. Yellow flame	1. Melts and drips. Drippings may burn. Acetic odor CELLULOSE ACETATE 2. Dense smoke. Flakes of soot in air (a) Odor of illuminating gas POLYSTYRENE (b) Acetic odor POLYVINYL ACETATE 3. Flame blue at edges (a) Melts and drips. Drippings may burn. Odor burnt sugar ETHYL CELLULOSE (b) Cracks and breaks

Table 22.2

SIMPLE TESTS FOR THE IDENTIFICATION OF THE MORE COMMON PLASTICS

<table>
<tr><td colspan="10">Cut thin sliver from edge of sample</td></tr>
<tr><td colspan="3">Powdery chips formed-indicates thermosetting resin.
HOLD SAMPLE IN LIGHTED MATCH, AND SMELL RESULTANT VAPORS</td><td colspan="7">Smooth sliver obtained indicates thermoplastic. Confirm by application of a hot metal wire or rod to the sample. Melting indicates thermoplastic
DROP SAMPLE ON TO HARD SURFACE</td></tr>
<tr><td rowspan="2">'Carbolic,' smell. Sample usually black or brown in color. Burns but extinguishes itself when flame removed = PHENOL-FORMALDEHYDE</td><td colspan="2" rowspan="2">Fishy smell-sample usually brightly colored (or white)
UREA-FORMALDEHYDE or MELAMINE-FORMALDEHYDE
TRY SCUFFING THE SAMPLE WITH FINGERNAIL</td><td colspan="2" rowspan="2">'Metallic' ring indicates presence of Styrene polymer
BURN A SMALL SAMPLE AND BLOW OUT FLAME. SMELL RESULTANT SMOKE</td><td colspan="5">Absence of 'metallic' ring precludes polystyrene (unless foamed) but may be high-impact polystyrene (containing butadiene rubber)
PLACE SAMPLE IN WATER (+ A FEW DROPS OFDETERGENT)</td></tr>
<tr><td rowspan="2">If sample floats, indicates a polyolefin (unless it is foamed polystyrene - easily identifiable)
(a) SCRATCH SAMPLE WITH FINGERNAIL
(b) BURN USING LIGHTED MATCH</td><td colspan="4">If sample sinks: not a polyolefin.
BURN SMALL SAMPLE. NOT EASE OF IGNITION AND TYPE OF FLAME</td></tr>
<tr><td>Self-extinguishing, black smoke. Sharp acrid odor Sample lighter in color than P.F.= EPOXIDE</td><td>Scuffing = UREA FORMALDEHYDE</td><td>No scuffing = MELAMINE FORMALDEHYDE</td><td>Characteris tic smell of styrene = POLYSTYRENE</td><td>Smell of styrene and bitter smell = STYRENE-ACRYLONITRILE</td><td>Burns with a clear flame, BLOW OUT FLAME AND RESULTANT VAPOR</td><td colspan="3">difficult to ignite and is self-extinguishing
NOTE COLOR OF FLAME</td></tr>
<tr><td></td><td colspan="2">The above test is not easy to interpret without experience, and definite conclusions can be drawn only from chemical tests</td><td></td><td>As above and smell of rubber = ABS copolymer</td><td>Glossy surface, does not scratch. Burns with smell of paraffin wax = POLYPROPYLENE</td><td>Fruity odor = ACRYLIC (PROBABLY POLYMETHYLMETHACRYLATE)</td><td>Flame has greenish tinge, REMOVE SAMPLE FROM FLAME AND SMELL VAPOR</td><td>Flame is yellow REMOVE SAMPLE FROM FLAME. SMELL VAPOR</td><td>Little flame. De composition of material but no charring. A cellular structure is developed be fore decomposition = POLYCARBONATE</td></tr>
<tr><td></td><td colspan="2"></td><td></td><td></td><td>Glossy surface, slight scratching. Burns and drips like sealing wax = HD/PE</td><td>Smell as for burning paper = CELLULOSE ACETATE OR CELLULOSE PROPIONATE (NO SIMPLE CONFIRMATORY TEST AVAILABLE)</td><td>Acrid smell. Material soft and flexible = PLASTICIZED PVC (IF FILM, COULD BE VINYLIDENE CHLORIDE COPOLYMER</td><td>Smell of formaldehyde = POLYACETAL</td><td></td></tr>
<tr><td></td><td colspan="2"></td><td></td><td></td><td>Not particularly glossy, scratches easily. Burns with smell of paraffin wax = LD/PE</td><td>Smell of rancid butter = CELLULOSE ACETATE BUTYRATE</td><td>Acrid smell. Material nonflexible (and glossy if in form of molding = RIGID PVC OR PVC/PVA COPOLYMER</td><td>Indefinite smell. Sample has slippery feel
PRESS COLD METAL POINT TO HEATED SURFACE THEN WITHDRAW IT</td><td></td></tr>
<tr><td></td><td colspan="2"></td><td></td><td></td><td></td><td></td><td></td><td>Threads easily formed = NYLON</td><td></td></tr>
</table>

(d) Nylon

The sample is burnt and a filter paper, moistened with a saturated solution of o-nitrobenzaldehyde in 2N sodium hydroxide solution, is placed in the fumes. Nylon 66 gives a deep mauve coloration. Other nylons give no color.

(e) Polyethylene Terephthalate

The sample is burn and a filter paper moistened with a saturated solution of o-nitrobgenzaldehyde in 2N soldium hydroxide solution, is placed in the fumes. A green-blue color is produced.

(f) Epoxide (based on diphenylolpropane)

The sample is dissolved in 1 cm^3 of concentrated sulfuric acid and 1 cm^3 of concentrated nitric acid is then added. This solution is then poured into 100 cm^3 of N sodium hydroxide solution. A bright orange red coloration is produced.

(g) Phenol-Formaldehyde

A reagent (known as Million's reagent) is first prepared by dissolving 10 g of mercury in 10 g of fuming nitric acid, without heating, and is then diluted with 20 cm^3 of water. Any precipitate which form is filtered off and discharged.

The sample is then boiled with 1 cm^3 of this reagent for 2 minutes. A red coloration is produced. This coloration is also given by some proteins.

(h) Urea and Melamine Formaldehyde

Reflux the sample with dilute sulfuric or phosphoric acid, and divide the solution in two parts.

(i) Add one drops of a saturated solution of xanthydrol. A white precipitate indicates urea formaldehyde.

(ii) Add a saturated aqueous solution of picric acid. A bulky yellow precipitate indicates melamine formaldehyde.

(i) Phthalates and Phthalic Acid

The sample is heated with 0.1 g of pure phenol and a drop of concentrated sulfuric acid until the melt turns organge or brown in color. When cooled the mass is triturated with 2 cm^3 of water and is then filtered. The filtrate is made alkaline with 10 per cent aqueous sodium hydroxide, when the characteristics red color of phenolphthalein is produced.

If in the test above, the phenol is replaced by recorcinol a green fluorescence is produced.

(i) Polyvinyl Acetate

An iodine reagent is prepared by dissolving 0.1 g of iodine and 1 g of potassium iodide in a mixture of 10 cm^3 water and 10 cm^3 ethyl alcohol and then making up to 100 cm^3 with 2N hydrochloric acid.

When sample is covered with 0.5 cm^3 of the above reagant, the solid becomes stained a deep red. This effect is enhanced if 10 cm^3 of water is added.

(k) Polyvinyl Alcohol

One drop of the iodine reagent described above is added to 1 cm^3 of a 0.5 per cent aqueous solution of the sample, when a blue color should result. If no coloration is observed, then one drop of a saturated aqueous borax solution be added to the mixture, and the blue color should then appear.

Polyvinyl alcohol containing more than 10 per cent acetate group gives a red coloration in this test.

(i) Polyvinyl Chloride and Vinyl Chloride Copolymers

The sample is dissolved in 5 cm^3 pyridine by boiling and, while still hot, 0.5 cm^3 of a solution of sodium hydroxide in methyl alcohol (2 per cent w/v) is added. A brown coloration is produced and eventually a brown precipitate is formed.

(m) Polyvinylidene Chloride and Vinylidene Chloride Copolymers.

The sample is heated on a water bath with 5 cm^3 of morpholine. After about two minutes, the solvent turns dark reddish brown, while after about five minutes both solvent and polymer turn almost black.

(n) Shellac

This polymer is readily recognised from the characteristic odor of sealing wax obtained on burning. It is soluble in dilute alkalis such as ammonium hydroxide. When heated to 150°C the polymer is convered to an alcohol-insoluble, horn-like mass in 20 to 60 min.

(o) Silicone

The white ash remaining after burning the sample is soluble in hydrofluoric acid and leaves no residue when the solution is evaporated. The presence of silica as a filler will, of course, invalidate this test.

Should any doubt exist after carrying out the above tests, further chemical tests may be applied which will determine the presence or absence of certain elements such as nitrogen, the halogens, or sulfur. The basic of this scheme is the Lassigne Sodium Fusion Test. Initially, 0.1 to 0.5 g of the polymer are decomposed by heating with metallic sodium in an ignition tube. When the reaction has subsided, and while the tube is still red-hot, the tube is plunged into about 10 cm^3 of distilled water contained in a small mortar. Care is obviously needed in carrying out this operation, and the ignition tube should be kept with the open end facing away from the operator at all times. The ignition tube and contents are carefully ground under water with a pestle and the mixture filtered.

The filtrate is divided into five portions which are then examined as follows :

1. *Nitrogen.* A portion of the test solution is placed in a boiling tube with several drops of freshly prepared ferrous sulfate solution and brought to boiling. After cooling, the contents are acidified with dilute sulfuric acid and a drop of ferric chloride solution is added. The formation of a blue precipitate (Prussian Blue) indicates the presence of nitrogen in the polymer under examination.

2. *Sulfur.* A few drops of freshly prepared sodium nitroprusside solution are added to the test portion contained in a boiling tube. The formation of a violet color indicates the presence of sulfur.

3. *Chlorine or Bromine* : A portion of the test solution is placed in a boiling tube and acidified with dilute nitric acid and boiled for 2 to 3 minutes. A few drops of silver nitrate solution are then added. A white precipitate, solution in ammonia, indicates the presence of chlorine while a yellow precipitate, insoluble in ammonia, indicates the presence of bromine Flourine does not a give precipitate.

4. *Fluorine.* An aqueous solution of 0.1 per cent zirconium nitrate and 0.3 per cent alizarin S is prepared, and this is used to impregnate a filter paper, which is then dried. The filter paper is then moistened with 50 per cent acetic acid. The test sample is neutralised with dilute hydrochloric acid and one drop placed on the moistened filter paper. The red color of the filter paper turns yellow if fluorine is present.

5. *Phsophorus.* The test solution is acidified with dilute nitric acid and an excess of ammonium molybdate is added. The formation of a yellow crystalline precipitate indicates the presence of phosphorus.

If the results from all the tests described above are correlated, it is usually possible to make a positive identification. As a guide to using the results of Lassaigne Test Table 22.3 lists the elements in many of the polymer commercially available.

Table 22.3

ELEMENTS PRESENT IN CERTAIN POLYMERS

Elements	*Present in*
Chorine	Chlorinated rubber: rubber hydrochloride; PVC; polychloroprene; polyvinylidene choride; PTCFE; VC/VA copolymers; chlorinated polyether.
Nitrogen	Cellulose nitrate; polyamides; polyurethanes; polyacrylonitrile; epoxides; urea- and melamine-formaldehyde; phenol-formaldehyde (due to the presence of hexamine).
Sulfur	Rubbers polysulfides; polysulfones.
phosphorus	Due to the presence of additives such as phosphate plasticizers (which must be extracted).
Chlorine and nitrogen	Vinyl chloride-acrylonitrile.
Chlorine, nitrogen, phosphorus	Phosphonitrilic chloride.
Chlorine and sulfur	Chlorsulfonated polyethylene (Hypalon).
Fluorine	Fluorocarbons.
Nitrogen, phosphorus, sulfur.	Cascin.

117. MANUFACTURE OF TIN CONTAINERS
118. MANUFACTURE OF STORAGE TANKS, PRESSURE VESSELS, HEAT EXCHANGERS
119. MARK II HAND PUMPS
120. MARUTI WORKSHOP CUM - SERVICE STATION
121. MECHANICAL JACKS
122. METAL CUTTING DIE DESIGN
123. METAL CUTTING OF AND GRINDING WHEELS (ABBRASIVE CUTTING WHEELS)
124. METAL HOOKS & CLIPS
125. METAL SEPARATION (COPPER, TIN, LEAD) FROM SPENT WASH ACID
126. METALLIC RING JOINTS
127. METALLIC GASKET (SPIRAL WOUND)
128. MICROVEE & ABSOLUTE FILTER
129. MICROWAVE OVEN
130. MILD STEEL INGOTS
131. MINI STEEL PLANT
132. MODERN VEHICLE WORKSHOP
133. MOPED
134. M.S.HINGES
135. M.S.INGOT AND HR. STEEL STRUCTURALS
136. M.S.INGOT BY INDUCTION FURNACES
137. M.S.PIPES
138. M.S. WELDING ELECTRODE
139. MUFFLERS & SILENCERS FOR THREE WHEELERS
140. NAIL CUTTER WITH FILER & MANICURE
141. NICHROME WIRE
142. NICKEL LINED SCREENS
143. NON-FERROUS ALLOY ROLLING
144. NON-FERROUS FORGING
145. NON-FERROUS FOUNDRY
146. NON PRESSURE
147. INCANDESCENT LAMP
148. NUMBER COMBINATION LOCKS FOR LUGGAGES
149. NUTS & BOLTS
150. PAPER COATED ALUMINIUM AND COPPER WIRE
151. PETROMAX CONTAINER
152. PHOTO ETCHING OF STAINLESS STEEL PLATES
153. PIPE GALVANIZING PLANT
154. PISTON RING-AUTOMOBILE
155. PLANT PROTECTION EQUIPMENTS
156. PLATINUM LABORATORY APPARATUS
157. PRESSURE COOKER & ALUMINIUM UTENSILS
158. PRESSURE COOKER (ALUMINIUM)
159. PRESSURE DIE CASTING
160. PRINTED ALUMINIUM COLLAPSIBLE TUBES
161. PRINTED TIN CONTAINERS
162. PRINTING PRESS (CYLINDER MACHINE)
163. PUMPS FOR CHEMICAL INDUSTRY (SPECIAL)
164. RAILWAY SLEEPERS (M.S.)
165. RAZOR TWIN BLADE
166. R.C.C SPUN PIPES
167. RECONDITIONING OF M.S. DRUMS/BARRELS
168. RE-ROLLING COPPER AND BRASS SHEET AND RODS
169. RE-ROLLING MILLS
170. RESIN COATED SAND
171. RESIN CORED SOFT SOLDER WIRES
172. ROLLING MILL (BY INDUCTION FURNACE) & MANUFACTURE OF BARS, ANGLES, SQUARES, TUBES AND OTHERS
173. ROLLER BEARING & FORGING
174. ROLLING OF STAINLESS STEEL PATTA
175. RUBBER INSULATED PLIERS (HAND TOOLS)
176. RUBBING COMPOUND FOR AUTOMOBILES
177. SCIENTIFIC LABORATORY EQUIPMENTS
178. SCOOTER ASSEMBLING
179. SECONDARY LEAD EXTRAC -TION BY SCRAP BATTERY PLATES,PIPES & SHEET
180. SEAMLESS M.S. TUBES & PIPES
181. SELF TAPPING STEEL SCREW
182. SEWING NEEDLES
183. S.G. IRON & ALLOY STEEL
184. SHEET METAL PRODUCTS, (FERROUS/NON-FERROUS)
185. SHIP/MARINE CONTAINER
186. SHOCK ABSORBERS
187. SHOE EYELETS
188. SHOT AND GRITS BY AUTOMIZATION PROCESS
189. SHOVELS
190. SILICO MANGANESE ALLOYS
191. SILENCERS (MUFFLERS) EXHAUST & TAIL PIPE FOR ALL TYPES OF VEHICLES
192. SINTERED BEARING
193. SINTERED BUSHES
194. SINTERED METAL PRODUCTS
195. SOFT AND HARD FERRITES
196. SPANNERS
197. SPARK PLUGS
198. STEEL PLANT (ELECTRIC ARC FURNACE BASED- EAF)
199. SPHERIODAL GRAPHITE CAST IRON
200. SPRAY DRYER
201. STAINLESS STEEL HINGES
202. STAINLESS STEEL SHEET ROLLING TO PRODUCE STAINLESS STEEL UTENSILS
203. STAINLESS STEEL UTENSILS
204. STAPLE PINS,PAPER PIN, GEM CLIPS ETC.
205. STEEL CASTINGS
206. STEEL CHAIN
207. STEEL FOUNDRY
208. STEEL FURNITURES AND ELECTRICAL APPLIANCES
209. STEEL PLANT (MINI)
210. STEEL RODS AND COILS FROM SCRAPS
211. STEEL ROLLING MILL
212. STEEL STRIPS (COLD ROLLED) SILICON WITH GRAIN RIENTED FOR ELECTRIC USE
213. STEEL TRANSMISSION LINE TOWERS & ROLLING MILL TO PRODUCE STEEL SECTION
214. STEEL FURNITURES AND ELECTRICAL APPLIANCES
215. STEEL WIRE DRAWING AND GALVANIZING
216. STEEL WOOL
217. SUBMERGED ARC WELDED PIPES
218. SUBMERSIBLE PUMP MANUFACTURING
219. SUPER ENAMELLED COPPER WIRE
220. THREE WHEELERS
221. TIE-ROD ENDS
222. TIN CONTAINERS
223. TOOLROOM AND SHEET METAL PRODUCTS
224. TRACTOR TRAILERS
225. TRANSMISSION POWER FITTING
226. TUBULAR POLES
227. SUPER ENAMELLED COPPER WIRES
228. TUBULAR POLES FOR ELECTRICAL TRANSMISSION (BY FABRICATION PROCESS)
229. TUBULAR POLES OF M.S. & HIGH TENSILE STEEL
230. VACUUM CLEANERS
231. VACUUM FLASK (STAINLESS STEEL)
232. VALVES FOR REFRIGERA TION AND AIR-CONDITION
233. VEHICLE WELDING & PAINTING
234. VENETION BLIND
235. WASHING MACHINES (AUTOMATIC & COMPUTERISED)
236. WATER CONTROLLER (AUTOMATIC)
237. WATCH STRAPS/CHAINS/ BRACELETS/BELT BRASS & STAINLESS STEEL
238. WATER COOLERS
239. WELDED WIRE MESH
240. WELDING ELECTRODES
241. WICK STOVES
242. WIND MILL WINDOW FRAME (FERROUS & NON-FERROUS)
243. WRIST WATCH

359. DI ETHYL OXALATE
360. DI METHYL ORTHOPHTHALATE
361. DI-METHYL PHTHALATE
362. DICLOFENAC GEL
363. DIOCTYL PHTHALATE (DOP)
364. DI PHENYL GLYCERINE
365. DI PHENYL OXIDE
366. DINITRO-CHLORO BENZENE
367. DISTILLED WATER
368. DODECYL BENZENE SULPHONATE
369. DUSTLESS CHALK
370. EDTA & ITS SALTS
371. ELECTROLESS NICKEL PLATING ON PLASTICS
372. ENDOSULFAN
373. EPOXY RESIN BASED COMPOUND
374. ETHYL ACETATE
375. EHTYL ETHER
376. ETHYL ALCOHOL (POTABLE LIQUOR)
377. ETHYL HEXANOL
378. EXTRACTION OF ESSENTIAL OILS BY SUGAR CRITICAL FLUID (CARBON DIOXIDE) METHOD FROM FLOWERS, HERBAL & SPICES
379. FERRIC ALUM
380. FERRO CHROME LIGNO SULPHONATE
381. FERRO MANGANESE
382. FERRO SILICONE
383. FERRO VANADIUM FROM VANADIUM SLUDGE
384. FERROUS SILICATE
385. FERROUS SULPHATE
386. FERTILIZER FROM ANIMAL BLOOD & LEATHER WASTE
387. FLUORESCENT TUBE LIGHT POWDER
388. FOAMED PVC COMPOUNDING & ITS PRODUCTS
389. FORMALDEHYDE
390. FRACTIONAL DISTILLATION OF D.M.O (DEMENTHOLIZED OIL)
391. FRACTIONAL DISTILLATION OF ESSENTIAL OIL & MEDICINAL PLANT EXTRACT
392. FRICTION DUST (LIQUID & POWDER) FROM CNSL
393. FRUIT FLAVOURS
394. FURFURAL FROM RICE HUSK
395. GARLIC ACID
396. GASKET SHELLAC COMPOUND
397. GEAR OIL
398. GIBBERELLIC ACID
399. GLASS PUTTY
400. GLYCERINE
401. GOSSYPOL (POLY PHENOL) FROM COTTON SEED OIL
402. GUAR GUM POWDER
403. HAIR FIXER (HAIR GEL TYPE)
404. H - ACID
405. HENNA PASTE MAKING
406. HEPTAL DEHYDE
407. HIGH CARBON FERRO CHROME
408. HYDRATED CALCIUM SILICATE BRICK
409. HYDRATED LIME FROM SEA SHELL
410. HYDROCHLORIC ACID
411. HYDRO FLUORIC ACID
412. HYDROGEN PEROXIDE (BY AUTO-OXIDATION PROCESS)
413. ICE PACKS (SOLUTIONS TYPE, WHITE GEL TYPE, VIOLET SEMI SOLID POLYMER TYPE)
414. IMPROVING DROP POINT PARAFFIN WAX FROM 45-50°C TO 75-80°C
415. INDUSTRIAL ALCOHOL
416. INTEGERATED COMPLEX OF EASTER & ALLIED PRODUCTS (D.O.P, D.B.P, ETHYL ACETATE WIRE ENAMEL & CABLE JELLY)
417. IMFL (WHISKY) & COUNTRY LIQUOR
418. IRON OXIDE FOR MAKING FERITTE
419. IRON SULPHIDE
420. JUTE BATCHING OIL
421. KESH KALA TEL (HAIR DYE LOTION) (VASMOL 33, BLACK NITE TYPE)
422. L-LYSINE MONOHYDROCHLORIDE
423. LACTIC ACID FROM WHITE SUGAR BY FERMENTATION PROCESS
424. LDPE GRANULES FROM VIRGIN (LDPE RESIN)
425. LEAD EXTRACTION FROM BATTERY SCRAP
426. LEAD OXIDE (A) LEAD MONOXIDE (B) LEAD TETRA OXIDE (C) GREYLEAD OXIDE
427. LIQUID GLUCOSE & ITS BY PRODUCTS
428. LIQUID OXYGEN BOTTLING PLANT
429. LIQUID SHOE POLISH
430. LIQUID FLOOR POLISH
431. LUBE OIL VISCOSITY IMPROVED FOR P.P.G/P.E.G.
432. LUBRICANTS ASHLESS 100% COMBUSTION
433. MAGNESIUM CARBONATE AND MAGNESIUM BICARMONATE
434. MAGNESIUM HYDROXIDE POWDER
435. MAGNESIUM SILICATE
436. MAGNESIUM SULPHATE
437. MALACHITE GREEN
438. MALEIC ANHYDRIDE
439. MANGANESE SULPHATE
440. MANUFACTURING OF CARBON MONO-OXIDE WATER GAS
441. MENTHOL BOLD CRYSTALS FROM FLAKES
442. MENTHOL CRYSTAL & MENTHA OIL
443. MERCURIC OXIDE
444. METAL PRE-TREATMENT CHEMICALS
445. METHANE GAS BY SODIUM ACETATE & SODA LIME
446. METHYL ACETYL RICINOLATE
447. METOL
448. METOL FROM HYDROQUI-NONE & METHYLAMINE
449. MICANITE
450. MICRO NUTRIENT MIXTURE
451. MINERAL WATER
452. MINERAL WATER AND PET BOTTILNG PLANT
453. MINERAL WATER IN BOTTLES, GLASS AND POUCHES
454. MINI CEMENT PLANT (BY ROTARY KILN PROCESS)
455. MIXED FERTILIZER
456. MOSQUITO & FLIES REPELLENT AGARBATTI (INCENSE STICKS)
457. MONO CHLORO ACETIC ACID
458. MONOCROTOPHOS (TECHNICAL)
459. MOSQUITO COIL
460. MOSQUITO COIL & MAT
461. MOSQUITO MAT
462. MOTHER TINCTURE & BIO CHEMIC MEDICINES
463. NAPHTHALENE & PHENYL (INTEGRATED UNIT)
464. NATURAL MINERAL WATER BY REVERSE OSMOSIS PROCESS
465. NICKEL PLATING BRIGHTNER (PRIMARY OR CARRIER BRIGHTNER & SECONDARY BRIGHTNER)
466. NICKEL SULPHATE
467. NICOTINE FROM TOBACCO WASTE
468. NICOTINE SULPHATE FROM TOBACCO WASTE
469. NITRO BENZENE
470. NITRO CELLULOSE SANDING SEALER/LACQUER
471. NITRO MUSK
472. NITROGEN & OXYGEN GAS PLANT
473. NON-IONIC SURFACTANT (WETTING AGENT)
474. NO-CARB PASTE
475. OCTANOL
476. ORTHO NITRO PHENOL
477. OXALIC ACID FROM MOLASSES
478. OXALIC ACID FROMRICE HUSK
479. OXALIC ACID FROM TREE BARK
470. OXALIC ACID FROM WASTE VEGETABLES
471. OXYGEN GAS PLANT
472. OXYGEN GAS PLANT (AIR SEPERATION METHOD)
473. PARA-AMINO BENZOIC ACID
474. PARA-AMINO PHENOL
475. PARA TOLUENE SULPHONIC ACID
476. PECTIN FROM RAW PAPAYA
477. PERFUME (LEMON & OTHERS)

478. PESTICIDE PREPARATION USING NEEM FRUIT & SEEDS (MARGOSA)
479. PET BOTTLES FROM PRE-FORM
480. PET PREFORM FROM RESIN FOR PET BOTTLES
481. PETROLEUM JELLY
482. PHENOL
483. PHENYL
484. PHENYL (BLACK) IN LIQUID FORM
485. PHTHALIC ANHYDRIDE
486. PHOSPHORIC ACID FROM ROCK PHOSPHATE
487. PHOSPHORUS BY CHEMICAL PROCESS
488. PHOTO EMULSION FOR ROTARY SCREEN PRINTING
489. PHTHALOCYANINE BLUE
480. PIGMENT EMULSION FOR TEXTILE
481. PIGMENT GUM
482. PLANT GROWTH REAGEN BASED CHLOROTHYL TRIMETHYL AMMONIUM CHLORIDE
483. PLANT HARMONES BASED ON 2,4-DICHLORPHENOXY ACENTIC ACID & NAPHTHALENE
484. PLASTICINE (MODELLING CLAY)
485. PLASTIC WASTE REPROCESSING
486. PLASTER OF PARIS BANDAGES
487. POLYESTER RESIN (G.P. GRADE LAMINATE GRADE, ELECTRICAL GRADE)
488. POLY VINYL ACETATE
489. POLYVINYL ACETATE EMULSION
490. POLYURETHENE FOAM
491. POTASSIUM DICHROMATE/ BICHROMATE
492. POTASSIUM IODATE
493. POTASSIUM NITRATE
494. POTASSIUM PERMAGNATE
495. POTASSIUM PER SULPHATE
496. POTASSIUM SULPHATE (FERTILIZER GRADE)
497. POTASSIUM PER OXY DI-SULPHIDE
498. POTASSIUM SILICATE
499. POTASSIUM STEARATE
500. POWER ALCOHOL
501. PVC RESIN FROM ETHYL ALCOHOL
502. PYRIDINE & ITS DERIVATIVES
503. RAPID FAST DYES (ONLY PROCESS)
504. REACTOR (CHEMICAL)
505. RECLAMATION OF USED ENGINE OIL (BY CLAY & VACUUM DISTILLATION PROCESS)
506. RECLAMATION OF SPENT BLEACHING EARTH
507. RECLAMATION OF NICKEL SPENT CATALYST FROM VANASPATI INDUSTRY
508. RECTIFIED SPIRIT FROM MOLASSES & MAHUA FLOWERS
509. RECTIFIED SPIRIT FROM RICE STRAW
510. RED OXIDE PAINT/PRIMER (ANTI CORROSIVE) BASED ORGANIC RED PIGMENTS
511. REMOVAL OF ANTIMONY FROM LEAD SCRAP
512. RESORCINOL
513. ROSIN SIZING AGENT
514. RESORCINOL
515. SALINE AND INJECTION WATER
516. SALICYLIC ACID
517. SANTONIN
518. SENNOSIDES FROM SENNO LEAF
519. SHOE POLISH
520. SILICA GEL (BLUE SELF INDICATING PROCESS)
521. SILICONE EMULSION
522. SILICONE FROM RICE HUSK
523. SILICON FROM SILICA (SEMI CONDUCTOR GRADE)
524. SILICONE RESINS
525. SILICONE SPRAYSILVER BRAZING FOIL
526. SILVER EXTRACTION FROM WASTE HYPO SOLUTION
527. SILVER NITRATE
528. SILVER PARTS FOR CERAMIC CAPACITOR SINGLE SUPER PHOSPHATE & MIXED FERTILIZER (NPK)
529. SINGLE SUPER PHOSPHATE (S.S.P) & SULPHURIC ACID
530. SODA ASH
531. SODA ASH FROM NATRON
532. SODA WATER BOTTLING PLANT (CARBONATED BEVERAGE)
533. SODIUM ALUMINATE
534. SODIUM BI-CARBONATE (BAKING SODA) FROM SODA ASH
535. SODIUM CHLORITE
536. SODIUM CHROMATE SODIUM CYCLAMATE
537. SODIUM DI-CHROMATE
538. SODIUM DI-CHROMATE & SODIUM SULPHATE AS BYE PRODUCTS
539. SODIUM HEXA META PHOSPHATE
540. SODIUM HYDROSULFITE
541. SODIUM HYPO CHLORIDE (BLEACH LIQUOR)
542. SODIUM ISO-PROPYL XANTHATE
543. SODIUM LAURYL SULPHATE
544. SODIUM LAURYL SULPHATE & SODIUM LAURYL ETHER SULPHATE
545. SODIUM NITRATE
546. SODIUM PETROLEUM SULPHONATE (EMULSIFIER)
547. SODIUM SILICATE FROM SILICA & SODA ASH
548. SODIUM SILICATE FROM (1) PADDY SILK HUSK 2) & SILICA
549. SODIUM CARBONATE & SILICA
550. SODIUM SULPHATE
551. SODIUM SULPHIDE BY BARIUM SULPHATE PROCESS
552. SODIUM SULPHIDE FROM AMMONIA & SODIUM CHLORIDE
553. SODIUM SULPHITE
554. SODIUM TRI-POLY PHOSPHATE
555. SOFTENER (CATIONIC ANIONIC & NON-IONIC)
556. SPIRIT FROM PINE APPLE
557. STANNOUS CHLORIDE
558. STEARIC ACID
559. STEARATES MANUFACTURE (CALCIUM, ZINC, ALUMINIUM, MAGNESIUM STEARATES)
560. SULPHUR FROM PYRITES & SLAG
561. SULPHUR CRYSTALS/LUMPS
562. SULPHURIC ACID
563. SULPHURIC ACID FROM DCDA PROCESS
564. SUPER PHOSPHATE (S.S.P)
565. SYNTHETIC IRON OXIDE (YELLOW)
566. SYNTHETIC RED & WELLOW IRON OXIDE FROM IRON FILLING & PICKLE LIQUOR
567. TARTARIC ACID
568. TOILET CLEANER
569. TOLUENE AND SBP FROM

CRUDE NAPHTHA
570. TRIMETHYL AMMONIUM CHLORIDE
571. TRIPHENYL PHOSPHITE (T.P.P)
572. ULTRAMARINE BLUE (LIQUID)
573. UREA FORMALDEHYDE & MELAMINE FORMALDEHYDE POWDER
574. UNDECYLINIC ACID
575. VINYL ACETATE MONOMER
576. VITAMIN C
577. VITAMIN E
578. WASTE WATER TREATMENT PLANT FOR INDUSTRIAL SECTOR IN INDIA (ONLY MARKER SURVEY)
579. WIRE DRAWING LUBRICANT
580. WIRE ENAMEL
581. XANTHATES
582. YELLOW DEXTRIN
583. ZINC CHLORIDE
584. ZINC OXIDE
585. ZINC PHOSPHATING BY COLD PROCESS
586. ZINC SILICATE
587. ZINC STEARATE
588. ZINC SULPHATE
589. ZINC SULPHATE MONOHYDRATE
590. ACID BLACK
591. AURAMINE'O'
592. AZO DYES STUFF
593. DYE & DYE INTERMEDIATE
594. DYE INTERMEDIATES
595. MALACHITE GREEN
596. METHYLENE BLUE
597. PHTHALOCYANINE BLUE
598. PHTHALOCYANINE BLUE & GREEN
599. REACTIVE DYES
600. SULPHUR BLACK DYE
601. VAT DYES
602. WATER CHILLING PLANT
603. WADDING OIL (100%) FOR WADDING OF COTTON HOSIERY CLOTH IN THE DYEING PROCESS
604. WHITE OIL
605. WAX FLOOR POLISH

ELECTRICAL, ELECTONICS, COMPUTERS AND INFOTECH/IT PROJECTS

606. AIR CONDITIONING
607. ALUMINIUM ALLOY CONDUCTOR
608. ALUMINIUM CABLE
609. ALUMINIUM ELECTROYTIC CAPACITORS
610. AUDIO CASSETTE ASSEMBLING & RECORDING
611. AUDIO CASSETTES DUPLICATING RECORDING
612. AUDIO CASSETTES & AUDIO STUDIO
613. AUDIO CASSETTES PLANE & RECORDED
614. AUDIO MAGNETIC HEADS
615. AUDIO MAGNETIC TAPE
616. AUDIO/VIDEO CASSETTES
617. AUTO BULB/LAMPS
618. AUTOMATIC VOLTAGE STABILIZER
619. BATTERY PLATES
620. BACK OFFICE (Rs. 5000/-)
621. B/W TV & COMPUTER MONITOR PICTURE TUBE
622. BREAD BOARDS
623. CALL CENTRE
624. CAMERA (35 MM)
625. CAPACITORS
626. CARBON ELECTRODE USED FOR BATTERY CELL
627. CARBON POTETIOMETERS
628. CEILING FAN
629. CERAMIC INSULATOR
630. CHILDREN INFOTECH TRAINING INSTITUTE (Rs. 5000/-)
631. CHOKE AND PATTI
632. CHOKE AND STARTER
633. CHOKE USED FOR FLUORESCENT LAMPS
634. COLOUR TELEVISION
635. COLOUR AND BLACK & WHITE TELEVISION
636. COMPACT DISC
637. COMPACT DISC PLAYER (AUDIO/VIDEO)
638. COMPUTER EDUCATION INSTITUTE
639. COMPUTER ASSEMBLY
640. COMPUTER HARDWARE
641. COMPUTER KEYBOARD
642. COMPUTER PERIPHERALS
643. COMPUTER PRINTERS
644. COMPUTER RIBBON
645. COMPUTER RIBBON REINKING OR REFILLING
646. COMPUTER STATIONERY
647. COMPUTER STATIONERY &

IMPORTED HARDWARE PARTS
648. COMPUTER TERMINALS
649. COMPUTERISED WASHING MACHINE (AUTOMATIC)
650. COMPUTER SOFTWARE
651. CONDENSER FOR MOTOR USING MPP FILM
652. CONTENT DEVELOPMENT CENTRE (EOU) (Rs. 5000/-)
653. CONTROL PANEL BOARD
654. COOLING COIL FOR AIR CONDITIONERS
655. COPPER STRIP COIL FROM SCRAP
656. CORDLESS TELEPHONES
657. CYBER CAFE
658. CYBERKIOSK (Rs. 5000/-)
659. DATA PROCESSING CENTRE (Rs. 5000/-)
660. D.C. MICRO MOTORS
661. D.G.SETS
662. DISH ANTENNA AND CABLE T.V. NETWORK EQUIPMENT
663. DISTRIBUTION TRANSFORMERS & REPAIRS
664. DOMESTIC ELECTRICAL APPLIANCES- ROOM COOLER, WASHING MACHINE, WATER HEATER, ELECTRIC ROOM HEATER
665. E-SCHOOL
666. E-COMMERCE/BUSINESS
667. ELECTRIC ENERGY METER
668. ELECTRIC FANS
669. ELECTRIC HORN FOR AUTOMOBILE
670. ELECTRIC LAMP/GLS (INCANDESCENT LAMP)
671. ELECTRIC MIXER
672. ELECTRIC MOTORS UP TO 10 HP. REWINDING OF ALL TYPES OF MOTORS WATER PUMPS
673. ELECTRIC MOTOR WINDING (FOR FAN, MIXIES, ETC.)
674. ELECTRIC STEAM IRON
675. ELECTRICAL APPLIANCES
676. ELECTRICAL FIXTURES
677. ELECTRICAL STAMPING
678. ELECTROLYTIC CAPACITORS
679. ELECTROMAGNETIC RELAY
680. ELECTRONIC BALAST/CHOK
681. ELECTRICAL CHOKE
682. ELECTRONIC DIGITAL WATCHES
683. ELECTRONIC DIGITAL WEIGHING MACHINE
684. ELECTRONIC FIRE ALARM
685. ELECTRONIC GAS STOVE LIGHTERS
686. ELECTRONIC PRESSURE INDICATORS, ELECTRICALS, ELECTRONIC LIQUID LEVEL INDICATORS, ELECTRONIC TEMPERATURE INDICATOR, DIGITAL TACHOMETER
687. ELECTRONIC TELEPHONE INSTRUMENTS
688. ELECTRONIC TOYS
689. ELECTRONIC WATCHES & CLOCKS
690. FAX MACHINES
691. F.H.P MOTORS
692. FLOPPY DISKETTES
693. FLUORESCENT LAMP STARTER
694. FLUORESCENT TUBULAR

LAMPS WITH INTRODUCTION TO MERCURY VAPOUR LAMP
695. FRANCHISEE COMPUTER EDUCATION CENTRE (Rs. 5000)
696. GAS DETECTOR (L.P.G)
697. GENERATOR SET & PUMP SETS
698. GENERATOR (BATTERY OPERATED)
699. GIS SERVICE CENTRE (GEOGRAPHICAL INFORMATION SYSTEMS)
700. HARDWARE FITTING FOR TRANSMISSION LINE (OVERHEAD LINE MATERIAL
701. HEADERS FOR TRANSISTOR ICS SEMI CONDUCTOR
702. H.T & L.T INSULATORS
703. H.T & M.V INDUSTRIAL CUBICAL SWITCH BOARD
704. INFORMATION MOVING DISPLAY (L.E.D TYPE)
705. INSURANCE CLAIM PROCESSING CENTRE (EOU) (Rs. 5000/-)
706. INTEGRATED CIRCUITS
707. INTERNET BASED STOCK TRADING (Rs. 5000/-)
708. INTERNET SERVICE PROVIDER (I.S.P.)
709. JELLY FILLED TELEPHONE CABLES
710. LAP TOP COMPUTERS
711. LEAD ACID BATTERIES
712. LEAD ACID BATTERY PLATES AND ASSEMBLING OF BATTERY
713. LEGAL TRANSCRIPTION & SECRETARIAL SERVICES CENTER (EOU)(Rs. 5000/-)
714. LIGHT EMITTING DIODES (L.E.D)
715. LINEAR ICS TRAINER KIT
716. LOUD SPEAKER
717. L.T TRANSFORMER REPAIRING
718. MEDICAL TRANSCRIPTION CENTRE
719. METAL FILM RESISTORS
720. METALLISED POLYPROPYLENE, POLYESTER FILM CAPACITOR
721. MICA BASE ELECTRONIC COMPONENTS
722. MICA PAPER WASTE PAPER FROM MICA WASTE
723. MICRO PROCESSORS TRAINER KITS BASED ON MICRO PROCESSORS
724. MINI COMPUTER (PERSONAL COMPUTER)
725. MINIATURE CIRCUIT BREAKER (M.C.B)
726. MINIATURE WATCH BATTERIES (BUTTON CELL)
727. MIXER/GRINDER (MIXI)
728. MONO CHROME COMPUTER MONITOR
729. MOTOR START ELECTROLYTIC CAPACITOR
730. MULTI LAYER P.C.B
731. MULTIPLE RELAY FOR LOW VOLTAGE
732. NEON INDICATOR
733. NEON SIGN MANUFACTURE
734. OPTICAL FIBRE CABLES
735. ON LINE SHOPPING MALL (Rs. 5000/-)
736. OPTO MECHANICAL & ELECTRICAL EQUIPMENTS
737. PHOTO COLOUR LAB
738. PICTURE TUBE (B/W)
739. PLAIN PAPER COPIER
740. PLASTIC FILM CAPACITORS
741. POLYESTER CAPACITORS
742. PORTABLE GENERATOR SET
743. PORTAL
744. PORTABLE TELEVISION(TV)
745. POWER CAPACITORS
746. POWER INVERTERS
747. POWER PLANT
748. POWER TRANSFORMERS UP TO 600 KVA
749. PRINTED CIRCUIT BOARD
750. PVC WIRES & CABLES
751. RE-CONDITIONING OF PICTURE TUBE
752. RESIN CAST CT & PT (1 KV)
753. SEMI CONDUCTOR DEVICE
754. SEMI CONDUCTORS FOR TRANSISTORS & DIODES
755. SETTING UP OF A VIDEO STUDIO
756. SMOKE DETECTORS
757. SOLAR CELLS
758. SOLAR MODULES
759. SOLAR PHOTO VOLTAIC SYSTEM
760. SOLDER FLUXES
761. SOLAR WATER HEATING PANELS
762. STEEL FURNITURE & ELECTRICAL APPLIANCES
763. STEREO AMPLIFIERS
764. STEREO CASSETTE RECORDERS/PLAYERS
765. STREET LIGHT FITTINGS SURGE SUPPRESSOR
766. TANTALUM CAPACITORS
767. TEFLON COATED ELECTRIC CABLE
768. TELEMEDICINE (DISTANCE HEALTH CARE) (Rs. 5000/-)
769. TELEPHONE CORD/CABLE
770. TELEPHONE (PUSH BUTTON TYPE)
771. TELEPHONE (PUSH BUTTON & CORDLESS)
772. TELEVISION (CTV & B/W)
773. TELEVISION (3-D)
774. TELEVISION DEFLECTION COMPONENTS
775. TELEVISION SIGNAL BOOSTERS
776. TELEVISION TUNERS
777. TRACTION BATTERIES
778. TRAINING INSTITUTE OF MEDICAL TRANSCRIPTION
779. TRANSFORMER FOR B/W TV
780. TRANSFORMER FOR VOLTAGE STABILIZER & E.H.T
781. TRANSMISSION POWER LINE FITTING
782. TRANSMISSION TOWER FITTING
783. TV AUDIO EQUIPMENT CABINETS & THEIR ASSEMBLING UNIT
784. UN-INTERRUPTED POWER SUPPLY (U.P.S)
785. VARIABLE FREQUENCY
786. VARIABLE VOLTAGE A.C. DRIVE
787. VIDEO CASSETTES (COMPLETE MANUFACTURING & ASSEMBLING)
788. VIDEO CASSETTES RECORDER (V.C.R)
789. VIDEO FILM STUDIO
790. VOLTAGE REGULATOR FOR AUTOMOBILES
791. VOLTAGE STABILIZERS
792. VOLTAGE STABLIZER & T.V. GAIN BOOSTER
793. WAX AND CHEMICAL COATED, BRAIDED TINSEL WIRE
794. WEBSITE DESIGN & E-MAIL REGISTERING
795. WELDING ELECTRODES
796. WIND ENERGY POWER PROJECT (10 MW) WIRE WOUND POTENTIOMETERS

FOOD, AGRO FOOD, PROCESSED FOOD, AGRO PLANTATION , CULTIVATION, FARMING, DAIRY/MILK, TOBACCO/PAN MASALA, BREWERY & DISTILLERY, EDIBLE OILS, EOU FOOD PRODUCTS AND ALLIED PRODUCTS

797. ALCOHOLIC BEVERAGES & VENEGAR FROM COCONUT WATER
798. ALCOHOL DRINKS FROM ETHYL ALCOHOL BY MIXING OF VARIOUS FLAVOURS
799. ANTI SCALE COMPOUND FOR ADDING INTO SUGAR JUICE BOILING
800. APPLE JUICE CONCENTRATED & DEHYDRATED FRUIT & VEGETABLES
801. ARTIFICIAL FISH MEAL FOR POULTRY FEED
802. AUTOMATIC BISCUIT PLANT
803. BABY CEREAL FOOD AND MILK POWDER
804. BACTERIA FOR CANE JUICE
805. BAKER'S YEAST
806. BAKERY INDUSTRY
807. BANANA PUREE
808. BEER & WINE
809. BEER PLANT (BREWERY)
810. BIDI
811. BIDI & CIGARETTE
812. BISCUIT PLANT

813. BREAD (AUTOMATIC PLANT)
814. BLACK PEPPER (SPICES)
815. BREAD AND BISCUITS
816. BREEDING FARM
817. BROILER CHICKEN
819. BUTTON MUSHROOM CULTIVATION & PROCESSING
820. CANNING OF RASAGULLAS IN METAL CANS
821. CAFFEIN FROM TEA WASTE
822. CANNING OF FRUITS & VEGETABLES
823. CASEIN AND BY-PRODUCTS
824. CASHEW FRUIT JUICE FROM CASHEW FRUIT APPLE
825. CASHEWNUT KERNEL EXTRACTION FROM CASHEWNUT FRUIT
826. CASHEWNUT SHELL LIQUID & KERNEL PROCESSING
827. CASHEW FENI
828. CATECHEU (BY CHEMICAL PROCESS)
829. CATTLE FEED FROM TAPIOCA
830. CHEWING & BUBBLE GUM
831. CHICKEN/SHEEP MEAT PROCESSING
832. CHOCOLATE (MILK)
833. CIGARETTE AND BEEDIES
834. COCOA BUTTER FROM COCOA MASS
835. COCONUT PRODUCTS & BY PRODUCTS PROCESS COMPLEX
836. COLD/SOFT DRINKS
837. COLLECTION OF MILK AND MILK MAKING POWDER
838. COLLECTION OF MILK AND PACKING IN POLYTHENE POUCH (1/2 KG.1 KG. & 2 KG.)
839. CONDENSED MILK (SWEETNED)
840. CONFECTIONERY INDUSTRY (TOFFEE & CANDY, SEMI-AUTOMATIC PLANT)
841. COUNTRY LIQUOR FROM MOLASSES
842. CIGARETTE
843. DAIRY FARM AND DAIRY (MILK) PRODUCTS (PASTEURISED MILK, BUTTER, GHEE, PANEER)
844. DAIRY FARM TO PRODUCE MILK & PACKING IN POUCHES (50%) & CAN(50%)
845. DAIRY FOR MILK PROCESSING
846. DAIRY FARM (BUFALO)
847. DAL (PULSE) MILL UNIT
848. DEHYDRATION OF CARROT & GARLIC
849. DEHYDRATION & CANNING OF FRUITS & VEGETABLES
850. DEHYDRATION OF FIGS
851. DEHYDRATION OF FRUITS AND VEGETABLES
852. DEHYDRATED ONIONS AND ONION POWDER
853. DRY ICE BY BREAKING OF AIR
854. DRYING OF RED CHILLIES, HALDI, DHANIA, AND GREEN PEAS
855. EGG POWDER (40,000 EGGS PROCESSING PER DAY)
856. EXPORT OF PROCESSED FOODS AND MARINE PRODUCTS
857. FISH CANNING & POUCHING
859. FISH FARMING (PRAWN & OTHER MARINE PRODUCTS)
860. FISH MEAL
861. FLOUR MILL AND MUSTARD OIL
862. FOOD COLOUR & ORASTED GROUNDNUT GRAM PEAS, ETC IN POUCHES
863. FROG LEGS PROCESSING
864. FROZEN MEATS PROCESSING
865. FOOD FLAVOURS (WHISKY) VODKA, GRAPE, BUTTER SCOTCH)
866. FOOD PRODUCTS COMPLEX (DEHYDRATED ONIONS, GARLIC POWDER & FLAKES, CATTLE FEED, TOMATO POWDER, TOMATO PRODUCTS, CANNED FRUITS & VEGETABLES, TOMATO PURE, GROUN NUT OIL, REFIND OIL, DEHYDRATED GRAPES, BANANA POWDER & WAFFERS)
867. FRUIT JUICE, JAM, JELLIES & ALLIED PRODUCTS
868. FRUIT JUICE, PICKLES PROCESSING AND CANNING
869. FRUIT JUICE MAKING & PACKING IN PLASTIC CONTAINER/POUCHES
870. FRUIT PROCESSING (JAM & JELLIES)
871. FRUIT PULP & JUICE CONCENTRATES
872. FRUIT & VEGETABLE DRYING (FREEZE DRYING METHOD)
873. GOAT & SHEEP FARMING
874. GRAM DALL/PULSE MILL
875. GRAPE DEHYDRATION
876. HARD BOILED CANDY (TOFFEE & CANDY)
877. HERBAL CIGARETTES
878. HONEY PROCESSING & PACKAGING
879. ICE CREAM OF DIFFERENT FLAVOURS
880. ICE CREAM STABILIZER
881. ICE MAKING PLANT
882. INDIAN MADE FOREIGN LIQUOR (I.M.F.L)
883. INSTANT FOOD (IDLI MIX, DOSA MIX, GULAB JAMUN MIX)
884. INSTANT FOOD (INSTANT FOOD & FAST FOOD PARLOUR)
885. INSTANT NOODLES
886. INSTANT TEA
887. INSTANT TEA FROM BLACK TEA
888. INTEGERATED STARCH BAKING POWDER/YEAST INDUSTRY
889. IODIZED SALT
890. IODIZED SALT (ORDINARY MOISTURE-LESS/FREE FLOWING IN PLASTIC BAGS AND CONTAINERS)
891. JAM, JELLIES, FRUIT JUICE & ALLIED PRODUCTS
892. KATHA AND CUTCH
893. KHANDSARI SUGAR
894. KHANDSARI SUGAR & IMFL
895. LACTIC ACID FROM WHITE SUGAR BY FERMENTATION PROCESS
896. LACTOSE & BY PRODUCTS PROCESSING FROM MILK
897. LIQUID GLUCOSE AND ITS BYE PRODUCTS
898. MACRONI AND VERMICILLI
899. MALT EXTRACTION FROM BARLEY
900. MANGO PROCESSING (MANGO PULP, JUICE & SLICES)
901. MAYUR BRAND TYPE CHEWING TOBACCO
902. MINERAL WATER
903. MILK PRESERVATION & MARKETING TO WHOLE SELLERS (INPOUCH PACKING BY UHT TECHNOLOGY)
904. MILK PROCESSING AND PACKAGING OF MILK PRODUCTS
905. MILK PRODUCTS (CASEIN, LACTOSE, GHEE & WHEY POWDER)
906. MILK TOFFEE
907. MINI FLOUR MILL
908. MINI SUGAR PLANT
909. MISRI (PEARL SUGAR CANDIES)
910. MODERN RICE MILL
911. MURABBA
912. MUSTARD OIL EXTRACTION & REFINING
913. MUTTON TALLOW
914. NAMKEEN INDUSTRY (BHUJIA, CHANA CHUR ETC.)
915. NAMKEEN & SWEETS
916. NON-BASMATI RICE FROM PADDY
917. OLEORESIN, ESSENTIAL OIL, DYES & POWDER OF SPICES
918. OLEORESIN EXTRACTION FROM DIPTERO-CARPUT TURMINATUS AND PINUS KHASYANA
919. OLEORESIN EXTRACTION FROM CHILLI
920. PAN MASALA AND POUCH

1059. BUFFALO HORN TIP, HOOF
1060. BANQUET HALL
1061. BUTTON
1062. CALCINED PETROLEUM (C.P) COKE
1063. CANVAS SHOES
1064. CANVAS SHOES, JUNGLE BOOTS
1065. CARBON BRUSH, BRUSH HOLDER & SLIP RING
1066. CEMENT SHEETS WITH COIR FIBRE & OTHER SEGMENTS
1067. CERAMIC TILES (GLAZED) BY DOUBLE FIRING/HEATING
1068. CHILDREN RECREATION CENTRE
1069. COAL BRIQUETTES
1070. COLD STORAGE & ICE
1071. COLD STORAGE FOR FRUITS AND VEGETABLES
1072. COMPRESSOR (HERMETIC) FOR AIR CONDITIONER
1073. COSTUME JEWELLERY/ IMITATION JEWELLERY
1074. DECORATIVE LAMINATED SHEET (SUNMICA)
1075. DIAMOND CUTTING & EXPORTS
1076. DRINKING STRAW FROM PROPYLENE
1077. ENGINEERING COLLEGE
1078. ENTERTAINMENT CLUB
1079. FASHION TECHNOLOGY INSTITUTE
1080. FAST FOOD PARLOUR
1081. FAST FOOD (INSTANT FOOD & FAST FOOD PARLOUR)
1082. FIRE EXTINGUISHERS (SODA ACID TYPE)
1083. FISH NET
1084. FLORICULTURE (CUT FLOWER ROSE) WITH GREEN HOUSE
1085. FLOOR COVERING SHEET
1086. FILM STUDIO (VIDEO)
1087. FLUSH DOOR, CHIP BOARD, WOOD WOOL & OTHER INSULATING BOARDS
1088. GAS DETECTORS OF L.P.G
1089. GEMS MANUFACTURING
1090. GLASS BOTTLE BY SCRAP
1092. GOAT & SHEEP FARMING
1093. GOLD ELECTROPLATING
1094. GOLD JEWELLERY (E.O.U)
1095. GOLD PLATED SILVER JEWELLERY & CUTLERY
1096. GRANITE SLAB AND TILES
1097. GREEN HOUSE
1098. HARD CHROMIUM PLATING
1099. HEALTH CLUB AND BEAUTY PARLOUR CUM HAIR SALOON WITH SONA BATH
1100. HEALTH CLUB CUM BEAUTY PARLOUR TRAININGINSTITUTE
1101. HORN TIP,HOOVE BUTTON
1102. HOSPITAL
1103. HOSPITAL (100 BEDS)
1104. HOSPITAL (200 BEDS)
1105. ICE MAKING PLANT
1106. IMITATION AND COSTUME
1107. JEWELLERY (NECKLACE, EARRINGS EAR TOP ETC.)
1108. INITMATE SCENT CHEMICALS FROM ALL TYPES OF FLAVOUR
1109. INVESTMENT CASTING
1110. JUTE, COIR, GLASS ROPE/ SUTLI
1111. JUTE TWINE
1112. L.P.G BOTTLING PLANT
1113. L.P.G REGULATOR (DOMESTIC PURPOSE)
1114. LAMINATED PARTICLE BOARD & HARD BOARD
1115. LAMINATED SAFETY AND TOUGHENED GLASS
1116. LEASING & HIRE PURCHASE
1117. LICHEN (CHARILA)
1118. MANILA ROPES
1119. MEDICAL COLLEGE
1120. MATCH UNIT FROM WAXED PAPER
1121. MEDIUM DENSITY FIBRE BOARD
1122. MELAMINE CROCKERY
1123. MINERAL WATER
1124. MINI CEMENT PLANT
1125. MIRROR SILVER, GOLDEN, PINK, BLACK & SMOKES
1126. MODERN ADVERTISING AGENCY WITH DTP & FILM STUDIO
1127. MOTEL/SMALL HOTEL
1128. MULTI COLOUR PRINTING
1129. MULTI STOREY COMMERCIAL COMPLEX ALONGWITH RESIDENTIALAND DELUX FLATS FOR FOREIGN TOURISTS & REVOLVING RESTAURENT AT THE TOP
1130. MULTIPLE LAMINATION INDUSTRY
1131. MUSHROOM GROWING AND PROCESSING (BY DEEP FREEZING METHOD)
1132. NEWS PAPER PRINTING
1133. NICKEL LINED INDUSTRIAL SCREEN
1134. OFFSET COLOUR PRINTING PRESS (SIX COLOUR)
1135. OFFSET PRINTING PRESS
1136. P.C.C ELECTRIC POLES
1137. PHOTOGRAPHIC DEVELOPER & FIXER
1138. PVC EXTRUSION PROFILE (DOOR & WINDOWS)
1139. POP-CORN
1140. PHOTO ETCHING OF S.S.
1141. PRE STRESSED CEMENT CONCRETE PIPES
1142. PILFER PROOF CAPS
1143. PILFER PROOF CAPS AND CROWN CAP
1144. POUCH MAKING & GRAVURE PRINTING (ROTO PRINTING)
1145. POULTRY & FISH FARMING (INTEGERATED UNIT)
1146. PRINTING OF TIN SHEETS
1147. READYMADE GARMENTS
1148. RESTAURANT
1149. ROSE PLANTATION AND ROSE OIL EXTRACTION
1150. ROTOGRAVURE PRINTING
1151. SAFETY BELTS
1152. SAFETY MATCHES
1153. SHOE LACES
1154. SILK COCOON CULTIVATION (GROWING OF SILK COCOON WARM)
1155. SILK SCREEN PRINTING FORMULATIONS FOR PLASTIC, PAPER & CLOTH
1156. SPIKENARD (JATAMANSI)
1157. STENCIL COATING SOLUTION
1158. SUGAR CANDY (MISRI)
1159. SUGAR CANE PLANTATION
1160. SUGAR CANE JUICE PRESERVATION
1161. SURAT ZARI
1162. SYNTHETIC SHOES & SOLES
1163. TEA PACKAGING INDUSTRY
1164. TENNIS BALLS
1165. THREE STAR HOTEL
1166. TRAVELLING AGENCY
1167. TRAYS, TROLLEYS FOR HOSPITAL WITH SCRATCHLESS COATING
1168. WAX EXTRACTS (TANNING POWDER)
1169. WIRE ROPE SLINGS
1170. WOOD WOOL SLAB
1171. WOODEN CANE FURNITURE WITH EXPORT POTENTIAL
1172. WOODEN FURNITURE
1173. WOODEN PANEL INCLUDING KILN SEASONING
1174. WOODEN FURNITURE
1175. WATCH CASE BUFFING
1176. WATCH DIAL
1177. WRIST WATCHES
1178. WATCHES (ELECTRONIC)
1179. ZEDOARY (KACHUR)

EDIBLE OILS, ESSENTIAL OILS LURICATIING OILS, GREASES, VEGETABLE OILS, WAXES, CAMPHOR, PERFUMES & PERFUMERY COMPOUNDS AND REFINED OILS ETC.

1180. AROMATIC PERFUMERY COMPOUND
1181. AEROSOL
1182. AGARBATTI PERFUMERY COMPOUND
1183. BEES WAX MANUFACTURE
1184. CAMPHOR
1185. CARDANOL FROM CASHEW NUT SHELL LIQUID
1186. CASTOR OIL
1187. CASTOR OIL DERIVATIVE OLEORESINS
1188. CHILLI OIL
1189. CITRONELLA OILS
1190. CLOVE OIL
1191. CONCENTRATE OF ROSE JASMINE & LILY ETC.
1192. COLOURED FLAME CANDLE

1193. CANDLES (SEMI-AUTOMATIC)
1194. CORN OIL (MAIZE OIL)
1195. DEHYDRATED CASTOR OIL
1196. EUGENOL FROM CINNAMON LEAF OIL
1197. EXTRACTION OF ESSENTIAL OIL (CARDAMON, JEERA, AJOWAN, GINGER OILS ETC. & PACKAGING OF GROUND SPICES)
1198. EXTRACTION OF JASMINE ESSENCE
1199. EXTRACTION OF ESSENTIAL OILS BY SUPER CRITICAL FLUID METHOD FROM FLOWERS, HERBS & SPICES
1200. EUCALYPTUS OIL
1201. EXTRACTION OF OIL FROM OIL SEED EXPANDEREXTRUSION TECHNOLOGY)
1202. FAT LIQUOR SULPHATED OIL
1203. FLAVOURS FOR FOOD
1204. GARLIC OIL & POWDER
1205. GINGER OIL, SANDALWOOD OIL AND NAGARMOTHA OIL
1206. GINGER OIL
1207. GINGER OIL & GINGER DUST
1208. INTEGERATED WAX COMPLEX
1209. IONONE FROM LEMON GRASS OIL
1210. JASMINE & LILLY FLOWER OIL
1211. LEMON GRASS OIL
1212. LIQUID PARAFFIN
1213. LUBE OIL & GREASE
1214. LUBRICATING OIL
1215. MENTHOL CRYSTALS
1216. MENTHOL OIL & CRYSTAL
1217. MICRO CRYSTALLINE WAX
1218. MUSTARD OIL (EDIBLE OIL)
1219. OIL FROM ARTEMISIA HERBS
1220. PALM OIL CRUSHING UNIT
1221. PAN MASALA
1222. PARAFFIN WAX
1223. PARAFFIN WAX FROM SLACK WAX
1224. REFINED OIL-SUN FLOWER OIL, GROUNDNUT OIL, STAFF FLOWER OIL & COTTON SEED OIL
1225. REFINED VEGETABLE OIL
1226. RECLAMATION OF USED ENGINE OIL
1227. RICE BRAN OIL (R.B.O)
1228. ROSE OIL EXTRACTION
1229. SMOKE LESS CANDLE
1230. SPICE OIL & OLEORESINS
1231. SOLVENT EXTRACTION PLANT (OIL CAKE BASED)
1232. SYNTHETIC ALMOND OIL
1233. SYNTHETIC TALLOW
1234. SYNTHETIC GHEE
1235. VEGETABLE OIL EXTRACTION & REFINING
1236. WADDING OIL (100%) FOR WADDING OF COTTON HOSIERY CLOTH IN DYEING PROCESS
1237 WAX EMULSION FOR TEXTILE
1238. WAX FLOOR POLISH

PAINT, ENAMEL, SOLVENTS, THINNERS, INKS & VARNISH

1239. ACRYLIC EMULSION PAINTS
1240. ALUMINIUM PAINT
1241 AUTOMOBILE PAINTS
1242. BALL POINT PEN REFILL INK
1243. BITUMINIOUS ROAD EMULSION
1244. BITUMEN
1245. BITUMINIOUS FELTS FOR WATER & DAMP PROOFING
1246. BITUMINIOUS ROAD EMULSION RAPID MEDIUM & SLOW SETTING
1247. BUFFING & POLISHING
1248. CEMENT PAINT FOR WHITE & GREY CEMENT

1249. DISPERSANT
1250. DRY DISTEMPER
1251. DRY DISTEMPER & CEMENT PAINT
1252. DUPLICATING INK BLACK FOR GESTNER DUPLICATOR
1255. EMULSION PAINTS (WATER BASED)
1256. HAMMERTONE PAINT
1257. INSULATING VARNISH & WIRE ENAMEL
1258. IRON OXIDE PIGMENTS
1259. INSULATING VARNISH (POLY VINYL BUTYRAL BASED, FFC GRADE)
1260. LIME COLOUR (CEMENT COLOUR)
1261. SYNTHETIC RED OXIDE FOR FLOORINGS
1262. SOLVENT & THINNERS
1263. MARKING INKS (WATER PROOF)
1264. METAL NAPHTHANATE (AS DRIER FOR PAINTS)
1265. N.C.PUTTY
1266. OFFSET PRINTING INK
1267. OIL BOUND DISTEMPER PAINT
1268. PAINT BRUSHES
1269. PAINT REMOVERS
1270. PAINT INDUSTRY
1271. PAINT & VARNISH
1272. PICTURE VARNISH
1273. POWDER COATING PAINT
1274. PRINTING INKS (OFFSET, FLEXO & ROTO GRAVURE)
1275. PRIMER PAINT & ENAMEL PAINT
1276. PUTTY & WATER PROOFING PAINT
1277. PRINTING INKS (FLEXO-GRAPHIC INK)
1278. PUTTY (METAL CASEMENT)
1279. RED OXIDE PRIMER (ANTI CORROSIVE)
1280. REFRECTORY PAINT (GRAPHITE BASED)
1281. SCREEN PRINTING INKS
1282. SILK SCREEN PRINTING INK FORMULATION FOR PLASTIC, PAPER, CLOTH
1283. STAMP & PAD INK
1284. STOVING PAINT
1285. SPIRIT SOLUBLE MALEIC RESIN
1286. TEXTURE PAINT
1287. THINNERS AND ITS ALLIED PRODUCTS
1288. TONER INK
1289. VARNISH THINNER (SOLVENT)
1290. VACUUM METALLIZING LACQUERS
1291. WOOD PRIMER

PHARMACEUTICAL, DRUGS, AYURVEDIC/HERBAL COSMETICS & MEDICINES, HOMOEOPATHIC MEDICINES, DISPOSABLE SYRINGE, DENTAL COLLEGE & FINE CHEMICALS ETC.

1292. AROMATIC PILLS
1293. ASPIRIN
1294. AYURVEDIC PAIN BALM OINTMENTS
1295. AYURVEDIC CHURAN AND TABLETS
1296. AYURVEDIC TABLETS (HAJMOLA TYPE)
1297. AYURVEDIC/HERBAL PHARMACY
1298. AYURVEDIC SHERBATS
1299. AYURVEDIC PRODUCTS
1300. BULK DRUGS (E.O.U)
1301. BLOOD BAGS
1302. CALCIUM GLUCONATE
1303. CAPSULE, TABLET & INJECTION WITH MODERN INSTRUMENTS
1304. CASHEW FENI
1305. CHLOROQUINONE PHOSPHATE (BULK DRUGS)
1306. CLINICAL THERMOMETER
1307. DENTAL CLINIC

Above all the "Detailed Project Reports" are available at *"ENGINEERS INDIA RESEARCH INSTITUTE"*. 4449, Nai Sarak (D), Main Road Delhi - 110 006 (India) ● Ph : 91-11-23918117, 2391 6431, 2384 0361 ● Fax : 91-11-2391 6431 ●E-Mail : eirisidi@bol.net.in ● WebSite : www.eiriindia.org

1308. DENTAL COLLEGE
1309. DENTAL GRADE EUGENOL
1310. DEXTROSE MONOHYDRATE, LIQUID GLUCOSE
1311. DEHYDRATED ONION & ONION POWDER
1312. DEXTROSE POWDER (ANHYDROUS FROM STARCH)
1314. DEXTROSE SALINE SOLUTION
1315. DISTILLERY (I.M.F.L)
1316. DISPOSABLE NEEDLES FOR SYRINGES
1317. DISPRIN
1318. DISTILLED WATER
1319. EMPTY HARD GELATINE CAPSULES
1320. FILLING & PACKING OF CAPSULES
1321. GLUCOSE - D - POWDER
1322. GLYCERINE
1323. HERBAL COSMETICS
1324. HERBAL SHAMPOO
1325. HERBAL HAIR OILS (AYURVEDIC)
1326. HOMOE & BIO-MEDICINES WITH MOTHER TINCTURE
1327. HOMOEPATHIC MEDICINES
1328. HYPODERMIC NEEDLES
1329. I.V. FLUIDS
1330. IBUPROFEN
1331. INFUSION & TRANSFUSION SETS (I.V. SET)
1332. INJECTABLE FOR PHARMACEUTICALS
1333. INJECTION AMPOULES PACKAGING BOX
1334. INTEGERATED SURGICAL COTTON
1335. ICE MAKING PLANT
1336. ICE & COLD STORAGE
1337. LACTOSE & BY PRODUCTS PROCESSING FROM MILK
1338. LICHEN (JATAMANSI CHARILA)
1339. LIQUID GLUCOSE AND ITS BY-PRODUCTS
1340. L-LYSINE MONOHYDRO CHLORIDE
1341. LIQUID GLUCOSE FROM POTATOES
1342. MEDICAL COLLEGE
1343. NICOTINE FROM TOBACCO WASTE
1344. OINTMENT-AYURVEDIC (YELLOW & WHITE)
1345. PHARMACEUTICAL AND FOOD GRADE GELATINE
1346. PHARMACEUTICAL INDUSTRY (TABLETS, CAPSULES, LIQUID, GEL, OINTMENT POWDER INJECTABLE)
1347. PHARMACEUTICAL UNIT (EOU) WITH FORMULA TIONS, INJECTABLES, ETC. PYRIDINE & DERIVATIVES
1348. SALT (IODIZED SALT)
1349. SALINE & INJECTION WATER
1350. SALINE WATER & DEXTROSE SOLUTION (I.V.FLUID IN PLASTIC BOTTLES)
1351. SORBITOL
1352. STARCH (MAIZE)
1353. SURGICAL ADHESIVE PLASTER
1354. SURGICAL BANDAGES
1355. SURGICAL GLOVES
1357. SURGICAL COTTON
1358. SURGICAL COTTON AND BANDAGE
1359. SYNTHETIC CAMPHOR POWDER
1360. TABLETS & CAPSULES
1361. TISSUE CULTURE
1362. TINCTURE FROM RECTIFIED SPIRIT
1363. TRIMETHOPIME
1364. VETERENARY MEDICINES (ONLY FORMULATIONS)
1365. VITAMIN 'C', SORBITOL' ANHYDROUS DEXTROSE, STARCH

PULP, PAPER, STRAW/GREY BOARD, KRAFT PAPER, PACKAGING, PAPER CARRY BAGE, PAPER FROM AGRO WASTE & STATIONERY ETC.

1366. AMMONIA PAPER
1367. AUTOMATIC BOOK BINDING
1368. ADHESIVE (FEVICOL TYPE)
1369. ALL PIN & GEM CLIPS
1370. CARBON PAPER
1371. CARD BOARD
1372. CARBON LESS PAPER
1373. CELLPHANE PAPER
1374. COMPUTER FORMS & SECURITY PRINTING PRESS
1375. CORRUGATED BOARD & BOX (PRINTED & LAMINATED)
1376. CORRUGATED BOARD AND BOXES FROM FROM CARD BOARDS
1377. CORRUGATED CARTONS FROM PLAIN PAPERS
1378. CORRUGATRED PACKING & MATERIAL (BULB & TUBES PACKING)
1379. DESK TOP PUBLISHING
1380. DEFOAMING AGENT FOR PAPER PLANT
1381. DRINKING STRAW PAPER
1382. D.T.P CUM OFFSET PRESS
1383. EGG TRAYS
1384. EXERCISE NOTE BOOK, REGISTER AND PAD
1385. FLEXOGRAPHIC INK
1386. GREETING CARD BY OFFSET PRESS
1387. HAND MADE PAPER FILTER PAPER
1388. HARD BOARD
1389. INJECTION AMPOULES PACKAGING BOXES
1390. INSULATIING PAPER
1391. KRAFT PAPER
1392. KRAFT PAPER FROM BAGASSE
1393. LAMINATED PACKAGING PAPER WITH PRINTING
1394. LAMINATION & COATING ON PAPER
1395. M.G. PAPER FROM WASTE PAPER
1396. MILL PAPER FROM WASTE PAPER
1397. MILL BOARD FROM RICE & WHEAT STRAWS
1398. MILL BOARD FROM WASTE PAPER
1399. MINI PAPER PLANT FROM SISAL
1400. MINI PAPER PLANT
1401. MULTI WALL PAPER SACKS
1402. NEWS PAPER FOR CHILDREN
1403. NEWS PRINT PAPER FROM RICE STRAW BAGASSE
1404. NEWS PAPER CHILDRENS
1405. NEWS PRINT PAPER
1406. OFFSET AND TREADLE TYPE PRINTING PRESS
1407. MILL BOARD BASED ON RICE STRAW
1408. PAPER AND BOARD FROM STRAW
1409. PAPER & PAPER PRODUCTS
1410. PAPER ENVELOPES
1411. PAPER CARRY BAGS
1412. PAPER BOARD CARTON
1413. PAPER CONES FOR LOUD SPEAKERS
1414. PAPER FROM AKRA
1415. PAPER FROM BAGASSE WITH CORRUGATED BOARD & BOXES
1416. PAPER FROM BAMBOO
1417. PAPER GLASSES FOR BEVERAGES
1418. PAPER FROM RICE HUSK & WHEAT HUSK
1419. PAPER FROM TREE BARK, EUCALYPRUS WOOD
1420. PAPER PRODUCTS
1421. PAPER PLANT (WHITE WRITING & NEWS PAPER FOR PULP & WASTE PAPER)
1422. PAPER PLATES, PAPER GLASS
1423. PAPER CONES & TUBES
1425. PAPER PLANT WITH DTP & PRINTING & PUBLISHING UNIT
1426. PAPER BASED PHENOLIC SHEET
1427. PAPER CUP FOR ICE CREAM
1428. PAPER TUBES SPIRAL WINDING COMPOSIT CONTAINER
1429. PAPER LABLE FOR BEER BOTTLES
1430. PARTICLE BOARD & BLACK BOARD WITH SANDING & LAMINATION OF PARTICLE BOARD
1431. PARTICLE BOARD FROM RICE HUSK
1432. POUCH FILLING & MAKING FOR TOMATO SAUCE
1433. POUCH MAKING &

GRAVURE PRINTING
1434. PROCESSING OF PAPER FOR FEEDING IN COMPUTER
1435. PULP FROM BAMBOO & WOOD
1436. PAPER FILES
1437. PLAYING CARDS
1438. ROSIN SIZING AGENT (FOR PAPER PLANT)
1439. SAND PAPER
1440. SANITRY NAPKINS
1441. SILICON COATED PAPER
1442. STENCIL PAPER
1443. STRAW BOARD AND GREY BOARD
1444. STRAW BOARD & MILL BOARD
1445. STRAW BOARD AND PAPER BOARD
1446. TISSUE PAPER FACIAL
1447. TISSUE MOIST TOILETERY CLEANSING TISSUE AND RELATED PRODUCTS
1448. TISSUE PAPER ROLLS
1449. TETRA PACK FOR MILK PACKAGING, GHEE & OTHER LIQUIDS
1450. TOILET PAPER ROLLS
1451. TOILET PAPER & NAPKINS
1452. WAX COATED PRINTED PAPER
1453. WET FACE FRESHNER TISSUE
1454. WHITE WRITING & PRINTING PAPER
1455. WRITING & PRINTING PAPER (PAPER MILLS)

PLASTIC, B.O.P.P, ACRYLIC, DISPOSABLE PLASTIC PRODUCTS, PET PRODUCTS, P.V.C, H.D.P.E, P.P, L.D.P.E., P.U, A.B.S, THERMOFOARMING, MASTER BATCHES, & POLYMER AND RUBBER PRODUCTS, TYRE, TUBE, ADHESIVE, SHEET, COIR & MANY OTHERS

1456. ABS GRANULES FROM ABS SCRAPS FROM OLD T.V. CABINETS, WHITE GOODS ETC.
1457. ACRYLIC BEADS
1458. ACRYLIC COPOLYMER EMULSION
1459. ACRYLIC LATEX
1460. ACRYLIC SHEET
1461. ACRYLIC SHEET & MOULDED PRODUCTS
1462. ACRYLIC TEETH
1463. AUTO TUBES
1464. AUTO FLAPS FOR TRUCKS & BUSES
1465. AUTO TYRES & TUBES
1466. BABY BOTTLES (PLASTIC) WITH WHITESILICON RUBBER NIPPLES
1467. B.O.P.P. FILM
1468. B.O.P.P. PRESSURE SENSITIVE SELF ADHESIVE TAPE
1469. BABY NIPPLE (SILICON)
1470. BABY NIPPLE (BIG SIZE)
1471. BALLOON PLASTIC ADVERTISING
1472. BLISTER FILM PVC
1473. BLISTER PACKAGING & POUCH PAKAGING
1474. BLOW MOULDING PLASTIC CONTAINER
1475. COATING ON METALIZED POLYESTER FILM/METALISED PAPER/ ALIMINIUM FOIL
1476. COATING ON PLASTIC (ELECTROLYSIS) & GLASS
1477. COIR FOAM (RUBBERISED)
1478. COLOUR COATING ON PLASTICS
1479. COLOUR MASTER BATCHES FOR VARIOUS PLASTICS
1480. CYCLE TYRES AND TUBES
1481. DISPOSABLE PLASTIC CUPS GLASSES, ETC.
1482. DISPOSABLE PLASTIC SYRINGES & NEEDLES
1483. DISPOSABLE PLASTIC SYRINGES
1484. DOUGH MOULDING COMPOUND (D.M.C)
1485. EPOXY RESIN
1486. EXPANDED POLYESTRENE MOULDING (THERMOCOLE)
1487. F.R.P AUTO,SCOOTER ROOFS & CEILINGS
1488. F.R.P PRODUCTS (HELMET, WASHBASIN SHEETS, ROOFING SHEETS)
1489. FIBRE REINFORCED PLASTIC (HIGH PRESSURE MOULDING WITH SMC BMC AND DMC)
1490. FIELD RUBBER CONVERTED TO THE 60% LATEX RUBBER
1491. FLEXIBLE P.U. FOAM
1492. FORMALDEHYDE CROCKERY & OTHER ITEMS
1493. FORMALDEHYDE RESIN (UREA, PHENOL,MELEMINE)
1494. GASKET SHEET
1495. GUM BOTTLE (PVC)
1496. GLASS BEADS
1497. HDPE COATED PAPER SACK
1498. H.D.P.E. BAGS
1499. H.D.P.E. CONTAINERS (BLOW MOULDING)
1500. H.D.P.E. CONTAINER, POLY JARS BY INJECTION MOULDING (FOOD GRADE)
1501. H.D.P.E. JERRY CANS
1502. HDPE MANUFACTURING FROM ETHYLALCOHOL
1503. H.D.P.E PIPE AND FITTINGS
1504. H.D.P.E. PIPES
1505. H.D.P.E PRINTED BAGS
1506. H.D.P.E TWINES AND ROPES
1507. H.D.P.E. & L.D.P.E PIPES AND FITTINGS
1508. H.D.P.E/PP BOX STRAPPING
1509. H.D.P.E/PP WOVEN SACKS
USING PLAIN LOOMS
1510. HOLOGRAM STICKERS-3D
1511. H.M BAG PLANT WITH PRINTING UNIT
1512. HAWAI CHAPPALS (RUBBER)
1513. I.V PLASTIC BOTTLE
1514. ICE CREAM CUP (PLASTIC)
1515. INJECTION MOULDED AUTO COMPONENTS
1516. INJECTION & BLOW MOULDED PLASTIC PRODUCTS
1517. INJECTION MOULDED PLASTIC PRODUCTS
1518. INTEGERATED COMPLEX ESTER'S & ALLIED PRODUCTS (D.O.P,D.B.P, & ETHYL ACETATE, BUYTL ACETATE, WIRE ENAMELS, JELLY CABLE COMPOUND)
1519. L.D.P.E. (LOW DENSITY POLY ETHYLENE) GRANULES FROM VIRGIN (L.D.P.E. RESIN)
1520. INTEGERATED SURGICAL RUBBER GOODS INDUSTRY
1521. INJECTION MOULDED PLASTIC BALLS
1522. L.D.P.E FROM ETHYL ALCOHOL
1523. LDPE MOULDED PRODUCTS
1524. LAMINATION OF COEXTRUSION MULTILAYER FILM IN ROLL FORM
1525. LATEX RUBBER
1526. LATEX RUBBER CONDOM
1527. MASTER BATCHES (COLOURED, P.V.C, L.D.P.E, H.D.P.E, ETC.)
1528. MELAMINE FORMALHYDE RESIN
1529. MOULDED LUGGAGE
1530. MULTI-LAYER (3 LAYER BAGS)
1531. MULTI-LAYER (3 LAYER) FILM WITH LAMINATION & PRINTING
1532. OIL SEAL
1533. PET BOTTLE/CONTAINERS
1534. PET BOTTLES FROM PRE FORM
1535. PET BOTTLE & MINERAL WATER
1536. PET PRE-FORM FROM PET RESIN
1537. PET PRE-FORM CUM PET BOTTLES
1538. PET PRE-FORM PET BOTTLES CUM MINERAL WATERS
1539. POLY CARBONATE RESIN
1540. PTFE COMPONENTS
1541. PU/PVC SOLE FOR SPORT SHOE BY IMPORTED M/C.
1542. PVC BATTERY SEPARATOR
1543. P.V.C COMPOUNDS (FRESH)
1544. P.V.C COMPOUNDS (SCRAP)
1545. P.V.C ELECTRICAL INSULATING TAPE
1546. P.V.C. EXTRUSION PROFILES
1547. P.V.C FITTINGS
1548. P.V.C FLEXIBLE FUSIBLE POWDER HEAT FUSIBLE POWDER
1549. P.V.C GRANULES (FOR

INSULATION & SHEETS GRADES)
1550. P.V.C GRANULES FROM PVC SCRAPS (WITH POLLUTION CONTROL)
1551. P.V.C HOSES
1552. P.V.C LEATHER CLOTH
1553. P.V.C FLEXIBLE PIPES
1554. P.V.C PIPES AND FITTINGS
1555. POLYTHENE BAGS (PRINTED)
1556. PVC PLASTICS FILM SHEET SOFT/RIGID
1557. PVC RESIN AND COMPOUND
1558. PVC RULAR
1559. PVC STABLIZERS (SINGLE PACK SYSTEM)
1560. PVC WIRE AND CABLES
1561. PAPER BASED PHENOLIC SHEET FOR ELECTRICAL
1562. PHENOL FORMALDEHYDE RESIN
1563. PHENOLIC RESIN
1564. PLASTIC BEADS FROM PLASTIC SCRAPS
1565. PLASTIC BUTTONS
1566. PLASTIC CANS
1567. PLASTIC COLLAPSIBLE TUBE
1568. PLASTIC CORRUGATED SHEET & BOXES
1569. PLASTIC FILM AND SHEETS WITH PRINTING FLEXO & ROTO/LDPE/HDPE/PP/HM/PVC
1570. PLASTIC FILTER MASTER BATCH & OTHER MASTER BATCHES FOR VARIOUS PLASTICS
1571. PLASTIC JERRY CANS
1572. PLASTIC GRANULES OR POWDER FROM PLASTIC SCRAP
1573. PLASTIC INJECTION MOULDED T.V. CABINETS
1574. PLASTIC ITEMS MANUFAC TURE FROM POWDER MELAMINE
1575. PLASTIC GOODS
1576. PLASTIC PIPES & TARPAULINES
1577. PLASTIC SHEET FROM SCRAP
1578. PLASTIC PLANT (BLOW MOULDING & INJECTION MOULDING)
1579. PLASTIC PRODUCTS (GOLD, SILVER, NICKEL)
1580. PLASTIC TOYS
1581. POLYESTER BEADING
1582. POLYESTER FILM
1583. POLYTHENE BAGS & AUTOMATIC PRINTING
1584. POLYTHENE PRINTED BAGS
1585. POLYURETHANE FOAM AND ITS PRODUCTS
1586. PROPYLENE FILM (PRINTED) & BAG MANUFACTURING
1587. PLASTIC MATS
1588. RAINBOW COLOUR ON PVC FILM & SHEET
1589. RED MUD PVC PIPES AND FITTINGS
1590. RE-RUBBERISED OF SOLID TYPE
1591. RESIN COATED SAND REXINE
1592. REXINE CLOTH & ALLIED PRODUCTS
1593. RUBBER ADHESIVE
1594. RUBBER AUTO PARTS
1595. RUBBER BELTING
1596. RUBBER MOULDING UNIT INCLUDING LINING RUBBER SHEETING
1597. RUBBER RECLAIMING
1598. RUBBER ROLLERS FOR TEXTILE MILLS & PAPER INDUSTRIES
1599. RUBBER & PLASTIC SHEETS, MATS & FLAPS
1600. RUBBER SHEET AND ALLIED HOSPITAL RUBBER GOODS
1601. RUBBERIZED PVC GASKET
1602. RUBBERISED COIR
1603. RUBBER COMPOUND FOR AUTOMOBILES
1604. SAFETY BELTS
1605. SILVER AND GOLD PLATING ON PVC AND NYLON-6
1606. SILICONE RUBBER NIPPLES/ TEATS
1607. SPECTACLE FRAMES (PLASTIC)
1608. SPUNGE RUBBER
1609. SURGICAL EXAMINATION GLOVES
1610. SYNTHETIC PEARL COATING ON POLYSTYRENE BEADS
1611. SYNTHETIC RUBBER ADHESIVE
1612. TEFLON MANUFACTURING
1613. TEFLON TAPE
1614. TEFLON TAPES & CABLES
1615. THERMOCOLE SHEET AND MOULDED PRODUCTS EXPANDED POLYESTERENE EXTRUSION PROFILES
1616. THERMOFORMED PACKAGING (BLISTER PACKAGING & POUCH PACKAGING)
1617. THERMOPLASTIC POLYURETHANE
1618. THERMOFORMED CUPS, PLATES & GLASS WITH HIPS SHEET
1619. THERMOCOLE
1620. THERMOCOLE BASED DISPOSABLE GLASS, CUPS & PLATES
1621. TOOTH BRUSHES
1622. TOY BALLOON, DECORA TIVE & INDUSTRIAL BALLOONS
1623. TREAD RUBBER
1624. TYRE RETREADING (HOT)
1625. TYRE RETREADING BY COLD PROCESS
1626. TYRE TUBES & FLAPS
1627. TYRE & TUBES
1628. UNSATURATED POLYESTER FOR REXINE
1629. V-BELT AND FAN BELT
1630. VINYL ASBESTOS AND PVC WALL PAPER
1631. VITON (FLUORO ELASTOMER)

SOAP, COSMETICS & PERFUMS

1632. ACID SLURRY, SYNTHETIC DETERGENT POWDER
1632. ACID SLURRY
1633. AGARBATTI SYNTHETIC, PERFUMERY COMPOUND
1634. AFTER SHAVE LOTION
1635. ANTISEPTIC CREAM
1636. BETA IONONE
1637. BLEACHING POWDER
1638. BLUE DETERGENT POWDER
1639. CLEANING POWDER (VIMTYPE)
1640. COLD CREAM
1641. COLOURED FLAME & PERFUMED CANDLES (RED, BLUE, GREEN FLAME)
1642. COSMETIC INDUSTRY (MODERN)
1643. COSMETIC INDUSTRY (SHAMPOO, SPRAY PERFUME, TALCUM POWDER
1644. DETERGENT POWDER (ARIEL TYPE)
1645. DETERGENT POWDER (NIRMA TYPE) FULLY AUTOMATIC PLANT
1646. DETERGENT WASHING POWDER
1647. FISH OIL SOAP
1648. GLYCERINE TRANSPARENT SOAP
1649. HAIR REMOVING CREAM
1650. HERBAL COSMETICS
1651. HERBAL SHAMPO & CREAM
1652. HERBAL/AYURVEDIC COSMETICS
1653. INCENSE POWDER,INCENSE STICKS & INCENSE CAKE
1654. OPTICAL WHITENERS
1655. ROSE OIL EXTRACTION
1656. SHAMPOOS (COCONUT OIL BASED COLD PROCESS)
1657. SHAVING CREAM
1658. SINDUR (KUMKUM)
1659. SOAP COATED PAPER
1660. SPRAY DRIED DETERGENT POWDER
1661. STAIN REMOVER
1662. TALCUM POWDER (FACE & TOILET POWDER)
1663. TOILET AND HERBAL SOAP
1664. TOOTH PASTE & POWDER
1665. WASHING DETERGENT POWDER AND WASHING SOAP
1666. WASHING POWDER LIQUID DETERGENTS,LOTION & SHAMPOO

TEXTILE INDUSTRIES, READYMADE GARMENTS, COTTON, DYEING, BLEACHING, CLOTH, HOSIERY, POWER LOOM, HAND LOOM, WOOLLEN, SILK, SOCKS, SURGICAL COTTON & MANY OTHERS

1667. ANGORA RABBIT WOOL
1668. BUCKRAM
1669. CANVAS SHOES, JUNGLE BOOT, BOOT RUBBER KNEES & BOOT COMBAT
1670. CARPET FROM COTTON WASTE
1671. CERAMIC THREAD GUIDE
1672. COTTON BUDS/SWABS
1673. COTTON FROM WASTE YARN
1674. COTTON ROLLS
1675. COTTON SPIDERS FOR LOUD SPEAKERS
1676. DENIM CLOTH
1677. DENIM CLOTH (INTEGERATED UNIT WITH BLEACHING, DYEING AND PRINTING)
1678. DISPERSENT FOR TEXTILE
1679. DYEING & BLEACHING
1680. DYEING OF HANK YARN
1681. EMULSIFIER FOR WOOL BATCHING OIL
1682. EMBROIDERY ON FABRICS
1683. GARMENT DYEING, WASHING & STITCHING (JEANS, JACKETS, SKIRTS & SHIRTS)
1684. GOVES KNITTING
1685. GUNNY BAGS
1687. HDPE WOVEN SACKS
1688. HDPE TARPAULINS USING PLAIN LOOM WITH LAMINATION
1689. HDPE/PP WOVEN SACKS USING CIRCULAR LOOMS
1690. HOSIERY CLOTH (COTTON) PROCESSING (BLEACHING, DYEING, FINISHING OF CLOTH)
1691. HOSIERY INDUSTRY
1692. HOSIERY MERCERISING
1693. HOSIERY PRODUCTS LIKE VEST, BRIEF, T-SHIRTS & SOCKS
1694. JACQUARD FABRICS
1695. JUTE COIR, GRASS ROPE/ SUTLI MAKING
1696. JUTE FELT
1697. JUTE TWINES
1698. KNITTED FABRICS
1699. LAMINATED JUTE BAGS
1700. LAMINATION OF HDPE WOVEN CLOTH (JUTE,COTTON, PAPER)
1701. NYLON YARN CRIMPING, DOUBLING AND BLEACHING
1702. PIGMENT BINDER FOR TEXTILE PRINTING
1704. POLYESTER RESIN FOR WIRE ENAMEL
1705. POLYESTER RESIN
1706. POLYESTER YARN FROM WASTE POLYESTER ZIP FASTENERS
1707. POWER LOOM
1708. READYMADE GARMENTS & HOSIERY
1709. READYMADE GARMENTS MERCHANDISE
1710. READYMADE GARMENTS & COVERS
1711. READYMADE GARMENTS & EMBROIDERY OF GOWNS, SHIRTS, BLOUSES, T-SHIRTS ETC. (ONLY LADIES)
1712. READYMADE SALWAR SUIT
1713. RECOVERY OF NYLON FROM NYLON WASTE
1714. ROTARY PRINTING AND DYEING ON COTTON, SYNTHETIC TEXTILE
1715. SANITARY NAPKINS
1716. SCREEN PRINTING ON COTTON CLOTH
1717. SEWING THREAD REELS & BALLS MAKING INDUSTRIES
1718. SCREEN PRINTING ON COTTON, POLYESTER & ACRYLIC
1719. SHAWLS (WOOLLEN)
1720. SHOE LACES
1721. SILK FABRICS ON HANDLOOM
1722. SOCKS KNITTING
1723. SPINNING, DOUBLING DYEING MERCERISING & BLEACHING OF COTTON YARN
1724. SPINNING & CARDING OF WOOL INTO YARNS
1725. STARCH BOOK BINDING CLOTH
1726. SURAT JARI
1727. SURGICAL COTTON & BANDAGE
1728. SYNTHETIC TEXTILE INDUSTRY(SUITING, SHIRTING, SAREES) TERRY CLOTH
1729. T-SHIRTS
1730. TOWELS, BED SHEET COVERS
1731. TERRY TOWEL
1732. TERRY FABRICS WEAVING UNIT
1733. TEXTILE AUXILLIARIES & CHEMICALS
1734. TEXTILE BLEACHING, DYEING & FINISHING & PRINTING OF COTTON FABRICS
1735. TEXTILE (HOSIERY)
1736. TEXTILE MILL
1737. TEXTILE DYEING & PRINTING
1738. TEXTILE PRINTING (JOB WORK)
1739. TEXTILE PIGMENT PRINTING BINDER
1740. TOWEL (TERRY)
1741. VELVET CLOTH BY FLOCKING PROCESS
1742. VISCOSE STAPLE FIBRE
1743. WADDING OIL (100%) FOR WADDING OF COTTON HOSIERY CLOTH IN THE DYEING PROCESS
1744. WEAVING OF DASUTI CLOTH WITH PRINTING, DYEING, EMBROIDERY & FINISHING
1745. WASHING OF JEANS & OTHER GARMENTS
1746. WORSTED WOOLLEN YARN CLOTH
1747. ZARI GLITTER SALMA SITARA OF PLASTIC FILM

INFOTECH/IT, HOSPITALITY, HOSPITAL, COLLEGE, SCHOOL, MEDICAL, ENTERTAINMENT CLUB, WARE HOUSING & REAL ESTATE, PROJECTS

1748. AMUSEMENT PARK
1749. AMUSEMENT PARK CUM WATER PARK
1750. BANQUET HALL
1751. CALL CENTER (DOMESTIC)
1752. CALL CENTER (INTERNATIONAL)
1753. CHILDREN RECREATION CENTRE
1754. COLD STORAGE
1755. COMMUNITY HALL
1756. COMPUTER EDUCATION INSTITUTE
1757. COMPUTER SOFTWARE
1758. COLLEGE
1759. CYBER CAFE
1760. DENTAL CLINIC
1761. DENTAL COLLEGE
1762. DIAGONOSTIC CENTRE
1763. E-COMMERCE/BUSINESS
1764. E-SCHOOL (Rs. 5000/-)
1765. ENGINEERING COLLEGE
1766. ENTERTAINMENT CLUB
1767. ENTERTAINMENT CLUB, HOLIDAY RESORT, 4 STAR HOTEL, AMUSEMENT PARK CUM WATER PARK, MUSHROOM & ITS PRODUCTS, FISH FARMING, LAKE FOR BOATING, DEER PARK
1768. FASHION TECHNOLOGY INSTITUTE
1769. FAST FOOD PARLOUR
1770. FIVE STAR HOTEL
1771. FOOD PARLOUR
1772. FRANCHISE TRAINING PROGRAMME FOR IIT & ENGINEERING ENTRANCE EXAMS.
1773. GOLF COURSE
1774. HEALTH CLUB, BEAUTY PARLOUR
1775. HEALTH CLUB AND FITNESS CENTER
1776. HEALTH RESORTS
1777. HOLIDAY RESORTS
1778. HOLIDAY RESORT CUM

ENTERTAINMENT CLUB WITH 4 STAR HOTEL
1779. HOSPITALS
1780. ICE CREAM PARLOUR
1781. INTERNET SERVICE PROVIDER (I.S.P.)
1782. MEDICAL COLLEGE
1783. MEDICAL COLLEGE, HOSPITAL & RESEARCH INSTITUTE
1784. MEDICAL TRANSCRIPTION CENTRE
1785. MENTAL RETARDATION HOSPITAL & CEREBRAL PALSY
1786. MOTEL/SMALL HOTEL
1787. MULTISTOREY COMMERCIAL COMPLEX
1788. MULTISTOREY RESIDENTIAL COMPLEX
1789. NURSERY SCHOOL
1790. NATURE CARE CENTRE
1791. NURSING HOME
1792. ONLINE SHOPPING MALL (RS. 5000/- REPORT)
1793. PORTAL
1794. REHABILITATION CENTRE FOR AGED & NEEDY PERSONS
1795. RESIDENTIAL CUM COMMERCIAL COMPLEX
1796. RESTAURANT
1797. RESTAURANT WITH PUB
1798. SCHOOL (PRIMARY)
1799. SCHOOL (HIGHER SECONDARY)
1800. THREE STAR HOTEL
1801. TOURIST CLUB
1802. TRAINING INSTITUTE FOR MEDICAL TRANSCRIPTION
1803. VIDEO FILM STUDIO
1804. WARE HOUSE
1805. WEBSITE DESIGN & E-MAIL REGISTERING

AGRO BASED INDUSTRIES

1806. COAL BRIQUETTES FROM AGROWASTE
1807. FURFURALFROM RICEHULL
1808. MUSHROOM CULTIVATION & PROCESSING (BUTTON)
1809. MUSHROOM GROWING & PROCESSING WITH AIR CONDITIONING
1810. MUSHROOM CULTIVATION & PROCESSING UNIT DEHYDRATION & PACKAGING OF OYSTER & PADDY STRAW MUSHROOMS
1811. ORGANIC MANURE
1812. PAPAYA CULTIVATION
1813. PAPAYA & TOMATO CULTIVATION
1814. PROCESSING & UTILISATION OF COCONUT
1815. PROCESSING OF SHEEP HAIR TO PRODUCE WOOL

BAKERY, CONFECTIONERY & FOOD PRODUCTS

1816. AGROLACTOR SOYA MILK
1817. APPLE FRUIT JUICE WITH CANNING BOTTLING
1818. AYURVEDIC SHARBAT
1819. BAKERY UNIT (PASTRIES, BREAD, BUNS, CAKE, TOFFEE ETC.)
1820. BAKING POWDER
1821. BANANA & ITS BY PRODUCTS
1822. BANANA POWDER
1823. BANANA WAFERS
1824. BANANA CULTIVATION
1825. BEER INDUSTRY
1826. DEHULLING OF JAUN FOR BEER
1827. BEER & WINE
1828. BEER, ALCOHOL, IMFL
1829. BESEN PLANT
1830. BISCUIT PLANT
1831. BREAD & BISCUIT PLANT
1832. BOTTLING PLANT COUNTRY LIQUOR FROM RECTIFIED SPIRIT
1833. BRANDY
1834. BREAD RUSKS
1835. CANNED FRUITS & VEGETABLES
1836. CANNING & PRESERVATION OF MEAT
1837. CANNING & PRESERVATION OF VEGETABLES
1838. CANNING OF MANGO PULP & MANGO SLICES
1839. CARBONATED BEVERAGS
1840. CASHEW FENI
1841. CASHEW NUT (DRIED & FRIED)
1842. CATTLE BREEDING
1843. CATTLE BREEDING & DAIRY FARM TO PRODUCE MILK
1844. CATTLE FEED FROM TAPIOCA
1845. CHEWING GINGER & AMLOKI
1846. CHEWING GUM
1847. CHILLI SAUCE
1848. CHILLI POWDER
1849. CHOCOLATE
1850. CIDER PLANT
1851. COCOA POWDER
1852. COCOA BUTTER & COCOA POWDER
1853. COCONUT SHELL POWDER
1854. COCONUT WATER
1855. COCONUT SWEET (WATERY)
1856. COCONUT MILK POWDER (DEHYDRATED)
1857. COCONUT PRODUCTS & BY PRODUCTS (INTEGRATED PLANT)
1858. COLD DRINK
1859. CURRY POWDER
1860. DAIRY FOR MILK PROCESSING (GHEE, BUTTER & PANEER)
1861. DAIRY PRODUCTS
1862. DAIRY PRODUCTS MILK PACKAGING IN POUCH (GHEE, BUTTER, ETC.
1863. DAIRY FARM TO PRDUCE MILK WITH PACKAGING (COW)
1864. DAIRY FARM TO PRDUCE MILK WITH PACKAGING (BUFALLOE)
1865. DAIRY FARM & MILK PRODUCTS
1866. DAL MOTH, CHANACHUR & BHUJIYA
1867. DEHYDRATION OF FRUITS & VEGETABLE
1868. DESICCATED COCONUT POWDER FROM COCONUTS
1869. DEHYDRATION & CANNING OF FRUITS & VEGETABLES
1870. DRY FRUIT ROASTING & PACKAGING
1871. DRYING OF RED CHILLIES, HALDI, DHANIYA, PEAS & GROUND NUT
1872. EGG POWDER
1873. FISH CANNING IN TIN & POUCHES
1874. FISH DEHYRATION (DRYING OF FISH)
1875. FISH MEAL
1876. FISH PROCESSING (BEAST FREEZING PROCESSES)
1877. FLAVOURS FOR FOOD INDUSTRIES
1878. FLOUR MILL (ROLLER)
1879. FROZEN MEAT
1880. FOOD DEHYDRATION (FRUITS & VEGETABLES)
1881. FRIED & ROASTED GROUND NUT, GRAMS, PEAR ETC.
1882. FRUIT JUICE MAKING & PACKAGING IN PLASTIC CONTAINER
1883. FRUIT JUICE IN TETRA PACK (DRINKS)
1884. FRUIT JUICE, SQUASHES, SAUCE & KETCHUP, JAM, JELLY, VINEGAR ETC.
1885. GARLIC FLAKES
1886. GARLIC POWDER
1887. GHEE & BUTTER
1888. GINGER (PULVERISED)
1889. GINGER GLAZING & PRESERVATION
1890. GINGER STORAGE
1891. GINGER PROCESSING
1892. GINGER OIL & GINGER DUST
1893. GINGER POWDER (DRY) & OLEORESIN
1894. GRAPE DEHYDRATION
1895. GRAPE CULTIVATION
1896. GRAPE JUICE
1897. HONEY PROCESSING & PACKAGING
1898. ICE CREAM & ICE CANDY
1899. ICE CUBE
1900. INVERT SUGAR
1901. IDLI MIX, DOSA MIX SAMBHAR MIX, VADA MIX, GULAB JAMUN MIX
1902. INSTANT COFFEE & INSTANT TEA

1903. INSTANT NOODLES
1904. INSTANT SOUPS
1905. IODIZED SALT FROM CRUDE SALT
1906. JAM CHUTNEY PICKLES & SQUASHES
1907. KATHA MANUFACTURING
1908. LECITHIN (SOYA BASED)
1909. LEMON & ITS PRODUCTS
1910. MACARONI MANUFACTURING
1911. MACARONI, SPAGHETTI, VERMICELLI & NOODLES
1912. MAIZE & ITS BY PRODUCTS MALTING PLANT
1913. MANGO PAPPAD (AAM PAPPAD)
1914. MANGO POWDER RIPE
1915. MANGO POWDER
1916. MANGO PROCESSING & CANNING (MANGO PULP)
1917. MEAT PROCESSING (CHICKEN MUTTON)
1918. MEAT PROCESSING (BUFFALO)
1919. MENTHOL BOLD FROM MENTHOL FLAKES
1020. MILK POWDER
1921. MILK POWDER & GHEE
1922. MILK POWDER, GHEE & SPICES
1923. MILK PRESERVATION & MARKETING TO WHOLE SELLERS
1924. MILK PRESERVATION & MARKETING TO WHOLE SELLERS (IN POUCHES)
1925. MILK TOFFEE MANUFACTURES
1926. MINERAL WATER
1927. MINERAL WATER IN POUCHES
1928. MINI FLOUR MILL ATTA MAIDA, SUJI & WHEAT BRAN
1929. MITHAI/HALWAI (SWEET & NAMKEEN)
1930. MUTTON PROCESSING
1931. PAN MASALA (MEETHA, SADA, ZARDA) MAKING & PACKING
1932. PAN MASALA AND POUCH MAKING
1933. PANEER (CHEESE)
1934. PAPAD & BARIYAN
1935. PAPAD PLANT
1936. PEPSICOLA IN POLYTUBES
1937. PETHA PACKAGING
1938. PICKLES
1939. PIGGERY/MEAT/CHICKEN PROCESSING
1940. PINE APPLE JUICE CANNING
1941. POTATO & ONION POWDER
1942. POTATO & ONION FLAKES
1943. POTATO CHIPS
1944. POTATO GRANULES
1945. POUCH FILLING FOR SAUNF SUPARI ILAICHI ETC.
1946. PRESERVATION OF RAWS MANGO JUICE
1947. PROCESSED CHEESE & MARINE PDTS.
1948. PULP FROM TARMARIND
1949. READYMATE PROCESSED FOOD
1950. RICE & CORN FLAKES
1951. RICE BASMATI (TRADING)
1952. RICE POLISHING & PACKAGING IN POUCH
1953. ROASTED/SALTED/MASALA/ CASHEW NUTS ALMONDS & PEA NUT
1954. ROLLER FLOUR MILL

INFOTECH/IT PROJECTS

1955. MEDICAL TRANSCRIPTION
1956. E-COMMERCE
1957. CYBERCAFE
1958. INTERNET SERVICE PROVIDER (ISP)
1959. COMPUTER EDUCATION CENTRE
1960. PORTAL (WEBSITE DESIGN)
1961. CALL CENTRE

TERMS AND CONDITIONS

FOR INDIA

1. Please ask for Quotations of Each *Market Survey Cum Detailed Techno Economic Feasibility Report.* Payable in advance through Draft/M.O./Cash in favour of 'ENGINEERS INDIA RESEARCH INSTITUTE', Delhi. Delivery by Regd.post within 2 Days. (Postage Free)

2. Ask for the Hi-Tech Projects Monthly magazine. Each Magazine covers many Project Profiles for selection of Industry.

FOR OVERSEAS

1. Please ask for Quotations in US $ of Each *Market Survey Cum Detailed Techno Economic Feasibility Report.* Payable in advance through Draft/M.O./Cash in favour of 'ENGINEERS INDIA RESEARCH INSTITUTE', Delhi. (Payable in India) Delivery by Regd.post within 4 Days.

2. Ask for "Hi-Tech Projects" Monthly magazine. Each Magazine covers many Project Profiles for selection of Industry.

ENGINEERS INDIA RESEARCH INSTITUTE

Add: 4449, Nai Sarak (D), Main Road, Delhi - 110 006 (India)
Ph:. 91-11-23918117, 23916431, 23840361, 98114-37895
Fax: 91-11-23916431 E-Mail : eirisidi@bol.net.in
Website:www.eiriinia.org
Also at : 4/27, Roop Nagar, Near Roop Nagar No. 1 School, Delhi - 110 007 (India) Ph:. 23840361